The Twilight of
French Eastern Alliances,
1926–1936

Piotr S. Wandycz

The Twilight of French Eastern Alliances, 1926–1936

French-Czechoslovak-Polish Relations

from Locarno to the Remilitarization of the Rhineland

PRINCETON UNIVERSITY PRESS

Princeton, New Jersey

Copyright © 1988
by Princeton University Press
Published by Princeton University Press,
41 William Street, Princeton, New Jersey 08540
In the United Kingdom:
Princeton University Press, Guildford, Surrey

This book has been composed in Linotron Sabon

Clothbound edition of
Princeton University Press books
are printed on acid-free paper,
and binding materials are chosen for strength
and durability. Paperbacks,
although satisfactory for personal collections,
are not usually suitable for library rebinding

Printed in the United States of America
by Princeton University Press,
Princeton, New Jersey

Library of Congress Cataloging-in-Publication Data
Wandycz, Piotr Stefan.
The twilight of French eastern alliances, 1926–1936 : French-Czechoslovak-
Polish relations from Locarno to the remilitarization of the Rhineland / Piotr
S. Wandycz.

p. cm.
"Sequel to . . . France and her eastern allies, 1919–1925"—Pref.
Bibliography: p.
Includes index.
ISBN 0–691–05528–9 (alk. paper)

1. France—Foreign relations—1914–1940. 2. France—Foreign relations—
Czechoslovakia. 3. Czechoslovakia—Foreign relations—France. 4. France—
Foreign relations—Poland. 5. Poland—Foreign relations—France. 6.
Europe—Politics and government—1918–1945. I. Wandycz, Piotr Stefan.
France and her eastern allies, 1919–1925. II. Title.
DC394.W36 1988
327.440437—dc19   88–5789
                                                    CIP

For
Kasia, Joanna, and Antoni

Contents

Preface / xi
Abbreviations / xv
Background: The French System / 3

Part One.   Post-Locarno Diplomacy
Chapter 1.   The Shadow of Locarno / 19
   The Powers / 19
   The Eastern Allies / 29
   Geneva, Berlin, Prague / 36

Chapter 2.   The Turbulent Year 1926 / 47
   Piłsudski's Coup d'Etat / 47
   Crisis in Prague, Union Nationale in Paris / 56
   Thoiry and Its Repercussions / 63

Chapter 3.   Eastern or Central European Locarno / 73
   Polish Diplomatic Offensive / 73
   Polish Advances and Czechoslovak Reserve / 82
   A Stalemate / 91

Chapter 4.   Toward the Evacuation of the Rhineland / 106
   Continuing Frustrations: Zaleski in Rome / 106
   Elusive Pursuits: Beneš in Berlin / 113
   Polish Moves Snubbed / 120

Chapter 5.   The End of an Era / 133
   Moves and Countermoves in Central Europe / 133
   Renewed Polish Efforts: The Hague Conference / 140
   The Aftermath of The Hague / 148
   An Overview / 156

Part Two. The Depression
Chapter 6. Revisionism and Briand's European Union / 163
  Rhineland Evacuated / 163
  Briand's European Union / 170
  Revisionism Rampant / 178

Chapter 7. Austro-German Union and Financial Diplomacy / 192
  The Curtius–Schober Project / 192
  Political Moratorium and the Soviet Angle / 203
  Annus Terribilis / 211

Chapter 8. French Initiatives and Failures / 222
  Plan Tardieu / 222
  French-Polish Malaise / 229
  Gleichberechtigung / 238
  An Overview / 252

Part Three. Responses to Hitler
Chapter 9. A Dilemma: The Four Power Pact / 259
  Disarmament or Preventive War? / 259
  The Four Power Pact / 273
  Hopes Deceived / 290

Chapter 10. At Crossroads, the German-Polish
  Declaration of Nonaggression / 300
  Alternatives / 300
  An Intermezzo / 315
  The Declaration of 26 January 1934 / 324

Chapter 11. Louis Barthou and His Diplomacy / 336
  Beginnings / 336
  In Warsaw and Prague / 347
  The Eastern Pact / 356

Chapter 12. Fronts or Façades? / 371
  Laval's First Steps / 371
  Toward the Stresa Front / 381
  Paris, Moscow, Prague / 395

Chapter 13. The Test of 7 March / 410
  The Impact of the Ethiopian Crisis / 410
  *Hodža Plan and the Ratification of
    the Franco-Soviet Treaty* / 422

Remilitarization of the Rhineland / 431
The Epilogue / 445

Appraisal: A Pattern of Relations / 448
Appendices / 479
Bibliography / 491
Index / 523

Preface

Ecartée de l'Europe centrale, la France resterait-elle
une grande puissance?
Victor de Lacroix to Delbos, 17 July, 1936

This book is chronologically a long-delayed sequel to my *France and Her
Eastern Allies 1919–1925* (Minneapolis, 1962). The delay proved a blessing in many respects, for during the last two decades the French archives
were made available for research as were several Polish collections scat-
tered around the world. In contrast to my previous, somewhat pioneering
efforts, I was confronted this time with an over abundance of sources, certain important gaps notwithstanding.

The past twenty years have seen a significant extension of our knowledge of European diplomacy in the 1920s and early 1930s. A "new international history" has appeared utilizing the freshly opened archives and
seeking a more integrated approach to the study of diplomacy. Several
valuable monographs and specialized articles on France and East Central
Europe have been published; however, no comprehensive treatment of the
French "system" has appeared.

The present work concentrates on France, Poland and Czechoslovakia
(and deals only tangentially with the Little Entente). In addition to considering bilateral relationships, I have attempted to place the political, military and economic intercourse between the three states within the changing international context. In the course of my research, many questions
had to be faced. To what extent can one speak of an integrated French
system of eastern alliances? Was such a combination one of the main options for the preservation of peace and status quo in interwar Europe?
How was it conceived by the three main partners? Did the interaction
between Paris on the one hand, and Warsaw and Prague on the other,
represent a paradigm of a great power–smaller states relationship that
transcends the 1920s and 1930s? Does the story throw a light on the West-
East rapports in general?

An investigation of events during the decade after Locarno appeared
particularly useful in providing an understanding of the eventual disinte-

gration of the French eastern alliances. Both December 1925, the date of the finalization of the Locarno pact, and March 1936 stand out as milestones of a process that culminated with the Anschluss, the Munich conference, and the invasion of Poland. Whereas these latter events have been extensively examined in many works, the former has not. To mention but one glaring gap, there is still no monograph on Locarno.

My research and writing would have been impossible without the generous support of several institutions and many individuals. Two years spent in Poland, Czechoslovakia, France, and Britain—1972–73 under the International Research and Exchanges Board program and 1977–78 as a Guggenheim Fellow—allowed me to do most of my research in European archives. Grants from the American Philosophical Society and the Hoover Institution in 1980 enabled me to do research in Stanford; a grant of the American Council of Learned Societies in 1982 gave me another opportunity to complete work in European archives. I acknowledge all this assistance with gratitude.

The Griswold Committee of the Whitney Humanities Center at Yale provided a generous stipend for the typing of this manuscript for which I am grateful.

Many friends and colleagues have assisted me in various ways, and I wish I could enumerate them all. Among those Czechoslovak historians who went out of their way to make my stay in their country fruitful and intellectually rewarding, Jaroslav Valenta and Zdeněk Sládek (and his wife) deserve special thanks. Colleagues and friends in France who patiently answered my numerous requests include Bernard Michel, Georges Mond, Zbigniew Rapacki, Henry Rollet, and Georges-Henri Soutou. I am obliged to Colonel Henry Fournier-Foch for copies of documents from Marshal Foch papers, now at Château de Vincennes. I would like to thank René Massigli, Ambassadeur de France, for permission to use his papers at the Quai d'Orsay. I am grateful to Jerzy Lukaszewski, rector of the College d'Europe in Bruges, who kindly located some documents for me in the Belgian Archives, and to Peter Krüger, who did the same in the Bundesarchiv. Alice Teichová graciously answered several of my queries. Among Polish historians, Henryk Bułhak kept me au courant of latest Polish publications, while Zbigniew Landau and Jerzy Tomaszewski were particularly helpful with regard to my research on economic issues. When visiting Poland I profited from conversations and discussions with many diplomatic historians. Let me mention only Henryk Batowski, Tadeusz Jędruszczak, Michał Pułaski Alina Szklarska-Lohmannowa, and Marian Zgórniak.

I am most grateful to several former Polish diplomats whom I consulted, particularly Count Edward Raczyński. I owe a special debt to Wacław Jędrzejewicz, a soldier and politician of interwar Poland, its historian in exile, and the *spiritus movens* of the Józef Piłsudski Institute of America. On many occasions I drew on his vast memory.

The contributions of several former graduate students at Yale to my diplomatic history seminars provided intellectual stimulus and a sense of the worthiness of the subject. I am indebted to Eva Balogh, M. B. Biskupski, Edward Keeton, MacGregor Knox, Williamson Murray, and Neal Pease. Also, I have greatly appreciated the sustained interest in my work shown by Anna M. Cienciala, a friend and fellow diplomatic historian, who was my first Ph.D. advisee. Finally, I wish to thank the staffs of the many archival collections in Poland, France, Czechoslovakia, Britain, and the United States in which I worked for their cooperation. The citations from Crown copyright records in the Public Record Office appear by permission of the Controller of H. M. Stationery Office. Those from the Stimson Papers and the Bullitt Papers are authorized by the Yale University Sterling Memorial Library.

New Haven, Connecticut

Abbreviations

AA	Auswärtiges Amt documents, Bundesarchiv, Bonn
AAN, Amb. Berlin	Archiwum Akt Nowych, Warsaw, Ambasada RP w Berlinie
AAN, BBWR	Archiwum Akt Nowych, Warsaw, Bezpartyjny Blok Współpracy z Rządem
AAN, DPLN	Archiwum Akt Nowych, Warsaw, Delegacja Polski przy Lidze Narodów
AAN, MSZ	Archiwum Akt Nowych, Warsaw, Ministerstwo Spraw Zagronicznych
AAN, Pos. Ateny	Archiwum Akt Nowych, Warsaw, Poselstwo RP w Atenach
AAN, Pos. Praga	Archiwum Akt Nowych, Warsaw, Poselstwo RP w Pradze
AAN, PPRM	Archiwum Akt Nowych, Warsaw, Protokoły posiedzeń Rady Ministrów
ADAP	Akten zur deutschen auswärtigen Politik
ANM	Archiv Národního Muzea, Prague
CA, CM, CAir/Sén	Commission d'Armée, Commission de Marine, Commission de l'Air/ Archives du Sénat, Paris
CAE/Ch	Commission des Affaires Étrangères, Archives de la Chambre des Deputés, Paris
CAE/Sén	Commission des Affaires Étrangères, Archives du Sénat, Paris
CD, NA	Czechoslovak documents in German translation, Captured German documents, National Archives, Washington, D.C.

CPP	Copies of Czechoslovak diplomatic documents in private possession
DaM	Dokumenty a materiály k dějinám československo-sovětských vztahů
DBFP	Documents on British Foreign Policy
DDB	Documents diplomatiques belges
DDF	Documents diplomatiques français
DDI	I Documenti diplomatici italiani
DiM	Dokumenty i materiały do historii stosunków polsko-radzieckich
DTJS	Diariusz i teki Jana Szembeka
DVP SSR	Dokumenty vneshnei politiki SSSR
FDR	Franklin D. Roosevelt Library, Hyde Park, New York
FO	Foreign Office documents, Public Record Office, London
FRUS	Foreign Relations of the United States
HIA, Amb. Paryż	Hoover Institution Archives, Stanford, Poland, Ambasada RP w Paryżu
J.O. Chambre	Journal Officiel de la République Française, Débats parlementaires, Chambre des Deputés
J.O. Sénat	Journal Officiel de la République Française, Débats parlementaires, Sénat
KV, CPP	Kroftový výklady na porádach, copies in private possession
MAE, P.A.	Ministère des Affaires Étrangéres, Archives diplomatiques, Papiers d'Agents
MF, F	Ministère des Finances Archives
MS, BJ	Dział rękopisów (manuscripts), Biblioteka Jagiellońska, Cracow
MS, BN	Dział rękopisów (manuscripts), Biblioteka Narodowa, Warsaw
MS, OSS	Manuscripts, Biblioteka Ossolineum, Wrocław
MS, PAN	Archiwum Biblioteki Polskiej Akademii Nauk, Cracow
MZV-VA	Ministerstvo Zahraničních Věci-Vystřižkový archiv, Státní ustřední archiv, Prague
PI, Amb. Londyn	Józef Piłsudski Institute of America, archives, Ambasada RP w Londynie
SDNA	State Department files, National Archives, Washington, D.C.

SHA, CSDN	Service Historique de l'Armée, Vincennes, Conseil Supérieur de la Défense Nationale
SHA, CSG	Service Historique de l'Armée, Vincennes, Conseil Supérieur de Guerre
SHA, EMA	Service Historique de l'Armée, Vincennes, État Major de l'Armée de Terre
SI, Amb. Londyn	Polish Institute and General Sikorski Museum, London, Ambasada RP w Londynie
SI, MSZ	Polish Institue and General Sikorski Museum, London, Ministerstwo Spraw Zagranicznych, Wydział zachodni files
SzD	*Studia z Dziejów ZSRR i Europy Środkowej*
YUL	Yale University Library, New Haven

The Twilight of
French Eastern Alliances
1926–1936

Background: The French System

The French policy of eastern alliances was a result of World War I. Having fought against the German bid for hegemony in Europe and to achieve a balance of power guaranteeing security and economic interests, France emerged in 1918 exhausted and deprived of its main continental ally, Russia. France was unable to secure American and British supportive cooperation, although the latter remained a constant goal of French diplomacy, and so sought to improve its position by relying on the "new" states bordering Germany in the east, Poland and Czechoslovakia. This alignment, conceived at first partly as a *cordon sanitaire* meant to separate Bolshevik Russia from Germany, became a new version of an "eastern barrier" designed to keep Berlin in check and preserve the status quo.[1]

The two French partners differed from each other with regard to postwar international organization. Czechoslovak plans of a belt of Slav states—Poland, Czechoslovakia, Yugoslavia—centered on Prague implied the existence of a small ethnic Poland unlikely to antagonize Russia or to seek dominance in the region.[2] The Polish leaders, however, believed that only a large and strong Poland could survive between a mighty Germany and a huge Russia, and attract the smaller neighboring countries within the Polish orbit. Thus, Czechoslovak and Polish foreign policy concepts were at odds from the beginning; a Warsaw-Prague rivalry became sharpened by a territorial dispute over Teschen (Cieszyn, Těšín).

At the eve and during the Paris Peace Conference, the French pursued a peace program that could be subsumed in three words—security, restitutions, and reparations; they sought systematically to strengthen territori-

1. See Hovi, *Cordon*, and Hovi, *Alliance*.

2. See Lundgreen-Nielsen, *Polish Problem*, 68; Radko Břach, "To the Origin and the Beginnings of Czechoslovak Foreign Policy," *Problems of Contemporary History*, 1 (1968) 1–55; Gajanová, "Ke vzniku," 44–46; Perman, 109–110.

ally both Czechoslovakia and Poland against Germany.[3] Their inability to achieve complete success in the Polish case was due to Anglo-American opposition to an aggrandized Poland, which was perceived as an instrument of French hegemonic designs. Paradoxically, the Treaty of Versailles, denounced by the Germans (especially because of the Polish settlement) as a *Diktat*, did not fulfill French goals. True, the Rhineland was to be occupied for fifteen years and its gradual evacuation would depend on German fulfillment of the treaty provisions, a measure designed to permit a French offensive into Germany until a total withdrawal of allied troops occurred. Disarmament clauses drastically cut the size of the German army and denied it heavy weapons. In the final analysis, however, the treaty by itself could not prevent eventual German recovery as a great power. There was no fundamental agreement between France and the Anglo-Saxon powers on reparations, interallied debts, and how to enforce peace. Economic collaboration did not survive the war. As for the League of Nations, both French nationalists and socialists found it, although for different reasons, a soulless body and a deceptive judicial frame. All this made the secretary general of the Quai d'Orsay, Philippe Berthelot, refer to Versailles as "a paix boche."

The French attitude toward Polish eastern borders, affected by the struggle during the Soviet-Polish war and the Pandora's box of nationalities, was ambivalent. Paris desired a collapse of the Bolsheviks but did not favor the plan of Poland's chief of state, Józef Piłsudski, to drive Russia back to its eighteenth-century borders and fill the vacuum in the Ukrainian-Belorussian-Lithuanian confines by a vast bloc connected with Warsaw. This "federalist" grand design eventually collapsed, but not before the Polish troops had pushed as far as Kiev and the Red Army had reached the gates of Warsaw.[4] After Piłsudski's victory, the war-weary Poles signed a compromise peace treaty of Riga with Soviet Russia; Lenin, having failed to make Poland communist, grudgingly accepted the settlement.

The French, while not identifying themselves with Warsaw's political goals, had assisted the Polish army during its campaigns. General Maxime Weygand acted as adviser to the high command during the climactic days, giving rise to the legend cultivated by the French and Polish Right, inimical

3. See Pierre Miquel, *La paix de Versailles et l'opinion publique française* (Paris, 1972), 546; compare Janusz Pajewski, *Odbudowa państwa polskiego 1914–1918* (Warszawa, 1978), 332–33; Hovi, *Cordon*, 174–75; Lundgreen-Nielsen, *Polish Problem*, 143, 176–77; and Poincaré, *Au Service* 11:97–98.

4. Main studies of this subject are Piotr S. Wandycz, *Soviet-Polish Relations 1917–1921* (Cambridge, Mass., 1969); M. K. Dziewanowski, *Joseph Piłsudski, a European Federalist 1918–1922* (Stanford, 1969); Norman Davies, *White Eagle, Red Star: The Soviet-Polish War 1919–1920* (New York, 1972). See also *La Guerre polono-soviétique de 1919–1920: Colloque* (Collection historique de l'Institut d'Etudes Slaves, 22, Paris-Lausanne, 1975).

to Piłsudski, that Weygand was the true savior of Poland. Czechoslovakia was openly critical of Poland's eastern ventures and pointedly distanced itself from the war. In mid-1920, the foreign minister Edvard Beneš exploited Poland's weakness to extract from the powers a favorable settlement of the Teschen dispute.[5] Piłsudski, whose advances to President Tomáš Masaryk in December 1918 had been rebuffed, and who was enraged by Prague's handling of the Teschen issue, grew increasingly anti-Czech.[6]

During the Soviet-Polish crisis in 1920, France was temporarily displeased with Czechoslovak policy. In one respect France was to blame, for the new secretary of the Quai d'Orsay, Maurice Paléologue, tried to promote a French-oriented Danubian union including and based on Hungary. This union raised a specter of territorial revisionism, and Czechoslovakia devised a counter-bloc that attracted Yugoslavia and, by 1921, Romania. Dubbed the Little Entente, the grouping was recognized by Paris after Berthelot resumed his functions and steered French policy back toward reliance on the victor states in East Central Europe.[7] A disoriented Warsaw was being told at first that Poland should stay away from the Little Entente, which did not carry French endorsement, and subsequently that it should become a member. The latter arrangement suited Romania, interested in a broader organization, but Beneš made it clear repeatedly that he did not want Poland in the Little Entente.[8] The French, operating in a somewhat confusing and confused situation, concentrated then on promoting Polish-Romanian rapprochement and trying to smooth over difficulties between Warsaw and Prague.

During this initial phase the French furthered their influence in East Central Europe through the use of military missions and economic initiatives. The mission in Czechoslovakia, whose head was made commander-in-chief of the Czechoslovak army by President Masaryk, was one of command. Its corresponding number in Poland was a counseling mission, al-

5. For views in Paris, see the somewhat one-sided Michael J. Carley, "The Politics of Anti-Bolshevism: The French Government and the Russo-Polish War, December 1919 to May 1920," *Historical Journal*, 19, 1 (1976), 163–89—with a rebuttal in Hovi, *Alliance*, 46–52—and Carley, "Anti-Bolshevism in French Foreign Policy: The Crisis in Poland in 1920," *International History Review*, 2 (July 1980), 410–31. For Beneš's anti-Polish views, see Kalvoda, *Czechoslovakia's Role*, 36–37.

6. The text of the little known letter of Piłsudski to Masaryk has been edited by Wandycz, "Listy Piłsudskiego," 108–10.

7. See Renouvin, "Origines," Ádám, "Confédération"; also see Magda Ádám, "France and Hungary at the Beginning of the 1920s," and Anne Orde, "France and Hungary in 1920: Revisionism and Railways," in Béla Király et al., eds., *War and Society in East Central Europe, 6: Essays on World War I, A Case Study of Trianon* (New York, 1982), 145–200.

8. See Lidia Buczma, "Z Genezy Małej Ententy," *SzD*, 6 (1970), 138–39; also Carmi, *La Grande Bretagne*, 30. For Polish thinking, see Tomaszewski, "Miejsce," 175; and Sapieha's circular in DiM, III, 410.

though some of the chiefs conceived its role very broadly and tried to intervene in the military-political life of the country.[9] French economic
penetration was seemingly connected with a grandiose plan, which existed
before the end of the war, of achieving control over key raw materials.
Partly designed to satisfy French needs, partly meant to deny these resources to potential enemies, this program also aimed to alleviate the existing disparity with Germany and serve as leverage against Berlin. Referring to East Central Europe, Premier Edouard Herriot expressly
recommended in 1924 that the "intervention of French capital not be left
to chance; I attach the utmost importance that it follow a concerted
plan."[10]

Thus, as Georges Soutou has argued convincingly, French economic
"imperialism" in this region was not a spontaneous expansion in which
financial and industrial goals shaped foreign policy, but rather the reverse.[11] Naturally, the government had to protect and satisfy the businessmen it had encouraged to enter this field; the latter in turn never hesitated
to pressure both France and the countries in which they operated, equating
their interests with patriotism.[12] With the possible exception of Eugène
Schneider, who sought to expand his East Central European empire in a
fairly consistent way, other companies were mostly interested in quick
profits, which were not intended for local reinvestment. Ruthless in their
dealings and arrogant in their behavior, they often made the Poles or the
Czechs believe in their power to affect France's foreign policies. Yet, their
omnipotence was doubtful, for even the steel industry "contrary to the
accepted myth, enjoyed little influence with the French government."[13]

The exact interdependence between economics and politics is not always easy to trace. Did Schneider's l'Union Européenne Industrielle et Fi-

9. For General Niessel's views, see Wandycz, "Colonel Beck," 121; and the detailed
treatment in Kukułka, *Francja*, 61–99.

10. Herriot to minister in Belgrade, 6 Dec. 1924, MAE, P.A. Massigli 4. Another note
affirmed that "the French business and financial policy abroad is sufficiently in the hands
of the state . . . to allow the government to direct this exportation . . . to the best political
interests of France" (MAE, Pologne 236:92–94).

11. Soutou "L'Impérialisme." See also Wurm, *Die französische Sicherheitspolitik*, 69–
100.

12. French financiers and industrialists kept reminding Paris that they were pursuing
the government's program of extending French influence in Central Europe and had
been drawn into these activities "on the express initiative" of the government. See correspondence in MAE, Tchécoslovaquie 79:113–15, and Pologne 214:129–34. When
Henry de Peyerimhoff accused the government of "lack of comprehension of economic
and financial realities," Poincaré's chef de cabinet commented ironically that these realities "seem to consist for M. de Peyerimhoff in allowing him to make good business (in
the Silesian mines) with the taxpayers' money." Cited in Soutou, "Mines," 152. Compare chapter 2 of Keeton, "Briand's Locarno Policy," Segal, "French State."

13. Schuker, *French Predominance*, 224.

nancière, which had large shares in Teschen metallurgy, support Czechoslovakia in its territorial dispute with Poland?[14] Soutou argues that this need not necessarily have been the case, because Schneider, having investments throughout the Teschen area, was more interested in unhindered circulation of coal and iron than in any specific frontier. Still, Beneš did intimate that in order to obtain French backing in Teschen, he had to make concessions with regard to a commercial treaty with France. So economic interests may have had an effect after all.[15]

One of the biggest achievements of French capital in Czechoslovakia involved gaining control over the Škoda concern, so as "to prevent this great arms factory" from falling "into enemy or even dubious hands."[16] In Poland, French economic penetration was affected by three considerations: interests of bankers and industrialists; the general policy of the government; and the exigencies of foreign policy. The dramatic increase in French investments in the Galician oil fields was seen in Paris as strengthening the hold over East European petroleum in order to assure French self-sufficiency, which "public opinion and the parliament so strongly insist on."[17] From Warsaw's perspective French investments were welcome as a guarantee of France's support for Poland's possession of the province, even though the price to be paid (high export quotas and privileges for the investors) appeared exorbitant.[18]

The case of Upper Silesia, whose fate was determined in 1921 by a plebiscite, provided a good example of interconnection between economics, diplomacy, and strategy. France wanted to deny this industrial basin to Germany and attribute it to Poland, but not without reaping its own economic advantages. The French industrialists found themselves wooed by their German counterparts, while Warsaw also made a desperate bid for France's support, offering extensive concessions.[19] The creation of a Société Fermière des Mines Fiscales de l'État Polonais (better known by the Polish abbreviation Skarboferm) to lease and administer the former Prussian state mines, and a subsequent establishment of a Franco-Polish bank did create a joint vested interest. But, if France stood by Poland during and

14. See Szklarska-Lohmannowa, *Stosunki*, 53.

15. Compare Soutou, "L'Impérialisme," 229; Campbell, *Confrontation*, 103; Gajan, "ČSR," 190–95.

16. Briand to Couget, 26 Feb. 1925, MAE, Tchécoslovaquie 84:201–202. See also Jíša and Vaněk, *Škodový závody*, and Teichová, *Economic Background*, esp. 56–62.

17. Cited in *Guerre polono-soviétique*, 79–80.

18. See Landau and Tomaszewski, *Gospodarka*, 1:315; Kukułka, *Francja*, 178, 186, 330; Soutou, "La Politique," 90.

19. In addition to Soutou, Landau and Tomaszewski, and Kukułka cited in n. 18 Przewłocki, *Stosunek mocarstw*, provides a rich literature on the subject.

after the plebiscite, the common economic establishment did not contribute in the long run toward cementing bonds between the two countries.[20]

The years 1921–24 saw the signing of formal alliances between France and Poland and also France and Czechoslovakia. In 1923–24 a serious attempt was made, in connection with Premier Raymond Poincaré's policy during the Ruhr crisis, to achieve a more integrated system through military coordination and a rapprochement between Poland and the Little Entente. In pursuing these plans French policymakers had to reckon with three facts of life. First, the Soviet-Polish peace treaty of Riga had traced the border farther to the east than Paris deemed justifiable, and although it recognized the frontier in 1923 France regarded it as a source of future complications. Second, the Little Entente treaties did restrict the French freedom of maneuver in the Danubian area. Third, despite continuous promptings, a Czechoslovak-Polish rapprochement appeared as elusive as ever, leaving a dangerous gap in the "system."

The Franco-Polish treaty, and particularly the secret military convention, resulted from Piłsudski's visit to Paris in February 1921. Although Marshal Ferdinand Foch and General Weygand objected to a military convention with a state not yet fully stabilized, and Berthelot was skeptical of commitments that would unduly increase foreign policy risks, President Alexandre Millerand, supported by the war minister Louis Barthou, overcame these objections on the ground that Poland would be a pivotal state in the nascent eastern barrier.

If the situation in Germany became a threat to peace, or in the event of German mobilization or German aggression, France and Poland agreed to reinforce preparations, to extend effective and quick aid, and to act in common accord. The signatories were to determine what constituted aggression and to decide on immediate military action. In case of a Soviet-Polish war, the French promised to send war material, maintain maritime lines of communications, and keep Germany in check. This promise fell short of Polish expectations, especially in case of a two-front war that involved both Germany and Russia (the so-called N plus R plan). Nor was Poland an equal partner; the diplomat Jules Laroche called Poland "une alliée de remplacement." The convention stipulated the length of Polish (but not French) military service and the size of the army. If Paris promised to extend armament credits worth four-hundred million francs, it also made the entire alliance operative on Warsaw's signature of several onerous economic accords.[21]

20. Soutou, "Mines," 146, 153–54.

21. For recent Polish treatment of the alliance, see Kazimiera Mazurowa, "Przymierze polsko-francuskie z roku 1921," *Najnowsze Dzieje Polski 1914–1939*, 11 (1967), 205–22; Ciałowicz, *Polsko-francuski sojusz*; and Cienciala and Komarnicki, *Versailles to Locarno*, 19–31. For French views, see Łaptos, "Dwa listy," and the detailed Bułhak,

With encouragement from France, the Poles proceeded to sign an alliance with Romania, accompanied by a military convention, on 3 March 1921. However, rapprochement with Czechoslovakia, which the French also encouraged, took several months. Prague's support for Poland during the Upper Silesian crisis contributed to the pro-Czechoslovak stand taken by Poland's new foreign minister, Konstanty Skirmunt, during ex-emperor Charles's attempts to regain the Hungarian crown. On 6 November 1921, the Beneš–Skirmunt pact, signed in Prague, brought the two countries closer together and even raised hopes for a military convention.[22] But an insignificant border dispute over Javorina, which Skirmunt hoped to see solved to his country's advantage and thus create a pro-Czechoslovak climate in Poland, caused the pact to fail.

A year later the question of French ties with East Central Europe became much affected by the overriding issue of an entente or even an alliance between France and Britain. Because London was unprepared to extend its security guarantee to France to include the eastern countries, Aristide Briand, then premier and foreign minister, may have been willing to subordinate the interests of France's friends to a Franco-British alignment. The delays in ratification of the Polish alliance seemed to indicate that Briand was none too eager to commit his country unreservedly to Poland.[23] Briand's dramatic resignation and replacement by Poincaré, however, changed the picture. Poincaré moved ahead with the ratification, and, although he went along with Prime Minister David Lloyd George's scheme of a conference on European reconstruction at Genoa which (included both Germany and Russia), he did his best to sabotage it.

The Genoa conference, which saw France, Poland, and the Little Entente present a common diplomatic front (even though Beneš still opposed Poland's entry into the Little Entente), proved a failure. The great event occurring on the margins of the conference at the neighboring Rapallo was the signing of a Russo-German pact on 16 April 1922. The treaty appeared a threat to Poland and the eastern barrier, indeed a challenge to the whole Versailles edifice. In France, the Left and Right clashed bitterly over foreign policy, supporting respectively collective security as embodied in the League of Nations and the more traditional alliances. The high command concentrated on working out common plans with eastern armies. In September 1922, the chief of the Polish general staff, General Władysław Sikorski, came to Paris, and Marshal Foch visited Czechoslovakia and Poland in May 1923. The second trip occurred following the dramatic

---

"Polsko-francuskie," and Bułhak, "La Pologne," 141–54. Also see Łaptos, *Francuska opinia*, 135–36.

22. See Szklarska-Lohmannowa, "Rokowania polsko-czechosłowackie w 1921 roku," *SzD*, 3 (1967), 187–206 and Valenta, "Vývojové tendence," 21.

23. Soutou, "L'Alliance," 297; compare Kukułka, *Francja*, 478.

French occupation of the Ruhr and witnessed not only an agreement on coordinated strategy against Germany, but also French proposals for a military alliance with Czechoslovakia.

In the course of the earlier discussions in Paris, the Poles argued that France assume the main burden of the war against Germany and quickly launch an offensive to relieve its allies. The French spoke of a thirty-day delay and outlined a plan of Polish-Czechoslovak offensive against Germany "in great style." Although during Foch's visit a general agreement was achieved, the Polish side insisted that Poland could not weaken unduly its position on the Russian front, in part because of commitments to Romania.[24] Foch's overtures to the Czechoslovak leaders were met with suggestions for exploring first a political accord. Masaryk and Beneš were critical of Poincaré's tough line toward Germany and condemned the Ruhr occupation. They were reluctant to identify too closely with France and especially with Poland. Yet, the international evolution was bringing Czechoslovakia closer to Paris, and after the visits of Masaryk and Beneš to the West negotiations gathered momentum.

The Franco-Czechoslovak Treaty of Alliance and Friendship, signed on 24 January 1924, contained no military convention; only secret letters exchanged between Beneš and Poincaré spoke of joint measures to counter aggression against either signatory by a common enemy. According to Prague's wishes, the treaty was essentially a political document providing for concerted action on foreign policy matters likely to threaten the security of the two partners or to undermine the European order. An exclusion of the Habsburgs and the prohibition of an Anschluss were specifically mentioned.[25]

The French viewed the pact with Prague as another step in the direction of a truly operative eastern barrier. The Quai d'Orsay spoke of the advantages of a "homogeneous organ" composed of the Little Entente and Poland. Poincaré seriously envisaged extending substantial financial aid to these states.[26] In February 1924, the war ministry recommended a joint session with the representatives of Polish, Czechoslovak, Romanian, and Yugoslav general staffs. Although a preliminary encounter with the Czechs, held in Prague, had already resulted in a protocol outlining the modalities of action in wartime,[27] attempts to develop a tripartite Franco-

24. See Bułhak, "Polsko-francuskie," 71–81, and "Rozmowy."

25. See Hartmann, "Ein Aspekt." The text of letters has now been printed in Wandycz, "L'Alliance."

26. See Soutou, "L'Alliance," 298–99; Wurm, *Die französische Sicherheitspolitik,* 27–30, 66, 81; and documentation in SHA, EMA/3, 7 N 3446/1 and 3, 7 N 3007. For a project of an accord between France, Poland, and the Little Entente, see MAE, Roumanie 64.

27. See especially Břach, "Francouzský."

Polish-Romanian military pact operating in case of the N plus R variant, as well as to bring French, Poles, and Czechoslovaks together to a conference table, proved impossible. It was obvious that Beneš wished to retain freedom of action vis-à-vis France while simultaneously retaining a special relationship to Paris. An integrated Polish–Little Entente alignment was likely to jeopardize both. "France can conduct its Little Entente policy through our intermediary," he asserted.[28]

The Czechoslovak foreign minister did not show much eagerness when told that France "greatly desired an intimate alliance" between Prague and Warsaw, and would do all possible to help in its realization.[29] The Poles appreciated the advantages of military cooperation with Czechoslovakia but had their own doubts about cooperation directed exclusively against Germany. They were annoyed at having been informed at a relatively late date of the Franco-Czechoslovak pact (which contained no reference to Polish military transit), and wished to ascertain how the pact would affect their obligations to France. The legal adviser at the Quai d'Orsay opined that Warsaw had in fact no "legal obligation" to come to France's aid if the latter went to war with Germany in the defense of Czechoslovakia. But it was imprudent to tell this to the Poles; one should rather insist that according to the French-Polish military convention a German mobilization represented a menace that would constitute the *casus foederis*.[30]

The intricate problem of interallied military collaboration was on the agenda of new talks with the chief of the Polish general staff, General Stanisław Haller, who came to Paris in early May 1924. The French acquainted him with the general nature of the Czechoslovak plan N (Germany), and agreed that in case of a two-front war a greater Polish and Romanian involvement against Germany would necessitate a considerable expansion of the Polish army. The four-hundred million credits would need to be activated fully.[31] Franco-Polish air force cooperation and the building of a harbor in Gdynia were subsequently discussed.

The Haller visit may have well represented the summit of French efforts to consolidate the eastern barrier. If Poincaré hoped that it would strengthen his hand in dealing with England and facilitate an entente, he was mistaken. The British labour government hated the very notion of

28. Břach, "Francouzský," 6; compare Gajanová, ČSR, 157.

29. See note, 18 October 1923, MAE, P.A. Millerand 56.

30. Comments by Laroche, 29 Feb. 1924, MAE, Tchécoslovaquie 42:51–53.

31. The first three installments were eventually scheduled for 1924, 1925, and 1926. See Ciałowicz, *Polsko-francuski sojusz*, 107. For the Haller talks, see Henryk Bułhak and Piotr Stawecki, "Rozmowy sztabowe polsko-francuskie w Paryżu (maj 1924)," *Przegląd Historyczny*, 66 (1976), 55–70; for the Czechoslovak angle, see Pułaski, *Stosunki*, 27.

sécurité, and the *New Leader* printed cartoons showing Poincaré feeding money to hungry vultures that bore the names of the French, Polish, Czechoslovak, and Romanian armies. Subjected to pressure of Anglo-American finance, the French government wavered. Under the slogan of "business not politics," the Dawes Plan was being born to regularize German reparations and open the gates for a flow of Western capital into Germany. Although Poincaré still hoped to maintain a connection between reparations and security, he was not destined to play the game to the end. Already during the Haller visit, the *cartel des gauches* won a resounding electoral victory. As a result, President Millerand was forced to resign and in June a leftist cabinet under Herriot was formed. A new period was beginning during which French external policy as a whole underwent a serious reorientation.

Herriot's concessions at the July 1924 London Conference related to the Ruhr, the reparations, and the Rhineland. They undermined the Versailles system and threatened French strategic interests. Paris still hoped, however, to achieve an entente with England through "internationalization of security," and in September Herriot launched, together with Prime Minister Ramsay MacDonald, the Geneva Protocol for the Pacific Settlement of International Disputes. A month later France officially recognized the Soviet Union; there was also renewed talk of Germany joining the League of Nations.

What impact did these actions have on the eastern alliances? Beneš, and the new Polish foreign minister, the anglophile Aleksander Skrzyński, cooperated at the League to make the Geneva Protocol a real guarantee of the status quo, and to implicate Britain in its defense. Simultaneously, they negotiated a series of Czechoslovak-Polish treaties. A danger appeared, however, that the Protocol would subordinate the working of the Franco-Polish alliance to the League; in fact, Herriot, who may have first heard of the 1921 convention upon assuming office, not only favored this approach but also wished to curtail French commitments to Poland.[32] Following a new round of interstaff talks in Warsaw, Poland's minister of war, General Sikorski, once again came to Paris to hold conversations between 5 October and 2 November. The main issue was naturally the convention. At the request of the Quai d'Orsay the French military prepared a revised version of the document, but it did not meet with the ministry's approval. The Quai d'Orsay really wished to remove all political provisions from the convention, making it just a technical agreement. Nothing was achieved, but it was a success on Sikorski's part to have gained the acceptance of a

32. See session, 15 Nov. 1924, SHA, CSDN 9, 71–89; compare Soutou, "L'Alliance," 300.

formula according to which the 1921 convention was legally binding until a new version was worked out.[33]

Sikorski's negotiations were affected not only by the defunct Geneva Protocol but also by the current plans for an Anglo-French-Belgian pact (possibly to be joined by Germany). Britain's foreign secretary, Sir Austen Chamberlain favored such a pact, but as previously East Central Europe constituted an obstacle. Hints were dropped that perhaps Poland could conclude a separate pact with Prague, and then the two groups could co-operate. Alarmed, Sikorski warned the Polish cabinet that a western pact would "force Germany to direct its main attack against Poland in war-time," and in peacetime "would facilitate, indeed incite Germany to act offensively against Poland while lessening friction with France." These were prophetic words.[34]

A western pact did not materialize, but on 5 February 1925, the German foreign minister Gustav Stresemann proposed a Rhineland security scheme that eventually became the Locarno pact. Only a few salient points of the negotiations that followed the German offer are noted here. Stresemann offered a reconfirmation of the territorial status quo along Germany's western but not eastern borders, with Britain and Italy acting as guaran-tors against a breach of peace. The scheme really implied a gradual dis-mantling of Versailles, especially in the east. To the British it represented a victory of their approach—"to remove a number of motives which might impel Germany to make war"—over the French system, which sought to secure that "German aggression should be met automatically by a superior army of allied Powers."[35] As for the eastern alignment, which Winston Churchill contemptuously called "a pack of small nations in leash of France," it was believed in London that, once a Rhine pact materialized, France "would gradually withdraw from or at least minimize her commit-ments to Poland," and Prague would be forced to draw closer to the Ger-man economic sphere.[36] The British had no objection to territorial revision in the east provided it was gradual and peaceful. The opinion voiced by Sir James Headlam-Morley the historical adviser at the Foreign Office that a new partition of Poland or a dismemberment of Czechoslovakia would throw all Europe into chaos, and that "even if we neglected to interfere to

33. See Ciałowicz, *Polsko-francuski sojusz*, 111–18, and Bułhak, "Rozmowy," and "Polsko-francuskie," 71–77.

34. Cited in Ciałowicz, *Polsko-francuski sojusz*, 118.

35. Retrospective memorandum by Owen O'Malley, 1 Dec. 1935, FO 371 200437 W 5075.

36. Churchill cited by Johnson, "Locarno Treaties," 110. The second quotation is in Schuker, *French Predominance*, 390.

prevent it happening, we should be driven to interfere, probably too late," was an isolated view.[37]

From the French viewpoint the Rhineland pact proposal did have several attractive features: prospects of economic cooperation with Germany, rapprochement with London, and the likelihood of German-Soviet estrangement. The price, namely a certain retrenchment in East Central Europe, did not appear too high. The French were hardly torn between loyalty to their allies and the need to cooperate with Germany, as has been sometimes asserted. Far from treating it as an agonizing choice, the Quai d'Orsay thought in terms of accommodating the former to the latter.[38] The existing idea of revising the alliance with Poland was now accompanied by the notion of using arbitration treaties in the east to eliminate the threat of an armed conflict there. If these goals were achieved, "our Polish and Czechoslovak alliances would be applicable only in circumstances that could hardly arise as long as Germany kept its engagements."[39] Both Chamberlain and Beneš believed that France would not stand in the way of a peaceful German revisionism in the east, and indeed many political leaders of the French Left thought that Poland should make some territorial sacrifices.

True, there were also strongly pro-Polish voices coming from Poincaré and some rightist and centrist quarters. French diplomacy sought to establish a link between the Stresemann scheme and the eastern alliances by proposing to guarantee German arbitration treaties with Poland and Czechoslovakia. Berlin, however, had no intention of allowing Paris to become a judge of what constituted German aggression, and in the last stages of the Locarno conference the French had to abandon this idea. They were also obliged to make another concession, namely to exempt Germany from the obligations arising out of article 16 (the sanctions clause) of the Covenant of the League of Nations. Berlin had argued that a disarmed Germany could not participate in sanctions; in fact, it sought to dispel Soviet fears of a Western conspiracy and maintain its bridges to Moscow. On 16 October 1925, simultaneously with initialing the Locarno pact together with Britain, Germany, Italy, Belgium, Poland, and Czechoslovakia (the last two signed only the arbitration accords and the final protocol), France concluded two identical mutual guarantee treaties with Warsaw and Prague.

French diplomacy sought to represent these two treaties, rather inaccurately, as part of the entire package. It also claimed that the Locarno pact

37. James Headlam-Morley memorandum of 11 March 1925 has been printed with minor stylistic changes in his *Studies in Diplomatic History* (New York, 1930), 171–72.

38. This view, expressed by Soutou, "L'Alliance," is borne out by existing evidence.

39. Note of direction politique, 26 Feb. 1925, MAE, Grande Bretagne 73:56–62; compare Wurm, *Die französische Sicherheitspolitik*, 252–55.

and all the negotiations that had preceded it had been in full agreement with Czechoslovakia and Poland. This statement was hardly exact. Skrzyński's conciliatory tactics resulted from his fear of Poland becoming isolated and from his concern lest the Polish alliance appear as a liability to France. General Sikorski pursued a harder line, accusing Paris of keeping Warsaw in the dark on occasion and of neglecting Poland's interest. This dual approach, at times embarrassing to Skrzyński, did not prove helpful, and the foreign minister's plea for a tripartite Franco-Polish-German (or even quadruple with the addition of Czechoslovakia) security treaty was unrealistic. A last-minute attempt by Skrzyński to include a statement in the German-Polish arbitration treaty banning war in all circumstances did not succeed.[40]

Throughout the period of negotiations, the Poles tried to strengthen their position through the creation of a common front with Czechoslovakia. When in April Beneš came to Warsaw to sign several treaties, the Polish government tried to convey the impression of full solidarity between the two states. In fact, Beneš did not intend to proceed to a military or even a political alliance with Poland. His attitude toward the proposed Rhineland pact was generally positive.[41] As the Czechoslovak envoy in Berlin noted, it was essential that Germany remain democratic, and this could only be achieved with the moral support of the rest of the world. A Franco-Czechoslovak-Polish bloc might contain Germany and even defeat it in war, but this would be a pyrrhic victory. A rapprochement with Berlin was desirable for Czechoslovakia not only on international grounds, but also because it could contribute to a domestic stabilization through a better understanding with the German minority.[42] Hence, Prague supported the line of the French diplomacy, a fact highly appreciated in Paris, while suggesting simultaneously that Czechoslovakia was not endangered by German revisionism and was in a different situation than Poland.

Looking back at the years that separate the Paris Peace Conference from Locarno, one sees that the French eastern "system" made relatively slow progress. The alliance with Poland was made operative only by 1922 and armament credits came even later. Czechoslovakia became involved only in 1924, at a moment when Paris pursued energetically the goal of a real political-military system. This heyday was indeed short-lived, and the reorientation of French diplomacy in 1924–25 represented a retreat also in

40. See Balcerak, *Polityka*, and, for the arbitration treaty, Krüger, "Schiedsvertrag." The Sikorski visit to London and his friction with Skrzyński is discussed in Ciałowicz, *Polsko-francuski sojusz*, 119–20; see Sikorski's biographers Kukiel, Korpalska, and Wapiński. See also Aleksander Skrzyński, "Istota i znaczenia paktu gwarancyjnego," *Bellona*, 18 (1925), 119–22.

41. See the most extensive review by Břach, "Locarno."

42. Unpublished article summarized in Krofta, *Z Dob*, 81–87.

the east. Officially, one could pretend that nothing had changed. Eastern alliances remained a useful element in the diplomatic game and even an object of military planning.[43] But their exact role in the changing international context and their impact on external relations of the three states did gradually alter. The chapters that follow seek to show how this occurred.

43. This chapter draws on my *France and her Eastern Allies 1919–1925* as affected by more recent documentation. Only the latter is cited in the footnotes.

Part One

Post-Locarno Diplomacy

Chapter One

The Shadow of Locarno

The Powers

The Locarno pacts were signed formally in London on 1 December 1925. These agreements, together with the Dawes Plan and the advent of the *Cartel des gauches*, marked a transition from the postwar division into victors and vanquished to an institutionalized concert of great powers presided over by Briand, Stresemann, and Chamberlain.

The policy of each of the three "locarnites," to use Chamberlain's expression, was based, of course, on different premises and corresponded to different domestic situations. To the British, Locarno was designed to "patch up the European concert and to allow Britain to concentrate upon domestic and imperial issues."[1] The Rhineland pact did not impose new obligations on London, which retained the right to decide what constituted a flagrant aggression in the west, or an unprovoked aggression in the east. The Foreign Office viewed the French eastern system as "an element not of security but of added apprehension and increased liability." Locarno, the British assumed, would enable France to limit its obligations in the east and eliminate some of the existing tensions. Another Foreign Office memorandum pointedly recalled, "as a matter of history," that "this country has never in the past taken up arms to resist the dismemberment of Poland." But, in an atmosphere of détente, "we hope to tempt both Germany and Poland to look to the West and resist whatever tempting offers Russia may make to break up the European family." If, the document concluded, "we can persuade France, Germany, Italy and Poland to continue to co-operate in giving effect to our Locarno policy, we shall have provided ourselves with the best and most effective protection against the common Russian danger."[2]

London knew that this would be no easy task. On occasion Chamber-

---

1. Kennedy, *Realities*, 269.

2. Respectively Foreign Office, Gregory and Tyrrell memoranda, 10 Jan., 10 April, 26 July 1926, DBFP, 1a, I:6, 857, II:177.

lain would fulminate against the "abominable" German behavior, and the Foreign Office speak of a gulf "which no bridge can span—between Anglo-Saxon and French mentality."[3] Nevertheless, the Locarno arrangements were seen as superior to the situation that had existed previously.

Seen from the perspective of Berlin, Locarno was the first step toward a recovery of freedom of action hampered by the occupation of the Rhineland (the "rope of the strangler," as Stresemann called it), disarmament, controls, and the French eastern alliances. By satisfying the French desire for security and economic cooperation, Berlin sought to create an atmosphere of conciliation that would be conducive to concessions in the fields of disarmament and revision.[4] These concessions were not seen as a reward for "good behavior" but as a logical sequel to Locarno. While the Rhineland evacuation was the first item on Germany's agenda, territorial revisionism in the east represented, in Stresemann's words, "not only the most important task of our policy but perhaps the most important task of European politics generally."[5] Poland, the principal target, was to be brought to its knees by relentless economic and political pressure, diplomatic isolation, and loss of credibility in Western eyes. Although the economic weapon was to prove ineffective after Poland's recovery in mid-1926, Germany fully exploited the national minority issue; the maintenance of a dissatisfied German minority in the contested areas became "a precondition for a satisfactory solution of the question of the Corridor and Upper Silesia."[6] Neither the German government nor the army was interested in minor border revisions that could jeopardize the goal of the recovery of the 1914 borders, a strategic more than an ethnic imperative.[7] As Staatssekretär Carl von Schubert put it, after being "reduced *politically* at Locarno," Poland ought to be "reduced *militarily*," for these were the two conditions for the final goal of territorial revisionism.[8]

This policy required some degree of German-Soviet collaboration to keep the Poles off balance. Stresemann did not intend to abandon Rapallo, although reconciling it with the Rhineland pact was no easy matter. Stalin condemned Locarno and, despite his desires to maintain a good working

3. Gregory memorandum, 10 April 1926, DBFP, 1a, 1:857.

4. On the change of German position see Krüger, "Politique extérieure," 274–76. For general treatment, Krüger, *Aussenpolitik*, esp. 505. For the argument that France should be given a "binding security against a German revenge," see Gasiorowski, "Stresemann," 303–304.

5. Cited in Höltje, *Weimarer Republik*, 254.

6. Norbert Krekeler, *Revisionsanspruch und Geheime Ostpolitik der Weimarer Republik: die Subventionierung der deutschen Minderheit in Poland 1919–1933* (Stuttgart, 1973), 113.

7. Post, *Weimar Foreign Policy*, 23.

8. Schubert's memorandum cited in Gasiorowski, "Stresemann," 294–95.

relationship with Berlin, had no intention of giving up a policy of exploiting the contradictions between the capitalist states. Berlin's goals in Central Europe were less clearly defined than those vis-à-vis Poland. Stresemann considered it useful for the Germans to speak loudly about an Anschluss, but it is doubtful that he treated this issue as a concrete task of German diplomacy. The thought of revising Czechoslovak borders was not seriously entertained in Berlin, and the role of the so-called Sudeten Germans was to assist in bringing Czechoslovakia into the German orbit rather than to work for its destruction.

Stresemann's insistence on peaceful change stemmed from Germany's inability to use force, not from pacifist inclinations. In 1924 he said that "in the last resort . . . great questions are always resolved by the sword." Nor did he exclude warlike measures altogether when speaking shortly after Locarno about the eastern territorial settlement.[9] By being a "good European" he meant pursuing his objectives within the framework of European politics rather than through unilateral actions. His program for the next two years, as he told the French ambassador in late 1925, included gaining France's consent to the evacuation of the Rhineland, an agreement with Belgium to recover Eupen and Malmédy, and the return of some former colonies. The Polish "corridor," he hoped, would "in the long run be settled amicably without depriving Poland of access to the sea," perhaps by compensating the Poles with Memel (Klaipeda) for the loss of Danzig. He asked, however, that the French not repeat this plan to Skrzyński.[10]

The Quai d'Orsay commented that Stresemann's program "revealed an audacity and a fertility of imagination that are well known and disquieting." He had already been warned that to raise such issues meant contradicting the terms of Locarno based on the respect of treaties.[11] The French government was particularly worried of possible effects that such views might have on the public, which desperately wanted to be reassured. Indeed, the mood of France was one of disenchantment mixed with illusions. Paris was still the cultural and artistic capital of the world. At the time of the signing of Locarno, some sixteen million people had passed through the International Exposition des arts décoratifs. Yet, not all the lights were burning in the Ville Lumière. Some leading writers, such as Romain Rol-

9. Cited in Turner, "Continuity," 514; also see his "Eine Rede Stresemanns." Compare Maxelon, *Stresemann*, 31; also Rheinbaben's remarks in Helmuth Rössler, ed., *Locarno und die Weltpolitik 1924–1932* (Göttingen, 1969), 47–51.

10. Laboulaye to Briand, 28 Nov. 1925, MAE, Grande Bretagne 87:188–91. The Danzig-Memel exchange was mentioned by Berthelot already in May 1925. See Patricia Gajda, *Postscript to Victory: British Policy and the German-Polish Borderlands, 1919–1925* (Washington, D.C., 1982), 205–206. Skrzyński heard about it as did the Polish ministry of finance. See Rataj, *Pamiętniki*, 310–11, and Landau and Tomaszewski, *Kapitały*, 91–93.

11. Briand to missions, 29 Nov. 1925, MAE, Grande Bretagne 87:211–12.

land and Henri Barbusse, horrified by the consequences of the war, turned to pacifism. Others voiced fears of the threat posed to traditional European values by American mass civilization. A spokesman of the bourgeoisie, Lucien Romier, wrote about the end of liberalism, extolling the virtues of nationalism and national egoism. Others saw communism as the panacea. The writers of the Royalist right, Charles Maurras and Jacques Bainville, fulminating against the inflation that they associated with the *cartel*, spoke of "collective theft." A fascist dissident from L'Action Française, Georges Valois, called dramatically in his pamphlet: "Bolshevism? Frenchmen you must choose!"[12]

France was strong because of its political prestige and the army, but these two power factors lasted only as along as they were truly maintained. The army, as the war minister admitted, was "in a state of *malaise*."[13] Dominated by generals steeped in the 1914–18 tradition who were still too young to retire, the officers' corps suffered from a slowness of promotion, inadequate pay, and cavalier treatment from a parliament ever suspicious of the military. The army had to accept an eighteen-month military service in 1923, and anticipate a further reduction to one year. Faced with cuts in personnel, the army demanded a new organization. The great issue was the adequate protection of borders, which had been ardently debated since 1920. At a special commission, transformed in December 1925 into a Commission de Défense des Frontières, Marshal Philippe Pétain and his collaborators emphasized security of French soil against an attack "brusquée," and advocated a continuous front strengthened by fortifications. Marshal Foch and General Marie-Eugène Debeney by contrast stressed the final objective—winning the war—rather than a strategy of repelling the enemy. A continuous line of fortified defenses seemed not only expensive but demoralizing for the troops.

Both sides were concerned with reducing casualties and concentrating the means of battle; they foresaw a war of movement intervening only during a second phase of operations. Whereas the mobilization plan A (January 1924 to June 1926) spoke of an "offensive solution," plan A-*bis* departed from the notion of concentration on the Rhine, and slowly abandoned the concept of a "firm and immediate" offensive.[14] General Charles Nollet was conscious of a "public opinion current that is little favorable

12. See Chastenet, *Histoire*, 5:146; La Gorce, *French Army*, 185–89. Valois's foreign policy program was summarized by Chłapowski in a dispatch, 30 Oct. 1926, AAN, MSZ 3789.

13. General Nollet on 30 Mar. 1925, SHA, CSG 50:36–52.

14. Tournoux, *Haut Commandement*, 335. This section draws heavily on Tournoux as well as on La Gorce, *French Army*, Keeton, "Briand's Locarno Policy," Hughes, *Maginot Line*. Already in 1921 Pétain had eliminated from army manuals the phrase that "only an offensive makes possible decisive results." Cited in Feller, *Le Dossier*, 186.

to the actual military system." Foch felt that it would be imprudent to speak of "mobilization" and "couverture" at a time when "pacifism was reigning." By talking too much about preparedness, one ran the risk of being regarded a militarist.[15] Indeed, the mentality of the army chiefs closely resembled that of the French bourgeoisie.

Military and political problems were, of course, inextricably linked with the economic situation of the country. War and reconstruction, accompanied by the declining value of the franc, provided a stimulus to production. Inflation stimulated the home market, the rising prices encouraged spending, but the modernization of industries was uneven as was the general growth of the economy. The greatly increased output of metallurgical and engineering industries enriched the entrepreneurial class but revealed an acute problem of dependence on foreign raw materials and markets. The metallurgists badly needed cartel agreements with their main partners and competitors, the Germans. Small producers, farmers, artisans, shopkeepers, and dealers felt ever more insecure as the economy modernized unequally and further industrialization took place. Inherent contradictions within the French economy were reflected in the society as a whole. The middle class was more frightened by inflation, the fall of the franc, and budgetary chaos than it was encouraged by favorable indices of industrial revival.[16]

Financial recovery was impeded by budgetary calculations that included the uncollected reparations and affected by expenses incurred during the Ruhr venture. In the absence of a tax increase, on which the parliament could not agree, the government relied on short-term bonds and a low level of currency in circulation. The year 1926 opened with a large budget deficit; advances from the Banque de France during the previous year had attained a dramatic figure of thirty-six milliards. As the franc continued to plummet—from 104 francs to a pound in December 1925 to 243 in July 1926—it seemed that only a substantial loan could resolve the situation. But as real as the financial difficulties were, one must stress the "paralysis of will and decision which gripped the ruling class as a whole."[17] The result was political instability. In November 1925, the socialists, unable to agree with the radicals on financial measures, left the government. A new cabinet of Briand fell in March 1926, and again in mid-June. Reconstituted as the

15. Nollet, 30 Mar. 1925 and Foch, 15 Jan. 1926, SHA, CSG 50:36–52, 122–42.

16. This section is based largely on Kemp, *French Economy*, and François Caron, *The Economic History of Modern France* (New York, 1978), and draws on Schuker, *French Predominance*, and Walter A. McDougall, *France's Rhineland Diplomacy 1914–1924* (Princeton, 1977). The standard work is, of course, the very detailed Sauvy, *Histoire économique*.

17. Kemp, *French Economy*, 84.

Briand-Caillaux ministry—Joseph Caillaux was in charge of finances—it sought to solve the financial difficulties through foreign policy schemes.

Much of the Right—its preferences for alliances and skepticism about the League notwithstanding—favored a rapprochement with Germany for material reasons, and those persistently opposed to Germany, such as Louis Marin, found themselves in a minority. Heavy industry badly needed an "economic Locarno," and politicians with industrial connections, including André François-Poncet and Pierre-Etienne Flandin, favored closer ties with Berlin. To the French Right, peace and détente was not only attractive because war carried with it the danger of revolution, but also because it meant lower military expenditures. One could see a rupture developing between the satisfied bourgeoisie and the army "that continued to harbor [anti-German] rancors which the rest of the nation had abandoned."[18]

The appeal of Locarno was strong for the peasant masses whose losses during the war had been disproportionately high, and to the socialist proletariat to whom international collaboration was a party creed. For workers in the metallurgical industries, expanded production removed the fear of unemployment. Good commercial relations with Germany, regularized by the 19 February 1926 treaty, were popular with the winegrowers of southern France, the backbone of the radical party, who successfully applied pressure to have their interests satisfied.

Briand had correctly gauged the mood of the country. Appealing with incomparable skill to different elements of the electorate, he succeeded in making his policy appear the best solution for France and Europe. He was the first to admit that the work accomplished at Locarno was, as all human efforts, imperfect,[19] but as he developed his arguments, using occasional half-truths or logic twisted to suit his purpose, the effect was overwhelming. Briandism became an outlook, a mood, nay a *Weltanschauung*.

Briand himself was a pragmatist who had moved from the Left toward the Right, and then swerved again more to the Left. He relied heavily on his powers of persuasion, although he might have "overestimated the effects of his skill as a conciliator."[20] His inner thoughts remain inaccessible, for he did not share them with others and left very little on paper; hence, there is room for controversy.

Briand believed that his country's weakness precluded a bold and risky policy. After a new war, he said, France would be a "poor and a disappearing nation." He saw no alternative to the Locarno policy, which had prevented the danger of a German-Soviet alignment, associated Britain in

18. La Gorce, *French Army*, 190–91.

19. 4 June 1926, J.O. Sénat, 1135.

20. Néré, *Foreign Policy*, 92.

the defense of France ("the Rhine has become an international frontier"), encouraged German democracy, and nurtured the new spirit of international relations.[21] Locarno was not the achievement of security, as the British viewed it, but the beginning of efforts to organize it. France could not be expected to bear all its costs: "One had not reached that degree of abnegation," Briand declared, "that means giving everything and receiving nothing."[22] Ready to bargain, the French foreign minister believed that France could further its aims through a friendly dialogue that would dull and emasculate German revisionist ardor. Time seemed essential to create a peaceful atmosphere and to give France a chance to recover from its difficult economic situation.

The French government and public opinion regarded the eastern aspects of the Locarno agreement as an integral part of the whole edifice. But the nagging question whether Locarno increased or weakened the security of the smaller allies remained very much alive. Publicly, Briand insisted that Prague and Warsaw profited by gaining the arbitration agreements, and he implied that Germany had engaged itself "to respect all the frontiers and not to undertake any act of force." He insisted that everything at Locarno had been done "in perfect agreement on all the points" with the Poles and the Czechoslovaks. "We lost none of our friendships," he asserted, "on the contrary they are strengthened."[23] Privately, Briand thought that the position of the two states was "the same after Locarno as before it;" neither better nor worse.[24] Taking this line, the French ambassador in Warsaw tried to persuade the Poles that the imbalance between the western and eastern state of affairs was not the result of Locarno; its roots were in the postwar settlement.[25] The asymmetry was, of course, not to be denied, and the Belgian foreign minister publicly said that one could not "close one's eyes on the difference which exists between the Rhine pact" and what the Poles called "a second-class guarantee."[26] Georges Bonnet, at Quai d'Orsay in 1938–39, went further when he wrote retrospectively that Locarno assumed a revision of the eastern borders, and "necessary sacrifices by Poland and Czechoslovakia to facilitate Germany's return to the European community." Briand allegedly thought he

21. Briand on 26 Feb., J.O. Chambre, 1017ff. and 4 June 1926, J.O. Sénat, 1135–39; 19 Jan. 1927, CAE/Ch; also Suarez, *Briand*, 6:136–43.

22. 23 Nov. 1926, CAE/Ch; also Paul-Boncour to Briand, 10 Dec. 1925 in Vaïsse, *Sécurité d'abord*, 21.

23. 4 June 1926, J.O. Sénat, 1138–39; compare 8 Nov. 1929, Suarez, *Briand*, 6:312; 1 Mar. 1926, J.O. Chambre, 1091–92.

24. See Bonnet, *Quai d'Orsay*, 91.

25. Laroche to Briand, 22 Jan. 1927, MAE, Pologne 136:1–4.

26. Vandervelde, 17 Nov. 1925, cited in MAE, Grande Bretagne 87:33.

could accomplish these goals through his adroitness, eloquence, and the prestige he enjoyed.[27]

What exactly was the effect of the French guarantee treaties with Poland and Czechoslovakia, signed in Locarno, on the relationship between Paris and its two allies? Briand explained to the cabinet that the treaty with Poland imposed no new obligations. In fact, France was not obliged to extend aid except in case of a common action under the auspices of the League. "We will march only if everybody marches with us."[28] According to the Quai d'Orsay, the aid to Poland depended on the decision of the Council, but it was less certain whether France had to await a recommendation (under article 16) before it could take any steps. If there was no unanimity (article 15, al.7) the French "reserved the right to act," although in practice "our attitude will be determined by consideration of immediate policy" and not the restraints (*ligotage*) of Locarno.[29] The Quai d'Orsay warned, however, that "it would be dangerous if one allowed this idea [that Locarno could block any independent French action] to take root, and if the silence of the press favorable to the government permitted Prague and Warsaw to think that this thesis is admitted here without being contested."[30]

Such a thesis was indeed developed by Pertinax in a series of articles that the ministry called "the most complete effort at a systematically hostile criticism." The noted journalist publicly assailed Locarno; privately he said that it meant war within ten years.[31] But, as a major debate in the chambers showed, the critics were a small minority. Some rightists spoke disparagingly of a pact that made Britain the arbiter of French destinies. Others, however, while admitting that Locarno brought no new guarantees to France, extolled its spirit and welcomed the chance to try a new approach in international relations. Millerand reflected the views of many when he said: "What we ask of Germany is not to abdicate, but to agree to follow its destinies within the framework of the new Europe as it had emerged from the great war."[32] Some centrist voices approving of Locarno

---

27. Bonnet, *Quai d'Orsay*, 114–15.

28. Bonnet, *Quai d'Orsay*, 88.

29. Laroche believed that France could act immediately, whereas Massigli opined that it had to await the decision of the League Council. Compare Briand's remarks, 19 Jan. 1927, CAE/Ch; 4 June, J.O. Sénat, 1139, 1 Mar. 1926, J.O. Chambre, 1092; Suarez, Briand, 6:137–38. Also compare second session, 15 Dec. 1925, J.O. Chambre, annex to procès-verbal, project of the law.

30. Note for Briand, 3 Feb. 1926, MAE, Grande Bretagne 88:180–93.

31. Phipps to Tyrrell, 28 Jan. 1926, FO 371 11270 C/330. Pertinax's articles in *L'Echo de Paris* appeared on 22, 30, 31 Jan. and 1 Feb. 1926.

32. 3 June 1926, J.O. Sénat, 1121. Millerand echoed Pertinax's point that Locarno would prevent Franco-British staff cooperation. Jacobson, *Locarno Diplomacy*, 35,

called for vigilance, and warned against illusions about German intentions.[33]

Several speakers brought up the disparity between provisions of the Rhine pact and arrangements in the east. The rapporteur, Joseph Paul-Boncour, a prominent socialist, admitted that although arbitration treaties with Germany had improved the position of France's allies, two incontestable weaknesses remained: German nonrecognition of eastern borders, and the difficulty of determining aggression in the absence of a demilitarized zone in the east. Recalling how Prussia's victory over Austria in 1866 had led to victory over France in 1870—"I refuse to forget that Sadova had preceded Sedan"—he stressed that security was indivisible.[34] One of the rightist deputies deplored that "our natural allies, Poland and Czechoslovakia," particularly exposed to danger, should be "deprived of the strongest guarantees"; another, fearing lest France lose the advantages derived from the alliances, called for an eastern Locarno, a demand echoed in the senate by an appeal that "France must have a policy on the Danube as well as a policy on the Rhine."[35] Millerand, in the speech previously mentioned, remarked on a basic contradiction between the French desire that the states of East Central Europe enjoy the benefit of article 10 of the Covenant (on territorial integrity), and the German revisionist goal.

The harshest criticism came from the maverick radical Henry Franklin-Bouillon and a leader of the rightist Union Républicaine Démocratique, Louis Marin. The latter called Briand's Locarno course "a complete change of policy" that could bring no advantages to France. When challenged by Briand to indicate an alternative, Marin spoke of alliances with Italy, Belgium, and the East European states. After an argument whether a real alliance system was feasible, Marin sounded a warning: "The day when the Germans will demand at the League of Nations a rectification of the frontiers of Silesia, the day when they will make a plebiscite in Austria to attach it to Germany . . . all this, gentlemen, will be a logical consequence of the [Locarno] pact."[36]

Still, the chamber ratified Locarno, 413 to 71 (plus some 60 absten-

---

tends to agree; the Quai d'Orsay note and Keeton argue that British help would in any case be ineffective assuming an "attaque brusquée," which was the main French concern.

33. A. Maginot, Jean Fabry, Paul Simon, 2 Mar. 1926 session, J.O. Chambre, 1135–37, 1139–40.

34. 25 Feb. 1926, J.O. Chambre, 964.

35. Louis Madelin, 2 Mar. and Marcel Plaisant, 26 Feb. 1926, J.O. Chambre, 1140, 1011–12; Chênebenoit, 4 June 1926, J.O. Sénat, 1135.

36. J.O. Chambre, 1083. The speech lasted from the 27 Feb. to 1 March session, 1041–62, 1075–86. Marin had been the founder in 1921 of the parliamentary club Les Amis de la Pologne from which the leftists departed in 1923. In 1925 they were instrumental in creating the Groupe parlementaire franco-polonais. See Ponty, "L'Attitude," 86–87.

tions), and in the senate only 6 votes were cast against it. In addition to some rightist and centrist deputies, the opponents comprised the communists who viewed Locarno as an anti-Soviet conspiracy.

The foreign ministry staff stood behind Briand. Indeed, right after the signing of the Locarno agreements, Jules Laroche spoke of a "euphoria" at the Quai d'Orsay. Berthelot began, however, to develop second thoughts, and differences of opinion between him and the minister became more noticeable.[37] There were also misgivings in high army quarters. General Charles Dupont of the military mission in Poland thought that at least Locarno enabled the Poles to enter the concert of the great powers. Others worried about the day when France would evacuate the Rhineland. "Locarno causes us to abandon a possible battlefield outside our borders," stated a member of the army commission.[38]

A French journalist and a Polish journalist submitted a questionnaire to a number of prominent scholars, writers, journalists, and members of parliament. The questions were: Did the spirit of Locarno conform to the existing international engagements? Was there evidence of a real progress in moral disarmament in Germany? Did Locarno offer new guarantees of legitimate states rights, or did it provide possibilities of pressure against certain states? Did it consolidate the Franco-Polish alliance? What could one expect of Locarno for French prestige in Central Europe?

The answers ranged from consistently positive (those given by a leftist deputy, Eugène Frot) to negative (those provided by Paul Lévy, the director of *Aux Ecoutes*). The journalist Jules Sauerwein was optimistic on virtually every count, whereas the writer Georges Bienaimé hoped that the Franco-Polish alliance would show its mettle at the first test, restoring to France the prestige it had "lost on the shores of Locarno." Saint-Brice of *Journal* called the spirit of Locarno one of "lassitude," which destroyed the alliance in practice. Louis Marin saw it "being realized at the expense of France and Poland." If moderately optimistic phrases predominated, there were enough notes of resignation and pessimism not to be lost on the Poles. The opinion of the rightist deputy Edouard Soulier that whereas in the past France and its allies were "masters of peace," Paris had now brought closer the day when Germany and Austria would unify and German-Russian pressures bear on Poland and Czechoslovakia, could not but sound disquieting to Poles and Czechs alike.[39]

37. See Laroche, *Au Quai d'Orsay*, 226. Compare Challener, "French Foreign Office," 83–84.

38. Edouard Soulier cited in Wurm, *Die französische Sicherheitspolitik*, 354; Col. Kleebeerg report cited in Ciałowicz, *Polsko-francuski sojusz*, 147–49. Also end of year report, 1925, SHA, EMA/2, Pologne 10.

39. Montfort and Piasecki, *La France*. An earlier survey can be found in Casimir Smogorzewski, *La Politique polonaise de la France* (Paris, 1926).

The Eastern Allies

Locarno did not represent a direct threat to Czechoslovakia; however, a combination of domestic and foreign developments contributed to a serious weakening of that country's position toward the end of 1925 and the beginning of 1926. The political stability of the Czechoslovak republic rested on two main pillars: the presidential *Hrad* (castle) and the governmental coalition system. The former operated on the basis of Masaryk's great prestige and his far-reaching influence. The latter was a quasi-permanent cooperation arrangement among the leaders of the main political parties, that depended on the partnership between the social democrats and the agrarians. The financial-industrial establishment assisted in the stabilization of the system.[40] The mid-November 1925 elections undermined this balance. The agrarian party was the winner at the polls, but although its leader, Antonín Švehla, was cooperating loyally with the Hrad, the agrarians were emancipating themselves from Masaryk's influence. The centrist Catholic people's party gained votes, while the social democrats, traditionally close to the Hrad, suffered a heavy defeat. The election not only hurt the Masaryk group but necessitated a rapprochement between the social democrats and the German socialists, permitting the latter's rise to power. It was clear that the Germans would have to be considered seriously as political associates.

The "all national" cabinet formed by Švehla, and ranging from national democrats to social democrats, was a shaky combination. The premier's opening speech was interrupted by hecklers and the singing of "Deutschland über Alles." In the government the agrarians sought protective duties on agricultural imports, and the populists demanded higher compensation to the clergy; both demands were bound to antagonize the remaining partners. The Švehla cabinet lasted only till mid-March 1926, and Masaryk had to appoint an interim "ministry of officials" headed by Jan Černý. The atmosphere of political strife, enhanced by economic difficulties contributed to communist and fascist manifestations; there were rumors of an impending *putsch*. Beneš was accused of subservience to the great powers and the League of Nations. The extreme Right equaled his policies with cosmopolitanism, parading its antagonism toward Freemasons and Jews.[41]

Long-forseen changes in the army command acquired a political signif-

---

40. See Mencl and Menclová, "Načrt podstaty," and several studies edited by Karl Bosl. For a comparison with Poland, see Wandycz, "Pierwsza Republika."

41. See Olivová, *Doomed Democracy*, 157–59; Gajanová, *Dvojí*, 45–46; Campbell, *Confrontation*, 165–68; Brügel, *Tschechen*, 179–80; César and Černý, *Politika*, 1:319–58.

icance. The transformation of the French military mission into a counseling organ took place on 1 January 1926. General Eugène Mittelhauser officially resigned as chief of staff and returned to France "disappointed and tired." A small mission headed by Colonel (Czechoslovak general) Louis-Eugène Faucher and directly dependent on the minister of national defense henceforth dealt with military instruction and proferred advice.[42] As Paris noted, the transformation took place "under the pressure of a movement of [Czech] opinion which seems to have been accelerated by the recent elections." Had one tried to prolong the former regime, it would have antagonized the Czechoslovak generals.[43] The French trusted Mittelhauser's successor, General Jan Syrový, but not his deputy, General Rudolf (Radola) Gajda, seen as an adventurer who at this point began to act as a protector of the Czechoslovak fascists. Jiří Stříbrný, the defense minister and Beneš's rival for leadership in the national socialist party, had made Mittelhauser's position very uncomfortable and was making pronouncements at odds with the pacific line of the foreign minister.[44]

If in late October, as the British envoy reported, there was universal enthusiasm in Czechoslovakia over Locarno,[45] the mood quickly changed. There was dissatisfaction that Beneš had delayed presenting the results of the Locarno conference to the parliament until mid-February 1926, and when the speech was given it was rudely interrupted. The communist leader Bohumír Šmeral responded to a remark about "our alliance with France [being] strengthened" with an onslaught on Czechoslovak diplomacy. It had formerly been a servant of France, he said, and was now one of England. A German deputy contemptuously declared that Locarno simply resulted from the fact that France could no longer oppress one hundred million Germans; Beneš, "the most faithful lackey of France," had to follow suit.[46]

The periodical *Přítomnost*, which stood close to the Hrad, criticized on 18 February 1926 the "si vis pacem para bellum" (if you want peace, prepare for war) approach displayed by national democrats, and extolled the spirit of Locarno. The organ of the foreign ministry and national socialist

42. See Břachová, "Francouzská vojenská mise" and Mareš, "La Faillite." General Joseph Le Blévec remained the commander of the higher military college in Prague. See reports of Mittelhauser, 28 Nov. 1925 and statute of the mission in MAE, SHA, EMA/2, Tchécoslovaquie and MAE, Tchécoslovaquie 22:178–79 and 183.

43. Quai d'Orsay–Couget correspondence, 28 Nov., 14 Dec. 1925, MAE, Tchécoslovaquie 22:173, 176–77.

44. See Zorach, "Gajda Affair"; also Dodd and Clerk to Chamberlain, 25 Jan., 17 Mar. 1926, FO 371 11230 C1259 and 3651.

45. Clerk to Chamberlain, 21 Oct. 1925, DBFP, 1a, 1:36–40.

46. See debates, 6 Oct., 18 Dec. 1925, 16, 19 Feb. 1926, Těsnopisecké zprávy, poslanecká sněmovna, sessions 371:1327–28; 3:36–37; 9:338; 10:433, and senat, 21 Apr., sixteenth session, 26.

papers discussed at length the Franco-Czechoslovak guarantee treaty—more precise than the 1924 alliance—and the arbitration convention with Germany. They concluded that Czechoslovak security was strengthened, and the alliance with France "super-guaranteed" by the signatories of the Rhine pact. They argued that France did not need anyone's consent—not even of the League Council—to bring aid to Czechoslovakia.[47] This assertion was dubious if we think of the views prevailing in Paris. It seemed incontestable that the Locarno concert of powers diminished the importance of Czechoslovakia, which had previously been able to maneuver between the powers. Beneš spoke of a "Central European Locarno" that would strengthen regional security with the participation of Hungary and Austria, a rapprochement with Russia, and good relations with Poland, but these were not easy goals to attain.

The idea of a Central European pact had been raised in Anglo-French talks in December 1925, and Chamberlain favored the scheme. Beneš told him that Poles and Yugoslavs were interested, the Romanians somewhat reserved, and the Hungarians needed to be exposed to a joint Franco-British pressure.[48] Rome, however, also needed to be convinced, and this was a much bigger problem, for Benito Mussolini had his own ideas about arrangements in the Danubian and Balkan areas. The French were treading cautiously. Delaying their already-initialed treaty with Yugoslavia, they played with the idea of a tripartite Franco-Italian-Yugoslav pact. Unwilling to be too harsh on Hungary, then embroiled in the forged francs affair, Paris simultaneously tried to cultivate Romania. The Little Entente, which met in Timişoara on 10 February 1926 advocated a firmer line vis-à-vis Hungary, but had to approve the ongoing talks between France, Italy, Yugoslavia, and Romania.[49]

With opposition to the Anschluss providing the only common ground between Paris, Rome, and Prague, Mussolini, ever suspicious of French activity in the Danubian region, rejected the tripartite pact. In this atmosphere of general mistrust, the chances of a Central European Locarno looked dim. A policy of rapprochement with Russia proved equally unsuccessful. The Timişoara meeting only acknowledged the right of each member of the Little Entente to pursue its own Russian policy. Beneš's own approaches to Moscow were based on the assumption that Russia, isolated after the German-Western reconciliation, would be willing to make far-reaching economic concessions in return for recognition. Apart from other considerations, Beneš needed those concessions to appease the Czech Right, which remained steadfastly opposed to a de jure recognition of the Soviet Union. But Moscow was not willing to pay a high price, and the

47. See *Zahraniční Politika*, 1925, 1353–55; *České Slovo*, 6 Jan. 1926.

48. Fleuriau to Briand, 4 Dec. 1925, MAE, Tchécoslovaquie 43:25–28.

49. Beneš's circular, 14 Feb. 1926, DaM, II, 243.

question of recognition was "adjourned sine die."[50] *Přitomnost* tried to minimize this diplomatic defeat by writing on 11 February that because Czechoslovak-Soviet relations functioned so well in practice, a formal recognition would make little difference.

These comforting remarks notwithstanding, the Czechoslovak government became increasingly aware that the country found itself "in a blind alley."[51] One could still play the Polish card, but this was by no means simple. In many respects Poland was worse off than its southern neighbor. The parliamentary regime, functioning under the 1921 constitution, modeled on that of France, exhibited all the weaknesses of a system that was not corrected, as in Czechoslovakia, by extra constitutional devices or a well-entrenched bureaucratic apparatus of the Third Republic. The Right and the Left found common language only at certain moments of crisis, and the vacillating Center did not serve as a balancer. A drastic transformation of a system in which the parliament was too powerful, the executive too weak, and factional strife bitter appeared necessary to many Poles. But the remedies proposed by the Right differed sharply from those advocated by the Left.

Structural weaknesses of the constitution were deepened by the growing dissatisfaction of the sizable national minorities and aggravated by economic difficulties that included rampant inflation and a tariff war with Germany. Berlin skillfully propagated an image of Poland as incapable of recovery except through massive foreign loans and claimed that such loans should be conditional on territorial revision. To cope with this critical situation a broad coalition ranging from national democrats to socialists emerged on 20 November 1925 under the premiership of Skrzyński, who retained the portfolio of foreign affairs. Because the parties continued to pursue divergent policies, the cabinet was hardly more than a palliative. Skrzyński's lack of membership made him almost an outsider in his own ministry.

The existing problems were dramatized by Piłsudski's stand. In his self-imposed exile, the marshal remained a towering figure. Treating attacks on him as assaults on the "moral interests of the army," he fulminated against constitutional arrangements that subordinated the army to unstable parliamentary controls. Some of his objections to the relationship between the government and the high command were justified.[52] But he went

50. See Couget-Quai d'Orsay exchanges, 13, 15 Feb. 1926, MAE, Tchécoslovaquie 64:99–100, Herman and Sládek, *Slovanská politika*, 63–67; also *Přehled dějin československo-sovětských vztahů*, 162–66.

51. Olivová, *Doomed Democracy*, 149. Compare Světlana Kalašniková, *Otázka uznání SSSR de iure v politice Československa v letech 1924–1926* (Praha, 1983), 111–13.

52. Ambassador Noulens opined in a lecture on 6 Dec. 1926 that the existing arrange-

farther in condemning the abuses of the parliamentary regime (*sejmo-cracy*), denouncing political parties, and calling for a "moral regeneration." The Left still saw Piłsudski as its one-time comrade; to the former legionnaires he was the only possible savior of Poland. In November 1925 a group of high-ranking officers visited Piłsudski in his Sulejówek home, and their spokesman in a belligerent speech placed the army's sabres at the marshal's disposal. By the end of the year, the French who carefully watched Piłsudski's rising star reported from Warsaw that he was already "the master of the situation."[53]

These circumstances made it difficult for Skrzyński to gain the acceptance of the Locarno policy by the government, army, parliament, and public opinion. The socialists, who for ideological reasons stood for the League of Nations, pacific settlement of disputes, and international conciliation, voiced support for Locarno.[54] One of their leaders thought the new situation was preferable to an exclusive dependence on Paris. "We had been as if married to France," he said, "while Czechoslovakia had been like a mistress who had to be wooed daily and put in a good mood."[55] The centrist parties ranged from a mildly positive to a negative attitude. The rightists were highly critical and viewed the Locarno pacts as removing the "real content" from "our alliance with France."[56] Their parliamentary spokesman and a noted francophile, Stanisław Stroński, was among the most outspoken critics; another critic was Piłsudski, to whose views we shall return later. Yet, all the dissatisfaction notwithstanding, Poland had no choice but to go along with the Western powers.

Skrzyński's defense of his pro-Locarno policy included optimistic prognostics along with more sober appraisals. He believed that he had gained the sympathy of London and of the French Left; an entente between Britain and Paris was essentially beneficial for Poland, for it would exorcise the ghost of a British-German rapprochement. The Franco-Polish alliance, he asserted "would emerge from Locarno strengthened, legitimized in the eyes of the world, endorsed by England." A more stabilized and secure Poland would have greater chances for obtaining foreign credits.[57] Skrzyń-

---

ment would have been unacceptable in France, SHA, EMA/2 Pologne 36. For constitutional-political problems and the May coup see works in Polish by Andrzej Ajnenkiel, Garlicki, *Przewrót majowy*, Holzer, *Mozaika polityczna*, and Pobóg-Malinowski, *Najnowsza historia*; in English by Polonsky, *Politics*, and Rothschild, *Piłsudski's Coup d'Etat*; and a recent biography of Piłsudski in both languages by Jędrzejewicz, *Piłsudski*.

53. See, for instance, Panafieu to Briand, 21 Dec. 1925, MAE, Pologne 53:114–17.

54. See Niedziałkowski, *Położenie*; foreign policy resolutions of the twentieth party congress in *Robotnik*, 4, 5 Jan. 1926; *Biuletyn Polityczny*, 1 (Apr. 1926).

55. Herman Diamand cited in Ziaja, *PPS*, 39.

56. See the populist party resolutions and the Christian national program in *Biuletyn Polityczny*, 1 (Apr. 1926).

57. Skrzyński to missions, 15 Oct., SI, Amb. Londyn, A.12.52/8; reports to cabinet,

ski believed in the wisdom of conciliatory policies. To a German scholar, Ludwig Stein, he spoke of Locarno as inaugurating a new era of mutual confidence.[58] Warsaw had already made a gesture toward Berlin by agreeing to suspend the expulsion of German "optants" (those who chose German citizenship), and hoped that Berlin would reciprocate. Publicly Skrzyński asserted that he wished to inspire confidence in Poland abroad.[59]

As a practical diplomatist, the Polish foreign minister expected that Locarno would give his country some respite in the prevailing difficult situation. Politics, he stressed, was "always the art of choosing one among several imperfect solutions."[60] At the same time, Skrzyński viewed Locarno as historically inevitable, marking the end of the first post-Versailles period of neither war nor peace. Even when he ceased being foreign minister, he dwelt on this broader aspect, calling Locarno an act "filled with the spirit of reconciliation, a telling proof of efforts toward accommodation between the *raison d'état* of individual states and that of the collectivity; a document of wisdom, moderation and foresight." Nations, he said, "which cease to serve the progress of humanity, perish."[61]

The immediate issues facing Poland after Locarno were the increased danger of German revisionism and the weakening French obligations toward Warsaw. The war minister asserted at a cabinet meeting on 6 March that the distinction made between the western and eastern German borders "simply encourages Germany to strive for a change of the frontier with Poland."[62] Skrzyński tried to minimize this threat, and he also argued, together with the judicial adviser to the ministry, that the Rhineland pact and the guarantee treaty left France full liberty to aid Poland.[63] This claim, as we know, was somewhat contrived.

The Polish army believed that two matters needed to be considered. First, in the opinion of the war ministry, the question of German disarmament underwent a major change, and concessions to Berlin, notably with regard to the Interallied Control Commission, were likely to be made. The Polish military tried to press their French colleagues to oppose them, but although Foch and the general staff saw the point, the whole issue was

---

19 Oct. 1925 and 10 Feb. 1926, AAN, PPRM, xxxi:85, xxxii:306–309; speeches in senate, 27 Nov. 1925, 3 Mar. 1926, Sprawozdania stenograficzne senatu xvii/9–10, cxxv/ 30–35. Also Balcerak, *Polityka*, 180–81.

58. See Laboulaye to Briand, 29 Nov. 1925, MAE, Pologne 112:164.

59. Panafieu to Briand, 27 Feb. 1926, MAE, Grande Bretagne 88:234–37.

60. Cited in Krasuski, *Stosunki 1919–1926*, 461.

61. Skrzyński, *Dwie Mowy*, 41, 45. Also, French text of one part in *Esprit International*, 7 (1927).

62. AAN, PPRM, xxxii:379.

63. See Krasuski, *Stosunki 1919–1926*; 445–46.

essentially political and could not be handled on the army level.[64] Second, and even more important, the actual working of the Franco-Polish alliance in case of war had to be reviewed. The Poles realized that the mutual guarantee treaty was far more restrictive than the military convention of 1921. War preparations, which were envisaged in the latter if the situation in Germany constituted a menace against either signatory (notably through mobilization) or endangered the Treaty of Versailles (article 1 of the secret convention), were not mentioned at all in the 1925 text. Also, the exact meaning of the expression "immediate aid and assistance" used in the guarantee treaty required clarification. The Poles were inclined to believe that France would provide it only after a decision of the Council of the League, and in their military studies began to assume a sixty- rather than a thirty-day delay in actual French military assistance.[65]

Because the 1925 treaty did not invalidate the 1921 convention, it was crucial for the Poles that the latter be in no way weakened. As the chief of staff put it, this document represented the only French engagement to "guarantee a practical application of the Franco-Polish alliance in case of need."[66] The French were perfectly well aware of this fact and had, as already mentioned, prepared a new project of a military convention, but deemed it prudent at that time not to submit it to the Poles.

The treaties of Locarno did cast a shadow on the French eastern alliances, even though the three governments concerned tried to deny or minimize the fact. In the political sphere Locarno indicated, as Bertrand de Jouvenel put it, that "France attached more importance to a reconciliation with Germany than to a consolidation of the position of its allies in the European east."[67] Bonnet wrote later that France was confronted with the following alternatives: maintain at any price the borders in the east, refuse to withdraw from the Ruhr, oppose German rearmament, and stay on the Rhine; or, if the eastern borders could not be maintained without a military effort "which we felt incapable of," espouse revisionism and even take the initiative in that direction. France, he concluded, proved incapable of making the choice.[68]

Such extreme alternatives, if logical, were unreal in the existing circumstances, but the problem of disarmament was real and pressing.[69] The

---

64. General Majewski to Skrzyński, 19 Nov. 1925, SI, MSZ, A.11/1. This explains the absence of formal attempts by the general staff to clarify the situation in Paris. See Ciałowicz, *Polsko-francuski sojusz*, 142.

65. See Bułhak, "Polsko-francuskie," 90–91; Wandycz, "Ocena traktatów."

66. Gen. Haller to Skrzyński, 27 Nov. 1925, cited in Kuźmiński, *Polska*, 21–22.

67. Jouvenal, *D'une guerre*, 2:74.

68. Bonnet, *Quai d'Orsay*, 116–17.

69. According to Sir Frederick Maurice's figures in the July 1925 issue of *Foreign Affairs*, French strength in peacetime was over 650,000 and after mobilization

French high command opposed concessions. General Mittelhauser wrote that "to disarm the nations of the Little Entente is to awaken German ambitions" and "tempt the devil."[70] Poincaré strongly objected to France disarming unless there existed a genuine security pact operating within the frame of the League of Nations.[71] The matter required careful handling, for a Preparatory Commission for a disarmament conference had been called in existence by a resolution of the League in December 1925. If no French political leader placed disarmament above security, a process began in which the old Roman dictum was paraphrased to "si vis pacem para pacem" (prepare peace). Briandism came to reflect and affect this mood in which lassitude, malaise, wishful thinking, and the inability to sustain the burden of international leadership were all present.

Geneva, Berlin, Prague

Three developments in early 1926 were of particular importance for France and her eastern allies: the question of a permanent seat for Poland on the Council of the League, the Russo-German treaty of Berlin, and a Skrzyński–Beneš rapprochement.

Worried by Quai d'Orsay's conciliatory tendencies toward Germany, which "grow at a tremendous pace," Ambassador Alfred Chłapowski was hardly reassured by the argument that Paris was deliberately making concessions so as to preserve the Locarno atmosphere. Chłapowski thought that Poland ought to strengthen its position by seeking a permanent seat in Geneva. French reaction toward Polish efforts would show whether Paris treated Locarno "exclusively from a narrow point of view" of pacifying Franco-German relations, or was seeking to establish a "new European system in which Poland would be one of the pillars."[72] The promises of Locarno could be fulfilled only, a governmental paper stated, if "Germany and Poland showed due consideration to one another."[73]

German entry into the Geneva organization, needed to make the Locarno treaties fully operative, came on the agenda on 8 February 1926, when Berlin formally submitted its application. That Germany would receive a permanent seat on the Council was taken for granted, and Warsaw insisted on being accorded the same privilege simultaneously. Otherwise,

1,200,000; Polish, 270,000 and 550,000; and Czechoslovak, 150,000 and 300,000. According to Ciałowicz, *Polsko-francuski sojusz*, 124, the Polish army on war footing would have over one million men.

70. Mittelhauser to Painlevé on the state of Czechoslovak army (also given to Foch, Pétain, Masaryk and Syrový), MAE, Tchécoslovaquie 22:204–220.

71. In *La Revue Belge*, Jan. 1926.

72. Chłapowski to Skrzyński, 19 Nov. 1925, SI, MSZ, A.11/1.

73. *Le Messager Polonais*, 28 Mar. 1926. Compare 19 and 20 Mar.

the Poles said, the government might not be able to have Locarno accepted; even a fall of the Skrzyński ministry could not be ruled out.[74]

Polish diplomacy concentrated its efforts on Paris, but it also sought British support. Chamberlain, although sympathetic toward Skrzyński's political line, was reluctant to take a definite stand; the Foreign Office was divided in its views. Impressed by Briand's strong advocacy of the Polish case—the Frenchman argued that it would be preferable for Poland and Germany to discuss their differences directly on the Council rather than to have France obliged to fight Poland's battles—Chamberlain decided to support Warsaw, although he made no official commitment.[75] Another, unpublicized reason for Briand's position was the fact that the term for Belgium on the Council was expiring, and the presence of another French ally would preserve the balance.[76]

In the course of parliamentary debates in late February and early March, Germany's entry into the League and its loudly voiced objections to a permanent seat for Poland came up in speeches of Louis Marin and Franklin-Bouillon. The former spoke of a "real danger" to Poles and Czechs, and attacked German "cynicism" and their ambition "to make the law at the League of Nations." The latter, loudly applauded, demanded a permanent seat for "our admirable ally." Briand tried to present the whole issue as a procedural matter. If the principle of enlarging the Council was accepted, he would be delighted to see "a great nation like Poland" granted a permanent seat.[77]

Briand's strategy probably deceived no one, for the issue was intensely political. An Auswärtiges Amt memorandum qualified a Polish entry into the Council as "an extraordinarily heavy blow to Germany." Poland's presence would be a major obstacle to policies of revisionism, and interfere with the goal of weakening the Franco-Polish relationship. Should Poland come closer to Britain, this would destroy hopes of combining German and British financial interests designed to weaken Polish resistance to future revisions. Noting Soviet overtures to Warsaw, the memorandum al-

---

74. See Laroche–Chłapowski conversation, 15 Jan., and Panafieu to Briand, 28 Feb. 1926, MAE, Pologne 75:1, and 53:133–34. On 25 Feb., the sejm demanded a permanent seat for Poland. The most detailed recent account is Henryk Korczyk, *Przyjęcie Niemiec i Polski do Rady Ligi Narodów w 1926 roku* (Wrocław, 1986).

75. Documentation in DBFP, 1a, 1:42, 122, 283–84; also xerographic copies of correspondence by Salter, Tyrrell, Cadogan, Drummond, and Chamberlain in Weinstein Collection, PI. Compare D'Abernon, *Diary*, 3:230, 235, 241.

76. The French realized that the German entry "could be interpreted by our friends of Central and Eastern Europe as a diminution of their influence and a menace for their future." Memorandum, 8 Nov. 1926, MAE, Grande Bretagne 89:104–19.

77. See second session, 27 Feb., first session, 1 Mar., and second session 2 Mar. 1926, J.O. Chambre, 1951, 1979, 1131.

ready visualized Poland emerging as a significant power in Central Europe.[78]

The Germans could afford to brush aside British suggestions of being more responsive to the Poles, knowing full well that London was above all intent on having Germany in the League while British opinion opposed an enlargement of the Council. If the Germans found Berthelot a strong defender of Poland's case, Briand seemed less firm. German diplomacy came to believe that he would not suffer a personal loss of prestige if the Polish candidacy failed. Despite Skrzyński's pleas to "prevent Germany [from] blackmailing everybody," the Polish position was weakening.[79]

There is no need to enter here into all the details of the Geneva imbroglio, which involved demands for permanent seats by Spain and Brazil, and Berthelot's attempts to find a solution. The French final position was that Poland receive one of the added seats with an assurance of reelection. On one occasion Briand told Stresemann that it would be best if "Poland did not exist at all," but because it did and he had given his word, a semipermanent seat was the only solution.[80] Skrzyński was allegedly "delighted with the combination that is offered to him," and the French representative in Geneva praised his adroitness.[81]

Throughout this tug-of-war Czechoslovakia, acting on behalf of the Little Entente, supported French efforts, but Beneš uncharacteristically avoided the center of the stage. His much-publicized offer to resign the Czechoslovak seat in favor of Poland was apparently the result of Stresemann's initiative conveyed through Briand,[82] which Beneš exploited partly for domestic reasons. It was clear that the Czechoslovak foreign minister did not wish to antagonize Berlin, and he was willing at one point to see Germany enter the Council in March, and Poland in September.[83] Still, he did provide some assistance to the Poles, who appreciated his generally positive attitude.

The postponement of German entry until September—the "Geneva fiasco"—strengthened rather than weakened Germany by demonstrating its

78. Herbert v. Dirksen memo, 9 Feb. 1926, ADAP, B, I/1:222–24.

79. See DBFP, 1a, 1:435–38, 486, 666; ADAP, B, I/1:237–38, 241–43, 258–60, 276–77, 291, 299–304, 313–14. Compare the Chłapowski telegram, 5 May 1926, HIA, Amb. Paryż, box 1.

80. Note, 13 Mar. 1926 on Briand–Stresemann conversation, ADAP, B,I/1:384–86.

81. Chłapowski telegram 11 Feb. 1926, HIA, Amb. Paryż, box 1. Compare Kozeński, "Próby zbliżenia." Also Grenard and Billy to Briand, 9 and 18 Feb. 1926, MAE, Tchécoslovaquie 69:163–65.

82. See Campbell, *Confrontation*, 176; Jouvenel, *D'Une Guerre*, 2:7–15; Note on Briand–Stresemann conversation, 14 Mar., ADAP, B, I/1:392–94; Lampson memo, DBFP, 1a, 1:538–39.

83. Notes of Luther and Schubert, 9, 26 Mar. 1926, ADAP, B, III:162, 195. Einstein to Secretary of State, 23 Mar. 1926, SDNA, 500.C001/362.

importance for the League and the desire of the "locarnites" to maintain unity. Still, for tactical reasons, Stresemann complained of the "severe injustice" inflicted on his country.[84] Simultaneously, he displayed his contempt toward the Poles. When Briand mentioned as evidence of his conciliatory labors a Skrzyński-Stresemann handshake in Geneva, the German foreign minister brutally retorted that he had met Skrzyński only once in a hotel and did not even speak to him. Privately, a ranking Wilhelmstrasse official jeered at "Briand's conciliation bacteria" that he had been spreading in Geneva.[85]

German attitude provoked some bitter words in France as well as renewed calls for closing ranks with the East Central European allies. Millerand considered this "more necessary than ever"; Sauerwein wrote an article printed in Poland about the need for solidarity and cooperation.[86] If there was criticism at the *sejm's* foreign affairs commission of Skrzyński for giving up a permanent seat, at least one deputy remarked that the Geneva strife proved that the Franco-Polish alliance was working in practice.[87]

At the time when Poland, seconded by France and Czechoslovakia, sought to improve its position through a permanent presence on the League's Council, complex maneuvers were underway in Eastern Europe that involved Poles, Romanians, Germans, and Russians. In early March, the Polish-Romanian alliance was due for renewal. Warsaw was careful to deal directly with Bucharest so as to avoid any arrangements that could make Paris an arbiter. The new treaty, signed on 26 March, contained a guarantee of existing borders that annoyed Berlin. In turn, Moscow, linking the Polish-Romanian alliance with Warsaw's diplomacy in the Baltic area, accused the Poles of organizing an anti-Soviet bloc.[88] Moscow was playing an involved diplomatic game. Worried by Locarno and its implications, it was exploring the possibility of resuming the Rapallo relationship with Germany while making simultaneous overtures to Paris and Warsaw. A Soviet proposal in mid-February 1926 of a nonagression pact with Poland floundered on Warsaw's desire to have the Baltic states and Romania included in it. Deputy foreign commissar Maxim Litvinov's overtures to the French were regarded by the latter as a maneuver to frighten Berlin into cooperation with Russia. Suspicions were not ap-

---

84. Stresemann circular, 20 Mar. 1926, ADAP, B, I/1:424–26.

85. Dirksen cited in Riekhoff, 130. On the handshake episode, Chastenet, *Histoire*, 5:157; Stresemann, *Vermächtnis*, 2:550.

86. 3 June 1926, J.O. Sénat, 1121; *Le Messager Polonais*, 23 Mar. 1926.

87. See *Robotnik* and *Le Messager Polonais*, 24, 25 Mar. 1926; Laroche to Briand, 27 Mar. 1926, MAE, Pologne 75:7–9.

88. See Bułhak, "Materiały do dziejów sojuszu polsko-rumuńskiego w latach 1921–1931," *Studia Historyczne*, 16 (1973), 424–26.

peased by an article in *Izvestia* on 5 March that tried to drive a wedge between France and Poland.

Indeed, after another complex Russo-German negotiation, the stage was set for the treaty of Berlin. The British ambassador to Germany, Lord D'Abernon, was told that the text would be innocuous and useful for stopping Soviet-Polish intrigues at German expense. He repeated, with seeming approval, a German view that "Poland allied to France and supported by Russia would become intolerable."[89]

Although London disliked the idea of a German-Soviet treaty, it believed that little could be done to prevent it. Paris was shocked. Even if initially Berthelot seemed "more contemptuous than upset" by what he called Stresemann's game of playing both ends, the Quai d'Orsay showed real concern. Briand agreed with Chamberlain that a protest in Berlin would be ineffective, but there was no need to hide the opinion that the "whole business" was "illtimed and unfortunate."[90] The French foreign minister admitted in the senate that the idea was initially unpleasant, but he opposed a motion to adjourn the entire Locarno ratification debate until Berlin provided a convincing explanation of its conduct.[91] Briand seemed to consider the matter primarily a British concern, and was prepared to follow London's lead, but did not wish to do anything himself that could harm his Locarno policy. The Czechoslovak envoy in Paris, Štefan Osuský, commented on the growing passivity of French diplomacy. He interpreted, however, the foreign minister's observation that the treaty was untimely and that Paris would be obliged to take certain steps to mean strengthening ties with East Central Europe.[92] But there were no indications of any such initiative.

Warsaw and Prague had been speedily informed of the forthcoming treaty, and London not only counseled restraint vis-à-vis Germany but applied pressure on French eastern allies to prevent any rash reaction on their part. The British were assuring the agitated Beneš and Skrzyński that the treaty was not contrary to Locarno or the Covenant, and telling them that "it is the coolest head which wins."[93] Obviously it was easier to be a stoic in London than in the East Central European capitals. In Osuský's opin-

89. D'Abernon to Chamberlain, 1 and 8 Apr. 1926, DBFP, 1a, 1:567, 587. On the German goal to prevent the long-range possibility of a Franco-Soviet-Polish alignment, see Krüger, "Politique extérieure," 278.

90. Crewe to Chamberlain, 13 Apr. 1926, DBFP, 1a, 1:607.

91. Sessions 3 and 4 June 1926, J.O. Sénat, 1106–12, 1138–40.

92. Osuský to Beneš, 25 Apr. 1926, CPP.

93. See correspondence in DBFP, 1a, 1:597–98, 603–605, 628–52, and Annual Report, Czechoslovakia 1926, FO 371 12009 C 3887/3887/12; also Couget to Briand, 15 Apr. 1926, MAE, Tchécoslovaquie 62:70–71; Skirmunt to Skrzyński, 12, 13 Apr. 1926, SI, Amb. Londyn, A.12.52/8. See also Korczyk, "Polska dyplomacja," 301–30.

ion, although "Rapallo treaty had been a surprise, this treaty signed after Locarno is frightening." Beneš characterized it as "a dangerous maneuver by Russia and Germany against Poland, England [and] the League of Nations," which would encourage Italian meddling as well.[94]

The Czechoslovak foreign minister prepared a questionnaire-memorandum that he passed to the British with the remark that it would be most dangerous to behave as "if nothing had happened." The questions read as follows: Would Germany give an assurance that the proposed treaty was not in contradiction to the Covenant? Would it apply economic sanctions even against Russia? Would it reaffirm its stand on article 16, and state that the treaty contained no secret clauses? If the Locarno powers did not raise these issues, Beneš said, they were bound to be introduced at the next session of the Council of the League in connection with Germany's expected membership of that body.[95]

The memorandum represented a joint position of Poland and Czechoslovakia, although Skrzyński deliberately played a supporting role behind Beneš. Still, he pointed out to London that the impending treaty meant a return to Bismarckian foreign policy, and might be also regarded as blackmail. Did Stresemann expect to get something from the West if he gave up the idea of cooperation with Russia?[96] Beneš's initiative—at least partly intended to improve his image at home after being damaged by Locarno— was based on the hope that the treaty would either be averted or significantly altered in accord with the Covenant.[97] To some extent, the latter did happen, and the final Treaty of Arbitration and Friendship signed on 24 April was legally unassailable. But this was due more to the superior skill of Germany diplomacy than to pressures exerted on Berlin.

The French who would have gladly probed deeper the matter of Beneš's questionnaire, were it only to appease their eastern allies, fell in step with London's cautious policy, much to Beneš's surprise. Their activity became eventually limited to a joint examination of the text by juridical experts of the Quai d'Orsay and the Auswärtiges Amt.[98] The former, while accepting

94. Osuský to Beneš, 8 Apr. and Beneš's circular 12 Apr., CPP, circular 15 Apr. 1926, DaM, II, 259–60.

95. Memorandum with comments in Beneš's circular, 17 Apr. 1926, CPP; compare Clerk to Chamberlain, 15 Apr. 1926, DBFP, 1a, 1:617–18.

96. Skrzyński telegrams to Skirmunt, 10, 15, 28 Apr. and his memorandum, 3 May, SI, Amb. Londyn, A.12.52/8 and MSZ, 82/12/18. Chłapowski telegram, 5 May 1926, HIA, Amb. Paryż, box 1.

97. Beneš's speech at cabinet meeting, 16 Apr. 1926, DaM, II, 260–62; analysis in Sládek, "Akce."

98. See reports of Jan Masaryk, Osuský, Krno, and Veverka, 17, 25, 27 Apr. and 20 May 1926, CPP; compare Chamberlain's circular and memorandum, 3 May 1926, DBFP, 1a, 1:704–11; also Morawski telegram, 10 May 1926, SI, Amb. Londyn, A.12.52/8.

the document as compatible with the Covenant, characterized it privately as "execrable." General Weygand wrote, albeit with gross exaggeration, that the treaty henceforth made "impossible any French intervention in Poland's favor."[99] Sauerwein commented that the treaty was "an extremely severe blow to the policy of Locarno and Geneva."[100]

There is no doubt that Stresemann had won a victory and demonstrated the possibility of exploiting the Locarno policy without sacrificing ties to Moscow. Conditions for a Soviet-German strategy of isolating Poland were preserved. Beneš, whose memorandum to Chamberlain had been leaked, was hard put to defend himself against Berlin's accusations of meddling in German-Western relations. Prague tried to explain the "misunderstanding" but with little success. The *Izvestia* came out with an article on "The Failures of Mr. Beneš."[101]

The Geneva imbroglio and the treaty of Berlin brought Czechoslovakia and Poland closer together. In several pronouncements, Beneš, Švehla, and Skrzyński referred to the very friendly relations between their countries. The pro-Czech envoy in Prague, Zygmunt Lasocki, was busy discussing economic, political, and military questions.[102]

Czechoslovak-Polish trade was not insignificant. In 1926 the Polish share in Czechoslovakia's imports stood at 7.1 percent and in exports 2; Czechoslovak shares in Poland's imports and exports were respectively 5 and 8.8 percent. Cattle, petroleum, and coal were among the chief products that went from Poland to its southern neighbor or in transit to Austria and Hungary. From Czechoslovakia came leather goods, textiles, and iron and steel products. The expansion of Škoda into a great car and plane factory had an impact in Poland where the Franco-Polish works were renamed Polish Škoda Works. The Poles also made attempts to direct Czechoslovak exports to the Gdynia and Danzig harbors and away from Hamburg.[103]

The existing difficulties stemmed mainly from customs regulations. Inflation in Poland led to higher custom tariffs, which delayed the ratification of the 1925 commercial treaty by Prague. Czechoslovak regulations in turn contributed to a virtual embargo on Polish cattle under the pretext

---

99. See DBFP, 1a, 1:698; Weygand, *Mémoires*, 2:332. On the dissatisfaction at the Quai d'Orsay, ADAP, B, 1/1: 509–11, 546–51.

100. *Le Messager Polonais*, 12 May 1926.

101. *Izvestia* cited in Gasiorowski, "Polish-Czechoslovak Relations," 503. See Gajanová, *ČSR*, 207; Campbell, *Confrontation*, 177; ADAP, B, III:250–51.

102. See Lasocki's article in *Národni Listy*, 13 Apr. 1926; Švehla's speech, 18 Dec. 1925, Těsnopisecké zprávy, Poslanecká sněmovna, third session, 36–37: article on the "corridor" in *Zahraniční Politika* (1925), 1469–72.

103. See Horejsek, *Snahy československé*; *Češi a Poláci*, 2:540–41; Jísa and Vaněk, *Škodový závody*, 209–11.

of hoof and mouth disease. Angry articles appeared in the press of both countries; French diplomatic reports spoke of a genuine economic conflict.

A liquidation of these disputes was essential for political and military reasons. The ratification of the commercial treaty which contained the all-important clause on the transit of war material, was viewed in Warsaw as a condition for a continuing rapprochement. Skrzyński was using the Polish-Czechoslovak army channels to apply pressure on the government in Prague. Interstaff talks, however, were to prepare the ground for a rapprochement but "not for a military alliance." By mid-1926 the foreign minister became more flexible. When he announced his intention to visit Prague, he instructed the military attaché, Colonel Jan Bigo, to tell the Czechoslovak chief of staff that the Poles favored commencing talks, although they still considered a precondition of any agreement the ratification of the commercial treaty.[104]

The prospect of closer ties between the two countries evoked great interest in Poland. Already in December 1925, the populist deputy Jan Dąbski had launched the slogan of an economic union, perhaps even a customs union. His ideas found support among populists, Christian democrats, and national democrats, partly because of the current agrarian difficulties. The campaign in which the Christian democratic paper *Rzeczpospolita* played an especially active role met with a favorable response on the part of many Czechoslovak agrarians, notably the Slovak leader, Milan Hodža. In a series of speeches and interviews, Hodža appealed to the peasant masses to lead the way to a Czechoslovak-Polish union that could later be enlarged by the neighboring countries.[105] Hodža's special interest was closely connected with his activities in the so-called Green International, centered on Prague, which promoted an East Central European bloc based on the common peasant denominator.[106]

The Polish government and the industrial circles were more skeptical about the possibilities of an economic union, and the conservative *Czas*, which was generally unfriendly to the Czechs, printed on 21 January 1926 ironic remarks about Hodža. On the Czechoslovak side, the agrarian, Catholic, and Slovak *l'udák* organs (*Venkov*, 23 December 1925; *Lidové Listy*, 1 January, 7 February, and 22 February 1926; and *Slovák*, 6 March 1926 took a strongly favorable position. The national democratic *Národní Listy* was unsympathetic and Beneš's *České Slovo* was critical about the

104. See draft of Skrzyński to Żeligowski (replying to 23 Sept. 1925 note), AAN, MSZ 55202. Also Bułhàk, "Z Dziejów," 134–35; Balcerak, "K Československo-polským," 452–53.

105. Speeches, lectures, and interviews in Hodža, *Články*, 4:239–56, 7:371–74. On May conversations between Polish and Czechoslovak agrarian leaders, see MS, PAN. Teki Zygmunta Lasockiego, 4091.

106. See Hodža, *Le Problème* and *Federation*.

practicalities of a union. This was also the view of Premier Švehla. The semiofficial *Prager Presse* was cool.[107] A German newspaper sounded a warning: it had nothing against these plans provided that German-Austrian-Czechoslovak issues found a simultaneous resolution.[108] Beneš's own position emerged clearly from a remark made to a British diplomat: should an official proposal along these lines come from Warsaw, Prague "would be embarrassed" and "not know what reply to make."[109]

On 16 February 1926, Skrzyński proposed to come to Prague to return Beneš's visit of the preceding year, ratify the outstanding treaties, and discuss such topics as the reorganization of the League Council, the preparatory disarmament conference, and economic problems.[110] His journey, however, had to be postponed because of the cabinet crisis in Prague. It fell to the new government of Černý to arrange Skrzyński's visit.[111]

The Polish foreign minister arrived in Prague on 13 April and stayed throughout the 15th. The reception was warm and large crowds applauded the visitor. The entire press, except for the communist *Rudé Pravo*, emphasized the importance of Skrzyński's presence for the Czechoslovak-Polish rapprochement. The *Prager Presse* published interviews with various Polish politicians to stress that all parties supported Skrzyński's foreign policy. The visit, the paper said (13 April), meant "the strengthening of the system of Central European politics as practiced by Czechoslovakia since its liberation." No wonder that the *Vossische Zeitung* entitled an article three days later: "Skrzyński's Journey to Prague— A Front Against Germany?"

Le Temps devoted a long commentary to the subject on 13 April; it spoke of "happy efforts" toward a definitive rapprochement that served the real interest of Europe and reflected the solidarity of the two countries. Recalling Beneš's article,[112] which had called for the closest collaboration necessary to strengthen the status quo, *Le Temps* fully endorsed this position. The status quo was untouchable, and when Germany entered the League it would be important for the voice of Poland and the Little Entente to be heard in Geneva. The paper cited a remark of Paul-Boncour during the latter's recent trip to Poland, that a Polish soldier on the eastern border was also a defender of the Western civilization. Poland, *Le Temps* con-

---

107. See press cuttings, MZV .VA, 478–1237 and 1238; also Max Muller and Clerk to Chamberlain, 27 Jan., 9 Feb., FO 371 11224 C 2029 and C 2030/44/12, and 8 Feb. 1926, FO 371 11224 C 2031.

108. *Kölnische Volkszeitung*, 16 Feb. 1926.

109. Dodd to Chamberlain, 25 Feb. 1926, FO 371 11225 C 2590.

110. Łukasiewicz to missions, 10 Apr. 1926, SI, Amb. Londyn, A.12/52/8.

111. The Polish side expressed great satisfaction that Beneš remained member of the Černý cabinet. See *Le Messager Polonais*, 24 Mar. 1926. Compare 5 Oct.

112. In the Easter issue of *Baltische Presse* devoted to Czechoslovak-Polish matters.

cluded, had strengthened its alliance with Romania and stood so close to Czechoslovakia that even without joining the Little Entente it was solidly with this group.[113]

During his stay in Czechoslovakia, Skrzyński ratified the arbitration and liquidation conventions (the commercial treaty would be ratified in June), conferred with Beneš, and visited Masaryk at his Lány residence. The Polish foreign minister assured the press that he was "in full accord" with Beneš, which should not be surprising because both countries were "threatened by common dangers." Misunderstandings had been merely temporary. Yet the goals of Skrzyński and Beneš were not identical, as was shown by their major speeches delivered at the great banquet in the Prague castle. Both addresses were extremely warm, and Beneš characterized his trip to Warsaw and Skrzyński's (his "dear colleague's") to Prague as symbolic of brotherhood and complementary interests in political, cultural, and spiritual spheres. "We have," Beneš said, "the same concept of general policy which we must pursue under the existing conditions in Central Europe." Both states strove to secure lasting peace, and worked to strengthen the political order based on the respect of the letter and the spirit of the League. They were reaching "a definitive, full and lasting stabilization of our friendly contacts." Beneš proposed a toast to "sincere and loyal friendship of our two nations."

In an extemporaneous reply, Skrzyński echoed his colleague's sentiments about mutual cooperation fortified through a defensive system relying on the League—"this new Holy Alliance concluded for the freedom of nations." But then, he went further. He invoked the tradition of the Jagiellonian kings who had ruled over the two countries, and of the Czech king George of Poděbrady who had advocated a European union. Skrzyński wanted to follow in their footsteps. "We have extended to one another," he said, "the hand in order to create in the heart of Europe a Slav bloc." Based on past experiences and fully committed to peace, it would preserve and defend the treasury of freedom.[114]

Apparently only the *Lidové Listy* singled out, on 17 April, the difference between the two speeches. Beneš wanted to strengthen the political order in Europe based on the Covenant; Skrzyński spoke of a bloc, although he placed it within the frame of the League. The paper noted that "our rapprochement (*spojení*) with Poland is thus far not an association (*spolek*), but, as Dr. Beneš has put it, a *common* policy." Even though the paper did not expressly state its preference for Skrzyński's approach, its position was

113. Prior to his departure from Warsaw, Skrzyński declared that there was no need for Poland to enter the Little Entente in order to work for a consolidation of East Central Europe; see *Národní Politika* and *Le Messager Polonais*, 12 and 14 Apr. 1926.

114. Both speeches in *Prager Presse* and *Národní Osvobození*, 15 Ap. and *Le Messager Polonais*, 17 Ap. 1926.

clear. Only two days earlier it had critically surveyed the evolution of Briand's foreign policy, which suggested that reliance on France could be problematic. Hence, a rapprochement with Warsaw was "imperative," and Skrzyński appeared to "be the first decidedly *European*-oriented Polish statesman who relies not only on native and allied bayonets, but is determined to pursue a sincere and *consistent policy of international cooperation.*" In other words, cooperation with Warsaw was less risky with Skrzyński than with anyone else.

Did the Polish foreign minister in his private conversations with Beneš translate the notion of a Slav bloc into a concrete offer of an alliance? There are indications that he did, although the form of his proposal is uncertain. Beneš apparently either turned it down or diluted a concrete idea into general phrases about brotherhood and friendship.[115] Perhaps Beneš doubted whether Skrzyński would maintain himself in power in view of the growing domestic strife in Poland, which indeed led to his resignation a few weeks later.[116] It is dubious, however, whether the Czechoslovak foreign minister would have accepted the idea of a Warsaw-Prague bloc in any case. True, at this point the coordination of policies vis-à-vis the forthcoming Berlin treaty, which the two statesmen discussed in Prague, brought Czechoslovak and Polish views on the German-Russian issue closer than ever before. A most favorable climate for a rapprochement existed. Did Beneš merely exploit it, to improve his position internally and externally, without being ready to take a step that would have earned Prague the enmity of Moscow and Berlin? This is possible. The fact remains that, as the *Journal des Débats* noted on 25 April, "the relations between Poland and Czechoslovakia have never been better and closer." The ratification of treaties opened the way for military conversations; hopes for a more permanent alignment persisted.[117]

115. Beck wrote: "in 1925 [?] Beneš turned down flat Count Alexander Skrzyński's attempt to conclude an alliance, invoking the fear to compromise his relations with Germany"; see Beck, *Dernier Rapport*, 108–109. According to the Yugoslav envoy Lazarević, the Poles had not forgotten how Skrzyński "offered to Mr. Beneš a pact of friendship and . . . met with a refusal," for leaders in Prague did not believe in the viability of Poland and wanted to be on good terms with Moscow. Laroche to Barthou, 4 Ap. 1934, MAE, Z 864.5, Tchécoslovaquie 2587.

116. See Balcerak, "Sprawa," 219.

117. For a campaign in favor of union with Czechoslovakia after Skrzyński's visit, see *Rzeczpospolita*, 21, 23, 26, 29 Ap. 1926.

Chapter Two

The Turbulent Year 1926

Piłsudski's Coup d'Etat

On 12 May 1926, Piłsudski marched into Warsaw at the head of his loyal troops. What seemed intended as an armed demonstration to force President Stanisław Wojciechowski to dismiss the week-old right-center cabinet of Wincenty Witos degenerated into a bloody struggle. After three days the president and the ministry resigned, and Piłsudski became master of the country. In addition to the post of commander-in-chief, the marshal became minister of war in the new cabinet, and he retained both positions until his death. Piłsudski's candidate, Ignacy Mościcki, was elected president of the Republic, and maneuvers by the parliament amounted to a legalization of the coup. Piłsudski disclaimed any intention of introducing fascism in Poland. In fact, the entire Left, including the communists, had supported his coup, having regarded the Witos cabinet as a prelude to a fascist revolution. Piłsudski's victory, however, was not a triumph of the Left. Rather than become dependent on any political party, the marshal sought to strengthen the executive, weaken the parliament, and install a regime of "moral cleansing" (*sanacja*) that transcended traditional party politics. The program of superimposing the state on a politically immature society was vague, and the prime minister Kazimierz Bartel tended to view the new system as a regime of technocrats whose job was to govern while that of the parliament was merely to control.

A constitutional amendment in August increased the prerogatives of the president, but the long-range goal of the Piłsudski camp was the introduction of a new constitution of an authoritarian type. The marshal himself was bitterly aware of the dilemma of authority versus liberty and realized that autocracy, rather than providing a lesson in civic virtues, breaks characters. Disillusioned with parliamentary democracy, he said that he would have to see if one could still govern Poland "without a whip." Although Piłsudski's followers did not constitute a political party that could gain a majority in parliamentary elections, they believed they had a mandate to govern because they represented the country's best. A loosely-knit movement of Piłsudski's supporters organized itself into the BBWR (the Polish acronym for the Nonpartisan Bloc of Cooperation with the Government). The marshal himself successfully wooed the conservatives, including the great landowners and upper bourgeoisie, and thereby weakened his national democratic opponents and discarded his image of a former socialist. Although the Piłsudski regime seemed set on a collision course with the major political parties, it also brought the country a certain social, economic, and even political stability. Economic improvement, which had begun already before the May coup, became more evident as the English coal strike opened new markets to Poland, and the new regime capitalized on such developments. Similarly, the national minorities, especially the Jews, who were worried by the nationalist overtones of the Witos cabinet, welcomed Piłsudski, whose progressive views they appreciated. The marshal's charisma and prestige made many Poles feel that he was indeed the man to lead the country into a better domestic and international future.

Piłsudski's personality defies easy description or classification. The closest analogy may be to Charles de Gaulle, with whom Piłsudski shared a passionate attachment to the greatness of his country and a conviction in its historic mission. Both men believed in their star and could not easily be labeled as belonging to the Left or the Right.[1] Piłsudski was a born leader. It was both his own and Poland's tragedy that he came to rule prematurely aged, embittered by party strife, and distrustful of people—almost a misanthrope. His masterful nature made it hard for him to suffer opposition; the boundless devotion of his followers, bordering on hero worship, provided him with trusted lieutenants rather than collaborators.

The May coup had not been inspired by Britain, as some historians and contemporaries suspected.[2] Still, the British generally welcomed Piłsudski's rise to power, although they would have felt better if the marshal had not been the man of the Kievan expedition and the Wilno seizure.[3] There is no evidence that the coup was "a response to Rapallo and Locarno." The international factor was marginal, although Piłsudski's preoccupation with Poland's security was real enough.[4] An assertion that the

1. See Roos, "Piłsudski."

2. 15 June 1926 entry, MS, PAN, "Dziennik Juliusza Zdanowskiego"; Leon Grosfeld, "Czy Anglicy rzeczywiście byli inicjatorami przewrotu majowego?" *Kwartalnik Historyczny*, 3 (1969) 677–81; compare reports of Gen. Dupont, 21 Dec. 1925, SHA, EMA/2, Pologne 7; Laroche, 28 May and Fleuriau, 23 June 1926, MAE, Pologne 54:66, 158–60.

3. Max Muller to Chamberlain, 25 May 1926, FO 371 11762/2276/41/55.

4. Gwido, *Polityka*, 12, believes in the foreign policy factor. For national democratic suspicions, see MS, BJ, Stanisław Rymar, "Moje wspomnienia," II, 146; and for a more pondered view, see MS, BN, Zofia z Grabskich Kirkor-Kiedroniowa, "Wspomnienia," III, 228.

event initiated a shift from a pro-French to a pro-British orientation in Polish diplomacy disregards the fact that Skrzyński had fully appreciated Britain's role.[5] A genuine British-Polish rapprochement, however, was not possible. Britain's Polish record in 1919–23 had been such that, as a British memorandum put it, "it is astonishing that he [Piłsudski] should preserve any regard for us at all."[6] The marshal was seemingly unaffected by past experiences and fully aware of the importance of cultivating Britain. But he realized that one could not rush. As he told the Polish minister in London, "we must not throw ourselves at the British, but act in such a way that they would recognize the need of closer relations with us."[7]

Regarding Piłsudski as an implacable enemy of Russia, the Soviets reacted almost hysterically to the May coup. Stalin and Karl Radek, the publicist-politician, assailed Piłsudski and his "fascism" in *Izvestia* and *Pravda*. Foreign commissar Georgii Chicherin described Piłsudski as "unpredictable," and his deputy Litvinov labeled him as enigmatic. The French ambassador in Moscow, frightened of the eastern repercussions of the May coup and of their impact on France, counseled Paris to attempt "to settle our relations with Russia in such a way that our security would not be at the mercy of changes that would occur in Eastern Europe." He even opined that France cultivate Russia rather than secondary states like Poland, for several allied countries do not equal one large power.[8] In Paris, Briand and Berthelot sought to dispel Soviet anxieties; they expressed disbelief that Britain was pushing Poland to further the exchange scheme involving the "corridor" and Lithuania and said they were giving counsels of moderation to the marshal.[9]

Warsaw was publicly asserting that it had no warlike designs upon Russia. Piłsudski told the Soviet envoy privately that the Russians must consider him stupid, for Poland could gain nothing from a new war, in which he personally could only risk losing his victor's laurels.[10] Indeed, one must

---

5. Conflicting interpretations in Zabiełło, *W Kręgu*, 179 and Starzeński, *Trzy lata*, 19. Also Jouvenel, *D'Une guerre*, 2:62.

6. Gregory memorandum, 17 May 1926, DBFP, 1a, 1:756.

7. See MS, BJ, Konstanty Skirmunt, "Moje wspomnienia," 143. Piłsudski ordered that reports from the London legation be sent to him. See the May to Dec. 1926 reports in AAN, Akta Józefa i Aleksandry Piłsudskich, 1: Adiutantura Belwederu, 4.

8. Herbette to Briand, 19 May 1926, MAE, Pologne 53:264–65; compare Borejsza, *Mussolini*, 154–55; also Keeton, "Briand's Locarno Policy," 260. For Soviet reactions, see Karol Poznański, "Wypadki majowe widziane od strony Moskwy," *Wiadomości*, no. 856 (23 June 1957); also Łopatniuk, "Przed Przewrotem," 167.

9. Briand to Herbette, and de Vaux, 23 July 1926, MAE, Grande Bretagne 89:71–72; audience du ministre, 3 Aug. 1926, MAE, Russie 359:58–59.

10. For Piłsudski's conversation with the Soviet envoy, see Zaleski's memoirs cited in

distinguish between Piłsudski's optimal long-range "federalist" solution of driving Russia out of the borderlands and creating a bloc assuring Poland's safety, and current diplomatic objectives. A clear distinction between *Realpolitik* and wishful thinking was shown by Roman Knoll, the Polish deputy foreign minister and a federalist himself, who said that the 1919–20 concepts "belonged to the past," and that Polish policy was based "on the Treaty of Riga and an economic rapprochement with Russia."[11]

As if to test Piłsudski, the Soviets suddenly presented in August a project of a nonaggression pact. Were they sincere? Moscow must have known that Warsaw would still insist on the inclusion of the Baltic states and Romania in such a pact, and on a satisfactory definition of aggressor. Shortly before, Litvinov was telling the Germans that "one must do everything to isolate Poland in the eyes of public opinion."[12] In late September the USSR concluded a treaty with Lithuania that had an anti-Polish edge to it. Were the Russians trying to keep Poland off balance? No wonder that Polish-Soviet exchanges proceeded very slowly.

Piłsudski thought that neither Russia nor Germany was in a position to attack Poland for a decade or so, and he seemed little perturbed by the treaty of Berlin.[13] The first canon of Polish foreign policy, the marshal told August Zaleski, the new Polish foreign minister, was that "Poland must maintain the strictest neutrality between Germany and Russia, so that these two states could be absolutely certain that Poland would not go with one against the other."[14] This concept, later described as the principle of a policy of balance, became an axiom of Warsaw's diplomacy in the years to come. Poland sought to convey this policy to Berlin, which on the whole had adopted a positive stance toward Piłsudski's coup. In the summer of 1926, a leading Polish socialist and an old acquaintance of Piłsudski, Herman Diamand, went to Germany to assure Stresemann of Poland's pacific intentions. If Diamand used the word "compensation," which Berlin understood to mean willingness to discuss territorial issues, Zaleski quickly removed all possible doubts on this subject. Stressing the need for peaceful relations and a settlement of economic problems, he stated that Poland had "agreed to make great sacrifices at Locarno in order to facili-

Wandycz, *Zaleski*, 35. For public pronouncements, see *Le Messager Polonais*, 23 May, 11, 22 June, and 24 July 1926; also Zaleski, *Przemowy*, 1:5–28.

11. See *Le Temps*, 27 May, 1926, and Roman Knoll, *Uwagi o polskiej polityce* (Warszawa, 1939), 23. Also Laroche to Briand, 11 Oct. 1926, MAE, Pologne 12:105–106.

12. See Schubert memorandum cited in Gasiorowski, "Stresemann," 302; also ADAP, B, II/2:229–31. On the Soviet war scare, Gen. Charpy report, 31 Aug. and Quai d'Orsay to war ministry, 23 Sept. 1926, SHA, EMA/2 Pologne 8 and 18.

13. See Laroche to Briand, 6 May 1926, MAE, Pologne 53:154–55.

14. See Wandycz, *Zaleski*, 36; compare Zaleski–Seipel conversation, 4 Mar. 1927 MAE, Pologne 75:158.

tate the realization of the accords," but there could be no concessions where the vital interests of the state were concerned.[15]

Shortly after the coup, the government publicly emphasized the continuity of Poland's foreign policy. Although Piłsudski disliked Skrzyński, he offered him a portfolio; however, Skrzyński refused, saying that he could not collaborate with people who had blood on their hands.[16] The foreign ministry was temporarily entrusted to Zaleski, the "imperturbable" former envoy to Rome. Zaleski was not, strictly speaking, a confidant of Piłsudski but he had been close to the marshal's camp during World War I. Less well-known than Skrzyński, he inspired confidence among foreign diplomats, and appeared the best candidate under the circumstances.[17] In June, Piłsudski, wishing to involve the conservatives in the government, proposed that Prince Janusz Radziwiłł lead the foreign ministry. Apparently Radziwiłł's political conditions were not acceptable; besides, the French, who were discretely consulted about the candidate, expressed an uneasiness about his alleged pro-German leanings.[18] Hence, Zaleski became a full-fledged foreign minister in the second Bartel ministry on 8 June. Although he had been at odds with Skrzyński on political and personal grounds, he continued his diplomatic course, which was of particular importance from the viewpoint of Franco-Polish relations.

Piłsudski's coup d'état, reported extensively on the first pages of the Parisian press, provoked mixed reactions in France. *Petit Parisien* compared the marshal with a Joan of Arc "chasing anarchy" (11 June); *L'Avenir* wrote that Piłsudski "had been intimately connected to Lenin" (19 June). A feeling of mistrust toward the man himself, mixed with fears about the role of the army in Polish politics, gradually waned, and there followed remarks about "national union" and return to legality. Piłsudski's interviews given to Sauerwein (*Le Matin*, 23 and 25 May) produced more balanced comments (*L'Echo de Paris*, 27 May) and a series of articles that expressed hopes about the growth of real democracy in Poland.[19]

The French government found itself on a good footing with Piłsudski, having anticipated his return to power early enough. During his April visit,

15. Speeches in *Le Messager Polonais*, 22, 24 July 1926; also Zaleski, *Przemowy*, 1:5–28. On the Diamand mission, see Gasiorowski, "Stresemann," 300–301; Riekhoff, *German-Polish Relations*, 321–22.

16. See Laroche–Skrzyński conversation, 16 June 1926, MAE, Pologne 54:126–29. Also Max Muller to Chamberlain, 7 June 1926, FO 371 11763 N 2737/41/45. Compare Wandycz, *Zaleski*, 26–27.

17. See Wandycz, *Zaleski*, 28–31; Laroche, *Pologne*, 48–50.

18. See Wandycz, *Zaleski*, 28, Władyka, *Działalność polityczna*, 22–23, 29. Also Laroche, *Pologne*, 47–48, and Laroche to Briand, 5 June 1926, MAE, Pologne 135:158–66.

19. See *Le Messager Polonais*, 6, 9 June, 22 July 1926, and press reports in AAN, MSZ 3788.

Paul-Boncour had met Piłsudski and had been impressed with "the man of tomorrow." Conveying his opinions to Briand, he advised that the French ambassador contact the marshal.[20] At that time Ambassador Hector de Panafieu, highly regarded by the Poles, was on the point of retiring, and Berthelot proposed the post to the political director at the Quai d'Orsay, Jules Laroche. The new ambassador visited Piłsudski at his Sulejówek retreat, and reported that the marshal was ever closer to gaining power. Still, both Laroche and the chief of the military mission seem to have been taken aback by the event of 12 May.[21]

After the coup, Piłsudski revisited Laroche on 20 May, and the two men discussed foreign policy and Franco-Polish relations. Laroche wanted to probe Piłsudski's alleged hostility toward Russia and his seeming inclination to reach an agreement with Berlin.[22] The conversation, taken together with other private and public statements by the Poles, was reassuring. In talking to Zaleski, Piłsudski formulated the second "canon" of Polish foreign policy, namely the alliances with France and Romania.[23] That the alliance with Paris was a cornerstone of Poland's diplomacy emerged clearly from many other utterances of Piłsudski. Laroche suspected that the marshal wished to rid himself of the reputation of a francophobe, a label assigned to him by his opponents, and to "deprive the national democrats of the monopoly [of francophilia] that they had arrogated to themselves."[24]

This last point merits consideration, for in the course of the next three years the nationalist Right would criticize the government's French policy and propagate its own alternative. During a tour of Paris, Rome, and London in the spring of 1926, the leader of the national democrats, Roman Dmowski advocated a Franco-Italian alliance that would contribute to a new order in Europe in which Poland could play her due part. Such ideas, colored by Dmowski's admiration for fascism and his belief in England's decline, were unfavorably received at the Quai d'Orsay, and helped to strengthen the links between the French government and the new Polish regime.[25]

20. Paul-Boncour, *Entre deux guerres* 2:170–71; Laroche, *Pologne* 25; MAE, Pologne 275:237–44; compare Borejsza, *Mussolini*, 137–38.

21. See notes in SHA, EMA/2, Pologne 26; Borejsza, *Mussolini*, 141.

22. See Laroche to Briand, 20 May, and Berthelot to missions, 16 May 1926, MAE, Pologne 43:270–75, Pologne 53:222–23.

23. See Wandycz, *Zaleski*, 36. Also Piłsudski's remarks at the Committee of State Defense, PI, Protokoł l-go posiedzenia Komitetu Obrony Państwa, 23 listopada 1926, copy.

24. Laroche to Briand, 28 May, and 18 June 1926, MAE, Pologne 75:40–41; 135:170.

25. See Blanchet note on Dmowski's journey, 22 Apr.; Laroche to Briand, 31 Dec.

The French, however, were concerned that a German-Polish détente might adversely affect (*fausse*) the working of the Franco-Polish alliance.[26] General Dupont, who had a low opinion of Piłsudski, did not exclude the possibility of abandoning the "corridor" or perhaps even Poznania to Germany. The marshal, he wrote, interpreted the alliance with Paris in a way that would leave him free to deal with Russia while France would serve as a guarantor against Germany. Laroche, who showed more understanding, even sympathy, toward the Piłsudski government, maintained that it was doing its best to cultivate France. The ambassador recommended that Zaleski's position be reinforced vis-à-vis the marshal by pointing to the credit he enjoyed abroad.[27] The French apparently appreciated the maintenance of Ambassador Alfred Chłapowski in Paris, despite a political gaffe he committed during the May conflict.

A good relationship with the new government in Warsaw was also advisable because it might reduce friction over economic and financial matters. From the autumn of 1925 to February 1926 a conflict had raged between the Poles and the Schneider concern over the armament works in Starachowice. Schneider was reluctant to provide promised funds; the Polish government threatened a breach of contract. Even Dupont mentioned the profound contempt displayed by French business toward the industrial capacities of Poland. The operation of Skarboferm produced incessant and reciprocal complaints about various financial and labor aspects.[28] At one point Warsaw threatened the French capitalists with higher taxes and even forced seizure of the enterprise. The Quai d'Orsay responded that such a move, without prior agreement with the French government, would be regarded as an "inimical act."[29] In late November 1926, the Polish government retreated, yet mutual recriminations continued unabated.

The Poles had also to make some concessions to the predominantly French consortium engaged in the building of the Gdynia harbor, where previous controversies had resulted in a temporary halt of the works.[30] The construction of Gdynia was connected with the larger issue of Polish maritime trade and the development of a navy. The French ministry of the

1926, MAE, Pologne 75:25, 103–104. Dmowski's letter to Corradini in Borejsza, *Mussolini*, 175–78; 8 Aug. entry in MS, PAN, Dziennik Zdanowskiego; for party platform, see Berezowski, *Polityka zagraniczna*, esp. 22–23.

26. Laroche to Briand, 28 May, MAE, Pologne 75:40–41.

27. Dupont report 1 June; compare with 1 Mar. and 17 May 1926, SHA, EMA/2, Pologne 7; Laroche to Briand, 5 Nov 1926, MAE, Pologne 75:93–94.

28. See Gen. Dupont dispatches, 13 Oct. 1925, 3 Feb. 1926, SHA, EMA/2, Pologne 7; also extensive material in MAE, Pologne 243:143–56, 224–43, 245–47, and Pologne 214:104, 129–34, 143–46, 198–207.

29. See Ministry to Laroche, 4 Aug. 1926, MAE, Pologne 214:212–13.

30. A new Franco-Polish agreement was signed on 30 Oct. 1926. See Landau, *Plan stabilizacyjny*, 45–48; Steyer, "Stosunki," 46–47.

marine was interested in the latter; the Quai d'Orsay thought it unwise "to encourage exaggerated ambitions" of the Polish navy, when land forces were essential for the working of the alliance. Eventually, the French naval mission was maintained, and in September 1926 a French squadron visited Gdynia in a display of seafaring solidarity.[31] The French were clearly interested in orders placed in their shipyards, although the question of credit occasioned difficulties, and in 1926 contracts were signed for the building of two destroyers (Burza and Wicher).[32] A Polish maritime company initiated a regular service between Poland and several French harbors. In 1926 the volume of Franco-Polish maritime trade occupied in terms of tonnage and number of ships the second place in Poland's sea commerce. It would decline systematically in the years to come.

The Polish government was fully aware of the impact the economic issues had on the working of the alliance between the two countries. Thus, although often frustrated and humiliated by the exigencies of the French capitalists, Warsaw regarded concessions as necessary in the general context of Polish diplomatic and military strategy.[33] Although Ambassador Laroche established a good personal rapport with Piłsudski, he had come to Poland with a mission that to a junior French diplomat in Warsaw seemed like "the funeral of the Franco-Polish alliance."[34] This comment referred to France's wish to revise the 1921 military convention to make it more compatible with Locarno and less likely to draw Paris into a Polish-Soviet conflict. Piłsudski's view of the alliance, as above all a military commitment, did not encourage such an initiative. What is more, the marshal was disinclined to follow blindly the new course of French diplomacy, which could either sacrifice Poland at the alter of Franco-German amity or unnecessarily expose Poland to Berlin's animus. Piłsudski viewed Locarno as an essentially harmful and dangerous accord that perpetuated, nay legalized the disequilibrium between the West and the East.[35]

In early 1926, the marshal had denounced the brutal way in which Poland's demands for real guarantees had been denied, and his annoyance with Skrzyński stemmed not so much from the latter's adherence to the

---

31. After Rear-Admiral Jolivet's death in 1926, Capitaine de Vaisseau Richard became the head of the naval mission until succeeded by Capitaine de Frégate Ceillier in 1929.

32. For correspondence concerning shipyards (Chantiers Navals Français, Chantiers de la Loire, and Chantiers et Ateliers Augustin Normand) that involved Crédit Lyonnais et Paribas, see MAE, Pologne 43:4–7, and AAN, MSZ 3810 and 3811 and HIA, Amb. Paryż, box 1. The first destroyer, Wicher, was handed over to Poland in July 1930.

33. On Bartel and Zaleski's willingness to resolve Franco-Polish economic disputes, see Laroche to Briand, 18 June 1926, MAE, Pologne 135:170.

34. Barbier, *Un Frac*, 270.

35. Beck, *Dernier rapport*, 5–6, 267–68.

pact, but because of his representation of it as satisfying Poland's need for security.[36] After the May coup, Piłsudski authorized Zaleski, in the absence of other options, to pursue a Locarno policy, and the foreign minister executed it loyally albeit without enthusiasm.[37] Piłsudski himself concentrated on military matters.

The French did not find it easy to cooperate with the marshal in this area. General Charles Charpy, who replaced Dupont as chief of the military mission, shared with most French professional soldiers a certain prejudice against the "dilettante" Piłsudski.[38] He found him "excessively proud," although he recognized the marshal's intelligence, capacity for hard work, and devotion to the country and the army. Charpy worried especially about structural changes that Piłsudski was introducing into the high command without consulting the dwindling and increasingly neglected French military mission.[39] Laroche regarded the Polish army as "one of the best in Europe," even though it lacked adequate war material and was affected by political divisions. It was "infinitely superior to the Czechoslovak army" in view of the latter's multiethnic composition.[40] Charpy shared these views. As for the strategic dispositions, the general learned, after a lengthy conversation with the marshal, that in the case of a two-front war two-thirds of Poland's effective forces would be deployed on the German front and only one-third on the Russian front. If this commitment was sincere, Charpy commented, it constituted a military assurance vis-à-vis Germany and eliminated worries about Poland's anti-Russian policy. The information given by Piłsudski about the planned offensive against Germany Upper Silesia also met with the general's full approval. The Quai d'Orsay and the war ministry regarded Piłsudski's statements with the greatest interest.[41]

If, by the end of 1926, Charpy still regarded the marshal as a "disquiet-

36. Interview in Piłsudski, *Pisma zbiorowe*, 8:289; compare Jędrzejewicz, *Kronika* 2:180–81; Komarnicki, *Piłsudski*, 61; and Juliusz Łukasiewicz, *Polska w Europie w polityce Józefa Piłsudskiego* (London, 1944), 13. Also Gawroński, *Moja misja*, 394; Wandycz, *Zaleski*, 26.

37. See MS, BJ, Skirmunt, 145; and Savery to Gregory, 26 May 1926, FO 371 11762.

38. See, for instance, Dupont dispatch, 17 May, SHA, EMA/2, Pologne 7; compare with Laroche to Briand, 17 June 1926, MAE, Pologne 41:171.

39. The reorganization involved the creation of the General Inspectorate of Armed Forces (GISZ), which relegated the general staff to a secondary position; the abolition of the War Council; and the establishment of the Committee of State Defense (presided over by the president of the republic and comprising the inspector general, premier, ministers of war, finance, and interior, and the chief of the general staff).

40. Laroche to Briand, 28 Sept. 1926, MAE, Pologne 21:146–47, also his letter of 30 Aug. 1926, MAE, Pologne 21:141–44.

41. Laroche to Briand, 30 Aug. and Quai d'Orsay to war ministry, 4 Sept. 1926, MAE, Pologne 135:174–77.

ing enigma," Warsaw seemed to follow a restrained policy toward both Germany and Russia. The N plus R plan was still binding, although the mission received no details about the *ordre de bataille*. The Polish army counted on Romania for the eastern front and Czechoslovakia for the western front. Charpy wrote that Poland was a "young, ardent and effervescent" nation and, all its difficulties notwithstanding, had to be reckoned with. Military expenditure claimed a large part of the annual budget. The French could be proud to have assisted in the creation of an army that "in case of a conflict with Germany [may] bring effective aid to France."[42]

Crisis in Prague, Union Nationale in Paris

Czechoslovakia found the Polish coup disquieting because of the ascendancy of Piłsudski's and as a precedent. To many Czechs the marshal epitomized Poland's anti-Russian policies; to the rightist bourgeoisie he was a "Red marshal." The national democrats stressed his Czechophobia and militarism. The socialist press, although less inimical, disapproved on principle of army coups. The comments of the German-Jewish liberal bourgeois organ, *Prager Tagblatt*, were sharply critical. The somewhat worried agrarian papers were more guarded. The *Prager Presse*, on 16 May contrasted the volatile situation in Poland with that of its own country, asserting that the latter must remain an oasis of order and democracy. Although a genuine concern for Poland's welfare was noticeable in many articles, the dominant note was that "Czechoslovakia must at all cost avoid being itself the victim of any similar violence."[43]

In the summer of 1926, the earlier-mentioned conflict between the agrarian-Catholic bloc and the socialists was being overshadowed by one between the Hrad and the combined forces of Karel Kramář and the profascist wing of the national democrats. Personal animosities apart, this was really a confrontation between liberal democracy and authoritarian nationalism. The Hrad singled out General Gajda as the object of its attacks, and rumors circulated about his plans to resort to a coup d'état. Masaryk seemed to contemplate drastic constitutional changes to increase presidential powers.[44] In the course of a vicious campaign Gajda was accused of

42. End of year 1926 report, SHA, EMA/2, Pologne 10. Compare Charpy to war ministry, 14, 28 Aug., 2, 18 Sept. 1926, SHA, EMA/2, Pologne 7.

43. See DBFP, Ia, II:11–13; compare Couget to Briand, 19, 21 May 1926, MAE, Pologne 53:266–67; 27:85–87; Faucher to Painlevé, 24 May, SHA, EMA/2, Tchécoslovaquie 2. Press cuttings in MZV-VA 478.1238; *Češi a Poláci*, 2:525; also Leczyk, "Polityka zagraniczna."

44. See *Masarykův sborník*, 2:174; Campbell, *Confrontation*, 169; Gajanová, *ČSR*, 216; Gajanova, *Dvojí*, 46–49; Herman and Sládek, *Slovenská politika*, 67–69.

innumerable, even improbable, misdeeds and was politically destroyed.[45] It is likely that Italian intrigues may have also been at work, as some quarters in Rome sought to replace French influence in Czechoslovakia with their own.[46]

The Right, as noted earlier, concentrated its fire on Beneš demanding an end of his Locarno diplomacy, and flaunting its own antibolshevism and anti-Germanism. Even Beneš's own party, swayed by Stříbrný, tried to force him out of the cabinet. Masaryk threw his prestige behind Beneš, and the foreign minister refused to resign.[47] The French proved precious allies to the Hrad. The envoy, Joseph Couget, when asked what impression Beneš's resignation would make abroad, replied that even if he stepped down temporarily "his country would lose at least fifty percent of the influence and authority he had gained for it in Europe."[48] Beneš was able to weather the storm, and he would later regain his standing in the national socialist party with the expulsion of Stříbrný, but he rightly complained that the press campaign waged against him not only confused the Czechoslovak public opinion "but compromised me and the state at home and abroad."[49]

In the autumn, the Hrad, assisted by Švehla, began to work out a compromise. Švehla refused to be a presidential candidate and gave instead his full backing to Masaryk. The president in turn made political concessions to the Center, which resulted in the socialists passing into opposition, but allowed the formation of a powerful coalition that included the agrarians, the Catholic party, the chastised national democrats, the Slovak populists, and for the first time German ministers representing the agrarians and Christian socialists. The so-called Gentlemen's Cabinet (*Panská vláda*), formed on 12 October 1926, was presided over by Švehla, Beneš retaining the ministry of foreign affairs. Although diplomatic successes such as the election of Czechoslovakia to the League Council had strengthened Beneš's standing, certain changes in the foreign ministry could weaken it. Kamil Krofta, a national democratic sympathizer and a well-known historian, became Beneš's deputy replacing Václav Girsa, destined to become envoy to Warsaw. Commenting on the transfer of Girsa—"absolutely

45. For full treatment of the Gajda affair, see Zorach, "Gajda Affair"; Gajanová, ČSR; Campbell, *Confrontation*; and Olivová, *Doomed Democracy*.

46. See Gajanová, ČSR, 212–14.

47. See Eisenlohr to Secretary of State, 16 Sept. 1926, SDNA, 860. F.00/253; Clerk to Chamberlain, 24 June 1926, FO 371 11227 C7168.

48. Couget to Briand, 22 June 1926, MAE, Tchécoslovaquie 69:177–78.

49. Couget to Briand, 29 June 1926, MAE, Tchécoslovaquie 33:42–45; compare articles in *Přitomnost*, 22 July, 14 Oct. 1926, 24 Jan. 1927; Masaryk's interview in *Gazette de Prague*, 8 Sept. 1926. Beneš's letter appeared in *Národní Osvobození*, 13 Sept. 1926.

committed to Beneš's foreign policy, particularly to close entente with France"—the new French minister in Prague, François Charles-Roux reported rumors about Beneš's eclipse.[50] The French military in turn worried about the presence of Germans in the cabinet and its impact on Franco-Czechoslovak cooperation.[51]

The 1926 crisis had weakened Beneš. His freedom to maneuver was likely to be restricted, not so much by Krofta, who proved a model of loyalty, but by the generally conservative tendencies of the cabinet. High agricultural tariffs, for instance, were bound to create difficulties with the Little Entente. French-Czechoslovak cooperation, according to the American envoy, was changing its character; as France's international position grew weaker, the need for French support appeared less urgent to many Czechs.[52] Even before the formal takeover by the Švehla cabinet, Beneš took an extended leave of absence and went abroad, partly to recuperate, partly to allow the passions to cool. In his absence (he came back on 12 January 1927), Czechoslovak diplomacy became somewhat passive.

It would be too easy, however, to blame this passivity for a continuing Czechoslovak reserve toward Polish overtures. After the May coup, Zaleski and Knoll went on record, publicly and in private, in favor of a rapprochement with Czechoslovakia. Even the critical Czechoslovak envoy, Robert Flieder, had to admit that the Poles had been displaying "constant goodwill" toward his country. Piłsudski "seems to have repudiated his old animosities against the government of Prague," Flieder said, and Laroche was pleased to hear it. The ratification of the Czechoslovak-Polish commercial treaty in late June was followed a few weeks later by a visit of the Polish military attaché at the Czechoslovak general staff with a proposal to begin negotiations. Laroche opined that such cooperation, which "corresponds to the wishes of the French general staff, . . . can only contribute to direct the principal effort of the Polish army against a possible aggression by Germany and not against Russia."[53] General Charpy commented that Poland "continues carefully to cultivate friendly relations with the states of the Little Entente."[54]

Beneš's responses were ostensibly positive. He had made pro-Polish remarks at the Bled Conference of the Little Entente in June in the presence of a Polish observer.[55] When the commercial treaty came up for ratifica-

50. Dispatches of Couget, 22 Nov.; Laroche, 31 Dec. 1926; Charles-Roux, 18, 27, Jan. Margerie, 3 Feb. 1927; MAE, Tchécoslovaquie 27:136–37; 5:204, 208, 210.

51. Dodd to Chamberlain, 18 Oct. 1926, DBFP, ia, ii:453–54.

52. Einstein to Secretary of State, 28 July 1926, SDNA, 860F.00/252.

53. Laroche to Briand, 11 Oct. 1926, MAE, Tchécoslovaquie 62:75–76.

54. Charpy to Painlevé, 10 Oct. 1926, SHA, EMA/2, Pologne 7.

55. See MAE, Tchécoslovaquie 69:178–81. There is no mention of Poland, however, in Beneš's circular on the Bled Conference, DaM, ii, 275–76. On Polish utterances, see

tion, he reiterated that good relations with Poland were important "politically as well as economically," but skillfully avoided being drawn into a discussion of the nature of a rapprochement.[56] The Yugoslav minister in Warsaw was skeptical and his Romanian colleague, recalling Piłsudski's bitter feelings toward Prague, thought that the Czechs ought to go out of their way to make advances to Warsaw: "Prague had taken enough advantages of Poland." Laroche seemed to agree, for he recommended that Briand extend good advice to Beneš, which would surely be heeded.[57]

Polish-Czechoslovak military talks appeared to hold some promise. The return of František Udržal as minister of defense in the "gentlemen's cabinet," and the maintenance of Syrový as chief of the general staff seemed a good augury. General Syrový reassured the Polish envoy that the German ministers would not affect conversations, for they were not included in the inner, decision-making cabinet. Udržal deemed a military agreement with Poland essential in view of the German danger, and explained that although Beneš had opposed it in the past and influenced Syrový against it, he would have now to adapt his views to those of the majority of the cabinet. Lasocki observed that a military convention might still have to be tied to a political agreement, of which Beneš seemed to disapprove, but Udržal was sanguine even about that aspect.[58] The Poles were interested in a comprehensive military-political accord, and the military attaché in Prague reasoned that Czechoslovakia's international weakness would make the government move closer to Warsaw.[59] His prediction, however, proved to be far too optimistic.

Polish overtures were answered by a formal letter of Syrový that expressed—"for reasons of pure courtesy," Faucher commented—hopes for inter-army talks. "This did not commit him to anything." On Piłsudski's orders, the Polish army responded by reiterating its interest in technical-military negotiations. Syrový's reply, which came only in December, was "even more colorless." The reason was an intervention by Masaryk, who grew alarmed lest Polish initiatives "lead us to the conclusion of a military agreement," which he absolutely opposed.[60] Beneš's speech, read in his

Zaleski in *Prager Presse*, 25 May; Laroche to Briand, 19, 24 May 1926, MAE, Pologne 75:34–39.

56. On debate in the senatorial foreign affairs commission, see *Prager Presse*, 26 June 1926.

57. Laroche to Briand, 22 June 1926, MAE, Pologne 75:46–48; also Laroche, *Pologne*, 72; compare Kozeński, "Próby," 316.

58. Lasocki to Zaleski 30 Oct. (copy to Piłsudski), 4 Nov. 1926, AAN, MSZ 5502.

59. See Bułhak, "Z dziejów 1921–1927," 136–37.

60. Faucher to Debeney, 12 Apr., SHA, EMA/2, Tchécoslovaquie 2. Compare Charles-Roux to Briand, 21 Jan. 1927, MAE, Tchécoslovaquie 62:78–79. Also survey 25 Apr. 1928, SHA, EMA/3, 7 N 3007 "Coopération polono-tchéque."

absence on 9 December 1926, mentioned ever more intimate cooperation with Warsaw unaffected by political changes in Poland. Collaboration with Zaleski was "very close and most friendly."[61] These words, however, were not accompanied by any concrete moves by Prague.

The stabilization of Czechoslovak politics came three months after a similar event in France: the formation of the cabinet of National Union on 23 July 1926. Presided over by Poincaré, the "grand cabinet" comprised several former premiers (Briand, Barthou, Paul Painlevé, Georges Leygues, Herriot) and such prominent figures of the Center and Right as André Tardieu and Louis Marin. Its main task was to achieve a balanced budget and stabilize the currency, and it was indicative of the subjective factor in the French economy that once an aura of confidence was recreated, the franc began to recover rapidly. The combination of Poincaré as premier and Briand as foreign minister appeared odd at first glance, but it corresponded to the political mood and the economic realities of the country. The two men differed greatly, but their views on domestic and even foreign affairs were not irreconcilable; in fact, they greatly needed one another.

The new cabinet was greeted in Warsaw with relief. The Polish ambassador reported that Poincaré, a "nationalist" in foreign policy, was above Briand and his policy derived from the cartel.[62] Still, Polish concerns about the extent of Franco-German rapprochement remained alive. The formation of a French-German Information Committee (which met in Luxembourg on 29–30 May) led by a Luxembourgois industrialist, Emile Mayrisch, and inspired by his French son-in-law, Pierre Viénot, caused anxiety. Its membership, which included such notables as Henri de Peyerimhoff and Théodore Laurent (respectively of the Comité des Forges and des Houillières), the duke de Broglie, and writers Henri Lichtenberger, André Siegfried, and Wladimir d'Ormesson, looked impressive.

A Quai d'Orsay memorandum sadly commented that Britain had wasted the possibility of directing European affairs in collaboration with France, and the latter had now to cooperate with Germany, although France had no illusions about Berlin's pacifist or amicable intentions. The French foreign ministry believed that German industry had not abandoned the goal of becoming the economic mistress of Europe.[63] The bureaux of the Quai d'Orsay took a dim view of such schemes—for instance, Arnold Rechberg's idea of a Franco-German military-economic alliance, presiding over a "corridor"-Memel exchange and placing Poland under a joint guar-

61. See Couget and Charles-Roux to Briand, 20 Dec. 1926, 16 Jan. 1927, MAE, Tchécoslovaquie 27:140–41; 4:126. Speech of 12 Jan. 1927 in Beneš, *Boj o mír*, 362–73.

62. Chłapowski to Zaleski, 3, 10 Aug. 1926, AAN, MSZ 3788.

63. Note on the Mayrisch committee, 15 June 1926, MAE, Grande Bretagne 89:42–54. Compare L'Huiller, "Allemands," and his *Dialogues* also Wurm, *Die französische Sicherheitspolitik*, 436–41.

antee of Berlin and Paris. When *Le Matin* commented that such notions were "by no means disapproved by Frenchmen who exercise a great political influence," the deputy-director of the Quai d'Orsay caustically remarked that no such persons were to be found at his ministry.[64]

German revisionism, as we know, was based on the notion of a link between economics and territorial change. Ambassador Pierre de Margerie learned from Stresemann that Poland should be strengthened as a bulwark against Russia, and the price the Germans expected for their assistance was "an amicable settlement of the question of the corridor and Danzig."[65] Was this to involve the "corridor"-Memel exchange? The idea seemed ludicrous if only because of Russia, and Stresemann denied that he ever took the scheme seriously. But he alleged that others, including Sauerwein did. Most likely, Berlin spread these rumors to create a state of uncertainty about the "corridor," sow discord between Warsaw and Moscow, and test the French, without necessarily regarding the plan as feasible. Zaleski indignantly rejected the very notion of such a "solution" on several occasions.[66]

The formation of the Poincaré cabinet prompted Zaleski to start an exchange with Paris. Chłapowski was instructed to explain that, although Polish opinion saw in Poincaré's premiership a certain guarantee against an excessive Franco-German rapprochement, it could not ignore some danger signals. French public opinion ought to realize that absurd stories about German-Polish talks on financial aid in exchange for border revision only played into Germany's hands by weakening Franco-Polish ties. Warsaw's position was clear, and Paris must not hesitate to support it "on the pretext that Poland may seek on its own a modus vivendi with Germany." The Franco-Polish community of interests was evident, as was "the mutual responsibility to adapt the behavior of both governments fully to the letter and spirit of the alliance."

In his conversation with the premier, Chłapowski was to dwell on economic-financial problems, and draw Poincaré's attention to a remark by

64. Seydoux to Berthelot, 22 Apr. 1926, MAE, Allemagne 389:5–6. Articles in *Le Matin*, 22 Apr. 1926 and 5 Dec. 1927 and *L'Avenir*, 21 Oct., 1 Dec. 1926, and 4 Feb. 1927.

65. Margerie to Briand, 28 June 1926, MAE, Pologne 113:25–30. The ambassador may have heard such a blunt statement for the first time, but his predecessor Laboulaye, and Briand's confidant, Hesnard, had heard it already in Nov. and Dec. 1925. See Bariéty, "Finances, 56–58. Also MAE, Grande Bretagne 87:211–12.

66. For Stresemann's denials, see DBPF, 1a, 11:569; ADAP, B, 11/2:315–16. Compare Laroche to Briand, 31 Dec. 1926, MAE, Pologne 113:92–94. Also Riekhoff, *German-Polish Relations*, 253–54. Although Berthelot seemingly favored the Danzig-Memel exchange, he opposed any concessions in Upper Silesia, Wurm, *Die französische Sicherheitspolitik*, 348. Zaleski rejected the idea for the first time in an interview reprinted in *Le Messager Polonais* 22 Aug. 1926.

the Reichsbank president Hjalmar Schacht that Berlin would be willing to assist Poland financially in exchange for a settlement in the "corridor." Pointing to a certain analogy between Polish and French financial issues, the ambassador was to express satisfaction that France was not counting on German assistance either. What was needed was "a clear, decisive and strong policy based on the permanent basis of existing treaties," and both countries should act in coordination. Chłapowski was to mention that Poland had not been kept fully au courant of Franco-German commercial *pourparlers*.

Having told Briand of his conversation with Poincaré, Chłapowski was to assure the foreign minister that Polish policy toward Berlin was neither tough nor aggressive. But Warsaw and Paris should resist German attempt to undermine the reparations articles of Versailles and insist on a clarification of the treaty of Berlin. They should work for the creation of a common diplomatic front that included Belgium and Czechoslovakia. The ambassador was to ask why Briand had used the term *entente* rather than *alliance* in a recent telegram to Warsaw, and express Poland's alarm over alleged German-Belgian talks over the cession of Eupen and Malmédy. Such actions could open the way to revisionism and become a threat to peace.[67]

The significance of Chłapowski's conversations proved greater even than Warsaw anticipated, as is discussed later. The encounter with Poincaré on 17 April was very cordial, and the premier showed particular interest in Schacht's remark and spoke of a tough line toward the Eupen-Malmédy scheme. The analogy between German revisionism vis-à-vis Belgium and Poland was perfectly clear to Poincaré, and he spoke strongly about it at a later cabinet meeting. According to Chłapowski, Barthou and Leygues supported the premier. What is more, Poincaré immediately informed the Quai d'Orsay about Schacht's utterance and drew it to Briand's personal attention.[68] Hence, when Chłapowski visited the foreign minister, the latter was full of reassuring statements. According to Briand "the premise of normalization of relations with Germany must be the closest contact between France, Poland, and the Little Entente." Collaboration with Germany could not in any way undermine it. There were no differences between the French and Polish views on reparations; the treaty of Berlin could be dismissed as unimportant, for even the Russians regarded it as a scrap of paper. As for the Eupen-Malmédy affair, it was short lived.[69]

67. Zaleski instructions, 7 and 19 Aug. 1926, AAN, MSZ 3788, and HIA, Amb. Paryż, box 1.

68. Note, 17 Aug., MAE, Pologne 113:49; Poincaré to Briand, 19 Aug. 1926, MAE, Allemagne 398:16–17.

69. Chłapowski to Zaleski, 21 Aug. 1926, AAN, MSZ 3788; telegram in HIA, Amb. Paryż, box 1.

The fact that Poland had not been informed about Franco-German commercial negotiations, which Chłapowski complained about, was not unusual. Two months later, France would sign a treaty of friendship with Romania without consulting Warsaw.[70] The Poles could not do much more than register their annoyance, for more important matters were at stake. The question of Poland's place on the League's Council was finally resolved through the granting of a semipermanent seat. Poincaré strongly supported Poland; Briand was more ambiguous. The election on 16 September for a three-year period and the assurance of reeligibility brought large majorities in Poland's favor. Somewhat unexpectedly, Czechoslovakia was reelected for a one-year term, and Beneš retained, at Stresemann's motion, the presidency of the Council.[71]

The Polish arrangement in Geneva was naturally overshadowed by the memorable act of German entry into the League. Briand surpassed himself in oratory when he exclaimed "down with cannons and machine guns," and declared that France and Germany were now collaborating in the work of peace. Two weeks later the West European Steel Cartel was signed—joined by Prague but not by Warsaw—followed on 29 December by a potassium cartel.[72] Both agreements strengthened the important lobby in France that supported continuing cooperation with the Weimar Republic.

Thoiry and Its Repercussions

The famous encounter between Briand and Stresemann on 17 September occurred in the little French village of Thoiry shortly after Germany's entry

70. The Franco-Romanian treaty provided for consultation and coordination of policies. A secret protocol provided for an exchange of views between the general staffs on cooperation should the situation call for it. For the protocol, see D. Tuţu, "Alianţe militare de României 1921–1939," *Probleme de politica externâ a României 1919–1940: Culegere de Studii II* (Bucureşti, 1977), 116; I am grateful to Henryk Bułhak for providing a translation. Compare note on treaties and conventions between France, Poland, and the Little Entente countries in Gamelin, *Servir*, 2:465–74. Romania proceeded to sign a treaty with Italy on 16 Sept. which annoyed Prague, although neither the Czechs nor the Yugoslavs knew at that time of the existence of secret clauses providing neutrality if either party was at war. See *O Československé zahraniční politice*, 140; compare Giampierro Carocci, *Politica estera dell'Italia fascista 1925–1928* (Bari, 1969), 59 and Cassels, *Mussolini's Early Diplomacy*, 339. Also Iordan-Sima, "La Roumanie.

71. See exchange of Zaleski–Chłapowski–Sokal telegrams, 11, 27, 28, 31 Aug., 1, 3, Sept. 1926, HIA, Amb. Paryż, box 1 and 6. On Beneš, several laudatory articles appeared in the French press; see, for example, *Journal des Débats* 9, Oct. 1926.

72. See telegrams of Chłapowski, Jackowski, and the economic attaché, 2 Oct. 1926, and 29 Jan., 2 Feb. 1927, HIA, Amb. Paryż, box 1 and 5. Monzie hailed the steel cartel as "the key to Franco-German peace"; see Planté, *Monzie*, 193. On the cartel in a wider framework, see Maier, *Bourgeois Europe*, 516–45.

into the League.[73] The initiative came from Briand, who considered an influx of foreign capital into France a precondition for economic recovery, and played with the idea of a "solution d'ensemble," which involved the payment of German annuities under the Dawes Plan—in the form of commercialization of German railroad bonds—in exchange for concessions in the Rhineland. As the German press put it, somewhat crudely, Berlin would pay France for a premature evacuation. Berthelot had mentioned such an idea already in November 1925, and told the British that a continued occupation of the Rhineland was nonsensical. Briand and General Pierre Desticker allegedly shared this opinion, but not Foch or Pétain.[74] Schacht, considering a commercialization of the bonds extremely difficult, thought that Germany should exact the highest price: revision in the "corridor" and Upper Silesia, return of the Saar, and the lowering of the total sum of reparations.[75] During the spring and summer of 1926, Berthelot conveyed to the Germans Briand's desire for a confidential talk with Stresemann. The Germans showed interest, but mentioned that a Franco-German understanding should not be limited to the execution of the existing treaties. Then the cabinet crisis in France brought delays, and in the new ministry Briand's and Poincaré's views differed considerably. The premier was in favor of a financial operation and even mentioned it to the Belgians and the Poles,[76] but without any political conditions attached.

On 5 August, Briand's confidant, Oswald Hesnard, virtually prepared the ground for a meeting, but the above-mentioned intervention of Chłapowski made Poincaré, Berthelot, and a ranking official René Massigli bring it to a halt. "I am determined to oppose it most categorically," Poincaré wrote Briand after the conversation with the Polish ambassador, referring to a link between finances and territorial revisions. Briand responded that he shared the premier's objections, but he seemingly saw no alternative to a deal with Germany, and was counting on his ability to circumvent the opposition in the cabinet.

Because the Thoiry conversations were not to engage France to a modification of the existing treaties, there was, as the Quai d'Orsay pointed out, "the risk of a *malentendu*" from the very beginning.[77] But, although

---

73. See Bariéty, "Finances"; Sieburg, "Les Entretiens"; Jacobson and Walker, "The Impulse."

74. See ADAP, B, I/1:10–11, 419–20. Also DBFP, Ia, 1:326–27.

75. See Stresemann to embassy in Paris, 8 Dec. 1925, ADAP, B, I/1:46–47.

76. See Chłapowski to Zaleski, 19 Aug. 1926, AAN, MSZ 3788; Grahame to Chamberlain, 28 Aug. 1926, DBFP, Ia, II:322.

77. See note of direction politique, 23 Nov. 1926, MAE, Allemagne 400:64. In the foreign affairs commission on 23 Nov., Briand barely mentioned Thoiry, and was clearly evasive on 19 Jan. 1927. CAE/Ch.

Briand had not been empowered to treat about the restitution of the Saar, the suppression of the Interallied Military Control Commission, an early evacuation of the Rhineland, or the transfer of Eupen and Malmédy in exchange for financial considerations, he did talk about these matters, intimating that arrangements were possible.[78] Briand acted in the hope of promoting an operation—expected to bring France about one milliard gold marks—that was qualified by Schacht as absurd, and by the Americans as most problematic.[79] By hinting to Stresemann that Poincaré might not remain in power, Briand engaged furthermore in rather dubious diplomatic double talk. No wonder he was reluctant to inform Paris about the conversation and kept misleading the Quai d'Orsay, which listened with some embarrassment to German accounts and tried to explain that the Germans must have misinterpreted the message.[80]

The reaction of French public opinion was mixed; several articles in the press referred to Thoiry as a funeral of Versailles. The revisionist tone of a Stresemann's speech to the German colony in Geneva aroused indignation. Senator Henry de Jouvenel rejected the idea of financial compensation for an early evacuation as illusory. "A German-French entente," he wrote, "can today only be an entente on the European east." Should Germany be disposed to enter into an economic entente with Poland, take engagements against the Anschluss, and provide security guarantees along the eastern borders similar to Locarno, the smaller European states would be reassured.[81] Sauerwein wrote in an analogous vein, although he was willing to contemplate some concessions to Germany. But the security gap left by Locarno had to be filled, he told a German diplomat. Reducing the length of the Rhineland occupation would cut the time the Eastern European states needed to consolidate. Piłsudski was "very reasonable," and both he and Beneš would gladly discuss these matters with the Germans, perhaps together with France.[82] Stresemann regarded Sauerwein's thesis as absurd, for Polish security had been achieved at Locarno, and "we cannot recognize a French right to maintain the occupation of the Rhineland to satisfy

78. See Bariéty, "Finances," 51–52; Stresemann's account and note, 17, 20 Sept. 1926, ADAP, B, I/2:188–91, 202–10.

79. On Schacht, see D'Abernon to Chamberlain, 7 Oct. 1926, DBFP, Ia, II:424; on American views Leffler, *Elusive Question*, 152–53.

80. See notes in MAE, Allemagne 398:54–58, 214–15; 399:2–6, 154–61.

81. *Le Matin* 9 and 24 Oct. 1926, Apparently these articles were inspired. See Olszowski to Zaleski, 26 Oct. 1926, PI, Amb. Londyn, reel 37; compare Jouvenel, *D'Une guerre*, 2:85.

82. Rieth to Auswärtiges Amt, 12 Oct. 1926, ADAP, B, I/2:325–27. Compare Sauerwein in *Le Messager Polonais*, 11 Dec. 1926.

Poland." Renewed efforts at a recognition of the eastern borders would naturally be rejected by Germany.[83]

In the French parliament, the Rhineland question became the center of attention, the deputies being somewhat confused whether the occupation was predominantly a security guarantee, a reparations pledge, or means of assuring the fulfillment of Versailles. The socialists tended to concur with the Germans that Locarno made a prolonged occupation unnecessary. The communists criticized Thoiry as an example of capitalist collusion. To some deputies, an early evacuation was possible only if France had other military substitutes; a representative of the Gauche Radicale argued that Germany should have enough sense to realize that Paris could not give up political rights for economic concessions. A moderate leftist spoke of the need for German guarantees to East European states to assure their security and inviolability of borders.[84]

The army's reaction was belligerent. General Debeney spoke publicly against a premature evacuation, and ranking officers close to Foch and the general staff told the Polish military attaché that a withdrawal from the Rhineland was at present unthinkable.[85] In *Revue de France* an unsigned article appeared (penned by Foch) that passionately argued that an evacuation would leave France vulnerable until the defense of frontiers was assured and the parliament voted the law on military organization.[86] At the Conseil Superieur de la Défense Nationale (CSDN) the marshal declared that to withdraw from the Rhineland meant abandoning substance for a shadow, and demanded that no concessions be made.[87] Giving Briand a memorandum on German disarmament evasions, he warned that if his position were ignored he would publicly disclaim all responsibility.

In two major speeches, at St. Germain-en-Laye and at Bar-le-Duc (26 and 27 September), Poincaré declared that a rapprochement with Germany, which he favored, had to be in accord with "our treaties and our alliances." France wanted tranquility in Europe, a stability on its frontiers, and the independence of "our diplomatic action." It wanted permanent safeguards and reparation payments. Privately, the premier admitted that he was not hostile to a premature evacuation, provided it occurred when

83. See Stresemann notes and telegrams in ADAP, B, 1/2:360–61, 373–75; 11/2:316.

84. M. Plaisant; compare the remarks of Fontanier, Berthod, and Marcel Cachin. J.O. Chambre, second session 29 Nov., and first session 30 Nov. 1926; 3878–82, 3885–87, 3899.

85. Col. Kleeberg to second bureau, 23 Sept. 1926, AAN, MSZ 2789.

86. "Un Crime de lèse-patrie: l'evacuation anticipée de la Rhénanie," *Revue de France*, Nov.–Dec. 1926.

87. SHA, CSDN, 3 Dec. 1926. The Conseil was presided over by the president of the Republic and included key ministers, vice-presidents of the CSG, and the Navy and Air Councils.

all military works on France's eastern borders were completed and involved complete mobilization of obligations under the Dawes Plan.[88] Poincaré avoided public criticism of Briand, and the cabinet reaffirmed its solidarity with the foreign minister. Clearly, the premier did not wish to bring differences into the open and concentrated on killing Thoiry quietly.[89]

Briand minimized the importance of articles appearing in France on the German-Polish borders. He told the German ambassador that it was the German press that was reopening issues regarded by Paris as definitely settled by the treaties and strengthened by Locarno. According to the German version of the conversation, Briand said that it was absurd to burden the Franco-German understanding with attempts at a German-Polish compromise.[90] In the foreign affairs commission and the CSDN, he stated that France would not give away something for nothing. Besides, it was not the evacuation that was on the agenda but the investigation commission in Germany acting under the auspices of the League.[91] The British were thus close to the mark when they opined that Berthelot's motto now seemed to be "festina lente," and suggested "no more Thoirys but a little sober English sense."[92]

Indeed, Berthelot and such top officials as Charles Corbin and Jacques Seydoux, visibly annoyed by Briand's proceedings, believed that each of the issues raised at Thoiry required a separate and detailed analysis. Because he thought that Briand had gone too far, Berthelot inspired a number of articles in *Le Temps* critical of concessions to Germany.[93] Several notes prepared at the Quai d'Orsay examined the East European implications of Thoiry, seeking a way to satisfy the legitimate concern of France's allies. The occupation, one note said, was meant to guarantee the execution of all the dispositions of Versailles, particularly the fulfillment of reparations, and was a pledge of security. If, after fifteen years, the allies considered

88. See conversation, 23 Sept. 1926: Moreau, *Souvenirs*, 111. Compare Poincaré–Hymans talk, 27 Aug. 1928, DDB, II, 530.

89. See Hoesch reports, ADAP, B, I/2:400–405, 504–505; Chłapowski reports, 26, 30 Sept. 1926, AAN, MSZ, 3789. According to the Belgian envoy, all the cabinet members, including Louis Marin, thought that conversation begun at Thoiry should be continued. Gaiffier to Vandervelde, 26 Sept. 1926, DDB, II, 377.

90. Briand–Hoesch conversation, 28 Oct. 1926, MAE, Allemagne 399:203–204. Compare Hoesch's account, ADAP, B, I/2:392; also 381.

91. 30 Nov. 1926, CAE/Ch; 3 Dec. 1926, SHA, CSDN.

92. Chamberlain minutes on Phipps report, 15 Dec. 1926, DBFP, Ia, II:655–57.

93. Massigli belonged to the critics of Thoiry; see Soutou, "L'Alliance," 307–308. On differences within the Quai d'Orsay, compare Chłapowski's dispatches, 4 and 22 Dec. 1926, in which he praised Berthelot as a good friend (AAN, MSZ 3791), with Hoesch to Schubert, 6 Nov. 1926 (ADAP, B, I/2:426–33). Berthelot told the British that he had inspired articles in *Le Temps*; see Phipps to Chamberlain, 23 Sept. 1926, DBFP, Ia, II:396.

that guarantees against German aggression were insufficient, the evacuation of the Rhineland could be postponed. "As long as we are on the Rhine we have effective means" to prevent a disruption of the territorial status quo and allow "the young States to have a respite to achieve their economic and political consolidation." If earlier withdrawal was to be contemplated, it would be opportune "to demand of Germany, in a way to be determined," new assurances of respect for the status quo. A new guarantee of peace "would have the advantage of proving to our allies of Warsaw and Prague that we do not separate our cause from theirs, and that we do not conceive of a French-German rapprochement in which their interests would be sacrificed."[94]

Another note examined the issue of Danzig and the "corridor," coming to the conclusion that the Germans had failed to demonstrate that they suffered from a separation of East Prussia from the Reich. As for Upper Silesia, the Poles could not do without it.[95] Still, another memorandum opined that because the German government would always seek to revise the status of the corridor, the problem had to be studied sooner or later. Poland's interest could be satisfied by a free port in Danzig, a neutralization of the Vistula River, and the right of permanent passage to the Baltic, for in case of war the Germans would occupy Danzig and cut off the "corridor" anyhow. What mattered most was for Poland to gain time in order to improve her position. Hence, Poland must establish economic ties with Germany, and France, far from being jealous, ought to welcome it.[96]

The memoranda pointing to a clear connection between the Rhineland evacuation and Poland emphasized the need to gain time, even, as in the last document, at the price of some territorial concessions. All this was extremely important from the Polish point of view. So was the fact that Thoiry, by bringing the Rhineland question into the open, made it more difficult for France to maintain a rigid and legalistic attitude. That in itself was a German success.

Beneš made no reference to Thoiry when talking shortly thereafter to Staatssekretär von Schubert. He dwelt instead on the absence of an anti-German sentiment in the Little Entente, and reminded the German that there were no points of friction between Prague and Berlin. As for Poland, Beneš explained that Czechoslovakia cultivated friendly relations without being bound by any special ties. When Schubert steered the conversation to issues concerning Danzig, the "corridor," and Upper Silesia and remarked that these problems, although not yet acute, would have to be

94. Note, 8 Oct. 1926, MAE, Allemagne 399:51–60.

95. Note by Blanchet, 15 Sept. 1926, MAE, Pologne 113:53–54.

96. Note from Seydoux's office, 23 Nov. 1926, MAE, Allemagne 400:64–81. Compare note on Seydoux–Walter Simons conversation, 23 Oct. 1926, MAE, Allemagne 289:116–32.

solved to Germany's satisfaction, Beneš "seemed to agree," except with respect to Upper Silesia.[97] Schubert may have used this conversation to inspire rumors spread by the German press about an alleged plan of Beneš concerning the rectification of the German-Polish borders; the Poles were understandably worried.

Warsaw naturally wanted to know if the Polish question had figured in the Thoiry talks, and if not, whether peaceful revision in the West (Eupen and Malmédy) would not create a precedent for the East. Because a premature evacuation of the Rhineland would unfavorably affect the Franco-Polish alliance, should not increased security in the East be considered a possible price Germany would pay for concessions on the Rhine? Such an arrangement would close the Locarno gap.

In reply to Laroche's inquiries concerning Thoiry, Paris cabled that "no allusion had been made to questions interesting Poland," and that the conversation contained nothing that could alarm or even "awaken the susceptibilities of the Polish government."[98] Becaue the Czechoslovak envoy Osuský had heard from Prague that there had been secret German-French talks on the "corridor" and Memel, the Quai d'Orsay instructed the missions to use every opportunity to reiterate that "the French government had never thought and does not think of lending itself to any revision of the territorial status quo in Eastern Europe."[99] Briand assured the Polish ambassador that the Thoiry talks had stemmed from Stresemann's initiative, and promised to pass on any information about subsequent conversations that could concern Poland, even in an indirect way. France would oppose any attempt to reopen the issue of the German-Polish frontier, which was "a matter settled once and for all."[100]

These protestations rang hollow. Briand could hardly claim credit for the fact that East Central Europe had not been discussed at Thoiry. It was Stresemann who had no desire to complicate the Franco-German dialogue by introducing the eastern issues. Chłapowski believed that Berthelot, rather than Briand, viewed the occupation of the Rhineland as crucial for European and especially Polish security. Commenting on the rumors about the "corridor," Memel, and secret Franco-German talks, Laroche wrote that "it would be an illusion to believe that concessions to Germany in this region would assure peace." He warned against moves that could under-

---

97. Note, 25 Sept., ADAP, B, III:394–97. Beneš regarded Schubert's statement as "grave." See Couget to Briand, 7 Oct. 1926, MAE, Tchécoslovaquie 39:33–35.

98. Laroche to Briand, 22, 24, 26 Sept., MAE, Pologne 134:181–85; compare Charpy report, 28 Sept., SHA, EMA/2, Pologne 8. Also Briand and Berthelot to Laroche, 28 Sept. 1926, MAE, Allemagne 398:200, and Pologne 134:186.

99. Briand to missions, 27 Oct. and note of Blanchet, 12 Nov. 1926, MAE, Pologne 113:67, 71.

100. Chłapowski telegram, 6 Nov. 1926, HIA, Amb.Paryż, box 1.

mine Poland's confidence in the French alliance. "The raison d'être of Poland from our point of view is that it is our outpost placed east of Germany." Although one naturally wants Poland to live in peace with the Germans, "we have no interest to see it either diminished or pushed into the arms of Germany, which would almost certainly happen if people here had doubts about our support."[101] Once again the Quai d'Orsay repeated that matters concerning Poland "had not been raised either at Thoiry or since then." A few weeks later, Poincaré said the same thing, and gave an assurance that France would remain true to its alliances and friendships.[102] Yet rumors persisted, including one about a revisionist statement made at the annual congress at the radical socialist party,[103] and naturally were publicized by the German press.

Zaleski sought to ally the nervousness of Polish public opinion. He affirmed that the Franco-German rapprochement at Thoiry and thereafter need not cause any anxiety. Voicing his confidence in France, the foreign minister expressed a desire for good relations with Germany, but also left no room for doubt that Poland would forcibly oppose any revisionism attempted at its expense.[104] Zaleski told the American envoy confidentially that it was desirable for France and Germany to settle their differences, for the "economic strength of France would be helpful to Poland." Thoiry and the continuing talks were not alarming, because the French could not permit Germany "to take advantage of the situation detrimental to the interests of Poland." Briand would consent to an earlier evacuation only if Germany gave sufficient guarantees that it would comply with disarmament provisions, guarantees that would act "as protection of Poland against German aggression."[105] While Piłsudski, according to Laroche, was inclined to act toward Germany in a circumspect and pacific fashion, and he wanted Paris to know it, the Polish government visibly desired to affirm its loyalty as an ally of France.[106]

101. Laroche to Briand, 8 Oct., MAE, Pologne 113:59–60. The Poles got an inkling of this telegram; see Chłapowski to Zaleski, 4 Dec. 1926, AAN, MSZ 3991.

102. Briand to Laroche, 13 Oct., MAE, Pologne 113:65; Poincaré's remarks in *Le Messager Polonais*, 10 Nov. 1926.

103. On the statement attributed to W. Bertrand, see Margerie to Briand, 19 and 27 Oct., MAE, Allemagne 399:135, 165; *L'Avenir*, 22 and 27 Oct.; Polish documentation in AAN, MSZ 3789 and 3790. On the uncritical handling of the French press by Polish journals, see Chłapowski to Zaleski, 30 Oct. 1926, AAN, MSZ 3789. On a pro-Polish resolution of the radical socialist party, see Chłapowski telegram, 18 Nov. 1926, HIA, Amb. Paryż, box 1.

104. Zaleski's utterances appear in *Le Messager Polonais*, 16, 28 Oct., an article written at the foreign minister's request, 8 Oct. 1926. For a brief synthesis of Zaleski's stand, see Wandycz, "La Pologne face."

105. Stetson to Secretary of State, 2 Nov. 1926, SDNA 751.60C./8.

106. Laroche to Briand, 16 Nov. 1926, MAE, Pologne 113:78–81.

The foreign ministry was mapping out a strategy to achieve Poland's participation in future decisions on an early evacuation of the Rhineland. Warsaw would base its claims on article 428 of Versailles, which spoke of the occupation as a "guarantee for the execution of the present Treaty," and on articles 2 and 4 of the 1921 Franco-Polish treaty, which referred to the maintenance of international peace and mutual consultation. Warsaw aimed at obtaining compensation for an early evacuation in the form of "firmer security for the borders between the Reich and Poland (Czechoslovakia)." A formula acceptable to the Locarno powers had to be found, and the memorandum recommended concerted diplomatic action in Paris and perhaps in Rome, London, and Washington.[107]

In early December, Zaleski went to Paris where he gave several press and radio interviews.[108] This visit was his second in the French capital in 1926; the first, in late August, had been overshadowed by recriminations surrounding Poland's seat at the League Council.[109] Now, the foreign minister concentrated on three issues: French policy on limitation of armaments (and he stressed that as France's military might declined the value of the alliance with Poland proportionately increased); coordination of policies toward the forthcoming abolition of the Interallied Military Control Commission in Germany; and new security guarantees in case of changes in the Rhineland status. Zaleski seemed pleased with the result of his conversations with Briand and Painlevé, who emphasized that these problems were linked to security guarantees in the West *and* the East. As for the effects of new French army laws on the alliance, the French ministers proposed the holding of a general staff conversation with the Poles.[110]

During his Paris visit, the Polish foreign minister met with Beneš on 6 December, and the two statesmen discussed the question of the planned withdrawal of military controls from Germany. The Czechoslovak foreign minister told his Polish colleague that he was trying to dissuade Briand from going too far in the direction of a compromise with Germany, but conversations with Briand were difficult because they always stayed in the realm of generalities.[111]

Polish efforts to safeguard their country's interests within the context of France's Locarno policy were being constantly undermined by Berlin, which assiduously worked to weaken the Franco-Polish alliance. In the

---

107. See "Pro Memoria," 7 Nov. 1926 printed in Grosfeld, "Polska," 7, 1 (1975), 191–93.

108. Notably for *Le Matin, Le Journal, Radio Agence*. See Chłapowski report, 11 Dec. 1926, AAN, MSZ 3791.

109. Zaleski's official declaration, *Le Temps*, 30 Aug. 1926. Also Jackowski, *W Walce*, 332–33.

110. Zaleski telegrams, 27 Nov., 3 and 4 Dec. 1926, HIA, Amb. Paryż, box 1.

111. Krasuski, *Stosunki 1926–1932*, 65.

anti-Polish strategy proposed at the Auswärtiges Amt, the emphasis was placed on France as holding "the key."[112] In the Reichstag, Stresemann claimed that the idea of guaranteeing Polish borders as a condition for an earlier evacuation of the Rhineland was considered absurd in French official circles, a statement that naturally caused a certain consternation in Warsaw and Paris.[113] Zaleski was also taken aback by the brutality of Schubert's remark made to him in Geneva, that a normalization of German-Polish relations would be impossible without a "solution of the border problem."[114] To make matters worse, German propaganda insinuated that Zaleski had talked about border revisions. The indignant foreign minister used the first opportunity to declare publicly and firmly that Poland would not give up one square inch of its land.[115]

As the year 1926 was drawing to a close, France and Czechoslovakia had regained their political-financial stability, and Poland was firmly under Piłsudski's control. A new cabinet presided over by the marshal was installed in October. Franco-German rapprochement proceeded. Thoiry may have been stillborn, but insofar as it brought the evacuation of the Rhineland to the forefront of international politics, it resembled a stone cast in a pond causing ripples that went wide and far. The eastern gap of Locarno was likely to widen, unless France, Poland, and Czechoslovakia were to act in unison to prevent one-sided concessions to Berlin.

112. Zechlin memorandum, 19 Nov. 1926, ADAP, B, II/2:345–51.

113. See *Berliner Tageblatt*, 24 Nov. 1926.

114. Compare ADAP, B, II/2:411–13; and Wandycz, *Zaleski*, 44–45.

115. See Wandycz, *Zaleski*, 45–47.

Chapter Three

Eastern or
Central European Locarno

Polish Diplomatic Offensive

The decision to withdraw the Interallied Military Commission from Germany, taken on 12 December, opened a new diplomatic phase. According to Stresemann all Germans expected that 1927 would bring a total evacuation of the Rhineland, and a gradual reduction of occupation troops was seen as a step in that direction.[1] German optimism, however, was premature, and the tactics of forcing the pace a mistake, as became apparent in a rather confused series of developments that involved Germany and the East.

If, as the French ambassador in Moscow thought, "the sun of Locarno" was really setting in the West, ought one not try to cultivate Russia, which alone could assure peace in the European East? Were the Soviet Union to move closer to Germany, it might exert such a pressure on Poland that France would become powerless to assist its ally.[2] But a rapprochement with Moscow was problematic, and Soviet diplomacy appeared more tortuous and perplexing than ever. Talks on a Russo-Polish nonaggression pact were resumed in March, but the Poles were dubious about real Soviet intentions. Litvinov's remarks about France being "a common friend" seemed to the Poles a hint to involve Paris as a mediator. Was Chicherin really aiming at some Russo-French-German understanding that could be prejudicial to Warsaw? Would France fulfill its obligations to Poland if the latter were attacked by Soviet Russia?[3]

These were not academic questions at a time when Polish-Lithuanian tension began to assume threatening proportions.[4] Piłsudski had been say-

1. See Stresemann circular, 18 Mar. 1927, ADAP, B, v:5–6.

2. Herbette to Briand, 8 Feb. 1927, MAE, Russie 359:117.

3. See Zaleski instructions for Patek, 31 Jan. 1927, PI, Amb. Londyn, reel 37; also Herbette dispatches, 12, 14, 16 Mar. 1927, MAE, Russie 359:128–34; and Brockdorff-Rantzau to Auswärtiges Amt, 22 Mar. 1927, ADAP, B, v:38

4. See Senn, "Polish-Lithuanian War Scare," and his *Great Powers*.

ing that he could not tolerate forever the "state of war" that, according to Kaunas, existed between the two countries. One could visualize the scenario of a Polish-Lithuanian conflict bringing about a Soviet intervention from which Germany might be tempted to profit. Stresemann actually said that the Russians suggested the possibility of such a development to him.[5]

Rumors about Piłsudski's warlike designs on Russia that emanated from Moscow seemed designed to embarrass Warsaw, for neither Chicherin nor the French diplomats took them seriously.[6] It is also hard to believe that Stresemann was really worried about the possibility of a Polish attack on East Prussia, as he pretended to be.[7]

Paris took Poland's side in its quarrel with Lithuania, but it also preached moderation to the Poles and sought to enlist Berlin's cooperation in resolving the Polish-Lithuanian conflict. The Germans could only gain diplomatically from a role of peacemakers in the east at a moment when their good faith was being questioned over the so-called eastern fortifications. The latter had been constructed in violation of disarmament clauses, and Briand had actually overcome Foch's objections to the withdrawal of the Interallied Military Commission by stressing its inefficacy: in six years it had failed to discover such fortifications in Königsberg, Glogau, and elsewhere. Stresemann tried to justify their construction by arguing that Germany had to protect itself against the Poles, who could in two day's time advance all the way to Berlin. But he realized that Briand was hard put to defend himself against the accusation of having "left the Poles in the lurch."[8]

There was a feeling in the Polish ministry of foreign affairs that if Briand were both premier and foreign minister, and there was no Foch, Germany might have gotten away with only a perfunctory inquiry into the issue of fortifications. Even as things were, the Poles had to multiply their efforts. Chłapowski recommended not to conceal a negative attitude toward the German-French rapprochement, and to argue against the theory of the "little states" of Eastern Europe, which reflected an attitude of condescension toward the "clients." In accord with Zaleski's instructions of 31 December 1926 a diplomatic offensive began. Memoranda were sent to Briand, Berthelot, and Massigli (then secretary of the Conference of Ambassadors) with copies to Marshal Foch. Throughout January and Febru-

---

5. See Stresemann–Chamberlain conversation, 12 Dec. 1927, DBFP, 1a, IV:182; and Hoesch visit, 30 Dec. 1927, MAE, Lithuanie 36:69–70.

6. See Schubert note, 2 Dec. 1926, ADAP, B, II/2:376; also Margerie and Laroche to Briand, 20 and 27 Dec. 1926, MAE, Allemagne 380:107–109 and Pologne 21:152–53.

7. See Chamberlain to Tyrrell, 6 Dec. 1926, DBFP, 1a, II:580–81.

8. See ADAP, B, I/2:583. The Quai d'Orsay warned Briand of the unfortunate effect that a glossing over the eastern fortifications would produce in Poland. Note, 12 Nov. 1926, MAE, P.A. Massigli 4.

ary 1927, the embassy reported almost daily contacts. The army, the press, and the deputies were exposed to a barrage of Polish representations.[9]

At home, Zaleski displayed an attitude of tranquility that prompted a rightist deputy to remark that "while Briand's optimism was incomprehensible, Zaleski's equanimity was puzzling." The minister's outward calm did not exclude his firm position on strict observance of treaties and a rejection of any tendency to differentiate between pacification in western and eastern Europe. Security was indivisible, and only if one accepted this axiom could one strive for understanding in Europe, which included Franco-German reconciliation.[10] Briand paid lip service to the Polish position, but kept telling Chłapowski that a German threat to Poland was not real for a long time to come. Chłapowski realized that while the French foreign minister "strove to strengthen my conviction that he is always our old friend on whom we could rely," he was in fact annoyed with Zaleski's pronouncements. This irritation showed in replies to questions about eastern alliances at the chamber's foreign affairs commission on 19 January.[11] Indeed, the French press took up the theme of sinister German intentions vis-à-vis Poland; Pertinax wrote about the preparations of a future battleground in the east. Several newspapers approved another declaration by Zaleski categorically rejecting the possibility of any territorial concessions.[12] Briand either knew or suspected that some of these articles were Polish inspired, and he complained about it when speaking to the German ambassador Leopold von Hoesch.[13]

The issue of eastern fortifications appeared thus as a warning against hasty and unilateral concessions to Germany, The Quai d'Orsay invoked public opinion that "is clearly growing restless at the apparent lack of response on the German side to M. Briand's policy of appeasement."[14] Marshal Foch spoke of the need for German "moral disarmament," which so far he had failed to notice. Without entering into the dragging exchanges on the eastern fortifications, one may recall that in May Briand insisted on the right of inspection, suggesting as a quid pro quo the reduction of the

9. See analysis of French trends in Chłapowski report, 11 Dec., as well as note for Zaleski, 31 Dec. 1926, and report, 5 Feb. 1927, in respectively, AAN, MSZ 3680, 3789 and 3792. Also Chłapowski telegram, 6 Jan. 1927, HIA, Amb. Paryż, box 1.

10. Speech, 4 Jan. 1927, in Zaleski, *Przemowy*, 1:46–47; for discussion in the foreign affairs commission, see *Kurjer Warszawski*, 5, 6 Jan. 1927; also Sprawozdania stenograficzne senatu, 9 Mar. 1927, CLI/3–15.

11. Chłapowski telegrams, 19 and 22 Jan. 1927, AAN, MSZ 3792.

12. Zaleski, *Przemowy*, 1:56–65.

13. Hoesch to Schubert, 9 Feb. 1927, ADAP, B, IV:269. Articles in *Journal des Débats*, *L'Avenir*, *La Victoire* and *Le Temps* had in fact been previously "discussed with" the Poles. See Chłapowski report, 27 Jan. 1927, AAN, MSZ 3792.

14. Chamberlain to Lindsay, 12 Jan. 1927, DBFP, 1a, II:716.

occupation troops in the Rhineland. He had already told the Germans that he favored an early evacuation but had to overcome the opposition of the cabinet and the army.[15] The Poles immediately pointed out that "any change affecting the occupation of the Rhineland is linked with the question of security and cannot be treated in isolation."[16] By July, the Conference of Ambassadors accepted German assurances that the fortifications had been demolished and officially confirmed the end of Allied military controls. Finally, by September 1927, Briand informed Stresemann that the French contingent in the Rhineland would be reduced, although not to the level that the German expected.

A premature evacuation of the Rhineland, while clearly not an immediate issue, continued to claim public attention. Between 3 and 12 January, *L'Echo de Paris* printed eight articles opposing evacuation, written by such prominent figures as Millerand, Frédéric François-Marsal, Georges Mandel, generals Edouard de Castelneau and Henri Mordacq, and others. The already familiar arguments—"moral blow to our military system"; loss of the last "gage de paix" France possessed; undermining French security, "the function of the security of our allies"—figured prominently in the articles. The occupation was also deemed important to allow the consolidation of the "resurrected Allies" and the firm establishment of republicanism in Berlin. Pertinax openly attacked French policy toward Berlin saying that the real issue that needed to be resolved was the "question Briand."

The socialist support of an unconditional evacuation represented a minority view, as did the belligerent position of *L'Action Française, Aux Ecoutes* or the Ligue des Patriotes at the other end of the political spectrum. The stand of the Right and Center was reflected in articles that observed that one could extract some German concessions now, but when the time came for the evacuation it would take place without any quid pro quo. Berthelot singled out Wladimir d'Ormesson's article "L'Occupation" in *Le Temps* on 15 February 1927 as most representative of the prevailing outlook in France.[17] It argued that it would be a waste of time to discuss the pros and cons of the Rhineland occupation in juridical, political, or psychological terms. No French government could allow an early evacuation without guarantees in the realm of security, reparations, and general policy. The end of the occupation was but a fragment of a larger whole: "After the Rhine, Danzig. After Danzig, Silesia. After Silesia, Austria." All

15. See ADAP, B, v: 143–46, 272–75, 295–99, 314–16.

16. Zaleski instructions, 10 May 1927, AAN, Amb. Berlin, 729. Chłapowski thought that Berthelot was more inclined to resist German pressures than Massigli; see reports 14, 20 May 1927, AAN, MSZ 3794.

17. See visit of ambassador, 17 Feb. 1927, MAE, Allemagne 400:150–53. The Polish embassy reported on the article, 18 Feb. 1927, AAN, MSZ 3793.

these questions had to be resolved through a joint and mutual accord, but none of them was yet ready for a solution. Hence, nothing would be gained by trying to rush.

The Germans thought otherwise. Working through the press, the Comité Franco-Allemand, and other channels, they sought to influence French public opinion.[18] The revisionist theme was dominant. As d'Ormesson later recalled, even the meetings of German and French Catholics always began with "Our Father" and ended with "Danzig and the Corridor."[19] Any French remark critical of the German-Polish border was eagerly reported. Thus, Peyerimhoff allegedly listened calmly to sharp criticism of Versailles; Poincaré seemed to agree with the francophile German Carl René that the "corridor" in its present form made no sense and should be settled amicably in the future, perhaps with Memel as compensation. Senator Henry Lémery's remark, which he later denied, that France would never be drawn into a conflict with Germany over the "corridor" was publicized, as was the private conviction of Robert Coulondre, a high-ranking official at the Quai d'Orsay, that the "corridor" was "a monstrosity."[20]

Given the obvious connection between an earlier evacuation of the Rhineland and Polish security, it was natural that Briand would be closely questioned at the foreign affairs commission by his political opponents. Such deputies as Franklin-Bouillon, Edouard Soulier, and the Alsacian Alfred Oberkirch were in the forefront with familiar warnings about a new Sadova and questions about "organic links of solidarity" with the eastern states. The foreign minister responded with the usual line that he had been in "intimate, almost daily collaboration with the representatives of Czechoslovakia and Poland," and he accused Franklin-Bouillon of being "more difficult than our Polish friends" who realized that the Locarno policy had given them greater security, and "they have thanked me for it."[21] Publicly Briand asserted again that Locarno did not prohibit France from crossing the Rhineland "to bring assistance to our Polish or Czech allies, if they were victims of aggression." A great bloc composed of France and its eastern allies was there, and even a fully rearmed Germany would not risk war against it.[22]

18. See Bariéty, "L'Appareil," 375–406; L'Huillier, "Allemands," 558–68; Kupferman, "Diplomatie parallèle," 80–81.

19. See *Le Figaro*, 3 July 1935.

20. See ADAP, B, IV:231–32, V:235–40, VII:211; also Barbier, *Un Frac*, 330, Laroche's correspondence 10 June, 7, 22 July 1927, MAE, Pologne 113:223–25, 239, 241, 249.

21. Sessions, 19 and 26 Jan. 1927, CAE/Ch. Chłapowski was well aware of Briand's difficulties with his opponents; see report 22 Jan. 1927, AAN, MSZ 3792.

22. Interview in *Le Petit Parisien*, 26 Feb. 1927.

Such pronouncements did not unduly worry Ambassador von Hoesch who wrote that it was not Briand who opposed a certain compromise over the German-Polish border but rather Poincaré and the army. This was also the opinion of Chłapowski who reported the premier's observation that "a German attack on Poland would be equivalent to an attack on France," and that cooperation between Paris and Berlin could only progress with a simultaneous improvement of German-Polish relations.[23] Indeed, Poincaré's speeches at Bar-le-Duc on 2 May, and Luneville on 19 June, even if partly motivated by domestic politics, sounded tough. He told the governor of the Banque de France that he did not favor a total commercialization of German bonds because this implied an evacuation of the Rhineland before France was militarily ready.[24] According to German sources this was also the view of Berthelot, who was "strongly influenced by Poland and who deplored that Briand always went unprepared to Geneva and was dancing there his 'Extratouren'."[25]

Was the Polish diplomacy right in refraining from openly challenging Briand's assertions? The editor of *L'Avenir*, Emile Buré, told Chłapowski that this approach only facilitated the minister's game vis-à-vis his opponents. The Poles should "*casser les vitres*," which would help Poincaré and affect the course of French foreign policy.[26] The Polish national democrats, exasperated by Briand's diplomacy—which seemed to justify "Piłsudski's attitude of open and contemptuous neglect of friendship and alliance with France"—shared this view. One of their party leaders, irritated by Zaleski's reticence, noted that the foreign minister "at last" took a stronger line in his speech.[27] Several Polish diplomats were annoyed with Briand's tactics, and Chłapowski displayed a calculated reserve toward the minister who "seeks tendentiously to exploit our courtesy in order to disarm the opposition."[28]

Yet "some cooling in the exclusive attachment of Poland for France" was, in the British opinion, not only due to Briand's policy but also to French treatment of the country as a colony; Laroche was allegedly "not the least exponent of this attitude."[29] This comment referred to economic friction much in evidence throughout 1927. A Polish decree regulating the

23. Hoesch reports in ADAP, B, IV:106–107, 194–96; Chłapowski to Zaleski, 5 Mar. 1927, AAN, MSZ, P.II,w.11,t.3 (old classification).

24. Moreau, *Souvenirs*, 320.

25. See ADAP, B, V:582.

26. Chłapowski report, 23 Dec. 1926, AAN, MSZ 3791.

27. MS, BJ, Rymar, II, 149; and MS, PAN, Dziennik Zdanowskiego, VI, p.I, 70, 131.

28. Chłapowski report, 11 Feb. 1927, AAN, MSZ 3793; compare MS, OSS, Alfred Wysocki, "Dzieje mojej służby," I, 456.

29. Max Muller to Palairet, 20 Apr. 1927, FO 371 12573 N 1872; also DBFP, 1a, IV:92, 185–87, 197–201. On Laroche see note 21 Jan. 1927, AAN, MSZ 3845.

employment of foreigners in industries raised French ire, and although Zaleski explained that the measure was principally anti-German, he could barely hide his irritation with French interference in Poland's legislative process.[30] The troubled affairs of the Skarboferm led to renewed representations, but even Laroche had to admit that French business interests were "not identical with those of the Polish government."[31] The Hotchkiss company negotiating a sale of their machine guns demanded that Paris make "the Polish government feel all the weight of the powerful intervention of France." Schneider wrote a terse letter to Piłsudski concerning the Starachowice works, a rather unorthodox procedure against which the Poles protested to the Quai d'Orsay.[32] In Upper Silesia, where the issue of local German participation led to mutual recriminations, Laroche had to lecture the French industrialists: "They must not forget that if we had wished to see the French element participate in the industrial and financial enterprises in Upper Silesia, this was surely not in order to play into German hands." The French should seek control but avoid giving the impression "that one exploits the industry without letting the country profit thereby." How would they react if similar proceedings took place in France?[33]

Pierre Quesnay told his chief, the governor of the Banque de France, that the egoism of the French businessmen in Poland was risking to hurt France's influence in the country. He characterized their policies as "exploitation."[34] There were also periodic clashes over trade relations, the existing convention being regarded as unsatisfactory on both sides.[35]

The economic dependence on France may have had something to do with the accommodating manner of Warsaw vis-à-vis Briand's foreign policy. But Zaleski was hardly passive. As part of the diplomatic-propagandistic offensive, he dispatched to Paris a special emissary, Anatol Mühlstein, whose talents for public relations were assisted by excellent contacts; he was shortly to marry Diane de Rothschild. Mühlstein conversed with, among others, Paul-Boncour, Louis Loucheur, Joseph Barthélemy, Henry de Jouvenel, and Auguste Champetier de Ribes. The Pole discovered that

30. Laroche–Quai d'Orsay exchange, 9, 18 May 1927, MAE, Pologne 252:22–23, 26, 34–36.

31. Laroche to Briand, 15 Dec. 1927, MAE, Pologne 214:305–306.

32. See Mar.–Sept. 1927 correspondence in MAE, Pologne 244:26–32, 60–62, 78–79, 88–94, 97–99, 102, 106–107, 194.

33. Laroche to Briand, 1, 13 Feb. 1927, MAE, Pologne 199:72, 87; also correspondence, 20 Nov., 1 Dec. 1927, Pologne 252:90. Compare Polish notes and reports, Oct.–Nov. 1927, AAN, MSZ 3671, and Jackowski, *W Walce*, 344.

34. See Moreau, *Souvenirs*, 438, 455.

35. French industrialists in Upper Silesia complained that out of the 12 to 15 million tons of foreign coal imported by France, only 325,000 came from the Polish (largely French-controlled) mines. See correspondence in MAE, Pologne 253:223–33.

Paul-Boncour, reputed to be the least pro-German politician of the Left, viewed the Rhineland as being of questionable military value, for no one in France thought in terms of an offensive against Germany to relieve Poland. Peace was the watchword, and an end of the occupation its precondition. Mühlstein found common language with Jouvenel who had opposed financial compensations for the withdrawal, and viewed German plans of neutralizing France as designed to facilitate a showdown with Poland. He repeated the catchword: no more Sadovas. Jouvenel understood by Eastern Locarno a security arrangement involving Germany and her eastern neighbors (principally Poland) which would fill the gap present in the Locarno pact. It would be the price Germany would have to pay for an early evacuation. He agreed with Mühlstein on the need to launch a vast propaganda campaign involving the chambers and the press.[36] Indeed, a campaign against the evacuation of the Rhineland began, and Jouvenel did become a champion of an "Eastern Locarno." In March 1927, thanks to Chłapowski's initiative, a group of Polish parliamentarians, representing all major political parties, visited France and unanimously defended the inviolability of Poland's borders and the need to guarantee them.[37]

The same month, Stresemann raised the Rhineland question with Briand in Geneva, despite earlier French warnings that the moment was inopportune. The result was a certain estrangement between the two statesmen. But while the evacuation issue momentarily receded into the background, the disarmament problem came to the fore. The Preparatory Commission for the Disarmament Conference had started its deliberation about limitations of armaments already in May 1926. The French tactics consisted of emphasizing the policy of cutting the length of military service as proof of peaceful intentions, while avoiding to appear unduly concerned with security. As for possible demands for guarantees in this area, the CSDN noted that "we can cover ourselves by the situation of Poland," which was far from secure.[38]

The key word was controls, for failing their introduction—as Paul-Boncour who represented France wrote Briand—an armament race would follow, and "neither our domestic policy nor our finances would permit us to embark on it."[39] Paul-Boncour praised the delegates of Poland, Czechoslovakia, and Romania for their loyal cooperation, but he did not fail to no-

36. Mühlstein to Zaleski, 8 Feb. 1927, AAN, MSZ 3794. Compare ADAP, B, v:596–98.

37. On the trip, see reports in AAN, MSZ 3793, 3794; Laroche to Briand, 3 Apr. 1927, MAE, Pologne 284:134–35; MS, PAN, Dziennik Zdanowskiego, 1, 96–98; Pamiętnik Hermana Liebermana, MS in private possession.

38. See session 22 Apr. 1926, SHA, CSDN, 90–113.

39. Personal from Paul-Boncour to Briand, 27 Mar. 1927, MAE, P.A. Massigli 5.

tice their extreme apprehensions.[40] Such apprehension was understandable in view of German goals at Geneva, namely a diminution of French and allied armaments combined with some rearmament for Germany. France was the main target, for "there can be no doubt," the Reichswehr stated, "that the political and military power of Poland and especially of Czechoslovakia is based only on the military aid of France." Weakening France and its allies was naturally a prerequisite for the liberation of the Rhineland and the Saar, the elimination of the "corridor," the recovery of Upper Silesia, an Anschluss, and the end of the demilitarized zone.[41]

Warsaw insisted that without broadened security even limited disarmament would endanger Poland.[42] The precise nature of security guarantees would depend on the development of the Rhineland question, but the Poles wanted a French promise that they would receive a satisfactory quid pro quo. Piłsudski, the Polish chargé d'affaires Mirosław Arciszewski told Berthelot, was satisfied as long as French troops stayed on the Rhine. He wanted an assurance that Poland could count on a continued occupation, and if Paris decided on an early end to the occupation, he would demand guarantees equivalent to an Eastern Locarno. Berthelot replied that an early evacuation was not yet an issue, but he implied that should France contemplate it, special guarantees might take the form of reparation payments or provisions for supervision in the Rhineland. Although no specific safeguards for Poland were mentioned, the Poles seemed to have understood that the French shared their viewpoint that the evacuation issue could be linked with the general security problem, and would react favorably if Poland raised this matter in Geneva. Zaleski even explored the possibility of common action, but the Quai d'Orsay was evasive. Perhaps this attitude should have made him more cautious when in September the Poles advanced concrete proposals at the League.[43]

Ambassador Laroche, who thought that the Polish government had good cause to worry because "our presence on the Rhine is the greatest obstacle to a German attack against Poland," explained what the Poles had in mind.[44] Warsaw thought of invoking article 429 of Versailles,

40. See session, 20 May 1927, CAE/Ch; also Paul-Boncour, *Entre deux guerres*, 2:192.

41. See ADAP, B, I/1:343.

42. Zaleski telegram, 27 Mar. 1927, HIA, Amb. Paryż, box 1. Compare Michowicz, "Realizacja," 111.

43. Exchange of Arciszewski–Chłapowski–Zaleski telegrams, 28, 31 Mar., 1, 8, 9, 13 Apr., HIA, Amb. Paryż, boxes 1 and 4; 9 and 23 Apr., AAN, MSZ 3794. Arciszewski's visit and the ministry's request for comments, 31 Mar. and 6 Apr. 1927, MAE, Pologne 75:170–74.

44. Laroche to Briand, 14 Apr. 1927, MAE, Pologne 75:180–93.

which said that the evacuation "may be delayed to the extent regarded as necessary for the purpose of obtaining the required guarantees" of the fulfillment of the treaty. Because Zaleski had no illusion that Berlin might provide a direct guarantee to Poland, he envisaged a German-Polish non-aggression pact guaranteed by France and Britain. This proposal did not appear unreasonable to Laroche, and if Germany refused it "would be a serious warning for us" and might justify the invocation of article 429. A Franco-British guaranteed pact would cover France against what "we have always feared," namely, German aggression against Poland without a direct anti-French thrust, a situation in which agreements made at Locarno would operate against France. If it seemed dubious that London would be willing to become a guarantor, the matter was worth exploring. Laroche wondered whether Poland, effectively protected against Germany, might not revert to an "adventurous policy" toward Russia, but thought that Germany would take precautions to prevent such developments; there existed, after all, the Russo-German treaty of Berlin.

Thus, Laroche not only favored a German-Polish treaty guaranteed by the West, but he even recommended an analogous accord between Berlin and Prague. Thus, the plans and role of Czechoslovakia had to be taken into consideration by Warsaw and Paris.

Polish Advances and Czechoslovak Reserve

As Beneš returned to Prague in early 1927, his position was still insecure. But he was determined to stay, for his departure, as he told foreign diplomats, would only harm Czechoslovakia's foreign policy; as long as Masaryk remained president, he would be foreign minister.[45] In May, Masaryk was reelected, although the behavior of the opposition, especially the communists, tarnished the solemnity of the occasion.[46] The French were pleased with the election, even if François Charles-Roux, Couget's successor, found Masaryk too much inclined to talking philosophy and morality. But he and Beneš complemented each other, and no one except Beneš "could guarantee the continuity of a policy the elaboration of which was his work as well as Masaryk's."[47]

The withdrawal of allied military controls from Germany had caused

45. See Dodd to Chamberlain, 28 Apr., FO 371 12097 C 3920; Charles-Roux to Briand, 1 July, MAE, Tchécoslovaquie 39:47–48; compare Einstein to Secretary of State, 7 Jan. 1927, SDNA, 860F.00/263; and report, 11 Feb., AAN, MSZ 3793.

46. The vote was 274 in favor and 56 (communists) against, with 104 abstentions. For anti-Masaryk demonstrations, see Charles-Roux report, 28 May 1927, MAE, Tchécoslovaquie 27:224–26.

47. Charles-Roux to Briand, 27 Mar., 1 July 1927, MAE, Tchécoslovaquie 27:162–63, 230–32.

some apprehension in Prague. The press agitated for a series of new arbitration pacts with Hungary similar to those between Germany, Czechoslovakia, and Poland concluded at Locarno, but Beneš refused to take this line.[48] Instead, Czechoslovak leaders went out of their way to stress good relations with Germany. The president termed them friendly; Beneš called them excellent (when talking to the British envoy), although he deplored that Locarno had not covered the eastern borders.[49] The Czechoslovak envoy in Berlin told the *Vossische Zeitung* that it was the duty of Germans in Czechoslovakia to build "a bridge between the two nations."[50] The German members of the Prague cabinet were doing just this, and more, with a vengeance. One of them (Franz Spina) observed to *Le Matin* that at a time when France was normalizing her relations with Germany, a Czech-German animosity could not exist. His colleague, Robert Mayr-Harting, after asserting that the principles of Locarno and Thoiry ought to apply to domestic Czech-German intercourse, declared that Czechoslovakia's role of a French gendarme vis-à-vis Germany was over.[51]

Such pronouncements worried Charles-Roux, even though Beneš assured him that he entertained no illusions about what one could expect from the Czech Germans in case of an international conflict. When it came, the Czechs would determine and pursue state policies without them. The French envoy was particularly perturbed by the possibility of German ministers affecting Czechoslovak military affairs; the Quai d'Orsay forwarded his report to the war ministry.[52]

Czechoslovak military developments did not cause, per se, any major worries in Paris. The military mission, staffed by twenty-two officers, could stay indefinitely, even if it was assumed that it would cease functioning by 1928–29, mainly for reasons of attrition. It was hard to find a sufficient number of French officers willing to spend long periods in Czechoslovakia, because it interfered with their normal military career.[53] The by-product of the Gajda affair was the creation of a post of inspector general, which went to General Alois Podhajský, formerly of the old Austrian

48. See DBFP, 1a, III:69–73. Allegedly Hodža wrote at this time to the Quai d'Orsay to urge closing French-Czechoslovak-Polish ranks (23 Apr. 1927 report, AAN, MSZ 3794). I failed to find this letter in French archives.

49. Respectively, interview in *8 Uhr Abendblatt*, 31 Jan. 1927; *Masarykův Sborník*, 2:348; Macleay report, DBFP, 1a, III:282–85.

50. See Charles-Roux to Briand, 19 Apr. 1927, MAE, Tchécoslovaquie 39:44–46.

51. See military attaché report, 31 Dec. 1926, AAN, MSZ 5421; Charles-Roux dispatches, 31 Jan., 20, 21 Apr. 1927, MAE, Tchécoslovaquie 33:57–58, 89–90, 92, 95. Compare ADAP, B, IV:456–59.

52. Charles-Roux to Briand, and Quai d'Orsay to war ministry, 10, 22, 25 Feb. 1927, MAE, Tchécoslovaquie 33:61, 64–65.

53. See Charles-Roux dispatches, 4, 18 May 1927, 3 Jan., 24 Sept. 1928, MAE, Tchécoslovaquie 22:221–22, 237–39, 249–50.

army. The French military mission, which always preferred ex-legionaries as more reliable, was alarmed. Faucher spoke of a German victory and feared lest the general lead the Czechoslovak army away from "the path we had traced for it."[54] The decline of the percentage of military expenditure in the budget (from 20.87% in 1926 to 18.21% in 1927) caused some concern, although legislation passed on 30–31 March 1927 preserved the eighteen-month service, and new defense laws were adopted in April.[55] The French viewed with approval the policy to "czechisize" war production industries as well as attempts to strengthen Škoda by domestic amalgamations and acquisition of new establishments in the Little Entente countries and Poland.[56]

Charles-Roux noted with some irritation that the image of Czechoslovakia in France was largely shaped by propaganda emanating from Prague. There was no French correspondent in the country and Havas agency drew all its information from Czechoslovak sources. The establishment of Czechoslovak-French parliamentary groups in 1926 and 1927 respectively in Paris and Prague contributed to warm feelings but not always to a deeper knowledge. "French journalistic zeal to justify, favor, and celebrate the influence of the Germans in Czechoslovakia," was "excessive."[57]

Not only the French envoy but Lasocki, his Polish colleague, was also worried by the German influence in Czechoslovakia. Mayr-Harting's organ took a strong stand against "a Polish orientation in our foreign policy," and Lasocki found Beneš's reticent about the issue of German eastern fortifications, which the deputy chief of staff regarded as a threat to Czechoslovakia as well as to Poland. Lasocki considered Masaryk and Beneš too intelligent to engage themselves blindly in a pro-German path, and he received assurances from both to that effect. But he could not fail to notice that the Czechoslovak foreign minister seemed oblivious of the fact that Polish confidence in Prague, never strong, needed to be nurtured. Unless new efforts were made to draw closer, stagnation would set in.

Lasocki tried to deal with this situation by intensifying the collaboration

54. Faucher to Painlevé, 9 May, and report 2 May 1927, SHA, EMA/2, Tchécoslovaquie 2,12.

55. See Faucher to Painlevé, 23 Nov. 1926, SHA, EMA/2, Tchécoslovaquie 2, and trimonthly report, 18 Apr. 1927, MAE, Tchécoslovaquie 27:166–213.

56. Plans for linking the Starachowice metallurgical works with Škoda, however, ran into difficulties. See MS, OSS, Wysocki, 1,b, 449; Charles-Roux to Briand, 27 Feb., 10 Aug. 1927, 9 July 1928, MAE, Tchécoslovaquie 84:264, 288–92, 296. Also Jíša, Vaněk, *Škodový závody*, 209–19.

57. Charles-Roux to Briand, 11 Apr. 1927, MAE, Tchécoslovaquie 33:81–82. The envoy cited *Le Monde Slave*, but an article on Czechoslovakia in *Le Temps*, 17 Feb., would also illustrate this point. See also Preissig, *Die Französische Kulturpropaganda*, which, although a Nazi propagandistic publication, contains interesting material.

with Charles-Roux, but the French envoy could learn little from Beneš that could be used to promote a Polish-Czechoslovak rapprochement. The foreign minister thought that the Poles should appreciate more the fact that their border with Czechoslovakia required no military protection. He sounded sympathetic toward the Poles, although Charles-Roux found him rather biased and overly critical. As for pro-German pronouncements, Beneš explained them as domestically motivated and therefore not very important. Prague sought no more than pacific relations with Berlin.[58]

The efforts of the Polish envoy to work through the minister of defense Udržal seemed encouraging at first. Udržal was definitely sympathetic; he assured Lasocki that Švehla and most of the cabinet favored closer collaboration with Poland and that he hoped a military convention would be concluded at some time. Lasocki was skeptical. His trust in Czechoslovakia was being weakened by pro-German trends and lack of concessions to the Polish minority in Teschen. But above all, he doubted whether Masaryk or Beneš would ever accept a military convention of which Germany disapproved. Udržal's arguments to the contrary notwithstanding, there was no glossing over the fact that Prague had not even submitted a project of a friendship pact. What is more, although the commercial treaty had become binding by November 1926, the transit protocol, so crucial for Poland, was not confirmed. Hence, Lasocki proposed a technical military conference to which Udržal agreed.[59]

At this point the envoy's efforts seemingly ran counter to Warsaw's policy. At Piłsudski's orders the general staff answered, on 3 February, General Syrový's earlier-mentioned noncommittal letter, leaving the initiative for a concrete proposal to the Czechoslovak side.[60] Lasocki, however, acting jointly with the military attaché proceeded to hold talks with Udržal, generals Syrový and J. Horák, and Colonel F. Bartoš. On 24 March he spoke to Beneš, and, as it turned out, the foreign minister's stand was negative. Udržal had to retreat from the position he had adopted, placing Lasocki in a most awkward situation. The Polish general staff was annoyed, and Zaleski agreed that the envoy had exceeded his instructions.[61] The denouement was Lasocki's recall from Prague. That was un-

58. See several dispatches of Lasocki in Jan. and Feb. 1927, AAN, MSZ 5501 and 5421; compare Charles-Roux to Briand, 18 Jan., 5, 19 Feb. 1927, MAE, Tchécoslovaquie 62:77, 81–84.

59. Lasocki to Zaleski, 5 and 28 Feb. 1927 (copy for Piłsudski), AAN, MSZ 5421, 5502.

60. That Syrový's letter was not as positive as the Czechs pretended was quickly discovered by the French. See Charpy to Painlevé and Laroche to Briand dispatches, Jan. through Apr. 1927, SHA, EMA/2, Pologne 7 and 18. Compare Lasocki to Zaleski, 3 Jan. 1927, AAN, MSZ 5502. Also Balcerak, "Sprawa," 220–21.

61. See Lasocki–Zaleski correspondence, 11, 22, 23, 25, 26, 28 Mar., 15 Apr., 7 June, and Piskor to foreign ministry, 26 Mar. 1927, AAN, MSZ 5501, 5502.

fortunate, for the envoy had wide political contacts and good relations with the press, and had followed a moderate line warning Warsaw against backing Slovak separatists. His interventions on behalf of the Poles in Teschen were tactful and often fruitful.[62] Lasocki's successor, Wacław Grzybowski, a close collaborator of Piłsudski, was convinced of Polish superiority toward the Czechs, and was letting the latter know that it was up to them to make advances. This attitude stemmed from Piłsudski's instructions, somewhat modified by Zaleski.[63]

On his departure, Lasocki was awarded the grand cordon of the White Lion Order, which the Prague government simultaneously gave to Bartel and Zaleski, but a bitter aftertaste remained of his mission. Beneš reproached Udržal; General Syrový criticized Warsaw for not creating a more favorable atmosphere for military collaboration. The chief of the French military mission reached the obvious conclusion that "the moment had not yet arrived when useful relations between the two general staffs could be established."[64]

A narrow, technical-military cooperation was possible. Representatives of the two general staffs met in Warsaw on 26–29 April to discuss general strategy, intelligence, and exchanges of military personnel (which interested the Czechs), as well as transit rights and Franco-Polish communications via Czechoslovakia (which interested the Poles). The result, however, was a limited agreement that involved a change in the transit protocol, making it less obviously anti-German and anti-Russian.[65] The next encounter took place in October in Prague and involved the respective intelligence sections, but the participants were not empowered to conclude any binding agreements.[66]

Charles-Roux and Laroche, in spite of all their sympathy and respect for Beneš, blamed the foreign minister for the lack of a real accord between Warsaw and Prague. Beneš continued to insist that his policy toward Poland was clear and logical, and opined that the time would come for an effort to influence public opinion in both countries toward a rapproche-

62. See MS, PAN, Teki Lasockiego, esp. 4091. Also Charles-Roux to Briand, 20 Apr., 20, 30 June 1927, MAE, Pologne 12:134, Tchécoslovaquie 62:116–19. Compare Kozeński, "Próby," 318–21. For Polish complaints in Teschen, Leon Wolff's speech, 18 Dec. 1925, Těsnopisecké zprávy, poslanecká sněmovna, 109–11.

63. See Wandycz, *Zaleski*, 129. On Grzybowski, see dispatches of Laroche, 12 Mar., 25 Aug. 1927, MAE, Pologne 55:28 and 12:134; and Charles-Roux, 31 Mar. 1928, 7 Sept. 1929, MAE, Tchécoslovaquie 62:174–75, 190–93.

64. Gen. Faucher to Gen. Debeney, 12 Apr. 1927, SHA, EMA/2, Tchécoslovaquie 2.

65. See Gen. Piskor to foreign ministry, 15 June (included protocol of conversations and copies of letters to Gen. Syrový and Polish minister of communications) AAN, MSZ 5502. Also Charles-Roux to Briand, 20 May 1927, MAE, Tchécoslovaquie 62:106–108. Compare Balcerak, "Sprawa," 222.

66. Bułhak, "Z Dziejów 1921–1927," 147.

ment. Charles-Roux was struck by Beneš's "apologetic tone" as the foreign minister surveyed the history of Czechoslovak-Polish relations since 1919. He also noted Beneš's use of harsh adjectives to describe the Poles: "sentimental, romantic," easily flattered, and unrealistic. Laroche commented that Beneš did not take sufficiently into account the fact that the Poles considered themselves mistreated by Prague over Teschen, Javorina, and the transit question. The foreign minister was contrasting "Czechoslovak wisdom with Polish vindictiveness," but surely the Poles had reasons for rancor and the Czechs should realize it. After all, it was Poland that wanted a military entente and Prague that was refusing it. If Czechoslovakia had cause to be prudent, Polish endeavors hardly testified to "mistrust and hostility" as Beneš seemed to believe.[67]

The activities of the Czechoslovak envoy in Warsaw, Václav Girsa, did not help to improve relations, Beneš had erroneously assumed that because Girsa came from a family settled in Polish Volhynia, which had been involved in the 1863 uprising, he would be a persona grata in Poland. In fact, the envoy, who nurtured a strong mistrust of Piłsudski, came to cultivate the opposition in such an obvious way that the marshal never received him. Laroche frequently complained about Girsa's unwillingness to take advice and lack of objectivity when reporting to Prague. Were Beneš's errors of judgment vis-à-vis Poland partly due to Girsa? Had the minister desired a rapprochement with Poland before Piłsudski's coup and then changed his mind? The French ambassador was not sure, but while he made allowances for Piłsudski's temperament, he expected greater flexibility from Beneš who had "a western comprehension." Laroche felt that rather than indulging in suspicions about Piłsudski's alleged eastern ambitions, Beneš should promote collaboration and cease treating Poland "as nonexisting and menaced with ruin." Paris ought to exert pressure on Prague.[68]

In the spring and summer, both Warsaw and Prague tried to maintain the appearance of good relations, the Czech press occasionally speaking of the need for collaboration. Sporadic observations by Masaryk and Beneš continued to vex the Poles. The minister's alleged reference to Poland as "the Balkan of the north" may have been fabricated by his opponents, but it probably reflected Beneš's true sentiments.[69] When the president men-

67. Charles-Roux and Laroche to Briand, 6 May, 8 June 1927, MAE, Tchécoslovaquie 62:92–93, 112–13.

68. Laroche to Briand, 16, 23 Dec. 1927, MAE, Tchécoslovaquie 62:140; Pologne 76:3–44; also Laroche, *Pologne*, 72–74.

69. Supposedly made at a press meeting and publicized in Stříbrný's paper. See chargé d'affaires to Zaleski, 26 Apr. 1927, AAN, MSZ 5501. Compare Charles-Roux and Laroche to Briand, 30 Apr., 7 May 1927, MAE, Tchécoslovaquie 62:89, 94–95. Press cuttings in MZV-VA, 478.1239.

tioned the possibility of a discussion about territorial revision, provided it was "objective and just," the Poles were hardly pleased.[70] During an incognito visit to Geneva in March, Masaryk "repeatedly brought up the question of the solution of the Danzig issue" in a long conversation with Stresemann. His mention of a free railroad and harbor assuring Polish access to the sea provoked Stresemann's reply that this was precisely what the Germans proposed. The president openly told his German interlocutor that Warsaw had lately sought "to effect a closer relationship" with Prague, but "he had no intention to become involved, for he would not consider pulling chestnuts out of the fire for Poland's benefit, if it came to a conflict [between Poland] and Germany."[71]

Evidently, an alignment with Poland that would antagonize Germany or Russia (or both) over issues that were not deemed essential by Prague made little sense to Masaryk and Beneš. The real issue to them was Austria's absorption by Germany likely to be followed by a "moral Anschluss" of Hungary, and a complete encirclement of Czechoslovakia. In view of the close economic ties between Czechoslovakia, Austria, and Germany, it might force Prague into intimate collaboration with Berlin. The Anschluss question was likely to come up at the first sign of trouble in the "danger zones"—Germany-Poland-Lithuania-Russia in the north and the Balkans in the south. To Beneš, the Anschluss was neither a purely political issue, as the French thought, nor an economic issue, as the British saw it, but both. To avert the danger, Berlin had to be reminded of the need to respect the treaties and deprived of economic arguments in favor of a union; Beneš's goal was a Danubian grouping beginning with a Prague-Vienna rapprochement.[72]

Talking to Stresemann, Masaryk observed that a formula could be found for the Austrian question providing for general cooperation between the successor states that "belonged together." In a conversation with Briand, the president suggested attaching Austria to a Central European grouping comprising Czechoslovakia, Yugoslavia, and Poland that could represent "a genuine force and an economic and political barrier opposing Germany's expansion." Masaryk did not envisage the grouping as a challenge; one could better control Germany through a rapprochement than by defiance. In fact, some concessions to Germany were unavoidable, and Masaryk said that one had to determine carefully what

70. Grzybowski to Zaleski, 3 Nov. 1927, AAN, MSZ, z.4,w.1, t.1 (old classification).

71. Stresemann's note, ADAP, B, IV:536–39. See also remarks on the "corridor" by Jan Masaryk and Krofta in Campbell, *Confrontation*, 184.

72. See Beneš's views as summarized by Einstein to Secretary of State, 23 Feb., 11 June 1927, SDNA, 760F.00/13 and 863.01/50; and by Macleay to Chamberlain, 10 May 1927, DBFP, ia, III:282–85.

needed to be defended. Because he followed this observation with a remark that he was not sanguine about Stresemann's dispositions toward Poland, the implication was that it was wiser to concentrate on the prevention of Anschluss rather than on the defense of the "corridor."[73]

Masaryk's mention of Poland as a member of the planned Central European grouping could have been hardly serious.[74] Laroche knew well that neither side desired it. He reported also that leading Poles, Zaleski included, did not hide their view that Anschluss might divert German attention from the "corridor" and Upper Silesia,[75] just as some Czechs (whom he did not name) were ready to sacrifice Danzig for Vienna. While the ambassador regarded revision in either case as "the beginnings of *revanche*," he differentiated between Anschluss—an infraction of principles—and a change in the corridor which would be "a veritable dismemberment."[76] Laroche criticized what seemed to be shortsightedness of the East Central European governments. Commenting on alleged Polish pro-Italian moves at the expense of Yugoslavia, he observed that Warsaw did not sufficiently appreciate "the solidarity of the new states for the preservation of the edifice erected by the different peace treaties."[77] This attitude contrasted with Beneš's program for a consolidation of the Danubian area, which he described as "the most important task of our common policy."[78]

The cohesion of the Little Entente was shaky at this point. Belgrade was in conflict with Italy and engaged in some talks with Budapest. While Rome stood by the Yugoslavs, the Romanians played their own game. Italy, having concluded a treaty of friendship and arbitration with Hungary, tried to detach Romania from its Little Entente partners and bring it closer to Budapest, hoping eventually to neutralize the Romanians in case of a Czechoslovak-Hungarian clash. Under these conditions, the Hungarians could hardly be interested in Masaryk's overtures and hints about the possible restitution of some territories "which contained important Hungarian population." Budapest's attempts to drive a wedge between Prague and Warsaw were anxiously watched by French diplomacy, even though the

73. Note of political director's office, 15 Mar. 1927, MAE, Pologne 113:165–67.

74. The Austrians and Germans thought that Masaryk said this for the benefit of the French; see ADAP, B, v:423–32. When *Čech* wrote in favor of Poland's entry into the Little Entente, Lasocki wondered if this was not French inspired. See 10 Jan. 1927 report, AAN, MSZ 5501.

75. See, for instance, the memo of Kazimierz Olszowski, Poland's envoy in Berlin, in Krasuski, *Stosunki 1926–1932*, 49.

76. Laroche to Briand, 28 Feb. 1927, MAE, Pologne 113:154.

77. Laroche to Briand, 13 Feb., also 24, 26 Mar. 1927, MAE, Pologne 12:124; 75:165–69. On the pro-Italian line, see Günther, *Pióropusz i szpada*, 84–85, 93–94.

78. For the 25 Oct. 1927 speech, see Beneš, *Boj o mír*, 385.

Poles affirmed that their friendship for Hungary had its limits, and that Piłsudski did not wish to meddle in this region.[79]

This complex diplomatic strife in the Danubian area absorbed a great deal of Beneš's attention.[80] During the encounter of the Little Entente ministers in Geneva, he tried to prevent the Romanians from giving an impression that they had departed from their basic foreign policy.[81] At the Jachymov meeting of the Little Entente, on 13–15 May, Beneš sought unsuccessfully to make the grouping an instrument of assistance to Austria through a consolidated economic regional cooperation. All that was achieved was a mere common statement opposing Anschluss. The conference went on record that the relationship of the Little Entente toward Germany was determined by Locarno; "the pro-French policy remains as ever the basis of the policy of the entire grouping." Lip service was paid to friendly relations and peaceful cooperation with Poland.[82]

Publicly Beneš sounded very optimistic over the developments: "If the Little Entente did not exist it would have to be invented," he declared paraphrasing František Palacký. But, Staatssekretär von Schubert gathered from Krofta that neither he nor his chief were fully satisfied.[83] The Quai d'Orsay saw at first in the Jachymov meeting "a splendid manifestation of the solidarity and vitality of the Little Entente." Charles-Roux found the formula that "the relations of our countries [of the Little Entente] with Germany are a function of German relations with France" very "interesting and satisfactory."[84] A different note was sounded by the envoy Mathieu de Vienne from his Budapest post: Jachymov did not alter the fact that the Little Entente has always been a defensive and largely negative arrangement. The grouping, which was "only a function of our policy and our security," must be made to understand, through French promptings and Beneš's guidance, that its role went beyond mere defense against Budapest. Also, one ought to involve Hungary, which was more important from the French point of view than the Little Entente, in the constitution of a French-influenced Central Europe "stretching from Poland to Yugo-

79. Laroche to Briand, 12 May 1927, MAE, Pologne 75:193–94.

80. On Beneš's appearance before the foreign affairs commission and his domestic worries, see chargé d'affaires to Zaleski, 9 Apr. 1927, AAN, MSZ 5421.

81. Beneš to ministry, 11 Mar. 1927, CPP.

82. See Beneš to missions, 17 May, CPP; Briand to missions, 20 July 1927, MAE, Tchécoslovaquie 70:133–38; Polish accounts of Jachymov in AAN, MSZ 3794.

83. Beneš's interview in *Prager Tagblatt*, 15 May; notes and reports in ADAP, B, V:353–56, 361–62, VII:422–24.

84. Charles-Roux to Briand, 22 May, and Quai d'Orsay to war ministry, 14 June 1927, MAE, Tchécoslovaquie 70:94–95, 120–21.

slavia and from Austria to Romania." If no action was taken, Hungary would become the pivot of a Danubian system opposed to France.[85]

Were Vienne's ideas, reminiscent of Maurice Paléologue's policy in 1920, to prevail in Paris, the difference between French and Czechoslovak approaches would become significant. A global plan involving Hungary was, obviously, not identical with Beneš's preference for bilateral agreements beginning with Austria. But even the latter policy was unlikely to succeed in view of the lukewarm attitude of the Little Entente partners. Yugoslavia still considered concessions to Germany in order to gain Berlin against the Italians, and Beneš himself briefly considered the idea of exploring the German option. In mid-June, he told the influential German representative in Bern that, given Germany's moral standing, he would welcome its support for the maintenance of peace in the Balkans, which Italy was disturbing. He suggested that Prague would be interested in going beyond its arbitration treaty with Berlin and conclude a treaty of friendship or nonaggression. The Germans were unresponsive.[86]

Thus, prospects for a regional grouping, advertised as a Central European Locarno, looked bleak. What is more Czechoslovak lack of response to Poland's advances, which no French coaxing could change, tended to isolate Poland. Hence, Polish diplomacy had to act alone when it presented its definite plan related to an "Eastern Locarno" on 3 June 1927.

A Stalemate

The Polish memorandum submitted to the Quai d'Orsay was preceded by a lengthy exchange between Chłapowski and Briand. Once again, the ambassador cautioned against Germany's ambitions; once more the minister stated that consideration of an early evacuation of the Rhineland was postponed. Chłapowski thought he detected a change of attitude on Briand's part toward rapprochement with Berlin and noted the foreign minister's renewed assurances of attachment to the alliance with Poland.[87]

As expected, the Poles built their case on articles 429 and 431 of Versailles, arguing in favor of a prolongation of the occupation if Germany failed to provide the Allies (hence Poland) with a sufficient guarantee against aggression, namely the already-mentioned nonaggression pact. Since 1925, the memorandum said, "the problem of Poland's security has

85. Vienne to Briand, 20 June, 1 Aug. 1927, MAE, Tchécoslovaquie 70:125–28, 141–42.

86. Müller's note, 22 June; Auswärtiges Amt to Koch, 5 July 1927, ADAP, B, VI:20–21.

87. Zaleski instructions, 9 May, Chłapowski telegram, 11 May 1927, HIA, Amb. Paryż, boxes 1 and 4.

made no progress," and a delayed evacuation would at least give the country a chance to strengthen its position through the League. A premature withdrawal, amounting to a recognition that Berlin had fulfilled all its obligations, would deprive Germany of any incentive to enter into negotiations with Warsaw.

Briand immediately responded with his favorite argument: Poland underestimated the significance of Locarno, which ruled out the possibility of a German "legal war" against Poland. He also explained that the Rhineland evacuation was tied to a number of international issues, and France had the right to take independent decisions in those matters. The ambassador tried to argue this point but without much success.[88]

Referred to the Quai d'Orsay, the Polish memorandum was demolished by the legal adviser, Henri Fromageot, who characterized it as "tendentious and inexact." If its interpretations were accepted, it would distort the provisions of Versailles and lead to "serious difficulties." The historical context of article 429, he said, made it applicable only to France and not to Poland; the Polish demand that Paris use its influence with the Allies to obtain German guarantees in exchange for shortening the occupation period was untenable, for Germany was under no legal obligation to do so.[89] In contrast to Fromageot, Massigli tried to salvage the political objectives of the memorandum. He agreed that Articles 429 and 431 could not be invoked, but article 428 might, because total fulfillment of Versailles, mentioned there, concerned Poland as well as other allies. If Polish legal argumentation was faulty, this shortcoming did not invalidate the thrust of the document. The Rhineland occupation did "to a certain extent" protect Poland, and if in the course of negotiations on its termination one raised the question of a German-Polish nonaggression treaty, Berlin might find it hard to refuse.[90]

Briand conveyed the impression of following Massigli's line of reasoning when talking to Zaleski on 10 June. He promised to make efforts to obtain a positive result, which Zaleski assumed to mean a British guarantee for a German-Polish nonaggression pact and a slow promotion of an Eastern Locarno. But, Briand also made it clear that Paris would, in the first place, look for a quid pro quo in the form of German reparations. The Polish diplomats thought they had secured a French promise that an early evacuation would not be carried out without Warsaw's knowledge, and that

88. Memorandum and aide-mémoire, 3 June 1927, MAE, Pologne 75:205–14; Chłapowski telegram, 3 June 1927, HIA, Amb. Paryż, box 4.

89. Observations, 9 June 1927, MAE, Pologne 75:220–21.

90. Note for the minister, 9 June 1927. For Massigli's authorship, see MAE, Pologne 75:222–25.

Paris knew exactly what the equivalents might be.[91] Laroche believed one could obtain a good deal from the Germans in exchange for an early withdrawal, and he repeated the familiar point: "we knew very well, and besides we have learned it from experience, that there is little likelihood of a French-German conflict being brought about by a direct attack" on France.[92]

Rumors reaching Paris and Warsaw that Germany was considering the possibility of a nonaggression treaty with Poland were not confirmed by any diplomatic moves. Rather, it was clear that Germany was promoting its case through commercial ties and pacifism, hoping to make France more amenable to "a gradual and practical" revision of Versailles.[93] French interest in a commercial agreement with Germany was also evident, and the accord signed on 17 August, represented "the triumph of the German point of view," causing some vexation in Poland and Czechoslovakia.[94] Briand, shortly after his talk with Zaleski, assured Stresemann that the idea of reconciliation was making headway in France, and that he had not departed from his former policies.[95] There is no indication that Briand attempted to plead Poland's case.[96] He obviously wished to find a way to eliminate the possibility of a German-Polish war, but seemed to regard cooperation with England, economic agreements with Berlin, and some token surveillance in the Rhineland as sufficient equivalents for the evacuation. And the Germans knew it.[97]

At this moment France was no longer in financial troubles as on the eve of Thoiry. The influx of foreign currencies, especially British pounds, placed Paris in competition with London on increasingly favorable terms and allowed a financial-diplomatic offensive led by the Banque de France. In late May, Poincaré had been advising the Banque's Governor Émile Mo-

91. Chargé d'affaires to Zaleski, 30 June 1927, AAN, MSZ 3795. There seems to be no record of Zaleski's conversations with Poincaré and Berthelot.

92. See Laroche report, and telegram, 18 and 22 June 1927, MAE, Pologne 76:6,8.

93. Margerie to Briand, 28 Feb. MAE, Allemagne 380:178–79; compare Stresemann to Hoesch, 16 March 1927, ADAP, B, IV:567–68. French wine producers clamored for the German market; see Bokanowski on 9 June 1927, CAE/Ch.

94. The citation is from Crewe, DBFP, 1a, IV:310. Compare ADAP, B, VI:250–51; also Krüger, "Beneš," 334; Schuker, *French Predominance*, 373; Polish ministry of industry and commerce notes, May–July, and reports from Prague, Aug.–Nov. 1927, AAN, MSZ 3724, 2882; cuttings, MZV-VA, 190.486.

95. ADAP, B, V:513–18.

96. German diplomats actually believed that Briand opposed Eastern Locarno, but even Poincaré never told the Germans that security in the east was deemed the proper equivalent for an early evacuation. See ADAP, B, VI:342–47.

97. See ADAP, B, VI: 131–32.

reau to assume a preponderant role in the countries of the Little Entente, "which in view of their hatred for England and their fear of Germany are now completely with us." A few months later, Moreau advised the French representative at the Financial Committee of the League of Nations to display greater activity: "one must reserve for France the financial influence in Poland, in Czechoslovakia, in Yugoslavia, in Romania and in Bulgaria." The governor said that both he and Poincaré were seeking to extend French influence over the Central European banks of issue.[98]

Indeed the French assisted Warsaw's search for a stabilization loan and tried to encourage their private investors, so that they could compete more successfully with Anglo-Saxon and German capital.[99] The loan negotiations led to a confrontation that pitted, Montagu Norman, governor of the Bank of England, and Schacht, who tried to obtain political concessions from Poland, against Moreau, who was determined to "support with all our strength our Polish friends against the financial imperialism of Great Britain, which in this case, has made an alliance with pangermanism."[100] With the assistance of the French banker Jean Monnet, who was active in the United States, and the American Federal Reserve Bank, the greatest contributor to the operation, Moreau won the battle. In June, Poincaré, who fully endorsed the governor's policy, informed the Quai d'Orsay of an appeal of the director of Mouvement Général des Fonds, Louis Moret, to the main figures in the French banking establishment to participate in the financial recovery of Poland. Poincaré deemed such participation "indispensable" on political and monetary grounds.[101]

The stabilization loan, finalized in October 1927, was handled through the Banque de France, even though the French share amount to only two millions dollars out of more than seventy-one. The amount was quickly bought out in France, and the Poles appreciated French role in the whole operation. Laroche saw great opportunities for a flow of French capital into Poland, which would strengthen the influence of Paris in the country.[102] By the end of 1927, financial diplomacy was in full swing, the Ban-

98. See Moreau, *Souvenirs*, 340, 410, 419; compare note on Avenol's visit to Seydoux, 31 Mar. 1927, MAE, Y 251:383–86.

99. Laroche to Briand, 21 Oct. 1927, MAE, Pologne 258:235–37.

100. Moreau, *Souvenirs*, 267.

101. Poincaré to Briand, 24 June 1927, MAE, 244:71–72. See also Moreau, *Souvenirs*, 268; compare Neal Pease, *Poland, the United States and the Stabilization of Europe 1924–1933* (New York, 1986). Also Monnet, *Memoirs*, 102–94.

102. See Laroche report, 11, 18 July, 17 Oct. MAE, Pologne 237:63–67, 93–95. The ambassador wondered also about Polish debts to France, which he calculated at 35 million dollars (875 million francs), but did not think the time ripe to raise the issue. On the notion of a stabilization loan as a whole, see Landau, *Plan stabilizacyjny*.

que de France discretely offering a fifteen-million-dollar loan to the Czechoslovak Národní Banka.[103]

As advantageous as this state of affairs was for Poland, it had as yet no direct bearing on the evacuation-security syndrome. Moreover, new complications arose in the east, when in late May, Britain had broken off diplomatic relations with the USSR, and some ten days later a white Russian emigré assassinated the Soviet envoy in Warsaw, Pyotr Voikov. Chicherin privately admitted that the murder "had no political significance" and was a "purely personal act,"[104] but Soviet diplomacy harped on Piłsudski's enmity to Russia and a potential war threat. The Polish government, which had no interest in antagonizing Russia at a time when its attention was focused on Germany, went out of its way to placate Moscow. General Charpy described Poland's attitude as "irreproachable, calm, and dignified."[105]

The Voikov incident briefly interrupted the lingering Soviet-Polish talks about a nonaggression pact. Resumed in July, they ran parallel to Franco-Soviet exchanges. In September, the Soviets proposed a nonaggression pact to France, and once again the Poles were suspicious lest Moscow planned to deal principally with Paris while isolating, "at least morally," Poland. Laroche recommended that a Franco-Soviet pact be tied to "our alliances"; Ambassador Jean Herbette affirmed to his Polish colleague in Moscow that France would always take Polish interests into account and act in agreement with Warsaw.[106] The Frenchman sought assurances from Litvinov that the Soviet Union had not assumed any engagements vis-à-vis a third state (i.e., Germany) bearing on the "corridor" or territorial revision. Litvinov declared that none had been assumed.[107]

In turn, Germany's ambassador Count Ulrich von Brockdorff-Rantzau accused Chicherin of pursuing a rapprochement with France "at our expense." Franco-Soviet negotiations, if combined with a Russo-Polish pact, could bring about an Eastern Locarno of sorts, making Germany appear to be the only power that opposed pacification in this part of Europe.[108]

---

103. Moreau, *Souvenirs*, 405, 448. For laudatory comments about the president of the Czechoslovak national bank, Vilém Pospíšil, see Couget to Briand, 17 Jan. 1926, MAE, Tchécoslovaquie 79:185.

104. See DBFP, ia, III:361; ADAP, B, v:519.

105. Gen. Charpy to Painlevé, 18 June 1927, SHA, EMA/2, Pologne 7. Compare Starzewski to Zaleski, 7 July AAN, MSZ 3795; Zaleski to Skirmunt, 27 May and [before 2 June] 1927, HIA, Amb. Paryż, box 1, and DiM, v, 157.

106. See Laroche to Briand, and Patek report, both 23 Sept. 1927, MAE, Russie 360:130–31 and PI, Amb. Londyn, reel 37.

107. Herbette to Briand, 28 Sept. 1927, MAE, Russie 360:156–57.

108. ADAP, B, VI:472–76.

The Germans were relieved to hear from Litvinov that Russia had no intention to enter a real collective pact that included Poland and Romania.[109]

Did Briand, as he told Zaleski and Chłapowski, seriously aim at some kind of an Eastern Locarno, and what did he understand by this term?[110] The Poles believed that a pro-London and a pro-Moscow line were competing in Paris, and Piłsudski did not wish to strengthen the latter by accelerating his own talks with Russia.[111] Indeed there were divergent estimates of the advantages that a Soviet-Polish nonaggression pact could bring either to France or Poland. While possibly contributing to a diminution of war risks in Eastern Europe, it could deprive the French of a useful argument in Geneva, namely that an endangered Poland was entitled to a higher level of armaments. In addition, a reduction of armaments would increase Polish need for greater French assistance in case of a war between Germany and Poland.[112] As for Eastern Locarno, its Polish version (a nonaggression pact with Germany obtained as a quid pro quo for an earlier evacuation of the Rhineland, that was guaranteed by France and hopefully Britain) seemed to contrast with Briand's concept of a nonaggression pact, purchased possibly at the price of some Polish concessions to Germany, and placed within a wider East European pacification scheme that included Russia.

Jouvenel, who believed that Briand really opposed an Eastern Locarno in its proper sense, clashed publicly with the foreign minister at a meeting of the Interparliamentary Union on 25–30 August 1927. Briand spoke from a prepared text, which indicated that he treated the matter very seriously.[113] Jouvenel's championship of the idea (in the Polish variant) combined with criticism of French foreign policy gained, however, only minor support. The Poles, unwilling to attack Briand directly, could not capitalize on the senator's remarks. But they were pleased that *Le Temps*, *L'Oeuvre*, *Journal des Débats*, and *L'Avenir* spontaneously voiced approval of an Eastern Locarno as the Poles understood the term.[114] Subsequently, Jouvenel proclaimed that the "salvation of our country and of Europe lies in the reconstitution of the Great Entente, allied to the Little Entente and Poland, who alone are capable of containing the devouring ambitions of the Reich."[115] Confronted by all these pressures, Briand had

109. See ADAP, B, VI:501–503, 512–13; VII:6–8, 46–48.

110. Zaleski telegram, and Chłapowski report, 8 and 29 Oct. 1927, HIA, Amb. Paryż, box 4, and AAN, MSZ 3795.

111. Knoll (in Zaleski's absence) to Patek, 22 Sept. 1927, DiM, V, 223.

112. Unsigned note on Soviet-Polish treaty, 8 Oct. 1927, SHA, EMA/2, Pologne 19.

113. Noted by Hoesch, see ADAP, B, VI:372–74.

114. Counselor Arciszewski disclaimed Polish inspiration; see his telegrams 27, 30 Aug. 1927, HIA, Amb. Paryż, box 4.

115. *L'Avenir*, 19 Aug. 1927.

to tell the British and the Germans that while an early evacuation made sense, it was not possible under the existing circumstances.

In September, the delicate web of Briand's diplomacy vibrated with a shock administered by the Polish delegate in Geneva, who proposed a universal nonaggression pact. This move should not have come as a surprise to the French, for the idea had been broached, as mentioned earlier, by Polish diplomats in Paris. A project was submitted to Briand in late August. True, the foreign minister was not keen, believing that the proposal was untimely and likely to antagonize the British.[116] The Germans saw in the Polish initiative an attempt to introduce an Eastern Locarno through a back door. To Chamberlain it appeared like a revived Geneva Protocol. The Soviets regarded it as directed against them, while Beneš, although regarding the principle as meritorious, was skeptical about its chances. Krofta assumed that Warsaw tried to force Germany to take a clear stand.[117]

Some members of the French delegation may have been trying to help the Poles, but Briand "loyally" (Stresemann's word) maintained his opposition to an extension of Locarno, and even pressured the Poles to abandon their original project. The emasculation of the Polish proposal by the "locarnites" and then its adoption in the form of a meaningless declaration on 24 September was a humiliating experience for the Polish diplomacy. Belatedly, Zaleski and his deputy tried to explain that they had never meant to act against the great powers or ignore their advice.[118]

The entire episode produced a certain commotion in the Polish and French press. *Kurjer Poranny* commented on 10 September that Paris was used to calling the diplomatic tune; any sign of Warsaw's independent action was unwelcome to the Quai d'Orsay and embarrassing to Briand. The French government denied that Briand had opposed the Poles because their initiative undermined Locarno. *L'Avenir* commented that if Locarno satisfied Warsaw, surely Poland would have no reason to advocate its eastern extension. The views of the Quai d'Orsay were probably best reflected in d'Ormesson's article "For a German-Polish Pact" in *Le Temps* on 14 September, which deeming Eastern Locarno premature and a general nonaggression pact too vague, advocated a nonaggression pact between Warsaw and Berlin.

Did French policy lack a certain clarity, as the British thought, and did

116. Tarnowski and Arciszewski telegrams, 24, 26, 27, 28, 30 Aug. 1927, HIA, Amb. Paryż, box 1 and 4. Compare, Wandycz, *Zaleski*, 49–50. The Polish memorandum of 3 June, also mentioned the need to strengthen the League.

117. Chargé d'affaires (Prague) telegram, 8 Sept. 1927, AAN, MSZ 5421.

118. See ADAP, B, VI:383–86, 396–400, 481; DBFP, 1a, IV: 356–57, 359–60, and FO 371 12676 Hm 9753. Also Alexandre Bregman, *La Politique de la Pologne dans la Société des Nations* (Paris, 1932), 218–20.

Briand in Paris and Paul-Boncour in Geneva speak with the same voice? The former was assuring London that "French public opinion would never countenance France going to war on behalf of the smaller States." The latter seemed to promote a revived Geneva Protocol trying to make Britain appear the villain.[119]

Around this time, in October, the Quai d'Orsay decided that the question of the revision of the 1921 military convention with the Poles should be considered. An altered text, we will recall, had been drafted in March 1926 with the cooperation of Marshal Foch and General Debeney.[120] Marshal Louis Franchet d'Esperey would go to Poland to decorate Piłsudski with the most prestigious Medaille Militaire and use this opportunity to propose a revision. To discuss the program of the visit, Piłsudski's chef de cabinet, Colonel Józef Beck, came to Paris, and Laroche warned that "one must scrupulously avoid appearing desirous of weakening the alliance." If Piłsudski "suspected us of trying to back out he might be tempted to look for support elsewhere." The ambassador had forewarned Beck of the presumed wishes of Paris: an elimination of political clauses from the convention, so that the governments could define the *casus foederis* in conformity with the Covenant of the League.[121] Laroche did not mention Locarno, which Piłsudski disliked, but it was clear that the French aimed at the subordination of the military convention also to the 1925 treaty (i.e., Locarno). As for Franchet d'Esperey, he was to take the line that the position of the French government had not changed since 1921; the object of the proposal was a simple "updating" of the document, giving it more precision and vigor.[122] This was obviously not the case, because the new project would no longer oblige France to act in case of a "danger of war" or a threat to the execution of Versailles, and would formally eliminate the obligation to assure the maritime communications with Poland. In case of a Soviet-Polish war, the issue of France's aid would be highly problematic.

The French marshal arrived in Warsaw on 17 November, and spent roughly nine days in Poland.[123] He returned to France via Czechoslovakia,

119. Phipps–Berthelot conversation, 12 Dec. 1927, DBFP, 1a, IV:184–85.

120. Projet de protocole franco-polonais, 30 Mar. 1926, SHA, EMA/2, Tchécoslovaquie 10. A note comparing it to the 1921 convention in SHA, EMA/2, Pologne 19.

121. See Blanchet note, 8 Oct., MAE, Pologne 26:22–23, and Laroche to Briand, 19 Oct. 1927, SHA, EMA/2, Pologne 18.

122. Exchange of letters, 4 and 10 Nov. 1927; aide-mémoire for Franchet d'Esperey with project of convention and ten-page memorandum, SHA, EMA/3, 7 N 3446/3. For a good summary, see Soutou, "L'Alliance," 315–17.

123. He was ordered to avoid a visit to Wilno and Lwów so as not to antagonize Russia. See Briand to Laroche, and Herbette to Briand, 9 and 28 Nov. 1927, MAE, Pologne 136:41 and 51–52.

where he stayed for five days (26 November to 1 December) but conducted no negotiations. In his report he noted that the Czechoslovak high command was less homogeneous than the Polish and plagued with intrigues. Also, German influences were noticeable, and the marshal was skeptical about Syrový's utterances about an offensive plan in Silesia.[124]

In Warsaw, Franchet d'Esperey talked to Piłsudski in private, participated together with his officers in three plenary sessions at which Piłsudski was accompanied by Polish staff officers, and held discussions in which only staff officers took part.[125] It seems that in the tête-à-tête conversations, Piłsudski "made a special effort to seduce the representative of France," who indeed was greatly impressed. As he recalled, the marshal revealed different facets of his rich personality. In private encounters he appeared as a "conspirator"; in larger sessions he was a "circumspect politician," an "adroit diplomatist," a "statesman," firm and decisive, who behaved with "the assurance of a leader who knew that, up to a point, he can speak as the master." Piłsudski discoursed at great length about Russia and his 1919–20 plans, drawing a comparison between his projected bloc and the Napoleonic Confederation of the Rhine. He reproached the French for often misunderstanding Polish policies, and professed in turn to be unable to comprehend Locarno. Poland was being forced to act alone, he said, and act alone it would. Piłsudski's monologues, interspersed with anecdotes and reminiscences, were not always easy to follow, and Franchet d'Esperey experienced occasional difficulties.[126]

The Warsaw conversations ranged widely. They touched on the French military mission, which was being kept outside any concrete work on strategic plans, even though, as its chief bitterly noted, it had forged all the mechanisms and prepared all the instructions.[127] Piłsudski showed more interest in the naval mission, to be granted an autonomous status, but

124. Franchet d'Esperey report, 5 Dec., SHA, EMA/3, 7 N 3446/3; compare with Faucher note for Berthelot, 22 Nov. and dispatch to Painlevé, 3 Dec., respectively, MAE, Tchécoslovaquie 2:88, 90; SHA, EMA/2, Tchécoslovaquie 2. Also Charles-Roux to Briand, 28 Nov. 1927, MAE, Lithuanie 34:290; and Einstein to Secretary of State, 22 Dec. 1927, SDNA, 760C.60M/210.

125. First private talk with Piłsudski on 17 Nov. was followed by a plenary session. On 18 Nov. there were staff talks followed by a plenary session; and on 19 Nov. staff talks, another personal talk between the two marshals, and a final plenary session. Documentation in SHA, EMA/3, 7 N 3446/3.

126. In addition to Franchet d'Esperey report, see also his "Souvenirs de mon voyage en Pologne en 1927: Pilsudski intime," *Pologne Littéraire*, 15 July 1935. On Piłsudski's objectives, see also the insightful annual report for 1927 of Gen. Charpy, EMA/2, Pologne 10.

127. Ibid. Operational studies undertaken in the Autumn of 1927 still assumed a French pro-Polish intervention, although considerably delayed by the Locarno procedure. See Bułhak, "Polsko-francuskie," 92–93.

above all he wanted to see a regular military attaché come to Warsaw.[128] It appeared that the marshal wished to put coordinated Franco-Polish operational planning on a new base. Alluding to the general strategic directives, as envisaged in the 1922–24 talks involving generals Sikorski and Haller in Paris, Piłsudski made it clear—either then or a little later—that he "wanted to hear no more about them."[129] In conversations with Franchet d'Esperey, he insisted on an annex to the procès-verbal stipulating that a study of frontiers and "couverture" be undertaken as an urgent matter at the periodic meetings between the two general staffs.

The crucial and central question was, of course, a revision of the military convention, which Franchet d'Esperey introduced at the first plenary meeting.[130] For the record, Piłsudski stated "most categorically" that this was a French initiative, and manifested a repugnance to have the military convention "locarnized" (Franchet d'Esperey recorded this expression). He did not seem impressed by assurances that the French general staff was determined not to diminish the military value of the pact, and agreed only to a preliminary exploration of the old text. Franchet d'Esperey proceeded by suggesting that it was not necessary to name explicitly Germany and the Soviet Union as aggressors. When Piłsudski remarked that this omission would deprive the convention of all precision, the French marshal somewhat lamely replied that such language would cover Poland against all possible aggressors. Because article 3 relating to security of maritime communications was de facto, obsolete, Franchet d'Esperey recommended possible use of Mediterranean and Balkan harbors. Piłsudski stated that one could not respond to these proposals without detailed studies, and requested that a written text of the amended convention be submitted the next day to the representatives of the Polish general staff. This the French did, giving the new text, piece by piece, for Franchet d'Esperey wanted to avoid the impression that "it had been prepared in advance." At the next plenary session, Piłsudski declared that he was unable to give any definite answer; consequently, the second meeting of staff officers could not produce any tangible result. The Polish marshal did not reject the possibility of further negotiations and suggested that the matter be handled through diplomatic channels. But it was obvious that as far as he was concerned, the answer was a polite no.

128. Laroche supported Piłsudski's request and also favored strengthening the naval mission. See diplomatic correspondence in MAE, Pologne 41 and Charpy military dispatches in SHA, EMA/2, Pologne 7.

129. Note for the chief of the general staff, 9 July 1929, SHA, EMA/2, Pologne 7.

130. Participants, in addition to the two marshals, included Lt. Col. Daille—Franchet d'Esperey's chief of staff—Maj. Limasset of the third bureau, the Polish chief of staff, Gen. Tadeusz Piskor, and his deputy, Gen. Tadeusz Kutrzeba, Col. Bolesław Wieniawa-Długoszowski, and Lt. Col. Beck. For a Polish translation of *resumé des entretiens*, see Wandycz, "Rozmowa."

The Franchet d'Esperey mission was a failure, and if the French had hoped that Piłsudski could be coaxed—after being flattered by the Medaille Militaire—into following their line, they were mistaken. Yet another opportunity for cultivating the marshal arose, as he decided to go to Geneva to attend to the Polish-Lithuanian controversy. The latter had been referred to the League by Lithuania's premier, Augustinas Voldemaras, and there was some fear that the marshal may resort to force and provoke a general conflagration in Eastern Europe.[131] Piłsudski's presence in Geneva created a sensation. At a secret session of the Council on 9 December, he confronted Voldemaras with a direct question: war or peace? On hearing the word "peace," he declared himself satisfied. His two-day stay provided ample chance for lengthy conversations with Briand, Paul-Boncour, Stresemann, and Chamberlain. The marshal appeared most friendly toward Stresemann, and Briand, although somewhat taken aback by Piłsudski's conversational style, eagerly seized on what he perceived to be the chance of a German-Polish understanding. Briand understood Piłsudski to say that he did not care much for the indefensible "corridor," and Chamberlain gathered a similar impression, not so much from what Piłsudski said but from his "general attitude." Briand regretted that Stresemann had not talked politics to the Polish leader who seemed to be accommodating, and the Frenchman mentioned again the idea of the Danzig-Memel exchange. Chamberlain also thought that Stresemann had missed a good opportunity, for Piłsudski was the only man who could rectify the mistakes committed at the Paris Peace Conference.[132]

The conversations between the three "locarnites" revealed a design of Briand, which had been in the making for some time. Based on the notion of a Polish-German accord, personally promoted by Stresemann and Piłsudski, it would amount to "a sort of Eastern Locarno," as Briand put it, diminishing tensions in the East that resulted partly from the fact that Russia was not a signatory of the Rhineland pact. Briand's Eastern Locarno would then take the form of a nonaggression pact between Germany, the Soviet Union, Poland, the Baltic States, and Romania. The scheme, as Chamberlain suspected, may have stemmed mainly from French domestic considerations. The forthcoming elections in 1928 were likely to strengthen the Left, which was clamoring for cuts in the army budget and military economies; hence, there was need to increase France's

131. On 21 Nov. Chicherin warned Warsaw that an attack on Lithuania would be regarded as an overture to an aggression against Russia. On French and especially Beneš's concerns, see dispatches in MAE, Pologne 9:160–62; Lithuanie 34:5–6, 56–57, 126–29, 237.

132. See minutes of secret session, SI, Ciechanowski Collection, 82/61/3; also Jędrzejewicz, "Rozmowa," 139–44. Also Chamberlain's account to Tyrrell, 12 Dec. 1927, FO 800 361 659–72. I am indebted to Thomas Dylan for pointing out this document. Compare DBFP, 1a, IV:180–83, 192–93, 196–97; ADAP, B, VII:483–84, 486–89, 552–53.

security through diplomatic means. The main obstacles to an Eastern Locarno, so conceived, were obviously the "corridor" and Bessarabia, but Briand listened calmly to Stresemann's argument that Poland could be included only if territorial issues were resolved. He said "not one critical word" about revisionism. The legal adviser of the Quai d'Orsay surprised his German counterpart by volunteering an opinion that the border issue between Germany and Poland would have to be solved.

Briand's project was obviously unacceptable to Warsaw. Piłsudski wanted to remove the razor-sharp edge of German-Polish relations, but neither he nor any other leader in Poland could countenance territorial revision.[133] That an unrealistic Danzig-Memel trade off could be seriously taken by anyone showed only how successful the Germans were in representing the "corridor" as a purely artificial creation designed merely to assure Poland's access to the Baltic. By obscuring the fact that this land was historically Polish and was inhabited by a Polish majority, one could argue that one corridor was as good as another. In a speech at Königsberg on 17 December, Stresemann rejected an Eastern Locarno. His goal was the corridor, and he thought that the road to its recovery led "through Paris and London." The French had to be cultivated so that they would "first lose the fear of a German threat, then recognize the impossibility of maintaining the present borders, [and] finally accept the revision of these borders in exchange for certain concessions in the financial sphere." Stresemann believed that great progress had been made, for "leading French politicians raised no objections to statements about the impossibility of the present frontiers."[134]

If prospects of an Eastern Locarno—either Poland's or Briand's version—looked dim, the idea of a Central European Locarno did not seem more promising in the last months of 1927. Here also there appeared to be a French and a Czechoslovak variant: Beneš's Danubian bloc based on preferential tariff treaties (beginning with a Prague-Vienna accord) and Briand's "great combination" linking economics and politics and providing a system of unilateral concessions to Austria by all the states of the region. The French foreign minister even contemplated some French concessions to Vienna and thought that Beneš should be encouraged to "begin a conversation with his Polish colleague" to further the entire scheme.[135] Indeed, at this point Warsaw went far in reappraising its atti-

133. We have at least two explicit statements of Piłsudski to this effect, on 21 Apr., and 8 June 1929. See Zacharias, *Polska*, 41.

134. See ADAP, B, VII:400–403, 521–26, 542–45. On Rechberg's activities (he managed to gain access to Briand, Foch, and Weygand), see comments in Col. Tournes to Painlevé, 9 Dec. 1927, MAE, Allemagne 390:117–31.

135. Briand to Charles-Roux, 22 Aug. (?), 1927, MAE, Autriche 79:127–34. For

tude toward Anschluss. A foreign ministry memorandum rejected the traditional arguments about the beneficial repercussions of an Austro-German union for Poland. It concluded that "Polish policy must openly and firmly oppose all Anschluss tendencies," for an annexation of Austria would strengthen Germany, deprive Poland and Czechoslovakia of the shortest transit route to France, place Hungary under Berlin's influence, and consistitute a precedent for treaty revisions. The embassy in Paris was informed of this new line and alerted to the idea of preparing the ground for an exchange of views between French, Polish, and Czechoslovak ministers at the September meeting in Geneva.[136]

The Polish initiative, lauded by Briand, met with a cool response in Prague, although the Czechs were not displeased to learn of Warsaw's interest in Austria. Polish diplomacy was vexed, and Charles-Roux criticized Beneš, who "instinctively withdraws into an attitude of reserve each time they [the Poles] approach him or make an overture."[137] While Ambassador Laroche tried to reassure the Poles that Czechoslovakia would help them against Germany, he had some doubts himself on that score.[138]

French concern over the Anschluss manifested itself in the press. Sauerwein even suggested that a formal German renunciation of union with Austria should be made a condition for the evacuation of the Rhineland. Yet the French and the Czechs continued to differ in their respective approaches to the problem. Krofta remarked that while France was applying pressure on Austria's neighbors to do something for Vienna, and wanted Czechoslovakia to make economic sacrifices, France itself was not prepared to make any.[139] The Poles commented that Paris was waiting for Prague's initiative, but the latter would "never adopt a constructive policy toward Austria."[140]

In early October, Berthelot came on a ten-day "courtesy" visit to Czechoslovakia, which naturally gave rise to speculations.[141] The secretary gen-

Beneš's ideas see the Marx–Stresemann–Seipel conversation, 14 Nov. 1927, ADAP, B, VII:251. Compare Ormos, *Problème*, 26.

136. Memorandum and foreign ministry to Paris embassy, 12 and 23 Aug. 1927, PI, Amb. Londyn, reel 38.

137. Charles-Roux to Briand, 1 Dec. 1927, MAE, Pologne 76:36–38; compare circular of western division of foreign ministry, 23 Aug., PI, Amb. Londyn, reel 38; Arciszewski telegram, 30 Aug. 1927, HIA, Amb.Paryż, box 4.

138. See Laroche report, 25 Nov. and telegram, 28 Dec., MAE, Pologne 76:33–34 and Tchécoslovaquie 62:141–48. On German influences, see Charles-Roux to Briand, 27 July, second bureau report, Oct. 1927, Tchécoslovaquie 39:49–56; 70:146–50. Compare Olszowski to Beck, 27 Dec. 1927, PI, Amb. Londyn, reel 38. See also Bułhak, "Z Dziejów 1927–1936," 104; Post, *Weimar Foreign Policy*, 129–30.

139. See ADAP, B, VI:120–21; briefing, 30 Sept. 1927, KV, CPP.

140. Bader to Zaleski, 11 Aug. 1927, PI, Amb. Londyn, reel 38.

141. His visit was filled with numerous conversations, and he spent some time in

eral reviewed the international situation. He voiced a conviction that democracy was growing in Germany, and he lauded Stresemann, although he regarded him as not above duplicity. Anschluss was not an urgent issue, and Berthelot agreed that Czechoslovakia could not "pay" Austria in order to induce it not to unite with Germany. Allegedly Beneš was far more pessimistic than Berthelot about the German developments, and he feared an all-out offensive against the peace treaties. Expecting a fiasco of the disarmament conference, Krofta echoed Beneš's view that Czechoslovakia was entering "one of the most difficult phases of our foreign policy."[142]

Beneš and the foreign ministry were aware of some tendencies in Berlin to try to draw Czechoslovakia closer to Austria and Germany, in order to loosen the French eastern alliances and outflank Poland.[143] They were astute enough to perceive the potential dangers stemming from German wooings assisted by pressures from Czechoslovak Germans, but Beneš was unwilling to counter such threats by reliance on Poland, although Krofta's views were rather different.[144] Nor was Prague willing to come closer to Rome, and it ignored the advice given by its envoy in Italy.[145] Beneš, like Briand, had very little respect for the duce.

Paradoxically, the rather ineffective Franco-Yugoslav treaty of 11 November was the only concrete evidence of French Danubian diplomacy in 1927. The accord antagonized Rome and earned criticism in London as "a retrograde step" with regard to Briand's Locarno policy. Why should France seek "minor advantages of tying herself up with small states whose interests would not always be identical with those of France and might involve her in continental complications?"[146] Trying to dull the criticism, Briand described the treaty as a pact of peace and denied that it contained a military convention.[147] This disclaimer did not convince the Polish lega-

---

Masaryk's residence at Topolčianky. See Macleay to Chamberlain, 13 Oct. and annual report 1927, FO 371 12095 C8431 and 12867 C238/2380/12; Gittings to Secretary of State, 17 Oct. 1927, SDNA, 751.60F/10; Polish reports from Prague and Paris, 15 Oct. and 15 Nov. 1927, AAN, MSZ 5421; ADAP, B, VII:102–103, 252–53.

142. Briefing, 13 Oct. 1927, KV, CPP.

143. See ADAP, B, VII:557–59.

144. See discussions, 27 Oct., 17 Nov. 1927, KV, CPP.

145. Briefings, 17 Nov., 1 Dec., KV, CPP; Mastný to Beneš, 11 May, 7 Nov. 1927, ANM, Mastný notebooks, 22–23. Compare memo on Central European Locarno, 15 Feb. 1928, DBFP, 1a, IV:262–67.

146. Tyrrell–Fleuriau conversation, DBFP, 1a, IV: 119–21; compare 101, 108.

147. 15 Nov. 1927 session, CAE/Ch. The military protocol attached to the treaty was so vague that the Quai d'Orsay responded negatively to Yugoslav offers to hold staff talks. See Gamelin, *Servir*, 2:465–74. A Yugoslav analysis of the military aspects of the treaty appears in Bogdan Krizman, *Vanjska politika Jugoslavenske države 1918–1941* (Zagreb, 1975) 44–48, and Vuk Vinaver, "Da li je jugoslovensko-francuski pakt iz 1927 godine bio vojni savez?" *Vojnoistori jski Glasnik*, 22 (Jan.–Apr., 1971), 178. I am grate-

tion, which deplored the likely consequences of the treaty on Franco-Italian relations that were seen as "the key to the entire political situation of Southern and even Central Europe."[148]

As the year 1927 was drawing to its end, French diplomacy seemed to have done little more than mark time. The concepts of an Eastern and Central European Locarno remained as elusive as ever. Prague continued to be little interested in Polish overtures; a Franco-Polish stalemate regarding the military aspects of the alliance was only put more sharply into relief by the mission of Franchet d'Esperey.

---

ful to my colleague Ivo Banac for drawing my attention to these works and for assistance in translating them.

148. Günther to Zaleski, 26 Nov. 1927, AAN, MSZ 4209.

Chapter Four

Toward the Evacuation
of the Rhineland

Continuing Frustrations: Zaleski in Rome

The triple issue of the Rhineland, reparations, and security "had not advanced one step" since Thoiry, as Briand noted at the beginning of 1928, and Stresemann decided to break the deadlock.[1] In two tough speeches on 30 January and 1 February, he demanded an early evacuation without any permanent civilian inspection. Asserting that Germany had fulfilled all the obligations under Versailles, he termed French insistence on security hypocritical. A disarmed Germany was no threat to its neighbors; even if it wished to use force, it could not simultaneously face France, Poland, and Czechoslovakia.[2]

Hesnard qualified this as a "vigorous renewal of hostilities," and indeed the mood of the Reichstag was belligerent.[3] In his response on the senate floor, Briand stated that the Rhineland was an allied problem that France could not resolve in isolation. He questioned the execution of the disarmament clauses by Berlin. As for reparations, he awaited concrete proposals of the German government. This last point struck Stresemann, for hitherto the French has spoken publicly only about security. German political circles also noted that the foreign minister had not expressly referred to an "Eastern Locarno."[4] This omission was encouraging, especially in view of Berthelot's remarks, both before and after the speech, deploring the 1919 territorial settlement and hoping for a solution to appease "justified Ger-

1. Briand quoted by Gaiffier to Hymans, 9 Feb. 1928, DDB, II, 465.

2. See Margerie to Briand, 1 Feb. 1928, MAE, Allemagne 390:163–65.

3. Hesnard to Berthelot, 15 Feb. 1928, MAE, Allemagne 390:268. At the Reichstag, not only the spokesman of the Deutschnationale attacked France for spinning the web of eastern alliances and rejected Eastern Locarno, but members of Stresemann's party and the Zentrum declared that peace was unthinkable with the existing borders in the "corridor" and Upper Silesia. See Stenografische Berichte, 30 Jan. 1928, B. 398:1250.

4. For Briand's speech, see J.O. Sénat, 2 Feb. 1928 session, 72. For German reactions, Margerie to Briand and Hesnard to Berthelot, 4, 15 Feb. 1928, MAE, Allemagne 390:213–15, 268.

man dissatisfaction." The secretary was clearly thinking of the idea of a Stresemann-Piłsudski deal.[5]

True, Briand had mentioned the need for improved guarantees to East European states, but he did so in reply to the speeches of senators Lémery and Jouvenel. The former has asked for an explanation of Stresemann's statement that demands for eastern security were deemed absurd in official French circles. The latter had harped on Eastern Locarno, seen as a quid pro quo for the evacuation of the Rhineland.[6]

To appreciate better Briand's position, one has to relate it to the main political trends in the country. The congress of Louis Marin's Fédération Républicaine had taken a stand, on 7 December 1927, against an early evacuation without adequate safeguards and in favor of close collaboration with Poland and the Little Entente. It spoke somewhat ambiguously about the insufficiencies of eastern alliances. The position of the Parti Démocrate Populaire (at its Orléans congress on 18–20 November) was similar. The electoral statement adopted by the centrist Alliance Républicaine Démocratique at Rouen (27–29 November) inclined toward more elastic formulas. It endorsed Locarno policies based on fulfillment of Versailles, and spoke of peace while remaining vigilant. According to a statement drafted by André François-Poncet, France ought to count on the League and on itself. A premature evacuation of the Rhineland was not yet an issue; the territorial integrity of Poland and Austria was inviolable.

The platform of the radical socialist party, torn by internal dissessions at the Paris congress (27–30 October), was influenced by Caillaux and stressed entente with Germany as the cornerstone of European cooperation. The qualifying statement "in the framework of our friendships," allegedly suggested by the French-Polish parliamentary group, was meant to show concern for the eastern allies. Both the Polish embassy and Franklin-Bouillon saw in the party stand a concession to the socialists. After declaring that the radicals had entered on a dangerous course that could bring war in a decade, Franklin-Bouillon resigned from the party and the presidency of the foreign affairs commission of the chamber.

The congress of the French Socialist party (SFIO) held in late December came out as expected for the evacuation of the Rhineland, although Paul-Boncour cautioned that it should not take place immediately and not without some controls. The majority of the socialists did not share these reservations as attested by the vote of their council in July 1928, which subordinated security to disarmament, evacuation, and treaty revisions. At

5. According to Berthelot, Stresemann's approach to Piłsudski offered the best chance, for the marshal did not like France and, as a dictator, could impose a solution. Hoesch to Auswärtiges Amt, 1, 3, 5 Feb. 1928, ADAP, B, VIII:129, 134–35, 138–39.

6. See J.O. Sénat, 31 Jan. 1928 session, 50 and 61. For German criticism of Jouvenel, see *Tägliche Rundschau* 12 Mar. 1928.

the International Socialist Congress in Brussels, the SFIO was vocal in favor of "immediate and unconditional evacuation." The socialists also advocated a small, purely defensive army, virtually reduced to a militia.[7]

The respective party positions on foreign policy were closely linked with their views on national defense and disarmament. As we know, the army chiefs, particularly Foch, had thought that the presence of French troops on the Rhine provided a real security guarantee. Briand admitted in late 1927 that the Conseil Supérieur de Guerre (CSG) had been delaying the construction of fortifications in the hope that the evacuation could be postponed even beyond 1935.[8] To the French public opinion, however, fortifications seemed the only justifiable solution to security problems.[9] Even the Right stood generally for a reduction of military service and a defensive strategy, a posture that hardly tallied with its criticism of Briand's diplomacy. The adoption of military laws in late 1927 and early 1928 resulted in a one-year service, a reorganization of the army, and the beginnings of construction of what became later known as the Maginot Line. The fortification, it is true, was originally conceived as a couverture—in the absence of a Rhineland buffer zone—for mobilization and concentration. Although its construction did not exclude a war of movement, the Maginot Line shortly became a pivot of French defensive strategy.

Without discussing again all the implications of the Maginot Line, it may be worthwhile to recall French President Gaston Doumergue's doubts and anxieties. "Our alliances are invoked," he said, "but . . . these alliances are valuable for the signatories from the security viewpoint only if each of them is in a position to assist the others." But if France further reduces its armaments, will not the states "which had hitherto counted on our material and military aid be tempted, in the presence of our military weakness, to turn to others? Will not Poland look toward Germany?" Briand's reply—that because everybody would be asked to reduce armaments, French relative position would not suffer and the value of alliances remain undiminished—did not sound very convincing.[10]

A Quai d'Orsay memorandum opined that if Germany tried to modify its eastern borders by force or affect the Anschluss, "we would be perfectly justified in prolonging the occupation of the Rhineland." Briand was willing to use article 428 of Versailles, as mentioned earlier, to obtain some additional security for Poland, but the French asked themselves whether the Germans would not respond to a promotion of a German-Polish non-

---

7. Excerpts of party platforms in Bourgin, Carrère, and Guérin, *Manuel*, 74–75, 88, 102, 146, 187. Compare Bonnefous, *Histoire*, 4:232–37. For interesting Polish and British reports, see AAN, MSZ 3796, and FO 371 12902 C 6247.

8. See Jacobson, *Locarno*, 138.

9. See SHA, CSDN, 4 June 1928 session, 130–37.

10. See SHA, CSDN, 13 July 1928 session, 145–52.

aggression pact by raising the "corridor" issue. As for the Anschluss, one could not ask Germany to give up its right to seek union with Austria through legal means. Perhaps there were other ways of satisfying the Reich. Time was running short, for all these matters had to be resolved through negotiations within the year.[11]

French policy toward Poland in early 1928 was characterized by three objectives: a change of the military convention, some appeasement of Polish fears over the anticipated evacuation, and a strengthening of Warsaw's position through cooperation with East Central European states. We shall deal here only with the first issue.

The Quai d'Orsay acknowledged Piłsudski's views, expressed to Franchet d'Esperey, that the revision of the military convention was a matter for intergovernmental negotiations. The latter would be fruitless unless some of Piłsudski's objections were taken into account, but one could initiate them by capitalizing on the good impressions that Piłsudski must have brought back from Geneva. Still, the Quai D'Orsay hesitated before giving its approval to Laroche.[12]

On 18 January, the French ambassador handed in the text of the revised convention.[13] Warsaw tried to ascertain if this initiative has the support of the French army, and Chłapowski reported that although the general staff had not been consulted, its approval would presumably be sought if any concrete changes were to be introduced.[14] Laroche in his explications covered the familiar ground, but he also stated that the French were willing to follow Piłsudski's wishes regarding article 2, namely that the government and not the general staff take the necessary decision to aid the other party, and article 6, referring to permanent contact between the general staffs. The French war minister also agreed to name a military attaché in Warsaw.[15]

11. Unsigned note for the Conference of Ambassadors "sur le plan d'une négociation rélative à l'évacuation anticipée de la rive gauche du Rhin," 17 Feb. 1928, MAE, Pologne 76:104–26. Compare views of Tirard in DBFP, 1a, IV:259–61.

12. Briand to Painlevé, 24 Dec. 1927, 31 Jan. 1928, SHA, EMA/2, Pologne 19 and EMA/3, 7 N 3446/3.

13. Text in SHA, EMA/2, Pologne 18 and SI, MSZ, A 11.49/F/2.

14. Exchange of Zaleski-Chłapowski telegrams, 16, 19 Jan. 1928, HIA, Amb. Paryż, box 1 and 2. Weygand's note of 26 Jan. 1928 appears to be the first bearing on this subject; see SHA, EMA/3, 7 N 3446/3.

15. There were also problems connected with the military mission; generals Debeney and Charpy wanted to withdraw the mission but the war ministry did not, probably in consideration of the impact such a withdrawal would have on the mission in Czechoslovakia. With regard to the personalities involved, General Bertrand Pujo took over the mission temporarily to be replaced by General Denain. See Ciałowicz, *Polsko-francuski sojusz,* 150–51; correspondence in MAE, Pologne 41 and 4. For the Czechoslovak angle, see MAE, Pologne 41:256, 260–61.

A close scrutiny of the French proposal revealed, among other elements, a new emphasis on "unprovoked aggression," and on decreasing obligations of France to assist its ally. For instance, the original engagement to keep Germany in check in case of a Polish-Soviet war was now qualified by the word "possibly" (*eventuellement*).[16] It was obvious that these changes would be unacceptable to Piłsudski, but the marshal decided first to ascertain how the French envisaged the actual execution of the military convention. One had to determine the modalities of "reinforced preparations" in case of a threat of war. When and how would French mobilization start and proceed, taking into account the government's decision? The marshal proposed sending to Paris a general staff delegation, headed by General Tadeusz Kutrzeba, to discuss all these matters. The French were embarrassed, for the new army laws would seriously impair the efficacy of their military aid to Poland. General Debeney was reluctant to reveal the mobilization plans to the Poles and the war minister Paul Painlevé expressly forbade it.[17]

In these conditions the Franco-Polish talks held in Paris (29 June–4 July) could hardly be a success. The final protocol signed by generals Kutrzeba and Jean Guitry and Rear-Admiral Mouget embodied three French-proposed amendments "in order to give satisfaction to the desiderata of the Polish general staff." According to the amendments, further staff talks would be held concerning the application of proposed article 3 (deliveries of French war materials), France promising to do "its best" to facilitate their arrival in Poland. In addition, proposed articles 4 and 7, which dealt with armaments, the military attaché, and the military and naval missions, would be somewhat changed. These proposals were rather vague. General Kutrzeba's project of creating an airbase on Polish soil fully equipped by France and remaining French property—"partly to compensate" Poland for the inability on France's part to protect the maritime Baltic route—was omitted from the protocol mainly because of the financial difficulties raised by the French. The project would resurface later.[18]

The Kutrzeba mission occurred in the summer of 1928, and we need to review the diplomatic and political developments that intervened in the

16. See commentary in Jackowski to Zaleski, and the letter of the legal adviser, S. Rundstein, 18, 28 Jan. 1928, SI, MSZ, 11.49/F/2. Compare Soutou, "L'Alliance," 317.

17. See Briand to Painlevé, 6 Feb., 10 June, and note of the chef de l'Etat Major de l'Armée, 19 June 1928, SHA, EMA/3, 7 N 3446/3.

18. On the Paris talks see "Note relative au projet de mise à jour de la Convention militaire franco-polonaise du 19 février 1921," 4 July 1928, SHA, EMA/2, Pologne 19. Notes of meetings in SHA, EMA/3, 7 N 3446/3; procès-verbal in MAE, Pologne 41:282–84. Compare Arciszewski telegram, 23 June 1928, HIA, Amb.Paryż, box 2. On the Kutrzeba proposal see "Note historique sur les questions de fourniture de matériel de guerre par la France à la Pologne," n.d. SHA, EMA/2, Pologne 19.

previous months. Briand's public response to Stresemann won Zaleski's approval. French views on guarantees of peace and security "seemed to conform entirely to Poland's particular interests," Laroche reported.[19] If Zaleski's speech of 9 January contained only a passing reference to the "ever growing" Franco-Polish friendship, the latter was stressed in President Mościcki's address (written by Piłsudski) to the sejm, and Piłsudski's own opening address to the senate in March.[20]

The March parliamentary elections in Poland were a success for Piłsudski insofar as the pro-marshal BBWR became the largest single group in the sejm and commanded a majority in the senate. But it had no absolute control of the chambers and was set on a collision course with the parties of the Left and Center, which were increasingly apprehensive of an evolution toward an authoritarian regime. The impact of this controversy was, however, only slightly felt in the field of foreign policy.[21] Criticism of Zaleski by the opposition was mild or directed against Piłsudski. As the French saw it, the policy of the foreign minister seemed to enjoy general approbation.[22] Naturally, the last word belonged to the marshal, a fact emphasized after his resignation as premier on 27 June, 1928.[23] Piłsudski, however, suffered a minor stroke in the spring, and although he quickly recovered, he was obliged to take a prolonged rest and he spent several weeks, from 19 August to early October, in Romania.[24]

The marshal's conversations in Geneva had neither brought an end to the Polish-Lithuanian controversy (exploited by Berlin and Moscow) nor began any rapprochement between Poland and Germany. The Germans, wrote the Polish envoy in Moscow, try to play both ends: "Stresemann directs the western policy and Count Brockdorff-Rantzau the eastern." The French ambassabor shared this view.[25] If Zaleski publicly professed

19. Laroche telegram, 11 Feb. 1928, MAE, Allemagne 390:259.

20. Zaleski, *Przemowy*, 1:101; for Piłsudski's speech, Sprawozdania stenograficzne senatu, 27 Mar. 1928, 1/3.

21. On political parties and foreign policy see the relevant parts in chapter 4 of Faryś, *Koncepcje*, Ziaja, *PPS*, and *Robotnik*, 1, 6 Nov. 1926, 1 Jan. 1928; Hemmerling, "Ludowcy"; Wapiński, "Myśl polityczna"; also *Gazeta Warszawska* 7 Oct., 18 Apr. 1928. Articles signed S[tanisław] K[ozicki] reflected the party line on foreign affairs.

22. See Laroche to Briand, 1 June 1928, MAE, Pologne 77:23.

23. In his interview in *Głos Prawdy*, 1 July 1928, Piłsudski said that, in agreement with the president and premier, he retained supreme control over foreign policy. The opposition criticized this statement as unconstitutional.

24. See Jędrzejewicz, *Kronika*, 2:305. Compare Adam Krzyżanowski, *Dzieje Polski* (Paris, 1973), 182. Also Laroche dispatches in late Apr. and May 1928, MAE, Pologne 9 and 77; Erskine reports, FO 371 2614 3764/8/55 and 2767.

25. Patek to Zaleski, 5 June 1928, PI, Amb. Londyn, reel 39; Herbette dispatches 10, 23, 30 Jan., 4 Mar. 1928, MAE, Pologne 76:50–61; Lithuanie 36:179–85; Russie 362:22–29. For unsuccessful private overtures to Stresemann by Prince Michał Rad-

his belief that Moscow would eventually sign a nonaggression treaty with Poland and its neighbors, Warsaw remained anxious and suspicious lest Paris complicate the game by an uncoordinated Franco-Soviet treaty. Briand's assurances that he envisaged such a treaty only as "an element in a system of treaties in which Poland's interests would be fully safeguarded" did not inspire absolute confidence.[26]

In late March, Zaleski decided to visit Rome. He may have intended to show that Poland "can have other friends,"[27] but his main concern was to explore the possibility of a common Italo-Polish policy within the framework of the slow-moving talks between Paris and Rome.[28] Although Zaleski had cleared his visit with Briand, and thus could not be accused of disloyalty, the trip aroused misgivings at the Quai d'Orsay and alarmed the Little Entente diplomats.[29] Zaleski was irritated. The foreign ministers of the Little Entente "spend all their time traveling," he told the French chargé d'affaires, "and I would not have the right to go to Italy."[30] He proceeded promptly, however, to reassure the Little Entente that Poland was united with it "through the common ideal of the maintenance of peace on the basis of inviolability and respect of the existing treaties." He emphasized the alliance with Romania, good relations with Prague, and the treaty of friendship with Yugoslavia. To pretend that Poland was disinterested in the territorial integrity of the Little Entente, he said, would be absurd.[31]

During two lengthy conversations with Mussolini in mid-April, Zaleski stressed his country's alliances, but also complained that Romania and France did not "always support us with solicitude." He said that it was only through a campaign of the conservative Parisian press that Poland was able to "straighten France's behavior in the German fortifications' affair." The minister characterized Poland's relations with Czechoslovakia as "cold." Mussolini later commented that Zaleski seemed "particularly

---

ziwiłł, see his account to Piłsudski, 7 Mar. 1928, AAN, Akta Piłsudskich 7, and to Stresemann, 12 Mar. 1928, ADAP, B, VIII:328–38.

26. Chłapowski telegram, 11 Feb. 1928, HIA, Amb. Paryż, box 2. Compare 16 Feb. report in Łopatniuk, "Nieznane dokumenty," 184–85. Also note on Frankowski's visit, 18 Jan. 1928, MAE, Russie 362:12, and Zaleski telegram, 6 Mar. 1928, HIA, Amb. Paryż box 6.

27. Erskine to Chamberlain, 27 Apr. 1928, FO 371 13300 N 2461/8/55.

28. See Zaleski, "Memoirs," his reports 9 Feb., 8 May, 24 June 1925, HIA, Zaleski Papers. Compare MS, BJ, "Pamiętnik Stanisława Kozickiego 1876–1939," III, part vii.

29. See numerous dispatches of Laroche, Tripier, Beaumarchais, and Charles-Roux in MAE, Pologne 4 and 76. Compare briefings, 13, 24 Apr. 1928, KV, CPP; Borejsza, *Mussolini*, 130; Kozeński, "Próby," 323.

30. Tripier to Laroche, 4 Apr. 1928, MAE, Pologne 4:36–44.

31. Zaleski's statement in Tripier to Briand, 7 Apr. 1928, MAE, Pologne 76:171–73. In Rome, Zaleski reaffirmed his position in an interview given to a Polish correspondent.

aggressive in his judgement of . . . both Prague and Belgrade, and very sympathetic whenever speaking of the Hungarians." Indeed, Zaleski seemed to advocate a rapprochement between Hungary and Romania, although it would have to proceed "only in small doses and not in the immediate future." Mussolini favored it also and observed that such a rapprochement "alone would make the Polish alliance with Romania effective." Both statesmen concurred on the need to work in this direction; they also shared the view that Anschluss should be opposed.[32]

The French Right called Zaleski's trip to Rome a Polish revenge for the excessively germanophile policies of Briand. This was an exaggeration. Obviously Warsaw wished to improve its international standing, but in that respect the results were meager: an agreement to upgrade the legations to embassies (which it took a year to do), and an accolade from Mussolini who referred to Poland as a "grande potenza." Nonetheless, the Quai d'Orsay showed signs of "bad humor," and there were indications of "panic" in some French circles. Chłapowski voiced suprise over this adverse reaction. Was Paris losing faith in Poland? Zaleski found it necessary to refer in his 18 May speech to "fantastic rumors" that were absolutely groundless.[33] But, if Paris frowned upon Zaleski's initiative, Prague was evern more directly affected by Polish activities bearing on the Danubian region. Still, outwardly at least, the government circles remained calm; the official *Československá Republika* denied any feeling of anxiety.[34]

Elusive Pursuits: Beneš in Berlin

As seen from Prague the diplomatic calendar of 1928 began with the Szentgotthárd affair, a discovery of arms being smuggled from Italy across the Austro-Hungarian border. The Little Entente raised an outcry over Hungarian violations of the disarmament provisions, and the incident, insofar as it affected Rome, was awkward for the British—then seeking to encourage Franco-Italian talks—and for Paris. When the machinery of the League was set in motion, the French showed a desire to avoid a crisis, and the Poles manifested a disinclination to join in any censure of Budapest.

---

32. See Mussolini to Amadori, 23 Apr. and to Majoni, 6 May 1928, DDI, 7, VI:212–13, 238, 270. I am indebted to Vera Grandi and Fabio Sampoli for help with the translation. Polish account in Zaleski telegram, 28 Apr., HIA, Amb. Paryż, box 1; Laroche telegram, 24 Apr., MAE, Pologne 76:213–18; Erskine to Chamberlain, 27 Apr. 1928, FO 371 13300 N 2461/8/55.

33. Zaleski, *Przemowy*, 1:132–133. For French reactions, see political director's note, 14 Apr., MAE, Lithuanie 38:47–48, and Arciszewski report, 20 Apr. 1928, PI, Amb. Londyn, reel 39.

34. See reports of Charles-Roux, 20 May, and Laroche, 21 Apr., MAE, Tchécoslovaquie 39:69; Pologne 76:208–10.

The affair was eventually patched up, but it demonstrated to Paris the flim-siness of the investigation procedures under the League, something worth remembering if one considered German evasions. In turn, the caution with which France had dealt with Rome was not lost on the Czechs. Beneš ex-plained his relatively moderate stand by saying that Hungary was a needed partner in his scheme of Danubian cooperation.[35]

To deal with stringent Hungarian revisionism, backed by Mussolini and promoted by the *Daily Mail*, owned by the conservative press magnate Lord Rothermere, Czechoslovak diplomacy continued to seek a rap-prochement with Austria, explore further the idea of a pact involving Cen-tral Europe modeled on Locarno, and improve relations with Germany. In February, Beneš attempted to win over Ignaz Seipel, the Austrian chancel-lor, by explaining to him that Prague did not contemplate a multilateral regional pact but rather bilateral treaties, which need not even involve abandonment of territorial claims but only a renunciation of war. Beneš was, of course, well aware of Italy's opposition to any scheme that ex-cluded it from Danubian cooperation but hoped to associate Italy some-how.[36]

In April, the Czechoslovak foreign minister visited London, Paris, and Brussels attempting to promote his ideas. British interest was limited, even though a Foreign Office memorandum had recognized the possibility of a Central European Locarno, provided it was built on Franco-Italian under-standing.[37] Somewhat optimistically, Beneš informed Prague that Lon-don—allegedly out of fear of the political and economic influence of Ger-many—was becoming more positive in its attitude toward France, the Little Entente, and Poland and cooler vis-á-vis Hungary and Mussolini.[38]

Beneš's attempts to bring the Little Entente partners in line with his pol-icy, however, proved difficult. Romania in particular was suspicious, and all the Czechoslovak minister eventually achieved was a certain reconcili-ation of views with regard to Germany, and a strengthening of the group-ing through an automatic prolongation of the Little Entente treaties.[39] As for Berlin, Krofta, for one, stressed that "we cannot abandon ourselves to

35. See Vaïsse, "Le Désarmement." On Beneš, see Einstein to Secretary of State, 18 Feb. 1928, SDNA, 760F.64/37.

36. On the obsession of Italian diplomats with a Danubian economic confederation, seen as a French-Czechoslovak plot engineered by the "subtle and perfidious Beneš," see Charles-Roux to Briand, 17 June 1928, MAE, Tchécoslovaquie 39:81–84.

37. Memorandum in DBFP, ia, iv:262–67. On Jan Masaryk's warnings not to count on Britain, see Gajanová, "Entstehung," 158.

38. See Briefing, 31 May 1928, KV, CPP. Compare Beneš' 6 June speech in *Boj o mír*, 397–413. On Hymans–Beneš conversation, 17 May, DDB, ii, 488–93.

39. On the Little Entente meeting, see Einstein to Secretary of State, 13 June, SDNA, 840.00/84; reports in MAE, Tchécoslovaquie 70:191–94, 199–201, 211–15, 257–59, 235. Also Beneš to missions, 25 June, and briefing 20 July 1928, KV, CPP.

illusions about a pacifist trend having triumphed in Germany," but he added that "at this moment Germany does not think about forcibly changing the status quo based on peace treaties." It was only after the evacuation of the Rhineland that the Germans could begin a diplomatic offensive, "which will certainly be directed in the first instance against Poland."[40] Thus, there was still time to make tentative approaches to Berlin, and indeed in March Beneš had opened his heart, as his interlocutor put it, to Max Beer, a confident of Schubert.

In the course of two long conversations, the Czechoslovak minister insisted that he was not anti-German and would have no objection to Berlin invoking more forcefully article 19 of the Covenant providing for peaceful change. He would have preferred to see Germany taking an openly negative attitude toward Eastern Locarno, for he had no use for it himself, and the matter left him completely indifferent. Again Beneš denied that he wished to use a regional system to prevent an Anschluss or to make Austria dependent on the Danubian grouping. If he opposed Anschluss, that was because Europe would not tolerate it; besides it would make Czechoslovakia completely dependent economically on Germany-Austria. Beneš agreed that the Germans had some moral right to seek a union but suggested that they seek compensation elsewhere. Did he have in mind the "Vienna or Danzig?" formula, Beer asked. Beneš replied that this was precisely what he was thinking of. Having thus taken an anti-Polish position, the minister added a few sharp words about the Hungarians who had to be taught a lesson.[41] Informed of this conversation, Schubert opined that Beneš was seriously worried about Anschluss and the fate of the Little Entente. He wanted to put Hungary "on a leash," but his ideas on Central European cooperation were still hazy.[42]

In May, the Czechoslovak foreign minister came, largely on his own initiative, to Berlin. The visit had a private character not to antagonize the Czech nationalists; Schubert, substituting for the ill Stresemann, acted as host. Beneš spoke to Chancellor Wilhelm Marx, Minister of Economics Julius Curtius, and Schacht.[43] In several conversations with Staatssekretär von Schubert, he repeated that his ideas about Central European Locarno—he actually avoided the term—were misrepresented. The main object had been a pact with Hungary, which he gave up because of Budapest's intransigence, but he was still interested in an economic accord. He was ready to sign a nonaggression pact with Austria; perhaps an Austro-

40. 26 Apr. 1928, KV, CPP.

41. Schubert's 12 Mar. 1928 note, ADAP, B, VIII:324–27.

42. Schubert's 23 Mar. 1928 note, ADAP, B, VIII:392–93.

43. See Campbell, *Confrontation*, 192–98; Brügel, *Tschechen*, 214–17; and Krüger, "Beneš," which differs from Brügel in the appraisal of Schubert's motivation. Also, see Krofta, *Z dob*, 91–92.

Yugoslav or an Austro-Italian treaty would be beneficial. Denying any intention of pressuring other states into cooperation to prevent an Anschluss, he spoke in general terms about a system of preferential tariffs (for instance) encompassing the Little Entente, Austria, Hungary, and Greece but not Poland. His opposition to Anschluss he explained in terms already familar from the conversation with Beer. Schubert commented that one should neither try to force Anschluss nor oppose it forcibly; as for Danubian agreements, they made little sense economically. One ought to strive after wider European cooperation, some form of United States of Europe, an idea that appealed to Briand and such French economic experts as Maurice Bokanowski and Daniel Serruys. But a gradual approach was advisable—for example, establishing first a German-Austrian-Czechoslovak economic unit. Beneš admitted that the idea had some merits on economic grounds but politically would produce an adverse reaction of France, Britain, and Italy. Berlin would be accused of pursuing a Great German design.[44]

The German envoy in Prague, Walter Koch, found it hard to believe that Beneš did not intend to use regional pacts to perpetuate the existing peace treaties in Danubian Europe. If the exact nature of the proposed preferential arrangements was hazy, that was because Beneš, being no economist, was unsure about it himself. Koch concluded that Beneš's motivation for the Berlin visit was largely domestic—disarming his political critics and driving a wedge between the Sudeten Germans and the Reich[45]—but there was more to it than that.

It appears that Beneš's main goal was to establish a direct contact with Germany within the framework of Briand's Locarno policy. Economic considerations played an important role, and the Prague press wrote of a great Franco-German economic system in which Czechoslovakia ought to find her proper place. Beneš's observations to Schubert that his country would be interested in a larger grouping in which France participated could be interpreted both as an objection to a tête-à-tête with Berlin and a desire to find a niche in the bigger edifice.

The Franco-German commercial treaty of 1927, combined with French tariff increases and the devaluation of the franc, had adversely affected Czechoslovak foreign trade. There were voices in Prague that France treated the country as a colony. Negotiations for a new trade accord that

---

44. There were three Beneš-Schubert conversations plus a super-secret session devoted to the issue of German rights in Czechoslovakia. Schubert notes in ADAP, B, IX:54–58, 65–78, 86–88. Compare Charles-Roux and Margerie reports 2 and 23 June, MAE, Tchécoslovaquie 70:202–203, 42:121–22; also Lindsey to Chamberlain, 24 May, DBFP, 1a, v: 74–75; briefing 31 May 1928, KV, CPP. For retrospective reference to the Berlin talks, see the speech of 21 Mar. 1934 in Beneš, *The Problem of Central Europe*, 37–38.

45. Koch to Schubert, 3 June 1928, ADAP, B, IX:123–27.

began in March 1928 were running into difficulties, and the Czechs may have wished to improve their bargaining position. Prague demanded the most-favored-nation clause; the French were reluctant to grant it, although France exported seven times more to Czechoslovakia than it imported, and a rupture could only profit Germany.[46] Calling attention to the political implications and stressing the German angle, Charles-Roux advised to provide "a good economic base to our relations with Czechoslovakia." Surely the French domestic and colonial market could absorb more Czechoslovak imports?[47] The commercial convention signed eventually on 2 July embodied a compromise: Czechoslovakia made concessions on customs duties, and France extended the most-favored-nation clause to all goods likely to be exported by the Czechs.

The French were intent on maintaining their economic and political influences in East Central Europe. When *Le Temps* seemed to admit the possibility of Czechoslovak-French relations becoming a function of good relations between Paris and Berlin, the envoy in Prague protested. "We have the right to be more ambitious," he wrote, "and consider that the contrary should be the case"—that is, that Czech-German relations be a function of those between France and Germany.[48] As for the envoy in Budapest, he emphasized that the Little Entente be treated as a means and not an end in itself. "If we work for it, it [the Little Entente] should, on its side, serve us." The group was not "an infirmary room one cannot enter except on tiptoes."[49]

In early 1928, Paris continued its policy of strengthening the Little Entente, particularly in the financial sphere;[50] reserved judgement on Beneš's plans; and once again explored the possibility of a military rapprochement between Prague and Warsaw.

Before going to Berlin, Beneš had told Zaleski that he had worked out a Central European Locarno project based on a nonaggression pact and arbitration treaties. It would comprise the Little Entente, Austria, and Hungary. Would it not end up by producing a rapprochement between Czechoslovakia, Hungary, Austria, and Germany wondered the Polish delegate in Geneva?[51] Grzybowski and Charles-Roux worried about the German

46. See articles in *Venkov*, 22 Mar. *Národní Listy*, 24 Apr., *Prager Presse*, 10 May, *Tribuna*, 24 June 1928. Compare Charles-Roux to Briand, 12 April and note, Relations Commerciales, 10 Mar. 1928, MAE, Tchécoslovaquie 83:148–49, 141–43.

47. Charles-Roux to Briand, 14 Mar. 1928, MAE, Tchécoslovaquie 83:144.

48. Charles-Roux to Briand, 18 Jan. 1928, MAE, Tchécoslovaquie 33:122–26.

49. Vienne to Briand, 27 Feb. 1928, MAE, Tchécoslovaquie 70:171.

50. See entries in Moreau, *Souvenirs*, 489, 493, 495, 499–500, 502, 506–507, 511, 514, 517, 523.

51. Zaleski telegram, 6 Mar. 1928, HIA, Amb. Paryż, box 6; Sokal report, 2 Apr. 1928, AAN, Pos.Ateny, 167.

angle.[52] The Frenchmen contrasted Masaryk's words about the Germans of Czechoslovakia being "an organic part of the state" with the president's reference to them in 1918 as "emigrants and colonists." Grzybowski saw a basic discrepancy between Beneš's representation of his country as a Slav bastion against Germandom, and Masaryk's comparison to Switzerland where the Germans were equal partners. Whom was one to believe?

Briand and Berthelot tried to reassure the Poles about the German implications of Beneš's plans. His activities were not to be taken "too seriously" for he was always "full of initiatives."[53] Nor was French diplomacy much impressed by Romanian ideas of enlarging the scope of the Little Entente through territorial guarantees, along with an involvement of Poland and to some extent Italy. A Danubian consolidation, if affected under the aegis of Rome, would be directed against France.[54] Laroche was skeptical about Poland's participation, for the Poles secretly despised the Romanians and had little in common with Yugoslavia. Some of these feelings were mutual. "The Little Entente," he wrote, "definitely does not have any luck with Poland." The ambassador deplored this state of affairs, because he believed that Poland needed friends in the region.[55]

French reminders to Beneš to show more comprehension of the Polish position usually produced the rejoinder that relations with Warsaw were good and he "wanted to keep them this way," or they elicited remarks about the bad faith of Piłsudski who fortunately was "not eternal." When the French envoy wondered why Prague did not seek a common platform with Poland on the Anschluss, Beneš answered that he knew the Polish habit of wanting a quid pro quo for any service they thought to have rendered. Aware of Czechoslovak views (which he did not share), Laroche redoubled his efforts to dissuade the Poles from flirting with Budapest, which only irritated Prague.[56]

In April, Beneš sought out Laroche, then in Paris, and made a number of statements the French considered most encouraging. The foreign minister explained at length why he wished to improve his relations with Warsaw, and admitted that some Polish grievances, notably those concerning

52. See Charles-Roux to Briand, 17, 26 Jan. 10, 12, 15 Feb. 1928, MAE, Tchécoslovaquie 33:127–28, 137–39; 62:162; Pologne 76:79–81, 100–101.

53. Chłapowski report, 5 May 1928, PI, Amb. Londyn, reel 39.

54. See dispatches of Laroche, 11 May; Japy, 15 June; and Vienne, 1 July 1928, MAE, Tchécoslovaquie 70:180–82, 185–89, 226–28. On ther eve of the Little Entente meeting in Bucharest, Mussolini suggested that Warsaw try to dissuade Romania from taking an anti-Hungarian line. See DDI, 7, VI:270.

55. Laroche to Briand, 28 Jan. 1928, MAE, Pologne 76:82–83; compare Leeper to Chamberlain, 27 Feb 1928, FO 371 13300 Hm 03820.

56. See the Briand–Charles-Roux–Laroche correspondence during the second half of January and early February 1928 in MAE, Tchécoslovaquie 62 and Pologne 76; also Beneš, *Boj o mír*, 411.

the activity of the Ukrainians in Prague, were justified. Should Poland be attacked by Russia, the incidents of 1920 (stoppages of munition trains in Czechoslovakia) would not recur. Beneš appeared to show an understanding of Polish attitude toward the Little Entente and Hungary; he was not worried by Zaleski's trip to Rome. While the Little Entente did not wish to be drawn into Polish difficulties with Germany and Russia, the existence of Poland "was a basic condition of European stability." Beneš had made similar observations to the French ambassador in Berlin, and affirmed that all the prejudices against Poland had disappeared in Czechoslovakia.[57] Because this last remark had been made during Beneš' visit to Berlin, reconciling it with what he was telling the Germans is difficult.

The French promptly relayed the conversation to Zaleski, who responded by making complimentary remarks about Beneš. In a speech on 18 May, the Polish foreign minister declared that the relations with Czechoslovakia were developing in a "spirit of neighborly cooperation," creating a firm basis for a "cultural and economic rapprochement between the two countries."[58] Did this exclude politics, and was a military rapprochement not to be seriously considered?

Before the Laroche–Beneš exchanges, the Quai d'Orsay had asked the war ministry whether the general staff could not facilitate a Czechoslovak-Polish military entente by proposing to both countries joint studies under the direction of France. This proposal sounded like a return to the 1924 plans. The main obstacle—the Hungarian question—was viewed as somewhat similar to the Russian issue in the Franco-Polish alliance; it could be overcome by concentrating on cooperation against Germany.[59] General Debeney agreed that a French initiative was needed. He foresaw no Polish objections, but noted that there was "certainly very little enthusiasm" on the Czechoslovak side. Charles-Roux concurred. The Czechs thought mainly in terms of passive cooperation, such as neutrality and transit facilities. If General Syrový was less cautious, he could not act without Udržal, who in turn had to consider the agrarians' policy of conciliation with the Sudeten Germans, and was obliged to refer to Masaryk. The discrepancy between the 14.7 percent allotted to military expenditure in the Czechoslovak budget and 30 percent in the Polish (a significant rise compared with earlier Polish expenditures) was symptomatic of current priorities. Given Beneš's preference for "successive and separate" military stud-

57. Laroche to Briand, 20 Apr., MAE, Pologne 76:202–205; compare Margerie dispatch 25 May 1928, Tchécoslovaquie 62:173.

58. Zaleski, *Przemowy*, 1:140. See also Laroche telegram, 24 Apr. 1928, MAE, Pologne 76:219.

59. Briand to Painlevé, 28 Mar., and for background, Charles-Roux report, 5 Feb. 1928, MAE, Tchécoslovaquie 62:165, 161. Also Bułhak, "Z dziejów 1927–1936," 100–102.

ies, French general staff would have to examine individually with its two counterparts the various hypotheses of French-Polish-Czechoslovak military cooperation and then communicate the findings to the other partner.[60]

This seemed like a cumbersome and complicated procedure. What is more, although the principle of triple military cooperation was fully accepted by French envoys and the general staff—Debeney being ready personally to supervise and assure coordination—a preliminary agreement between Warsaw and Prague on the object of the studies was a precondition of military talks.[61] Such an agreement was unlikely; once again only technical staff conversations, dealing with intelligence matters, took place between the Poles and the Czechoslovaks in Zakopane, in September 1928. Perfunctory, lip-service cordiality, punctuated by recurring minor friction was still the characteristic feature of Czechoslovak-Polish relations.[62] When Beneš assured Grzybowski that he had behaved loyally toward Poland during his Berlin talks, just as Zaleski had done vis-à-vis Czechoslovakia in Rome, he accurately described the very narrrow confines of the loyalty that prevailed between the two countries. French efforts to compensate for their own declining military might by forging a Czechoslovak-Polish link in the alliance chain remained unsuccessful.

Polish Moves Snubbed

Stresemann and Briand had agreed in March to delay conversations about the Rhineland and related matters until after the elections in their respective countries. The French elections, held in April, registered a defeat of the radical-socialists, and a success of the centrist and rightist parties supporting Poincaré. This result was a check to Briand's German policy, and indeed the governmental statement of 7 June omitted the usual mention of the spirit of Locarno, expressing instead concern over French security and treaty rights. On 25 June, France officially stabilized the franc (franc Poincaré) at one-fifth of its prewar value. The country's strong financial position permitted the lifting of the ban on exportation of capital, making the French capable of investing abroad (until 1932) around 890 million gold francs annually. The importance of this fact for East Central Europe

60. See note 25 Apr. 1928, SHA, EMA/3, 7 N 3007, "Coopération polono–tchéque"; compare Charles-Roux to Briand, 19 Apr. and Quai d'Orsay to war ministry, 12 May 1928, SHA, EMA/3, 7 N 3446/1. Also Soutou, "L'Alliance," 322.

61. War ministry to Quai d'Orsay, 1 July 1928, SHA, EMA/3, 7 N 3446/1.

62. Friction with the Poles in Teschen was one example; see 2 May briefing, KV, CPP, and Charles-Roux reports, 14, 31 May 1928, MAE, Tchécoslovaquie 62:174–75, 185. On the other hand, there were friendly manifestations; Polish planes participated in the Little Entente aeronautic competitions, and the press occasionally printed amicable statements. Hodža's appeals for a larger East Central European union including Poland did not reflect the government's position. See Hodža, *Clánky*, 7:177.

hardly requires emphasis.[63] German elections, which followed in late May, resulted in losses for the nationalists and the centrists, and gains for the social democrats. A new cabinet, formed after serious difficulties by the socialist chancellor Hermann Müller, and facing grave domestic problems, was held together largely through Stresemann's foreign policy. This responsibility imposed new strains on the minister. His health was impaired, and the conduct of German diplomacy devolved for several months on Schubert.

The European security debate became affected at this point by protracted negotiations about a peace pact originally conceived in Paris as a bilateral treaty but changed into a broadly conceived multilateral accord following a proposal offerred by U.S. Secretary of State Frank Kellogg. As Senator Lémery put it: "The declaration of love that we expected from the United States transformed itself into a declaration of universal friendship."[64] The proposed pact carried with it a potential threat to the French system of alliances. Because the French had anchored the latter on article 16 of the Covenant, the Germans were interested in preventing an expressly stated connection between that article and the peace pact.[65] Beneš on his side wanted to make sure that the Kellogg proposal did not conflict with either the Franco-Czechoslovak treaty, or Locarno, or the agreements of the Little Entente. Although occasionally dubious about French tactics, Beneš approved the conditions Paris had proposed: the pact would be binding only after its universal acceptance; the right of self-defense would be retained; signatories would be released from their obligations vis-à-vis a member who violated the document; prior commitments arising out of the Covenant and Locarno would be preserved.[66]

The Poles thought that the Kellogg proposal "represented certain dangers," the most important of which was "that in the absence of a general security guarantee, the system of our defensive alliances would be deprived of practical significance." They were worried that Paris did not immediately approach Warsaw, as if ignoring that the American scheme "affected in the first place our agreements with France." But before Chłapowski could ask how Paris intended to reconcile the proposed pact with "our interests," Laroche inquired if the Polish government planned to join the

63. See Girault, "L'Europe centrale," 122.

64. Cited in Bonnefous, *Histoire*, 4:340.

65. See Krüger, "Friedenssicherung," 252–54.

66. See 6 June speech in Beneš, *Boj o mír*, 401–405; briefings, 31 May, 8 June 1928, KV, CPP; Charles-Roux to Briand, 2 June 1928, MAE, Tchécoslovaquie 42:121–22; Beneš–Hymans conversation, 17 May 1928, DDB, 11, 448–93; Einstein to Secretary of State, 17 Jan. 1928, SDNA, 711.5112 France/160; also Lawrence E. Gelfand, ed., *Louis Einstein: A Diplomat looks Back* (New Haven, 1968), 202.

pact and what alterations it wished to see.[67] Indeed, the French had already intimated to the Americans that if would be difficult for them to sign a document from which Poland, Czechoslovakia, and Yugoslavia were excluded. Warsaw, however, disliked the idea of dealing with Washington via Paris, and Zaleski approached the United States directly.[68] If Paris thought it was doing its best to assist Warsaw, the Poles were distrustful. As a junior French diplomat in Warsaw saw it: "We have once again given the Poles an impression, deplorable in itself and humiliating to us, that France considers them henceforth a deadweight which it only awaited the opportunity . . . of dropping."[69]

Piłsudski might contemptuously dismiss the proposed Kellogg pact as another scrap of paper, but Polish diplomacy resented being excluded from the secret talks held by French, British, and German jurists. Prestige was not the only consideration, for the Germans succeeded in gaining the acceptance of their interpretation of clauses relating to the Rhineland.[70] Under the Kellogg pact, France would keep its right to resort to military action in case of a flagrant violation of the Rhineland status, but only if there was a "nonprovoked act" of German aggression.[71] In practice this clause meant a further restriction of the French freedom of action, a matter that directly affected Poland. The jurists agreed, however, that the right of self-defense, on which both the French and the Poles insisted, would not be affected. The Kellogg-Briand Pact (or the Pact of Paris) was solemnly signed on 27 August, and the Parisian press described it poetically as "a spiritual wedding of Briand and peace."[72] Laroche told Zaleski that thanks to the efforts of the French government, Poland received through the pact a virtual nonaggression engagement from Germany, which had eluded it so far. The leftist radical socialist Pierre Cot wrote that the pact was bringing new assurances to Poland and Czechoslovakia through the obligation

67. See Zaleski telegrams, 5, 10 May 1928, SI, Amb. Londyn, A.12.52/10; HIA, Amb. Paryż, box 1.

68. See Houghton to Secretary of State, and Stetson–Kellogg correspondence, 7 and 14–17 May 1928, FRUS 1928, I, 63–65. Compare Zaleski telegram, 14 May 1928, PI, Amb. Londyn, reel 39.

69. Barbier, *Un Frac*, 335. Compare Zaleski in Wandycz, *Zaleski*, 51–52. On conversation with Laroche, see Zaleski telegram, 20 May 1928, HIA, Amb. Paryż, box 1.

70. Ciałowicz, *Polsko-francuski sojusz*, 147n.; Wysocki, *Tajemnice*, 64–65. On the Franco-Polish aspect, see telegrams of Zaleski, Chłapowski, Wysocki, Arciszewski, respectively 28, 30 June, 12, 15 July, HIA, Amb. Paryż, box 2.

71. This meant "crossing of the frontier, or opening of hostilities, or assembling armed forces in the demilitarized zone . . . if the assembling of troops constituted a nonprovoked act of aggression." See Krüger, "Friedenssicherung," 251; compare DBFP, 1a, v:764–67.

72. Cited in Bonnefous, *Histoire*, 4:274.

on the part of signatories to resolve all their disputes by pacific means.[73] Stresemann was closer to the mark when he concluded that the pact would weaken the French alliance system and assist Germany in its demands for disarmament.[74]

Zaleski put little faith in the efficacy of the Kellogg–Briand pact, but the foreign ministry had to stress, for domestic consumption, its contribution to stabilization, completion of the Covenant, and the possibility of American participation in European economic cooperation.[75] Asserting publicly that Franco-German normalization could not cause any anxiety in Warsaw, Zaleski was fully intent on pressing Paris not to make any new concessions to Berlin.[76] During his visit in early June which the French had not encouraged, the foreign minister aired privately and in public his opinions on the early evacuation of the Rhineland. Underscoring full identity of views with France, excellent relations with the Little Entente, and cordial "neighborly relations" with Czechoslovakia, Zaleski assailed revisionism as the greatest threat to peace. Without naming Germany or the Rhineland, he warned that it was easy to evacuate an area but hard to reoccupy it if the other side did not keep its engagements.[77] In press interviews, he labored the theme: "We see in the occupation a guarantee of general security."

The French were vexed by Zaleski's pronouncements, which raised a storm in Germany. By what right, the German press asked, did the minister speak about the evacuation, which was no business of Poland? Ambassador von Hoesch pointed out at the Quai d'Orsay that his government would never consent to discuss these matters with Warsaw, nor would Germany recognize the Polish borders. "Horse-trading"—namely, evacuation for eastern security—did not correspond to what Briand had been

73. Laroche to Briand, 24 Aug, MAE, Pologne 113:314. For Cot's article, see *La Rennaissance*, 22 Dec. 1928.

74. See Jacobson, *Locarno*, 192.

75. Cabinet meeting, 18 Jan 1929, AAN, PPRM, XLVI, 81–82.

76. On 18 May, he declared that "we are certain that our old friend France with whom we are bound by so many common interests, will proceed on this path [of normalization] with due caution, guarding, together with us, peace and inviolability of treaties on which peace is unequivocally based." On 25 May, he recalled that a pacified Europe ought to include its eastern part. See Zaleski, *Przemowy*, 1:130 and 146–62. Laroche reported extensively on the first speech on 19 May and 1 June 1928, MAE, Pologne 77:4–5, 23.

77. See *Le Temps*, 14 June, which left out, however, Zaleski's allusions to the Rhineland, mentioned by *Gazeta Warszawska*, 20 June 1928. Compare Crewe to Chamberlain, 13 June 1928, FO 371 12902 C 4578; also Zaleski, *Przemowy*, 1:175–81. During his visit Zaleski spoke to President Doumergue, Briand, and Berthelot and addressed the Franco-Polish parliamentary group and the press. For French lack of enthusiasm, see Zaleski telegram, 17 May 1928, HIA, Amb. Paryż, box 1.

telling the Germans, and Berlin had to be reassured that French views remained unchanged. The political director at the Quai d'Orsay, Charles Corbin, was visibly embarrassed.[78] Briand, faced with a request for a formal disavowal, refused to discuss the Polish stand by saying that it would be impolitic of the ambassador to insist on a French governmental appraisal of "political concepts attributed to the Polish government." Hoesch understood what Briand meant, smiled and renounced any intention to execute his instructions. The foreign minister then proceeded to make it clear that he did not propose to involve Poland in the negotiations.[79]

The British who were not sure at first how Paris would treat the incident, noted that Berthelot "spoke rather impatiently" of Zaleski and his "too many declarations." They concluded that Zaleski had "evidently been snubbed in Paris, which is all to the good."[80] Thus, Zaleski's attempt to be more outspoken only produced an adverse reaction in France and elsewhere. Understandably the foreign minister was greatly upset.[81] Reverting to greater caution, the Poles continued to watch for any signs of pro-German moves in France. The formation of a Franco-German parliamentary group of studies under Briand's patronage aroused anxiety. So did the trip to Germany of the radical-socialist deputy Jean Montigny, who on his return spoke of the "weak spot" of Franco-German cooperation—namely, the "corridor," which needed to be removed.[82] Similar remarks were made by some French deputies in the course of the ratification of the Kellogg-Briand pact. And, as always there were economic strains in Franco-Polish relations that were worrisome.

Profiting from Zaleski's visit, Berthelot complained about the Polish treatment of Skarboferm. A serious conflict was brewing with the Marcel Boussac group (Comptoir de l'Industrie Cotonnière à Paris) which the Polish government was accusing of financial irregularities and squeezing profits out of the textile mill at Żyrardów without any regard for Poland's economy or workers' intersts.[83] The deputy foreign minister was telling the

78. Note 19 June 1928, MAE, Pologne 77:31.

79. Note d'audience, 22 June 1928, MAE, Pologne 77:39. Compare Schubert–Hoesch correspondence, ADAP, B, IX; 185–88, 204–206.

80. Chamberlain note, conversation with Berthelot, and Erskine to Chamberlain, 28, 29 June 1928, DBFP, 1a, v: 123, 143–44, 147. Also Grahame and Henderson to Chamberlain, 15 and 19 June 1928, FO 371 12902 C 4605 and C 4747/969/18.

81. Laroche telegram, 29 June 1928, MAE, Pologne 77:41.

82. See note of political director, 19 June, MAE, Allemagne 391:103–104; Chłapowski report, 24 June, AAN, Amb. Berlin 73. Compare Hoesch report, ADAP, B, IX:171–73.

83. See Quai d'Orsay correspondence with embassy in Warsaw, MAE, Pologne 136, 215, 252, 258. Also Landau and Tomaszewski, *Sprawa*.

remonstrating Laroche: "Let the ambassador come one afternoon, not as the protector of Skarboferm, Częstochowa, or Żyrardów, but as the representative of France, our friend and ally, and I will devote as much time to him as will be needed."[84] True, the Schneider–Starachowice rapport had improved, and although the French grumbled about "financial sacrifices," this meant a reestablishment of the Schneider–Creusot influence in Poland, and an evolution toward producing uniform artillery material in France and Poland.[85] As for general French investments, the Quai d'Orsay agreed with the ministry of finance that the most important and profitable ventures in Poland were new businesses and attempted takeovers of already existing establishments. Floating Polish shares on the French market seemed less desirable.[86]

Because the 1924 trade convention became obsolete, new and difficult negotiations began in the commercial field. The Poles pressed for higher quotas of scrap iron (eight million tons monthly—to which the Comité des Forges objected—and complained that France was more generous to Italy, a potential adversary, than to Poland, which needed iron for national defense purposes. Eventually, a trade protocol was accepted on 8 July 1928, but a full-fledged convention had to wait until 24 April 1929. The Poles were hoping that it would reduce their unfavorable trade balance with France.[87]

While promoting economic interests, the French diplomacy was careful not to separate them from politics. Recognizing that France's economic stakes were high (around ten milliard francs) and existing problems vexing, Laroche insisted that Zaleski, "of whom I have great need," be treated with consideration. France should let other states oppose Warsaw's postulates regarding an extension of the Briand-Kellogg pact to all members of the League and appear at least to go along with Zaleski's ideas. In the case of Rhineland evacuation, although it was evident that Poland must not be involved, Polish claims should not be rejected overtly. "This is above all a mattter of being adroit in sparing the sensitivity, always on edge, of a young and still weak state."[88]

These disingenuous tactics rendered more difficult the task of Polish diplomacy. True, Chancellor Müller's demand on 3 July for the evacuation of the Rhineland was rejected by France and Britain, but Zaleski worried

84. MS, OSS, Wysocki II, 144.

85. Blanchet note, 26 Jan. 1928, MAE, Pologne, 244:122–24.

86. Finance ministry to Quai d'Orsay and Briand to Laroche, 6, 15 Oct. 1928, MAE, Pologne 232:142–43, 163–64.

87. See Quai d'Orsay–Laroche correspondence between March and June in MAE, Pologne 250. Compare cabinet session, 24 Apr. 1929, AAN, PPRM, L, 502.

88. Laroche to Corbin, 24 Aug. 1928, MAE, Pologne 215:95–97.

about the possibility of new French concessions. He wondered if a German renunciation of Anschluss might not be deemed a sufficient compensation for an early withdrawal. "Since Locarno France attempts constantly to accommodate Germany at our expense," he wrote, and "stresses at every opportunity Germany's position as a great power to our disadvantage." He wished these views to reach Briand.[89] The French foreign minister denied the existence of any tendency to link Anschluss with the evacuation: Zaleski's views amounted to a lack of faith in France, which, however, could not abandon its peaceful policy toward Germany for Poland's sake. An early evacuation was an interallied affair, and Briand avoided any precision about his stand.[90] Thus, uncertainty prevailed.

New conversations between Stresemann, Briand, and Poincaré were inconclusive. The French foreign minister acknowledged the official German demand for total evacuation, but made no comment about Stresemann's complaint that "two precious years" had been lost. Nor did he refer to East European problems. Poincaré kept clear of the Rhineland issue, limiting himself to a remark that the matter could only be resolved jointly with reparations and a debt settlement. He thought to discern a trace of blackmail in Stresemann's observations about the "corridor," and was not satisfied with the German's explication of the Anschluss issue.[91]

The existing state of Czechoslovak-Polish relations did not permit a coordinated action by Warsaw and Prague. Chłapowski not only felt that Czechoslovak diplomacy was timid and secretive, but he suspected Beneš of disloyalty.[92] Krofta seemed rather dispirited and pessimistic in his analysis of the situation. He was critical of French handling of Central European issues, and regarded a permanent prohibition of Anschluss impossible. The existence of a strong Poland and a "healthy" Russia, he remarked, would be of the greatest importance to Czechoslovakia, but a rapprochement with Poland was difficult and would entail the risk of all possible complications.[93] The following months brought no improvement in the relationship. Piłsudski's interest in Romania as an ally against Russia predicated a certain Romanian-Hungarian détente, which went against the pol-

89. Zaleski telegram, 19 Aug. 1928, HIA, Amb. Paryż, box 2.

90. Chłapowski telegram 22 Aug., HIA, Amb. Paryż, box 2. Compare telegram, 8 Sept. 1928, PI, Amb. Londyn, reel 39.

91. See Stresemann note 27 Aug. 1928, ADAP, B, IX: 631–34; for conversations, see DBFP, IA, V:271–72 and DDB, II, 523–30, 533. Compare Schmidt, *Statist*, 151–54. For German belief in a coordinated French-Polish-Czechoslovak press campaign against the Anschluss, see Auswärtiges Amt circular, 10 Sept. 1928, ADAP, B, X:34–36.

92. Chłapowski telegram, 8 Sept. 1928, PI, Amb. Londyn, reel 39.

93. Briefing, 2 Aug. 1928, KV, CPP.

icy of Prague.[94] The visit to Warsaw of the Hungarian foreign minister, Lajos Walkó, at the beginning of December alarmed Paris and the Little Entente. The episode testified once more to the incompatibility of Czechoslovak and Polish goals. A prominent national democratic adversary of Piłsudski jotted down in his diary: "Everything commands us to love the Czechs and to stand together with them unequivocally in the face of common dangers. But one cannot overcome a certain feeling that makes a rapprochement impossible."[95]

At the September session in Geneva, Müller officially demanded an early and unconditional evacuation of the Rhineland. His attack on "double-faced" French policy irked Briand, who responded with a sharp indictment of Berlin's policies. The Poles voiced their satisfaction, but as Laroche noted they became less insistent on their right to participate in the Rhineland negotiations.[96] This change in attitude probably resulted from Zaleski's failure to persuade Lord Cushendun (deputizing for Chamberlain) to admit Poland to such talks.[97]

Cushendun turned down a similar request made pro forma by Beneš. As the Czechoslovak foreign minister explained, public opinion at home would be dissatisfied "if it were to appear that he lagged behind his Polish colleague in this matter."[98] Thus, French eastern allies were successfully kept out of the talks among the representatives of the great powers in Geneva, which resulted on 16 September in an agreement to establish a committee of experts to discuss reparations, and a Commission of Verification and Conciliation to deal with the Rhineland issue. But, if the deadlock that had existed since Thoiry was broken, a good deal of ambiguity remained. Müller believed he had achieved a separation of the evacuation and repa-

94. See Laroche to Briand, 28 Aug. 1928, MAE, Pologne 77:43–45. Piłsudski told the deputy foreign minister on 27 Dec. that he wanted the alliance with Romania to bring full benefits to Poland. "They say that this will break up the Little Entente. I do not care. Czechoslovakia is an artificial creation . . . [and] it is not worthwhile to occupy oneself with this state or base on it our program of action." Cited in Ciałowicz, *Polsko-francuski sojusz*, 158.

95. 11 Nov. 1928 entry, MS, PAN, Dziennik Zdanowskiego, VI, p.2, 22. On the Walkó visit, see reports in MAE, Pologne 77:131–33, 141–42, 164–65. Compare briefing, 6 Dec. 1928, KV, CPP. Walkó was received by Piłsudski on 1 Dec. See Jędrzejewicz, *Kronika*, 2:321.

96. See Laroche to Briand, 21 Sept. 1928, MAE, Allemagne 391:247–48. *Gazeta Warszawska*, however, opined on 10 Oct. that because there was no likelihood of compensations for Poland, the only way out was not to evacuate the Rhineland before 1935.

97. Zaleski telegrams to Paris embassy and missions, 12 Sept. 1928, HIA, Zaleski Papers; SI, Amb. Londyn, A.12.52/10. On Cushendun–Zaleski conversation, 13 Sept., DBFP, 1a, V:321–23; Polish account, Zaleski telegram, 14 Sept., HIA, Zaleski Papers.

98. Cushendun–Beneš conversation, 21 Sept. 1928, FO 371 12904 C 7291.

rations issues, but the French considered that this was not so. Briand told Zaleski that the wording of the communiqué was purposefully vague so that he could use it to guarantee Polish interests as affected by the anticipated withdrawal.[99]

"The Poles are visibly worried," Massigli wrote to the Quai d'Orsay. They had not believed that an accord would intervene and thought that it was dangerous for Poland. He warned that their apprehension would be echoed in the pro-Polish press in France. Zaleski, Massigli thought, realized that Warsaw's position was weak, and he seemed mainly concerned to persuade public opinion at home that the country was not abandoned and that western and eastern European problems were not treated separately.[100] Laroche also believed that the foreign minister, who insisted that Paris and London did not fully appreciate Polish anxieties, could be appeased by some comforting formula.[101] General Sikorski conferred privately with Foch, who shared Polish apprehensions concerning the consequences of an early evacuation.[102] With or without Polish promptings, Millerand declared once again at Clermont-Ferrand that allied presence on the Rhine provided security for East European states.

Whether Zaleski's main concern was face-saving or whether he merely wished to convey this impression is not clear. On 12 October a sharper tone crept into Polish representations. A memorandum submitted by Chargé Arciszewski, while displaying the familiar arguments about Locarno, indivisible security, and German revisionism, demanded with some insistence that Poland be kept informed of future negotiations and that French influence be used to facilitate Poland's participation in the work on general security and reparations, as well as in signing final accords. The accompanying comments of Arciszewski struck Berthelot as "unbelievable." This was not the language of Zaleski, he opined. Was it influenced by the military circles?[103] If this was a reference to Piłsudski and his alleged animus against France, Laroche disputed the point. "The marshal is certainly not francophile," he wrote, but he does not detest France; rather "he does not know us well."[104]

Berthelot concealed his feelings so well, that the chargé got the impres-

---

99. Zaleski to missions, 17 Sept. 1928, SI, Amb. Londyn, A.12.52/10.

100. Massigli to Corbin, 17 and 19 Sept. 1928, MAE, P.A., Massigli 4.

101. Laroche to Briand and Massigli, 26, 27 Sept. 1928, MAE, Pologne 77:53–54, and P.A., Massigli 6.

102. See Sikorski, "Foch," 188.

103. Text of memorandum, 12 Oct. 1928, MAE, Pologne 77:58–60 and SI, MSZ, A.11/2. See Massigli to Laroche, 16 Oct. and to Berthelot, 23 Sept. 1928, MAE, P.A., Massigli 4 and Pologne 77:50–51.

104. Laroche to Briand, 19, 25 Oct. 1928, MAE, Pologne, 136:90, 94.

sion that the secretary actually welcomed the Polish note.[105] As to the merit of the case, the Quai d'Orsay adopted delaying tactics. When Arciszewski finally saw Briand, the latter extended vague assurances, but they were so persuasively presented that the Poles believed that Paris treated Polish requests with "full understanding" and would try to win over Chamberlain as well as work for German-Polish détente.[106] This was wishful thinking, and the French written reply contained little that was concrete. It claimed, however, that it was thanks to France that Poland became a signatory of the Kellogg–Briand pact, which brought "to your country new and precious guarantees of security."[107] All this meant that France would not jeopardize its position in future negotiations with Britain and Germany by insisting on the Polish angle, but it was trying to sweeten the bitter pill. At Laroche's recommendation, General Louis Maurin came—bringing a Consular sabre to Piłsudski—to represent France at the tenth anniversary of Poland's independence. His visit had been preceded by that of General Pierre Hering, commander of the École Supérieure de Guerre.[108]

Polish anxieties were shared, although to a lesser extent, by the Little Entente. The Yugoslav foreign minister wished that France associate more closely the "small Allies with its general policy," which would encourage the vacillating Romania.[109] Beneš deemed Czechoslovak and Polish involvement in the Rhineland negotiations of limited practical interest, but of great "political and moral value." He speculated on whether the fact that both countries had been signatories of Locarno would provide a sufficient justification for admitting them to the negotiating table. Czechoslovakia and Poland had every right to take part in the work on reparations, but claims to participation in political debate appeared to Beneš illusory on juridical grounds. Thus, he agreed to influence Warsaw in a sense desired by the French—that is, to moderate its demands.[110]

---

105. Arciszewski telegram, 13 Oct. 1928, HIA, Amb. Paryż, box 2.

106. Zaleski, Arciszewski and Chłapowski telegrams, 19, 25, 30 Oct., HIA, Amb. Paryż, box 2; 2 Nov., PI, Amb. Londyn, reel 39; SI, Amb. Londyn, A.12.52/10. Polish written statement, 25 Oct. 1928, MAE, Pologne 77:80–81. In his souvenirs, Zaleski recounted a conversation with Briand in which the latter, after telling the Pole that surely France and its eastern allies held Germany militarily in check, opined that they must make concessions to Germany in order to keep England convinced that they had done all to avoid a war with Germany. See Wandycz, *Zaleski*, 74.

107. Quai d'Orsay to Chłapowski, 6 Nov. 1928, MAE, Pologne 77:107–108, also SI, MSZ, A.11/2.

108. On the visits, see reports and notes in MAE, Pologne 77:120–21, 126–28, 148–59; and Pologne 21:187–88; and Pologne 43:124–25. The French visitors noted that Piłsudski visited for the first time the naval forces in Gdynia, and opined that Warsaw was more preoccupied with Germany than with Russia.

109. Note of political director, 25 Sept. 1928, MAE, Tchécoslovaquie 70:260–65.

110. Massigli to Berthelot, 23 Sept. 1928, MAE, Pologne 77:50–51. For Beneš's views

In the 4 October speech, Beneš's usual optimism was less marked than one could have assumed from the press. The minister concentrated on three major questions: reparations (a revision of the Dawes Plan), evacuation of the Rhineland, and limitation of armaments.[111] In the discussion that followed, German deputies called Czechoslovakia "France's slave," and deplored the "vassal relationship" between Prague and Paris. They made it clear that they did not oppose the Anschluss. As on similar occasions in the past, Charles-Roux urged the government to react against the aspirations of the Germans to influence Czechoslovak foreign policy. He also criticized the naiveté of some French circles that extolled Czechoslovak-German cooperation as the "most beautiful thing in the world."[112]

On 3 November, Stresemann, having recovered sufficiently from his illness, resumed control over the foreign ministry. Two weeks later he demanded an early evacuation of the Rhineland irrespective of reparations and debts negotiations, which threatened to upset the delicate arrangements arrived at in Geneva in September. A few days later a crisis in France led to the formation of Poincaré's new cabinet, on 11 November, which comprised no radical-socialists, a rare occurrence in interwar French politics. Although the crisis was mainly domestic in nature, foreign policy issues were not absent from the debates in which Briand stressed a basic identity of his views with those of Poincaré. The only difference, he asserted, was that of temperament. The foreign minister contrasted the German notion that Locarno would be indefinitely stretched with the French assumption that while working for an ever growing rapprochement, one had to retain "a certain prudence." German domestic politics resembled "moving sands," and the Reichswehr was in reality a cadre for an army, four million strong. Briand emphasized the need to defend native soil and left unanswered the question of the rightist deputy Stanislas de Castellane: "Do you think that the Germans, for example, will always accept the situation created by the corridor of Danzig?"[113]

Despite a rejection of Stresemann's demands by Paris and London, the fact remained that Britain favored an early withdrawal, and the growing Franco-German economic ties also operated in favor of a settlement. At the Lugano meeting of the League's Council in early December, there was a growing feeling that progress was in sight. Lugano witnessed also a sharp

---

on financial compensation, see his conversation with Hymans, 17 May 1928, DDB, II, 488–93.

111. Beneš, *Boj o mír*, 414–28.

112. See Charles-Roux to Briand, 9 Oct. 1928, MAE, Tchécoslovaquie 33:159–61.

113. See 9, 14, 23 Nov. sessions, CAE/Ch. The inevitability of Anschluss and the subsequent turn of Poland was stressed at the time by Maj. Charles de Gaulle. His letter is cited in Noël, *La Guerre*, 58.

verbal clash between Zaleski (acting under Piłsudski's order) and Stresemann over the issue of the German minority in Poland, used by Berlin as an instrument of revisionism.[114] The French criticized Zaleski for his "brutal evocation of this problem," which complicated the tasks of Briand's diplomacy. The representatives of the Little Entente shared the French viewpoint.[115] The episode was characteristic of the widening gap between the strategies of Warsaw and Paris toward Berlin. The Quai d'Orsay felt that Zaleski should have sought approval of his move by Paris, or at least coordinated his activities. His rejoinder that some Poles feared that France was allowing itself to be drawn into a policy of reconciliation with Germany at Poland's expense elicited a lecture about "excessive sensitivity" and lack of faith in France. This reproach was becoming an ever more frequently recurring admonition. Laroche warned Poland against creating an unfortunate impression that it wanted "to impede egotistically and without real cause a policy that conformed to our essential interests." Profiting from Polish discomfiture, he interjected a complaint about Skarboferm. "After the incidents of Lugano, and after the reverberations they had caused in Germany and all over Europe, the Polish government ought to care less than ever to have a conflict with the French government over an issue that affects the very essence of the Upper Silesian question."[116]

The Poles had to back down. They decided to proceed more cautiously in Geneva, and to satisfy France on Skarboferm, because "without the sincere and energetic support by France," Poland "would not be in a position to defend its interests effectively."[117] As the British assessed the situation: "Poland was beginning to wonder whether the day may not come when France, on friendly terms with Germany and definitely assured against German aggression, may have no further use for her." Hence, Poland was making attempts at greater independence, which were "not altogether to the liking of France."[118] It was otherwise for Czechoslovakia. Noting the

114. See Carole Fink, "Defender of Minorities: Germany in the League of Nations, 1926–1933," *Central European History*, 5 (Dec. 1972), 330–57. Also see an interesting note by Bülow, 13 Dec. 1927, ADAP, B, VII: 502–503.

115. See dispatches of Massigli, Margerie, and Laroche, as well as Quai d'Orsay to Laroche, 15, 19, 20 Dec. 1928, MAE, Pologne 201:163–66, 177–89.

116. Laroche to Briand, 20 Dec. 1928, MAE, Pologne 136:108–109; 215:156.

117. See Zaleski telegrams, 10, 21 Feb. and Chłapowski, 20 Feb. 1929, SI, Amb. Londyn, A.12/52/10. A motion of the foreign ministry to the cabinet justified concessions to the French by stressing the need of preserving good rapport at the time when the evacuation of the Rhineland, the Dawes Plan, and disarmament were under discussion. See meeting, 18 Jan. 1929, AAN, PPRM, *XLVI*, 50–51, 95–96. Also Korespondencja w sprawach Skarbofermu, AAN, Prezydium Rady Ministrów, Akta Tajne, part VII, 11. For relevant French correspondence, see MAE, Pologne 215:98–257.

118. Annual Report, 1928 Poland, FO 371 14027 N 2176/2176/55.

"unending stream" of French politicians, generals, scholars, and artists coming to Prague, and the privileged treatment of Czechs and Slovaks visiting France, the British legation speculated whether all this was not due to French fears lest improved relations between Czechoslovakia and Germany "may lessen the value" for Prague of the alliance with Paris.[119] It is hard to improve on this succinct summation of the essence of Franco-Polish-Czechoslovak relationship in late 1928.

119. Annual Report, 1928, Czechoslovakia, FO 371 13580 C 2322/2322/12.

Chapter Five

The End of an Era

Moves and Countermoves in Central Europe

By late 1928 it was obvious that Germany would experience difficulties in fulfilling the Dawes Plan without an influx of new capital and increased exports. Poincaré favored a comprehensive arrangement that would link reparations and interallied debts. After lengthy negotiations, a committee of experts was established in January; headed by Owen D. Young it embarked on preparing recommendations that would be ready five months later.

Defining Prague's stand, Krofta said: "We are naturally for the French position," although "we must not expose ourselves more than necessary, because it lies in our political and economic interest that Germany's burden be alleviated rather than increased." The Czech diplomat feared adverse effects on his country's economy if Germany were to be impoverished. He also noted the potential dangers accompanying a reparations' debate that by arousing German resentment, might lead to a deterioration of Franco-German and Polish-German relations.[1] Prague's cautious stand reflected the closeness of commercial links with Germany and the important place that German-owned industries occupied in the Czechoslovak economy.[2] Warsaw had somewhat different concerns. Zaleski was pleased with Briand's and Chamberlain's position that the Young Committee must stay clear of political issues,[3] but Warsaw was also aware that Berlin would seek to introduce them in the deliberations of the economic experts.

1. Briefing, 2 May 1929, KV, CPP.

2. Allegedly, of 1121 enterprises employing 100 or more workers, 848 were German and 149 had mixed German-Czech capital. See Grzybowski reports, 29 Jan., 25 Feb. 1929, AAN, Amb. Berlin 50. Also Zgórniak, "Sytuacja międzynarodowa Czechosłowacji," 10. Still, during the period from 1919 to 1929 only three German banks survived. See Dobrý, *Hospodářská krize*, 21.

3. See Laroche to Briand, 15 Mar. 1929, MAE, Pologne 77:211. Zaleski was also pleased with the handling of the national minorities issue in Geneva by the West and the Little Entente.

Indeed, Schacht argued that the loss of agricultural lands to Poland and the decline of productivity of East Prussia (separated from the Reich) imposed severe strains on the German economy. The Poles protested, and Zaleski complained that Paris was not keeping him informed. Talking to Hoesch, Berthelot expressed his disapprobation of German attempts to use the Young Committee as a springboard for revisionism. The Foreign Office was also annoyed. Any unilateral attempt to reopen the territorial question, it said, would be "a direct menace to peace."[4] Schacht's initiative was clearly untimely, but it was indicative of the growing German frustration over lack of success in foreign policy. A domestic political crisis was brewing, and in the months to come Stresemann would use it to apply pressure on Paris and London.

The relative effectiveness of Czechoslovak and Polish diplomacy in dealing with the situation was to some extent connected with internal developments. Provincial elections held in December 1928 strengthened the national socialists—now securely under Beneš's control—and further undermined the position of Kramář. Udržal, who became premier in February 1929, excluded from his cabinet Beneš's chief rival Milan Hodža.[5] Bitter attacks of the communist party, sovietized in the course of 1929 under Klement Gottwald's leadership, did not seriously embarrass the government. As the Polish chargé d'affaires noted, Masaryk now held the key to the situation.[6]

Nationality problems, while becoming more intense, did not yet pose an acute problem to the republic. The condemnation for state treason of a leading Slovak populist, Vojtech(Béla) Tuka, served as a warning to the l'udák party of Father Andrej Hlinka not to espouse separatism, although the event contributed to the rise of a nationalist and intransigent Slovak stand. Warsaw showed some interest in the Slovaks but was devoting more attention to the Polish minority in Teschen, extending financial assistance and encouraging its political unity. Prague espoused a policy of firmness. As Masaryk wrote in the army journal *Naše Vojsko*, nations just as individuals had the right of self-defense, and Czechoslovakia would use it if endangered.[7]

Beneš's concept of Central European cooperation were supported by the industrial-financial establishment, symbolised by the director of Živnostanská Banka Jaroslav Preiss, but as always opposed by the protectionist-

4. See British memorandum 4 May 1929, DBFP, 1a, VI:272–73. Also, note, 8 May 1929, MAE, Pologne 77:223–25. For Polish protests, Zaleski telegrams, 22 Apr., 7 May 1929, HIA, Amb. Paryż, box 2.

5. An interesting characterization of Hodža in 21 Feb. 1929 briefing, KV, CPP.

6. Karszo–Siedlewski report 28 Dec. 1928, AAN, Amb. Berlin 50.

7. See Charles-Roux to Briand, 2 July 1929, MAE, Tchécoslovaquie 29:42–77.

minded agrarians.[8] When Romania and Yugoslavia began to promote a scheme of closer economic cooperation within the Little Entente, to be extended later to Austria and Hungary, Beneš brought it to a halt. Both domestic considerations and the expected opposition of the great powers dictated this policy.[9] Besides, Krofta was right to doubt the chances of creating an economic bloc when the Little Entente did not have even a real railroad agreement.[10] The French envoy, who favored economic cooperation in the region, also had to admit that so far such cooperation was nonexistent. His colleague from Berlin feared that all regional combinations without Germany would be unworkable and thus would invite penetration.[11]

A new demonstration of the vitality and solidarity of the Little Entente was badly needed. At the conference in Belgrade (20–22 May) Beneš hoped to replace the three political treaties by a single pact, discuss again economic cooperation, achieve a joint de jure recognition of the USSR, and prevent Warsaw's rapprochement with the grouping. He was only partly successful with regard to a joint pact, and unsuccessful in the matter of recognition of Moscow. A conference of economic experts would meet in Prague in September. As for Poland, it was agreed to keep her at a distance.[12]

The stand of the Little Entente toward Poland, partly a result of the baffling state of Soviet-Polish relations, was undoubtedly affected by Zaleski's visit to Budapest, which coincided with the opening of the Belgrade Conference. Oddly enough, the dragging Polish-Lithuanian controversy and the recurring rumors of Piłsudski's anti-Russian designs—spread periodically by Soviet propaganda—were not preventing Moscow's new overtures to Warsaw and Paris.[13] On 29 December 1928, Litvinov pro-

---

8. The agrarians' protectionist stand did not exclude their advocacy of a large East Central European bloc, comprising Poland and based on the common peasant denominator. See Hodža's speech before the International Agrarian Bureau, 24 May 1929, Hodža, *Články*, 4:283–86.

9. See Sládek and Tomaszewski, "Próby w latach dwudziestych," 20–21. Also Ormos, *Problème*, 29.

10. See Charles-Roux to Briand, 24 May 1929, MAE, Tchécoslovaquie 71:73–74.

11. See Charles-Roux and Margerie to Briand, 23 Mar., 24 May 1929, MAE, Tchécoslovaquie 83:241; 71:114–15.

12. See reports of Charles-Roux, Puaux, and Dard, between 10 and 23 May, and a Yugoslav memorandum 29 May, MAE, Tchécoslovaquie 71:69, 76, 78, 92–94, 124; also Charles-Roux to Briand, 6 May, Pologne 77:220–22; and briefing 23 May, 6 June 1929, KV, CPP.

13. For Czechoslovak feelings about these rumors, see 24 Jan. 1929 briefing, KV, CPP. As an example of the war scares, in late May *Moskauer Rundschau* and *Izvestia* printed the text of an alleged Franco-Polish military convention of 1922 directed against Russia. See the numerous dispatches of Herbette in MAE Russia, 362; and French-Polish cor-

posed to Poland the signing of a protocol making the provisions of the still unratified Kellogg-Briand Pact applicable to their mutual relations. The Germans were alarmed, and when the Russians suggested a triple arrangement (with the inclusion of Germany) Schubert dismissed it as smacking of an Eastern Locarno. Warsaw's acceptance of the Russian offer appeared to Stresemann as creating "an impossible situation, which we have always feared"—namely, of providing Soviet protection for Poland's eastern border, its rear (*Rückendeckung*).[14]

The Litvinov Protocol of 9 February 1929 represented a departure from the previous Soviet position on multilateral pacts in the region, for it included—at Warsaw's insistence—the Baltic states and Romania. Amounting to a de facto recognition of the eastern borders, it did not put an end to Soviet attacks on Poland. They alternated with attempts to continue talks on a nonaggression treaty and a commercial accord. As the Polish minister in Moscow wrote, the Soviet government, despite signing pacts and protocals and carrying on a disarmament campaign in Geneva, still had a revolutionary war on its program.[15]

If the Little Entente wished to stay clear of the perplexing moves in the Soviet-Polish arena, it found Zaleski's journey to Budapest disquieting. The Polish minister arrived at the Hungarian capital in the footsteps of Dino Grandi, undersecretary at Palazzo Chigi, which conveyed the impression of a coordinated action. The Czechoslovak foreign ministry had heard in March of alleged Polish attempts to detach Romania from the Little Entente and steer it in the direction of a Polish-Hungarian-Romanian combination.[16] Was Zaleski's trip a step in this direction?

The Hungarians were seeking assurances that Poland would not join the Little Entente, and wished Warsaw to act as a broker between Budapest and Paris. In exchange, they were willing to entertain Polish requests for transit facilities of war material.[17] Zaleski who favored caution and tried to avoid giving offense to France and the Little Entente, allowed himself to be maneuvered into a press conference where his remarks were construed as an offer of mediation between Budapest and Paris. His private and public denials did not repair the damage.[18] On 24 May, *Le Temps*

---

respondence resulting in a Briand-Zaleski agreement to issue an official *démenti*, MAE, Pologne 131:140–59.

14. Schubert notes, 29 Dec. 1928 and Stresemann to Ambassador in Moscow, 18 Jan. 1929, ADAP, B, x:581:84, XI:43.

15. Patek to Piłsudski, 25 Feb. 1929, AAN, Akta Piłsudskich 6.

16. See briefing, 14 Mar. 1929, KV, CPP.

17. See Endre Kovács, *Magyar-lengyel kapcsolatok a két világháború között* (Budapest, 1971). I am indebted to Eva Balogh for the translation.

18. See dispatches of Matuszewski, Ciechanowiecki, and Zaleski, 18, 19, 29 May, AAN, MSZ 6594; Zaleski denials, 27 May, AAN, Akta Świtalskiego, 70; reports of

tried to calm the troubled waters by saying that the visit "ought not to arouse suspicions in any of the Central-European capitals," for it signified no change of Polish policy. But Belgrade and Bucharest were uneasy. Only the government and the press in Czechoslovakia affected calm, making reassuring statements of Zaleski's loyalty,[19] although the real view was quite different. Beneš told Charles-Roux that Zalenski's trip was meant to demonstrate to Paris and the Little Entente that Poland was "a great power" that could proceed on its own and pursue several independent approaches. The French envoy, while inclined to agree, persisted in his opinion that the visit as such was simply a clumsy move.[20]

French diplomacy decided, however, to find out if Poland had concluded an arms transit agreement with Hungary as Prague has alleged.[21] Laroche's inquiries elicited a formal denial from the deputy foreign minister. Speaking in the marshal's name, he assured the ambassador that no agreement had been signed, which was true, and that if any military arrangement had been contemplated, France would have been consulted beforehand.[22] This was not the whole truth, for the Poles had been exploring the possibilities of transit for themselves and for Romania. Budapest made the latter conditional on a significant improvement of relations with Bucharest. It was more willing to consider transit to Poland, but asked Zaleski not to inform the French or the Romanians about these conversations. The foreign minister assured the Hungarians he was not planning to mention it to Paris but might have to let the Rumanians know if the situation should warrant it.[23]

The French did not probe any farther, but suspicions on the part of the Little Entente were not dispelled. What is more, the three countries became angry with France when Hungary's premier István Bethlen was warmly received in Paris and held conversations with Doumergue, Poincaré, and Berthelot. The Yugoslav foreign minister told the Czechoslovak envoy Štefan Osuský that the Little Entente "ought to show its claws and make Paris feel that France needed the Little Entente no less than the Little Entente

---

Laroche, Vienne, Beaumarchais, and Rivière, 4, 14, 23, 25, 30 May 1929, MAE, Pologne 77:217; 78:3–4, 17–18, 31–33, 40–42. Zaleski's interview, *Neue Freie Presse*, 23 May 1929.

19. Grzybowski report, 8 June, AAN, Amb. Berlin, 50; Charles-Roux to Briand, 1, 6, 21, 25 June, MAE, Pologne 78:48; 71:137–38; 78:158–64, 169.

20. Charles-Roux to Briand, 15 July 1929, MAE, Pologne, 78:192–93.

21. Briefing, 27 June 1929, KV, CPP, and Laroche and Charles-Roux, June dispatches, MAE, Pologne 78.

22. Laroche to Briand, 15 July 1929, MAE, Pologne 78:192–93.

23. Walkó-Belitska exchange and Bethlen letter to Zaleski, 25, 29 May 1929, in Dezsö Nemer, ed., *Iratok az ellenforradolom történetéhez* (Budapest, 1967), 4:281–83. I am indebted to Eva Balogh for the translation of these documents.

needed France."[24] Zaleski's journey to Romania in late October, during which he went out of the way to cultivate his hosts, somewhat improved the Polish-Romanian relationship. But, as the French diplomats remarked, there was little real warmth in it, and it was known that Piłsudski did not hold Romania in great esteem.[25]

Did Poland have at this time something resembling a dual government—as Girsa speculated—with the cabinet and Zaleski for "foreign consumption" and a secret government directed by Piłsudski that would assert itself at a given moment? And was it the latter that entertained sinister plans of an eastern expansion?[26] This was a distorted but not a totally false picture of the situation. The real controversy was not between Zaleski and the political forces in the country, but between them and Piłsudski, who was ever suspicious of "foreign agencies." The marshal not only viewed the communists as paid by Moscow, but also the socialists as financed by Germany, and the national democrats as quasi-agents of France.[27] In the existing power structure there was a distinction between the *real* Piłsudskiites from the first brigade, to whom Zaleski did not belong, and other high officials. The former often took direct orders from Piłsudski, and their importance was not always commensurate with the positions they occupied in the state hierarchy.

Zaleski's own conciliatory line was at certain times modified, as we have seen, by direct intervention of Piłsudski, who reserved for himself all decisions on such matters as Russia (Lithuania) and those that affected the military. But Zaleski was still far from being "a front." His own policy of loudly proclaiming a trust in France while quietly agitating in Paris continued. In a major speech on 15 January 1929, he asserted once more that "we never have and never will obstruct the Reich's efforts toward an understanding with France, because we are absolutely convinced that the goal and the result of French-German friendship cannot and will not be a weakening of Franco-Polish friendship." He believed that "gradually the German public opinion will come to understand that precisely because France had Poland as an ally, this makes possible her rapprochement with the Reich."[28] Zaleski was addressing the French more than the sejm's foreign affairs commission, although he also tried to reassure the latter. His statement that the evacuation of the Rhineland was scheduled for 1935

24. Cited in Gajanová, *ČSR*, 254.

25. See speech in Zaleski, *Przemowy*, 2:17–18; Laroche to Briand, 30 Oct. 1929, MAE, Pologne 78:162–65. For Piłsudski's views, see 18 Apr. 1929 entry in AAN, Akta Świtalskiego 70; Beck, *Dernier rapport*, 7.

26. See briefings, 24 Jan., 26 Sept., 7 Nov. 1929, KV, CPP.

27. See penetrating observations in 8 Apr., 3 May 1929 entries, PAN, MS, Dziennik Zdanowskiego, VI, part 2, 27–28.

28. Zaleski, *Przemowy*, 1:211.

(and the importance of the issue must not be overestimated) was clearly disingenuous.[29]

The foreign minister knew that overt Polish attempts to create difficulties over the Rhineland evacuation would have "a disasterous effect on public opinion in Great Britain and would inevitably alienate all sympathy for Poland."[30] But it also seems that not only Zaleski but also General Sikorski, then in oppositon, believed that a policy built on the assumption of a permanent Franco-German estrangement and hatred would be suicidal.[31] But could a genuine rapprochement between Germany and France be achieved without endangering Poland? The Poles kept asking themselves this question as they followed German activities in France. Rechberg's widening circle of contacts created uneasiness, even though Polish diplomacy did not overrate his importance.[32] More attention was paid to Paul Reynaud, Schneider's son-in-law, belonging to Union Républicaine Démocratique, who conferring with Schubert spoke of cooperation between French and German conservative parties. France, he said, could obviously not force Poland to give up the "corridor," but it could, if Franco-German relations gained a certain degree of intimacy, proffer friendly advice and apply gentle pressure.[33] The rightist Parti Démocrate Populaire declared at its congress at Nancy on 9–11 February that it was in favor of close cooperation with Germany. On the left side of the political spectrum, Herriot's speech in Zurich on 26 May was free from revisionist accents, but his ardent plea for a Franco-German rapprochement did not escape Polish notice.[34] It was symptomatic for the existing atmosphere that the former political director at the Quai d'Orsay, Jacques Seydoux, was asked to resign from the Franco-German committee of studies after his article in *Le Petit Parisien* on 24 February, which opposed Germany's claims to the "corridor."[35] Polish fears about the pro-German trends in France were not groundless, and once again the need was felt for diplomatic countermeasures.

29. For the debate and connected articles on foreign policy, see *Gazeta Warszawska*, 16, 23 Jan., 23 Feb., 2 Mar. 1929.

30. See Erskine-Chamberlain exchange, 7, 18 Jan. and Perowne memorandum, 21 Jan. 1929, DBFP, ia, VI:47–48; FO 371 13616 C 308 and C 843/45/18.

31. Sikorski's views in his *Polska*, see Kuźmiński, *Polska*, 28. For Müller's comments on Zaleski, see Krüger, Aussenpolitik, 501.

32. See reports in MAE, Allemagne 392:140–41, 147–56, 167–70, and 393:13, 16, 23. Also Chłapowski to Zaleski, 4 Aug., 2 Sept. 1929, AAN, Amb. Berlin 74. Rich documentation can also be found in ADAP, B, XI.

33. Schubert note, 26 Apr. 1929, ADAP, B, XI:449–51.

34. Laroche to Briand, 1 June 1929, MAE, Allemagne 392:203.

35. See Bessenheim note, 1 Mar. 1929, ADAP, B, XI:227–28. Compare Seydoux, *Mémoires*, 28–32.

Renewed Polish Efforts: The Hague Conference

A new Polish diplomatic offensive, which gathered momentum in the late spring and early summer of 1929, took place in a changing international situation. In Geneva, the preparatory disarmament commission ended its first round of discussions on a draft convention in early May. Briand's position had been that France could justify large sums for defensive fortifications more easily than an increase in the army budget—another argument for the Maginot Line. Poincaré worried about the possible effects of this policy on France's means to assist Poland, but he concurred with President Doumergue that the Polish case did not "imply special efforts." Surely, "the menace of a mobilization on our part would stop a German offensive against Poland."[36]

The formation of Ramsay MacDonald's Labour cabinet on 5 June, in which Arthur Henderson took over the Foreign Office, did not facilitate the tasks of French diplomacy. MacDonald not only favored, as the conservatives did, a limitation of armaments, reconciliation with Germany, and a speedy evacuation of the Rhineland, but his views were tinged with anti-French and pro-German sentiments. His pronouncements replete with criticism of East Central European governments produced consternation in Paris and Warsaw. Beneš alone seemed unperturbed, feeling that he could find a common language with the British Left whose coolness toward Italy and Hungary he appreciated.[37]

The submission of Young Report on 7 June, represented an important step in the evolution of the reparations' issue. If the amounts appeared huge on paper and angered the Germans, the possibility of collecting them was small. The distinction between realities and expectations was blurred, and what is more, the fulfillment of the plan depended exclusively on the good will of a Germany freed of foreign economic controls, because the reparations commission would exist no longer.

The outburst of German nationalism on the tenth anniversary of the Treaty of Versailles shook the French. They felt that the time had not yet come to accept a premature evacuation of the Rhineland. Briand, responding to Hoesch's question about French conditions for the latter, invoked "good will, clearly and loyally demonstrated by Germany with regard to the fulfillment of its obligations."[38] There could be no doubt that financial

---

36. Session 30 Jan. 1929, SHA, CSDN, 153–61. The unhappiness of the army representatives emerges quite clearly from the protocol.

37. Charles-Roux to Briand, 6 Oct., MAE, Tchécoslovaquie 39:108–11; compare 6 June 1929 briefing, KV, CPP. Also Jouvenel, *D'une Guezze*, 2:253. For Piłsudski's dissatisfaction with the MacDonald government, see AAN, Akta Świtalskiego 70.

38. Audience du ministre, 1 July 1929, MAE, Y 38:45–50.

considerations were uppermost in French minds. The fact that Paris insisted no longer on the Verification Commission stemmed largely from the fact that the Rhineland ceased to figure in French military thinking as a springboard for an all-out offensive in Germany.

What new approach could Polish diplomacy devise under these circumstances? A position paper of the foreign ministry recognized that France treated the evacuation issue mainly as a trump card in its negotiations over reparations. Poland, standing no chance to participate in the evacuation discussions, ought to seek compensations elsewhere. It should concentrate on getting rid of all financial burdens under Versailles and Saint Germain (in exchange for abandoning its own claims) and strive for monetary assistance including the placement of a loan on the French market. In the military sphere, the document proposed studies by the respective general staffs aimed at the improvement of security in the postevacuation period. Finally, the ongoing international negotiations ought to be exploited to advance German-Polish trade and financial talks so as to achieve a settlement. Also, for the sake of German and Polish public opinion, efforts should be made to obtain, on the occasion of the evacuation of the Rhineland, a solemn declaration on the indivisibility of European security.[39]

Another memorandum[40] dwelt on a new formula for an Eastern Locarno, and came up with a proposal to use the so-called model D of the Collective Treaty of Mutual Assistance—elaborated on and approved in Geneva—as a basis for a tripartite Franco-German-Polish pact. According to this model, which provided for regional accords, the signatories engaged themselves to renounce war, submit their differences to procedures for pacific settlement, and lend each other assistance immediately after the Council of the League had found that an act of aggression had occurred. But, because the model lacked clear provisions regarding flagrant aggression or obligatory aid in case of an attack by a third party, and was ambiguous about the unanimity rule on the Council, it was felt that these gaps had to be filled.

Still another memorandum listed three basic postulates regarding an early evacuation of the Rhineland. These were a participation of all Allied and Associated Powers in the preparation of the formal act; a Polish signature on this document; and an unequivocal French guarantee of aid to Poland in case of flagrant German aggression. This last engagement was to represent a compensation for Poland's consent to the evacuation. Zaleski thought, however, that since great powers would never accept such

39. See "Uwagi dotyczące ustosunkowania się Polski do ewakuacji Nadrenii," 18 Feb. 1929, SI, MSZ, A.11.49/F/1/7. Compare Chłapowski telegram, 14 Feb. 1929, HIA, Amb. Paryż, box 2.

40. Kulski memorandum, 14 Feb., and comments by Western Division, 17 Feb. 1929, SI, MSZ, A.11/2.

demands, he was ready to be satisfied with a statement in the document on evacuation affirming the indivisibility of European security.[41]

Paris was not very receptive to these ideas. When Zaleski first mentioned the model D to Briand, in March 1929, the foreign minister was unimpressed. The Quai d'Orsay showed little desire to find a mutually satisfactory solution, and it combatted Polish proposals with legalistic arguments. When the new embassy counselor and high-ranking Piłsudskiite, Tadeusz Schaetzel, engaged in conversations with the French, he felt like "a creditor meeting his debtor who is neither ready nor inclined to do anything concrete about their relationship."[42]

The Quai d'Orsay proceeded from the assumption that Germany would be disinclined to consider a tripartite pact unless it involved "at least an apparent" weakening of Franco-Polish obligations arising out of the 1921 military convention and the treaty of 1925. Reexamining these obligations, the French stressed their inner ambiguities. The treaty of 1925, for instance, defined *casus foederis* as nonprovoked "recourse to arms"—that is, mobilization—while article 16 of the Covenant spoke of "resort to war." Which definition was to guide French action? It was recalled that French assistance to Poland depended not only on the League but also on some form of accord of the Locarno powers.

The French note concluded that the existing obligations were onerous and likely to produce a conflict between the views of the government and the parliament, not to mention the varying interpretations of *casus foederis*. Hence, the argument in favor of limiting and modifying them would be compelling. If France were to replace these obligations by those arising out of a tripartite pact, it could no longer be accused of conducting a policy of alliances, but would not such a change create a precedent affecting other French treaties? A tripartite pact would not bring Poland a guarantee of its border with Germany, but it would introduce more precise assurances against nonaggression than those under the Kellogg–Briand pact. If no clause of flagrant aggression were inserted, French aid to Poland would be limited to a specific case of German aggression recognized as such by a unanimous vote of the League Council. Polish assistance to France, should the latter be directly attacked (which seemed unlikely) would also depend on the Council's decision. But, because Poland was—by virtue of the combined provisions of the 1921 and 1925 treaties and the Treaty of Versailles—a de facto guarantor of the demilitarized Rhineland, and because a German aggression against France would bring an intervention of the

41. See "Postulaty polskie w związku z ewakuacją Nadrenii," and note of the Western Division on Zaleski's letter, 16 June 1929, SI, MSZ, A.11.49/F/1/6.

42. Schaetzel to Lipski [?], 18 May, SI, MSZ, A.11.49/F/1. See also Zaleski telegram, 18 May 1929, HIA, Amb. Paryż, box 4. Compare notes and circulars of Corbin, 14, 24 May 1929, MAE, Pologne 78:2, 19–24.

Locarno powers, the French assumed that Poland would at least order a
general mobilization and contain a part of the German Army. The inser-
tion of a flagrant aggression clause would not be helpful, for in the absence
of a demilitarized zone in the east it would be difficult to define what constituted flagrant aggression.

In brief, a tripartite pact might have some merit but it would necessitate
the abrogation of the 1925 treaty and at least some modification of the
military convention of 1921.[43] All this meant that Paris understood the
Polish proposal as a suggestion to substitute the tripartite pact for the 1925
treaty; and the French added to it the idea of modifying the military convention. Although Warsaw may not have been greatly opposed to the former, it was adamantly against the latter. Once again, while one side wished
to strengthen the alliance, the other was seeking to dilute it.[44]

The Polish general staff had its own views on what would be a suitable
compensation for the evacuation of the Rhineland, namely a political declaration by the great powers combined with an arrangement making the
military convention more operative, especially through material aid from
France.[45] Piłsudski emphasized this last point. "By constantly crying out
that it is endangered by Germany, and by seeking to invent ever new for-
mulae of security, Poland," he wrote "only needlessly exposes itself to the
accusation that its alarms are excessive because the Covenant of the
League, Locarno, and the Kellogg pact bring it sufficient safeguards."
Hence, Warsaw should neither insist on a declaration nor a representation
on the Verification Commission, but engage in talks with the French on
the creation of artillery, munitions, and planes stocks in Poland; an ampli-
fication of General Kutrzeba's proposal made vainly in Paris in 1928. A
French armament loan appeared to Piłsudski a matter of lower priority.
The marshal approved the idea of a modified model D pact—comprising
at least Poland, France, and Germany—and suggested periodic allied conferences to examine the German situation from the point of view of general
security. It is likely, however, that he did so on tactical grounds. He was
more serious when he urged Zaleski to try to resolve quickly all the financial disputes with Germany so that both countries could resume normal
relations.[46]

An opportunity for renewed Franco-Polish military talks presented itself

43. See "Traité eventuel entre la France, l'Allemagne et la Pologne (Obligations d'assistance mutuelle)," 24 June 1929, MAE, Pologne 78:80–86, stamped "directeur politique." Compare note of Service Français de la SDN, 12 July, MAE, Pologne 78:99–
103.

44. See Massigli to Corbin, 13 June 1929, MAE, Pologne 78:61.

45. Note "Okupacja Nadrenii a bezpieczeństwo Polski"; Pełczyński telegram, 31 May
1929, HIA, Amb. Paryż, box 8.

46. Wysocki note, 3 July 1939, IS, MSZ, A.11.49/F/1/8.

when the French high command, worried lest Poland move away from the 1922–24 concepts of a joint strategy against Germany, invited representatives of the Polish general staff to Paris. The French had heard that Piłsudski, concentrating his thoughts on the eastern front, was allegedly viewing the German flank as "the business of France." According to General Victor Denain, chief of the military mission; Polish assistance promised in the early stages of the war "did not correspond to the Polish military power," although Warsaw invoked shortages of war material. He recommended that Paris "seek to overcome the natural repugnance of our allies to direct their efforts and their studies toward a possible struggle with Germany."[47]

A high-ranking delegation, headed by General Tadeusz Kasprzycki, held conversations with their French colleagues from 26 to 28 July. It tried to probe matters, evaded thus far, connected with army organization, mobilization plans, and peacetime deployment. The French high command, while willing to envisage cooperation regarding liaison, air force and material aid, did not wish to conduct joint "staff map exercises."[48] General Jean Guitry gave the Poles the kind of information "that any well-informed public could have." Proffering somewhat vague assurances, he mainly questioned the Poles about their military preparedness. General Debeney made Kasprzycki admit that Germany was Poland's most dangerous enemy. The French chief of staff explained that after the evacuation of the Rhineland a sudden German attack would be contained by a system of permanent defensive fortifications. In case of an invasion of Poland, France could only relieve the Polish front by marching up to the Rhine. He hoped that the Poles could hold out until then.[49] Kasprzycki was not informed that the new plan B was clearly defensive. If the Polish staff suspected it, the insistence on the creation of French artillery and ammunition stocks in Poland, air force cooperation, and an armament loan of 1.5 milliard francs (1 milliard in nature and 0.5 in cash) becomes fully understandable.[50]

The same demands figured in a long diplomatic note presented to the Quai d'Orsay on the eve of the military conversations. Recalling that international guarantees constituted, together with armed forces and the al-

47. Denain to Debeney, 21 Feb. 1929, SHA, EMA/2, Pologne 11; also correspondence in Pologne 19, and MAE, Pologne 136:161, 164.

48. See note for the Chef de l'Etat Major de l'Armée, 9 July 1929, SHA, EMA/3, 7 N 3446/3.

49. See note of the second bureau, 24 May, and resumé des entretiens, 26–28 July 1929, SHA, EMA/2, Pologne 19.

50. For a summary of plan B—which foresaw a gradual withdrawal but not, as in the past, in preparation for a counteroffensive—that was valid until July 1930 and, with some alterations, until May 1931, see Tournoux, *Haut commandement*, 335–36.

liance with France, the basis of Poland's security, the document argued that the Young Plan and the evacuation of the Rhineland would necessitate supplementary safeguards: the above-mentioned material assistance and the tripartite pact with a flagrant aggression clause.[51] Briand was skeptical about the latter but more positive about the former, which made Chłapowski wonder whether the interests of the French armament industry did not play a role here.[52] The Quai D'Orsay, however, perceived great difficulties in satisfying any Polish requests. Collaboration in the field of aviation would be complicated; establishing stocks of artillery and munitions would raise financial and constitutional problems. A tripartite pact could be contemplated only if the military convention were modified. If Warsaw insisted, Paris could not refuse to transmit this proposal to Berlin but would not make it a condition for the evacuation of the Rhineland.[53]

In the subsequent conversation with Zaleski, Briand tried to be mildly encouraging. Poland would be invited to the forthcoming conference, and one could hope that difficulties with credits and armament stocks would be resolved to mutual satisfaction. The foreign minister, however, disposed of Zaleski's suggestion that France and Poland agree among themselves before approaching the Germans with a tripartite pact proposal, by saying that the Germans would be likely to demand the abrogation of the Franco-Polish alliance as a precondition for such a pact.[54]

The Conference for the Final Liquidation of the World War, as the first Hague Conference was grandiloquently referred to, lasted from 6 August until 31 August. Only its barest outline can be presented here. Briand hoped to achieve a definite settlement of the Young Plan, to exclude the Saar from the conference agenda, and to avoid being rushed into a total withdrawal from the Rhineland. The Verification Commission was used largely for tactical purposes to gain delays, as Briand sought political and financial advantages in exchange for his consent to an early evacuation. A showdown with the British over the distribution of reparations endangered the French position, and hopes of exerting financial pressures on London proved illusory. Threatened by Henderson that Britain would unilaterally evacuate the Rhineland, Briand intimated that France would be

---

51. See aide mémoire, 23 July 1929, MAE, Pologne 78:105–10, also Lipski to Schaetzel, 23 July, SI, MSZ, A.11/2.

52. Chłapowski telegram and report, 23, 24 July 1929, SI, MSZ, A.11/49/F/1.

53. French doubts about the tripartite pact had been forcibly expressed to the Poles already before the aide mémoire. See notes, 11 and 19 July, and then 25 and 30 July 1929, MAE, Pologne 78:96–98 and 104, and Pologne 21:199–200 and 78:112. On various Polish ideas and on cooperation regarding disarmament in Geneva, see Lipski's correspondence with Lechnicki and Schaetzel, and Wysocki's with Chłapowski in July 1929, SI, MSZ, A.11.49/F/1 and 10a.

54. Zaleski telegram, 27 July, HIA, Amb. Paryż, box 2. See also note, 26 July, and Briand to Tripier, 6 Aug. 1929, MAE, Pologne 28:204–206.

willing to begin the evacuation by 15 September without, however, indicating the time of its completion.

The foreign minister was fully aware of the opposition of the army circles and the governmental coalition to an early date for the evacuation. The actual work on the Maginot Line would not start until 1930. Foch's saying that the withdrawal would be a crime was recalled and publicized.[55] But Briand's delaying tactics at The Hague proved of no avail, and on 27–28 August he was forced to agree to vacate the Coblenz zone between September and November, and the zone of Mainz between 20 May and 30 June 1930. These decisions, together with the approval of a somewhat modified Young Plan, and followed by a final agreement of 30 January 1930, which closed the second Hague Conference, represented a watershed in postwar international relations.

Efforts of Polish diplomacy must be seen against this background. Poland had been allowed to participate only in the work of the economic commission at The Hague and excluded from political deliberations.[56] Partly to placate Polish public opinion, Zaleski protested against this exclusion and made vain efforts to insert in the final resolution of the political committee a reference to the necessity of territorial status quo. In the financial field, protracted German-Polish negotiations, in which the French played a certain role, pressing both sides to reach agreement, resulted in the so-called Liquidation Accord.[57] Although this represented a certain success for Warsaw, the Poles were not jubilant.

Political matters at The Hague could only be discussed bilaterally with the French. Realizing that the tripartite project was dead, Zaleski and the high-ranking foreign ministry official, Józef Lipski, attempted to persuade Briand, Berthelot, and Massigli to introduce the concept of flagrant aggression into the French-Polish treaty of alliance, which would have made French aid to Poland under the Covenant articles automatic and instantaneous. Massigli, who considered a flagrant aggression clause impossible, because Paris could not act without consulting London, tried to convince the Poles that in actual practice French military preparations would not be delayed by deliberations in Geneva. But what would trigger the mobilization, the Poles inquired? The answer that the 1921 convention covered this contingency elicited a Polish comment that Laroche had advocated its modification on the grounds that it was legally dubious. Berthelot tried to

55. Notably by deputy Reibel on 29 Dec. 1929, see J.O. Chambre, 4714–15.

56. On the question of Poland's invitation, see Tripier and Beaumarchais dispatches, 30, 31 July, 4 Aug. 1929, MAE, Y 38:217, 243–44; Y 39:42–43.

57. On French involvement, see Briand–Curtius conversation, 4 Jan and Schubert to Rauscher, 21 Jan. 1930, ADAP, B, XIV:20–21, 101–102. Extensive treatment in Krasuski, *Stosunki 1926–1932*, 179–96.

question this interpretation, which incidentally he shared, and the discussion was becoming circuitous. Perhaps, Laroche suggested, one could promise the Poles an immediate mobilization, called "preparatory measures," so that France would be ready to act by the time the Council of the League adopted a decision.[58]

Regarding an armament loan—and Zaleski later claimed that Briand had promised him two milliard or even two to three milliards francs[59]— the French were willing to talk about Polish orders in French armament factories financed through a rather complex arrangement, based on the "assurance-crédit" bill of 1928, which would not require parliamentary approval. The ministry of finance definitely opposed a loan for a buildup of Polish arms production, because it would not benefit French industry. As for the creation of military stocks in Poland, it was regarded as too costly and establishing a dangerous precedent.[60] Zaleski's efforts at The Hague thus produced rather limited results, which made him all the more desirous to have a joint Franco-Polish communiqué, reaffirming the solidarity of the alliance, issued at the end of the conference. The French were reluctant, but eventually went along with an innocuous statement referring to possible financial agreements, published on 30 August.[61]

Czechoslovakia's presence at The Hague was justified by the French on the grounds that this country had formal rights to German reparations, and its formal assent to the Young Plan was required. It was also necessary to settle the Czechoslovak "liberation debt" to the Allies; and there were aspects of the "eastern reparations"—Austrian, Hungarian, and Bulgarian—that concerned Prague. The latter were settled only at at the second Hague Conference (3–20 January 1930), following protracted preparatory negotiations. A Czechoslovak-Hungarian controversy occupied an important position, and the French diplomacy, trying to mediate, invited Beneš together with Bethlen to Paris, much to the Czech's annoyance. Fearing that Prague's refusal to ratify the agreements would cause consid-

58. On Franco-Polish negotiations at The Hague, see Ciałowicz, *Polsko-francuski sojusz*, 158–60; Jędrzejewicz, ed., *Lipski* 15–18. Compare note, 19 Nov. 1932 and "projekt traktatu polsko-francuskiego," SI, MSZ, A.11.2. Also Massigli note and Laroche and Berthelot letters, 16, 18, 28 Aug. 1929, MAE, Pologne 78:124–30, 133–36. Also DTJS, II, 14–15.

59. See Wandycz, *Zaleski*, 81–82.

60. See memorandum, 29 Aug. 1929 describing the ideas of Farnier from Mouvement Général des Fonds, HIA, Amb. Paryż, box 8; Kirkor to foreign ministry and memo, 2, 21 Sept., SI, MSZ, A.11.6. Also Kirkor, "Próby dozbrojenia Polski," 34–40. Compare Ministère des Finances to Quai d'Orsay and Briand to Laroche, 31 Aug. and 17 Sept. 1929, MAE, Pologne 244:193–98; 28:213.

61. See MAE, Pologne 78:137–40. For British comments, see Broadmead to Henderson 5 Sept. 1929, FO 371 14018 C 4060/8/55.

erable delays in the ratification of the Young Plan, the French proved accommodating, agreeing even to take over a portion of Czechoslovak payments.[62]

Czechoslovakia's financial concern at The Hague contrasted with Polish political preoccupations. In two major speeches of 30 January and 30 May 1930, Beneš devoted most of his presentation to economic problems. His reference to the Rhineland evacuation was laconic. He stressed "full and unreserved" support by France; The Hague conference, he said, provided a real peace following the armistices after World War I.[63] The fact that Czechoslovak debts had not been completely canceled, while the small reparations that Germany owed to the Czechs were, provided the opposition with an excuse to attack Beneš. "Our foreign policy had suffered a defeat" wrote an extreme rightist paper. Prague, it demanded, should reorient its diplomatic course, remake the alliance with France on the Franco-Polish model, reorganize the foreign ministry, and dismiss Beneš.[64] Such extravagant demands were, of course, untypical and isolated. With the formation of the so-called Great Coalition cabinet on 7 December 1929, Czechoslovakia was entering a period of greater domestic stability. Yet, in the wake of The Hague conference, there was need to rethink the whole question of matters international and of the place that the French-Czechoslovak-Polish relationship occupied in them.

The Aftermath of The Hague

The Hague conference was Stresemann's victory and Briand's defeat. Germany had reached its goal, an early evacuation of the Rhineland, in exchange for the Young Plan, which would shortly turn out to be a scrap of paper. As Georges Bonnet put it many years later, this was a "decisive turning point of allied policy." The evacuation was approved without "the slightest settlement of pending problems in Eastern Europe."[65] Britain's responsibility for that state of affairs was considerable. The threat of a unilateral British withdrawal—in fact British troops left by mid-December 1929—combined with American insistence on the Young Plan, not to

62. On Czechoslovak issues at The Hague conferences see Gajanova, *ČSR*, 263–66; and Juhász, *Foreign Policy*, 96–97. French documentation in MAE, Y 38, 40, 41; Tchécoslovaquie 77; P.A. Tardieu 25(631); also HIA, Loucheur Papers, 6:252. For the Czechoslovak perspective, see 5 Sept. 1929 briefing, KV, CPP, and letters in ANM, Mastný 7 and Kramář 2.3. For British documentation, see DBFP, 1a, VI and VII.

63. Beneš, *Boj o mír*, 438–524.

64. *Fronta*, 30 Jan and 10 Apr. 1930. For the paper's place in the political spectrum, see Petr Pithart, "První republika: jak jí viděla opozice," *Svědectví*, 71–72 (1983) 278–81.

65. Bonnet, *Quai d'Orsay*, 103; compare Henry de Jouvenel, *La Paix française* (Paris, 1932).

mention Italian operations in the Danubian area and the attraction of economic cooperation with Germany, left Briand the narrowest of margins
for diplomatic maneuver. If the foreign minister himself had not regarded
the occupation as a great instrument of security, his colleagues in the cabinet like André Maginot and André Tardieu did. Yet, they went along with
Briand who received a standing ovation in the chamber after his 8 November speech devoted to The Hague. The previous fall of his cabinet on 22
October did not signify a lack of confidence in the foreign minister, who
retained his post in the Tardieu government formed on 3 November 1929.

The new premier was rather cool and haughty, a fairly typical representative of the upper bourgeoisie, and lacked Briand's persuasive
charm.[66] He was impatient with the Right, which was split on foreign policy; by making difficulties for the government, it was opening the way for
a new leftist cartel. He chastized the Left, which, while opposing the cabinet on domestic issues, tolerated it only because of Briand's presence at
the Quai d'Orsay. But, if the basic line of French foreign policy remained
unchanged, Tardieu quickly asserted his authority over the administration
and contributed to a different tone and atmosphere. Berthelot was on the
decline, and his future successor Alexis Léger began his ascension to
power.[67]

The decisions made in the Dutch capital were a blow to Poland. "The
date of The Hague conference," wrote *Gazeta Warszawska* on 19 August,
"will remain in history as the date of the collapse of the *sanacja* [Piłsudski's
regime] policy in the realm of foreign affairs." Rhineland, "the first line of
trenches," had been abandoned without a fight. The Polish nationalists no
longer drew a clear-cut distinction between the unfriendly French Left and
the polonophile Right. They saw the French policy as leading to a future
war, and described the struggles in the chambers as concerned only with
the rate of velocity of France's decline.[68] Could the Polish diplomacy be
blamed for this state of affairs? When a nationalist senator, Stanisław Kozicki, exclaimed: "One should have done everything to prevent this [evac-
uation] or obtain compensatory guarantees," and a progovernment senator shouted back: "Tell us how," there was no answer.[69] Indeed, it would
have been difficult to find fault with Zaleski's efforts.

66. A good characterization of Tardieu appears in Bariéty, "Der Tardieu-Plan," 371–
73.

67. Penetrating analysis by Hoesch, ADAP, B, XII:477–80. Briand's relative isolation
was noted by the influential journalist B. Koskowski; see *Kurjer Warszawski*, 29 Dec.
1929.

68. See *Gazeta Warszawska*, 13, 18, 19 Aug., 3 Sept.; Kozicki's articles 15–31 Oct.
1929, 1 Jan. 1930. Compare Laroche reports, 5, 10, 23 Feb. 1930, MAE, Z 698.12,
Pologne 2198, and Z 698.1, Pologne 2099.

69. See Sprawozdania stenograficzne senatu, 12 Mar. 1930, XXX/26.

The British embassy (the legation was raised to embassy following the example of Italy and Turkey in 1929 and preceding the United States by a year) commenting on "Poland's impotence at The Hague," wondered if Warsaw would try to lean more heavily on France. Other British diplomats thought that there was really nothing that Berlin could offer Paris to make it acquiesce in a revision in the east. But, in view of the intensified German revisionist propaganda and a Franco-German rapprochement, one could not exclude the possibility that "some ingenious solution might prove acceptable to Poland and Germany if France stood sponsor to it."[70] While the Poles followed anxiously all signs of German attempts to influence the French, Zaleski enjoined on the press to react with moderation. The French embassy in Warsaw reported on governmental efforts "not to displease us even in questions of secondary importance."[71]

From early November to late December 1929 a foreign policy debate was going on in the French parliamentary chambers and the commission on foreign affairs. East European and especially Polish problems figured in it as usual. Franklin-Bouillon and Millerand continued to dwell on the discrepancies between security in the West and the East.[72] Briand emphatically denied that France had ever lost interest in Poland. "Never had my Polish friends put forward the thesis" that there was an equivocation between the French stance in favor of the status quo and German revisionism. If such opinions were occasionally voiced in the sejm, Zaleski quickly corrected them.[73]

Franklin-Bouillon challenged the minister's assertion that the Poles were happy with the existing situation by citing excerpts of a speech by Janusz Radziwiłł, the chairman of the sejm foreign affairs commission. Radziwiłł, while stressing his confidence in the French government, had pointedly remarked that Franco-German arrangements "must not be made to Poland's detriment." The Poles had not received a territorial guarantee at Locarno, and this omission is "what they held against this treaty."[74]

Briand was visibly annoyed, and declared "I know very well of the work that is being carried on by certain Polish elements, and I am not sure that it is favorable to the maintenance of peace." To Franklin-Bouillon's re-

70. See Broadmead, Erskine, and Rumbold dispatches, 5 Sept., 3 and 11 Oct. 1929, FO 371 14018 C 4060/8/55 and C 4530/8/55 and DBFP, 1a, VIII:44.

71. See reports of Tripier and Laroche, 28 Nov., 28 Dec. 1929, MAE, Pologne 78:167–69, 197–98. Compare Chłapowski reports, 14 Aug., 27 Dec., and Schaetzel to Zaleski, 12 Oct. 1929, AAN, Amb. Berlin, 74, 75.

72. See J.O. Chambre, Nov. 8, 3071; Sénat, 20 Dec., 1311–12; CAE/Ch, 22, 27 Nov. 1929, also 21 Mar. 1930.

73. Briand speeches, 8 Nov., 20 Dec. 1929, J.O. Chambre, 3049–58, Sénat, 1312–13.

74. For Radziwiłł speech, see *Czas*, 6 Dec. 1929.

buke—"This is a singularly imprudent phrase. . . . You shall see the effect it will produce in Poland tomorrow"—Briand replied "For me it is only the Polish government that counts, and it had been associated with the work of Locarno."[75]

The next day, Georges Mandel invoked not only Radziwiłł but also a vote of the Polish sejm asking for compensations for the evacuation of the Rhineland. "This proves that all our allies do not have the same conception of the defensive value of the Rhinish security as the [French] minister of foreign affairs."[76] Paul Reynaud, citing a different passage from the Radziwiłł speech and quoting Zaleski, defended Briand's position as well as his own, for he had been accused of having discussed the "corridor" with German rightists.[77]

The Quai d'Orsay tried to counter the effect of Polish criticism by hastily collecting Zaleski's pronouncements approving the French-German rapprochement.[78] Well briefed, Briand got on a high horse on 26 December. After enumerating all the remarks of the Polish government testifying to its trust in the French government, he asserted that Paris had never conducted "a policy of egoistic security." Amid great applause by the deputies, he exclaimed grandly: "It is not the habit of France to sacrifice its friends and its allies."[79]

The Radziwiłł incident was trivial, but it showed Briand's touchiness regarding the Polish aspect, as well as the willingness of the deputies—a few members excepted—to be swayed by Briand's rhetoric. The parliament did not wish to have the image of France as a staunch and benevolent protector of its eastern allies damaged or destroyed. It was easier to close one's eyes to unpleasant realities.

A genuine malaise in Poland was, of course, a fact. It was loudly voiced by the rightist opposition and shared by certain pro-governmental groups.[80] Yet, Zaleski felt that he had no option except to affirm his trust in France's loyalty. He repeated that "just as Polish-German collaboration

75. J.O. Chambre, 23 Dec. 1929, 4621.

76. J.O. Chambre, 24 Dec. 1929, 4668.

77. J.O. Chambre, 4640–45. On 27 Dec., *Journal des Débats* ascribed to Reynaud the view that seventy million Eastern allies were merely "a source of complications." The paper called this "an aberration."

78. See telegram between Quai d'Orsay, Blanchet, and Laroche, 24–26, 28, 31 Dec. 1929, MAE, Pologne 78:174, 177–78, 191–92, 203–208, 219. Compare Barbier, *Un Frac*, 348–49. Laroche elicited a statement from Zaleski deploring the use of foreign policy issues in domestic French political controversies.

79. J.O. Chambre, 4677–79.

80. See *Gazeta Warszawska*, 21, 25 Feb. 1930. Compare Laroche reports, 5, 10, 25 Feb. 1930, MAE, Z 698.12 Pologne 2190; Z 698.1 Pologne 2099.

would be unthinkable without fully respecting French interests, so French-German rapprochement could not take place at the the the expense of Poland's interests."[81] Radziwiłł, as if to correct the use made of his former speech, echoed Zaleski's stand.[82] Briand was appreciative of such pronouncements, which "conformed so well to the policy that we have jointly pursued."[83] Probably many Poles shared the view of a socialist deputy, Kazimierz Czapiński, that Poland must not try to hinder the Paris-Berlin collaboration, for it was not a private initiative of Briand, but "the policy of all of France."[84] Indeed, the overwhelming majority by which the French chambers ratified The Hague accords in late March and April seemed to confirm the correctness of this appraisal.[85]

Zaleski's determination to be agreeable to Briand was undoubtedly affected at this stage by hopes attached to the bilateral negotiations conducted at The Hague. The visit of a French parliamentary delegation to Poland and the speech of the minister of commerce and industry, Georges Bonnefous, were understood as an indication of Paris's desire to strengthen the ties between both countries.[86] Schaetzel opined that after The Hague France remained alone with its concessions and the "applause of the Geneva gallery." He thought that Poland, thus far badly underestimated by Paris, could now become more valuable to France. Hence, one must emphasize again and again that only the Polish alliance and "a [French] relationship with Germany seen through the prism of this alliance, could be a valid line of French foreign policy."[87]

The last Polish move at The Hague had been a project tying the alliance to model D and the Kellogg–Briand Pact and making French aid to Poland concurrent with an appeal to the League. The final version had been submitted for approval to Piłsudski who, however, decided to await an initiative from France. Consequently, Laroche prepared a new variant of the treaty based on the assumption that France must avoid compromising "the capital work of Franco-German rapprochement," but also find a formula

81. See Zaleski, *Przemowy*, 2:23–25, 31–64, 69–85. Compare Laroche to Briand, 6 Jan. 1930, MAE, Z 698.1 Pologne 2099.

82. Sprawozdania stenograficzne, LXXV/73 session, 7 Feb. 1930.

83. Briand to Laroche asking him to thank Zaleski 1 Mar. 1930, MAE, Z. 698.1 Pologne 2099.

84. Sprawozdania stenograficzne, LXXV/67, session 7 Feb. 1930.

85. Chłapowski reported that only the Marin and Wendel faction in the Union Républicaine Démocratique (URD) opposed Briand. See his and Frankowski reports, 18 Jan., 12 Apr. 1930, AAN, Amb.Berlin, 75.

86. See Lipski's private letter to Schaetzel, 23 Sept. 1929, SI, MSZ, A.11.49/F/1. Compare Laroche to Briand, 5 Sept. 1929, MAE, Pologne 276:205–206.

87. Schaetzel's private letter to Lipski, 27 Sept. 1929, SI, MSZ, A.11.49/F/1.

satisfactory to the Poles. The ambassador called Poland "a trump in our game, as are our Czech, Yugoslav and Romanian clients." The value of these trumps he argued must not be diminished; "They will only make us stronger when dealing with Germany." Laroche liked the idea of anchoring the new text on the Kellogg–Briand pact and wondered if the French-Czechoslovak treaty might not be similarly adjusted. But he shared the view of Paris that a modification of the military convention was a prerequisite. Immediate assistance must not mean that "one charges head down and without delay into the demilitarized zone." To assume such an obligation would be an "impardonable imprudence" in view of the actual state of the French army.[88]

Laroche proposed in his project—which he showed to the Poles—that if France or Poland became a victim of unprovoked flagrant violation of the Kellogg–Briand pact, which would entitle it to demand immediate assistance in accord with the 1925 treaty, the other signatory, after having determined that a violation did occur, would immediately take all the necessary dispositions and preparations in order to fulfill the engagements.[89] This formula, far from dissipating Polish doubts, only strengthened them. Chłapowski pointed out that France would only pledge itself to take imprecise measures and act only after a decision of the League. What was needed was an accord unequivocally stating the obligation of instantaneous aid that could be defined in a secret agreement.[90]

It was the same story all over again. While agreeing on the usefulness of tying an alliance to the Kellogg–Briand pact, Warsaw wanted its automatic functioning; Paris opposed it. The Quai d'Orsay recalled, which was ominous under the circumstances, that neither the 1921 not the 1925 treaty "contained any guarantee by France of the current borders of Poland."[91] While technically correct, such a reminder indicated that Paris wished to have a free hand even in that respect. In such circumstances, Franco-Polish talks in November did not advance matters.[92]

The Quai d'Orsay explained to Tardieu that the Poles were worried about the "policy of appeasement pursued between France and Germany," and feared that the latter, freed on the Rhine would turn against the "cor-

88. Laroche to Berthelot, 5 Oct. 1929, MAE, Pologne 78:151–58. Compare Wysocki to Chłpowski, 8 Oct. 1929, HIA, Amb. Paryż, box 8.

89. Text in Laroche to Berthelot, 5 Oct. 1929, MAE, Pologne 78:151–58 and in SI, MSZ, A.11.2. Article 1 printed in DTJS, II, 15.

90. Chłapowski to Zaleski, 22 Nov. 1929, SI, MSZ, A.11.49/F/1/38. Compare Gen. Kutrzeba's project on the modalities of cooperation in case of aggression, SI, MSZ, A.11.49/F/1.

91. Note of political director, 10 Sept. 1929, MAE, Pologne 78:143.

92. See Zaleski to Chłapowski, 15 Nov. 1929, HIA, Amb. Paryż, box 8.

ridor" and Upper Silesia. Summarizing Polish requests, the document suggested that perhaps one could assist Poland's aeronautical industry.[93] An armament loan would antagonize Anglo-Saxon public opinion and be unfavorably viewed by the chambers. The "assurance-crédit" operation, however, was still a possibility. The acceptance of a text providing for automatic aid would weaken the existing treaties and harm "the efforts made by the French government to orient its relations with Germany in a sense favorable to the strengthening of peace."[94] No wonder that Chłapowski found Tardieu vague and evasive when he came to plead for closer intercourse between the two states.[95]

The French-Czechoslovak relationship posed no similar problems and difficulties. In early 1929, Charles-Roux had recommended an introduction of Škoda shares on the French financial market in order, everything else apart, to interest the public in Czechoslovak industry, which it "ignores almost completely."[96] The fact that Škoda, as we know, was mainly French-controlled made such a move doubly attractive. In the military field, Beneš made it clear to Briand that he wanted to retain the French mission; collaboration between General Faucher and the Czechoslovak general staff was of definite "political significance."[97] The importance of the mission was attested by Marshal Pétain who attended Czechoslovak army maneuvers toward the end of August. The visit, coinciding with the last phase of The Hague conference, appeared calculated to produce a certain political effect; probably for that very reason Pétain eluded an invitation to come to Poland as well. The Polish military attaché called it a demonstration of force under the aegis of France.[98] Indeed, the Czechoslovak press devoted unusual attention to the event attended not only by the chiefs of staff of the Little Entente but by President Masaryk himself.

Pétain was greatly impressed with Czechoslovak armed forces, created and organized "in the image of the French army." He noted, however, inadequacies of armament—there were only twenty armored cars and five tanks—and wondered whether soldiers of German nationality would be

93. See the exchange between Quai d'Orsay and war ministry, 9, 21 Oct. 1929, SHA, EMA/3, 7 N 3446/3.

94. Note for Tardieu, 30 Nov. 1929, MAE, Pologne 136:190–92. Compare Zaleski to Chłapowski, and Chłapowski to ministry, 19 Nov. 1929, SI, MSZ, A.11.49/F/1. On Polish debt to France, which, with interest included, would come to 1,897,389 francs by 1931, see correspondence in MAE, Pologne 215, 244.

95. Wysocki's instructions to Chłapowski, 19 Nov., HIA, Amb. Paryż, box 8. Excerpt of Chłapowski to Zaleski, 2 Dec. 1929; Lipski to Zaleski, 12 Jan. 1930, SI, MSZ, A.11.49/F/1. Lipski's Jan. note, SI, MSZ, A.11/6.

96. Charles-Roux to Briand, 29 Mar. 1929, MAE, Tchécoslovaquie 84:327.

97. Charles-Roux and Beneš to Briand, 22 and 28 Dec. 1929, MAE, Tchécoslovaquie 22:354–56 and 362–63.

98. See Bułhak, "Z Dziejów 1927–1936," 105.

reliable. The Czechs, he thought, underestimated German political activities "dissimulated under an apparent loyalty." By contrast, their preoccupation with Hungary seemed excessive. The marshal recommended the appointment of a high-ranking officer as military attaché and organizing a regular exchange of officers. He hoped that the fine Czechoslovak army would not be left alone at the beginning of hostilities; France ought to forge solid links between it and the armies of the Little Entente, and if possible Poland. "It is the whole question of our military relations with the states of Central Europe, remaining under our influence, which has to be resolved."[99]

As always, the Polish-Czechoslovak aspect was crucial. If the French were for a rapprochement between Warsaw and Prague before The Hague, wrote Charles-Roux, "we can only be more so since then."[100] Periodically, there were encouraging signs. A Czechoslovak delegation headed by L. Novák, the minister of commerce, and Přemysl Šámal, the influential chief of Masaryk's chancellery, visited the Poznań fair and was received by President Mościcki. The Polish government, characterizing Czechoslovakia as "the natural market for our agricultural products and cattle," and a significant importer of coal and oil, described it as "an ultraloyal partner" in commercial dealings.[101] Occasionally, some Czechoslovak papers asserted that Warsaw had more in common with Prague than with Budapest, and invoked the need for strengthening security in view of the approaching evacuation of the Rhineland.[102] But, there was no progress after the inter-staff military meeting in July, and Krofta opined that if political talks were to be initiated, old differences would resurface.[103] The respective attitudes of the envoys hardly contributed to a better atmosphere. To Girsa, even the Polish socialists were guilty of chauvinism. "The Czech national socialists [Girsa's party] call it nationalism when they practice it themselves," Laroche drily commented. Charles-Roux believed that Grzybowski would not oppose a rapprochement but would make no effort to further it. Beneš's dark hints that he knew what to think of the Pole's attitude may have indicated that Grzybowski's dispatches were being read, the Czech-

99. Pétain report, 11 Sept. 1929, MAE, Tchécoslovaquie 22:343–47. Compare Charles-Roux and military mission reports, 10 Sept., 8 Oct. 1929, MAE, Tchécoslovaquie 22:237–39 and 29:121–36. Also Faucher reports in SHA, EMA/2, Tchécoslovaquie 2 and 6.

100. Charles-Roux to Briand, 7 Sept. 1929, MAE, Tchécoslovaquie 62:190–93.

101. See the foreign ministry motion for the ratification of a trade protocol, 16 Mar. 1929, AAN, PPRM, XLVII, 75. Compare *Słowo Polskie*, 11 May 1929.

102. See Charles-Roux and Laroche dispatches between 25 Aug. and 12 Sept. 1929, MAE, Tchécoslovaquie 62:186–98; 29:83–87; Pologne 78:141–42, 144–48. Also briefing, 5 Sept. 1929, KV, CPP. Several articles in *Národní Politika* and *Národní Listy* in Aug.

103. Briefing, 13 Sept. 1929, KV, CPP.

oslovak intelligence having apparently broken the Polish code. French diplomats wondered whether they themselves should not take precautions against Prague's excessive "curiosity."[104]

There seemed to be no place for Poland in Beneš's political thinking.[105] As for Masaryk, he expressed a hope that the Germans and the Poles would reach an accomodation. "The ways are perhaps not yet clear, but an agreement would come even over this difficult ["corridor"] problem."[106] This comment sounded like a pious wish of a disinterested third party contemplating the German-Polish issue from Olympian heights.

An Overview

By 1930 the Locarno era was drawing to its close. Stresemann had died in October 1929; Chamberlain was out of office; Briand had passed his political prime. The Wall Street crash, which at first was hardly noticed in France, was heralding the end of an epoch characterized by prosperity and high hopes of stabilization and peace. During the four years that followed the signing of the pacts on the shores of Lago Maggiore, an important evolution had taken place in European relations; its impact on the French system of eastern alliances was profound.

The policies associated with Briand's name sought to resolve France's political, economic, and strategic problems through a revival of the entente cordiale, a reconciliation with Germany, a defensive military strategy, and a maintenance of a sphere of influence in East Central Europe. If the principal goal of French diplomacy was the creation of a Paris-Berlin axis, around which Europe's international relations were to resolve, eastern alliances were a liability condemned to insignificance if not oblivion. This is how the British saw their fate after Locarno. If, on the other hand, the purpose of conciliation was to enmesh, even at the price of important concessions, Germany in a cobweb of collective arrangements and to associate it with the Versailles system, then the alliances, especially with Poland, retained their value. It appears that both goals and attitudes coexisted side by side; the differences between Poincaré, Briand, the army leaders, the economic establishment, and public opinion reflected the degree of emphasis on one or the other.

For many influential groups in the country, Franco-German reconcilia-

104. See dispatches of Charles-Roux, 1 Nov. 1929, 11 Feb. 1930, MAE, Tchécoslovaquie 62:205–206 and Z 864.5, Tchécoslovaquie 2586; and of Laroche 3 Oct., 2 Nov. 1929, MAE, Tchécoslovaquie 62:200–201; Pologne 56:187–88.

105. Intercepted Marek reports, 17 Sept. 1929 and 13 Feb. 1930, SHA, EMA/2, Tchécoslovaquie 14; also Charles-Roux to Briand, 20 May 1930, MAE, Z 864.1, Tchécoslovaquie 2568.

106. Interview in *Berliner Tageblatt*, reprinted in *Prager Tagblatt*, 1 Oct. 1929.

tion claimed primacy, and a large part of French public opinion believed in it. The eastern alliances were to be adapted to the changing circumstances and used as important trumps in the diplomatic game played by rules dictated from Paris. Already before Locarno the Quai d'Orsay had sought to limit French military obligations to Poland, but after the Rhineland pact imposed political legal restraints on France's freedom of action, continued aid became a real and insoluble problem.

Reconciling the eastern alliances with a policy of rapprochement with Berlin was comparable to the squaring of a circle.[107] No doubt, French attitude toward German revisionism was evolving between 1925 and 1930. As Hoesch observed, Paris had originally regarded a threat to the Polish borders as tantamount to a threat on the Rhine. Then voices began to be heard that France would accept a freely negotiated German-Polish border settlement. Finally, the French government was giving the Germans to understand that it would actually welcome it.[108] In a way, Paris was playing for time, hoping that a democratic Weimar Republic, ever more closely associated with the West, might forgo if not the claims themselves, at least the forcible means of achieving them.

Assuming that Briand's main goal was to "tame" Germany, without making crucial French political and military concessions, he did not achieve his objectives in the 1925–30 period. By entangling Germany into collective security, France was losing some of her own maneuverability. All French cabinets regarded collaboration with London as vital, and were prepared to make concessions to gain it. Yet association with London brought no tangible increase of security, for regardless of Locarno the British had recognized that the border was on the Rhine, provided that they could decide when to defend it. Chamberlain did not wish to see a violent change of the existing borders in East Central Europe; his successors were less worried by such prospects. All British governments saw the French system as a dangerous relic of the past, an irritant, and a manifestation of French militarism. In that sense, reliance on Britain was virtually incompatible with the policy of eastern alliances.

The frequently mentioned contradiction between an offensive French diplomacy and a defensive military strategy may be more apparent than real, for Briand's policy was hardly offensive, although the political rhetoric tended to obscure this fact.[109] France's economic weakness was one of the reasons for it, but financial redress after 1926 did not result in a

107. Sargent opined in a letter to Rumbold, 24 Feb. 1930, that "except on the remote hypothesis of the acceptance by France of German ambitions for a modification of her Eastern frontier, the rapprochement cannot have concrete results of any magnitude." DBFP, ia, VII:474.

108. Hoesch to Auswärtiges Amt, 6 Mar. 1931, ADAP, B, XVII:11–12.

109. This point is well argued by Soutou, "L'Alliance," 346–48.

basic reorientation of Briand's diplomatic course. Domestic constraints connected with the socialist stand and the volatile part played by the radical socialists were real enough, but Poincaré showed that one could govern the country without the latter. De Gaulle had asked once the rhetorical question whether "a grand national vision (*rêve*) is not essential for a people to sustain its activity and maintain its cohesion?"[110] Briand's vision of peace tended to strengthen a process of spiritual disarmament. The average Frenchman, who opposed an increase in taxes and wanted a small defensive army, and the businessman who pursued relatively narrow interests, saw a legitimization of this position through a relaxed vigilance in the name of noble humanitarian goals.

From the Polish viewpoint, the shadow cast by Locarno was real enough. Worries about the "eastern gap" were compounded by ambiguities about the actual working of the alliance with France. Both Skrzyński and Zaleski hoped that as a result of a Franco-British rapprochement, Poland might become a ward not only of Paris but also of London. Their timid overtures showed, however, that Britain's determination to avoid responsibilities in the eastern part of the continent was unshakable.

From late 1926, as a premature evacuation of the Rhineland became a real danger, Warsaw sought to delay the withdrawal or obtain a quid pro quo in the form of an Eastern Locarno (involving a guaranteed German-Polish nonaggression pact or later a model D tripartite treaty) combined with French financial assistance. Simultaneously, the Poles opposed a weakening of the military alliance, wishing instead to make reciprocal aid automatic. Polish diplomacy had to tread carefully not to appear as an obstacle to Franco-German reconciliation and a burden to Paris. It had to be defensive and tactically accommodating. Piłsudski, who believed that the first five years after his ascension to power would bring no major international upheavals necessitating active Polish interventions, planned to use this period to consolidate the country politically and militarily.[111]

Paris felt unable to heed Polish demands for increased security. If an Eastern Locarno was ever seriously envisaged by France, it was in the form of a larger grouping of the eastern allies reinforced by a rapprochement with Soviet Russia. The French dialogue with the Poles became more frustrating. A feeling of malaise was compounded by economic friction. The impact of French business and finance was by and large detrimental to the development of the eastern system. Financial assistance on a large and imaginative scale, supported by Poincaré and Moreau, proved to be another insoluble problem for domestic French and international reasons.

The point made shortly after World War I by Jacques Bainville that Poland's security depended to no small degree on a strong Danubian organ-

---

110. Cited in Chastenet, *Histoire*, 5:317.

111. See Beck, *Dernier rapport*, 3.

ization remained valid during the 1920s. Yet attempts to bring Prague and Warsaw closer together, made repeatedly by French diplomacy and partly designed to alleviate France's own burden, proved futile. Except in such matters as disarmament and the national minority question—where a joint Czechoslovak-Polish front existed in Geneva—the two countries pursued their separate and incompatible policies. Prague spoke of a Central European Locarno that, in the final analysis, meant bringing Austria and Hungary within the sphere of influence of the Little Entente through nonaggression and economic pacts. Paris shared Prague's concern over the Anschluss, but was less taken with a Central Locarno. It also worried lest Czechoslovakia gravitate toward the German economic orbit. Schubert's ideas of a German-Austrian-Czechoslovak bloc were unacceptable to Beneš and Briand alike, but Prague's stress on friendly relations with Berlin was only partially welcomed by the French. To the Poles it appeared a sign of Czechoslovak disinterest in Poland's fate. The desire of Beneš's diplomacy to deflect German expansion from Vienna to Danzig was only in part matched by feelings recurrent in Warsaw that the Anschluss may not be an unmitigated evil.

During this period, the more exposed Poland made advances to Prague rather than vice versa, and these ill-fated attempts only revealed the limits beyond which the Czechoslovak government was unwilling to go. A military alliance was out of the question; close political collaboration between Poland and Czechoslovakia was foundering on several rocks: German, Hungarian, Russian, Italian. A certain Polish animosity against the Czechs, reciprocated by the latter, did not help matters. Warsaw never seriously thought of joining the Little Entente, but it was interested in collaborating with it and transforming it into a regional grouping that could provide protection against Germany and Russia. This was exactly what Prague did not want the Little Entente to become. French diplomacy did not take a clear-cut position on the respective projects of regional cooperation in East Central Europe; its main concern was to maintain France's influence in the region. The Little Entente seemed the best possible option; Poland's inclination to associate Italy with the region was viewed with suspicion.

If Polish diplomacy could claim few if any successes during the post-Locarno years, Czechoslovak achievements were more apparent than real. None of the issues in the Danubian area was really resolved. The Anschluss remained a threat; economic cooperation made no progress; and the strain on Czechoslovak-Polish relations was not removed. The Hague conference achieved a final liquidation of World War I, but from the viewpoint of the eastern alliances it marked a further decline of the French system. Chances of its revitalization were not readily apparent as the Great Depression struck Europe and the world.

Part Two

The Depression

Chapter Six

Revisionism and Briand's European Union

Rhineland Evacuated

When the last French contingents left the Rhineland on 30 June 1930, the great depression had already begun. Following the Wall Street crash in late October 1929, it spread widely, although the effects on individual countries varied as did the time of their occurrence. The fall of world prices of agrarian products was already noticeable in early 1929; a crisis in industry, characterized by declining production and mass unemployment, came roughly a year later. The financial crisis deepened the existing problems. A tendency toward protectionism and autarchy contributed to the rise of blocs and imperialist expansion. State intervention assumed massive proportion in international trade, whose volume greatly diminished. The radicalization of social and political life affected diplomacy, although a Mussolini-type foreign policy marked by aggressiveness and belligerence predated the depression era. Invocation of peaceful solutions and indignant denial of the use of force, so characteristic for the Locarno period, made room for unabashed saber-rattling. A brutalization of domestic politics went hand in hand with a lowering of respect for treaties and open contempt for the rights of weaker nations.

France with its balanced industrial-agrarian economy could at first weather the storm better than most countries. It was only by late 1931 that the first symptoms of a financial crisis appeared. The French government tried to cope with it through deflationary measures and strengthened protectionist policies. Domestic instability increased, bringing with it a growing despair of the future and a draining of energy of the bourgeoisie. In early 1930, however, France was still in an unusually strong financial position—having accumulated gold and foreign money amounting to over twenty percent of the world reserve—and able to practice a financial diplomacy to advance its foreign policy goals. In fact, it was imperative on monetary grounds that France export some of its capital.[1]

1. See Sauvy, "Economic Crisis," John C. de Wilde, "Franch Financial Policy," *For-*

Czechoslovakia, as compared with its neighbors in East Central Europe, enjoyed the advantage of being industrially developed and almost self-sufficient in agricultural products. A creditor rather than a debtor, it was at no time threatened by insolvency. By raising taxes and customs duties the government succeeded in keeping the budgets fairly well balanced. Czechoslovakia was more vulnerable in trade. In 1932, however, with a drastic reduction of export levels, a nearly sixty percent drop of industrial production, and a crisis in agriculture (although state intervention prevented a sharp fall of prices), the country hit the bottom of the depresison. Because the affected industries were largely located in the predominantly German-inhabited Sudeten areas, the ensuing high rate of unemployment fanned their anti-Prague sentiments. Similar phenomena could be observed among the Poles in Teschen Silesia. In Slovakia, hidden unemployment in the countryside, which could not be alleviated by the weak industrial sector, contributed to a radicalization of the masses. At the meeting of the populist party in Ružemberok in January 1930, the demand for autonomy figured prominently in the program. More aggressive younger politicians like the polonophile Karol Sidor or Ferdinand D'určanský moved to the forefront of the Slovak autonomist movement. Udržal's "great coalition" was, however, in control of the situation and remained so for its two years in office. In 1930, Czechoslovakia could boast of being an oasis of economic and political stability in a Europe battered by mounting waves of nationalism and radicalism.[2]

Poland was grieviously affected by the depression. A recession in agriculture and the beginnings of a crisis in industry appeared already in 1929. The agrarian crisis remained after it had been overcome by most European countries; the worst year for industry was 1932. Given the phenomena of hidden unemployment and "price scissors," the peasantry suffered badly. Decline in the production of capital equipment and a fall in coal output hurt the economy. Unemployment figures were high. Anxious not to antagonize the western investors, Poland did not try to prevent the flight of foreign capital and continued to adhere to the gold standard. The consequences were costly.[3] All this exacerbated the existing political and social tensions. Piłsudski met the challenge posed to his regime by the center-left (Centrolew) congress in Cracow in June 1930 by brutal measures: the sejm was dissolved, and in September a number of opposition leaders were arrested and imprisoned in the Brześć fortress. This notorious affair rever-

eign Policy Reports, 8 (1932); Neré, *La Crise*. On capital exports, compare Bonnefous, *Histoire*, 5:44.

2. See relevant parts of Faltus, "Rozwój gospodarczy," also Pryor, "Czechoslovak Economic Development," esp. 198–215; and relevant parts in Dobrý, part III of Olšovský et al., *Přehled*.

3. See Landau, "Depression," 337–54.

berated through the country, tarnishing the image of the marshal and sanacja. The painful effect was compounded by "pacifications" in Eastern Galicia undertaken in retaliation for Ukrainian territorist acts. The subsequent victory of the pro-Piłsudski bloc in heavy-handed elections in late 1930 was purchased at a high political and moral price.

The great depression undoubtedly fertilized the ground for the growth of extremist forces, but it created neither the ground nor the forces.[4] This was true for France, Czechoslovakia, and Poland and for Germany. Already at The Hague, Stresemann was saying that a German failure at the conference might result in a right-oriented radical government in Berlin.[5] After the November 1929 elections in Germany, Tardieu thought that either Alfred Hugenberg or Hitler was likely to gain power.[6] Commenting on the Nazi electoral triumph ten months later, Sir Horace Rumbold, the British ambassador in Berlin, wrote that it was "a revival of the national spirit and the hope of the rebirth of Germany that carried them to victory." Similarly, his Polish colleague Alfred Wysocki noted that Hitler appealed to his followers not by speaking about the economic crisis but by calling on them to sacrifice their lives to free Germany from the shackles of bondage and to create "a new religion and a new state."[7]

The fall of the Müller coalition cabinet in March 1930 led to the formation of a shaky ministry presided over by Heinrich Brüning. The new chancellor, a somewhat ascetic figure, authoritarian, fiscally conservative, and a revisionist offered a telling contrast to Stresemann. Engaged in complex domestic political juggling, he exploited to the full the argument that unless serious concessions were made to Germany the very system of the Weimar Republic would collapse and be replaced by a radical-nationalist regime. He told Hitler, Hugenberg, and the Reichswehr chiefs that he welcomed sharp opposition from the Right so that he could appear as a moderate abroad.[8] This was playing with fire, and his foreign minister, Julius Curtius, was not above riding the revisionist wave either. The new team in charge of German diplomacy—Bernhard von Bülow, Ernst von Weizsäcker, and Konstantin von Neurath—opposed Locarno and stressed free-

---

4. More recent studies include Herman van der Wee, ed., *The Great Depression Revisited* (The Hague, 1972); Kindleberger, *Depression*; Josef Becker and Klaus Hildebrand, eds., *Internationale Beziehungen in der Weltwirtschaftskrise 1929–1933* (München, 1980); Girault, "Crise économique et protectionisme hier et aujourd'hui," *Relations Internationales*, 16 (1978); Julian Jackson, *The Politics of Depression in France 1932–1936* (Cambridge, 1985). Also the complete issue of *Dzieje Najnowsze*, 6,2 (1975).

5. See ADAP, B, XII:349.

6. See 29 Mar. 1930, J.O. Chambre, 1396.

7. Respectively Rumbold to Henderson, 31 Oct. 1930, DBFP, II, 1:527, and Wysocki cited in Ajnenkiel, "Rozmowa," 133–38.

8. Bennett, *German Rearmament*, 49.

dom of maneuver.[9] A "veritable explosion of nationalism," in the words of a leading French diplomat Robert Coulondre, was taking place in Germany. As Robert Vansittart, the permanent undersecretary at the Foreign Office, diagnosed it, the question was not whether Germany would pursue all the revisionist goals, but how belligerently and under whose guidance: the Volkspartei, the Zentrum, or the extreme nationalists of the Hitler brand.[10]

It mattered a great deal to Paris that the evacuation of the Rhineland be a symbol of Franco-German reconciliation and a triumph of the spirit of Locarno.[11] If the Germans showed a proper spirit of appreciation, wrote the British ambassador in Paris, Briand would be "enabled to continue his policy of *rapprochement*." But if they used the occasion to present fresh demands they would "weaken his position" and play into the hands of his opponents.[12] The German reaction surpassed all the worst premonitions of Briand. Newspapers rejoiced over the end of the "era of shame and tribulation," and displayed "cool contempt" toward so-called French generosity. Rhineland, they said, was evacuated not five years too early but many years too late. Reporting these "ungracious comments," Ambassador Rumbold thought that one could not be surprised by French disappointment. Referring to allusions that the Rhineland was not yet freed of all "servitudes"—meaning its demilitarized status—he wrote that "no sooner is one grievance redressed than the Germans come forward with another."[13]

Spontaneous manifestations had a counterpart in governmental statements. President Hindenburg's manifesto made no reference to Stresemann or Franco-German reconciliation, but instead paid a tribute to the long-suffering Rhinelanders, spoke of the "day of liberation," and recalled that the Saar still awaited its reunification with the Reich.[14] Three days after the evacuation, Curtius "went out of his way" to declare to the British ambassador "in particularly energetic terms" that Germany "could not rest content with her present frontier in the East." He added that "he would not leave the French under any illusion on that point."[15] No wonder

9. Krüger, *Aussenpolitik*, 512–23.

10. Coulondre to Tardieu, 26 March 1932, MAE, P.A. Tardieu 25 (631). Memorandum in DBFP, ia, VII:834–52, referred to in Vansittart, *Mist Procession*, 405.

11. Numerous representations of Briand and Tardieu appear in ADAP, B, XIV:399–40, 463; XV:84–85, 242–43.

12. Tyrrell to Henderson, 3 July 1930, DBFP, II, 1:479.

13. Rumbold to Henderson and Sargent, 3 July, 16 Oct. 1930, DBFP, II, 1:480–86, 518.

14. Rumbold characterized the manifesto as epitomizing "two of the besetting weaknesses of the German character, ingratitude and tactlessness"; DBFP, II, 1:480–86.

15. DBFP, II, 1:490.

that the position of Briand as "the father of the policy of German-French reconciliation and of the evacuation of the Rhineland had become at this moment extraordinarily difficult," Hoesch wrote.[16]

The French foreign minister, although badly shaken, tried to make the best of a bad situation. Apart from a plan for European union, which is discussed later, his possibilities were limited. An entente with Rome was still beyond reach, and remained so for the rest of the year, partly because of the Yugoslav angle, which Briand tried to minimize when addressing the foreign affairs commission. In his remarks he argued more vigorously than usual for France's eastern alliances, bearing out Vansittart's earlier opinion that, despite everything, they were "still a cornerstone of her cosmos."[17] France was not isolated, Briand said, for it had such friends as Poland, Czechoslovakia, Romania, and Yugoslavia. This fact "was not negligible," and after all "cannons and machine guns counted for something"—an odd phrase in Briand's mouth. The foreign minister mentioned his frequently awkward position between Germany and Poland, but claimed that it was he who brought Berlin and Warsaw together in the matter of the commercial treaty. Although he did not believe in the threat of a Habsburg restoration, he could assure the Little Entente that French policy had not changed. He knew that they entertained no doubts about French "loyalty and firmness."[18]

This last remark was applicable to Prague more than to Warsaw.[19] The Poles sought Italian friendship as a reinsurance and the June conversations between Grandi, Piłsudski, and Zaleski aroused some anxiety in Paris and Prague.[20] The Polish-Italian rapprochement, however, was skin-deep, even though Warsaw was probably unaware of the fact that Mussolini regarded the "corridor" as the number one item for revision.[21] As always the Poles

16. ADAP, B, xv:386–87. The British thought that Briand had to be supported at this juncture; see DBFP, ii, 1:389–90.

17. See 1 May 1930 memorandum, DBFP, ia, vii:843–47.

18. 10 July 1930 session, CAE/Ch.

19. See 13 Feb. briefing, KV, CPP; compare Mastný to Beneš, 20 June 1930, ANM, Mastný, notebook 122–23. On the Polish angle, Vansittart commented that it was likely that "any attempt to push Franco-German political understanding too far upstream would be wrecked on the Polish snag." Paris was weighing the risk of supporting Poland, appearing more like a liability than an asset, "in a quarrel no longer of vital interest" to itself. DBFP, ia, vii:843–47.

20. On the Grandi visit, see Borejsza, *Mussolini*, 471; Sierpowski, *Stosunki*, 268–71; Günther, *Pióropusz i szpada*, 108. For French distrust of any Polish pro-Italian moves, see Nov. 1930–Feb. 1931 correspondence in MAE, Z 698.1, Pologne 2099; also Polish reports from Paris, 6 Feb., 11, 23 Mar. 1931, AAN, MSZ 3797.

21. Mussolini said that to René Pinon. See Laroche and Beaumarchais to Briand, 15 and 29 May 1930, MAE, Z 698.1, Pologne 2099; MAE, P.A. Tardieu 81 (689). I found no indication that the French repeated Mussolini's remarks to Warsaw.

worried about the growth of German revisionist propaganda in France. In March, a strongly pro-German book by René Martel, *Les Frontières orientales de l'Allemagne* appeared in Paris, and in the summer *La Volonté* published an article describing the German-Polish border as "illogical and unjust." The alliance with Poland, the paper said, was only profitable to the Poles; for the French it could only mean the danger of a new war.[22] More serious from the Polish standpoint was Sauerwein's article in *Le Matin* suggesting the possibility of a compromise in the "corridor," for the Poles wondered if it was not inspired by the Quai d'Orsay, although the official circles criticized it.[23]

The French general staff meanwhile prepared two studies, respectively, on the military convention and the "corridor." The first, dated January 1930, surveyed the history of the alliance since 1921, and emphasized that the army had consistently and fully informed the Quai d'Orsay of the various developments. Until a new order, the document concluded, "the secret military convention of 1921 remains valid." As for the "corridor," the second study (of July) established the following points. From an ethnic viewpoint the area was "indisputably Polish." It played a vital part in Poland's economy, and the alleged hardship of the separated East Prussia was due more to economic factors than to the Versailles border. Germany's claims were "neither juridically nor economically valid," and its revindications were motivated by political-historical and sentimental factors. But for that very reason, a peaceful resolution of the conflict seemed extremely difficult, although time was clearly working for Poland.[24]

It is possible that the second study was connected with Polish efforts to attract new French capital into the "corridor." After the consolidation of Poland's wartime debt to France on 24 January 1930, the cabinet authorized the signing of an agreement with a French consortium for the completion of the second round of works in the Gdynia harbor.[25] Negotiations also began to create a Franco-Polish company that would build and exploit a railroad linking Silesia with Gdynia. Piłsudski and the chief of the general staff drew General Denain's attention to the economic and strategic importance of this line, and wished the French war ministry to en-

22. Albert Saurat, "La France et la Pologne," *La Volonté*, 30 July 1930.

23. See note on Zaleski–Laroche conversation, 6 June, SI, MSZ, A.11/6 and on Laroche–Lipski talk, 12 Aug. 1930, AAN, MSZ 3763. On speculations whether the Sauerwein article was a trial balloon launched at Briand's behest, see Wiley to Secretary of State, 8 Oct. 1930, SDNA, 760C.6215/520.

24. See Etude relative à l'accord militaire franco-polonais, Jan. 1930, SHA, EMA/3, 7 N 3446/3, and Etude sur le corridor polonais, 31 July, 1930, SHA, EMA/2, Pologne 21. Compare an interesting note in ADAP, B, xv:397–401.

25. See cabinet session, 7 Feb. 1930, AAN, PPRM, xlix, 486–94. The French groups involved were: Société de Construction de Batignoles, Schneider et Co., Société anon. Hersent, Achermans et van Haaren, Højgaard et Schultz.

courage Parisian banks to advance the funds needed. The French minister of public works, Georges Pernot, who visited Gdynia in August, reported on urgent requests from Poland and added that French diplomats and military officials believed that France ought to finance Poland's reconstruction.[26]

Paris wished to avoid any excessive manifestations of Franco-Polish solidarity. The Quai d'Orsay opposed the idea of an exchange of state visits between the respective presidents, and vetoed Marshal Pétain's participation in ceremonies commemorating the tenth anniversary of the battle of Warsaw. It was feared that prominent French visitors could be exposed to Polish requests.[27] Indeed, already in early April, Piłsudski had ordered Zaleski to renew diplomatic pressure on France to strengthen cooperation in the field of security and to obtain armament credits.[28] The Poles received a confirmation of Briand's promises made at The Hague, but concrete arrangements regarding military supplies were to be dealt with by the respective general staffs. Paris, however, was ready to restore the fourth installment of the loan that Skrzyński had renounced in the spring of 1925.[29]

In Warsaw, representatives of the foreign ministry, army, and treasury agreed that Poland request one milliard frances in goods and half a milliard in cash (partly through governmental loans). Piłsudski appeared somewhat skeptical about the chances of the entire operation, and he opposed any onerous conditions that the French might attach to it.[30]

Paris was careful not to admit the existence of a formal link between the loan to Poland and the evacuation of the Rhineland. Laroche explained that while his government recognized a de facto connection, it wished to avoid an ambiguous legal situation. The Polish foreign minister on his side responded by downplaying, for tactical reasons, the urgency of the loan.

26. See Denain note, 30 July, SHA, EMA/2, Pologne 11; Pernot's "Relation du voyage," 6 Aug. 1930, MAE, Z 698.12, Pologne 2197; compare Wiley to Secretary of State, 8 Oct. 1930, SDNA, 751.60C/23.

27. See exchanges between Laroche, the Quai d'Orsay, and the war ministry, Mar. to June 1930, MAE, Z 698.12, Pologne 2198.

28. Negotiations with the French were to be on "a footing of equality," and Piłsudski was particularly interested whether General Weygand would assist Polish efforts. See Lipski undated note, SI, MSZ, A.11/6.

29. Zaleski to Piłsudski, 14 May 1930, SI, MSZ, A.11/F/1.

30. See protocol of interdepartmental meeting, 24 May; Col. Pełczyński to foreign ministry, 14 June 1930, SI, MSZ, A.11/6 and A.11/49/F/1. The one and a half milliard was to be realized through a triple operation: a Polish loan floated in France (to which Warsaw attached great importance, hoping to overcome the prejudices of the financial circles), a direct French governmental loan (for which Poland offered the income from state forests in the Toruń region as security), and deliveries in kind financed under assurance-crédit. The army insisted on a priority for armor and heavy artilery. Treasury's views in 3 July 1930 memo, SI, MSZ, A.11/6.

He believed that if the Poles showed too much alacrity, they would receive less advantageous terms. Hence, delaying tactics seemed advisable. It may well be that Warsaw committed an error of judgement, for matters came to a standstill and the Poles were finally driven to complain about Quai d'Orsay's silence.[31] Talks were resumed in September in an atmosphere that, as we shall see, was greatly changed.

Briand's European Union

Some six weeks before the evacuation of the Rhineland, Briand had come forward with what may be regarded as his last major initiative—the project of a European Union. The idea had been first expressed in his speech in Geneva, on 5 September 1929, when recalling old European unity and invoking article 21 of the Covenant, which referred to regional associations, the foreign minister declared that the peoples of Europe should establish "some kind of a federal bond." The envisaged grouping would be "primarily economic." Following a favorable reaction in Geneva, Briand addressed a memorandum to European governments on 1 May 1930 that stressed security as the key to the continent's pacification and progress. National sovereignty of member states was not to be affected, and the entire organization, subject to the League of Nations, was presented as a further step on the Locarno road.[32]

The project, far from being a quixotic scheme, represented Briand's attempt to promote his German policy through a novel type of international cooperation. The emphasis on economics in the initial version corresponded to the recommendations of the 1927 world economic conference and had the support of Stresemann. France's industrial and especially financial circles were much interested in a vast European system that, based on Franco-German economic harmony, would improve their country's position through cartels and other accords, and mobilize the continent against Anglo-Saxon influences. The idea of a continental collaboration under the aegis of Paris and Berlin had a strong advocate in Briand's economic adviser, then minister of national economy, Louis Loucheur.

The British saw in the original proposal the beginnings of a system com-

31. Briand asked Chłapowski not to leave with him the Polish memorandum that contained the phrase about the need for "accelerated completion of the organization of Poland's defenses" in view of the Rhineland evacuation. Briand said he would be in an awkward position if he had to summarize this at a cabinet meeting. See Polish text, 15 July, SI, MSZ, A.11/6; Chłapowski telegram, 26 July, HIA, Amb. Paryż, box 4. An amended memo was handed in late in Aug. For Zaleski–Laroche talks see 6 Aug., note, SI, MSZ, A.11/6. Also, Zaleski to Mühlstein, 18 Aug., and Mühlstein and Chłapowski telegrams, 27 Aug., 1 Oct. 1930, SI, MSZ, A.11/6.

32. Text in DBFP, II, 1:312–24. The authorship is usually ascribed to Alexis Léger. Compare Suarez, *Briand*, 6:327, 332–34.

parable to that envisaged by the Geneva Protocol of 1924, and encompassing "the French network of alliances, assistance and arbitration treaties." Noting the emphasis on security in the May memorandum, the Foreign Office thought that the object was "to reinforce French political hegemony in Europe."[33] London judged the project unacceptable to Berlin, and indeed *Deutsche Algemeine Zeitung* jeered that Paris tried to translate its imperialism from French into esperanto.[34] Although Schubert and Hoesch saw merit in the plan provided it restored the original stress on economics, German leadership unanimously condemnded Briand's proposed union as likely to impose new restraints on Germany in the name of European consolidation. The question was not whether to reject it but how to reject it without incurring discredit.[35] All of Briand's arguments that the union would be based on the great powers and might in fact facilitate revisionism in an atmosphere of general trust were to no avail.[36] Thus, the skepticism of Berthelot and Massigli[37] about the chances of the project was justified, and the plan was virtually buried in Geneva through its transfer to a Commission for the Study of European Union especially created for this purpose.

What were the reactions of French eastern allies to Briand's project? In their formal reply, the Poles "rejoiced" at this "happy initiative," but in fact, there was no enthusiasm and the proposal was regarded as unrealistic.[38] Some Poles viewed it as illustrative of Briand's idealism; others thought it was bluff designed to impress European and French public opinion. The Polish delegate in Geneva, Franciszek Sokal, assumed that Briand's goal was to promote a rapprochement with Germany, paralyze Italy's aggressive policies, oppose America's economic expansion, and develop an anti-Soviet bloc. Within such a scheme, France, together with its eastern allies, could achieve greater security. The proposal could also serve as an alibi in case peace could not be maintained.[39] Zaleski qualified his public approval by warnings, explicit or implicit, against a great powers'

33. Respectively, DBFP, 1a, VII:460, and II, 1:324–33.

34. Chastenet, *Histoire*, 5:201.

35. See ADAP, B, xv:93–96, 126–30, 168, 169, 208–15. Compare Krüger, *Aussenpolitik*, 523–30.

36. See ADAP, B, xv:67–69, 239–40, 343–45.

37. See Chłapowski to Zaleski, 19 July 1930, AAN, Amb.Berlin, 1518.

38. Polish reply, 10 July, AAN, Amb. Berlin, 1518; comments in Lipski to Chłapowski, 1 July, SI, MSZ, A.11/6; Laroche, *Pologne*, 101; Denain annual report, SHA, EMA/2, Pologne 11; Erskine to Henderson, 6 Aug. 1930, FO 371 14983 and minutes W 7402; ADAP, B, xv:413–16. On Polish skepticism, MS, OSS, Wysocki, II, 125, 157.

39. See MS, BJ, Skirmunt, 148; MS, PAN, Dziennik Zdanowskiego, VI, part 2, 37 and Sokal to Zaleski, 2 May 1930, AAN, Amb.Berlin, 1518.

directorate, revisionism, and, in a more discrete way, Franco-German economic hegemony on the continent.[40] Just as the Germans feared that Briand's union would amount to a petrification of the European status quo, so the Poles were suspicious lest the contrary prove to be the case.[41] Aware of these apprehensions, the French government tried to imply that the projected union would make East European borders with Germany more secure: "In this sense Paneuropa was to be a correction of Locarno."[42]

Briand's original speech in Geneva had appeared "nebulous" to the foreign ministry in Prague; Beneš gave an interview in which he opposed the possibility of revising postwar treaties.[43] Officially, Czechoslovakia "gladly accepted" the May memorandum but emphasized that it could not be prejudicial to the principle of national sovereignty and equality of states. Prague extolled the notion of regional organization for peace and expressed some doubts about the practicalities of a larger plan. The British described the Czechoslovak reply as "a discussion essay rather than a statement of fact."[44]

Naturally, Czechoslovak diplomats speculated about the objective of Briand's proposal. Osuský assumed that it meant to give a new impetus to the League in its efforts to promote disarmament, security, and economic cooperation, because lack of success in these areas endangered Briand's policy. The envoy felt that Berthelot was less involved in the plan than Léger and that Tardieu did not favor it. According to Krofta, the project stemmed both from general postwar idealism and more concrete French desires. He mentioned the opposition to an excessive economic dependence of Europe on the United States, the need for a larger customs area, the belief that within a unified Europe minority problems would become less acute, and that within the League of Nations the influence of overseas countries would be curtailed. An all-European Locarno and a customs union were "of great political importance" for the Czechs, and insofar as the project aimed to uphold the status quo and promote economic cooperation, it had the support of Prague. Krofta was less certain whether a European association would not endanger the Geneva organization; he had no doubts that Germany would raise serious obstacles to the whole scheme.[45]

---

40. Zaleski's speech and article in Zaleski, *Przemowy*, 2:99–102, 108–109. Also Zaleski telegram, 19 June 1930, HIA, Amb. Paryż, box 4.

41. See Wiley to Secretary of State, 20, 21 June 1930, SDNA, 840.00/188 and 189.

42. Gajanová, *ČSR*, 270.

43. 31 Sept. 1929 briefing, KV, CPP. Even Charles-Roux was skeptical. Beneš's interview was reported by *Gazeta Warszawska*, 6 Apr. 1930.

44. Foreign Office minute, FO 371 14983 W 7402.

45. See 22 May, 3, 10, 24 July 1930 briefings, KV, CPP.

Beneš did not seem "to think much of the Briand plan in itself" except that it might lessen the chances of the great powers indulging "in the luxury of another war." A European political union that excluded Russia and the United States, and most likely Britain, did not appeal to him. He may have even thought that the plan represented a French endeavor to gain greater security at the expense of the East European allies.[46] Hence, Beneš's public pronouncements on the Briand project were unusually sober. He warned that its realization would take decades, and remarked that a European association ought not to exclude the existence of regional groupings (the Little Entente). Speaking to journalists in September, he used the term *přestavka* ("pause") to characterize the stage reached in Locarno diplomacy.[47]

Beneš's reticence was also connected with a development that paralleled the Briand proposal and directly affected the Danubian region. In mid-May, Loucheur undertook a two-week journey that took him to Prague, Bucharest, and Budapest. He came with a plan for economic redress of Central Europe based essentially on the notion of recreating in some form the prewar Austro-Hungarian market.[48] Although his conversations with Masaryk and Beneš were cordial enough the national democratic press raised alarm about Loucheur's forceful promotion of the interests of the Western industrialized states. Krofta denied this, but he had to admit that the Frenchman's views on Austria and Hungary could cause concern.[49] Beneš tried to dismiss the portent of Loucheur's plan saying that the French minister was "talking about something he did not understand." Only an idle dreamer could imagine that the region could be economically reconstructed without a prior political settlement.[50] Beneš feared that the plan would operate politically to the advantage of Hungarian revisionism, and it was no secret that Budapest was pursuing assiduously a rapprochement with Paris and seeking to weaken the French support for the Little Entente.[51]

A connection between the Loucheur and Briand plans became clearer

46. See Addison to Henderson, 4 July, 29 May, and annual report, Czechoslovakia 1930, FO 371 14983 W 7337; 14981 Hm 03702, and 15179 C 362/1203/12.

47. For public utterances, see Beneš, *Boj o mír*, 60–61; compare 11 Sept. 1930 briefing, KV, CPP.

48. Press cuttings, speeches, etc., in HIA, Loucheur Papers, 7a. Also Loucheur, *Carnets*, 168. Compare Sládek and Tomaszewski, "Próby latach trzydziestych," 382–83.

49. See 6 May 1930 briefing, KV, CPP; Marek report (intercept), 25 May, SHA, EMA/2, Tchécoslovaquie 14; Ratshesky to Secretary of State, 26 May 1930, SDNA, 840.00/163.

50. Addison to Henderson, 16 May 1930, FO 371 14981 C 5463.

51. See ADAP, B, xiv:235–38. On Beneš's uncertainty whether the French did not seek to accommodate Vienna at Prague's expense, see Marek report, 25 May 1930 (intercept), SHA, EMA/2, Tchécoslovaquie 14.

when the former was developed at the Commission for the Study of European Union. It anticipated a meeting of the East Central European states to discuss the issue of cereal surpluses; while noting the Yugoslav and Romanian predilection for preferential tariffs, it proposed the creation of a committee to study customs regulations.[52] These proposals suggested the possibility of a Danubian customs union placed under French or even broader West European aegis, an arrangement that would likely endanger Prague's position in the area. The British envoy wrote in his typical facetious manner that the Czechs appeared "suddenly to realize that they were not the favourite wife, but the most insignificant concubine who was being flattered not for her looks but for her skill in the kitchen."[53]

In view of the catastrophic fall of agrarian prices, their protection was indeed the major preoccupation of East Central European states. Governmental involvement in the grain trade, through state monopoly as in Czechoslovakia, or state purchases and state-directed exports as in Poland, indicated the seriousness of the problem.[54] But, a combination of agrarian states, including Romania and Yugoslavia, would cut across the Little Entente, and this fact, combined with the potential dangers of the Loucheur plan, made Prague determined to strengthen the cohesion of the triple grouping.

Centrifugal tendencies within the Little Entente certainly existed. Bucharest was grumbling about the Czechoslovak suggestions of a Hungarian threat; by crying "wolf," they "want to keep us in a state of alert," a Romanian diplomat complained.[55] Prague's partners considered the possibility of a rapprochement between the Little Entente and Hungary, and even an eventual association with Poland, as steps in the direction of a European union,[56] but the sudden return of Carol to Romania and his resumption of the royal crown raised fears of a Romanian deviation from a pro-Little Entente and a pro-French line.

The meeting of the Little Entente at Štrbské Pleso (25–27 June) agreed that the handling of the Briand memorandum required circumspection,[57] although officially it welcomed the document as corresponding to the political objectives of the group. Beneš succeeded in achieving a tripartite complementary accord-statute, through which the members decided to co-

52. See Massigli to Briand, 21 Jan. 1931, MAE, P.A. Puaux 255 (29).

53. Addison to Sargent, 9 July 1931, FO 371 1518 Hm 03698.

54. See Ivan T. Berend and György Ránki, *Economic Development in East Central Europe in the 19th and 20th Centuries* (New York, 1974), 242–64; Raupach, "Great Depression," 236–45.

55. See Vienne to Briand, 25 Feb. 1930, MAE, Z 684.10, Tchécoslovaquie 2601.

56. See Leczyk, *Polityka*, 263–65; also Olivová and Kvaček, *Dějiny Československa*, 160–62.

57. Briefing, 3 July 1930, KV, CPP.

ordinate their foreign policies and, in the case of an attempted restoration of the Habsburgs in Budapest, break off diplomatic relations with and blockade Hungary, as well as to call for a session of the League of Nations. A statement by the Czechoslovak minister of defense that in view of the Italian and Hungarian maneuvering, Central Europe was in greater danger of war than ever before created quite a sensation.[58] Was Prague crying "wolf" once again?

The reorganization of the Little Entente was naturally represented as corresponding to the spirit of the Briand memorandum. Beneš declared that the grouping was no longer "a combination directed against Hungary" but pursued a "much broader mission" aspiring to be "an instrument of collaboration in Central Europe, indeed in all of Europe."[59] The French minister in Prague was not much impressed by the new provisions for regular meetings and a certain streamlining of procedures that seemed to "consecrate what was alreday being practiced."[60] Only military cooperation seemed to have made some progress with the conference of the chiefs of staff, scheduled for September, to study the case of an Italian attack on Yugoslavia.[61]

The Štrbské Pleso conference did not put an end to divergences within the Little Entente. Yugoslavia and Romania moved toward closer economic cooperation and, instead of including Czechoslovakia first and only much later Hungary in the negotiations, invited the latter to the Bucharest grain conference. There was consternation in Prague, anxious articles in the press, and a discrete demarche by Beneš.[62] The conflicting interests between agricultural states and the industrialized Czechoslovakia were also reflected in a Polish initiative to organize an agrarian East Central European bloc. Seen as a partial answer to Briand's union, it was based on the assumption that the agrarian states had to present a common front in order to win preferential treatment. The Czechoslovak agrarians, notably Milan Hodža, supported this position.[63] Not so the Czechoslovak government which was cool to a Polish proposal for a conference in Warsaw

---

58. Cited in Vondracek, *Foreign Policy*, 319.

59. Charles-Roux to Briand, 10 June 1930, MAE, Z 864.10, Tchécoslovaquie 2601.

60. Charles-Roux and Puaux to Briand, 2 July, 29 June 1930, MAE, Z 864.10, Tchécoslovaquie 2601. New statute in *Zahraniční Politika*, 1930, II, 1003–1004.

61. See the main studies: Kiszling, *Kleinen Entente*, and Batowski, "Sojusze."

62. See note, "La Petite Entente," 9 Dec. 1930, and Seguin to Briand, 29 July 1930, MAE, Z 864.10, Tchécoslovaquie 2601; briefing, 24 July, KV, CPP; Karszo-Siedlewski and Kobylański reports, 17 July, 11 Aug 1930, AAN, MSZ, Z.4, w.2, t.6 (old classification); also Gajanová, *ČSR*, 275, and Leczyk, *Polityka*, 265–66.

63. See article, 27 July 1930 in Hodža, *Články*, 4:310–12; also his *Federation*, 103–104; and articles in *Národný Hospodar* (cited in *Gazeta Warszawska*, 3 June) and *Národnie Noviny*, 25 July 1930.

which Beneš did not expect to be a success. Moreover, a Polish-led agrarian bloc might undermine the Little Entente and be viewed askance by Poland's great neighbors.[64] Indeed, Moscow regarded the forthcoming conference as a "purely political act" directed against Russia and Germany. The Auswärtiges Amt also stressed Polish political motivation stemming from anxieties about the evacuation of the Rhineland and fears that a southeastern bloc could reach an understanding with the West, leaving Poland isolated.[65]

The Warsaw conference held on 28–31 August postulated the creation of a bloc with annual conferences and a standing committee of economic research. It demanded the regulation of surpluses, the elimination of internal competition, custom tariff preferences within the bloc and in dealing with outside countries, and credits for agriculture.[66] Although Czechoslovakia did participate (together with its Little Entente allies), as did Hungary, Bulgaria, Latvia, and Estonia, and attended the subsequent conference in Bucharest, Prague's predictions that there would be no real sequel proved justified.[67] Insofar as the agrarian bloc initiative represented an attempt to wrench the leadership in the region from Czechoslovakia, Poland was not successful.

The French attitude toward the agrarian bloc activities was ambivalent. Paris strongly opposed a preferential regime that could interfere with France's commercial policies and raise havoc with the entire system of most-favored-nation clause. Nor were the French prepared to absorb East Central European grain surpluses given the concern for their own farmers and arrangements with the empire and overseas producers. But they could not remain completely indifferent to the plight of their allies and friends in the east, especially as they had been engaged in financial operations in East Central Europe, bolstering the currencies of Romania and Yugoslavia.[68] Moreover, the French were urging Prague and Warsaw once again to engage in military cooperation.

Between June and August the commander of the École Supérieure de Guerre, General Gaston Dufour, the former Czechoslovak chief of staff, General Mittelhauser, and Marshal Franchet d'Esperey visited Czechoslovakia. The last two held talks with the leading figures in the country.[69]

---

64. See 17, 24 July 1930 briefings, KV, CPP; Tomaszewski, "Miejsce," 183; Sládek and Tomaszewski, "Próby w latach trzydziestych," 380.

65. See ADAP, B, xv; 426–27, 440–41.

66. See Starzewski, "Zarys dziejów," 3:65–66.

67. 4 Sept. 1930 briefing, KV, CPP.

68. Montagu Norman "inweighed in forcible terms against the financial activities of France in Central and Eastern Europe," DBFP, 1a, VII:507.

69. See reports of generals Dufour and Mittelhauser, 15, 30 July 1930, SHA, EMA/2,

Speaking to the Polish chargé d'affaires, the marshal insisted on the need of military cooperation between Warsaw and Prague. Jan Karszo-Siedlewski replied that such an idea would encounter the opposition of the Czechoslovak government, which feared to be drawn into a conflict with the USSR and was pursuing an ambiguous line vis-à-vis Berlin. Undeterred Franchet d'Esperey asked the chargé to deliver his personal message to Colonel Beck, then minister without portfolio in the Piłsudski cabinet, to the effect that a military convention between Poland and Czechoslovakia was "most desirable." Charles-Roux, informed of the conversation, concurred with the Polish diplomat that if France was really serious, the French general staff would have to act as an intermediary. Laroche recalled that he had been already recommending it for some time.[70]

The chances of Prague being willing to submit to France's military guidance and pressure were slim. Addison may have exaggerated only a little when he wrote that "in theory France is still the patron saint, and homage is duly paid at her shrine on state occasions"; under the surface, however, the Franco-Czechoslovak friendship was showing "some signs of wear and tear." Certain officers of the French military mission regarded the Czechoslovak army as not a worthy fighting force. The Czechs, in their turn, showed signs of irritation "at the incessant advertisement of French protection, with its implication of superiority." They felt that Czechoslovakia was "only a pawn in the French game, which the player will sacrifice without hesitation to gain a move."[71]

Basic Czechoslovak-Polish differences with regard to Germany and Russia remained unchanged. The Poles conveyed their displeasure over the signing of a treaty of friendship and arbitration between Czechoslovakia and Lithuania on 3 March 1930, and Charles-Roux did not altogether blame them.[72] Laroche found Prague's concern with Eastern Galicia, perceived as a bridge to Russia, deplorable. French interest required that Czechoslovakia be oriented "toward the Western problems." It would be "a fatal blow to our policy of equilibrium and perhaps even a fatal blow to Central European civilization to see a triumph of the panslav idea which

Tchécoslovaquie 10. Grzybowski saw in Franchet d'Esperey's visit an indication of an increasing tendency on the part of Czechoslovak political circles to stress close cooperation with France. See 30 June 1930 report, AAN, MSZ 5422.

70. See report of Karszo-Siedlewski, 1 Sept. 1930, AAN, MSZ 5422; also Charles-Roux and Laroche to Briand, 7 and 29 Sept. 1930, MAE, Z 864.5, Tchécoslovaquie 2856 and Z 864.10, Tchécoslovaquie 2604. See also Bułhak, "Z Dziejów 1927–1936," 107.

71. Annual report 1930: Czechoslovakia, FO 371 15179 C 2362/1203/12. For Franco-Czechoslovak trade relations, see Lubaczewski's comments, 12 Oct. 1930, AAN, MSZ 5491.

72. Charles-Roux to Briand, 10 Mar. 1930, MAE, Z 864.1, Tchécoslovaquie 2568.

would tie Czechoslovakia . . . to Russia." It was essential for France that Eastern Galicia serve as "a barrier" between Prague and Moscow.[73]

Fundamental differences were accompanied by minor irritants. The question of the Polish minority in Teschen began to figure more frequently in the press, and in 1930 polemics acquired a more stringent tone. In April, Polish national minority parties voiced their grievances mainly over educational and civic matters at a meeting in Karvina. But they also asserted, through deputy Karol Junga, that only unhinged minds could imagine the existence of a Polish threat to the Czechoslovak Republic. The role of the Polish minority, *Prawo Ludu* asserted, was that of "a bridge of friendship between the two nations." While at this stage the contacts between the Polish minority and the consulate in Moravská Ostrava grew more intimate, the former on occasion asked the latter not to aggrevate local friction.[74] The Poles manifested their loyalty to the Republic during Masaryk's visit to the region in July, and even after the population census of December introduced the category of "Silesian-Czechoslovaks" (which resulted in some pressure on Poles to register as such) the minority blamed mainly the provincial administration for abuses.[75] For all the antagonism, typical for a border region and fed by nationalist feelings, the situation in Teschen was far from explosive. The Polish government, fully conscious of the use made by Germany of its national minority issues for revisionist propaganda, was not prepared to follow the example of Berlin. Nor was Warsaw interested in intensifying transient economic friction, for the existing relationship had produced a favorable trade balance to Poland and assured transit facilities for exports destined for Austria, Hungary, or the Middle East.[76] As before the real cause of the Czechoslovak-Polish inability to close ranks was international, with Soviet Russia and Germany occupying the center of the stage.

Revisionism Rampant

In the summer and autumn of 1930, Europe watched anxiously the course of events in Germany. The electoral campaign, the first without the "shadow of the Rhineland" occupation, brought into the open "all that

73. Laroche to Briand, 7 Aug. 1930, MAE, Z 864.1, Tchécoslovaquie 2568. For Beneš's argument that his Slav policy was strictly subordinated to a Czech policy, and that he approached the Ukrainian question with an open mind, his main concern being good Soviet-Polish relations, for the "only great danger for peace was Germany," see Grzybowski to Zaleski, 11 Feb. 1931, AAN, Amb. Berlin, 51.

74. See Consul R. Ripa to envoy, 12 May 1930, AAN, MSZ, Z.4, w.2, t.6 (old classification)

75. Chrobot's interview in *Duch Czasu*, 30 Mar. 1931; compare the more belligerent Junga in *Nasz Kraj*, 27 Feb. 1931.

76. See southern division of foreign ministry note, 3 Sept. 1930, AAN, MSZ 5522.

Germany hopes for and intends to strive for in the field of external affairs," wrote the British ambassador. And he concluded: "The snowball of 'revision' continues to roll down the electoral slopes, and, as it rolls, it is gathering speed and size."[77] Not to be outdone, a member of the Brüning cabinet, Gottfried Treviranus, called in a fiery address on 10 August for the mobilization of the German nation to do something about the "open wound in Germany's eastern flank." Condemning the "unjust boundaries," he exclaimed, "Away with all idle talk of a catastrophe! What we need is the courage to banish our distress!"[78]

The Poles responded by a wave of demonstration and a public subscription for the building of a submarine, to be called "The Answer to Treviranus." Zaleski alerted Paris, and was assured that France was unanimous with Poland in the condemnation of Treviranus and of the revisionist campaign. Briand was particularly upset by the implication in the speech that Germany pursued peaceful revision because it was not strong enough to use other means. He called this *un peu fort*, and felt that "some china had been broken." What disturbed him greatly was the adverse effect it would have on his foreign policy.[79] *L'Echo de Paris, L'Intransigeant*, and even *Le Temps* sharply upbraided Treviranus; Poincaré and Barthou took a strong public stand against revisionism.[80] The deputy political director at the Quai d'Orsay, André Lefebvre de Laboulaye, repeated the by now familiar formula to the German chargé d'affaires: all sensible men agreed that the drawing of Germany's eastern borders was "not very happy," but one could not expect the Poles to give up the "corridor," which was mainly inhabited by them. As for Danzig, it was under the League of Nations protection.[81]

The German diplomats were conscious of the fact that the speech was a serious tactical mistake. The envoy in Warsaw even argued that a policy of tension with Poland was counterproductive. At best it led to such suggestions as d'Ormesson's advice to Poland to improve communications across the "corridor" and make small corrections along the Vistula; at worst it made people like Reginald Leeper of the Foreign Office predict that Germany would end up by losing East Prussia as well.[82] Brüning, Curtius, and Bülow favored a policy of gradual revisionism, utilizing the Rus-

77. Rumbold to Henderson, 29 Aug. 1930, DBFP, II, 1:502.

78. Cited in Erich Eyck, *A History of the Weimer Republic* (New York, 1970), 2:276.

79. See Mühlstein to Zaleski, 18, 21 Aug. 1930, SI, Amb. Londyn, A.12.52/11. Also ADAP, B, xv:473, 476–77, 442–45, 506–508; DBFP, II, 1:491–93.

80. Poincaré Meuse speech, in *L'Illustration*; Barthou in *Annales*.

81. See ADAP, B, xv:473, 476–77. Still, *Le Temps*' remark that German hopes for revision were in the nature of things was seen in Warsaw as a tacit acceptance of revisionism. See MS, OSS, Wysocki, II, 165–66.

82. Rauscher to Bülow, 13 Aug. 1930, ADAP, B, xv:448–51.

sian and Lithuanian connections but always remembering that France held the key. It would not do to engage in an excessive revisionist campaign that would be weakening Briand's position.[83] At first glance this approach looked like a continuation of Stresemann's policy, but the style and methods were very different.

The Treviranus speech caused apprehension in Czechoslovakia, and the leading papers—*Národní Politika, Lidové Listy, Československá Republika,* and *Venkov*—stressed that a revisionist threat to Poland could not be indifferent to the Czechs and Slovaks. Beneš's *České Slovo* and the official *Prager Presse* printed Sauerwein's article that spoke of Hitler's shadow cast over Germany, a menace to the country and the outside world.[84] The Slovak *Národnie Noviny* referred to secret German-Soviet military cooperation, and called for an expression of Czechoslovak friendship to Poland.

In early September, the Polish minister of industry and commerce, Eugeniusz Kwiatkowski, came to visit the Prague fair. The trip may have been made in response to the earlier-mentioned appeal by Franchet d'Esperey to the Poles, for Kwiatkowski came on Piłsudski's express orders to sound out the Czechoslovak leaders. In talking to Kwiatkowski, Masaryk deemed an effective collaboration with Poland difficult as long as Polish policy toward Russia remained unchanged. The existence of a German-Soviet front against Poland made Prague most reluctant to engage in serious conversations.[85] During Kwiatkowski's visit the Brześć affair took place, and although it did not directly affect the conversations, the arbitrary arrest of opposition deputies deepened Czech distrust of and antagonism toward the Piłsudski regime.[86]

The astounding success of the National Socialist German Workers Party (NSDAP) in mid-September elections in Germany took Beneš by surprise. Electoral gains by communists raised the specter of extremist groups dominating German politics and led to substantial withdrawals of foreign capital, thus aggravating the financial situation of the country. The conclusion drawn by the Czechoslovak foreign minister was that it made all the difference whether a conflict with Germany occurred in three or in twenty

---

83. See ministerial conference, 20 Aug. 1930, ADAP, B, xv:470–72.

84. See Karszo-Siedlewski report, 18 Aug. 1930, AAN, Amb. Berlin, 51.

85. See accounts in Ciałowicz, *Polsko-francuski sojusz,* 167–68 and in Bułhak, "Z Dziejów 1927–1936," 108–109 (both based on information from Kwiatkowski); 11 Sept. 1930 briefing, KV, CPP; Charles-Roux to Briand, 20 Sept. 1930, MAE, Z 684.5, Tchécoslovaquie 2586.

86. *Přítomnost* sharply criticized Polish politics on 5 Nov.; Beneš voiced his disapproval privately, see MS, BJ, Kozicki, III, part VII, 95. The socialist speaker of the senate, František Soukup, addressed an open letter to Kwiatkowski pointing out that the Brześć affair had damaged the Polish image in Czechoslovakia and demanding an end of reprisals. See Annual Report 1930 Czechoslovakia, FO 371 15179 C 2362/1203/12.

years' time, hence it was imperative to delay it. Publicly, Beneš denied the possibility of a Franco-German war. Were it to take place, the Bolsheviks would be the real victors, and the Germans knew it.[87] Privately, he agreed with a British view that a German aggression "need not be feared for the next ten years."[88] The Polish "corridor" and Hungary appeared to Masaryk to be the two danger spots in Europe, and the president once more aired his critical opinions about the "corridor," placing the Czechoslovak government in an awkward position.[89] Asked to comment, Krofta "shrugged his shoulders, looked even more miserable than usual, and said that he hoped that the President's utterances would not be taken seriously."[90] Naturally, the opposition vigorously exploited the incident. In an open letter to "Brother Poles," the extreme rightist "three musketeers," Gajda, Stříbrný, and Karel Pergler, distanced themselves from Masaryk and asserted that "the Polish sea is a Slav and therefore a Czech sea."[91] In late September, Czech nationalists instigated anti-German riots in Prague that caused embarrassment to Beneš, then attending a session of the League. On the other side of the political spectrum, the all-out pacifists glorified in "cowardice," forcing the president to intervene and assert that certain values, the fatherland included, had to be defended with arms.[92]

Referring to the brutal nationalism that had penetrated Czechoslovakia, Krofta remarked that if the Czechs were foolhardy, France would abandon them. "Our security lies in a Franco-German modus vivendi," which Czechoslovakia dare not obstruct. As for Poland, he opined that France would not expose itself. "We must keep this in mind," he said. "Our people incorrectly assume that France wants us to carry an anti-German pol-

87. See 18, 30 Sept. 1930 briefings, KV, CPP.

88. See DDB, II, 631.

89. Masaryk's remarks made in a conversation with Polson Newman appeared in the *London General Press*, 30 Oct. and were reprinted among others in *Neue Freie Presse* and *Prager Tageblatt*. See briefing, 2 Oct. KV, CPP; and Ratshesky to Secretary of State, 30 Sept., 13 Oct., 1930, SDNA, 760F.6415/23 and 24. Zaleski's attempts to calm down public opinion (see *Le Messager Polonais*, 4 Oct.) were acknowledged by *Československá Republika*. See also Zaleski interview in *České Slovo*, 26 Nov. 1930.

90. Addison to Henderson, 15 Oct. 1930, FO 371 14329 C 7819; Charles-Roux and Laroche reports, 30 Sept., 1, 2 Oct., MAE Z 864.1, Tchécoslovaquie 2568; briefings 2 and 9 Oct., KV, CPP; also *Gazeta Warszawska*, 30 Sept., 3 Oct. 1930. Masaryk found it hard to abstain from expressing his opinions, for several months later he explained to the French envoy that while he had approved of the "corridor" at the time of the peace conference, he had been asking himself whether he had not been wrong. Would not a different border be better, because the existing one provided the Germans with amunition for their revindications? Charles-Roux to Briand, 13 Jan. 1931, MAE, Z 864.1, Tchécoslovaquie 2568.

91. See press cuttings in MZV-VA, 478.1242.

92. See articles in *Přitomnost*, 22 Sept., 10 Nov., 10, 17 Dec. 1930. Also references in Bláha, *Branná politika*, 183.

icy, and one directed against our German minority. This is an error. France wants us to neutralize and to control the minorities, so that we would, by [cultivating] good relations with Germany, alleviate [France's] own position."[93]

Although there was a note of pessimism in the assessments of Krofta and Beneš concerning the international situation, the foreign minister tried to appear his optimistic self again.[94] Charles-Roux felt that Beneš played with words when he asserted that Czechoslovakia had no international disputes; surely the Hungarian issue was unresolved and the Anschluss remained a threat. There was German nationalism, the German-Polish controversy, German-Soviet military collusion, and a strain in Franco-German relations. Surely all this affected Prague. The discord between Paris and Rome was hardly a matter of indifference for the Little Entente. The envoy wondered how the sentiment of solidarity with France—on which Beneš insisted—would be translated into practice "if a grave tension or conflagration occurred in which we would find ourselves implicated?"[95] Beneš's characterization of the Czechoslovak-Polish relationship as "the most amicable in the world" elicited Charles-Roux's wry comment: "As the department knows, this is the reply that M. Beneš invariably gives when his attention is drawn to the Polish-Czechoslovak relations."[96] Bemoaning the fact that the two countries that were entitled "to expect help from us" were unable to arrive at a cooperation "that would serve them as a supplementary safeguard," the envoy repeated the advice, by now given ad nauseam, to recommence efforts in Warsaw and Prague "to achieve a better entente between the two states."[97]

French promptings may have accounted for the overtures made in late 1930 to the Poles by the deputy chief of staff General Alois Eliáš and the chief of the second bureau, General Vladimír Chalupa. Their suggestion of a meeting between General Syrový and his Polish counterpart General Tadeusz Piskor met with skepticism on the part of the Poles.[98] The Czechoslovak officers had to admit that the army and the government did not see eye to eye on the question of cooperation with Poland, Beneš being still

93. See briefings, 30 Sept., 9 Oct., 13, 27 Nov. 1930, KV, CPP.

94. See speech in Beneš, *Boj o mír*, 529–50. The minister sounded fairly optimistic when talking to Maynot of the Agence Havas. See Charles-Roux to Briand, 15 Dec. 1930, MAE, Z 864.1, Tchécoslovaquie 2568.

95. Charles-Roux to Briand, 24 Oct 1930, MAE, Z 864.1, Tchécoslovaquie 2568.

96. Charles-Roux to Briand, 18 Oct. 1930, MAE, Z 864.1, Tchécoslovaquie 2568. On Beneš's evading a question about cooperation with Poland, see Charles-Roux to Briand, 24 Oct.; *Pražský Večerník*, 28 Oct., and 23 Oct. 1930 briefing, KV, CPP.

97. Charles-Roux to Briand, 19 Oct. 1930, MAE, Z 864.5, Tehécoslovaquie 2586

98. See Bułhak, "Z Dziejów 1927–1936," 109–10.

unwilling to go beyond a formal neutraliation of the common border. In the event of a Polish-German conflict, Czechoslovakia would stay neutral, except when France became a participant.[99]

The electoral success of the Nazis produced a profound impression in Poland. Circles around Piłsudski thought, however, that this development might not be altogether disadvantageous. The rapid German evolution from Stresemann to Hitler, wrote *Gazeta Polska*, was bound to disappoint those who had placed their hopes on Locarno and The Hague. The vastness of Hitler's demands might mean that he was bent on "a *Drang nach Westen* rather than a *Drang nach Osten*."[100] True to his predilection for super-secret, almost conspiratorial diplomacy, Piłsudski dispatched a special emissary to the NSDAP leader. The marshal may have been aware that the Nazis, while vociferous against Poland, had a certain respect for him as a strong man.[101] The emissary spoke to the chief of staff of the S. A., Otto Wagener, and then to Hitler himself. Piłsudski's overture was allegedly meant to convey to the Nazi leader the idea that the marshal would be prepared to seek, together with Hitler—once he came to power—a mutually satisfactory arrangement to avoid a conflict. Impressed by the fact that the virtual head of a foreign state approached him on such a basic matter of foreign policy, Hitler told Wagener that he was determined to respond to this initiative.[102]

Piłsudski's personal diplomacy in no way interfered with the main Polish thrust—an acceleration of talks with Paris about the finalization of an armament loan. The Poles speculated how the Nazi victory would affect Briand and French public opinion. Was this a good moment to strengthen Franco-Polish ties? Would difficulties, likely to arise in connection with German opposition to the Young Plan, make it easier to speed up the financial transaction? The Polish minister of finance suggested the use of the

---

99. Charles-Roux to Briand, 27 Jan. 1931, MAE, Z 864.5, Tchécoslovaquie 2586.

100. Cited in Krasuski, *Stosunki 1926–1932*, 301.

101. See Rumbold to Henderson, 17 Dec., DBFP, 1a, VII:261.

102. The episode is mentioned in Ciałowicz, *Polsko-francuski sojusz*, 168 (also in *Sprawozdania z komisji posiedzeń Komisji Oddziału PAN w Krakowie*, styczeń-luty 1961). English summary of Wagener's note in Henry A. Turner, *Hitler: Memoirs of a Confidant* (New Haven, 1985), 49–50. The full text, made available to me by Professor Turner, appeared in a Polish translation: Wandycz, "Próba nawiązania przez Marszałka Piłsudskiego kontaktu z Hitlerem jesienią 1930 r.," *Niepodległość*, XI (1978), 127–38. Polish historians suggest that the emissary may have been Witold Prądzyński, who had previously been engaged in commercial negotiations with the Germans. It is conceivable that the desire of Ernst Röhm, Wagener's successor, to visit Poland in Mar. 1921 and to speak with Piłsudski was somehow connected with the earlier initiative. The Polish foreign ministry ignored the overture. See Schimitzek, *Drogi*, 208.

argument that to alleviate the economic crisis it was essential to assist not only Germany but also Poland, which was likewise afflicted.[103]

Zaleski was pleased to learn that Briand now seriously considered placing a Polish loan on the French market, the first of such loans to be extended to East Central European states.[104] Tardieu favored a comprehensive program of credits, which in the words of Briand would "assist in a particularly effective way our external activity," and "stabilize in the most direct manner the European economy, consolidating the state of affairs created by the treaties." The foreign minister expressly referred to aid to Romania, to support its agriculture, and to Poland, to help with the Silesia-Gdynia railroad.[105] In October, the minister of commerce, Pierre-Etienne Flandin, went on a tour of Danubian and Balkan capitals with proposals of financial assistance for their grain exports. Here was another example of financial diplomacy that France could practice in the early stages of the great depression.[106]

Concrete Franco-Polish financial negotiations, however, made little progress. The Poles were partly to blame, for they confused the issue by giving priority to the railroad project over the armament loan. It proved impossible to float a loan in view of parliamentary difficulties, and a French governmental loan was also likely to meet with opposition.[107] Subsequently, Zaleski blamed Piłsudski for missing a favorable moment out of fear that the credits would place Poland in a state of increased dependence on France.[108] While the marshal's dislike of foreign loans was well known,[109] the basic difficulties existed on the French side. How could Briand affirm that the Rhineland evacuation was a step toward pacification of Europe and simultaneously justify armament credits?[110] We have noted this predicament already in an earlier passage.

Increased tension between Berlin and Warsaw made the French general staff reflect again on the danger France would face if she wanted to aid Poland before a verdict of the League of Nations. This consideration would have "to influence the decisions of the government when it would have to interpret and execute the engagements contracted vis-à-vis Po-

---

103. See note, 6 Oct. AAN, MSZ 3762, and Matuszewski to foreign ministry, 14 Oct. 1930, SI, MSZ, A.11/6.

104. Zaleski's letter to the foreign ministry, 17 Sept. 1930, SI, MSZ, A.11/6.

105. Briand to Tardieu, 22 Oct. 1930, MAE, Y 251:289–91.

106. See Kaiser, *Economic Diplomacy*, 20–21, and Flandin, *Politique*, 97–98.

107. Mrozowski to the cabinet, 16 Dec. 1930, SI, MSZ, A.11/6. Compare Chłapowski telegram, 2 Mar. 1931, HIA. Amb. Paryż, box 4.

108. See Wandycz, *Zaleski*, 82.

109. Numerous statements to that effect appear in AAN, Akta Świtalskiego, 70.

110. See Chłapowski retrospective report, 23 Dec. 1930, SI, MSZ, A.11/6.

land."[111] In turn, General Denain, in a note handed personally to the minister of war, André Maginot, gave serious thought to this problem.[112]

Denain wrote that Warsaw, had "sulked" for a time because of what it regarded as unfulfilled promises made during the previous talks between military leaders. But Poland, worried by the possibility of a German attack in collusion with the USSR, was turning again to France. The Poles, the general wrote, would fight and perish before giving in, but they wished to have their doubts dispelled whether France would make war for the "corridor." If it would not, they would be obliged to come to some kind of a settlement with one of their mighty neighbors, for a country with forty-two infantry divisions could hardly sustain a two-front war. Denain admitted to a certain contradiction between Poland's determination to fight and an alleged willingness to resolve its differences with Berlin (the more likely partner of the two). He perceived even a "trace of blackmail" vis-à-vis France, but it was dangerous to disillusion the Poles if one wanted to preserve "our diplomatic and military influence in Central Europe." Warsaw wanted a revision of the convention but in the sense of having a new accord registered with the League and a secret agreement between the two general staffs authorized by the governments. The agreement would define the nature and modalities of reciprocal aid, ensure common staff work, and protect maritime routes by the French and Polish navies. This goal contrasted, as Denain recalled, with France's unaltered wish to harmonize the convention with the Covenant, Locarno, and the Kellogg–Briand Pact. Practical close cooperation between the two armies was fine, but new obligations were not. There was a willingness to extend armament credits, but, the general reminded his superiors, Polish requests for 1.5 milliard francs had encountered opposition in Paris. It would be "neither honorable nor adroit to maintain obligations that we should not keep," Denain wrote; however, something tangible had to be done to "prove to the Poles that our friendship is real." Armament credits were a pledge of good faith, and indeed in November, Paris consented to reactivate the fourth installment of the old loan. The final agreement, signed on 18 February 1931, provided for deliveries of material for Polish artillery, air force, and navy totalling 113 million francs.[113]

In late 1930 and early 1931 the French general staff prepared studies on

111. Note au sujet de l'éventualité d'un conflit armé germano-polonais, Oct. 1930, submitted to generals Weygand, Armengaud, and Gamelin, SHA, EMA/2, Pologne 21. Compare Castellan, *Le Réarmement*, 469–71; and Gauché, *Le 2e Bureau*, 114.

112. Note personelle et secrète, also resumé, both 4 Nov. 1930, SHA, EMA/2, Pologne 22 and 11.

113. On the reactivation of the loan, see Ciałowicz, *Polsko-francuski sojusz*, 163–64; Soutou, "L'Alliance," 340; Chłapowski reports, 8 Nov., 24 Dec. 1930, 21 Jan., 18 Feb 1931, HIA, Amb. Paryż, box 4.

military and political aspects of a limited German aggression in the "corridor" and Upper Silesia. Posing the question whether Germany had an interest in precipitating matters, the first note advanced arguments for and against it. On the one hand, considering the growing German influence over French public opinion, one could say that time worked for Germany. Taking into account the demographic trends in the "corridor," however, the opposite was true. Germany would undoubtedly wish to end the demilitarization of the Rhineland and seek through the disarmament conference a reduction of French and Polish armaments. If Germany thought that it could act with impunity, and believed that "a German attack against Poland would not immediately provoke a French military reaction," Germany would carry out its revisionist objectives, which "it was determined to fulfill one way or another."[114] The second study concerned the scenario of a European conflict started against Poland either by Germany alone or in cooperation with the USSR. Berlin would try to make the war appear to be a Polish provocation and wage it first with irregular Stahlhelm units. The conflict would then spread, with Romania, Hungary, the Little Entente, Bulgaria, and Italy becoming involved. In the final phase, a German offensive against Poland and an Italian attack on Yugoslavia would trigger a general mobilization in France. In conclusion, the authors of the study stressed that Germany must not be allowed to augment its effectives or shorten the duration of military service. Otherwise, in five years' time its armed forces would be stronger than they had been in 1914.[115]

While the army was examining different hypotheses of a future war, the politicians kept arguing about the direction of French foreign policy. The Left blamed French nationalism for the political evolution in Germany, although Herriot himself rejected this position.[116] The radical socialist congress, held in Grenoble in early October, operating on the assumption that the party would play a key role in a new cabinet, did not espouse general disarmament (advocated by Cot) but strongly approved a concili-

114. Note au sujet de l'éventualité d'un conflit germano-polonais (2eme partie), 5 Nov. 1930, SHA, EMA/2, Pologne 21.

115. Hypothèse sur la forme et le development d'un conflit européen, 26 Feb. 1931, SHA, EMA/2, Pologne 21. The note was a "tableau d'ensemble" to be followed by a more detailed study. According to French figures, the respective armed effectives were: Poland—286,000 (1.5 million after mobilization to be completed in 30 days) with 60 old tanks and 300 planes; Czechoslovakia—500,000 (1.5 million after mobilization in 20 to 30 days) with 23 tanks and 656 planes. German forces when mobilized (after 6 months) would comprise 2 million men with some 50 planes adapted to war usage but no tanks. See "Resources de guerre," 20 Feb. 1931, SHA, EMA/2, Pologne 21.

116. Soulié, *Herriot*, 329.

atory policy toward Germany.[117] *La République* went farther on 4 November, with a front-page article "Contre la guerre!" Edouard Daladier argued that when the alliance treaty with Poland expired in two years' time [?][118] one should think twice before renewing French promises "to make war for the Polish corridor." Léon Blum advocated in *Le Populaire* a revision of the "corridor" while some socialists and radicals thought that the Poles must be advised to liquidate the causes of German complaints.[119] The maverick publicist Gustave Hervé appealed to Hitler, via Rechberg, for a Franco-German alliance based on satisfaction of German demands in the Saar, colonies, and Austria and involving French intervention in Warsaw to induce the Poles to cede the "corridor." Somewhat ironically the *Völkischer Beobachter* asked against whom was the alliance to be directed.[120]

Although Curtius seemed bent on departing from the Stresemann line, Briand's policy of rapprochement with Germany and of support for Brüning remained valid even if it became more vulnerable to criticism.[121] The *Revue des Deux Mondes* wrote on 15 October that the Germans who had "never fixed the limits of their revindications in the east" seemed to hope that France had forgotten Sadova and would one day "become anemic and mad enough not to understand that a Polish defeat would be a prelude to her own" collapse. The article ended with "Quo vadis Germania?" On 6 November Franklin-Bouillon delivered one of his most eloquent attacks on German eastern revisionism. Recalling his predictions concerning the evacuation of the Rhineland as well as his past pleas, he asked for a public statement that France would never permit a revision of frontiers established by Versailles. Once concessions started, the whole edifice would collapse, and how "would we then dare to look in the eyes of our admirable allies, particularly the Poles?" The frontier of Poland "is the frontier of France" he exclaimed.[122] Briand responded feebly by reiterating old arguments about the merits of Locarno and by invoking his belief in a Euro-

---

117. See Bonnefous, *Histoire*, 5:44; compare *Gazeta Warszawska*, 11, 12, 15 Oct. 1930.

118. A reference to an apocryphal text of a Franco-Polish treaty allegedly signed by Foch and Sikorski in 1922 providing for a ten-year alliance. The "text" was published by *Revue Parlementaire* and reprinted by *Zahraniční Politika*, (1930) 2:1248–49.

119. Particularly Cot, Grumbach, and Emile Borel. See 5 Nov. 1930 session, CAE/Ch.

120. See comments in *Gazeta Warszawska*, 25, 26 Oct. 1930; briefing 30 Sept. 1930 KV, CPP.

121. Curtius on conversation with Briand, and Hoesch telegram, Nov. 22; ADAP, B, XV:533–37; XVI:183–85. Also Mühlstein and Chłapowski to Zaleski, 13 Oct., 6 Dec. 1930, AAN, Amb. Berlin, 75.

122. See 6 Nov. 1930 session, J.O. Chambre, 3271–78.

pean union. Tardieu seconded him by emphasizing the unanimity of views in the cabinet.[123] For all its applause for Franklin-Bouillon, the chamber supported the government; the Right because it feared the fall of the cabinet, the Left because it believed in Briand. Besides, as the British ambassador opined, at least fifty percent of Frenchmen were afraid to be dragged into a war over Poland; the only bad thing, Sir William Tyrrell added, was that the Germans were well aware of it.[124]

In early February 1931, the new cabinet of Pierre Laval again excluded the radicals. The only important change in France occurred in the high command where Weygand replaced Pétain as vice-president of the Conseil Superieur de Guerre (CSG), that is, as commander-in-chief designate. General Maurice Gamelin became chief of the general staff. Laval declared himself a "disciple and an unconditional supporter of Briand" (who remained foreign minister), determined to remove all Franco-German friction. If there was a certain stiffening of the government's position under the impact of nationalist forces, this was with regard to disarmament. After contrasting German efforts with French weakness, the rapporteur of the military budget declared that "the military value of a country, believe me, is still its best guarantee of peace."[125] Franklin-Bouillon spoke of a policy "vitiated by illusion which today results in deception and tomorrow in danger." The Left responded to his warnings with cries of "down with war." Briand was still able to sway the opinion of the chamber, particularly with regard to French–East European policy. Once again, he disingenuously assured the deputies that the ties with France's allies "had never been so close, had never been so solid."[126]

"A strange campaign in favor of a general revision of treaties," one deputy remarked, was undermining Europe.[127] A new series of Hervé's articles in *La Victoire* (12, 27 February; 2, 8, 24, 27 March 1931) stressed that as brave as the Poles and the Czechs might be, they could not satisfy France's need for allies among the big powers. Moreover, "nonrevision means war," Hervé asserted. Such opinions, even if they corresponded to an important trend on the Right, were not universally held; still, both the Germans and the British believed that the majority of Frenchmen would welcome a settlement in the east based on some concessions on the part of Warsaw. Such prominent Catholics as François-Marsal and d'Ormesson,

123. See summary in Bonnefous, *Histoire*, 5:47.

124. Gaiffier to Hymans, 12 Nov. 1930, DDB, II, 624.

125. Bouilloux-Lafont at 24 Feb. 1931 session, J.O. Chambre, 1105–1107.

126. See 3 Mar. session, J.O. Chambre, 1518–21, 1523–31.

127. 24 Feb. 1931 session, J.O. Chambre 1105–1107.

and radicals like Cot, were involved with this issue "not without the knowledge" of the Quai d'Orsay.[128]

The Germans tried to gauge the real thinking of leading Frenchmen through informal channels. A former diplomat, Kurt von Lersner, used his stay in France, in December 1930, to converse with, among others, Tardieu, Painlevé, Loucheur, François-Poncet, d'Ormesson, Laboulaye, and Stanislas de Castellane. He reported that fear of war with Germany permeated many French circles, although some of his interlocutors argued that the German appetite was insatiable. Most Frenchmen, he felt, privately favored a return of the "corridor" to Germany as inevitable in any case. Perhaps Poland could be compensated with Memel (Laboulaye) or a corridor through the "corridor" could be established (Painlevé)? Tardieu wondered about the possibility of a Franco-German-British accord leaving all the "ticklish questions" in abeyance for a five-year period.[129] Flandin, approached by Franz von Papen, the future chancellor who came to Paris in early 1931, seemed to favor a Franco-German-Polish entente fully defensive in character and including a common guarantee of Polish eastern borders. Papen concluded that while the French were thinking hard how to establish closer cooperation with Germany, they also strove "with all their means" to maintain their position in East Central Europe.[130] Critical of the German methods of pursuing revisionist objectives, Briand told Ambassador von Hoesch that had the Germans acted with prudence and moderation, they could have gained a decisive influence in the Upper Silesian industry and obtained transit facilities through the "corridor."[131]

How did the Poles see the situation? According to Lipski, developments in Germany had a "sobering effect" on the Western powers, and enhanced Poland's standing as a factor of peace between Russia and Germany. He thought that the West was seeking to strengthen "reasonable elements" in Berlin, and that Warsaw should do the same not to be out of step.[132] Zaleski publicly reaffirmed that Polish policy met with an increasing understanding in France, while Radziwiłł repeated the cliché that the Poles

128. See Nichols memorandum, 7 Jan., and Tyrrell to Vansittart, 17 Feb. 1931, FO 371 15221 C 173 (and also Hm 04150); compare ADAP, XVII:8–10.

129. ADAP, B, XVI:240–44. *Le Temps* rejected on 17 Feb. 1931 the idea of exchanging the "corridor" for Lithuania and demanded that this be made plain to Berlin. For Weygand's interest in some arrangement in the "corridor," see his penciled annotation on "Complement à l'étude sur le corridor polonais," prepared by Capt. Vialet, 6 Dec. 1930, SHE, EMA/2, Pologne 21.

130. ADAP, B, XVI:562–67.

131. ADAP, B, XVII: 31–32. Hoesch heard that Briand had allegedly told Chłapowski "mais arrangez-vous donc avec les Allemands." Compare Kaiser, *Economic Diplomacy*, 101.

132. Lipski to Wysocki, 23 Feb. 1931, Jędrzejewicz, *Lipski*, 25–31.

must never take the positions that a Franco-German rapprochement could endanger either Poland or its alliance with Paris.[133] Laroche surmised that the Poles, while opposing revisionism, were showing a better appreciation of French foreign policy and of the need for a Franco-German dialogue.[134] This was hardly true for the Polish government, and certainly not true for the nationalist Right, which called for plain speaking and open voicing of grievances in Paris.[135]

Intimating that Piłsudski was not inspiring confidence in the West, deputy Stroński wittingly remarked that "Zaleski may be as clean shaven as can be, but he is being seen abroad with a droopy mustache and bushy eyebrows"[136]—an unmistakable allusion to the marshal's appearance. Indeed, Piłsudski, having consolidated his power at home, proceeded to establish a firmer grip over external policy. In December 1930, he appointed his trusted lieutenant Józef Beck deputy foreign minister, which heralded a tougher course.[137] Laroche was worried by this appointment, which appeared to be the first step toward the replacement of Zaleski. Ugly rumors about Beck, circulated by the socialist press, increased French apprehensions about the number-two man in the foreign ministry. These worries were also shared by Prague.[138]

Beneš regarded Franco-German cooperation as crucial and was ready to act as an intermediary. Sharing his thoughts with Wilhelm Regedanz, the confidant of the grey eminence of German politics, General Kurt von Schleicher. Beneš hoped that Germany would discard the Russian connection, and France would draw away from Italy. He insisted that the Franco-Czechoslovak alliance, originally directed against Germany, lost this char-

133. 23 Feb. 1931 speech in Zaleski, *Przemowy*, 2:209; Radziwiłł cited in Krasuski, *Stosunki 1926–1932*, 206.

134. Laroche to Briand, 25 Feb. 1931, MAE, Z 698.1, Pologne 2099.

135. See Piestrzyński cited in *Gazeta Warszawska*, 22 Feb. 1931; Seyda on 17 Mar. in the senate, see Sprawozdania stenograficzne senatu, xv, 37 and 41.

136. *Gazeta Warszawska*, 21 Feb. 1931. The Brześć affair, Ukrainian "pacifications" and tough methods used in the elections that brought the governing camp 55.6 percent of seats in the sejm and 67.6 in the senate provoked adverse reactions in the West. For Paul-Boncour's and Loquin's letters of protest to Piłsudski, see Chłapowski to Zaleski, 3 Mar. 1931, AAN, MSZ 3763.

137. At a conference on 18 Nov. attended by the president, Premier Sławek, and Beck, Piłsudski criticized Polish diplomacy for licking the boots of the West (his expression was even stronger) and neglecting eastern issues. See AAN, Akta Świtalskiego, 71.

138. Laroche regarded Beck as overly ambitious, sly, and unfamiliar with Western mentality. He would have prefered Wysocki as the future foreign minister. See reports, 17 Dec. 1930, 22 Jan., 17 Feb. 1931, MAE, Z 698.1, Pologne 2099. Also Laroche, *Pologne*, 102, 104. Rumors about Beck centered on his alleged complicity in the disappearance of Piłsudski's adversary, General Zagórski, and involvement in the Brześć affair. For Czechoslovak misgivings, see Charles-Roux to Briand, 12 Jan. 1931, MAE, Z 698.1, Pologne 2099.

acter after 1925. The Little Entente was not a French instrument. Czechoslovakia "had never relied on France financially, because as experience had shown, the French were always seeking to attach political conditions to financial transactions."[139] While Koch in Prague was disinclined to take Beneš's remarks at face value, Regedanz was impressed. Noting Beneš's anti-Polish remarks, he reported that the minister not only criticized Warsaw's policy toward Berlin, but also volunteered the information that in the last few years he had been approached by Poland, but had "rejected all these attempts at a rapprochement." Beneš advised Berlin against raising the "corridor" issue, for the matter would solve itself within a Franco-German system, Poland becoming obliged "to give in to German wishes."[140]

The year of the evacuation of the Rhineland had witnessed a high tide of German revisionism and extreme nationalist manifestations. French attempts to cope with the situation by classical Briandism—enmeshing Germany in international cooperation (the European union) and strengthening the French sphere of influence in East Central Europe—proved vain. Chances for advancing such policies by financial diplomacy were seized too timidly, and plans such as Loucheur's awakened suspicions of economic vested interests. Studying repeatedly the issue of military cooperation with Poland, the French general staff could do little more than urge the government to be vigilant, provide war material, and try to close the Czechoslovak-Polish gap. Polish diplomacy showed no outward signs of a change, but Piłsudski was getting ready to seize the initiative should an opportunity present itself. The continuity in Czechoslovak policy remained evident; competition over the agrarian bloc with Warsaw provided yet another example of the incompatibility between their foreign policies. The year 1930 was marking a transition in which new elements appeared but not markedly enough to change the previous pattern of international relations dominated by the Franco-German dialogue.

139. See Regedanz's reports on conversations with Beneš, 18, 20, 21 Jan., 21 Feb. 1931, AA, 4606/E 192 047–57/2375, and ADAP, B, XVI:421–24, 439–41, summarized in Campbell, *Confrontation*, 220–21.

140. The anti-Polish accents do not appear in the 12 Feb. and 5 Mar. 1931 briefings, KV, CPP. Beneš's strong anti-Hungarian feelings, however, emerge clearly from his letter to Loucheur, 3 Jan. 1931, HIA, Loucheur Papers, box 10.

Chapter Seven

Austro-German Union
and Financial Diplomacy

The Curtius–Schober Project

On 21 March 1931, Europe was stunned by the announcement of a projected customs union between Germany and Austria. Less than a week earlier Briand had told the chamber that the Anschluss was a remote contingency; Masaryk had no fears that it would happen soon.[1] The French government and parliament were shocked. President Doumergue denounced the project in a speech in Nice on 9 April; *Le Temps* described it as a threat to a policy of peace based on treaties. Some senators called it a "thunderbolt" out of a clear sky, and compared the customs union project to such prewar coups as Tangier and Agadir.[2] Members of the foreign affairs commission spoke of an Anschluss in disguise and a first step toward the revival of Mitteleuropa.[3] Franklin-Bouillon saw the move as a result of Briand's "constant blindness" in the face of realities, and a rightist deputy described it as a blow at the very foundations of French diplomacy.[4]

Briand barely concealed his annoyance in public. Privately, he sounded bitter. His conciliatory policy toward Germany, he told the American ambassador, had been a gamble but well worth the risk. Now, that was how Berlin repaid him. The customs union project "discredited him with the Chamber and wiped out overnight his political capital in the country."[5] Briand felt hurt and publicly humiliated. As a Foreign Office memo put it,

1. Briand, 3 Mar., J.O. Chambre, 1525: Masaryk's views reported by Charles-Roux, 12 Jan. 1931, MAE, Z 864.1, Tchécoslovaquie 2568.

2. Senators Berard, Lémery and Henessy, 28 Mar. 1931, J.O. Sénat, 682, 685–89.

3. 25 Mar., 1 Apr. 1931 sessions, CAE/Ch. Ybarnegaray and Soulier argued for the closing of ranks with Central European states.

4. Franklin-Bouillon and Scapini, 8 May 1931, J.O. Chambre, 2562, 2665, 2644–45.

5. See Walter Edge, *A Jerseyman's Journal* (Princeton, 1948), 194. Sir Walford Selby commented that "Germany had destroyed the reputation of the French statesman who had served her interests best." Note, 6 Dec. 1931, FO 800, 285. Compare Bonnefous, *Histoire*, 5:84–88; Chastenet, *Histoire*, 5:209–10; Scott, *Alliance*, 10. The affair contributed to Briand's failure in his bid for the presidency of the republic in May.

192

this "was the last straw as far as France and the succession States were concerned."[6]

What prompted Berlin to throw "this stone to ruffle the waters"?[7] The idea of a union between Germany and Austria was, of course, part of the German revisionist program, and it had been freely discussed between Berlin and Vienna in 1930. Curtius and Bülow showed particular interest and were willing to go ahead even in the teeth of French and Czechoslovak opposition. Serious reservations by Schubert and Hoesch were ignored; adding insult to injury, it was decided to "dress the matter up in a Pan-European cloak."[8]

The agreement in Vienna aimed at political objectives through economic means. The wish to assist the Austrian economy occupied a relatively minor place in German thinking, even though Berlin did regard the project as a countermove to the agrarian bloc.[9] Bülow viewed the customs union as "the beginnings of a development that would be likely to lead to a solution scarcely conceivable by other means, of vital political interests of the Reich." Once Austria was included in the German sphere, Czechoslovakia would be compelled to enter it also. Poland would be isolated, and "we should have her in a vise that could perhaps in the short or long run make her willing to consider further the idea of exchanging political concessions for tangible economic advantages." Bülow admitted that these were still "castles in the air," but he was devoting a good deal of thought to long-range ramifications and possibilities.[10]

If successful, the so-called Curtius–Schober project (Johannes Schober was Austrian chancellor) could indeed have revolutionized the entire situation in Central Europe. No wonder that Czechoslovak diplomacy alerted Paris just before the official announcement was made. France proceeded to approach London and Rome, which—together with Czechoslovakia—were signatories of the 1922 Geneva Protocol concerning Austrian independence. The British were averse to the union mainly because of the harm it would do to Briand's conciliatory Germany policy, but they had their own views on how to handle it. They also began to explore their own plan for stabilizing the Danubian situation.[11] Italy's attitude was one of reserve, so France assumed the leadership of the campaign enlisting Poland's support and exerting some pressure on Belgrade and Bucharest, then negoti-

---

6. Selby note, 6 Dec. 1931, FO 800, 285.

7. Briand's expression cited in DBFP, ii, ii:18.

8. See Stambrook, "Customs Union Project," 24–33; compare Krüger, *Aussenpolitik,* 531–33; also Bennett, *Germany,* 53.

9. See Bariéty, "Der Tardieu Plan," 368.

10. Bülow to Koch, 19 Apr. 1931, text in Stambrook, "Customs Union Projects" 43–44.

11. See especially Carmi, *La Grande Bretagne,* 171–78; Bennett, *Germany,* 56–62.

ating commercial agreements with Berlin. It also made overtures to Hungary.[12] The French and the Czechs pursued two objectives: a nullification of the customs union project, and the elaboration of an alternative plan that would assist Austria within the framework of a general Danubian economic reconstruction.

Beneš seemed sanguine about the chances of torpedoing the Curtius–Schober concept. On 26 March and 21 April, he termed the project legally, politically, and economically unacceptable. Far from being a step in the direction of a European union, it would lead to the emergence of two rival blocs on the continent. Economically, it would endanger Czechoslovakia, destroy the Little Entente, and adversely affect all of Europe. Politically, it would eventually undermine the independence of his country. But, not wishing to be purely negative, Beneš outlined an alternative scheme involving industrial and agrarian states; we shall discuss it a little later.[13]

The Czechoslovak foreign minister referred to Polish solidarity in opposing the customs union, and indeed Warsaw took this line, although not without initial hesitations. Krofta correctly surmised that the Poles did not immediately feel that the Curtius–Schober plan affected their interests, and they even thought that to deflect German attention from the "corridor" was not a bad thing. Prague would be driven much closer to Warsaw, Paris, and Rome. This "short-sighted policy," Krofta said, was quickly abandoned, and he praised the legation in Prague for realizing that in this affair Poland had to go together with Paris and Prague.[14] Zaleski's first reaction had been that Poland ought to reserve its judgment until a study of the implications of the union project. Learning, however, of Briand's decision to move forcibly and of his request that Poland manifest its displeasure, as well as of the adverse economic effects of the union on Polish economy, he decided to take a firm stand.[15] Beck was inspiring the Polish press to stress the economic consequences of the Curtius–Schober agree-

12. For the Hungarian angle, Ormos, "Problème," 30–32; Juhász, *Foreign Policy*, 98–100, For Bethlen's views, see Quai d'Orsay to Puaux, 16 Apr. 1931, MAE, P.A. Puaux 255(25).

13. See Beneš, *Boj o mír*, 544–619; for economic consequences, see Houštecký, "Plán rakousko-německé," 34–35 and Olšovský, *Světový obchod*, 240. Compare Gajanová, *ČSR*, 281; Stambrook, "Customs Union Project," 43; Grzybowski telegram, 23 Mar. 1931, HIA, Amb. Paryż, box 6; on Beneš's determination, DDF, I, VI:957. According to Krofta, Prague as an ally of France could retain its political independence, but it would lose it if drawn into a bloc with Germany and Austria. See 9 Apr. KV, CPP.

14. Briefing, 9 Apr. 1931, KV, CPP.

15. See Zaleski telegrams, 23, 24, 25 Mar., and Beck, 27 (or 28) Mar. 1931, HIA, Amb. Paryż, box 4. A joint study of the foreign ministry and the ministry of industry and trade concluded that the project would affect Polish exports to Austria and the Danubian region as well as cattle transit to Italy, and destroy the Polish-sponsored agrarian bloc plan.

ment while avoiding references to Anschluss and politics. Simultaneously he hoped that a more active French policy would consolidate international opinion, which was particularly necessary in view of some disorientation in Romania and Yugoslavia.[16]

Warsaw believed it advisable, for tactical reasons, that France and the Little Entente, especially Czechoslovakia, take the lead.[17] Deploring the union project, Beck intimated to foreign diplomats that Europe might be obliged to make the best of it, for it could be very difficult to force Berlin and Vienna to back down.[18] Zaleski struck a similar chord in his conversations with Briand and Berthelot. Perhaps he detected a wavering at the Quai d'Orsay and observed a certain French repugnance to take the initiative without the backing of a strong anti-Anschluss coalition.[19] The Polish foreign minister used this opportunity to develop the following argument. Should it prove impossible to oppose effectively the idea of an Anschluss, one ought to try to obtain additional guarantees for Poland against German revisionism. Talking to the British ambassador, he gave his argument a somewhat different twist: one of the conditions for the acceptance of the Austro-German union could be a German recognition of Polish frontiers. He mentioned a scheme that Brüning was allegedly prepared to consider—namely, an exchange of some German-inhabited districts in Upper Silesia for Polish-speaking areas in East Prussia; a return of Danzig to Germany with a free zone for Poland; and a railroad connection through the "corridor" placed under exclusive German management. Zaleski hinted that personally he would not oppose examining such a settlement; the Foreign Office, however, found it hard to believe that Brüning would accept this solution.[20]

Hence, Warsaw and Prague, while objecting, together with Paris, to the Curtius–Schober project, did not see eye to eye on the Austrian question. The differences grew as countermeasures were contemplated. Financial developments played into the hands of the French, and after the failure of the Creditanstalt bank Paris made it clear that any assistance to Austria would depend on its abandonment of the union project.[21] Placed in a hope-

16. Beck telegrams, 23, 26 Mar.; compare with those of Szembeck and Babiński, 23 and 24 Mar. 1931, HIA, Amb. Paryż, box 4. Also Bader's 23 Mar. telegram, box 6.

17. Unlike France and Czechoslovakia, Poland was not a signatory of the 1922 Protocol.

18. See Wiley to Secretary of State, 26 Mar. 1931, SDNA, 682.6331/65; compare Quai d'Orsay to Puaux, 28 Mar. 1931, MAE, P.A. Puaux 255(25).

19. See Chłapowski telegram, 10 Apr. 1931, HIA, Amb.Paryż, box 4.

20. See Riekhoff, *German-Polish Relations*, 230–31, 286. Also minutes FO 371 15222 Hm/B 862. Erskine never believed that a compromise was possible; see his note for Sargent, 19 Jan. 1931, FO 371 155221 C 560.

21. See Kaiser, *Economic Diplomacy*, 36–38; compare Gehl, *Austria*. Beneš pressed

less situation, Vienna agreed to have the Permanent Court of International Justice examine the legality of the union in view of Austria's other international treaties. During the Geneva debates Zaleski kept in the background, much to the annoyance of the Czechs, but he did so as a result of an agreement with France. Paris did not wish to antagonize Germany through a Polish involvement; as it was, tension between Berlin and Warsaw ran high over the minority issue.[22] The final verdict of the Permanent Court in September declared the Austro-German union contrary to the Geneva Protocol, but it proved easier to demolish the project than to propose a constructive plan for Austria and the Danubian area. Consideration of such attempts bring us back to Czechoslovak and French initiatives.

In Prague, one of the first reactions to the Curtius–Schober plan was public criticism of Beneš for allowing himself to be caught off guard, combined with renewed demands for rapprochement with Poland. The rightist *Národní Listy*, the agrarian *Venkov*, and the Slovak papers led the campaign, and the Polish rightist and populist press responded favorably.[23] Hodža revived his advocacy of a Central European organization based on Czechoslovak-Polish cooperation.[24] Gratified by the fact that the attempted Anschluss "had as its immediate result a rapprochement between Poland and Czechoslovakia," the French army renewed pressure for military cooperation between the two states.

In late April, General Faucher prepared, at the request of the general staff, a wide-ranging study on Czechoslovak war potential and strategy. He felt that Beneš's position had been dictated by domestic difficulties, a prudent policy toward Germany, the assumption that even without a military convention French support to Prague was assured, and fears of being pushed toward closer cooperation with Warsaw. Such a cooperation, Faucher admitted, "would have been undoubtedly the main [French] interest in a convention" [with Prague]. The German-Austrian project marked a certain change in Prague's attitude. "The necessity of common action appears to be only too evident" to the Czech military, but a lot of effort would be required to make both governments appreciate this fact. Regarding Czechoslovak policy toward the Germans, Warsaw was partly right when it reproached Prague for "wanting to be too clever and nursing illusions that could carry certain dangers to both countries." In case of a

---

Paris to make a repudiation of the union a condition for loans; see Houštecký, "Plán rakousko-německé," 43.

22. See Laroche, *Pologne*, 75; compare *Češi a Poláci*, 2:352, also Beneš's circular 21 May, and Krofta's briefing, 20 (?) May, 1931, KV, CPP.

23. See Houštecký, "Plán rakousko-německé," 37–38, Mar.-Apr. press cuttings, MZV-VA 478.1224; military mission reports, SHA, EMA/2, Tchécoslovaquie 8. Briefing 9 Apr. 1931,KV, CPP.

24. Lectures and interviews in Hodža, *Članky*, 4:384, 417–31.

conflict with Germany, Beneš wanted, through a neutral stance, to gain time to liquidate Hungary with the aid of the Little Entente partners. Only then would Czechoslovakia turn against Germany, its operations being greatly facilitated by a French offensive south of the Main River. Faucher agreed that in view of Hungary's strategic location it would be necessary to find a pretext for occupying that country. But he still regarded a joint Polish-Czechoslovak effort in Upper Silesia as a higher priority, unless this operation and the occupation of Hungary could be carried out simultaneously. Hence, a comparison of Czech and Polish operational plans was essential and had to be followed by common studies.

Nobody asked the Czechoslovak army to win the war on its own, Faucher wrote, although certain "civilian strategists" in Czechoslovakia assumed that this was the case. France wanted the Czech forces only to do their best. Hence, one had to build a bloc of the defenders of the treaties, and France "had a preponderant part to play" in it. One had to educate French public opinion and bring France and Czechoslovakia closer to one another. If, in case of real danger, "we are still in the present situation, we shall be in a pretty bad fix."[25]

The French army took the task seriously. It is likely that it encouraged the signing of the new military pact of the Little Entente on 11 May, which extended that of 1923. It was partly due to its efforts that for the first time the Polish and Czechoslovak intelligence chiefs (Colonels Tadeusz Pełczyński and Jaroslav Soukup) met in Warsaw to study the German situation.[26] But it was an uphill struggle, for in December the French were still complaining about the Czechoslovak army's obsession with the "strangling of Hungary" in the first phase of a future conflict. The Czechoslovak general staff was slow in realizing that the probability of a strife with Budapest was at present "almost nil." Worse, counting on a long period of peace with Germany, Prague refrained from any military activities that could appear to be directed against Berlin. No maneuvers had been held along the Germans borders since 1927. The question of a joint command of the Little Entente armies had been explored timidly, and if General Syrový showed a better understanding of the problems involved, he resigned himself "all too easily" to narrow staff work that no longer corresponded to the realities. True, Syrový realized, as did to a greater extent his deputy, General Lev Prchala, that Germany was the principal opponent and that military ties with Poland were essential. But he meekly accepted Masaryk's and Beneš's view that, as long as Piłsudski remained in control, even military collaboration was difficult. Seriously worried, General

25. Contribution à l'étude de potential de guerre de la Tchécoslovaquie, 25 Apr.; with Gen. Faucher to Gen. Guitry, 26 Apr. 1931, SHA, EMA/2, Tchécoslovaquie 2.

26. See annual report, 1931, SHA, EMA/2, Pologne 11. Also Bułhak, "Z Dziejów 1927–1936," 111–12.

Faucher felt that Syrový should be made to appreciate more the importance of the Polish factor. Perhaps he should be brought to Paris in order to discuss the entire military situation in Central Europe.[27]

Faucher's critical observations were borne out by Beneš's confidences to Lersner. Describing himself as a "faithful friend of France until death," the foreign minister also declared that he would not let himself "be goaded (*hetzen*) into a war by anyone." And he repeated: "I will never wage war against Germany except when drawn into a world war." Once again, he expressed his willingness to serve as an intermediary between Berlin and Paris.[28]

With respect to Beneš's thinking about East Central European political arrangements, the foreign minister's allusions to a possible customs union with Poland were tactical in nature—to impress Germany—and Krofta, referring to it as a riposte to the Curtius–Schober project, deemed "such a combination difficult." From Prague's point of view it was imperative to concentrate on Yugoslavia and Romania, for if they were attracted to a German-Austrian grouping, this would be the end of the Little Entente. But, Krofta said, Beneš "had a plan."[29]

Beneš's plan was essentially similar to the agrarian bloc concept as complemented by the postulates of the Czechoslovak agrarian party. Already on 4 April the foreign minister told Charles-Roux that it was urgent "to elaborate in agreement between Paris and Prague a system one could oppose to the German economic project." Beneš envisaged a regime of preferences for the exports of agricultural surpluses to the West without corresponding preferential treatment of Western exports. Two separate conferences—one consisting of agricultural, the other of industrial states—would work out the whole scheme, and Beneš placed the Little Entente, Hungary, Poland, and possibly other countries in the first gathering. The French envoy opined that this plan would correspond to the views of the Polish government.[30]

Satisfied with the French reaction, Beneš suggested that Warsaw, as the sponsor of the agrarian bloc, take the initiative to promote the plan. This would allay the misgivings of Budapest and Rome, and enlist the support of Bucharest.[31] Paris headed this advice, and the Poles responded with

27. Gen. Faucher to war ministry, 29 Dec. 1931, SHA, EMA/2, Tchécoslovaquie 2.

28. ADAP, B, XIX:72–75. Compare the appraisal of the Czechoslovak situation by Addison to Simon, 17 Dec. 1931, FO 371 15178 C 9568/221/12.

29. Briefing, 9 Apr. 1931, KV, CPP; also Charles-Roux to Briand, and Briand to Puaux, 9 Apr., MAE, P.A. Tardieu 85(693), P.A. Puaux 255(26).

30. See Sládek and Tomaszewski, "Próby integracji w latach trzydziestych," 383–384; Gajanová, *ČSR*, 282–83; also Quai d'Orsay to Puaux, 7 Apr. 1931, MAE, P.A. Puaux 255(25)

31. Quai d'Orsay to Puaux, 7 Apr. 1931, MAE, P.A. Puaux 255(25).

alacrity. Beck expressed full agreement with the French emphasis on the agrarian bloc as the only effective countermeasure to the German-Austrian customs union. He also wished to involve Bulgaria, Greece, and the Baltic countries in the plan, and was particularly happy that Czechoslovakia, which as a semi-industrial country had been hesitant before, seemed to have changed its views. Warsaw did not fully realize that Poland was to be used as a front for a Czechoslovak-French plan. Laroche recommended that the Poles be maintained in the belief "that their action is considered as the effective element," but one had to direct the Poles "with precision in order to avoid ill-considered initiatives," and not forget that the key part was to be played by Prague.[32]

The division of roles implied that the Czechoslovak government stayed in the background, but accepting this status was difficult for Beneš, who enjoyed being in the diplomatic limelight. When the French envoy criticized the foreign minister's public references to his efforts, Beneš, ill pleased, spoke of the expectations of Czechoslovak public opinion. He agreed finally to follow the French suggestion of attaching his study to the previous French initiatives and the agrarian bloc resolutions. Charles-Roux and Laroche were particularly intent to avoid all possible friction between Warsaw and Prague, and if possible exploit this chance of a rapprochement.[33]

In mid-April Beneš gave the French his memorandum on the economic organization of Europe. Its principal objectives were a provisional solution of the agrarian crisis in Poland, the Little Entente, Hungary, and Bulgaria; an adoption by the leading industrial countries (France, Germany, Italy, Austria, Czechoslovakia, and possibly Switzerland, Belgium, and the Netherlands) of "a different way of looking at the fundamental problems of the European crisis"; and inducing such industrial states as Britain, and possibly Belgium and the Netherlands, to attempt a European approach toward industrial production. The implementation of these objectives—involving among others features preferential agreements, a customs truce, and a stabilization of tariffs—was to be pursued by the conference of the agrarian states, a conference of the industrial countries (called by France), and through normal diplomatic channels.[34]

Briand's reaction was not uniformly positive. He agreed that the industrial states should not exact concessions in exchange for their purchases of cereal surpluses but thought that such concessions might eventually be un-

---

32. Laroche to Briand, 13, 14 Apr. 1931, MAE, P.A. Puaux 255(25). On Polish trade with the five Danubian countries, see Laroche to Briand, 23 Mar., MAE, P.A. Tardieu 84(692); compare Zaleski telegram, 7 Apr. 1931, HIA, Amb. Paryż, box 4.

33. Charles-Roux to Briand, 13, 14 Apr. 1931, MAE, Z 864.10, Tchécoslovaquie 2601.

34. Charles-Roux telegram, 15 Apr. 1931, MAE, P.A. Puaux 255(25).

avoidable to induce these states to grant preferential treatment. He personally favored new government-sponsored cartels as a means of tackling the problem. German-French industrial cartels appeared especially desirable.[35] Osuský argued that economic and financial cooperation would be unsuccessful without political and psychological foundations. With the financial tools at its disposal, France was in a position to organize a system of European cooperation. Briand explained to Osuský how the narrow vested interests of French farmers, industrialists, traders, and financiers made practical results difficult thus far. He thought, however, that the ministries of commerce, agriculture, and finance acting in unison could resolve the problems. What is more, Laval allegedly realized that the impact of the German-Austrian plan had provided an impulse for domestic and international consolidation.[36]

For the first time Paris was willing to consider preferential treatments for East Central European cereals, but did not wish to abandon compensations altogether. Nor was France prepared to endorse fully an agrarian bloc, and Warsaw began to entertain doubts. The embassy reported from Paris that the Quai d'Orsay seemed to be in constant touch with Beneš, who had in mind a vast plan including Germany and Austria. This appeared suspicious to the Poles, and Zaleski asked the French to be informed of the nature of the plan under consideration.[37]

The French constructive plan of 1 May singled out four major problems in need of a solution: the disposal of East Central European cereals surpluses, which it proposed to handle through a preferential system entailing Western sacrifices but also including later unspecified compensations; the market crisis affecting the industrialized countries, which was to be treated through industrial and agricultural cartels and the lowering of customs tariffs; the lack of credits in East Central Europe, which France would seek to remedy through financial collaboration; and the special position of Austria, which Paris proposed to deal with by granting special preferential treatment to all Austrian products. The note made it clear that France was willing to consent to exceptions regarding the most-favored-nation clause only for the benefit of the agricultural states and Austria, and that the creation of an atmosphere of trust and peace in Europe was a precondition for French financial aid.[38]

35. On this point, see especially Bariéty and Charles Bloch, "Une Tentative," 437–38.

36. Osuský telegram to Beneš, 19 Apr. 1931, CPP.

37. See Chłapowski and Frankowski reports, 18, 25 Apr., AAN, MSZ 3797; Zaleski telegrams, 21, 23 Apr. SI, Amb. Londyn, A.12.52/11; Laroche telegram, 28 Apr. 1931, MAE, P.A. Puaux 255(25).

38. See text in DBFP, II, 11:40–42; Briand to missions, 30 Apr. 1931, MAE, P.A. Puaux 255(25), Compare Bennett, *Germany*, 93–94. The special advocate of cartels was François-Poncet—hence, the occasional references to the Briand–Poncet plan.

The plan seemed to offer some inducement to Austria to abandon the Curtius–Schober project, but it held no attraction for Germany. The mention of the possibility of financial assistance and perhaps facilities for German exports to the region in return for Berlin's preferential treatment of eastern cereals sounded vague to the British and potentially dangerous to the Poles because it could open the way for bargaining with Germany.[39] Berlin, which had underestimated the extent of Czechoslovak opposition to an Austro-German union, continued to send trial balloons to Prague.[40] In late March and April, Regedanz, acting allegedly on his own, held long conversations with Beneš. The Czechoslovak statesman was imprecise in his comments and suggestions, which sounded pro-German but were meant to obscure Beneš's principal objective, an exclusion of Germany from the Danubian area.[41]

Much more serious than this verbal fencing was the meeting of the Little Entente in Bucharest (3–5 May) at which Beneš wanted to persuade the Romanians and the Yugoslavs to take a joint stand against the Curtius–Schober project and to appraise the Czechoslovak and French plans positively. The two foreign ministers were not prepared to follow blindly Paris and Prague. Mindful of the difficulties they had encountered when trying to obtain loans from France (contrasted with the ease with which Czechoslovakia obtained a small conversion loan), they insisted on economic concessions from Prague and on French credits as a condition of their cooperation. Beneš had to promise to overcome the agrarians' opposition to lower tariffs and to represent in Paris Yugoslav-Romanian objections concerning compensations and a privileged treatment of Austrian products.[42]

The communiqué of the Bucharest conference, which spoke of unanimity of views among the three states and with France, thus concealed real differences. Paris was vexed by what it called the Little Entente's unwillingness to subordinate its egotistic concerns to "vital interests at stake."[43]

39. See DBFP, II, II:50–51; Chłapowski to Zaleski, 29 Apr. 1931, AAN, MSZ 3797.

40. In late Mar., Beneš refused suggestions for Czechoslovak participation in the German-Austrian scheme and for acting in Paris for a compromise solution. See Campbell, *Confrontation*, 222–23; Gajanová, *ČSR*, 281; Charles-Roux to Briand, 24 Mar. 1931, MAE, P.A. Puaux 255(25).

41. See Regedanz-Bülow correspondence, 28 Apr., 1 May 1931, ADAP, B, XVII:262–63, AA, 4601/E 188 651–52, 4601/E 192 429–30. Also Brügel, *Tschechen*, 223–24 and his *Czechoslovakia*, 101–102. Compare Sládek, *Pozycja międzynarodowa*, 65.

42. See dispatches in MAE, P.A. Puaux 255(25) and MAE, Z 864.10, Tchécoslovaquie 2601; briefings 7 and 20(?) May 1931, KV, CPP. Compare Gajanová, *ČSR*, 284, 288; Campbell, *Confrontation*, 234; Vondracek, *Foreign Policy*, 337. The loan to Czechoslovakia was around fifty million dollars.

43. See Seguin to Briand, 5, 7 May, and Quai d'Orsay to Charles-Roux, 10 June 1931, MAE, Z 864.10, Tchécoslovaquie 2601. Beneš's idea of an Austrian settlement was that the country be neutralized (and guaranteed not only by Austria's creditors but also by

The Quai d'Orsay was grateful to Beneš for having made "a veritable effort . . . to rejoin almost completely our position" during the discussion of the French constructive plan in Geneva.[44] An effort it was, for Prague was hardly keen on the plan, which seemed "nebulous and difficult" to Krofta. France, while remaining protectionist, was pushing others to conclude tariff agreements. At first France had seemed helpless when facing the Curtius–Schober affair but then expected others just to follow its lead.[45] A Prague newspaper wrote that if France stopped buying cheaper cereals in Canada and purchased them in Yugoslavia and Romania instead, the annual difference would amount to a mere ninety million francs. If France and Czechoslovakia joined forces, the cost would be small as compared to the danger of a distintegration of the Little Entente.[46]

Poland volunteered to support the French constructive plan in all the capitals of East Central Europe and to coordinate its action with that of the French diplomacy. Zaleski suggested, however, that should it prove impossible to prevent the German-Austrian union, one ought to promote a grouping of states that comprised Poland, the Little Entente, perhaps Bulgaria and Greece, as well as France and Italy.[47] Poland's willingness stemmed partly from political reasons (although Piłsudski thought that Warsaw "should at present avoid anything that might in the future restrict its freedom of action"[48]) and partly from economic considerations. On 30 March, Poland and France signed an agreement (finalized on 29 April) that provided for a concession to Compagnie Franco-Polonaise de Chemin de Fer to build and exploit for forty-five years the Upper Silesia-Gdynia line.[49] Such an involvement of French capital in an area exposed to German revisionism was viewed in Warsaw as extremely important. The French shareholders would become "determined opponents of any change of Polish borders."[50] The American ambassador was skeptical. The amount was

---

the Little Entente, Poland, and Hungary) and sign a commercial convention with the Little Entente and possibly France and Italy. See Charles-Roux to Briand, 29 May 1931, MAE, P.A. Puaux 255(25).

44. Telegrams from Geneva, 19 May 1931, MAE, P.A. Puaux 255(25)

45. Briefings 7 and 20(?) May 1931, KV, CPP.

46. *Pražský Večerník*, 8 June 1931.

47. Laroche to Briand, 8 May, 6 June, MAE, P.A. Puaux 255(25); note on Zaleski–Laroche conversation and Zaleski reply 2 and 8 May, AAN, MSZ 1518. Zaleski to missions, 4 May, 1931, SI, Amb. Londyn, A.12.52/11.

48. Lipski to Wysocki in Jędrzejewicz, *Lipski*, 31–32.

49. The board of directors comprised two Frenchmen and two Poles and a French chairman. French capital represented eight out of fifteen million francs, and the company was to issue bonds guaranteed by the Polish treasury. The first issuance took place in 1931, but others did not follow, and in 1933 the Polish State Railroads took over the line. For some of this information, I am indebted to Zbigniew Landau.

50. See cabinet session, 18 Apr., AAN, PPRM, LVII, 30–31; compare 27 Apr. 1931

not sufficiently large "to materially change French policy in the event of being called upon to defend Poland in a war which would not involve the defense of French territory." Only if subsequent large investements and loans followed (which did not), "the course of French policy toward the east might be affected."[51]

After the dust settled on the Curtius–Schober plan, political relations between Poland and Czechoslovakia became "a little more sweet-sour." The Czechs who "discovered Poland" right after the announcement of the customs union project, forgot it just as rapidly. Economic talks came to a standstill, minority issues resurfaced, and the Poles complained about Ukrainian activities in Czechoslovakia. Zaleski, returning from a cure at Karlovy Vary, went through Prague but did not stop to confer with Beneš. Disgusted, Charles-Roux commented on the petty chicaneries both countries indulged in at a time when their united forces would barely suffice "to contain the growing might of Germany." Surely collaboration, particularly in the military sphere, lay in the interest of both, apart from "alleviating the responsibilities of France in Eastern and Central Europe."[52] In early July, Briand qualified Czechoslovak-Polish relations as a weak link in the general system. The Polish ambassador assured him that Warsaw would make efforts "to comply with the wishes of the French government," and Beck, commenting on the "negative attitude" of Prague, made similar affirmations to Laroche. The latter felt that Warsaw at least was trying to improve the relations with its southern neighbor.[53]

Political Moratorium and the Soviet Angle

In late spring and summer, while plans for dealing with the economic crisis were under discussion, the eye of the storm shifted to Germany. On 20 June, viewing the German financial collapse as threatening international monetary stability, President Herbert Hoover proposed a one-year moratorium on all intergovernmental payments. This initiative, taken without consultation with Paris, angered the French. Prague welcomed it and War-

---

discussion, Sprawozdania stenograficzne senatu, XVIII, 4–38; also Steyer, "Stosunki," 45.

51. Willys to Secretary of State, 28 Apr. 1931, SDNA, 860C.51,Creusot Consortium 5 and 7.

52. Charles-Roux to Briand, 26 June 1931, MAE, Z 698.1, Pologne 2099.

53. Laroche to Briand, 26 June MAE, Z 698.1, Pologne 2099; note of Briand–Chłapowski conversation, 1 July and Laroche to Briand, 8 July 1931, MAE, Z 864.5, Tchécoslovaquie 2586. Beneš's maneuvers at this point were ambiguous, for late in June he told the Polish envoy that he intended to propose an eternal security pact along the Czechoslovak-Polish border, and later intimated to the Romanians that he had reached some agreement with Zaleski. However, Warsaw denied the knowledge of either the proposal or the agreement. See Beck telegram, 10 July 1931, HIA, Amb. Paryż, box 4.

saw reacted with mixed feelings, but both decided to withhold their final consent pending Franco-American negotiations.[54] France was more interested in maintaining the principle than in collecting the money (which was unlikely), and sought to use its financial leverage for political ends. Thus, the French made their participation in a large international operation designed to assist Germany financially conditional on Berlin's consent to relax political tensions. "We have never been in a stronger position" wrote Berthelot, and Mühlstein commented on a "great increase of [French] conciousness of their own strength with regard to Germany and Britain."[55]

Paris wished to achieve its goals through a dialogue with Berlin rather than through coercion. Herriot contrasted Briand's "policy of equilibrium of rights" founded on pacific motivation with Franklin-Boullion's "policy of alliances" in the traditional prewar style, and the chamber clearly preferred the former.[56] François-Poncet told Hoesch that a defeat of either France or Germany over the Anschluss issue would split Europe and have dangerous repercussions. But Germany had to show some good will; Briand and Laval fully agreed on this point.[57] It appeared that France would be willing to assist Austria and Germany financially, but Germany would have to abandon its "ceaseless demands for changes in political conditions that are not in themselves obstacles to economic progress."[58] Pierre Quesnay, the French director of the Bank of International Settlement, thought that some political results could be achieved through purely economic diplomacy. For instance, the German-Polish problem was insoluble, hence one had to try to lessen the significance of frontiers and stress economic advantages. The handling of the customs union erred by bringing political aspects to the fore. What Quesnay really advocated was an intensified Franco-German economic cooperation that would dull the edge of political conflicts. At this point Paris should concentrate on Berlin, not on Warsaw or Bucharest.[59]

Implementation of such a policy was easier said than done, for the crux

54. See Leffler, *Elusive Question*, 234–40; compare Wiley, Ratshevsky, and Sokołowski dispatches 24, 17, 27 June, 3 July, SDNA, 462.00 R296/4297 and 4582, and FRUS 1931, I, 200–201, 227.

55. Berthelot on 18 Aug. 1931 cited in Bréal, *Berthelot*, 233; Mühlstein report, 14 Aug. 1931, AAN, MSZ 3732.

56. See session, 8 May 1931, J.O. Chambre, 2661–62, 2673–74.

57. See Bennett, *Germany*, 96–100, Hoesch telegrams, ADAP, B, XVII:222–23; AA, 2406/D 509 646–47; also DBFP, II, II:152.

58. DBFP, II, II:153; Chłapowski telegram, 24 June 1931, HIA, Amb. Paryż, box 3.

59. Quesnay to René Mayer, 8 Apr. 1931, Archives Nationales 314, AP 32. For this document, I am indebted to Lubor Jílek. See also MS, BJ, Zygmunt Karpiński, "Wspomnienia," III, 67.

of the matter was how to reconcile measures designed to assist German economic recovery with devices susceptible to bring about political stabilization. Furthermore, a proposal that Brüning agree to a minimum program of revision would imply the acceptance of the principle of revisionism per se. In *L'Esprit International*, d'Ormesson outlined certain possible arrangements: Poland would hand over to Germany a railroad line across the "corridor"; bring the East Prussian border to the Vistula River; internationalize the commission of the Vistula; and work out an agreement on the Polish population in East Prussia. Perhaps one could also add some provisions about demilitarization of both the "corridor" and East Prussia.[60]

The alleged Polish approval of this article, taken together with the earlier mentioned hints dropped by Zaleski, may have indicated Warsaw's desire to show that the German-Polish controversy was not insoluble and the Poles were not unreasonable. It did not signify acquiescence in revisionism. In fact, Warsaw agreed with Chłapowski that Poland should continue to seek a guarantee of its borders but without mentioning the term Eastern Locarno. Because the German economic crisis had political foundations, aid to Germany must be accompanied by demands for political stabilization.[61] In view of Briand's isolation in the cabinet and a certain disenchantment with his German policy, Chłapowski hoped that the need for closer cooperation with Poland and the Danubian states would dawn on Paris.[62]

Briand told the ambassador that the French government would not fail to mention the question of Polish security in the forthcoming conversations with the German government, but the weakness of the latter did not offer great hope for success.[63] Actually, Berlin leaked to the press proposed projects linking economic recovery with security pledges, and there was indignant talk about a revival of an Eastern Locarno. Berthelot had to deny that this was intended.[64] Because he thought that time was working for Poland, given the declining number of Germans in the "corridor" Zaleski suggested a twelve-year moratorium on revisionism as a condition of French help to Germany. As a signatory of the final protocol of Locarno

60. 18 Apr. 1931 issue. For summary and comments, note du Service Français de la Société des Nations, 29 June 1931, MAE, P.A Massigli 4.

61. See Beck telegram, 26 June, HIA, Amb. Paryż, box 4; Chłapowski report 3 July 1931, AAN, MSZ 3797.

62. Chłapowski report, 27 June 1931, AAN, MSZ 3797. Still, Senator Iwanowski returning from Paris opined that the French would make every concession to Germany to avoid war. 10 June 1931, PI, MS, Dziennik Kazimierza Świtalskiego, copy.

63. Chłapowski telegram, 1 July 1931, HIA, Amb. Paryż, box 4.

64. See Bennett, *Germany*, 230–31.

and of the Kellogg–Briand pact, Warsaw attempted to be included in the Western negotiations with the Germans, but to no avail.[65]

During conversations with Brüning and Curtius, held first in Paris on 18–19 July, and then in a more formal setting in London (20–23 July), Laval, François-Poncet, and Flandin (with Briand in the background) pressed the Germans to accept a ten-year moratorium as part of a package deal that included a nonaggression and consultation pact and a loan.[66] The Germans refused, and the French found themselves isolated. Prime Minister MacDonald "would not support France's demand for the perpetuation of all the iniquities which were done by her little allies." U.S. Secretary of State Henry L. Stimson was suspicious of French attempts "to secure her hegemony as against Germany" on the basis of the territorial status quo.[67] *L'Echo de Paris* rightly complained that the Anglo-Saxon powers had prevented France from exploiting Germany's financial weakness to obtain political concessions.

The Poles were told at first merely that the Germans would never be reconciled with the "corridor."[68] Actually, the Polish question had figured in several conversations. Advocating a political moratorium François-Poncet argued that at a later stage the French would be willing to mediate in the German-Polish controversy. "Already for some time," he said, there existed in "French governmental circles" a plan to talk with the Germans and the Poles "openly about the possibility of revision. The question was naturally extremely delicate, but one had to tackle it sometime." Laval evaded a discussion with Curtius, who falsely asserted that Piłsudski and Zaleski had not wanted the "corridor" after World War I, and received it only as a gift from Woodrow Wilson, who needed Polish votes. But Laval did tell Stimson that if the Polish "corridor" could be solved, "France would have no other trouble with Germany." The secretary made a mental note of this remark.[69]

Germany neither gained nor made concessions in the Paris and London talks, but both the Germans and the French concluded that a continued dialogue was necessary. A new attempt at rapprochement was likely to center on economics, particularly cartels, and Mühlstein thought that the negotiations would be "more realistic and more calculated" than Briand's

65. Zaleski and Beck telegrams, 12, 15, 16, 17 July 1931, SI, Amb. Londyn, A.12.52/11. Compare Höltje, *Weimarer Republik*, 215–16; correspondence in Jędrzejewicz, *Lipski*, 36–39, 41–42. On the Chłapowski–Laval conversation, Wiley telegram, 17 July, SDNA, 462.00 R 296/4588.

66. See Bennett, *Germany*, 265–71; François-Poncet, *Souvenirs*, 22–23; Scott, *Alliance*, 21, 24; Pertinax, *Gravediggers*, 375. Also Vaïsse, *Sécurité*, 108–109.

67. Stimson–MacDonald conversation, 7 Aug. 1931, FRUS 1931, I, 516.

68. Mühlstein to Zaleski, 25 July 1931, AAN, MSZ 3798.

69. See ADAP, B, XVIII:41–44, 128–31, 147–50, 290–96. Also FRUS 1931, I, 549.

previous policies. If Flandin seemed less interested, Laval appeared as the main advocate of the new approach.[70] So did François-Poncet, a typical representative of the *haute bourgeoisie* with close ties to the Comité des Forges, who decided at this point to abandon a brilliant political career at home to become ambassador in Berlin. Because Franco-German conciliation as practiced by the French Left had failed, it might succeed, he hoped, when tried by the Right.[71] Briand asked the Polish envoy in Berlin to cooperate with François-Poncet, for "both of you must somehow reach an understanding with Germany."[72]

Direct approaches to Berlin were not the only weapon in the French diplomatic arsenal, for roughly two weeks after the London conference, Paris initialed a nonaggression treaty with the Soviet Union. To understand this occurrence, we need to recall past events. Exchanges between Soviet Russia and France began in 1926, and for the next two years Moscow made overtures for a nonaggression pact to both Paris and Warsaw. A breakdown in Franco-Soviet exchanges occurred in 1928, and although Poland signed the Litvinov Protocol in 1929 further talks were deadlocked.[73] In late June 1930, Stalin referred to France as the most aggressive and militaristic country; at the preparatory disarmament commission, Soviet policy went consistently counter to French and Polish endeavors. *Pravda* and *Izvestia* showed malicious joy at French and East Central European discomfiture over the Curtius–Schober project. On 24 June a German-Russian protocol renewed the Berlin Treaty. The Germans regarded their continuing cooperation with Russia as "the needed counterweight against the aggressive anti-German policy promoted by France." Only "the menacing and uncertain attitude of Russia prevents Poland from being more demanding and impudent in her attitude toward us."[74] Moscow, however, was far too astute to rely only on Germany. Moreover, worries about a German–West European combination directed against Russia became compounded by grave domestic problems and, above all, by a threatening situation in the Far East. It was under these circumstances that between October and December 1930, Moscow renewed its overtures to Warsaw for a nonaggression pact.[75]

Piłsudski, while deeply distrustful of Russia, always believed that it was

70. Mühlstein report, 25 July, AAN, MSZ 3798.

71. For a characterization of François-Poncet, see Bérard, *Ambassadeur*, 109.

72. See MS, OSS, Wysocki, II, 207, also 239.

73. See Girault, "Les relations." Also Michowicz, "Realizacja," 123–25.

74. See Memorandum, 5 Feb. 1931, ADAP, B, XVI:515.

75. For Soviet denials of the existence of the October overtures, see Mikhutina, *Sovetsko-polskie otnosheniia*, 26; also Jonathan Haslam, *Soviet Foreign Policy 1930–1933* (London, 1983) 68–69. Compare Zaleski telegram, 10 Jan. 1931, HIA. Amb. Paryż, box 4; Laroche to Briand, 28 Dec. 1930, 3 Jan. 1931, MAE, P.A. Puaux 255(25).

essential for Poland to reach direct agreements with its two great neighbors in order to strengthen Poland's freedom of diplomatic maneuver. Judging the moment ripe, he gave the green light to Zaleski, who informed the French, the Baltic countries, and Romania of a Soviet offer to conclude a political pact (and a commercial treaty) amounting to a broadened Kellogg–Briand accord.[76] The Poles were mostly concerned with a Soviet neutrality guarantee and the participation of all European states bordering on Russia in a nonaggression treaty. Negotiations were likely to be arduous, and the absence of Piłsudski, who went to Madeira (12 December–29 March 1931) to repair his health, indicated that no decisions would intervene soon.

Meanwhile in France, the government's interest in a nonaggression treaty—accompanied by similar treaties between Moscow, Warsaw, and Bucharest—began to grow. Pressure by big business, concerned with access to the Russian market, was a factor, but the main goal was to drive a wedge between Moscow and Berlin. In January 1931, Briand authorized Berthelot's conversations with Ambassador Valerian Dovgalevsky, and serious talks ensued in March and April.[77] French public opinion was cool, and as a rightist senator put it, many Frenchmen feared that "the Russian card is dangerous for the person who uses it."[78] Litvinov on his side, mentioning Berthelot's overtures, told the Germans that the Soviets were willing to talk but were dubious of French intentions.[79]

Informed of the Franco-Russian conversations, Warsaw invoked its long experience in dealing with Moscow and proffered some counsels. The French government found this contact useful for countering the accusation that conversations with the Soviets were menacing French eastern allies.[80] In early July, the Quai d'Orsay consulted the Poles on issues that had a bearing on possible Soviet-Polish conflict and French attitude toward it.[81] Finally, the draft of a Franco-Soviet pact of nonaggression was initialed, as mentioned, in early August 1931.

French-Soviet negotiations had been conducted independently of any

76. The American chargé d'affaires commented that Warsaw seemed to have embarked on a policy of "appeasing" Russia and obtained a free hand from Paris. Wiley to Kelley, 5 Jan. 1931, FDR, Wiley Papers, box 1.

77. See historical survey in DDF, 1, x:75–76. Compare Girault, "Les relations," 245–47; see Laboulaye's explanations in Chłapowski report, 23 May 1931, AAN, MSZ 3797.

78. Lémery on 28 March 1931, J.O.Sénat, 687.

79. ADAP, B, XVII:312–13.

80. See Leczyk, *Polityka*, 279; relevant material in HIA, Amb. Paryż, box 4; AAN, MSZ 3798 and Amb. Berlin 76; Laroche dispatch, 4 July 1931, MAE, P.A. Puaux 225(25).

81. Quai d'Orsay to Laroche, 6 July 1931, MAE, P.A. Puaux 255(25).

exchanges between the Polish and Russian diplomats, although Paris kept Warsaw informed. The Russians were not told that a formal link between the two envisaged treaties—western and eastern—existed, or that France deemed it desirable.[82] In mid-August, Laboulaye asked Mühlstein about the state of Soviet-Polish pourparlers, and remarked that a Soviet-French pact would in no way restrict France's obligations to Poland or Romania. The Poles were rather skeptical. They deduced from an observation by François-Poncet that he and Berthelot had insisted on keeping Warsaw informed of the negotiations while others had opposed it. Would France, seeking a direct link to Russia, be inclined to desert Poland? Did the campaign in the French press emphasizing that a rapprochement with the USSR must not be achieved at the expense of the eastern allies help to keep the Quai d'Orsay loyal to Warsaw? Chłapowski tended to think so.[83]

By late August, the French started to make their treaty with Russia dependent on the conclusion of eastern pacts, and applied pressure on Poland to negotiate in earnest. On 23 August, Warsaw officially submitted the project of a nonaggression pact to the Russians. Shortly thereafter a Havas Agency communiqué appeared in *Le Temps* (27 August) that gave a Quai d'Orsay-inspired version of the history of the pourparlers, establishing a connection between the two parallel negotiations. Tass, the Soviet news agency, contested this account. In September, the French intimated that the signing of a nonaggression pact between Warsaw and Moscow was virtually a condition of further Franco-Soviet negotiations; Warsaw would be pressed not to be dilatory. Briand told Curtius that the French parliament would not ratify a pact with Russia unless the eastern allies signed their treaties first.[84] Thus, even if there was a tendency in Paris to proceed to final signature without waiting for the outcome of Soviet-Polish negotiations, this approach became impossible for domestic reasons. Fear of East European complaints and a distrust of Russia also played their part.[85]

Confronted with the ever more threatening situation in the Far East—in September the Mukden incident opened the way to Japanese control of

82. See Briand, Berthelot, Massigli, Litvinov in ADAP, B, xviii:377n., 405, 483–84.

83. See Mühlstein report, 14 Aug. 1931, AAN, MSZ 3798 and Chłapowski in Łopatniuk, "Nieznane dokumenty," 185–86; compare Schaetzel–Świtalski conversation on 3 Sept., AAN, Akta Świtalskiege, 71. On the press, see Scott, *Alliance*, 15; articles in *L'Ordre*, 4, 5, 9 Sept. 1931. Sikorski's article on a false Eastern Locarno condemns a Franco-Soviet pact independent of Poland; see *Kurjer Warszawski*, 20 Sept. 1931.

84. See DVP SSSR, xix, 535–36; ADAP, B, xviii:405.

85. Soviet Russia mistrusted France equally. Launching a trial balloon of a tripartite Soviet-German-French pact excluding Poland, Litvinov justified the exclusion on the grounds that otherwise "France would gain the possibility of playing Germany against Soviet Russia and vice versa." Dirksen to Auswärtiges Amt, 23 July 1931, AA, K290/K 101 487–90.

Manchuria—Moscow wanted to stabilize the situation on its western borders. Negotiations were not easy. Warsaw, although pressed by the French, wished to demonstrate its own ability to conclude a nonaggression pact with Russia and insisted on signing simultaneously with the Baltic states and Romania. The text of the Franco-Soviet accord was communicated in deepest secrecy to Warsaw in October; Zaleski had been only informally acquainted with it in late August. The accompanying note by the legal adviser of the Quai d'Orsay pointed out that the treaty would deprive Germany of the hope that in the event of a conflict with Poland, Russia would intervene on Germany's side. Should a Soviet-Polish pact follow, Berlin's expectations of a Moscow-assisted revision of Versailles would collapse. The treaty would also contribute to a stabilization of Franco-German entente, and show the same path to Poland. "Nothing more erroneous than [seeing here] a wish to transform the treaty into a *renversement des alliances*," the legal adviser commented. The pact, serving as counterweight to Rapallo and Berlin, marked simply the birth of a new equilibrium. Soviet Russia evidently desired to remain neutral between France and Germany, and "one could not demand more of her."[86]

The Polish embassy observed that French policy toward the USSR would "have no undesirable effect on Polish-French relations."[87] Warsaw, however, did not wish merely to copy the text of the Franco-Soviet treaty, even if Zaleski seemed more accommodating than Piłsudski, Beck, and the envoy in Moscow, Stanisław Patek. The marshal was reluctant to tolerate any close supervision by Paris of the negotiations with Russia. He also insisted that territorial violation be made the criterion of aggression. As for the Romanian angle, the Poles viewed it as their affair in which French interference was resented.[88]

Bucharest feared that a Paris-Moscow pact would diminish the value of eastern alliances. Seeing little benefit in a treaty with USSR, unless it brought a recognition of their possession of Bessarabia, the Romanians suspected Moscow of wishing to drive a wedge between them and Poland.[89] Having been informed by Warsaw of Sovet-Polish exchanges in May, and receiving an offer of assistance in the negotiations, Bucharest adopted dilatory tactics. The Romanians noted that Piłsudski showed no

86. Note of Lyon, 26 Aug. 1931, AAN, MSZ 3798.

87. Mühlstein report, 24 Oct. 1931, AAN, MSZ 3798.

88. See Beck–Mühlstein exchange of telegrams, 18, 21, 22, 28 Oct. 1931, HIA, Amb. Paryż, box 3; also MS, OSS, Wysocki, II, 33. Compare Budurowycz, *Polish-Soviet Relations*, 13. For the French pressure on Patek, see Leczyk, *Polityka*, 290; compare Wiley to Secretary of State, 23 Nov. 1931, SDNA, 760C.6111/20. Also, DiM, v, 562–65.

89. See Schulenburg to Heeren, 12 Jan. 1932, AA, K290/K 101 982–85.

inclination to press them, so they were surprised and chagrined when talks between the Russians and the Poles began to accelerate in late November 1931.⁹⁰ They were particularly worried by the Polish abandonment of the original demand for simultanous conclusion of all pacts with Soviet neighbors, which became unrealistic in view of bilateral negotiations between Moscow and the Baltic states.

Foreign Minister Dimitri Ghika began to explore the possibility of direct talks with Russia, but his tactics evoked criticism in Paris and Warsaw. Berthelot encouraged the Romanians to "work hand in hand with the Poles," and the latter applied pressure.⁹¹ Paris wished to conclude its own final treaty with the Soviets, so as to improve its position vis-à-vis Germany; Piłsudski who had dropped his original policy of dragging out the negotiations to assure parallelism with Poland's neighbors, now decided to make the Soviet-Polish pact an example for them to imitate.⁹² In January 1932 the text was initialed, the last minute haste on Poland's part stemming largely from the signing of the Soviet-Finnish pact on 21 January, and the scheduling of the Latvian-Soviet accord for 5 February. The Poles felt that they have now reached the same position as France.

The chief of the French military mission to Poland saw in the Polish-Soviet pact not only an assurance that Russia would not be on Germany's side in case of a conflict, but also that Poland had renounced any aggressive designs on the Soviet Union in the eventuality of a Russo-Romanian conflict. This was "a double and precious assurance of peace."⁹³ For the Soviets, however, the nonaggression pact with Warsaw was tantamount neither to a recognition of Versailles nor to a guarantee of Poland's borders.⁹⁴ What is more, delays in the final signing of French and Polish treaties with the USSR, caused by Romania, would, in the months to come, result in new friction and bitterness between France and her two eastern partners.

Annus Terribilis

Czechoslovak involvement in the French strategy of neutralizing the Soviet Union had been minimal. Prague adopted an attitude of reserve, even though the Hrad and leftist groups in the country extolled the advantages of an economic rapprochement with the Soviet Union. Yet chances of rec-

90. On this phase, see Bacon, *Closed Doors*, 10, 49–51, 143, 151.

91. See Puaux exchanges with Paris, 7, 9 Dec. 1931, MAE, P.A. Puaux 255(28), 255(25); Bacon, *Closed Doors*, 56.

92. See Laroche telegram, 20 Dec. 1931, MAE, P.A. Puaux 255(25).

93. Annual report 1931 by Col. Prioux, SHA, EMA/2, Pologne 11.

94. Stalin's remarks to Emil Ludwig in Budurowycz, *Polish-Soviet Relations*, 12.

ognizing the USSR were still slender, and Krofta, for one, regarded Soviet interest in pacts with France, Poland, and Romania as dictated by necessity. Russia, he felt, mainly wanted financial aid from France, now that German and American sources were no longer available.[95] Czechoslovak-Polish relations registered no change for the better. Sharp polemics—in which the Cracow *Ilustrowany Kurjer Codzienny* excelled—centered on the issue of the Polish minority in Teschen. An improvement of their lot, Piłsudski told Beck, was a condition for détente with Prague.[96] Some efforts to reduce tension through a press accord produced only temporary results.[97] Beneš's mistrust of the Polish government transpired from his talks with the envoy.[98] As before, the Warsaw card was not the one that Prague intended to play.

Telling the French that Czechoslovakia was the only country in East Central Europe that was holding out in the midst of the economic depression, Beneš pointed out that its importance as "France's auxiliary" had in fact increased. This conviction prompted Beneš, after the virtual failure of the French constructive plan, to elaborate a new Danubian project himself, although its newness and exact nature remained hazy.[99] By and large, it entailed the advocacy of a grouping comprising the Little Entente plus Austria and Hungary without the participation of any great power.[100] Between July and October Beneš made overtures to Hungary, which in August received a contingency loan from France, and the responses were encouraging.[101] Approaches to Vienna proved less successful, but a possibility of an agreement between Czechoslovakia, Hungary, and Austria existed. Prague, however, was in no position, nor did it wish, to confine it to these countries. On their side, neither Vienna nor Budapest wanted to be associated with the Little Entente as a whole, and their economic accords with Italy (at Semmering) provided them with other options. All this may have explained Beneš's unwillingness to formulate his program with greater precision. Besides, as he told an Italian diplomat,

95. See *Přehled dějin československo-sovětských vztahů*, 234–35; briefing, 26 Nov. 1931, KV,CPP; Košek to ministry, 18 July 1931, CPP.

96. Beck, *Dernier rapport*, 9–10.

97. See press cuttings in MZV-VA, 478.1244 and 1245.

98. See Bułhak, "Z dziejów 1927–1936," 112.

99. See Charles-Roux to Briand, 30 Sept., 17 Oct. 1931, MAE, Z 864.1, Tchécoslovaquie 2568. Compare DaM, II, 543; briefing, 29 Oct. KV, CPP.

100. See Koppens report, 22 Sept. 1931, AAN, Amb. Berlin, 51. Krofta thought that the politically unhealthy economic dependence on Germany could only be lessened by a rapprochement of Central European states. See 12 Nov. 1931, KV, CPP.

101. See Bystrický and Deák, *Európa*, 51; Juhász, *Foreign Policy*, 100–101; Campbell, *Confrontation*, 234–35; Gajanová, *ČSR*, 290–91; Ránki, *Economy*, 82–83, 94–96; Ormos, *Problème*, 32–33; briefings, 24 Sept., 3 Dec. 1931, KV, CPP.

each time he took a formal initiative, this only aroused mistrust in Rome.[102]

French involvement in Beneš's diplomatic maneuvers in late 1931 was evident, although the economic and financial assistance extended by Paris to the Danubian region was far too limited. Vested interests of the farmers allowed France to conclude only restricted preferential agreements with Hungary, Yugoslavia and Romania (between September 1931 and January 1932), which did not make their products competitive with either North American or North African cereals. Big business in turn was not keen on strengthening Czechoslovakia financially, a competitor on the French market.[103]

Prague's efforts to float a loan in the winter of 1930–31, subscribed mainly by French banks, had been unsuccessful. When negotiations started anew in the autumn of 1931, two operations were simultaneously discussed: credits of 200 million francs to the Czechoslovak banking system, and a larger loan floated by French private banks guaranteed by the government.[104] The French government tied the talks to the larger issue of Franco-Czechoslovak commercial relations, and it succeeded in gaining new advantages through the trade agreement of 1 December and additional protocols (signed in March 1932).[105] Secondly, the question of the French-controlled Škoda armament factories quickly came to the foreground. As the Quai d'Orsay explained to the ministry of finance, Škoda had been executing large orders to Romania that remained unpaid.[106] The concern had also suffered from the withdrawal of French and British short-term loans, and the Czechoslovak government was reluctant to assist it without additional French monies. The Quai d'Orsay recalled the importance of Škoda "as the principal factor of our economic influence in Czechoslovakia and the supplier of the three countries of the Little Entente." Aid was thus indispensable, and it could also be used to pressure

102. See Gehl, *Austria*, 40; Charles-Roux dispatches, 1, 12 Nov., 21 Dec. 1931, MAE, Z 864.10, Tchécoslovaquie 2601; Z 864.1, Tchécoslovaquie 2568; P.A. Tardieu 84(692).

103. See Kaiser, *Economic Diplomacy*, 41–43.

104. For the various stages of the negotiations: Quai d'Orsay to finance ministry, 6 Mar. 1931, MAE, Z 684.10, Tchécoslovaquie 2604, dossier 11; Charles-Roux to Briand, 11 Nov. MAE, P.A. Tardieu, 85(693); Tardieu's explications, 5 Mar. 1932, J.O. Chambre, 1134–36. Peacock to Vansittart, 2 Apr., and Guerney to Reading, 15 Oct. 1931, FO 371 15 C 2412 and C 7799. *Národní Osvobození, Lidové Listy* and *České Slovo*, 12, 18 Dec. 1931 and 30 Dec. 1932. Analysis in Teichová, *Economic Background*, 374–76; Girault, "L'Europe," 130–31.

105. See Osuský to Bizon and Flandin, 13 Feb. 1932; Deputy A. Duval to finance ministry, 10 Feb. and reply from Movement Général des Fonds, 21 May, 1932, MF, F^{30}, 2052.

106. See Jan Masaryk's letter, 14 Sept. 1932, ANM, Mastný 8/527–528.

Prague to end the campaign waged mainly by German but also by some Czech papers against Škoda and the French capital.[107]

All these considerations notwithstanding, negotiations moved slowly, and Osuský had to lobby incessantly. In would surely be unfortunate, the envoy wrote Briand at one point, if Czechoslovakia were to gain the impression that "France does not interest itself sufficiently either in the fate of my country or in the future of Central Europe."[108] Such argument coupled with the danger of Škoda being taken over by the Czechoslovak government, finally convinced the ministry of finance. A loan of 600 million francs was approved, provided the question of Škoda was resolved with the aid of Prague. Schneider's Union Européenne began to work on a formula associating the Czechoslovak government with the management of the concern without, however, giving it effective control.[109] The cabinet gave its final approval in December, the chamber ratified it on 5 March 1932.[110] In presenting the case "on grounds of general policy," Tardieu (then premier and foreign minister) praised the unfailing loyalty of Czechoslovakia to France as well as its economic stability. "Never had a loan been more justified," he exclaimed. If French socialists and radicals decided to abstain from the vote, this was not because they were critical of Czechoslovakia but because they opposed financial diplomacy promoting rival blocs in Europe and imposing a burden on the French taxpayer.[111] Their position was symptomatic of the mood in the country.

The loan did not all go to the Czechoslovak treasury. Almost one-third of it was kept in France to pay for deliveries of French industrial exports to Czechoslovakia. The Prague government vigorously denied that 150 million out of the 600 were to cover Škoda's outstanding accounts with Schneider, but there is little doubt that a state credit of 250 million crowns extended to the concern was part of the whole operation. Foreign observers ascribed the success with the loan to Osuský; Krofta attributed it to the foreign minister, and *České Slovo* on 24 January called it "a proof of

107. Berthelot to finance ministry, 14 Nov. 1931, MF, F[30], 2052. Tardieu cited Briand's saying that it was in the interest of "French policy to enhance the prestige and the influence of Czechoslovakia." 5 Mar. 1932, J.O. Chambre, 1135. For the complex maneuvers by Prague, Paris, and Schneider (playing its own independent game), see Segal, "French State," 254–97, also 135–41.

108. Osuský to Briand, 3 Dec. 1931, MF, F[30], 2052.

109. See notes, 4, 16 Dec. 1931, MF, F[30], 2052.

110. The loan agreement was signed by Flandin and Osuský on 20 Jan. 1932, and was endorsed in Feb. by foreign affairs commission. See retrospective note, 26 Feb. 1932, MF, F[30], 2052.

111. See discussions, 10 Feb., 4 Mar. 1932, CAE/Ch and 5 Mar., J.O. Chambre, 1132–41. Comments in *L'Ere Nouvelle*, 2 Mar., *La Volonté, L'Oeuvre, La Libertæ, Journal des Débats*, 3 Mar., *La Croix*, 8 Mar. See Osuský to Flandin, 1 Apr. 1932, MF,F[30], 2052.

confidence in Beneš's policy."[112] Yet the delays in obtaining the credits and the commercial difficulties made some Czechs, especially among the opposition, wonder about the degree of French commitment to their country.[113]

This uncertainty was even more justified in the Polish case. Endeavors to obtain monies for agriculture, Warsaw's commercial bank, potash development, capital investments in Upper Silesia, and armaments ran into endless difficulties.[114] Platonic declarations of love contrasted with harsh realities. When Zaleski visited the colonial exhibition in Paris, he pledged Poland's unswerving loyalty and expressed full confidence in French policies. Acting as host, the minister of colonies Paul Reynaud invoked in reply a letter of Colbert to Louis XIV saying that he would never grudge millions to Poland even if he had to sell everything and impoverish his wife and children. Yet a month later, when Zaleski, accompanied by Adam Koc, the head of the treasury, visited Flandin, the minister of finances, the latter was reticent.[115]

Poland feared particularly the effects of French protectionist measures, for the interests it paid for servicing French loans could come from increased exports. Should the balance become negative again (as in 1929–30), Polish monetary equilibrium would be endangered. The Poles expressed incomprehension of French commercial policies toward them, especially since France had granted some tariff concessions to other East Central European countries.[116] Polish negotiators dealing with their French counterparts were frustrated. Zaleski was told by the minister of commerce, Louis Rollin, that the blame rested with Tardieu, but according

112. See briefing, 3 Mar. 1932, KV, CPP; *Algemeine Zeitung* (Chemnitz), 1 Apr., *New York Times*, 31 Jan. The loan was at five percent with high servicing rates. Czechoslovakia pledged as security the income from the state monopoly on tobacco. Banks involved in the operation included L'Union Parisienne, Paribas, Lazard Frères, Crédit Lyonnais, Société Générale pour favoriser le développement du Commerce et de l'Industrie, Comptoir National Escompte, Société Générale du Crédit Industriel, Banque des Pays de l'Europe Centrale, Banque des Pays du Nord. For analysis see Teichová, *Economic Background*, 206, 374–76. On the Škoda aspect: 3 Mar. 1932, KV, CPP; Charles-Roux to Tardieu, 27 Feb., MF, F[10], 2051; Finance ministry to Quai d'Orsay, 26 Feb., MAE, P.A. Tardieu 85 (693). A governmental denial appears in *Venkov*, 9 Apr. 1932.

113. See Charles-Roux to Tardieu, 27 Feb. 1932, MAE, Z 864.1, Tchécoslovaquie 2568; criticism in *České Slovo* and *Národní Politika*, 16 Mar., 6 Apr. 1932.

114. See Ciałowicz, *Polsko–francuski sojusz*, 164; Chłapowski and Mühlstein reports, 13 June, 8 Aug. 1931, AAN, MSZ 3797, 3814.

115. Description of visits in AAN, MSZ 3764. Proposals for a commission to study matters of financial, commercial, and industrial cooperation with France in note, 4 Sept., and Chłapowski reports, 3 and 10 Oct. 1931, AAN, MSZ 3813.

116. See Beck to Zaleski, 22 Sept.; note, 19 Nov., memo, 28 Nov. 1931, AAN, MSZ 3813.

to Berthelot the difficulties stemmed from Rollin's department.[117] Negotiations between the Polish army and Fiat aroused the ire of Citroën; Paris resorted to political pressure to force Warsaw to turn toward the French automobile industry. A Polish proposal to set up a joint economic committee met with French coolness on the grounds that a Franco-German committee had been established and France did not want to diminish its importance.[118] No wonder Mühlstein spoke of the paradox of having close political and bad economic relations.[119]

The Franco-German committee had been set up during a Berlin pilgrimage of Laval and Briand in late September 1931, which created some consternation in Poland and annoyance in French opposition circles. In *L'Ordre* (27 September), Emile Buré wished the travelers ironically "bon voyage" and warned "beware of pickpockets." D'Ormesson speculated what could be profitably discussed and concluded that it mattered most to clear the air and make sure that "Europe felt protected against surprises."[120] Laval assured Zaleski that nothing that could affect Poland would be discussed in Berlin, and repeated—as did Briand and Berthelot—after the visit that the conversations had an "exclusively economic and mainly theoretical character."[121]

Still, a connection between economics and politics there was. As Brüning told the British, France was the only country to provide the credits for the afflicted countries in Central Europe. But, "if she stepped into the breach, she might try to create a customs union with Czechoslovakia, Austria, Hungary, and Yugoslavia, to the detriment of Germany and England."[122] A feeling of anxiety and uncertainty pervaded Europe. In September, Britain, governed now by the national cabinet of MacDonald, was forced off the gold standard. In Germany, Curtius resigned, and Brüning took over the Auswärtiges Amt amidst conditions bordering on financial catastrophe.

In October, Laval went to Washington to discuss the entire economic and political state of Europe, hoping to arrive at some common policy with

117. Sokołowski report and notes on conversations, 20 and 25 Nov. 1931, AAN, MSZ 3813.

118. Lipski–Laroche conversation, 15 Dec. 1931, AAN, MSZ 3813; on the Citroën affair see Mühlstein and Chłapowski telegrams 26 Aug., 15 Sept., HIA, Amb. Paryż, box 3.

119. Mühlstein letter to Lipski, 28 Dec. 1931, AAN, MSZ 3813.

120. *Revue de Paris*, 15 Sept. 1931; compare Chłapowski report, 21 Sept. AAN, Amb. Berlin, 77.

121. Zaleski to ministry, 29, 30 Aug. 1931, AAN, Amb. Berlin, 77 and HIA, Amb. Paryż, box 3. Compare Wysocki circular, 29 Sept. SI, Amb. Londyn, A.12/52/12. Also Massigli to Berthelot, 20 Sept. 1931, MAE, Z 698.12, Pologne 2198; François-Poncet, *Souvenirs*, 22–29.

122. Rumbold to Reading, 30 Oct. 1931, DBFP, II, II:314.

the United States. According to Berthelot, he would try to make Washington understand that Germany could not manage without French aid, and the latter was predicated on Berlin's renunciation of revisionism.[123] This was a difficult task, for Stimson thought that France was aggravating the crisis by trying to exact political concessions from Berlin. The secretary contrasted the French notion of security—consisting of a "perpetual freezing" of the status quo, maintenance of "unjust" provisions, and use of military force to guarantee them—with the American idea of solving one by one the problems that prevented Europe "from settling down."[124] The views at the State Department insofar as they reflected understanding of and sympathy for the French position had little impact on Stimson and the White House.[125] A strong statement made in Piłsudski's name by Ambassador Tytus Filipowicz to the effect that if Germany invaded the "corridor" the Polish army would fight whether the League liked it or not, annoyed Hoover. A strong Germany, he said, was Poland's best defense against Soviet Russia. "The sooner you will reach an agreement with Germany in the matter of the corridor, the better for you and for the rest of the world."[126]

During Laval's first conversation on 23 October, Hoover plunged immediately into a discussion of Central Europe; Stimson reminded the Frenchman of his remark that if the "corridor" issue were solved, there "wouldn't be any trouble at all between Germany and France." Laval explained that Poland would fight, hence a solution was a "political impossibility." He admitted that the "corridor" looked absurd on the map, and that the Treaty of Versailles had unfortunate effects on Central Europe, but it was simply impossible to change it now. But even if a solution of the "corridor" were possible, he said, it "would only whet Germany's appetite." Hoover regarded this as a "conventional French argument" with which he had no patience. As for Stimson, he was only confirmed in his views that France was "rich, militaristic and cocky." There seemed no

---

123. Zaleski to ministry, 2 Oct. 1931, HIA, Zaleski Papers.

124. Memorandum on Stimson's conversation with Senator Morrow, 2 Oct. 1931, SDNA, 033.511 Laval, Pierre/257. On American attitudes toward France, Leffler, *Elusive Question*, 261–63.

125. See memoranda: Division of Western European Affairs, 5 Oct., SDNA, 033.511 Laval, Pierre/98/1/8; Hugh Wilson's and Thomas W. Lamont's (for the President), 19 and 20 Oct. 1931, Herbert Hoover Presidential Library, 1-E/884.

126. See Zaleski and Filipowicz telegrams, 2, 22 Oct. 1931, HIA, Zaleski Papers; on Polish nervousness concerning the Laval visit and the Filipowicz–Castle conversation, see FRUS 1931, II, 597–99, 599–601; compare Wiley to Secretary of State, 2 Dec. 1931, SDNA, 760C.6215/572; YUL, MS, Stimson Diary, XVIII, 160. For a general assessment, see Pease, "The United States and the Polish Boundaries, 1931: An American Attempt to Revise the Polish Corridor," *The Polish Review*, 27 (Winter, 1982), 122–37; Leffler, *Elusive Question*, 265; Link, *Stabilisierungspolitik*, 506.

other prospect for the future "but a line-up between Germany, Britain, and perhaps ourselves against France."[127] As if to emphasize this attitude, the powerful chairman of the foreign relations committee, Senator William E. Borah, held a press conference at which he advocated a revision of the "corridor," of Upper Silesian borders, and of the Hungarian frontiers. Irrespective of whether he acted with the tacit approval of the administration, which found his bluntness embarrassing, it was clear that Borah said publicly what many leading Americans were saying in private.[128]

Politically, Laval's trip was a failure, although the premier tried hard, after his return, to represent it as a success. The chief French postulate, a ten-year political moratorium and a consultative pact with the United States, had been brushed aside. When the premier told Chłapowski that he thought he had convinced the Americans "of the correctness of the French thesis" on security, he either deceived himself or the Polish ambassador. He was closer to the truth when he claimed to have "acted completely along the lines of our interests," for he did defend the "corridor" and criticized Borah.[129]

Annus terribilis, to borrow Arnold Toynbee's term, was drawing to its end, leaving in its wake an expanding economic depression and social unrest. Contemporaries noted "a gradual, but quite distinct stiffening of the military spirit in Germany."[130] Revisionism was rampant and becoming more strident. During the November foreign policy debates in the French chamber antirevisionists and revisionists clashed with greater force. The former recalled the Sadova-Sedan sequel and demanded that France make it clear that the frontiers of Poland, Czechoslovakia, Romania, and Yugoslavia were "sacred for us." The latter, mainly socialists and communists, were receiving increased support from the radicals.[131] At the radical con-

127. YUL, MS, Stimson Diary, XVIII, 168–69, 175–76, 179; also FRUS 1931, II, 254; DBFP, II, II:287–90.

128. On the Borah incident: YUL, MS, Stimson Diary, XVIII, 181–82; Willys to Secretary of State, 26, 27 Oct., 2 Nov., and memo 19 Nov., SDNA, 760C.6215/553, 560, 561, and 564; Filipowicz telegram, 23 Oct., HIA, Zaleski Papers; Mühlstein report, 7 Nov., AAN, Amb. Berlin, 77. On Borah's revisionism, Claudel to Briand, 30 Mar. 1931, MAE, P.A. Puaux 255(29); on Polish press praising Laval for his stand against Borah, and for Czechoslovak representations to the senator, see Bressy and Charles-Roux to Briand, 29, 30 Oct., MAE, Y 61: 85–88, 110°–110°¹. For general appraisal, see Robert H. Ferrell, *American Diplomacy in the Great Depression: Hoover–Stimson Foreign Policy, 1929–1933* (New Haven, 1957), 202–203.

129. Zaleski and Chłapowski telegrams, 28 Oct., 6 Nov. 1931, HIA, respectively Zaleski Papers and Amb. Paryż, box 3.

130. Col. J. H. Marshall-Cornwall, 9 Dec. 1931, DBFP, II, II:522.

131. Foreign policy interpolations, 6 Nov.; speeches, 7 and 13 Nov. 1931, J.O. Chambre, especially 3312–15, 3317–18, 3321, 3363, 3369; and for Briand's speech in which he asserted yet again that in difficult times "Poland had always had France" at its side, 3373–78.

gress held in early November, Cot insisted that a European organization could only be built on Franco-German collaboration, hence the necessity for a détente in the "corridor," perhaps through internationalization of transports and a free zone in Danzig. The rising young vice-president of the party, Jacques Kayser, echoed Cot's sentiments. True, Herriot, who assumed the party's presidency, was unwilling to follow the left wing, and the final platform mentioned a revision of treaties without sacrificing Polish rights. It did ask, however, both Germans and Poles to listen to the voice of moderation and reason.[132]

Openly revisionist utterances combined with pacifist feelings provoked an extreme rightist backlash. In late November, the militants of the Croix de Feu broke up the International Congress of Disarmament held in Trocadéro. But there was also an atmosphere of hopelessness and gloom in Paris. It seemed useless to go farther in cooperation with Brüning, because the advent of Hitler could upset all the arrangements. People talked about Bolshevism and war; the morale of the industrial and financial circles was low. A prominent Frenchman, asked what France would do in the present situation, replied that it would do precisely what Britain and the United States had done when they had the power to act, namely nothing.[133]

Was Poland drifting away from France? Zaleski's comforting pronouncements drew the criticism of the Right and the Left, which accused him of indulging in vague generalities Yet, his position vis-à-vis his critics remained relatively strong.[134] Seeking to strengthen Poland's international standing and to ascertain to what extent Warsaw could count on British support against revisionism, the foreign minister went to London (10–11 December). The results of the visit proved to be meager. Zaleski's explanations why Poland could not consent to territorial concessions in the "corridor" seemed to interest the foreign secretary Sir John Simon much less than Polish views on the current state of Warsaw's relations with the USSR.[135] Zaleski had told the French that his London trip would be an

132. See *La République*, 7 Nov. 1931; Polish reports on the congress, AAN, MSZ 3701 and 3798; Höltje, *Weimarer Republik* 151–52, Laroche to Briand, 18 Nov., MAE, Z 698.12, Pologne 2198; Wiley to Kelley, 28 Nov. FDR, Wiley Papers, box 1. Revisionist articles multiplied in *Revue des Vivants* and *Notre Temps* (Jean Luchaire). See L'Huiller, "Francuzi," 55.

133. Bullitt to House, 13 Dec. 1931, YUL, William C. Bullitt Papers 1891–1967 (fragment). Compare Bullitt, *Correspondence*, 17; also Laval to Briand, 10 Dec. 1931, MAE, Z 698.12, Pologne 2198.

134. Zaleski spoke on 30 Oct. and 17 Dec.; for comments, see Laroche to Briand, 19, 20 Dec 1931, MAE, Z 698.1, Pologne 2099; compare Wiley to Secretary of State, Nov. 9, SDNA, 760C.00/48. *Gazeta Warszawska*, 18 Dec. 1931.

135. See Nowak-Kiełbikowa, "Wizyta." Compare Wandycz, *Zaleski*, 91–94. Also Simon to Erskine, 10 Dec. 1931 FO 371 15586 Hm 03795; Zaleski telegram, 11 Dec., SI, Amb. Londyn, A.12.52/12; Fleuriau to Briand, 15 Dec. 1931, MAE, Z 698.1, Pologne

attempt to alleviate Franco-British difficulties stemming from France's support of Poland. Did this mean a desire to lessen the French charge of Polish affairs, Laroche wondered? The ambassador worried that some Poles seemed to begin viewing the alliance as a façade that concealed a "disquieting unknown." Poland did not wish to abandon the alliance but wanted to make the French understand that it was not completely dependent on France's mercy. Laroche commented that although one might welcome a certain diminution of the charges that the alliance imposed, were it to disappear, a greater French freedom would be purchased at "a loss of a trump which after all has its importance." Worse still, a dissolution of the alliance would be "the first blow at the system on which France had relied since the conclusion of peace." Would such loss be "inconsequential for its authority and prestige even vis-à-vis Germany?"[136]

The report was characteristic for the perennial French dilemma of how to ease the burden of the alliance without losing Warsaw's allegiance altogether. The London trip, however, was not sufficient to force Paris to rethink the matter seriously. Zaleski, as the French saw it, was really trying to assure himself a place in the Paris-London dialogue.[137] But what about Piłsudski? The marshal's emotional outburst about Poland's future, in front of a young aide in October 1931, may have resulted from a fit of depression, but Piłsudski increasingly worried about the course of international events.[138] Around Christmas 1931, he told Beck that as collective security was weakening Poland would have to follow a more independent course, trying to settle on its own such issues as Danzig, the minority treaty, Lithuania and Teschen. Once again, he wondered whether Austria or Czechoslovakia would be first stricken off the map. The Teschen question could be resolved only as part of an international upheaval; biding its time Warsaw could meanwhile strengthen the Polish minority there and establish links with the Slovaks.[139] This sounded like a policy of *farà da se* with a definite anti-Czech component. But, because Piłsudski was above all a pragmatist, this need not be necessarily seen as a rigidly set long-range program.[140]

2099. For French interest in the "corridor" aspects of the conversations, London embassy report, 16 Jan. 1932, AAN, MSZ 3799.

136. Laroche to Briand, 1 Dec. 1931, MAE, Z 698.1, Pologne 2099. It seems that Zaleski had forewarned Laval and Berthelot of the visit on 21 and 25 Nov.

137. Fleuriau to Briand, 23 Dec. 1931, MAE, Z 698.1, Pologne 2099.

138. See Jędrzejewicz, *Kronika*, 2:400.

139. Beck, *Dernier rapport*, 8–10. There is no other source for this conversation. For beginning Polish subsidies to Slovak newspapers, see Kozeński, *Czechosłowacja*, 45.

140. For a different view of Valenta, namely that the subseqeunt periods of détente with Czechoslovakia were merely the result of Polish tactics—the anti-Prague goals remaining unchanged—see *Češi a Poláci*, 2:353.

There was much unfinished business as the year 1931 ended. Neither Paris nor Prague had succeeded in elaborating an acceptable program of Danubian cooperation; the French and Polish nonaggression pacts with the USSR were merely initialed. Proposals for a political moratorium proved vain, and German revisionism continued unabated. At times French diplomacy showed a lack of imagination and seemed to work at cross-purposes. In a sense, it was a year of missed opportunities, for Paris succeeded neither in Berlin nor in Rome. Financial diplomacy had offered possibilities that were not fully exploited. If the French government perceived them clearly, it lacked the courage to pursue vast objectives rapidly enough in the teeth of domestic opposition. True, France was both a creditor and a debtor, which was awkward; the Anglo-Saxon powers constantly applied brakes. Paradoxically, if French wealth was a mighty political weapon, so was German misery, which aroused much sympathy and understanding in Washington and London.[141] With the first effects of the depression visibile in France and the accelerated German drive for revision, the future looked none too bright.

141. This concluding paragraph is influenced by and convergent with the views of Vaïsse, *Sécurité*, 98–104, 123.

Chapter Eight

French Initiatives and Failures

Plan Tardieu

In early January 1932, Chancellor Brüning let it be known that Germany would not resume reparation payments. In mid-February, Austria appealed for aid to assist its economy, expressing willingness to cooperate with its neighbors. It became imperative to propose concrete measures to deal with the situation. A British suggestion of a Danubian customs union, however, aroused unjustified suspicions in Rome and Berlin that it was French-inspired.[1] The Italians continued to voice their preference for an Italo-Austro-Hungarian combination; the Germans had not abandoned their notion of an alignment with Vienna and Prague. Beneš's idea of a five-states economic group (the Little Entente, Hungary, and Austria)—"a kind of a League of Nations in miniature"—aroused criticism at the Quai d'Orsay on the grounds that it would be opposed by Italy and in the long run permit German penetration of the region. A narrower Czechoslovak-Austrian-Hungarian bloc, based on preferential tariffs and quota arrangements seemed preferable. If it cut across the Little Entente, the community of its political interests coupled with French influence in Prague was believed a sufficient safeguard against a disintegration of this grouping. True, there would be opposition from Czechoslovak industrial and agrarian circles, which had already delayed the Czechoslovak-Hungarian trade negotiations, but this barrier was not insurmountable. It was important, however, to gain Italy's support, for whenever it was lacking Beneš took refuge in an attitude of prudent reserve.[2]

Governmental changes in Paris interfered with the formulation of a con-

1. See Stambrook, "British Proposal"; Carmi, *La Grande Bretagne*, 171–78. For conflicting French and British views, see Girault, "Korreferat zu Jacques Bariéty," 389–92.

2. See Bourdeillette, "Note sur le rapprochement économique des pays danubiens," 20 Jan., and "Situation financière et économique de l'Europe Centrale," 11 Feb. 1932, MAE, P.A. Tardieu 84(692). For Berthelot's lookwarm attitude toward Danubian entente see Girault, "Crise," 373. Relevant correspondence in MAE, P.A. Tardieu 84(692) and 85(693) and P.A. Puaux 255(29).

crete program, much to Prague's chagrin.[3] Briand's death in March symbolized the passing of Briandism, although its basic concepts never completely disappeared. The advent of Tardieu, as premier and foreign
minister, whose personal ambition combined with the need for success before the May elections, hastened the formulation of a plan of action in the
Danubian region. It was essential to devise a system offering financial security to France and strengthening its economic and political influence in
the area. Tardieu had explored Czechoslovak reactions to a new French
initiative already before the formation of his cabinet; now an interrelated
activity began.[4]

Beneš insisted that Paris secure British backing and affect a rapprochement with Italy. He succeeded in convincing Sir John Simon of the imprac-
ticability of a Danubian customs union; a greatly impressed Massigli
wrote that Prague alone "had a policy." Beneš's program to which he had
won over the Romanians and the Yugoslavs was based on the following
elements: the Little Entente would work for an economic agreement with
Austria and Hungary starting with a Czechoslovak-Hungarian commercial accord; to achieve a cohesive single group, both agrarian and industrial preferences would be accepted; and, while a detailed plan was being
worked out, there would be no negotiations with the great powers, the
latter being asked only for their general approval of intra-Danubian negotiations. This plan did not eliminate the participation of Germany and
Italy; in fact, they were expected to divide between themselves much of
their industrial exports, which Czechoslovakia and Austria would be unable to supply to the Danubian market.[5]

The Quai d'Orsay, regarding the three-state alignment as easier to
achieve and more firmly grounded in economic realities, was not ready to
accept Beneš's program in toto. Paris felt that it had the right to expect
Beneš's compliance with French wishes especially at a moment when the
Czechoslovak loan was being approved.[6] Still, there were important arguments against a narrower group: it would not resolve the problem of
Czech and Austrian industries, and by excluding Romania and Yugoslavia

3. See Chłapowski report, 1 Feb. 1932, AAN, MSZ 3799; compare 7 Jan. briefing,
KV, CPP.

4. See Bariéty, "Der Tardieu Plan," 374–75. On fears that a worsening Danubian
crisis "will be very prejudicial, because we will no longer receive the interest on the
money we have invested in all these countries," see minister of finance to Tardieu (?), 28
Feb. 1932, MAE, P.A. Tardieu 85(693). Views of Stanislas de Castellane in Chłapowski
report, 13 Feb. 1932, AAN, MSZ 3799.

5. See Bystrický and Deák, *Európa*, 57–59; Massigli and Charles-Roux to ministry,
17 and 25 Feb. 1932, MAE, P.A. Tardieu 84(692).

6. Tardieu to Massigli, 22 Feb. 1932, MAE, P.A. Tardieu 84(692). On Massigli–Beneš
conversations and on Quai d'Orsay attitude toward Prague, see Bariéty, "Der Plan Tardieu," 376–77.

would make them even more dependent on Germany. That was also the viewpoint of Massigli, who felt that the Little Entente was a reality and had to be "treated with consideration."[7] It fell to Beneš to convince Tardieu—who had with him a project for a "féderation danubienne" involving credits to Austria and Hungary—that only a preferential system worked out by the five interested states without the participation of the great powers was acceptable. After the conversation, Beneš cabled Prague: "having reached an agreement with me, Tardieu elaborated his memorandum." Krofta could thus tell his collaborators that the Tardieu Plan was "in fact our plan, the plan of Minister Beneš."[8]

The document that Tardieu submitted to Britain, Italy, the Danubian states, and Poland (between 2 and 7 February) foresaw a system of mutual tariff reductions in the Danubian area leading possibly toward an elimination of economic barriers. Because Czechoslovakia and Austria could not absorb the agricultural surpluses of the remaining three countries, these products would be granted unilateral preferential treatment by outside powers without any quid pro quo. A special international fund would be established to assist the process of organization and adjustment.

The drawbacks of the plan, an outgrowth of the 1931 French and Czechoslovak projects, were numerous.[9] Czechoslovak agriculture and certain branches of Hungarian production would be endangered by foreign competition. The predominantly agrarian states would find their economy dominated by Czechoslovak and Austrian industries. The great powers would not only have to make some sacrifices but also be expected to contribute financially. The large overseas exporters, such as the United States and Argentina, were bound to resent the competition of the Danubian countries on the European market.

The French expressed their willingness to accept some derogations to the most-favored-nation clause, although this could have an impact on trade relations with Germany, and to contemplate financial aid. They were less eager to absorb extra agricultural imports.[10] The British, moving toward an imperial economic bloc (culminating in the Ottawa Conference), did not want to tie their hands. The Labour Party criticized the Tardieu Plan as an anti-German French scheme of dominating Europe.[11] Germany

---

7. Massigli to Tardieu, 27 Feb. 1932, MAE, P.A. Tardieu 84(692).

8. Krofta to missions, 6 Mar., and briefing, 10 Mar. 1932, KV, CPP. Chłapowski heard at the Quai d'Orsay that it had favored a tripartite arrangement, but gave in "to categorical demands of Min. Beneš who considered that [it] . . . would be fatal for the existence of the Little Entente." 11 Mar. 1932 report, AAN, MSZ 1521.

9. For a good analysis, see Bariéty, "Der Tardieu Plan," 378–79.

10. On positive reactions of the French press, see Edge to Secretary of State, 8 Mar. 1932, SDNA, 640.0031, Danub/23, 660H.6331/66.

11. *Daily Herald*, 30 Mar. 1932; see also Carmi, *Le Grande Bretagne*, 185–88.

took a negative stand arguing, with some justification, that the plan would not satisfy the needs of the agrarian countries.[12] The Italians, whose support the Quai d'Orsay tried hard to obtain, quickly came to regard the plan as a political maneuver sponsored by Beneš, and designed to place Hungary and Austria at the mercy of Czechoslovakia while diminishing Italian influence in the Danubian region. On 8 March, Rome infomed Paris and Prague of the conclusion of preferential treaties with Vienna and Budapest, a move that appeared to Beneš almost as dangerous as the defunct Curtius-Schober project. Vexed with Italian policies, Tardieu assured the Czechoslovak minister that the French would remain "maîtres du jeu."[13]

Despite the basic Czechoslovak identification with the Tardieu Plan, Prague was somewhat critical of the improvisations and even opportunism inherent in it. What is more, when Krofta spoke of the necessity of accepting the whole scheme for "political reasons," he had in mind the connection between the Tardieu Plan and the concurrent program of Flandin, which seemed to aim at rebuilding the prewar Austro-Hungarian market even if under a Franco-Czechoslovak aegis.[14] This may explain the critical comments in the Czechoslovak press, which also reflected vested interests of the agrarian and industrial circles. Paris did its best to persuade the Czechoslovak government to promote the plan, and it publicly extolled Czechoslovakia as the cornerstone of a Danubian organization.[15] Beneš, although not overly optimistic about the scheme's chances, did advertise it in parliament, while playing down his own involvement and carefully avoiding remarks that could give offense to the powers. Presenting the Tardieu Plan as a step in the direction of Briand's European union, he denied its anti-German edge and deemed Italian apprehensions as unjustified. But he also declared that if Rome and Berlin rejected the proposal, it stood no chance of being realized.[16]

12. See Campbell, *Confrontation*, 238–39; Ormos, "Problème," 33–35; Kühl, *Föderationspläne*, 46–47; Antonín Basch, *The Danube Basin and the German Economic Sphere* (London, 1944), 63–65.

13. Beaumarchais to Tardieu and Quai d'Orsay to Massigli, 11 and 10 Mar. 1932, MAE, P.A. Tardieu 84(692); compare dispatches of Charles-Roux, Massigli, Tardieu, and Vienne, 8, 9, 15, 20 Mar., MAE, P.A. Tardieu 84(692); also Przeździecki report, 18 Mar., AAN, MSZ 1521; compare Bystrický and Deák, *Európa*, 65; Bariéty, "Der Plan Tardieu," 380.

14. See Sládek and Tomaszewski, "Próby w latach trzydziestych," 386–87; compare Chłapowski report, 11 Mar. 1932, AAN, MSZ 1521; briefing, 10 Mar. KV, CPP.

15. See statements of Tardieu, 4 Mar., CAE/Ch; 5 Mar. 1932, J.O. Chambre, 1136.

16. 22 Mar. 1932 speech in Beneš, *Boj o mír*, 637–48; comments in Seguin and Charles-Roux reports, 18, 22, 24, 26 Mar., MAE, P.A. Tardieu 84(692). On Beneš's lack of enthusiasm, Wysocki report, 16 Mar., PI, Amb. Londyn, reel 44; memorandum by Castle, 29 Mar., FRUS 1932, I, 851. On Beneš's "low profile," see *Gazeta War-*

Beneš, who had previously showed no desire for a French mediation in the Czechoslovak-Hungarian commercial deadlock, concluded that the Tardieu Plan had improved Prague's position to the extent that "finally we shall have Hungary where the Little Entente wanted it to be for years."[17] Indeed, on economic grounds, Budapest could ill afford to antagonize Paris. As for the merits of the plan, the Hungarians were divided in their opinions.[18] French diplomats urged Prague to reestablish trade relations with Budapest so as to "bar economically the road" to Germany and Italy and provide a strong basis for the Tardieu Plan. But commercial talks dragged on, the Hungarian attitude being, in the Czech view, determined by the slogan "money from France, revisionism from Italy."[19]

The Little Entente, guided by Beneš, adopted a friendly but cautious attitude toward the French initiative. They did not wish to offend Berlin and Rome and saw no replacement for the German market. There was also a recurring concern lest the Tardieu Plan resurrect French ideas (first broached in 1920) of a Danubian federation.[20] The Little Entente went along with Tardieu when he conceded to the British that the four-powers conference held in London should precede any intra-Danubian negotiations. Beneš suggested, however, that general principles established by the powers be translated into concrete arrangements by the smaller states. He insisted that Paris refuse to accept any definite measures without the consent of the Little Entente.[21] In a confidential aide-memoire for Tardieu, Beneš spelled out once again his postulates: no participation of any great power in the Danubian preferential system; equality of treatment for the five states concerned; and the disappearance of special Italo-Austro-Hungarian arrangements while leaving an open door for Vienna to deal with Rome and Berlin. If financial aid to the Danubian countries required additional guarantees, his country would be willing to provide them.[22]

The four-powers conference held in London on 6–8 April turned out to

---

szawska, 16 Mar. 1932; also Hamilton Fish Armstrong, *Peace and Counterpeace: From Wilson to Hitler, Memoirs* (New York, 1971), 495.

17. Beneš to Udržal cited in *O Československé zahraniční politice*, 189. Compare briefing, 7 Jan. 1932, KV, CPP; Charles-Roux report, 25 Feb. 1932, MAE, P.A. Tardieu 84(692).

18. See Juhász, *Foreign Policy*, 101–102; Kühl, *Föderationspläne*, 46–47; Ránki, *Economy*, 105–107; Bystrický and Deák, *Európa*, 64–65; Gajanova, *ČSR*, 294–95; Ormos, "Sécurité," 312; Stephen Borsody, *The Tragedy of Central Europe* (New York, 1962), 57–58.

19. Cited in Gajanová, *ČSR*, 295. See also Vienne and Charles-Roux reports, 20 Mar., 2 Apr. 1932, MAE, P.A. Tardieu 84(692).

20. See Bystrický and Deák, *Európa*, 71–72; Carmi, *La Grande Bretagne*, 189–93; Campus, *Mica Înțelegere*, 102.

21. Beneš telegram to missions, 24 Mar. 1932, CPP.

22. Charles-Roux to Tardieu, 2 Apr. 1932, MAE, P.A. Tardieu 84(692).

be "a miserable failure" in Jan Masaryk's words. The envoy wondered how the French might have assumed that it could be otherwise.[23] British unwillingness to back France on financial aid to the region destroyed the only trump Paris had. Italy took a negative stand and so did Germany, characterizing the Tardieu Plan as a political attempt to constitute with the help of French gold "a bloc of Danubian states over which France would exert a dominating influence, either directly or through the intermediary of Czechoslovakia."[24] Krofta thought that because France had no chance of establishing a political hegemony in the Danubian area having only limited economic relations with the region (loans were an insufficient instrument of control), all it could do was to seek to prevent German domination. Perhaps one could still gain Italian cooperation.[25]

Exploring various ways to salvage the Tardieu Plan, Beneš sought a reaffirmation by the Little Entente (meeting in Belgrade on 13–15 May in the presence of Zaleski as an observer) of its adherence to the project. He promised his associates to obtain French financial assistance, and they agreed to oppose aid to Austria and Hungary before a solution of the general Danubian problems.[26]

Continuing French efforts in the region were adversely affected by Tardieu's loss of general elections, although his cabinet continued to function as a caretaker until the formation of the Herriot ministry in June. Herriot's interest in this field was limited, and he experienced difficulties with an international loan floated by the Austrians and approved by the powers in July. The Tardieu Plan was dead, but despite real differences of approach between Paris and Prague, Franco-Czechoslovak collaboration had passed this test remarkably well. The Quai d'Orsay lauded Prague as a faithful and loyal ally that had "brought the most reliable support" to France.[27]

The Polish case was different. Poland had not been consulted during the preliminary exchanges, and when the Polish chargé d'affaires complained about being faced with a fait accompli, he was told that only a general

23. Masaryk to Mastný, 9 Apr. (compare his pessimistic letter, 14 Apr.) 1932, ANM, Mastný, 7/491 and 492.

24. Telegram from embassy in Berlin, 10 Apr. 1932, MAE, P.A. Puaux 255(26).

25. Briefings, 21 Apr., 4 May KV, CPP; compare Charles-Roux and Beaumarchais dispatches, 11, 23 May 1932, MAE, P.A. Tardieu 85(963) and Puaux 255(29). On Beneš's thinking about the London conference, see his telegram to missions, 13 Apr., CPP.

26. Dispatches of Charles-Roux, Puaux, Dubail, and Naggiar, 3, 18, 20, 27 May 1932, MAE, P.A. Tardieu 85(693) and Z 864.10, Tchécoslovaquie 2601; compare briefing, 19 May, KV, CPP, Bystrický and Deák, *Európa*, 74–75; Campbell, *Confrontation*, 242. Also Marek report, 22 June (intercept), SHA, EMA/2, Tchécoslovaquie 14.

27. Note, 9 May 1932, "Politique extérieure de la Tchécoslovaquie," also Charles-Roux to Tardieu, 16 May, MAE, Z 684.1, Tchécoslovaquie 2568.

project existed, which Tardieu had discussed solely with Beneš.[28] Two days later, however, the Quai d'Orsay instructed Laroche to stress the importance "we attach to the assistance that the government in Warsaw would give to this work so consequential for the recovery of Central Europe."[29] Beck felt that although the French proposal was inspired by the same concern that had made Poland promote the agrarian bloc, Polish economic interests in the Danubian area needed to be protected. Moreover, the Poles wanted to be associated with the negotiations on the great powers' level. Laroche recommended care be taken not to aggravate Poland's position or offend its sensibilities, especially as the opposition press claimed that Poland's interests were being ignored. The fact that Prague seemed to be treated as the number-one ally in Central Europe, and that Berlin had been notified of the Tardieu Plan earlier than Warsaw, did provoke some annoyance.[30]

Beneš assumed that the Poles strove after a loose association with the nascent grouping, not unlike the way in which Poland had been connected with the Little Entente. This assumption was incorrect, for Warsaw's principal concern was to be involved in the negotiations.[31] Hence, Poland's exclusion from the London conference rankled, being viewed as a blow to the country's prestige.[32] Speaking of Berlin's interest in Poland's attitude toward the Tardieu Plan, Beck dwelt on German machinations, which under a friendly guise aimed to "undermine and weaken the Polish-French relations."[33] Thus, if German and Polish negative views on the economic aspects of the Tardieu Plan happened to converge, one can hardly speak of Warsaw and Berlin jointly killing the project.[34] Warsaw, for all its objections, was aware of the political desirability of a Danubian group, and

28. Chłapowski telegram, 4 Mar. 1932, HIA, Amb. Paryż, box 3.

29. A copy of the Tardieu Plan was given "à titre personel" to Zaleski in Geneva, and to the ministry only on 7 Mar. See Quai d'Orsay to French delegation and Laroche, 6 Mar.; Laroche to Tardieu, 7 Mar. 1932, MAE, P.A. Tardieu 84(692).

30. Laroche to Tardieu 8, 9, 10 Mar. 1932, MAE, P.A. Tardieu 84(692); Beck to missions, 8, 9 Mar., SI, Amb. Londyn, A.12.52/12; also telegram 11 (or 12) Mar., HIA, Amb. Paryż, box 3. On Polish public opinion, see Girsa reports, 8, 11, 23 Mar. 1932, CPP; Willys to Secretary of State, 9 Mar., SDNA, 640.0031, Danub/14. Compare *Gazeta Warszawska*, 8, 11, 26 Mar., 1 Apr. 1932.

31. Briefing, 25 Feb. 1932, KV, CPP; compare Beck telegram, 1 Apr.; Skirmunt dispatches, 24, 30 Mar., Zaleski–Moltke conversation, 7 Apr., SI, Amb. Londyn, A.12.52/12 and AAN, MSZ 1521; J. Kostanecki memo, 1 Apr., PI, Amb. Londyn, reel 45. Compare Willys to Secretary of State, 16 Mar. 1932, SDNA, 640.0031, Danub/33.

32. See FRUS 1932, I, 853, 855–56; compare briefing, 21 Apr. 1932, KV, CPP, also Beck–Mühlstein exchange 1 and 5 Apr., HIA, Amb. Paryż, box 3.

33. Beck telegram to missions, 13 Apr. 1932, AAN, MSZ 1521.

34. For a different view see Valenta in *Češi a Poláci*, 2:533; compare Pułaski, *Stosunki*, 41; Krasuski, *Stosunki 1926–1932*, 288–90; Schimitzek, *Drogi*, 229–30.

it continued, unlike Germany, to voice its approval of the plan were it only because of its relationship to France.[35] After the London conference, Zaleski suggested that the issue of Danubian reconstruction be treated as part of a larger scheme including reparations, American debts, and general European monetary problems. Paris "appreciated the willingness of the Polish government to collaborate" with France.[36]

The fluctuations of the Tardieu Plan awakened an echo in the Polish-Czechoslovak relationship. A Czech national democratic deputy questioned Beneš why nothing was being done to associate Warsaw with a Central European organization.[37] After the failure of the London conference, Beneš decided to revive the idea of a Polish-Czechoslovak customs union through inspired articles in the press. His motivation, as once before, was purely tactical. As he told Charles-Roux "except in the case when Czechoslovakia would find itself completely isolated, it would not seriously envisage such a device."[38] No wonder that Polish governmental circles wished for such an isolation to occur. In these circumstances Krofta's public lecture at the Jagiellonian University and Zaleski's remarks that a balance of power in Central Europe depended on Czechoslovak-Polish cooperation were deprived of political significance.[39]

French-Polish Malaise

If the Tardieu Plan had produced some ripples in Franco-Polish relationship, the Romanian aspect of the nonaggression pacts with Russia contributed to more serious friction. France, as we remember, had initialed its treaty with the USSR in August 1931, delaying the final signing until the conclusion of a Polish-Soviet pact. The latter, initialed in January 1932, was to be finalized when Romania would complete its negotiations with

35. Zaleski to Skirmunt, 2 May 1932, PI, Amb. Londyn, reel 44. Zaleski viewed the Tardieu Plan as "quite muddled," and Polish diplomacy was aware of Berthelot's and Coulondre's skepticism. See Chłapowski and Zaleski telegrams, 8, 11 March, and 13 Apr., HIA, Amb. Paryż, box 3. Compare briefing, 21 Apr., KV, CPP.

36. See Polish aide-mémoire, 9 May (Chłapowski dates it 7 May) and French reply 13 May; also Zaleski to Beck, 15 Apr., SI, MSZ, A.11/49/F/3/3; Charles-Roux to Tardieu, 14 May, MAE, P.A. Tardieu 85(693); Chłapowski telegram, 7 May 1932, HIA, Amb. Paryż, box 3.

37. See Grzybowski report, 2 Apr. 1932, PI, Amb. Londyn, reel 45.

38. Charles-Roux to Tardieu, 9 Apr. 1932, MAE, P.A. Tardieu 85(693). For the Czechoslovak press, see cuttings in MZV-VA 478.1246. On Krofta's views, which were somewhat divergent from Beneš's, see report from Prague, 9 May 1932, AAN, Amb. Berlin, 51, and Grzybowski letter, 17 May, AAN, MSZ 5505.

39. See Girsa to Beneš, 28 May 1932, and Krofta's mention of Polish efforts to give his Cracow visit a political significance it did not have, in briefing, 14 June, KV, CPP. Compare Charles-Roux to Tardieu, 9 Mar. 1932, MAE, P.A. Tardieu 84(692).

Moscow. There was no unanimity of views in Paris on the desirability of these accords. Weygand grudgingly admitted that a treaty between War-saw and Moscow made sense, but was dubious about a Franco-Soviet pact. According to Berthelot, Laval was not opposed to the nonaggression pacts but did not exaggerate their importance. Still, the conclusion "of a chain of peace pacts along the western frontiers of Russia" was not re-garded as negligible.[40] When Tardieu came to power, Litvinov surmised that an improvement of relations with the Soviet Union was not part of his government's main tasks and objectives.[41] As far as Paris was concerned, Bucharest could procrastinate. This placed Poland in an awkward posi-tion, lessening its possibilities of applying pressure on the Romanians.[42]

At first Zaleski, Piłsudski and Beck were willing to give Bucharest—for the sake of the alliance—ample time to resolve its difficulties with Mos-cow. But, as time went on, Piłsudski grew impatient with Romanian dila-tory tactics. Returning from his Egyptian visit in mid-April via Bucharest, the marshal brutally told the Romanians that Poland could not afford fur-ther delays. His diatribe was partly directed against the French leaders who, as he put it, changed "the political line from one day to the next, Tardieu throwing into the garbage pail what Briand did." After all it was France that had "put in motion this Polish-Soviet train." Piłsudski went on: "I am not French! If I make policy with twenty people who change tomorrow what they did yesterday, you'd like that a lot, wouldn't you?" Warsaw followed a consistent course based on alliance with Romania and a sphere of influence in the Baltic region, and Piłsudski wanted Romania to abandon its "present negative position."[43]

The Romanians complained to Paris. Did the Quai d'Orsay believe, they asked, that Poland would sign without Romania and without informing France? Laroche was instructed to lecture the Poles on the virtue of soli-darity between all border states, but this remonstrance had little effect. Piłsudski had made up his mind that if after a certain period efforts to find a way out of the Soviet-Romanian embroglio failed, Warsaw would pro-ceed with the signature of the pact. This decision amounted to an ultima-tum, and Warsaw refused to join France in making a demarche in Moscow

40. See Zaleski and Chłapowski telegrams, 2, 7 Jan. 1932, HIA. Amb. Paryż, box 3; Chłapowski reports, 11 Jan. PI, Amb. Londyn, reel 44; 31 Jan., in Łopatniuk, "Niez-nane dokumenty," 188–89; compare Berthelot to Puaux, 3 Feb., MAE, P.A. Puaux 255(26).

41. See DVP SSSR, xv, 213; compare Zaleski to Beck, 26 Feb. 1932, SI, MSZ, A.11. 44/F/3/11. Also Bystrický and Deák, *Európa*, 70; Scott, *Alliance*, 36–38.

42. See Bacon, *Closed Doors*, 62, 93, 96–97; compare Massigli to Berthelot, 11 Feb., 10 Mar. 1932, MAE, P.A. Massigli 4; also Zaleski telegrams, 26 Feb., 11 Mar., SI, MSZ, A.11.49/F/3/11 and HIA, Amb. Paryż, box 3.

43. 13 Apr. meeting, Bacon, *Closed Doors*, 97–99; numerous dispatches in MAE, P.A. Puaux 255(29); Girsa report, 2 Mar. 1932. Also Bułhak, "Polska a Rumunia," 325–26.

to help the Romanians. The delays, it said, were not caused by Russia but by Bucharest. The distance between Warsaw and Paris was growing.[44]

Nicolae Titulescu, the real power behind Romania's diplomacy, did everything to play Paris against the Poles.[45] Somewhat perplexed, Tardieu wished to make Bucharest aware of "the delicate situation in which the French government would find itself if Poland gave effect to Piłsudski's warning." Simultaneously, he was telling Warsaw "to maintain a united front," and tried to avoid giving the impression that "we are disinterested in these negotiations."[46] This "elaborately devious policy" angered Zaleski, for it enabled the Romanian government "to pretend that France not only did not encourage it to conclude [the treaty], but seemed to prefer that it not be concluded."[47] When in early June, the Romanians protested against another Polish ultimatum, Laroche, while deploring such high-handed methods (which he ascribed to Beck), observed that if Paris wanted Romania to sign, it had to say so in a way "that would leave no room for any doubt about our point of view." He recalled how a few months earlier "we had been pressing the Polish government" to conclude a pact with Russia; now Warsaw was placed in "an absolutely false position" vis-à-vis Moscow.[48]

The replacement of Tardieu by Herriot brought no clarifications. The new premier and foreign minister did not show a full grasp of the negotiations with the USSR, and was unable to answer Ambassador Dovgalevsky's query whether France made its own nonaggression treaty dependent on the successful conclusion of Russo-Romanian talks.[49] In these conditions the Poles waited no longer. On 25 July, they signed the nonaggression treaty with the USSR leaving Bucharest with a vague promise not to ratify the pact until Romania signed its own accord.

Warsaw regarded the treaty as a great success. It provided for mutual

44. See Bacon, *Closed Doors*, 99; Laroche and Tardieu telegrams, 19 Apr. 1932, MAE. P.A. Puaux 255(26); also Beck telegram, 24 Apr., HIA, Amb. Paryż, box 3. Also Skrzypek, "Zagadnienie rumuńskie," 192–93, and his "Polsko-radziecki pakt," 27–28.

45. Bacon, *Closed Doors*, 101–104; 11 May 1932 telegram from Geneva, MAE, P.A. Puaux 255(26). For Polish views: 3 Mar. session in the senate, Sprawozdania stenograficzne, xxxii/18–20. See also Lungu, "Titulescu," 185–213.

46. See Bystrický and Deák, *Európa*, 222, 230–32; Kvaček, *Nad Evropou*, 45–46, and his "Ke genezi," 302; Campus, *The Little Entente and the Balkan Entente* (Bucureşti, 1978), 52–54; also DDF, I, II:244 and 704; ADAP, C.I/1: 66–67; SDNA, 770.00/229; Massigli to Coulondre, 16 Feb. 1933, MAE, P.A. Massigli 4.

47. Laroche telegram, 7 June 1932, MAE, P.A. Puaux 255(26). On Tardieu's deviousness see J. D. Greenway memorandum on French-Polish-Romanian negotiations, 13 Feb. 1932, FO 371 17234 1611.

48. See Laroche telegram, 13 June 1932; compare with Puaux's dispatches, 10, 14 June, and Quai d'Orsay to Puaux, 13 June, MAE, P.A. Puaux 255(26) and (28).

49. See DVP SSSR, xv, 440–41 and DDF, I, 1:105. Compare Herriot, *Jadis*, 2:312.

renunciation of war and aggression; neutrality in case of attack by a third party; maintenance of international engagements; and a promise not to enter into accords directed against the other signatory. Existing alliances with France and Romania remained untouched; the German-Soviet pincers were pried open. Warsaw thought it had proved its ability to reach a direct settlement with one of the mighty neighbors without outside (French) assistance.[50] If a similar pact could be achieved on the German side, Piłsudski's cardinal tenet of balance between Berlin and Moscow would be realized. Thus, the marshal did not look upon the treaty as a first step toward an alignment with Russia; in that sense, Polish objectives were limited, not to say negative.

The reaction in France was largely adverse.[51] Recalling that the original impulse for the pacts had come from Paris, the Poles complained at the Quai d'Orsay. In response, the French spoke of the Romanian angle and dwelt on the fact that the Poles were at first reluctant to enter into negotiations and then became too eager. Chłapowski suspected that French displeasure stemmed from the belief that France would have to face now the finalization of its own treaty with Moscow. Herriot admitted that much, mentioning intensified Russian pressure.[52] Paris was also annoyed with the new manifestation of Polish independence and toughness. Herriot opined that if Warsaw hurried with the ratification, leaving Romania in the cold, this would alter the character of the policy concerning nonaggression pacts, and unfavorably affect Franco-Polish relations.[53] Paris's own efforts, however, to force Bucharest to clarify its position proved vain; Romanian-Soviet negotiations ground to a halt. On 29 November, under vastly changed international conditions, France signed her treaty with Russia; Poland had ratified its own nine days earlier. During this last phase the Poles kept the French closely informed of the developments, a fact Paris appreciated.[54]

A certain amount of ill feeling produced by the Soviet-Romanian aspect was augmented by friction in a bilateral Franco-Polish relationship. Listing

50. Piłsudski allegedly told the Romanians that their two countries ought to arrange their own own affairs outside of France. See DDF, I, 1:103–104.

51. On French reaction, Scott, *Alliance*, 57–58. Stroński assured the "French friends" in *Kurjer Warszawski*, (7 Aug.) that the pact did not change one iota in the Franco-Polish alliance. On Polish press see, DDF, I, 1:109–110.

52. Chłapowski reports, 30 July, 13 Aug. 1932, AAN, MSZ, P.II, w.65, t.4b (old classification) and DiM, v, 596–98; also Bacon, *Closed Doors*, 146–47.

53. Herriot to Warsaw and Bucharest missions, 3 Aug. 1932, DDF, I, 1:142–43.

54. A useful overview of the Franco-Soviet and East European-Soviet negotiations appears in "Note pour le Président du Conseil" 23 Nov. 1932, DDF, I, II:53–61. There may have been some guilty feeling at the Quai d'Orsay, for Berthelot wondered if Polish moves occurred because the French had "meddled a bit in the Romanian negotiations." See Mühlstein telegram, 2 Nov. 1932, HIA, Amb. Paryż, box 3.

several points of discord a Quai d'Orsay note concluded: "It is indubitable that a general malaise reigns at present in French-Polish relations," which could have adverse effects on French economic interests, not to mention "untoward political repercussions from which our influence would inevitably suffer."[55]

At this time long-standing Polish grievances over the activities of the French-controlled Żyrardów textile mills exploded. Żyrardów had been showing deficits since 1931; the mishandling of workers by the French management led to the assassination of one of the directors and to violent press attacks described by Paris as an "abominable defamation campaign against French capitalists." Only strong pressure forced Warsaw to stop a public scandal.[56] Less dramatic were French-Polish confrontations over the Fiat contract, and the failure of the second installment of railroad credits to arrive as promised by Schneider. The Poles argued that they had made far-reaching concessions to attract French capital without a significant result. The "abandonment of the greatest work of French expansion in Poland . . . would not fail to exert a disastrous influence on the general situation in Central Europe." It could only strengthen German beliefs that France was renouncing its traditional policy in that part of the continent.[57] Indeed, what General Sikorski characterized as Poland's humiliating "begging" for credits was producing no results.[58]

In the military sector, Piłsudski was demonstrating his dissatisfaction by dispensing with, in a cavalier manner, the services of the French mission. The marshal never had a rapport with France's military establishment, which (with few exceptions) barely concealed its contempt for the self-taught "dilettante." Weygand allegedly called Piłsudski "an usurper even in his legend."[59] In turn, the Polish high command reciprocated occasionally with pin-pricks.[60] The contract of the military mission was due to ex-

---

55. "Note pour le Ministre," 28 May 1932, MAE, Z 698.12, Pologne 2198. On the difficulties of French capitalists, see DDF, I, 1:668–70.

56. Detailed treatment in Landau and Tomaszewski, *Sprawa*, 110–56.

57. Note for Herriot and aide-mémoire for President Lebrun, 25 May 1932, SI, MSZ, A.11. 49/F/3 nos. 6 and 7; compare Zaleski to Beck, 26 Feb., SI, MSZ, A.11.49/F/3/11; also Herriot, II, 291, Girsa report, 16 Apr., 10 Sept. 1932, CPP; *Gazeta Warszawska*, 25 Mar. 1932.

58. Sikorski to Paderewski, 19 May 1932, AAN, Archiwum Ignacego Paderewskiego, 29558. Compare DDF, I, 1:137–38, 359–60; I, II:96–97. According to Senator Targowski, the 1932 efforts were the last to work out a close economic relationship with France. Already in 1931 Premier Prystor concluded that the endeavors were hopeless. I obtained this information from Professor Landau who cites Adam Koc's testimony AAN, BBWR, t.115, 56.

59. Sikorski to Paderewski, 30 June 1929, AAN, Archiwum Ignacego Paderewskiego 29556.

60. The Poles sent only a minor general and no honor guard to Foch's funeral. See

pire in late 1932, and the French were startled to learn in April that the Poles not only wished no extension but decided to terminate the naval mission as well. This was a blow to "our amour propre," the French confessed, and sharp words were exchanged.[61] In August, Polish officials bid farewell to the two missions in a most perfunctory way.[62] In October, Piłsudski received Colonel (shortly to become general) Charles d'Arbonneau, the first genuine French military attaché, for his predecessor, Major Geoffroy du Périer de Larsan, named in 1928, had been restricted in his functions by the existence of the military mission. The marshal addressed d'Arbonneau "as a soldier to a soldier" with a frankness that verged on rudeness. If the attaché was likely to meet with coolness, Piłsudski said, this would stem from the "regretable policy that France had conducted toward Poland." Yes, the marshal declared, "France will abandon us, France will betray us! This is what I think, and this is what I should tell you."[63] Analyzing Piłsudski's long-standing mistrust of France, Laroche opined that the marshal did not wish to do away with the alliance because he had nothing else to put in its place. But while maintaining it, he did so "without enthusiasm and even with skepticism."[64]

The events in France during early 1932 did nothing to dispel this skepticism. The replacement of Briand by Laval in January had aroused some Polish hopes, but the advent of Tardieu quenched them.[65] Indeed, the head of the Truppenamt, General Kurt von Hammerstein, thought that Germany could reach an understanding with Tardieu more easily than with Briand. On 29–30 April, unofficial representatives of Tardieu and Brüning were present at a secret meeting in Luxembourg of prominent French and German industrialists and Catholic notables. Naturally, the question of the "corridor" and Upper Silesia figured in the conversations, the Germans arguing that if their grievances were satisfied, Berlin would be willing to guarantee Poland's borders with Russia. A tripartite Franco-German-Polish military accord was also mentioned. The French participants were ret-

---

comments in MS, PAN, Dziennik Zdanowskiego, 2, 26, 28; Stanisław Kirkor's letter, *Zeszyty Historyczne*, 21 (1972), 230–32; Ciałowicz, *Polsko-Francuski sojusz*, 165, 167. For Polish resentment over the French failure to inform the general staff about matters pertaining to the Rhineland and of interest to Poland, see correspondence between Gen. Denain and war ministry, 14 Dec. 1939–3 Jan. 1930, SHA, EMA/2, Pologne 21.

61. See correspondence in SHA, EMA/2, Pologne 19. Compare exchange of notes verbales, 7, 28, 30 April; and Beck to Chłapowski, 2 May 1932, HIA, Amb. Paryż, box 3. Also Girsa reports, 14 May, 10 Oct., CPP. Compare *Gazeta Warszawska's* polemic with *La République*, 10 June 1932.

62. See DDF, I, 1:145–46; also Wysocki to Zaleski, 6 Aug. 1932, AAN, MSZ 2767.

63. D'Arbonneau to Paul-Boncour, 26 Oct. 1932, DDF, I, 1:593.

64. Laroche in DDF, I, 1:591–92. His opinion accorded with that of Col. Prioux; see annual report, SHA, EMA/2, Pologne 11.

65. See Chłapowski report, 13 Feb. 1932, AAN, Amb. Berlin 78.

icent at first, but they came away convinced that a Polish settlement was a precondition of a French-German entente.[66]

The Poles did not know for certain, but they suspected the existence of intimate contacts between French and German industrialists.[67] The old diplomat and president of the Banque des Pays de l'Europe Centrale, Jules Cambon, voiced his conviction that while Poland would preserve its independence "your western frontiers would have to be nibbled."[68] There remained, of course, pro-Polish voices among the Right. Bainville recalled his remarks to Zaleski and Beneš, that their professed satisfaction with Locarno had not helped their countries' cause.[69] But an attachment to allies in the east was on the wane, and *L'Oeuvre* was not far wrong when it wrote on 31 May that the French electorate no longer believed that France's border was on the Vistula.

Before and during the general elections, the radicals made ample use of the unpopular East European loans to attack the government. The party's "young Turks"—Cot, François de Tessan, Emile Roche, Jacques Kayser, and Edouard Pfeiffer—were particularly vocal. Reviving the rumor that the Franco-Polish alliance was due to expire in 1932, Pfeiffer expressed doubts about its very purpose.[70] When Polish papers questioned his claim that he spoke for the party, *La République* accused Warsaw of trying to split the radicals. The French nation, the paper said, "would not permit its profound devotion to Poland to drive it into an armed conflict."[71] Some of the fervor of *La République* was due to the electoral campaign, for the paper later approached the Polish embassy with an offer of collaboration in exchange for concealed subsidies.[72] Cot, however, tried to convince Zaleski that the Left, once in power, would try to mediate the German-Polish controversy, and Poland would have to make some territorial concessions. The foreign minister retorted that if Poland contemplated concessions, it

66. See Bariéty and Bloch, "Une Tentative," 439–51; Girault, "Crise," 375–76; Link, *Stabilisierungspolitik*, 521. French participants included René Duchemin, Jean Parmentier, Louis Marlio, and Wladimir d'Ormesson.

67. See Chłapowski report, 8 Mar. 1932, AAN, Amb. Berlin, 78.

68. Sobański to Paderewski, 25 June 1932, *Archiwum Polityczne Ignacego Paderewskiego*, III, 206.

69. Article cited in *Gazeta Warszawska*, 19 Apr. 1932.

70. See Mühlstein to Berthelot, 23 Feb. 1932, MAE, Z 698.12, Pologne 2198; *Le Temps*, 20 May, discrediting the rumor about the expiration of the alliance. On "Young Turks," see Serge Bernstein, *Histoire du parti radical* (Paris, 1980–82) 2:104–106.

71. See Pfeiffer interview in *Kurjer Warszawski*, 31 Mar. 1932; *Gazeta Polska*, 3 Apr. *La République*, 5 Apr. Relevant Laroche reports in MAE, Z 698.12, Pologne 2198 and 698.1, Pologne 2099; Chłapowski report, 28 May, PI, Amb. Londyn, reel 44. For Polish peasant party efforts to influence the French Left, see Borkowski, "Stronnictwo ludowe," 152–53.

72. Chłapowski report, 25 Nov. 1932, AAN, MSZ 3766.

would not need a French mediation, and implied that an abandoned Warsaw could turn to Berlin.[73] Undiscouraged, the radicals prepared a study of the "corridor" that proposed its exchange for a band of territory along the Lithuanian frontier.[74] Even a generally pro-Polish deputy thought that it would be wise to return Danzig to Germany; uncertainties about what France would do in case of a German attack on Poland were set out clearly by Pertinax.[75] Not only the Poles, but the British ambassador in Paris thought that "never was the stage in France more favourably set for a Franco-German rapprochement."[76]

Still, the Polish press welcomed the formation of the Herriot ministry of the Left on 3 June. Chłapowski listed several cabinet members—Paul-Boncour, Painlevé, Albert Sarraut, and Leygues—with whom the embassy had a good rapport. Herriot himself was less reliable, but he would not personally act against Polish interests. Although Chłapowski commented on the mood of resignation in France vis-à-vis Germany, he did not anticipate any drastic changes in the political course.[77]

Herriot inherited a situation not dissimilar to the one he had faced in 1924. Once again, France was experiencing financial difficulties; German problems (reparations and disarmament) required a solution; the dependence on Britain was increasing; the French socialists, who stayed outside the cabinet, pressed for appeasing Berlin.[78] True, there were also voices critical of French policies toward Germany since 1925. If German financial distress was obvious, the question remained whether Berlin should not pay for assistance with a political moratorium. The French, however, who had favored the idea two years earlier, were now divided in their counsels.[79]

On 31 May, Franz von Papen formed an ultraconservative "cabinet of barons." He stood for a rapprochement with France, and, while personally no rabid polonophobe, he had to depend on the support of General Schleicher and the Reichswehr whose hatred of Poland was no secret. An anti-Polish warlike hysteria was fueled by publications and radio programs.[80] The tension focused on Danzig, where a dispute raged over Poland's right to use the Free city as a "port d'attache" for her navy. The

73. Zaleski's reminiscences in Wandycz, *Zaleski*, 101–102; compare Laroche to Tardieu, 11 May 1932, MAE, Z 698.12, Pologne 2198.

74. Study by Varenne with map, dated 1932 June, MAE, Pologne 351:167–68.

75. Pezet on 6 July 1932, CAE/Ch; Pertinax in *The Baltimore Sun*, 24 June.

76. DBFP, II, IV:463.

77. See Chłapowski reports, 13 June 1932 and 8 Feb. 1933, AAN, MSZ 3690 and 3801; also Laroche to Herriot, 9 June, MAE, Z 698.12, Pologne 2198; for uncertainties about Herriot's course: Hoesch in ADAP, B, xx:221–23.

78. See analysis in Vaïsse, *Sécurité*, 248.

79. See DBFP, II, III:94–96, 135–39; compare Herriot, *Jadis*, 2:317.

80. See Roos, *Polen*, 39–44; Castellan, *Reich*, 472–73; DDF, I, 1:76.

French backed the Polish position, praised the Poles' sang-froid, and advised prudence so that Warsaw would be in the right if a confrontation occurred.[81] On 14 June, on the eve of the Lausanne conference, the Polish destroyer *Wicher* sailed into the Danzig harbor ostensibly to act as host to a visiting Royal Navy flotilla, but also carrying orders to open fire on the nearest official building should Danzig offer an insult to the Polish flag. This was a typical Piłsudski coup, a notice served on the powers that Warsaw would not tolerate the slightest derogation to its rights and interests, and was not afraid to act forcefully.[82] The decision to move was so swift that Zaleski, then in Geneva, had not been forewarned.[83]

The *Wicher* episode exploded like a bomb at the League. Although justifying the Polish act was difficult, Zaleski maneuvered adroitly. He alerted the powers to the dangerous situation that could arise when the German ship *Schlesien* would, as announced, visit the Free City. If the "port d'attache" issue were resolved, Zaleski promised that there would be no incident during *Schlesien*'s call. He won his point, and a procedure was set in motion that led to a Danzig-Polish agreement on 13 August.[84] The French were vexed by the whole affair, yet, when the agreement intervened, chargé d'affaires in Warsaw Pierre Bressy congratulated Zaleski. The Polish minister responded that although the means employed were not to his taste, "one had to recognize that under the circumstances Marshal Piłsudski had had a happy inspiration."[85]

Clearly, Piłsudski had intended to test both Berlin and Paris, but he seemed less concerned with a German threat to Poland than with a Franco-German deal prejudicial to Warsaw.[86] Indeed, Papen came to Lausanne with an offer to France of an accord amounting to a customs union, military entente, and consultative pact open to other great powers, as a quid

---

81. See Beck telegram, 4 May 1932, SI, Amb. Londyn, A.12.52/12; Note, 23 May, MAE, Z 698.1, Pologne 2099; Laroche and François-Poncet to Tardieu, 1, 2 June, MAE, P.A. Tardieu 81(689); Chłapowski report, 3 June, AAN, MSZ 3799. Compare ADAP, B, xx:204–205.

82. See MS, OSS, Wysocki, II, 240. For the commander's account, see Tadeusz Podjazd-Morgenstern, "Wejście ORP 'Wicher' do Gdańska w 1932 r.," *Bellona*, 1 (1953), 44–48.

83. See Wandycz, *Zaleski*, 103. Beck writes that he had been forewarned, in *Dernier rapport*, 18.

84. See Wandycz, *Zaleski*, 105–106; Wojciechowski, "Polska," 119–20; Simon to F.O., 17 June; Carr memorandum, 20 June; Drummond–Zaleski conversation, 20 June 1932, FO 371 16309 N 3779 and N 3823 and N 3824.

85. See DDF, 1, 1:206–207; Quai d'Orsay note of 6 July 1932 stressed the lack of coordination between "the evolution of Polish and French political thinking," MAE, Z 698. 1, Pologne 2099. Compare Chłapowski report, 25 June, AAN, MSZ 3799. For criticism of Polish foreign policy by Girsa, see reports, 8, 28 May, 18 June, CPP.

86. Text of Piłsudski–Wysocki conversation published by Ajnenkiel, "Rozmowa."

pro quo for the end of reparations and the recognition of Germany's equality of rights regarding disarmament (*Gleichberechtigung*). The thrust of the proposal was anti-Soviet.[87] Herriot, however, did not trust Papen, and the publication at this point of Stresemann papers conveying the impression that the late German statesman had deceived the French and had a particularly low opinion of Herriot did not help matters. The French premier opposed concessions and Beneš shared his position.[88] Had Herriot even been tempted to work with the Germans, a British counteroffer of a consultative accord (accord de confiance) seemed so much more attractive. Reliance on London made it easier to accept the elaborate scheme concerning German reparations, but the Franco-British accord proved to have very little substance. London assumed no new commitments; Warsaw resented the fact that it had not been consulted beforehand.[89] The subsequent accession to the accord by all European states (the USSR excepted) made it a meaningless document.

Herriot had not succumbed to German wooing, and he had fewer illusions about the republican spirit in Germany than many Frenchmen. At the same time his reliance on the Anglo-Saxon powers (again, a parallel with 1924 comes to mind) pushed him in the direction of ultimate concessions to Berlin. This became evident as the disarmament question came to the fore.

Gleichberechtigung

Of all the international issues in 1932, that of disarmament was the most difficult and portentous. The preparatory commission concluded its work with a project on limitations rather than reductions of armaments, and it was a French success in what it prevented rather than in what it achieved. The unavoidable consequence, as General Albert Niessel put it somewhat cynically, was that "these palavers [in Geneva] be dominated from the beginning by the hypocrisy of all the governments, each trying to reduce significantly the military means existing in other countries, while carefully preserving its own advantages."[90]

German insistence on the principle of equality of rights meant that part 5 of the Treaty of Versailles be replaced by an agreement providing either

87. See Franz von Papen, *Memoirs* (London, 1952), 175–76. Compare, Herriot, *Jadis*, 2:322; Bariéty and Bloch, *Une Tentative*, 452–53; Vaïsse, *Sécurité*, 264–65.

88. For Beneš's stand, see Campbell, *Confrontation*, 243; compare Gajanová, *ČSR*, 300.

89. See Beck to Chłapowski, 19 and 21 July, and Zaleski circular telegram, 29 Aug. 1932, SI, Amb. Londyn, A.12.52/12. Also Laroche dispatch, DDF, 1, 1:39–40.

90. Gen. Albert Niessel, *Le Déséquilibre militaire* (Paris, 1937), 37. For comparable views, see Beck, *Dernier rapport*, 261–64.

for general disarmament (down to the German level) or a limited rearmament of the Reichswehr. Either alternative spelled dangers to France and its allies, and it was clear that Berlin's attitude toward Poland largely governed the German stand on disarmament. Vansittart wrote that Germany's case, on grounds of morality and equality, "happens largely to coincide with our own [British] interests. We desire disarmament and we do not desire a perpetual [French] hegemony."[91] The American and Italian points of view came close to those of Britain. The Soviets, using the slogan of total disarmament, supported in fact the German stance. They also continued their clandestine military collaboration with Berlin of which the French and Polish intelligence were well aware.[92] Thus, France was isolated among the great powers.

For the French disarmament was not an end in itself, but "a means to arrive at a solid international organization of peace within the League of Nations."[93] They agreed on the need to maintain their stock of arms and delay practical measures of disarmament in the name of "security first." Important differences, however, existed between Weygand, who opposed not only a limitation of armaments but even budgetary cuts, and the government, particularly Paul-Boncour who believed that France had to show good will so as not to become internationally isolated when Germany regained her military strength.[94] In the course of heated debates at the CSDN in the winter of 1931–32, Weygand, preoccupied with the retention of forces capable of defending the country (especially when the "hollow years" would diminish the number of conscripts), battled over army figures and financial appropriations.[95]

East European problems naturally entered into these calculations. A special commission entrusted with the study of disarmament officially recognized as "desirable" an extension of the Locarno guarantees to the eastern borders of Germany. Paul-Boncour thought future international forces could be permanently stationed in the Rhineland and along the German-Polish frontier.[96] The senate army commission carefully reviewed the ar-

91. Cited in Bennett, *German Rearmament*, 109.

92. The Polish intelligence is credited with supplying most of the evidence. See Castellan, *Reich*, 186–95; compare 4 Sept. 1930 briefing, KV, CPP.

93. "Note pour le Président du Conseil," 7 June 1932, MAE, P.A. Massigli 5.

94. Paul-Boncour's testimony, 9 Mar. 1948 in *Evénements survenus en France*, 3:785–87.

95. Weygand at 13 Oct. 1931 session, SHA, CSDN 9. For differing views, see sessions 20 Jan., 3 Feb. 1932, CAE/Ch. Military issues are discussed in Minart, *Le Drame*, 12–21, and in relevant parts of La Gorce, *French Army*; Vaïsse, *Sécurité*; Bankwitz, *Weygand*; Gen. André Prételat, *Le Destin tragique de la ligne Maginot* (Paris, 1950); Feller, *Le Dossier*.

96. Session 5 Dec. 1932, SHA, CSDN 9, and MAE, P.A. Paul-Boncour 253(2); compare Vaïsse, *Sécurité*, 137.

maments of Poland and the Little Entente.[97] On the floor of the chamber, a rightist deputy asserted that the East Europeans were not a negligible quantity and could not be dismissed even from a military standpoint.[98]

Zaleski learned with satisfaction that Berthelot regarded real disarmament a folly at a time when the USSR was on the offensive, Germany was revisionist, and Italy was rearming. Order in Europe could only be maintained by France and its allies.[99] In mid-January 1932, Massigli reported, after a visit to Warsaw, Prague, and Belgrade, that while there was a general consensus of opinion, each country had its own special concerns. The Poles insisted that their current level of armaments needed to be raised rather than lowered, particularly in view of their geographic position. Moreover, disarmament had to be not only physical but also moral. While France's plans appeared somewhat imprecise to the Poles, its delegation in Geneva planned to concentrate on combatting the demagogic Soviet approach to disarmament.[100] Czechoslovakia, whose armament policies included a fixed budgetary ceiling, was prepared—despite the opposition of its Little Entente partners—to reduce the military service to fourteen months as it eventually did. Beneš intended to pursue a line parallel to France, allowing for flexibility and some concessions in exchange for increased security for the smaller European states and controls over armaments. By and large, Czechoslovak and Polish interests converged, and their general staffs cooperated loyally, sharing a somewhat pessimistic view about the outcome of the Geneva deliberations.[101]

The disarmament conference opened on 2 February, under the presidency of Arthur Henderson, a defeat for France which had supported Beneš's candidacy. Three days later, Tardieu submitted the French plan that combined the proposal for an international force under the League—to which member states would contribute certain contingents and their

97. Gen. Bourgeois presentation, 19 Jan. 1932 sessions, CAE and CA/Sén.

98. E. Soulier, 22 Jan. 1932, J.O. Chambre, 116.

99. Zaleski to ministry, 2 Oct. 1931, HIA, Zaleski Papers.

100. See Massigli note, 19 Jan. 1932, MAE, P.A. Paul-Boncour 253(2); also Komarnicki report, 11 (?) Jan., PI, Amb. Londyn, reel 44. On Polish military budget (thirty-five percent of total) and armaments, see annual reports SHA, EMA/2, Pologne 11; also Zaleski to missions, 9 Jan., AAN, Pos. Ateny, 167. Compare Michowicz, "Realizacja," 126–30; and his general *Konferencja.* Also see Stawecki, "L'Attitude"; an enlarged Polish version appears in *Acta Universitatis Lodziensis: Folia Historica,* 28 (1986).

101. For agreement of the general staffs of the Little Entente to act in solidarity with France and Poland, see Seguin and Charles-Roux reports, 1, 15, 23 Dec., and Quai d'Orsay to Seguin, 7 Dec. 1931, MAE, Z 864.10, Tchécoslovaquie 2604. Compare Bystrický and Deák, *Európa,* 219–20; Vaïsse, *Sécurité,* 121–22. Beneš's instructions appear in Maria Čuláková, "Pakt čtyř," Thesis, Karlova Universita (1967). See also comments of Gen. Stanisław Burhardt-Bukacki, in Bułhak, "Z Dziejów 1926–1937," 117.

heavy weapons (especially air force)—with a strengthened security system reminiscent of the still-born Geneva Protocol of 1924. The plan was above all a tactical gambit meant to gain Britain's support. The Quai d'Orsay assumed that it could rely on Poland and the Little Entente, even if there were some differences among them, notably on qualitative disarmament, and indeed Zaleski and Beck supported the Tardieu plan. The same was true for the Czechs.[102]

Faced with the opposition of the great powers, Tardieu assured the foreign affairs commission that France would make no concessions without new guarantees of security.[103] His successor, Herriot, caught between the socialists and the army at home, found the situation increasingly difficult. As a way out, Beneš suggested in mid-June a modified plan, but a week later President Hoover proposed a one-third cut of land forces with armor, bombers, and heavy artillery to be eliminated, and substantial reductions in naval tonnage. Beneš believed that this impossible proposal only "increased the confusion among the great powers." The French and the Poles shared his viewpoint, but not wishing to oppose Washington, they agreed, together with the Little Entente representatives, to consider the Hoover plan. They hoped that during the recess, presidential elections in the United States would clarify the picture.[104]

The conference formally separated in late July, but Beneš's compromise resolution, designed to relegate political issues to later sessions, did not satisfy the Germans. Berlin stated that it could not promise to participate in further debates if Gleichberechtigung were not granted. The French government considered various options to break this deadlock. Was a strengthening of eastern alliances one of them?

In May, Berlin had received reports about French military talks with the eastern associates that could result in a full-scale alliance should Germany withdraw from the reparations of disarmament conferences.[105] This inaccurate information probably related to conversations within the Little Entente and studies by the French general staff. As far back as January, Beneš told Charles-Roux of Yugoslav proposals to make the military accords valid against German or Italian aggression, proposals that he had rejected.

102. See note, 19 Feb., and "Note pour le Président du Conseil," 7 June 1932, which praised Poland's and Little Entente's loyalty "même lorsqu'il n'y avait pas parallélisme absolu des intérêts," MAE, P.A. Massigli 4 and 5. Compare 21 May, Franco-Polish meeting, Vaïsse, *Sécurité*, 121.

103. 4 Mar. 1932 session, CAE/Ch.

104. See Herriot, *Jadis*, 2:304–305; on Beneš's suggestions, Vaïsse, *Sécurité*, 261; quote from Bystrický and Déak, *Európa*, 138. Zaleski–Paul-Boncour conversation, 1 July 1932, AAN, DPLN, 196. Also Michowicz, "Rozbrojeniowy plan."

105. See Post, *Weimar Foreign Policy*, 279.

This negative attitude seemed to the French as characteristic of Beneš's policy toward Berlin or Rome.[106]

The thinking of the French command emerged from a study by the second and third bureaus of the general staff annotated by Gamelin and approved by Weygand.[107] Dealing with the hypothesis of a conflict between France, Poland, and the Little Entente on the one side, and Germany, Russia, Italy, Hungary, and Bulgaria on the other, this long document examined alternative military operations, and concluded that a unified command in the east would be essential. The commander-in-chief "could obviously be no one but a Frenchman," but would the allies, particularly the Poles, accept such an arrangement? Reading the study one can easily understand the extreme reluctance on the part of the French general staff, particularly Weygand, to consent to any significant measures of disarmament, which would make this type of military planning completely unrealistic. Even so, the actual state of military cooperation in East Central Europe hardly justified the hopes for coordination and joint command. General Prchala's overtures to the Poles in February 1932, presumably French inspired, for "quiet" joint operational planning found no response for two months. The Poles wanted to know "what Czechoslovakia would do in the case of a Polish-German armed conflict." Prchala eventually had to admit that his gambit represented only the army's viewpoint. Hence, only technical military contacts continued throughout the year: a meeting in Prague in July and in Warsaw in December.[108]

Beneš told the cabinet that "we are going through the most dangerous and difficult period since the signing of the peace treaties."[109] Developments in Germany—secret army modernization (*Umbau*), liquidation of the Prussian government, and Nazi victories—were viewed with alarm in Prague and elsewhere. The French believed that Piłsudski was secretly obsessed with the German threat.[110] In France, Buré sounded the call: "Back

106. Charles-Roux to Laval, 28 Jan. 1932, MAE, Z 864.10, Tchécoslovaquie 2604. A new military convention of 9 May prolonged merely the existing Little Entente provisions.

107. "Note et étude au suject de la coopération militaire de la Pologne et de la Petite Entente dans le cas d'un conflit européen," 10 May 1932, SHA, EMA/2, Pologne 21. Also Gamelin to Weygand, 11 July, EMA/3, 7 N 3446/1. It would be instructive to relate this study to mobilization plan C; see Tournoux, *Haut commandement*, 336.

108. Col. Czerwiński reports, 11 Jan., 18 Feb., 8, 25 Apr., 12 May 1932, AAN, MSZ 5502; compare Bułhak, "Z Dziejów 1927–1936," 113–16; Girsa report, 27 Apr. CPP; Faucher to Piétri, 19 Apr., SHA, EMA/2, Tchécoslovaquie. On German assumption that Czechoslovakia would be neutral in a German-Polish war, see Castellan, *Reich*, 491; also d'Arbonneau report, 5 Feb. 1933, SHA, EMA/2, Pologne 12.

109. Noël to Herriot, 30 July 1932; compare his dispatches 27 June, 8 July, and Charles-Roux, 16, 27 May, MAE, Z 864.1, Tchécoslovaquie 2568.

110. See DDF, I, 1:150.

to alliances." When a radical socialist deputy pessimistically contrasted Germany, Italy, and Russia with the exhausted France, his rightist colleague exclaimed: "Should one declare oneself defeated in advance?"[111] Yet, just as Beneš continued to favor caution, so Herriot could hardly try to return to the unpopular concept of relying on the East European alliances.[112] As the Quai d'Orsay observed, it was true that Poland and the Little Entente stood by France, but this bloc could not successfully compete for international influence with such powers as Britain or the United States.[113]

France could chose between a continued rejection of Gleichberechtigung, at the risk of an armaments race and open conflict, and a compromise arrangement that one hoped would restrain Germany. On 29 August, Berlin tried to force the issue by secretly proposing an entente based on the acceptance of the equality of rights. Herriot saw this move as a test of allied solidarity, and Zaleski fully agreed with Herriot's negative stand toward Berlin's overture. A revision of Versailles, which is what this proposal amounted to, was not a proper subject of either bilateral Franco-German conversations or talks among certain powers. Piłsudski adamantly opposed a repudiation of part 5 of Versailles. If it took place as a concession to Germany, Poland would demand to be released from the minority treaty, and the Treaty of Versailles would be dismantled piece by piece.[114] Beneš on his side believed that Gleichberechtigung must follow and not precede an agreement on disarmament between France, Britain, and the United States. While the French and allied position was legally strong, resistance to German demands had to take a form that would not antagonize British and American public opinion. In any case, he thought, the dialogue could not be continued along Franco-German lines, but must be transferred to Geneva.[115]

French rejection of Berlin's overtures made foreign minister von Neurath declare that Germany would not attend the disarmament conference. The Reichswehr was flexing its muscle holding its biggest maneuvers yet near Frankfurt am Oder. Simulated tanks, which participated in the exercise, symbolized the demand for forbidden weapons.[116] Herriot's speech at Granat was a riposte that the Polish embassy characterized as sharp in

---

111. Exchange between H. Guernut and E. Soulier, 29 June 1932, CAE/Ch.

112. Chłapowski report, 20 Aug. 1932, AAN, MSZ 3800; compare DiM, v, 496–598.

113. Note, 28 Aug. 1932, DDF, I, 1:227–33.

114. See Bressy to Zaleski, 3 Sept., and Laroche to Herriot, 5 Sept. 1932, AAN, MSZ 3690, and DDF, I, 1:267. Also Zaleski and Mühlstein telegrams, 10 and 12 Sept., HIA, Amb. Paryż, box 3; Laroche, *Pologne*, 111; Girsa dispatch, 7 Sept., CPP.

115. Noël dispatches, DDF, I, 1:200, 280–81.

116. See Roos, *Polen*, 51; also DDF, I, 1:362, 394–95.

form but disappointing in content. The French were thinking of concessions, even though Herriot assured Chłapowski that this was not so, and
that he would not desert Poland and the other allies at the forthcoming
conference in London.[117] The premier deluded himself that he had reached
an agreement with the Anglo-Saxon powers on banning Germany to
rearm. "And what if it does?" a deputy asked. Herriot could only invoke
the use of juridical means.[118]

In an already familiar pattern, the international tension registered on the
barometer of Czechoslovak-Polish relations. Once more, the opposition
papers criticized Beneš's Polish policy, asserting that a strong Prague-Warsaw combination under the leadership of France would bring security to
both countries. Hlinka's Slovaks, more autonomist in their stand, notably
after the Zvolen meeting, voiced a pro-Polish line. The Polish nationalist
and populist press responded, which made an Italian paper speak of the
emergence of a French-Czechoslovak-Polish military alliance.[119] The
French renewed their representations in Prague.[120] Girsa admitted that in
view of the international developments Piłsudski seems to have changed
his inimical attitude toward Czechoslovakia. Poland was taking "the first
step," but "a normal democratic state" could not rush into an alliance with
Piłsudski's authoritarian regime, which would be "a difficult partner."
Warsaw wished to commit Prague to an anti-German alignment, but
Czechoslovakia might want to remain neutral. Polish strivings to deprive
it of freedom to maneuver were inadmissible. In brief, an alliance might be
advantageous to Poland but create complications for Prague. Girsa's views
carried weight, especially as they corresponded to the thinking at the Hrad
and the views of the Left.[121]

As new disarmament proposals were feverishly worked out by the
French in October, Beneš played a major role promoting his own project

117. See Chłapowski and Zaleski telegrams, 5, 8, 21 Oct. 1932, HIA, Amb. Paryż,
box 3; compare Frankowski report, 30 Sept., and Chłapowski's 13, 15 Oct., PI, Amb.
Londyn, reel 44. Compare alarmist article in *Gazeta Warszawska*, 21 Sept.

118. 10 Oct. 1932 session, CAE/Ch. Herriot did say, however, that for Poland this
was "a matter of life and death."

119. *Lavoro Fascista*, 4 Oct. 1932. See *Národní Politika*, 15 Sept., 18 Oct.; *Národní
Listy*, 17 Aug.; *Slovák*, 11 Nov.; Hodža's speech in *Články*, 7:337. Report on Slovaks,
DDF, I, 1:642–44. On Polish press, Girsa report, 21 Sept., CPP.

120. The Poles assumed that Painlevé, who visited Prague, and Gen. Faucher exerted
pressure. See Czerwiński report, 1 Oct. 1932, AAN, MSZ 3960. Compare Noël and
Laroche telegrams, 18, 19 Oct., MAE, Z 864.5, Tchécoslovaquie 2568. Also Bystrický
and Deák, *Európa*, 227; Koženski, *Czechosłowacja*, 46–48; *Češi a Poláci*, 2:536;
Bułhak, "Z Dziejów 1927–1936," 118.

121. Girsa reports, 1, 19 Oct. 1932, CPP. For leftist criticism of Piłsudski's regime,
see Jaroslav Vozka, *Polsko, žalář národů, nebezpečí pro světový mír* (Praha, 1932).

and encouraging Herriot and Paul-Boncour to conciliate the Anglo-Saxon powers.[122] The Poles were being less and less consulted, perhaps because it was feared that their opposition would further complicate the controversy in France between the government and the army.[123] Paul-Boncour's project of mid-October (based on the so-called maximum plan) provided for the transformation of armies into militias, international controls, an international force under the League, and a mutual ssistance pact completing the Locarno agreements. It implied Gleichberechtigung and assumed British and American guarantes. Weygand, whose relations with Herriot and Paul-Boncour were strained almost to the breaking point, considered that the plan would either prove purely utopian or destroy the French army. Yet, the general, when overruled, did not go to the extreme of submitting a resignation.[124] In the parliament, supporters and opponents of the government exchanged heated, and familiar, arguments. Once more, Franklin-Bouillon recalled Sadova and Sedan, exclaiming that "there is no French security [but only] the security of France and its allies." The leftists countered with a condemnation of the eastern alliances. "Poland and Romania are military nations and predatory nations," one deputy cried. The socialists added they were attacking the Piłsudski regime, not the Polish people.[125] In the senate's army commission, Paul-Boncour's plan was defended on the grounds that France must avoid isolation. "Facing the great powers, can we lean on our small allies?" the chairman asked rhetorically.[126]

The plan of Paul-Boncour, presented on 14 November, was more flexible than Tardieu's plan of February. The Poles complained that they had not been fully consulted and viewed the plan as endangering the Franco-Polish alliance.[127] Beneš, who thought that he had gained MacDonald's support, quickly discovered that the British, not to mention the Americans,

---

122. See Rollet, "Deux mythes," 329; Vaïsse, *Sécurité*, 292–300; DDF, 1, 1:432–33, 439.

123. Mühlstein reports, 29 Oct., 4 Nov., 1932, AAN, MSZ 3800 and PI, Amb. Londyn, reel 44, and his telegrams, 29, 30 Oct., HIA, Amb. Paryż, box 3. Mühlstein learned at the Quai d'Orssay that Osuský was also kept uninformed.

124. See DDF, 1, 1:476–81, 614–41; also Vaïsse, *Sécurité*, 297–302; Minart, *Le Drame*, 33; Bankwitz, *Weygand*, 63–70.

125. Chasseigné and Franklin-Bouillon speeches, and Louis Marin's clash with Longuet and Reynaudel on 28 Oct. 1932, J.O. Chambre, 2904, 2911–16, 2927. For Polish reactions, see Mühlstein and Laroche to Herriot, respectively 29 Oct. and 3 Nov. 1932, MAE, Z 698.12, Pologne 2198.

126. 18 Nov. 1932 session; compare with 8 Dec., CA/Sén.

127. Text, DDF, 1, 1:710–18; Mühlstein and Szembek telegrams, 1, 13 Nov. 1932, HIA, Amb.Paryż, box 3. Polish complaints in Laroche to Paul-Boncour, DDF, 1, 1:593. Note de S.R., 20 Jan. 1933, SHA, EMA/2, Pologne 37.

were unwilling to assume any guarantees. As for the Germans, they made their return to Geneva conditional on Gleichberechtigung. Panicky, the French government first turned to direct conversations with the new Schleicher cabinet, the British assuming the position of an arbiter, and then to negotiations within the restricted circle of the great powers.[128] Indeed, already on 23 October, Mussolini had launched his idea of a four-power consortium, an ominous notion when seen from the perspective of Prague or Warsaw.

The great powers' deliberation in Geneva resulted in the 11 December communiqué that recognized German equality of rights within a regime of security. This was Herriot's formula, which the French tried to interpret as a recognition of a principle, and the Germans as a basic revision of Versailles. The second was really closer to the truth, for in the eyes of the international public opinion the military clauses of Versailles had ceased to exist.[129]

This agreement was a serious blow to Poland. Piłsudski, who had been telling d'Arbonneau in October that France would desert Warsaw, now opined that the "structures of international life as it had existed in the preceding ten years" would be profoundly shaken.[130] The resignation of Zaleski on 2 November, while related not to the Geneva developments but rather to the minister's incompatibility with Beck, indicated a serious change in Polish diplomacy.[131] Zaleski had stood for a certain line, and in the changing conditions the marshal needed a different man, a disciple and executor to preside over a new course. Just as Zaleski's departure caused regrets in Paris and Prague, so the person of his successor, Colonel Beck, provoked anxiety. The Czechs expected no radical departures but thought that Beck would imprint Polish foreign policy with a different style. He seemed "a dangerous man" endowed with "an officer's mentality." French papers of the Right and Left revived rumors about Beck's alleged recall from Paris in 1923 when serving as military attaché (*Le Figaro*, 17 November). *Le Populaire* called him a "hangman of Brześć" and an assassin of

128. See Vaïsse, *Sécurité*, 325–30. On Beneš; Campbell, *Confrontation*, 246; DDF, I, 1:709–10; also 19 Oct. 1932 briefing, KV, CPP.

129. See Duroselle, *La Décadence*, 43. Compare Vaïsse, *Sécurité*, 341–47; DDF, I, v:876.

130. Recalled by Beck in his *Przemówienia*, 327.

131. For the resignation, see Wandycz, *Zaleski*, 108–24; for press cuttings, see PI, Jan Weinstein Collection, xxiv. Girsa commented that although Zaleski was no czechophile he tried to avoid friction and was a loyal partner in Geneva. His departure was "a great loss for Poland." See reports, 19 Oct., 7 Nov., 5 Dec. 1932; also briefing, 3 Nov., KV, CPP. Appraisals by Jan Šeba, *Rusko a Malá dohoda v politice světové* (Praha, 1936), 852; Fiala, *Soudobé Polsko*, 143–44; Noël to Herriot, 11 Nov., MAE, Z 698.1, Pologne 2099. Compare analysis in *L'Europe Centrale*, 12 Nov.

General Zagórski (3 November). He was branded a francophobe desirous to detach Poland from France.[132]

Laroche characterized Beck as a dynamic, ambitious, and overconfident young man (he was thirty-eight) who believed in tough diplomacy, as epitomized by the Romanian episode and the *Wicher* incident. Laroche worried lest Poland continue to indulge in such methods. It was absurd to accuse Beck of germanophilia, but he had no sentimental attachments to France, which he regarded as "a trump in the political game." But he was intelligent enough to realize that nothing could replace the French alliance.[133]

To reassure Paris, Beck's first public statement stressed continuity in external policy. Herriot was informed that he could count on Poland. During the Polish national holiday parade on 11 November, Piłsudski singled out Laroche for a friendly conversation.[134] A tour by Beck's deputy, Jan Szembek, which included Paris, London, Brussels, Berlin, and a little later Rome, was partly designed to counter adverse reactions to the ministerial change at the Brühl Palace.[135] Beck's own conversations with Herriot in Paris and Paul-Boncour in Geneva resulted in a somewhat perfunctory declaration of similarity of views.[136] A harsher tone, however, appeared in Beck's circular, on 1 December, in which he stated that Poland would not be bound by any decisions affecting its interests and taken without its participation. Hence, Beck criticized the 11 December declaration on Gleichberechtigung not only because it operated in Germany's favor, but also because it was arrived at by a small group of powers—an unhealthy development for the League of Nations.[137]

Concessions made in Geneva to Berlin did not lessen international ten-

132. Beck was also attacked by *L'Action Française, Journal des Débats, L'Echo de Paris,* and *L'Ordre.* See *Gazeta Warszawska* and *Kurjer Warszawski,* 28 Nov., 1 Dec. 1932.

133. Laroche to Herriot, 2, 3, 10 Nov., and to Berthelot 3 Nov., MAE, Z 698.1, Pologne 2099; also DDF, I, II:453. For German and Soviet opinions that Beck's nomination signified Warsaw's resolve to weaken dependence on France, see François-Poncet dispatch, 3 Nov., MAE, Z 698.1, Pologne 2099 and Dirksen–Stonomyakov conversation, 14 Nov. 1932, AA, 9292/E 65 944–48.

134. See statement, 3 Nov. 1932 in Beck, *Przemówienia,* 37; Laroche to Herriot, 4, 15 Nov., MAE, Z 698.1, Pologne 2099 and 2198, also Laroche, *Pologne,* 117.

135. See Ciałowicz, *Polsko-francuski sojusz,* 177; Roos, *Polen,* 56; Note de S.R., 20 Jan. 1923, SHA, EMA/2, Pologne 27; Laroche to Herriot, 11 Nov. 1932, MAE, Z 698.1, Pologne 2099; Girsa report, 19 Jan. 1933, CPP. The foreign ministry resided in the historic Brühl Palace.

136. *Le Temps,* 30 Nov. 1932; compare Laroche dispatch in DDF, I, II:451–53.

137. DTJS, I, 5; Beck, *Przemówienia,* 42–43. For Beck's view that a German government that relied on the army could hardly accept real disarmament, see DDF, I, II:174–75.

sions. Rumors about the imminence of a German-Polish conflict circulated, and a new study of German and Polish military capabilities was prepared in Paris.[138] The Auswärtiges Amt thought that the recently signed French and Polish nonaggression treaties with the USSR provided no guarantees for Poland's borders. German-Russian military collaboration was not affected; indeed Karl Radek, then a major writer on Polish and international affairs in *Izvestia*, thought that Moscow would assist a German attack on Poland by applying pressure on Polish eastern borders.[139] Litvinov allegedly predicted that the Franco-Soviet pact would lead to a "weakening of the bonds between France and Poland."[140]

Developments in Geneva shook Beneš, and his major address "Will Europe decide for peace or for war?" attested to the seriousness with which he viewed the situation.[141] The 11 December declaration did not surprise him, although he complained about not having been consulted.[142] He called it "a small step forward"—even if partial and open to varying interpretations—and he may have been later strengthened in this optimistic outlook by Paul-Boncour's assurances to Osuský.[143] While Kramář bitterly criticized the French, Beneš merely expressed concern about an evolution toward a great powers' directorate advocated by Mussolini, and hoped that France "would not agree" with such policies. Still, he fully realized the need for Little Entente discussion and joint preparation of devices to prevent the small states from becoming an instrument of the great. Perhaps even Poland could be associated with such an undertaking.[144]

The mention of Poland was no harbinger of a drastic policy revision. Still, Krofta thought that in the matter of the "corridor," a vital question for Poland, it lay both in Czechoslovak and French interests to maintain a

138. See briefing, 15 Dec. 1932, KV, CPP; compare Campbell, *Confrontation*, 249. See "Possibilités de mobilisation de l'Allemagne contre la Pologne au début de 1933," 23 Dec. 1932, SHA, EMA/2, Pologne 21. For views that it was by no means certain that Germany would attack Poland before attacking France, see Gen. Bartier to Massigli, 3 Dec., MAE, P.A. Massigli 5.

139. See Köpke circular, 23 Dec. 1932, AA, 6616/E 499432, 437–47. Compare DDF, I, II:101–103 and 664–65.

140. Aloisi, *Journal*, 39. For Czech appraisals, see Girsa report, 19 Oct. 1932, CPP, and *L'Europe Centrale*, 3 Dec.

141. For the 7 Nov. 1932 speech, see Beneš, *Boj o mír*, 653–81; briefings, 3, 11 Nov., KV, CPP.

142. See DDF, I, II:421.

143. See Beneš to missions, 17 Dec. 1932, CPP; for Beneš's statement and Paul-Boncour's remarks to Osuský, see Bystrický and Deák, *Európa*, 158–60 and DDF, I, II:343; also Noël to Paul-Boncour, 3 Jan. 1933, MAE, Z 864.1, Tchécoslovaquie 2569.

144. Kramář in *Národní Listy*, 26 Dec. 1932; comments in Noël to Paul-Boncour, 27 Dec., MAE, Z 864.1, Tchécoslovaquie 2568. On Beneš, see Massigli to Herriot, 17 Dec., MAE, Z 864.1, Tchécoslovaquie 2568, also briefing, 15 Dec., KV, CPP.

common front against Germany. He refused, however, to speculate on his country's reaction to a German-Polish war, and was reticent about military collaboration with Poland.[145] As for a political rapprochement between Poland and the Little Entente, Beneš intended to explore it at its 18–19 December conference in Belgrade.

The reasons for holding a second Little Entente meeting in the course of the year were closely connected with the ramifications of the Geneva declaration. The great powers had made their decision without consulting the Little Entente; moreover, certain French economic policies, which could in effect facilitate German and Italian activities in the Danubian area, filled the Czechs with apprehension.[146] At the beginning of the conference, Beneš himself spoke of the need to resist endeavors of the great powers to "order about [the smaller states] like colonies." He singled out Italy, Germany, and to some extent Britain as the culprits.[147] The Czechoslovak foreign minister aimed at transforming the Little Entente into a single diplomatic unit with a uniform policy. This meant in practice exerting greater control over Romanian diplomacy, which on occasion followed a separate course.[148] Beneš proposed the creation of new organs for the Little Entente, which gained approval, and represented this move as "a new step toward the strengthening of a common front and a rejection of all kinds of revisionism."[149] The three foreign ministers agreed on a common approach toward disarmament but made no decisions with regard to economic cooperation.[150] The idea of a link between the Little Entente and

145. Krofta's remarks to journalists, 17 Nov., and briefings, 3, 24 Nov. 1932, KV, CPP; also Noël to Herriot, 19 Nov., MAE, Z 864.1, Tchécoslovaquie 2568.

146. See Bystrický and Deák, *Európa*, 230–32; Kvaček, *Nad Evropou*, 45–46, and his "Ke genezi návrhu na," 302; Campus, *The Little Entente and the Balkan Entente* (Bucureşti, 1968), 52, 54. Also DDD, I, II:244 and 704; ADAP, C, I, 1:66–67. On economic aspects, see Massigli to Coulondre, 16 Feb. 1933, MAE, P.A. Massigli 4.

147. See "Záznam o jednání ministrů E. Beneše, B. Jeftiče a N. Titulesca na konferenci Malé dohody v Bélhrade," 18–19 Dec. 1932, CPP (hereafter cited as "Záznam"). Beneš declared a little later that the Little Entente was "tired of being a plaything of their great neighbours," which provoked a comment that it did not mind being a French instrument in the past but with France weakening "it was no longer so pleasant." Eden to Foreign Office and minutes, 11 Feb. 1933, FO 371 16676 C 1200.

148. This had been true in the case of the Mussolini–Averescu letters exchanged on the signing of the Romanian-Italian treaty of 1926, which provided for neutrality in case of an attack by a third party and for consultation between the general staffs. Czechoslovakia and Yugoslavia had been kept in the dark about this arrangement. See "Záznam," and O *Československé zahraniční politice*, 197; also DDF, I, 1:46.

149. Beneš to missions, 21 Dec. 1932, CPP; English translation in Bernstein to Secretary of State, 16 Jan. 1933, SDNA, 770.00/230. Compare DDF, I, II:298–99.

150. See Naggiar to Paul-Boncour, 3 Jan. 1933, MAE, Z 864.10, Tchécoslovaquie 2604; compare DDF, I, II:103–195. It was only at this time that the French discovered

Poland received little encouragement. Titulescu, still peeved by Warsaw's behavior in the Soviet-Romanian affair, accused the Poles of being disloyal and envious of Beneš. For once the roles were reversed: Prague showing interest in a connection with Warsaw, Romania opposing it.[151]

The Organizational Pact of the Little Entente, agreed upon at the Belgrade conference, was finally adopted in Geneva on 16 February 1933. Its signature was hastened by the so-called Hirtenberg affair involving arms smuggling to Hungary and by Hitler's accession to power in Germany. The reorganized Little Entente (Beneš's proposal to rename it the Central European League was not adopted) became endowed with a permanent council of foreign ministers, whose unanimous consent was needed for "every unilateral act changing the actual situation of one of the States of the Little Entente in regard to an outside State." An economic council, and a seretariat based in Geneva, were to be established, and the original treaties extended for an indefinite period. The pact was open to accession by others "under conditions applicable to each particular case." Beneš claimed to have created a "veritable *Staatenbund*" with "a single foreign policy." The semiofficial *L'Europe Centrale* commented on 18 February that "a great power is born. It would treat on an equal footing with other European powers."[152]

Opposition parties in Poland reacted favorably to a revitalized Little Entente, some leaders even asking Girsa whether Poland would be welcomed to join.[153] Paul-Boncour assured the foreign affairs commission of Poland's sympathetic attitude toward the grouping even though Poland's association with the group was an open question.[154] In fact the Polish government was upset by Bucharest's failure to consult Warsaw, for the pact's provisions for coordinated policies had a bearing on the Polish-Romanian alliance. Beck regarded the pact as an "unfavourable development" be-

---

the existence of preferential tariffs accorded by Czechoslovakia to Yugoslav and Romanian cereals. See Noël to Herriot, 13, 15 Dec. 1932, MAE, P.A. Puaux 255(26).

151. See "Záznam," CPP; DDF, 1, ii:280–81. A little later Belgrade mentioned the possibility of Polish adherence; see Naggiar to Paul-Boncour, 17 Feb. 1933, MAE, Z 864.10, Tchécoslovaquie 2601.

152. DDF, 1, ii:469; Čulaková, "Pakt Čtyř," 51; Kvaček, *Nad Evropou*, 47; Olivová, *Doomed Democracy*, 167. Krofta thought that the pact would strengthen Prague's hand vis-à-vis Poland. See DDF, 1, ii:647–48, and Noël dispatch, 22 Feb. 1932, MAE, Z 684.5, Tchécoslovaquie 2586.

153. Girsa report, 12 Jan. 1933, CPP; Laroche to Paul-Boncour, 22 Feb. 1933, MAE, Z 864. 10, Tchécoslovaquie 2601; note, 18 Sept. 1933, "La Pologne et la Petite Entente," Z 698.12, Pologne 2200; *Češi a Poláci*, 2:544–45. Also *Gazeta Warszawska*, 18 Feb. and *Chwila*, 3 Mar. 1933.

154. 1 Mar. 1933 session, CAE/Ch.

cause it heightened tensions between the two blocs in Central Europe; Poland's possible adhesion would require "careful consideration."[155] Warsaw was clearly unenthusiastic.

Massigli thought that France could profit from a strengthening of the Little Entente; any unpleasant surprises were unlikely because Prague was too firmly attached to Paris.[156] When shown confidentially the final text, the French diplomat was less positive. The changes did not amount to much in practice, but the pact could compromise efforts for a Franco-Italian détente.[157] Consequently, the new foreign minister, Paul-Boncour, went out of his way to tell the Italians that they must not believe that it was France that had pushed the three states toward "this federation."[158] Responding to parliamentary interpellations, he asserted that just as the Little Entente had come into existence without French inspiration, and collaborated with Paris on an equal footing, so it made the recent changes on its own.[159] In the more restricted circle of the foreign affairs commission, Paul-Boncour said that the organizational pact had not been worked out "behind our backs" nor was it directed "against us." At a time when "some other [countries] may seem to be deserting us," France must be firmly attached to this grouping. One could count on Beneš to permeate it with "a spirit of moderation."[160]

Indeed, according to the French envoy in Prague, the Czechs considered the pact as reinforcing the international position of France, corresponding to "our conception of peace, and fitting into the political frame" of French plans for the limitation of armaments.[161] Hence, Paris told the Poles that the pact represented a major victory of French policy; an antagonistic attitude toward it on the part of the Polish government created a bad impression.[162] Actually, as reported by Osuský, who was known for his critical views of the current French policy, leading circles in France viewed the pact "as a warning and a lesson." The envoy opined that the stronger and

155. See DDF, I, II:825–26 and Erskine to Simon, 28 Feb. 1933, FO 371 166 76 C 2029/21/62. Also Rucker's note, 1 Mar. 1933, SI, MSZ, Z.11.4.

156. Massigli to Herriot, 17 Dec. 1932, MAE, Z 864.1, Tchécoslovaquie 2568.

157. See DDF, I, II:554–55; compare 628–29, and for analysis pointing toward a mainly demonstrative character of the pact, see 679–82.

158. See Aloisi, *Journal*, 74, who also noted Litvinov's negative position toward the Little Entente (p. 71), Compare Košek report, 23 Feb. 1922, CPP.

159. See Quai d'Orsay briefing paper, 4 Apr. 1933, MAE, Z 864.10, Tchécoslovaquie 2602.

160. 1 Mar. 1933, CAE/Ch.

161. Noël to Paul-Boncour, 20 Feb. 1933, MAE, Z 864.10, Tchécoslovaquie 2601.

162. Chłapowski telegram, 19 Feb. 1933, HIA, Amb. Paryż, box 3; compare his 22 Feb. report, AAN, MSZ, P.II, w.65, t.4c (old classification). Also DTJS, I, 7–10.

more independent the Little Entente would be, the greater the support it would receive in Paris.[163]

All things considered, the organizational pact, which Beneš represented as a major achievement, hardly marked a revolutionary departure. The Little Entente neither became a cohesive bloc nor did it extend its obligations to defend its members against a great power. Paradoxically, the pact was in a sense "a sign of relinquishing further attempts to organize all of Central Europe."[164] By antagonizing the powers, it may have contributed inadvertently to the Four Power Pact.[165] Up to a point the pact reflected a growing East European realization that "the balance sheet of . . . [French] foreign policy in 1932 is mediocre not to say distressing," as a report for the Chamber of Deputies in Paris noted.[166] There was undoubtedly much truth in this statement.

An Overview

The period of the Great Depression offered an increasingly sharp contrast to the early post-Locarno years. The relative compatibility that had existed between Briand, Chamberlain, and Stresemann was replaced by a more antagonistic relationship between Paris, London, and Berlin. Italian and Soviet roles in international relations increased. As European economic stability was called into question, aggressive nationalism and revisionism asserted themselves. "The weight of France's gold on the scales of diplomacy"—to borrow the title of an article in the *New York Times* on 13 October 1931—proved sufficient to prevent a Curtius–Schober project but not to extract a political moratorium from Berlin. Tardieu's economic plan foundered on the opposition of the great powers, as did French constructive plans in the realm of disarmament. The United States and Britain, bent on saving Brüning and the tottering Weimar Republic through concessions to Germany (especially in East Central Europe) shared the responsibility for French failures. As the position of Paris weakened between 1931 and 1932, the dependence on Britain grew correspondingly.[167] Attempts to use Russia as a card in the diplomatic game varied in intensity with the changing cabinets in Paris; the Italian card still proved difficult to play. A growing tendency to approach the most important European issues through a

---

163. Cited in Bystrický, "Pokus," 168–69. Chłapowski ascribed the favorable reaction of the French press to Czech subsidies, 8 Mar. 1933 report, AAN, MSZ, 3776.

164. Gajanová, *ČSR*, 305.

165. See Carmi, *La Grande Bretagne*, 204–207.

166. Report of Adrien Darien, J.O. Chambre, Documents parlementaires, annex 1535, 514.

167. Hoesch contrasted French strength in early 1931 with the "increasingly defensive position" coupled with dependence on Britain by late 1932. Cited in Gehl, *Austria*, 44.

great powers' consortium—from the London April 1932 conference to the five-powers declaration on Gleichberechtigung—went hand in hand with a crisis of self-confidence in France. By 1932, as most observers noted, the French were tired, disillusioned, and incapable of providing support for a coherent policy toward Germany.[168] French diplomacy could pursue neither military hegemony nor concrete economic and political collaboration with Berlin. The result was a series of half-measures.

Policies of reconciliation seemed to work neither under the patronage of the Left nor when attempted by the Right. The reason, in Krüger's words, was that "German policy from 1930 to 1932 represented an attempt, as determined as it was risky, to use without taking account of the dangers, the world economic crisis in order to recover total freedom of action."[169]

French domestic weaknesses were affecting the continuity of external policy. The five foreign ministers—Briand (losing his grip), Laval ("all involved in combinations), Tardieu (remarkably intelligent but full of pique), Herriot (displaying all his cards),[170] and Paul-Boncour (barely making his impact)—all realized that security came first on the French diplomatic agenda. But they were neither free agents nor overly consistent in the pursuit of their goals. The ministerial instability worried the eastern allies. Referring to a permanent cabinet crisis, Osuský reported that many people spoke of the need for a dictatorship.[171] The rift between the Left and the Right and between the government and the army, plus the heavy deficit and mounting socioeconomic problems darkened the political scene in a way reminiscent of the pre-Locarno days.

French eastern alliances, as a deputy observed, suffered from a double malentendu. In France, public opinion viewed the alliances in terms of generous protection extended to the weak, a contribution through sacrifices to the cause of peace. The outside world assumed that "France sought above all to gain a political clientele for narrowly egotistical interests."[172] At the beginning of this period it seemed that French financial power could breathe a new life into the system. This hope proved largely an illusion. Loans to East Central European states were not of sufficient magnitude to strengthen decisively their economic and military capabilities. By refraining from a policy of large-scale economic build-up of Poland, which would have placed Germany in a disadvantageous position, the French may have paid a high price politically in the long run.[173] Problems developed even

168. See Goguel-Nyegard, *La Politique*, 313.

169. Krüger, "Politique extérieure," 290.

170. Bérard, *Ambassadeur*, 168.

171. Cited in Kvaček, *Nad Evropou*, 17.

172. Rapporteur Viénot, 29 Dec. 1932 session, J.O. Chambre, 5753.

173. This point in made by Krüger, "Politique extérieure," 294.

with the Czechoslovak loan. The electoral campaign of 1932 showed how bitterly the socialists and many radicals opposed financial aid that burdened the taxpayer to further what they regarded as old-fashioned alliances.[174] The efforts of the French army to improve the military chances of the eastern allies proved exceedingly difficult; a growing malaise characterized the Franco-Polish relationship.

Despite Laroche's efforts to interpret Piłsudski for the benefit of Paris and to cultivate the Polish leader, distrust was mounting, not diminishing.[175] Piłsudski saw how the Japanese aggression in the Far East exposed the powerlessness of the League. He watched collective security being undermined and observed the unabashed pretense of the great powers to make decisions that affected other nations' fate. He was increasingly convinced that Poland had to maneuver on its own. Warsaw resented not being consulted over such basic issues as disarmament, and found the vacillations of France's Soviet policy disconcerting. In turn, Paris was vexed by such Polish moves as the *Wicher* episode and "ultimatum" to Romania. The termination of the military and naval missions was a blow to French prestige; the nomination of Beck signaled the use of harsher diplomatic methods.

The intimacy between Paris and Prague did not significantly decrease during this period. Yet, for all his involvement in French plans and initiatives, Beneš grew more pessimistic. He too sensed the approach of an era of the great powers' hegemony, within which France's role would necessarily dwindle. His trust in Paris notwithstanding, the foreign minister followed its leadership with open eyes, attempting to influence French policies toward Italy or a Danubian confederation, and resisting any endeavors to be pushed closer to Poland. In strengthening the Little Entente, he increased his watchfulness but revised neither his political strategy nor tactics.

Czechoslovak-Polish relations, the improvement of which remained a constant and vain French preoccupation, oscillated between fleeting instances of rapprochement and phases of marked coolness. The former occurred in moments of international tension, was promoted by Czechoslovak opposition, and appeared more and more platonic to Warsaw. Prague wished to maintain good relations with Poland, but consistently resisted efforts to join in a common anti-German front. Beneš deemed it highly imprudent to take a stand that would burn bridges to Berlin and restrict his freedom of maneuver. Dislike for the Piłsudski regime and differing economic interests prevented cooperation on such matters as the agrarian

174. See Louis Marin and Viénot on East European loans, 29 Dec. 1932, J.O. Chambre, 3750, 3752.

175. See Girsa's reports, 2 and 18 Feb. 1932 in CPP and CD, NA, T 120, 1316/D 497188–89.

bloc or the Tardieu Plan. Military circles in Paris, Warsaw, and Prague were well aware of the need for a Polish-Czechoslovak alignment, but the Hrad, while approving limited technical cooperation, shied away from the thought of an alliance. In view of the weakening of the French army, the military basis of the eastern system was being eroded. The gap between planning and practical execution was widening; eastern alliances were becoming slowly little more than a facade.[176] Yet neither of the three states had anything else to put in their place. Assurances of friendship for France, as well as pro-Czechoslovak and pro-Polish pronouncements in Paris, were still de rigueur. But they had an increasingly hollow ring.

176. For French doubts and apprehensions, see Albert Mousset, "La France et ses alliés d'Europe orientale," *L'Europe Centrale*, 24 Dec. 1932.

Part Three

Responses to Hitler

Chapter Nine

A Dilemma:
The Four Power Pact

Disarmament or Preventive War?

On 30 January 1933, Adolf Hitler became the chancellor of Germany. His foreign policy goals went well beyond the revision of the Treaty of Versailles. Thinking in terms of race, space, and might, Hitler regarded lesser border rectifications as a by-product of his bid for the unification of people of the Germanic race, the acquisition of a *Lebensraum*, and the dominant role of the *Herrenvolk*. France, the hereditary foe, would have to be smashed in order to embark on such grandiose projects; Britain and Italy might hopefully be won over. Hitler's aims could only be achieved by force, which to the Nazi leader was the decisive element of domestic and international relations. But until Germany disposed of a mighty army, short-range objectives had to be couched in traditional diplomatic terminology. This consideration necessitated a projection of Hitler as a reasonable statesman, and a blurring of the distinction between familiar German demands and the Nazi targets.[1] Many observers stressed at first Hitler's dependence on Hindenburg, the conservatives, and the army. The rantings of *Mein Kampf* could hardly reflect the real program of the German government; a national socialist revolution, even if successful, would force the new regime to concentrate on domestic issues. Even so, some British and American diplomats began to think that Germany was preparing for war and needed peace only to gain the necessary strength.[2]

1. Out of the huge literature on Hitler, particularly relevant works are: Weinberg, *Foreign Policy*; Hildebrand, *Foreign Policy*; Jäckel, *Hitler's Weltanschauung*; Charles Bloch, *Hitler und die europäische Mächte 1933-1934. Kontinuität oder Bruch* (Frankfurt a/Main, 1966); H. Trevor-Roper, "Hitlers Kriegsziele," *Vierteljahrshefte für Zeitgeschichte*, 8 (1960); 121-33; Knipping, "Frankreich"; and Jacobsen, *Aussenpolitik*. Most of these authors successfully challenge Taylor's interpretations in *Origins*. On the East European aspects of Hitler's policy as affected by Pangermanism, annexationism, and geopolitics, see Kaiser, *Economic Diplomacy*, 57–59.

2. See Vansittart, *Lessons*, 216; the views of Moffat and Bullitt appear in Weinberg, *Foreign Policy*, 143, 167.

Hitler's rise to power took the French government by surprise.[3] Public opinion, split and confused over domestic issues, failed to grasp the Nazi phenomenon and react to it in any way approaching unanimity. If the internal policy of the new German government was "a challenge to every principle of the French Republic,"[4] there was no talk of countermeasures in the press. François-Poncet's dispatches showed hesitance in assessing the new development, although the ambassador termed it "grave." He advised a wait-and-see attitude without abandoning hopes for a rapprochement, which d'Ormesson, for instance judged impossible. To Flandin, the new chancellor seemed less dangerous than his immediate predecessors. As Franklin-Bouillon put it: "Hitler is the romantic and mad violence. Von Papen and Schleicher are the methodical and organized violence of Prussia." Both Daladier and the steel magnate François de Wendel thought that the Nazi revolution (which Wendel regarded as transient) would open the eyes of the world to the German danger. The second bureau considered *Mein Kampf* as a document "that was capital, fundamental and perfectly valid."[5]

Hitler's writings, which contained many virulent passages about France, said little about Poland, even though the Nazis were in the foreground of anti-Polish revisionism. The Poles, while traditionally alert to the German danger, were not unanimous in their appraisal of Hitler. The socialists took an inimical position on ideological grounds, calling Hitler a menace to Poland and the world. The populist congress described nazism as a "call to the German nation for new murders and new conquests." Both parties agreed on the need for a rapprochement with Czechoslovakia.[6] A few of the national democratic leaders, including even briefly Roman Dmowski himself, felt a certain ideological affinity with the "nationalist revolution" in Germany. The party organ, however, had already in 1931 warned that Hitler's conception of Germany's international role was bound to lead to a conflict with Poland. Prominent nationalist deputies made this point forcibly in the sejm. The governmental circles viewed Hitler as less dangerous to Poland than Stresemann had been; they preferred to see the "abscess break" than to deal with an unclarified situation. The vast goals of nazism

3. Compare ADAP, C, I/I:134 and Chłapowski telegram, 2 Feb. 1933, HIA, Amb. Paryż, box 3.

4. Tyrrell to Simon, 20 March 1933, DBFP, II, IV:465. Compare Vaïsse, *Sécurité*, 356.

5. Chargé Wendl report, 4 Feb. 1933, in Berber, ed., *Europäische Politik*, 19, with a full version in CD, NA, T120, 1316/D 496 934–36; Scott, *Alliance*, 101–102; d'Hoop, "Frankreichs Reaktion"; compare Vaïsse, *Sécurité*, 357–60; Duroselle, *Décadence*, 59–63; Gauché, *Le 2e Bureau*, 32; Franklin-Bouillon's remark, 28 Oct. 1932, J. O. Chambre, 2914. Characteristic dispatches of François-Poncet, DDF, I, II:543, 545–53.

6. See Jachymek and Szaflik, "Myśl polityczna," 231–32; Faryś's *Koncepcje*, 280–82, 307–308; Schimitzek, *Drogi*, 272; Ziaja, *PPS*, 187–94. Also Wojciechowski, *Stosunki*, 21–22; Roos, *Polen* 85–86, Weinberg, *Foreign Policy*, 14.

were likely to make those in France who had believed in the possibility of a rapprochement with Berlin at Poland's expense face the facts. What is more, an isolated Nazi regime might be more prone to reach a modus vivendi with Poland than its Prussian-dominated predecessor.[7]

Addressing the foreign affairs commission on 15 February, Beck declared that the attitude of Poland toward Germany would be exactly the same as Germany's toward Poland. A reasonable relationship depended more on Berlin than on Warsaw. This statement was both a warning and an overture, the Poles were ready to be tough but did not exclude the possibility of bilateral talks. For all the anxiety prevalent in Poland, and the distaste for Hitler among the Left and the conservatives and in governmental circles, Warsaw adopted an attitude of reserve in evaluating the consequences of Hitler's rise to power.[8]

The Czechoslovak government reacted calmly and without overt hostility to the Nazi ascendancy. *Národní Politika*, which spoke of a threat to peace, was an exception among the Czechoslovak papers.[9] Press organs close to the Hrad opined at first that Hitler would have to moderate his more extreme views because of the strength of the "republican social classes" in Germany. Beneš and Masaryk did not believe that the Third Reich could last for more than a few years. Among big business and the financiers, there were traces of positive sentiments about the chancellor.[10] If the long-range implications of the Nazi program of uniting all Germans were to be taken seriously—and Hitler did envisage the inclusion of a colonized Bohemia and Moravia in his future empire—there was certainly cause for alarm. At this juncture, however, one could hardly perceive a threat in the Czech-German friction over the trials and sentencing of Sudeten German Nazis. Hitler told their leaders that the Reich could not help them for a long time. German ministers in the Prague cabinet emphasized their loyalty to the Czechoslovak Republic.[11] Thus, Beneš was able to state

7. For Dmowski's views, see Zarnowski, *Dyktatury*, 212; Andrzej Micewski, *Roman Dmowski* (Warszawa, 1971), 399; *Archiwum Polityczne Ignacego Paderewskiego*, III, 215, 219; Faryś, *Koncepcje*, 339–41, 364–65; Wapiński, "Myśl polityczna," 207. Kozicki, Stroński and Radziwiłł utterances cited in Kozeński, *Czechosłowacja*, 52. Also DDF, I, II: 585–88; Gawroński, *Moja misja*, 20; Zabiełło, *W kręgu*, 193; Beck, *Dernier rapport*, 24.

8. Beck, *Przemówienia*, 54–59; compare Girsa report, 2 Feb. 1933, CD, NA, T120 1316/D 497 183.

9. See Noël to Paul-Boncour, 31 Jan. 1933, MAE, Z 864.1, Tchécoslovaquie 2569; Compare Weinberg, "Czechoslovakia and Germany," 764–67.

10. See Campbell, *Confrontation*, 253–54, and his "The Castle," 248–49; Kvaček, *Nad Evropou*, 26–27.

11. See Kvaček, *Nad Evropou*, 19–21; Kaiser, *Economic Diplomacy*, 60–61; Brügel, *Czechoslovakia*, 107. Also Krüger, "Staatensystem," 238.

in the parliament that he hoped to have the same kind of relationship with the new Germany that he had enjoyed with the Weimar Republic.[12]

In France, at the beginning of 1933, the weak radical-left centrist cabinet of Daladier (with Paul-Boncour at the Quai d'Orsay) strove hard to balance the budget. Exposed to socialist pressure to make heavy cuts in defense, the ministry was unable to avoid a conflict with Weygand. From this point on, a military historian asserts, one can legitimately speak of a "foreign policy of the general staff" seeking an "espace de maneuvre" outside of France and a continental power as an ally.[13] Continuing to warn about the dangers confronting France in the near future, Weygand requested a definition of "what France demands of its armed forces." A purely defensive army "was doomed to failure." If Poland, for example, was invaded by Germany, was France to enter German soil to enforce treaties and take "securities"? Without mobilization, such action was impossible. And what were the military obligations of the Little Entente? French action, implied by the network of alliances, required the resolution of two issues: coordinated war planning and communications. Without a "physical liaison"—the only wartime contact could be established through Saloniki—one could do nothing. If no serious studies were undertaken and the army was emasculated through budgetary pressures and international blackmail, French forces would be "unable to fulfill their mission when the day of danger would come."[14]

Premier Daladier sought to allay the fears about the projected economies. He saw no essential difference between the policies of Hitler and Schleicher or Brüning, and he questioned Weygand's view that "since the armistice we have never been so close as now to the possibility of war." Although there were dissenting voices, the CSG agreed that in view of the existing resources France had to content herself with "a defensive front."[15] Indeed, whereas mobilization plan D, adopted in April 1933, foresaw a delayed offensive to relieve the pressure on the eastern allies (confronting the bulk of German forces), a later study considered a firm control of the Rhine, up to the Netherlands, an indispensable condition of an offensive

---

12. Speech, 1 Mar. 1933, Beneš, *Boj o mír*, 695.

13. Dutailly, *Problèmes*, 26.

14. See Weygand note and letter, DDF, I, II:357–59, 597–600. For the Saloniki transit, see notes, 30 (?) Dec. 1932, SHA, EMA/2, Pologne 21; 26 Jan. 1933, MAE, Z 864.10, Tchécoslovaquie 2604, and DDF, I, IV:551–54. Compare "Conduite de la guerre en Europe Centrale dans les différentes hypothèses du conflit," 31 Jan. 1933, SHA, EMA/3, 7 N 3446/1. For more general issues, see Bonnefous, *Histoire*, 5:133–59; Vaïsse, *Sécurité*, 366–67; La Gorce, *French Army*, 252–56, Tournoux, *Haut commandement*, 337; Gamelin, *Servir*, 2:98–100.

15. See respectively sessions, 14 Feb., CA, CM, CAir/Sén; 15 May 1933, SHA, CSG 50.

directed at southern Germany.[16] Could the air force offer a solution? Already in 1932, General Paul Armengaud had developed this point in his *L'Aviation et la puissance offensive de l'instrument de guerre de demain*. With bombers based in Czechoslovakia and fighters in Poland, France could provide immediate aid to the allies, while heavy bombers flying from home bases would join in the operation.[17] But a discussion of these ideas at joint sessions of the senatorial military commissions only led to controversies about the tactical use of the French air force.[18]

Air force cooperation and coordinated planning constituted the major item on the agenda of conversations between the French and the Czechoslovak chief of the general staff, General Syrový, brought to Paris in late January 1933. The discussants recognized the need to study various strategies, and the Czechoslovak side finally consented to treat Germany as the principal foe (after the liquidation of Hungary). A closer military cooperation between the Little Entente states as well as Polish-Czechoslovak staff talks, both directed against Germany, were deemed important objectives. The principle of stationing an unspecified number of French air squadrons in Czechoslovakia was accepted. A more detailed study, made in Prague by the chief of the French second bureau, Lieutenant Colonel Marie Koeltz, followed by late April and early May.[19]

All these plans had a certain aura of unreality given the weak attitude of the French government and the state of public opinion. The British had no doubts that if "Germany attacks Poland, France will let her and will not move. There is no French minister, either of the Left or Right, capable of making the French take up arms for Poland." The "discouraged and hesitant" government "lost confidence in the satellite system as a means of containing Germany."[20]

Hitler's advent to power gave a new urgency to the disarmament question. The French position was unenviable, for having "ceded virtually everything in 1932" France "was starting from zero in 1933."[21] The Brit-

---

16. Study 1933, Aug. SHA, EMA/2, Pologne 21. Plan D is summarized in Tournoux, *Haut commandement*, 337.

17. See Paul F. Armengaud, *Batailles politiques et militaires sur l'Europe: témoignages 1931–1940* (Paris, 1948), 18, 25–26.

18. See session, 14 Feb. 1933, CA, CM, CAir/Sén. Compare Le Goyet, "Evolution," and Truelle, "La production."

19. On Syrový and Faucher visit, 28–31 Jan. 1933, and Gamelin to chief of the Air Force, 15 Jan. in SHA, EMA/3, 7 N 3446/2; compare "Analyse des dispositions nous liant à la Tchécoslovaquie," 2 June 1938, SHA, Cab. du Min. de Guerre, 5 N 579/6. Also Marès, "*La Faillite*," 52–53; DDF, I, III:418–21 and ministry to legations in Prague, Vienna, and Budapest, respectively 17, 25 Apr., MAE, Z 864.10, Tchécoslovaquie 2604.

20. See respectively DDB, III, 58 and DBFP, II, IV:466.

21. Duroselle, *Décadence*, 67.

ish believed that the deadlock could only be broken through negotiations between the five powers; the Germans were warning that if collective security were made a condition of equality of armaments they would raise the issue of territorial revision.[22] The French government thought it had to stress its positive stance toward disarmament, a position supported by a large majority in parliament.

The specter of a great powers' directorate and the threat of revisionism caused anxiety in Czechoslovakia and Poland. Paul-Boncour agreed with the worried Beneš on the need of a close contact between Paris, the Little Entente, and Warsaw. He explained that only a slow and progressive realization of German equality of rights was envisaged.[23] Krofta noted that if Polish borders were to be discussed, those between Hungary and Czechoslovakia would follow. As Beneš prophesied, "the year 1933 will see the appearance of the great offensive of revisionism."[24] Would Paris contemplate territorial revision as a price for the acceptance of its ideas on disarmament? Although Paul-Boncour denied any connection between the two, the Quai d'Orsay felt that "one could not exclude a priori" the examination of territorial issues if raised jointly with military matters and bearing on "partial improvements," not "radical modifications" likely to overturn the "very foundations of peace."[25] Czechoslovak diplomacy seemed aware of such views, but as always it chose the part of exerting its influence through close collaboration with Paris. The Poles, more directly endangered, adopted a more defiant posture.

On the eve of the reopening of the disarmament conference, Chłapowski warned Paul-Boncour and his deputy Cot against great powers' conversations, as contrary to the spirit of the Covenant and the Franco-Polish alliance, and voiced concern over prorevisionist tendencies of the French press. He reported on Paul-Boncour's passivity toward international as well as domestic matters.[26] In Geneva, Beck repeated Polish reservations and expressed preference for a limited technical disarmament convention; however, the French understood that he would go along with their tac-

22. See DBFP, II, IV:483–84; Leeper minutes on 1 Feb. 1933 note, FO 371 17227 N 704; Černý dispatch (extract) in Berber, *Europäishe Politik*, 21; briefing, 5 Jan. 1933, KV, CPP.

23. Conversation notes, 24 Jan. 1933, DDF, I, II:520–22.

24. Briefing, 5 Jan. 1933, KV, CPP; Girsa report on revisionism, 26 Jan., CD, NA, T120, 1316/D 497 176; DDF, I, II:378–81, 490; Hankey memo, Simon to Tyrrell, Vansittart to Hankey, 1, 10, 13 Feb. 1933, FO 371 16715 C 934/316/18, and C 1200/316/18 and C 1348.

25. Project of instructions, MAE, Z 864.10, Tchécoslovaquie 2602; Paul-Boncour statement, session 1 Mar. 1933, CAE/Ch.

26. Chłapowski reports, 18, 28 Jan. 1933, AAN, Amb. Berlin, 80 and MSZ 3801.

tics.[27] Thus, they were startled when the Polish delegate, Edward Raczyń-ski, informed Paul-Boncour and the Little Entente representatives that Poland would advocate a limited accord banning, among others, heavy weapons and air bombardment. For the first time the Poles were to differ publicly from the French. "If your objective was . . . to produce a certain psychological shock," wrote Mühlstein to Beck, "this aim was fully achieved." Paul-Boncour spoke of Polish ingratitude; Herriot called the Polish move "a grave event"; the editor of the pro-Polish *Petit Parisien* declared that Beck was "not a friend of France."[28]

Laroche expressed surprise over Polish "dissident action" and pointed to "serious consequences" of this "grave tactical mistake."[29] Beck retorted that he had explained to Paul-Boncour that it was impossible to achieve a comprehensive scheme rapidly without allowing Germany to raise revisionist matters. Even the French minister was under no illusions about the chances of his plan, which was worked out, incidentally, without any consultation with Warsaw.[30] Foreign diplomats agreed that Raczyński's stand was "dictated by fear of French concessions as regards article 19 [of the Covenant] in return for some German security concessions." There was "certainly a feeling among certain Frenchmen that the Corridor is going to be raised." Had Beck been able to get full French support, he would not have taken this line.[31] The Polish minister argued that Paris, by clinging to vast schemes, was undercutting the conference's chances. He admitted, however, that the idea of banning arms his country did not possess stemmed also from Polish "sacred egoism."[32] Simultaneously repeating that great powers' decisions taken without Poland's participation were not binding, and that this position was not contrary "to our alliance [with France] which remains one of the primary bases of our policy," Beck was drawing a distinction between the alliance as a permanent factor and the day to day Franco-Polish collaboration. The governmental *Gazeta Polska* made this crystal clear. If the current line of the French government depended on the policy of the socialists, Poland had no obligation to follow suit.[33]

27. DDF, I, II:451–53, 523–24, 569–70.

28. DTJS, I, 7–10; compare Vaïsse, *Sécurité*, 380.

29. Instructions to Laroche, 8 Feb. 1933, DDF, I, II:577–78.

30. Laroche dispatches in DDF, I, II:593–95, 737–39.

31. See Wigram to F.O. 9 Feb. 1933, FO 371 17350 W 1732; Bastianini report in Borejsza, *Mussolini*, 205–206; Girsa report, 2 Feb. 1933 (abbrev.), CD, NA T120, 1316/D 497 183.

32. Beck, *Dernier rapport*, 45, 262–64; compare DTJS, I, 10.

33. See Beck, *Przemówienia*, 58, 62; compare comments in *Gazeta Warszawska* and *Ilustrowany Kurjer Codzienny*, 16, 25 and 24 Feb. 1933; senate debate 24 Feb., Spra-

The Raczyński incident was echoed in press polemics. While several Polish papers deplored a policy that could oppose Warsaw to Paris, the pro-government *Kurjer Poranny* criticized the defeatist tendencies at the Quai d'Orsay. Paul-Boncour was annoyed by what he termed a "perfidious, tendentious and unjust campaign." Laroche opined that its objective was to convince the Polish public opinion that one could not count on France, and at the same time force Paris to take more account of Poland. The ambassador was sarcastic about Beck trying to play at Talleyrand, for he knew well that the French alliance could not be replaced by any other combination.[34] This observation occurred frequently in Laroche's reports.

With the exception of Pertinax, who on 9 February approved in *L'Echo de Paris* the Raczyński declaration, the Parisian press took Poland sharply to task. Beck complained to Laroche of being "dragged in the mud" by the French newspapers. *La République* wrote that surely Poland and the Little Entente knew that "there have been no French statesman among those in power since the war who would dare to mobilize the French people in case of a conflict on the Vistula, the Danube or in the Balkans," and if he tried "most of us would not march."[35] Prorevisionist utterances multiplied.[36] On 28–30 January, several French and German industrialists and politicians who had participated in the 1932 Luxembourg talks resumed informal exchanges in Paris and reached general consensus about the need to modify borders in the "corridor" and Upper Silesia. Compensation for Poland would include Memel and free zones in Danzig and Gdynia. France and Germany would then jointly guarantee all Polish borders and work for a comprehensive Franco-German-Belgian-Polish security pact based on general staff cooperation and following a common policy on disarmament. One of the participants, René Duchemin, allegedly told the Germans that the French government had seen and approved the final protocol of the meeting, and although this possibility is not corroborated by other sources, it cannot be ruled out. The Poles who had learned about the meeting suspected it in any case. Neurath, however, regarded the recommendations as unacceptable to Germany. Hence, Hitler was not informed, and the encounter had no sequel.[37]

---

wozdania stenograficzne senatu, XLVI/5, 11-21, 36. Also Laroche dispatches DDF, I, II:627–28, 683 and 24 Feb. 1933, MAE, Z 698.1, Pologne 2099.

34. See Laroche–Paul-Boncour exchanges, 8, 9, 10, 21 Feb. 1933, MAE, Z 698.12 Pologne 2198 and Z 698.1, Pologne 2099. Also 1 Mar. note, SI, MSZ, A.11/4.

35. Paper cited in DTJS, I, 10–11.

36. Among others of Jouvenel, Albert Bayet, Pierre Dominique, Marcel Déat, Jean Luchaire, Pfeiffer, Gaston Bergery, Suarez. See Jan Weinstein, "Polska polityka zagraniczna w krzywym zwierciadle historyka," *Niepodległość*, 9 (1974), 369–70. Compare Vaïsse, *Sécurité*, 360.

37. See Bariéty and Bloch "Une Tentative," 457–61; Wojciechowski, *Stosunki*, 17; ADAP, C, I, 1:2–4.

The British noted the following paradox. In principle the French opposed a revision of Versailles and would revolt against the idea if confronted with it. At the same time, they felt that the "corridor" had to be somehow disposed of to prevent the conflagration they feared.[38] Even Weygand regarded it as an insoluble problem resulting from the errors committed in 1919. Paul-Boncour thought that a revision was unavoidable in the future.[39] Laroche's remarks to his German colleague went along similar lines, although the ambassador also thought that if a Warsaw-Berlin rapprochement occurred, it could—while serving the cause of peace—entail certain risks for France.[40] It was symptomatic that the head of the Quai d'Orsay press bureau took alarm when a Polish journalist requested permission to conduct an opinion poll on the "corridor," for he feared that interviews with Léon Blum, Herriot, or even Paul-Boncour might only confirm that "the French statesmen were quite indifferent and even generally quite negative with regard to this burning problem."[41] In these circumstances, Laroche's denials that any responsible French circles inclined to revisionism at Poland's expense sounded rather hollow.

Meanwhile events at the disarmament conference were taking a discouraging turn as France was obliged to substitute the "myth of controls" for the "myth of collective assistance."[42] On 16 March, MacDonald proposed for the first time concrete figures for the major continental armies: 200 thousand for France, Italy, Germany, and Poland organized as national militias. Daladier voiced his bitterness to Beneš, but both agreed, for tactical reasons, to treat the proposal as a basis for deliberations.[43] Beck refused to be convinced by MacDonald's argument that the choice lay between concessions and letting Germany repudiate the whole treaty.[44] The British plan did not have much of a chance anyway, for Hitler was only interested in the legalization of a 600 thousand strong army, then in the process of being organized, and German diplomacy maneuvered so as to shift on others the responsibility for the collapse of the conference.

The alternative to concessions was force. From Britain came Winston Churchill's lonely voice: "Thank God for the French army." He continued with a warning: "As surely as Germany acquires full military equality with her neighbours while her own grievances are still unredressed and while

38. Tyrrell to Vansittart, 24 Mar. 1933, FO 371 16683 C 2680; compare Johnson to Roosevelt, 12 May, Nixon, *Roosevelt*, 2:121; compare DDF, I, III:246, 327.

39. Col. Heywood report in Tyrrell to Vansittart, 13 Jan. 1933, FO 371 16715 C 573; see also Mühlstein to Beck, 17 Apr., DTJS, I, 13.

40. See ADAP, C, I, I: 71–72; DDF, I, II:452–53.

41. Note of Pierre Comert, 10 Feb. 1933, MAE, Z 698.12, Pologne 2198.

42. Minart, *Le Drame*, 37.

43. See Kvaček, *Nad Evropou*, 23; Vaïsse, *Sécurité*, 389–99; DDF, I, III;20, 30–31.

44. Beck–MacDonald–Simon conversations, 17 Mar. 1933, DBFP, II, V:61–62.

she is in the temper which we have unhappily seen, so surely should we see ourselves within a measurable distance of the renewal of general European war." Calling France the "guarantor and protector of the whole crescent of small states which runs right round from Belgium to Yugoslavia and Rumania," Churchill predicted that if the French force be weakened "they will be at the mercy of the great Teutonic power."[45] Weygand painted a similarly bleak picture of the future. Referring to German breaches of the disarmament provisions, he felt the only way to respond would be to tell Berlin "now, straight away, that we would not have it."[46]

The story, based on circumstantial evidence, that Marshal Piłsudski proposed on one or more occasion to the French in 1933 a preventive war against Germany appears in several variants.[47] There are those who maintain that Piłsudski did seriously consider it and proposed it unsuccessfully to Paris; those who believe he sounded the French only in order to frighten Germany and make it amenable to a direct settlement with Poland; those who feel that he weighed the pros and cons of a preventive war without making any proposals; and finally those who deny he had any such plans, and ascribe the widely circulating rumors to the Poles, the Germans, even to Mussolini. The term "preventive war" appears to be a misnomer, for Piłsudski had seemingly in mind a wide range of options including a demonstration or use of force justified by incidents in Danzig or German violations of part 5 of Versailles. "Preventive war" may also have been a means more than an end in itself epitomizing Piłsudski's bold strategy combined with native caution.[48]

There is little doubt that many politicians recognized that preventive measures may be the only logical course of action, whether practicable or not, to stop German rearmament. Mussolini, Undersecretary Fulvio Suvich, and Ambassador William Bullitt mentioned it, although with the proviso that France would not take the risk.[49] The British ambassador in

45. Churchill, *Storm*, 75–76. Churchill stressed that the "corridor" was Polish by history and population.

46. Tyrrell to Simon, 18 Mar. 1933, FO 371 16706 C 2627.

47. See Jędrzejewicz, "Preventive War"; Kuźmiński, "Wobec zagadnienia"; Gasiorowski, "Pilsudski"; Roos, "Präventivkriegspläne"; Boris Celovsky, "Pilsudskis Präventivkrieg gegen das national-sozialistische Deutschland," *Die Welt als Geschichte*, 14 (1954) 53–70; also Roberts, "Beck," 612–14; Mazurowa, *Skazani*; and the most recent Rollet, "Deux mythes."

48. For Piłsudski's native caution and intensified personal involvement in foreign policy, see Girsa reports, 26 Jan. and 10 May 1933, CPP. The latter emerges clearly from Jędrzejewicz, *Kronika*, 2:433–38.

49. See Aloisi, *Journal*, 143; Romer report, 11 Sept. 1933, PI, Amb. Londyn, reel 46; Komarnicki–de Soregna conversation, 29 Sept., AAN, MSZ 108; Pertinax, *Gravediggers*, 382.

Berlin wrote that if one regarded Hitler solely as the author of *Mein Kampf*, the preventive war idea was prefectly logical.[50] Hitler told his generals on 3 February that the most dangerous time for Germany would be the early phase of rearmament. "If France has capable statesmen, it will attack us during the period of [our preparations], not itself, but probably through its vassals in the cast."[51] The head of the Quai d'Orsay press bureau mentioned the alternatives: "attack Germany or wait tamely for Germany to attack us," conveying the impression that he favored the former. According to a Foreign Office minute, such views were supposedly held by "responsible circles" in France.[52] British Ambassador Tyrrell reported on "much ill-judged talk of preventive war even among circles which should know better," but the military were against it. Besides, the French recognized that there were "no good legal grounds for military sanctions." It was also believed in Berlin that "responsible people [in Paris] are talking of a preventive war," and they are holding the Poles back, for Warsaw would certainly opt for an invasion of Germany.[53] Similarly, the German ambassador wrote from Paris that the thought of forcibly preventing the growing German might was gaining ground.[54] The Polish representative at the League later asserted that he had learned from Paul-Boncour that a preventive war had been the subject of secret deliberations on the cabinet level and unanimously rejected.[55]

It seems that the German military decree of 22 February, seen as a clear violation of the disarmament clauses, made Paris contemplate forcible action. Article 213 of Versailles, which spoke of investigation of disarmament breaches, could be invoked. Should Germany refuse an investigation, preventive measures might be considered legitimate. Yet, there were doubts about the legal grounds. Soundings of the British were discouraging, and Weygand considered a long and bloody war unthinkable without British cooperation.[56] Tardieu's exclamation that if he were still in power he would authorize "an immediate promenade of our soldiers in Germany" might have been a bravado. Daladier's remarks about a preventive

---

50. Phipps to Simon, 21 Nov. 1933, DBFP, II, VI:90.

51. Weinberg, *Foreign Policy*, 27.

52. Harvey to Vansittart, 19 Sept. 1933, FO 371 16709 Hm 03936.

53. Rumbold and Tyrrell to Simon, 7 Apr., 19 May, 1933, DBFP, II, V:28, 268–69.

54. Köster to Auswärtiges Amt, 11 Mar. 1933, ADAP, C, I/1:135.

55. Komarnicki, *Piłsudski*, 78. Massigli said years later that he never heard anything about it but could not rule out the possibility of private conversations between individual ministers. See Mazurowa, *Skazani*, 204–205.

56. See Vaïsse, *Sécurité*, 375-76. Also DDF, I, VI:290; compare DBFP, II, V:196–99, 289–98. Hymans said that "L'idée d'une guerre préventive a été à maintes reprises repousée par le Gouvernement et les hommes d'état français." DDB, III, 361.

war, made to the British, were explained as calculated to gauge their re-action and to intimidate the Germans.[57]

The French leaders, while secretely playing with the idea of a preventive war, deemed it an impossible undertaking for a democratically governed country.[58] As Premier Albert Sarraut said in November 1933, this was a solution that everyone in France "rejects with horror." For such a policy, Paul-Boncour wrote later, one would not have found ten voices in the chamber. As Blum admitted thirteen years later, a preventive operation in 1933 might well have been the "unique" way of averting World War II, but the socialists, himself included, found the idea horrifying. Even the most ardent foes of Germany—Georges Mandel, Jean Fabry, or Franklin-Bouillon—had to deny in parliament that the tough policies they advo-cated could lead to a preventive war.[59]

According to Beck, Piłsudski had "carefully examined the pros and the cons of chances of a preventive war before taking the decision to negotiate with Germany; and he abandoned the idea in view of the weakness of our possible allies."[60] Beck's secretary wrote that the marshal had made such suggestions "in a most discrete form," and a high-placed member of the *sanacja* recalled that although Beck had been skeptical about exploring the matter Piłsudski "ordered him to seek stubbornly the possibility of making simple logic prevail."[61] The marshal allegedly told an aide de camp that even if Poland were to attack Hitler, it would still be a measure of de-fense.[62] It was widely believed in Geneva that Piłsudski favored the use of article 213 as a pretext for coercive action.[63] But did he approach the French?

In early 1933, two emissaries were dispatched to Paris on missions the character of which had never been satisfactorily explained. The first, Jerzy Potocki, Piłsudski's former aide de camp who was soon to become ambas-sador to Italy, came armed with oral instruction from the marshal. He was

57. See Vaïsse, *Sécurité*, 407–408, 445, and Jacques Dinfreville (on Daladier) "De Lattre chez Weygand," *Revue des Deux Mondes* (July 1970), 75–76.

58. See DDB, II, 361; DBFP, II, V:600; DDF, I, III:572.

59. 9, 14, 30 Nov. 1933, J. O. Chambre, 4041–43; 4110, 4124, 4127, 3845. Also Osuský report, 21 Oct., CD, NA, T120 1316/D 496 970; Paul-Boncour, *Entre deux guerres*, 2:344; Bariéty, *Relations*, 33.

60. Beck, *Dernier rapport*, 66. A brief reference to preventive war also appears in Rydz-Śmigły's reminiscences, 129, 139.

61. Starzeński, *Trzy lata*, 82; Miedziński, "Pakty wilanowskie."

62. Cited in Jędrzejewicz, "Preventive war," 83.

63. Piłsudski's confidant Sokolnicki (cited in Jędrzejewicz, "Preventive war," 89) rules out the notion of preventive war in the strict sense of the term. Compare Weinberg, *Foreign Policy*, 60. Piłsudski's interest in using article 213 is mentioned by a high-rank-ing League official and a well-informed journalist (who relates it to "preventive war"): Harold Butler, *The Lost Peace* (London, 1941), 83, and Dell, *Geneva Racket*, 200–202.

to talk directly to Paul-Boncour, bypassing the Polish embassy, and to convey an "avertissement" apparently in connection with the developments at the disarmament conference. The mission was in keeping with Piłsudski's predilection for secret diplomacy, but its avowed purpose does not explain the emissary's stay in Paris for over two months.[64] It is likely that Potocki, while not being the carrier of any specific proposal, may have, without realizing it himself, been sent to test the French resolve and provide Piłsudski with appraisals he needed in order to orient his policy.

On 6 March, while Potocki was still in Paris, the marshal decided on a dramatic move, namely strengthening the small Polish garrison on Westerplatte in Danzig. Ostensibly this was Poland's reply to the Free City's repudiation of an accord on the harbor police, but the unilateral act, technically violating international agreements, was above all a demonstration of Poland's will to defend its interests, even by forceful means. The French found the incident embarrassing, and helped formulate a compromise in Geneva that eventually entailed the withdrawal of the Polish reinforcement.[65] The German envoy in Warsaw, Hans von Moltke, opined that Piłsudski's main objective had been "to give a warning to the supporters of revisionist thinking in Europe." Grzybowski told his French colleague in Prague that Piłsudski wanted to show that the real problem was not the "corridor" but Danzig; the Westerplatte was meant to be the first but not the last of the moves he contemplated.[66] General d'Arbonneau actually used the term "preventive war" to describe the affair.[67] Both François-Poncet and Wysocki wrote retrospectively that the Westerplatte incident was a trial balloon to test French and British reactions. The French diplomat thought that Piłsudski was in fact offering an opportunity to the Western powers to exploit the incident for a move against Berlin.[68]

The Westerplatte affair and the appearance in Paris of Piłsudski's confidant Colonel Bolesław Wieniawa-Długoszowski, seemingly sent to ex-

---

64. See DDF, I, II:451; DTJS, I, 3–4; Wandycz, "Trzy dokumenty," and "Jeszcze o misji." The letters to the author from Countess Alfredowa Potocka, Józef Potocki, Jan Weinstein, Roman Dębicki, and Michał Łubieński indicate that Potocki was not the carrier of a preventive war proposal. Compare Ciałowicz, *Polsko-francuski sojusz*, 184. Jacques de Launay's story that in Feb. 1933 Beck as Piłsudski's emissary brought to Paul-Boncour a preventive war proposal (*Histoire contemporaine de la diplomatie secrète*, Lausanne, 1965, 235n.) corresponds to no sources know to me. Rollet, "Deux mythes," 236–40 concludes that Potocki's mission was only concerned with disarmament matters.

65. See DDF, I, I:742–43, 755, 811-12.

66. See respectively ADAP, C, I/1:128, 144–45 and DDF, I, II:823.

67. Report Nov. 1932–Feb. 1934, SHA, EMA/2, Pologne 12. The Italian envoy Giuseppe Bastianini ruled out, however, the possibility that the Poles contemplated a preventive war. See Laroche to Paul-Boncour, 30 Apr. 1933, MAE, Z 698.1, Pologne 2099.

68. MS, OSS, Wysocki, II, 301; François-Poncet, *Souvenirs*, 165.

plore the views of the French army,[69] coincided with the earlier-mentioned French soundings of the British. Mühlstein reported that rumors about Polish plans of a preventive military action were circulating among "very serious political circles" in Paris. Top ministers, including Daladier and Paul-Boncour, were talking about it. The Westerplatte coup appeared as a "prepared incident." Visibly worried, the veteran politician Joseph Caillaux told Mühlstein: "Do not orient yourselves toward war. This country will not march."[70] French intelligence reported a growing German-Polish tension.[71] Laroche did not believe that Warsaw was seeking an opportunity to use force, and the military attaché generally shared this view, but he reported that many people in Poland believed that if war with Germany was inevitable, it was better to "make it now than later." This feeling also existed among the military.[72]

The German envoy in Warsaw, while failing to observe military preparations, mentioned several reasons that might push the Poles toward forceful action. They were concerned about French unwillingness to fight for the "corridor," but were inclined to think that if Poland resorted to a fait accompli, France would not abandon its ally. As for Czechoslovakia and the Little Entente, Warsaw reckoned only with the possibility of indirect aid. Moltke concluded that everything depended on Piłsudski, and "nobody knows what he thinks."[73]

There are indications that the idea of a preventive war was present in the minds of some Czechs. A diplomat startled his French colleague by remarking that the proceedings of Nazi Germany would justify a preventive war; he wondered if France would take the initiative. Koch wrote from Prague that the idea was "carefully considered" at the Hrad, Polish influence being exerted in that direction. The envoy ruled out any Czechoslovak desire to become actively involved, but he also noted Masaryk's remarks about the certainty of war in the near future. Beneš also made references to conversations concerning preventive war.[74] Such information accounted for beliefs on the German government level that preparations were underway along Polish and Czechoslovak western borders; Hitler

---

69. See Ciałowicz, *Polsko-francuski sojusz*, 181–82; Pobóg-Malinowski, *Najnowsza historia*, 2:550; Gawroński, *Moja misja*, 31; Jurkiewicz, *Pakt wschodni*, 42.

70. Mühlstein's private letter to Beck, 17 Apr. 1933, DTJS, I, 12–13.

71. Colonel Koeltz note, 14 Mar. 1933; intelligence reports of late Apr., SHA, EMA/2, Pologne 37.

72. Laroche in DDF, I/III:172–73, 707; d'Arbonneau report, 5 Apr. 1933, SHA, EMA/2, Pologne 12; Compare Girsa report, 2 May 1933, CPP.

73. See ADAP, C, I/I:326–31; also 149, 288, 399–40, 349, and Girsa report, 2 Mar. 1933, CD, NA, T120, 1316/D 497 190.

74. Clement-Simon to Paul-Boncour, 28 Apr. 1933, MAE, Z 864.10, Tchécoslovaquie 2602; compare ADAP, C, I/I:340 and Král, *Spojenectví*, 39.

took the rumors of Polish overtures to France seriously.[75] The German press was filled with alarmist articles accusing Poland of preparing to strike.

Stories about Polish proposals to France persisted throughout the spring and they revived in the autumn; the British as well as the Russians lent credence to them.[76] Except for an occasional article in the socialist *Robotnik*, which advocated preventive action, the Polish press and diplomacy denied and ridiculed the rumors.[77] This does not exclude, of course, the possibility that Warsaw originated them. But it is also plausible that the German papers gave the preventive war deliberate publicity in order to discredit and embarrass the "war-mongering" Polish government. Unless some new evidence to the contrary is forthcoming, one can assume that Piłsudski's hints and soundings, and well as his provocative acts such as the Westerplatte demonstration, may be collectively subsumed under the "preventive war" heading. The object was to make it clear to the French where Piłsudski stood, and to serve notice on Berlin of Warsaw's determination.[78]

The Four Power Pact

The "preventive war" moves coincided in time with a diplomatic negotiation concerning a Paris-Rome-London-Berlin pact. At the beginning of 1933, Paul-Boncour had named Henry de Jouvenel ambassador to Rome to work for "a lasting entente" linking the interests of both countries. The division between the pro-French and pro-Italian groupings in the Danubian and Balkan regions was to be effaced, and Rome's economic involvement in the area was to be permitted, without, however, making it completely dependent on Italy. Instructions to Jouvenel recalled that French foreign policy strove "to preserve the status quo in Europe" in close cooperation with England through "the maintenance of our ties of particular friendship with Poland and Little Entente."[79] An abatement of anti-Italian

75. See ADAP, C, I/1:340; also Otto Meissner, *Staatssekretär unter Ebert–Hindenburg–Hitler* (Hamburg, 1950), 334; compare DDF, I, II:821, III:190; DBFP, II, IV:452. For German fears also 17 May 1933, CAE/Ch.

76. See Phipps to Simon, 21 Nov. 1933, DBFP, II, VI:80–81. Probably this and similar dispatches made Vansittart speak of Polish proposals to France in *Mist Procession*, 412, 468–69. For Litvinov's belief in their authenticity, see DBFP, II, XII:786. Only Flandin, *Politque*, 118, and François-Poncet in Mazurowa, *Skazani*, 179, accepted the story of preventive war proposals.

77. See DDF, I, III:415. Compare d'Arbonneau report, 2 May 1933, SHA, EMA/2, Pologne 12; also *Gazeta Warszawska*, 29 Apr.; Pułaski, *Stosunki*, 57. For Wysocki's denials to Hitler, see DTJS, I, 49.

78. See Szembek's retrospective view cited in Jędrzejewicz, "Preventive War," 79.

79. DDF, I, II:610–14.

prejudices at the Quai d'Orsay was associated by the British with the rise of Alexis Léger to secretaryship general.[80]

Mussolini was interested in a rapprochement with France to facilitate the realization of Italian postulates in colonial, naval, and Danubian matters, but he had no wish to commit himself fully against Germany and lose his freedom of maneuver. His goal was a four-power directorate through which Italy, thus far outnumbered in Geneva by the French-led bloc, would become one of the states determining the course of European affairs.[81] The duce told Jouvenel on 2 March that certain international matters required revision, and he named the Polish "corridor." A transfer to Germany of a Polish strip along the Baltic, ten to fifteen kilometers wide, would connect Germany with East Prussia; although Gdynia would pose a problem, the alternative was war. Mussolini also favored some adjustment of borders to Hungary's advantage. His guiding motto was: "Let us avoid above all that the little nations make the great ones fight among themselves."[82]

The Mussolini–Jouvenel conversation moved the Franco-Italian negotiation from a bilateral to a European level, a possibility foreseen by the Quai d'Orsay. Jouvenel did not appear shocked, and if one remembers his championship of an Eastern Locarno in the 1920s, it is obvious that his opinions had significantly changed.[83] He admitted that "one would have to spare the amour propre of the Poles," and that revision in the Danubian area raised more problems, for one was dealing here not with one state but with three.[84] Still, a revision of treaties was unavoidable, and if one said no to Rome, an Italo-German rapprochement could materialize, leaving an isolated France "to carry the burden of the little nations and of their security." True, the acceptance of Mussolini's ideas might fatally injure French authority vis-à-vis its allies, but a choice had to be made. A resolution of the "corridor" issue would avoid a potential European war; surely France had guaranteed peace to the Poles and not guaranteed their borders. Poland would have greater guarantees, bought "at a relatively low price," and France's gain would largely compensate the "risk of a temporary dissatisfaction on Poland's part." Cooperation with Italy would also protect Austria. As for Hungary, some revision might be possible in view of Masaryk's earlier references to border modifications. Jouvenel recommended precautions and the conclusion of three accords: a Franco-Italian-British agreement on the limits of planned revisions (the criterion being

80. See Tyrrell to Simon, 16 Mar. 1933, FO 800 288; Chłapowski report, 7 Mar. AAN, MSZ 3801; Duroselle, *Décadence*, 23–25; 71–73; Cameron, "Léger," 384.

81. See Aloisi, *Journal*, 75.

82. Jouvenel to Paul-Boncour, 3 Mar. 1933, DDF, I, II:730–32.

83. See Binion, *Defeated Leaders*, 173–74.

84. See Aloisi, *Journal*, 79; compare Borejsza, *Mussolini*, 441.

avoidance of the danger of war); an agreement between the three powers on disarmament and security; finally, a Franco-Italian agreement preceding any attempted revision of treaties. Revision, with France involved in the process, would appear "as a voluntary concession to peace, guaranteeing to our allies," who owe so much to France, "the security of their future."[85]

Mussolini's formula on the "corridor" and his support of Hungarian revisionism evoked "most serious reservations" on Paul-Boncour's part.[86] The foreign minister was particularly worried lest the Poles find out about the talks, and agreed with the Italian diplomat Pompeo Aloisi that France must not insist on bringing the smaller countries "into all these questions."[87] The Four Power Pact, as outlined by the duce in the second week of March, revolved around a Rome-London axis, the Italians bringing in Germany, and the British winning over France. Mussolini told the Germans of his worries about a preventive war waged by France (although French masses were pacifist) and its allies against both Germany and Italy. While supporting Berlin's position on the "corridor," he urged patience, for the Reichswehr was not yet a match for the Polish army.[88]

Hitler could hardly be enthusiastic over a plan that sought to stabilize Europe at the price of limited revision. As for France, Tyrrell cautioned London that revisionism in France could "only thrive in an atmosphere of calm."[89] Mussolini's formal version of the Four Power Pact, presented during the visit of Prime Minister MacDonald and Foreign Secretary Simon to Rome on 18–19 March, invoked the Kellogg–Briand pact and the five powers' Geneva declaration. The Covenant of the League was not mentioned, and the possibility of the signatories imposing their will on others was implied. It was recognized that Germany's Gleichberechtigung would be progressively realized should the disarmament conference end in failure. Similar concessions would be made to Austria, Hungary and Bulgaria. The British introduced some amendments to make the proposed pact more palatable to France. "The pill of revision" would be "sweetened by the reaffirmation of the doctrine of sanctity of treaties." But even so, as MacDonald pointed out, "the effect of a special agreement on the part of

85. Jouvenel in DDF, I, II:758–60; compare Osuský report, 22 June 1933, CD, NA, T120, 1316/D 469 952.

86. See DDF, I, II:776; compare DBFP, II, IV:529.

87. Aloisi–MacDonald–Simon conversation, 14 Mar. 1933, DBFP, II, IV:528.

88. ADAP, C, I/1:157–59; compare Aloisi, *Journal* 83–84; Jarausch, *Four Power Pact*, 34–39.

89. Tyrrell to Vansittart, 15 Mar. 1933 and Sargent's minute, FO 371 16683 C 2680. For Germany see DDF, I, III, 38–39; Wysocki report, 8 June, AAN, MSZ, z.2, w.36, t.18 (old classification); Jarausch, *Four Power Pact*, 47, 50–53; Mazur, *Pakt Czterech*, 163–71, 217–21, 257–58.

Germany not to attack France was to some extent an implication of her intention to attack Poland." France might also object to the fact that while in the League it was not isolated, it might consider itself to be so within the pact. Still, on 21 March the British ministers went to Paris to convince the French to go along.[90]

The French raised a number of pertinent questions. Daladier remarked that "it was difficult to dispose of the property of others without consulting them," and when MacDonald suggested some conversations with Beneš and Beck, Paul-Boncour asked what would happen if the two opposed revision. How could such a pact be justified before Europe? Would it not be contrary to the League? The British countered that, the alternative being unlimited German rearmament and territorial revisionism, the pact would provide the means of "getting the machinery of revision into order." As Paul Reynaud put it later, the idea was that France and Britain would join Hitler and Mussolini at the table not to share their meal "but in the hope of moderating their voracity."[91]

Paris stood at the crossroads, for as the Quai d'Orsay opined, it was impossible either to reject the pact or to accept it as formulated. The former would lead to accusations that France destroyed a peace initiative. The latter would be a fatal blow to the League policy, subordinate Paris to a majority within the pact, eliminate the possible advantages of a direct Franco-German rapprochement, and "ruin our system of alliances." Poland, "which does not intend to be treated any longer as a secondary power, and the Little Entente, which had constituted itself into a political entity, would not easily accept being pushed aside." The Quai d'Orsay recommended efforts to associate Warsaw, and if possible other states, with the pact and make it subordinate to the League, France might also consider playing the Russian card.[92]

From late March until 7 June, when the Four Power Pact was initialed, the French government worked feverishly to dull its revisionist edge and to reconcile it with the eastern alliances. Simultaneously, it strove to gain domestic approval and convince the Little Entente and Poland that they should trust France's loyalty. Even though French public opinion was preoccupied with financial problems and domestic scandals, the Four Power Pact gave rise to sharp arguments in the press, in the foreign affairs commission, and in the parliament. The editor of *L'Homme Libre*, E. Lautier, dubbed the pact "a butchers' club" (club des charcutiers), in view of its pretense to carve up other states. *Journal des Débats* called it—even in

90. See DBFP, II, v:73–75, 86-99, 101; also Simon to Foreign Office, 19 Mar. 1933, FO 371 16683 C 2682.

91. Reynaud, *Au Coeur*, 53.

92. Note, 19 Mar. 1933, DDF, I, III:21–25.

its diluted form—a "criminal act" and the "most dangerous operation performed since 1919."[93] *L'Ere Nouvelle, L'Echo de Paris,* and *Journal* were critical; *Le Temps* wavered; the communist *L'Humanité* attacked the pact, while *Le Populaire* became sympathetic toward the idea; *La Volonté* and *La République* were generally in favor.

Within the government Daladier played the crucial role, seconded by Paul-Boncour, with Jouvenel as the driving force behind the foreign minister. Daladier's departure from his original skepticism had to do with hopes of improving Franco-German relations; he tried to represent the proposed pact as being in the tradition of Locarno and the Kellogg–Briand. He kept denying that France would adhere to a "directory" of powers or further a new Holy Alliance. For Paul-Boncour the raison d'être of the pact was rapprochement with Italy and a détente between Rome and the Little Entente. He also asserted that France would strive to prevent a hegemony of the four substituting for the League. Although it would be somewhat isolated within the group, "I prefer to have Italy and Germany in front of me than to feel them join each other behind my back."[94]

The adherents of the Four Power Pact included people of varying orientations: Anatole de Monzie, Pierre Cot, Georges Bonnet, and Senator Henry Béranger. Caillaux's advocacy of it went so far that he threatened to overthrow the cabinet if it did not conclude the accord. General Gamelin favored it mainly because of its potential for Franco-Italian military cooperation. The socialists were uneasy about a directory of great powers but saw the pact as a step toward peace and away from the old-style alliances. The radicals were split, with Herriot, mistrustful of Italy and of the pact's implications, voicing his doubts in the parliament and urging Daladier's government not to sign. The opponents numbered several leading figures of the Right and Center, for instance Tardieu, Millerand, and Barthou, the last two being the only members of the senatorial foreign affairs commission to speak against the pact.[95]

The parliamentary critics assailed the pact on general grounds and by referring specifically to the French eastern alliances. The "Rome intrigue" and German revisionism worried Poland—"an essential element of European reconstruction," Franklin-Bouillon asserted. Recalling that the French border was on the Vistula, he warned that if France adopted the

93. Cited in Jarausch, *Four Power Pact,* 167; compare Micaud, *French Right,* 26–27.

94. See Daladier at 6 Apr. 1933 debate, J.O. Chambre, 1929–1950. For Paul-Boncour, see DDF, I, III: 523, 566–67, 580. For extensive explanations, see 8 Nov. session, CAE/Ch; the last point was made on 22, 29 Mar., 5 Apr., CAE/Ch.

95. See Paul-Boncour, *Entre deux guerres,* 2:349–50; Scott, *Alliance,* 127–28; Bystrický and Deák, *Európa,* 196; Mazur, *Pakt czterech,* 184–95; Soulié, *Herriot,* 424, 430; Gamelin, *Servir,* 2:94.

thesis that the great powers had the right to decide the fate of the smaller states, "it would discredit itself for ever and bring about its own ruin." Louis Marin called Mussolini's scheme "the most abominable act which could endanger peace and security." Jean Ybarnegaray asked Paul-Boncour about the government's position on a partial elimination of the "corridor" and an aggrandizement of Hungary.[96]

Although the chamber rejected by a large majority a motion of "no confidence," uneasiness remained. Jouvenel could write that "it is not with the Little Entente and Poland that we shall succeed, but with England and America," and argue that the smaller states might one day reproach France for exposing them to risks they could not handle, and "which we are not capable of helping them face."[97] Similarly, Hubert Lagardelle of the French mission in Rome may have believed that France was becoming a plaything of the Little Entente and its "first-rate prestigitator" Beneš, and that the smaller states constantly intrigued "to put the world on fire."[98] The Quai d'Orsay, however, did not subscribe to such simplistic views but thought that the attitude of Poland and the Little Entente "obliges us, because of our engagements and in the very interest of peace, to display a good deal of prudence."[99]

Prague had closely followed Jouvenel's mission in Rome and the first Italo-British-French exchanges. It found the flirtation with Mussolini perturbing despite Paul-Boncour's assurances that the policy of collaboration with Czechoslovakia remained unchanged.[100] Beneš, speaking to Simon, denied both fears of Germany and a military dependence of his country on France, but he was critical of Italy and admitted that the French Left was beginning to regard the Little Entente as "a burden."[101] The Czechs learned from Jouvenel about his conversations with Mussolini, but Osuský's attempts to elicit more information from the Quai d'Orsay proved vain. Even so, the Czernin Palace correctly appraised the trends in Paris. While recognizing that negotiations with Rome could be beneficient, especially to lessen the Italo-Yugoslav tension, it deemed the revisionist over-

96. See Pezet, Franklin-Bouillon, Marin, 28, 31 Mar. 1933, J.O. Chambre, 1614, 1702–12; Ybarnegaray and Bergery, 29 Mar., 5 Apr., CAE/Ch.

97. Jouvenel to Paul-Boncour, 25 Mar. 1933, DDF, I, III:76–79.

98. Lagardelle to Anatole de Monzie, 29 Apr. 1933 in Planté, *Monzie*, 177–78.

99. DDF, I, III:105–107. Compare Duroselle, *Décadence*, 73; Carmi, *La Grande Bretagne*, 221–22. On close contacts with East Central European governments, see ministry to Laroche, 3 Mar. 1933, MAE, Z 864.10, Tchécoslovaquie 2604.

100. See Chvalkovský report, 4 Feb. 1933, CD, NA, T120, 1316/D 497 158–60; Bystrický and Deák, *Európa*, 194–96; Kvaček, *Nad Evropou*, 28; Noël, *Illusions*, 21; compare Hubert Ripka in *Lidové Noviny* 8 Jan. On worries in Prague, see Noël to Paul-Boncour, 20 Mar., MAE, Z 864.1, Tchécoslovaquie 2569.

101. 17 Mar. 1933 conversation, DBFP, II, v:64–65; compare Bystrický and Deák, *Európa*, 202.

tones of the pact and the way the matter was being discussed in France "scandalous."[102]

Efforts by the Poles to obtain elucidations at the Quai d'Orsay also met with evasions, and they learned of the Mussolini-Jouvenel conversation (including references to the "corridor") from Pertinax.[103] Through London they discovered that Franco-British conversations had touched on that issue and understood that France seemed little inclined to oppose revisionism. Paul-Boncour's denials that the "corridor" had been discussed only increased suspicions; the Poles saw some analogies to the pre-Locarno Western talks. As for mounting opposition in France and the negative stance of the Little Entente envoys, Warsaw was kept informed by Chłapowski.[104]

On 21 March, Beck spoke critically about Mussolini's ideas to Laroche, but otherwise seemed unperturbed and even surprised by nervous reactions of the French press.[105] Three days later, however, his attitude underwent a dramatic change, caused probably by more information and most likely by Piłsudski's return to the capital. The marshal considered the situation grave and ordered Jerzy Potocki, just named Poland's ambassador to Rome, to resign and motivate his decision by the impossibility of promoting—under the circumstances—good relations between the two countries. Characterizing the proposed pact as "contrary to Poland's interests," Beck informed the missions of the need to "modify our position toward the states of the Little Entente," and of his intention to visit Paris and Prague.[106] The next day, he summoned the French ambassador and the Little Entente envoys, conveying a misleading impression, through a press communiqué, of a collective meeting and the emergence of a united Franco-Polish-Little Entente front. Speaking in the name of Piłsudski and Mościcki, he informed Laroche that before taking a position toward Mussolini's proposal, Poland wished to establish contact with the French government. Beck would be in Paris to talk with Daladier and Paul-Boncour, and the subject of the conversations would transcend the Four Power Pact. He wanted to explain in particular how "one sees from here the situation in Germany." The foreign minister also mentioned a rapprochement with

102. Jouvenel informed Chvalkovský on 4 Mar., see Ádám, "Les Pays," 5. On Osuský's efforts, see his 22 Mar. note, HIA, Osuský Papers, box 22; compare report, 20 Mar. CD, NA, T120, 1316/D 496 937. Also briefing 23 Mar., KV, CPP.

103. See Chłapowski and Romer telegrams, 11, 20 Mar. 1933, AAN, Amb. Berlin, 80 and 43, and HIA, Amb. Paryż, box 3. Pertinax article in *Le Matin*, 19 Mar. See Ruecker note for Dębicki, 15 Mar., SI, MSZ, A.11.49/F/3; Mazur, *Pakt czterech*, 131.

104. See telegrams, 22, 23, 24 Mar., HIA, Amb. Paryż, box 3, and reports, 24 Mar., 6 Apr. 1933, AAN, Amb. Berlin, 43.

105. Laroche to Paul-Boncour, 21 Mar. 1933, DDF, I, III:49–50.

106. Telegrams to missions, 23, 24 Mar. 1933, DTJS, I, 26–28.

Czechoslovakia, and Laroche understood that he intended to visit Prague. This was actually what he proposed to Girsa.[107]

Did Piłsudski want to strengthen Paris's resolve or, if one thinks about the preventive war rumors circulating at this moment, was he ready to make some concrete proposals? Whatever his intentions, three days later Beck suddenly announced that he was obliged to postpone his trip to Paris.[108] Was the change caused by an exchange of dispatches between Warsaw and Paris that suggested that either Daladier was cool to the idea of Beck's visit or that Chłapowski had misunderstood the nature of the French response? Subsequently Paul-Boncour wrote Laroche that the premier and he had been awaiting the Polish minister.[109] Could such a trivial misunderstanding have thwarted Warsaw's initiative? By 25–27 March, Beck deduced from a note handed in by Laroche and a telegram from London that the French would not reject Mussolini's proposal. This information, combined with the ambiguity of the French government's reaction to his own visit, may have made Beck feel that a Polish move at this point would court failure. Furthermore, because Piłsudski had told Beck not to rush, and the marshal fell seriously ill on 24 March, the minister, left without guidance, may have decided to wait.[110]

Krofta deemed the postponement of Beck's visit to Paris and Prague a demonstration against Paul-Boncour and not Beneš.[111] The latter, although leaving to Titulescu to declare that revisionism meant war and the Four Power Pact "the isolation and chaining of France," was not passive.[112] In a confidential note for the French foreign minister, Beneš wrote that if he were in the place of the French government he would reject both this "perfectly ridiculous" proposal and conversations outside the League.

107. Laroche to Paul-Boncour, 24 and 27 Mar. 1933, MAE, Z 698.1, Pologne 2099 and DDF, 1, III:93. Also Girsa telegram, 24 Mar., CPP.

108. Beck telegram, 28 Mar. 1933, HIA, Amb. Paryż, box 3.

109. Exchange of Laroche–ministry telegrams, 27, 29, 30 Mar. (compare 8 May) and Naggiar–ministry, 25 Apr. 1933, MAE, Z 698.1, Pologne 2099. Compare Chłapowski telegram, 28 Mar., HIA, Amb. Paryż, box 3.

110. See DTJS, 1, 24–26; Beck, *Dernier rapport*, 41; for Piłsudski's illness, Jędrzejewicz, *Kronika*, 2:440; compare Weinstein to Raczyński, 5 Aug. 1972, PI, Jan Weinstein Collection, reel 415; also Laroche to Paul-Boncour, 11 and 27 Apr. 1933, MAE, Z 864.5, Tchécoslovaquie 2856.

111. Briefing, 11 May 1933, KV, CPP. Girsa for one was pleased with the adjournment of Beck's visit, for he feared lest Poland tried to drag Czechoslovakia too far. For bitter remarks about Paul-Boncour, see Beck, *Dernier rapport*, 42; also DTJS, 1, 12–13; Dębicki to Mühlstein, 13 June 1933, SI, MSZ, A.11.49/F/3/26.

112. See Giurescu, "La Diplomatie," 81–86; Bystrický and Deák, *Európa*, 323–24; Kvaček, *Nad Evropou*, 28; Aloisi, *Journal*, 102; Chłapowski telegram, 4 Apr. 1933, HIA, Amb. Paryż, box 3. On the great antirevisionist demonstrations in the Little Entente states, see reports in MAE, Z 864.10, Tchécoslovaquie 2602.

There was a basic distinction between adjustments that had been made constantly over the last fourteen years and revisionism elevated to a political objective. The latter could only lead to complications for France, at home and in its dealings with the anxious Little Entente. Indeed on 25 March, the Little Entente, despite Italian hopes that Paul-Boncour would keep it in check, published a strongly worded communiqué in Geneva criticizing accords designed to dispose of the rights of others as contrary to the League of Nations.[113]

Urging the French to resist and the British to dilute the Four Power Pact by making it subordinate to the League, Beneš also promoted the Little Entente's efforts to make its weight felt on the international scales.[114] There was talk about a bloc of fifty million people, a fifth European power, and manifestations of annoyance, even on Beneš's part, with the constant references in the West to the "small countries." It looked as if, for once, there was a real convergence of views between Warsaw and Prague and a genuine possibility of cooperation in a common fight.

When Beck had announced that he wished to go to Prague, the French and the Czechs viewed it as indicating a drastic change of Piłsudski's policy.[115] A French diplomat went farther when he wrote retrospectively: "If M. Beneš and Colonel Beck had exchanged the visits . . . negotiations between Rome, Paris, and London would have come to a halt."[116] When notified of Beck's intention (by Raczyński in Geneva and through Girsa), Beneš had responded with alacrity: the Pole would be assured a warm welcome, and the character of the visit adjusted to his wishes.[117] For the time being the news was kept secret with Beneš informing only Paul-Boncour, whom he told that the visit was to be a "courtesy gesture," which "in view of the recent state of Polish-Czechoslovak relations had a happy significance."[118] According to Beck, Piłsudski was ready at this point "to demolish the wall erected between us and Prague, in spite of the profound distrust he had for Beneš's policy."[119]

The term *wall* seems exaggerated, for precisely at the beginning of 1933 Poland seemed closer to Czechoslovakia than before. A Czechoslovak-Pol-

---

113. For text of communiqué and Beneš's note, see DDF, I, III:80 82–83; also, Aloisi, *Journal*, 102–104.

114. See Simon-Beneš conversation, DBFP, II, v:106–108; briefing, 30 Mar. 1933, KV, CPP; Čulaková, "Pakt Ctyř," Ripka's article appeared in *Lidové Noviny*, 20 Apr. 1933.

115. See DDF, *I*, III:74–75; and 30 Mar. 1933 briefing, KV, CPP.

116. Charles-Roux to Barthou, 19 Mar. 1934, MAE, Z 864.5, Tchécoslovaquie 2586.

117. See Raczyński, *od Narcyza*, 60; Noël and Laroche to Paul-Boncour, 25 Mar. 1933, MAE, Z 864.5, Tchécoslovaquie 2586 and Z 698.1, Pologne 2099.

118. Note, 25 Mar. 1933, DDF, I, III:82–83.

119. Beck, *Dernier rapport*, 41.

ish press meeting in Warsaw in mid-January led to a campaign in favor of collaboration. Technical military conferences (12–13 January, and 31 January–4 February) resulted in a convention on communications. General Prchala, who viewed the Little Entente as anachronistic, thought that Czechoslovakia needed an alliance either with Germany or Poland, and he opted for the second. Czechoslovak general staff desired to start joint studies of an operational nature, and the minister of national defense recommended cooperation with the Polish air force. Generals Faucher and d'Arbonneau did their best to encourage this trend, which they realized would have to be initiated by the governments in Prague and Warsaw.[120]

In a retrospective defense of his diplomacy, Beneš asserted that he had thrice offered a pact to Poland in late 1932 and early 1933, but this claim is misleading.[121] Krofta's briefings reflected the familiar theme: "we have no intention of assuming the risks of Polish foreign policy," the best formula being Little Entente and Poland. The secretary of the foreign ministry, Arnošt Heidrich, stated later that "an alliance for common defense was not considered suitable for our policy in view of the acute danger of a conflict over the corridor."[122] What Beneš and Krofta favored was a rapprochement, especially because the consolidation of the Little Entente had placed Prague in a stronger bargaining position. On the eve of a meeting with Beck in Geneva on 3 February, Beneš told Léon Noël, the new French envoy, that he was planning to propose "a pact of perpetual friendship."[123]

The two foreign ministers had apparently met already on 26 January, but the content of their conversation is not mentioned in any known document. On 3 February, Beneš assured his Polish colleague that the Little Entente would oppose German expansion in Central Europe, and suggested that Poland and Czechoslovakia refrain from any mutually prejudicial moves and sign a pact of eternal friendship providing for a demili-

120. See numerous dispatches in MAE, Z 698.1, Pologne 2099 and Z 864.5, Tchécoslovaquie 2586 and 2588; Girsa reports, 2, 3, 20, 25 Feb. 1933, CPP; press cuttings in MZV-VA 478–1247a and 1249; DDF, I, III:164 and d'Arbonneau reports 7 Feb. and 25 July, SHA, EMA/2, Pologne 12. Also Bułhak, "Z Dziejów 1927–1936"; Kvaček, *Nad Evropou*, 29–30; Kozeński, *Czechosłowacja*, 56.

121. See Beneš, *Memoirs* 7 and 33, and the slightly different Beneš, *Paměti*, 11, 15. Beneš wrote that in "September 1932 at Geneva" he offered "Beck, the Polish Foreign Minister, a political agreement which was to pave the way for a military treaty." He repeated in a letter printed in Namier, *Europe in Decay*, 281–85, and in the 27 Oct. 1941 memo printed in Ladislav K. Feierabend, *Ve vládě v exilu* (Washington, 1966), 2:172. However, in Sept. 1932 Beck was not yet foreign minister and was not in Geneva. See Tomaszewski and Valenta, "Polska," 700.

122. Briefings 6 Feb., 9 Mar. 1933, KV, CPP. Krofta repeated his doubts about an alliance with Poland in "Hřichy naší dřívější zahraniční politiky," ANM, Půzostalost Krofty, III, 1, 32. Arnošt Heidrich's testimony is cited in Káňa and Pavelka, *Těšínsko*, 38.

123. Noël to Paul-Boncour, 3 Feb. 1933, MAE, Z 864.5, Tchécoslovaquie 2586.

tarization of their common border. This proposal was an old idea of Beneš, now cloaked in a high sounding name. The minister emphasized that he was thinking aloud rather than making a proposal; no wonder that Beck was reserved.[124] During subsequent meetings in Geneva and Paris in mid-March, only pleasantly banal remarks were exchanged about the usefulness of these contacts.[125] Beneš told the French that he offered Poland neither an adhesion to the Little Entente nor an alliance. Talking to the British he asserted that he "had already declined an alliance with Poland"—implying that such an offer had been made—and explained that "Czechoslovakia would not make an alliance" because "it would be very dangerous to give Germany clear cause for fearing encirclement."[126]

Irrespective of whether Beck had actually made a proposal, which seems unlikely, a basic distinction between a military alliance and a pact of friendship was obvious. The former was concrete, the latter, at least from Warsaw's viewpoint, largely meaningless.[127] Could Piłsudski's interest in a military alliance with Prague be taken for granted?[128] Probably not, if one remembers his doubts about Czechoslovakia's viability. Everything seems to indidicate that the purpose of Beck's intended visit to Prague was to gain Beneš's consent not for a military alliance but for a Warsaw-led united diplomatic front against the Four Power Pact. In fact, Grzybowski later confirmed the purpose of the mission to Krofta. Would the next step have been an alliance? Perhaps, but this is only a speculation. At any rate, if the Czechs welcomed Beck's initiative, they were less enthusiastic about accepting Poland's lead in the unfolding diplomatic game.[129]

United in their opposition to Mussolini's proposals, each country chose a different way of handling the issue. Beck declared that he would not join even if invited, and hinted that his country might leave the League.[130] Al-

---

124. See Bystrický and Deák, *Európa*, 238; Tomaszewski and Valenta, "Polska," 701. Anon. (Beneš), *Polsko a Československo*, 24–25, mentions only a pact of friendship.

125. Laroche to Paul-Boncour, 11, 27 Apr. 1933, MAE, Z 864.5, Tchécoslovaquie 2586. The supposition that the idea of Beck's visit to Prague may have been discussed during these meetings (Tomaszewski and Valenta, "Polska," 703) is not borne out by evidence.

126. See DBFP, II, IV:521, V:64. For efforts of British diplomacy to ascertain whether Poland had proposed anything concrete (which seemed doubtful), see Erskine–Oliphant–Simon correspondence, 12 Apr., 12 May 1933, FO 371 16676 C 341 and 400. Also DDF, I, III:139–40.

127. See Kahánek, *Beneš*, 177. Kahánek was strongly pro-Polish.

128. See Erskine to Simon, 10 May 1933, FO 371 1660 623 C 1272.

129. Grzybowski to Beck, 28 June 1933, AAN, Amb. Berlin, 51; for the perception of Beck's aims of a Polish-led Central Europe, see 13 July briefing, KV, CPP.

130. DDF, I, III:142–47, 149–53; d'Arbonneau report, 2 May 1933, SHA, EMA/2, Pologne 12; Beck-Chłapowski exchange in early Apr., HIA, Amb. Paryż, box 3; Chłapowski to Beck, 7 Apr., AAN, MSZ, z.2, w.38, t.18 (old classification).

though Poland's pride was hurt by the exclusion from the great powers' circle, prestige was not the main consideration. Beck gave Laroche to understand that his country preferred the risk of isolation to constant interference by the big four. He insisted that the German situation be clarified "now rather than after two or three years of consolidation of the Hitlerite regime."[131] Because he also mentioned Poland's determination "to make guns speak," if anyone encroached on Poland's territory, there was a consistency in Warsaw's approach.

Revisionism aimed at Poland was increasingly seen as a matter of concern to Prague. Even Masaryk, who had previously believed in the possibility of a solution in the "corridor," now changed his mind.[132] Osuský warned Paul-Boncour that if the Four Power Pact were anchored on article 19 of the Covenant, and Poland refused to cede the "corridor," a German attack on Poland could be legitimized. Once territorial revision started along German-Polish borders, it could be the beginning of the end, as it had been at the time of the eighteenth-century Polish partitions.[133] All this showed the existence of a certain community of interests between Czechoslovakia and Poland that would have justified closer cooperation were it not for the divergent attitudes toward Paris and its policy.

The French government decided to propose a diluted version of the Four Power Pact, but before submitting its 10 April draft to Rome it endeavored to have its policy endorsed by the chamber. The debate on 6 April was a replay of familiar arguments and counterarguments ending with a comfortable majority for the government. As the Polish ambassador observed, the cabinet passed the responsibility to the chamber, which simultaneously rejected revisionism and displayed illusions about great powers' collaboration. Counteraction by Poland and Little Entente, he opined, might produce some results with regard to revisionism but could not affect the direction of French policy shaped for so many years by the outlook of the radical camp.[134]

The French draft, which with minor change became the basis of the final text, clarified that signatories would concern themselves only with questions affecting them. As for revision—and the term itself disappeared—it was weakened by an invocation of the Covenant's articles that spoke of

131. MS, OSS, Wysocki, ii, 301; DDF, i, iii:153.

132. See briefing, 30 Mar. 1933, KV, CPP; Ripka's analysis in Monicault to Paul-Boncour, 20 Apr., MAE, Z 864.10 (11?), Tchécoslovaquie 2604; compare DDF, i, iii:138–39; *L'Europe Centrale*, 13 May, defending Polish rights in the "corridor."

133. Memo and note for Paul-Boncour, 31 Mar. 1933, HIA, Osuský Papers, box 20. Osuský was very outspoken in his criticism of the Four Power Pact.

134. 6 Apr. debate, J.O. Chambre, 1929–50; Chłapowski reports, 8 Apr., 6 May 1933, AAN, MSZ, z.2, w.36a, t.18 (old classification); AAN, Amb. Berlin, 80: compare Paul-Boncour, 4 May, J.O. Sénat, 800–801.

territorial integrity and sanctions against aggression. The emphasis was on the League and the disarmament conference, although the four powers reserved for themselves the right to examine questions related to limitations of armaments.[135]

In his major speech on 25 April, Beneš sounded, as always, reasonable and cooperative.[136] He praised France whose alleged decline he disbelieved, and whose alleged hegemony in East Central Europe he denied. In turn, the states of this region did not pressure France to obtain the unachievable. Great powers' cooperation could be useful; even more so if Germany cooperated with Poland, and Italy with the Little Entente. Arbitrary revision he opposed, and if anyone sought to impose decisions on Czechoslovakia, his country would know how to defend itself. A Four Power Pact seemed to "represent the Italian idea of a hierarchy of states and would provide an opportunity for the now isolated Germany to sign an important diplomatic document." The Czechs were clearly suspicious of the ongoing negotiations among the powers and resented that they had not been consulted prior to the dispatch of the French proposal of 10 April.[137]

Beneš singled out Poland as a country Europe ought to reckon with, and with which he hoped to sign a pact of perpetual friendship. Speaking of Beck's visit to Prague, which according to Grzybowski was simply postponed, he explained to the Polish envoy that he saw it not merely as a demonstration of their common opposition, but as "an expression of a lasting rapprochement." He anticipated his own return visit to Warsaw and the signing of a political pact. He said that "once I march, I am faithful forever, and one can trust me."[138] Presumably Beneš thought that the course of international events was pushing Poland toward cooperation with Czechoslovakia, and he hoped to convince the Poles to follow his lead. His overtures for the "eternal pact of friendship" fully conformed to his avowed "policy of pacts and friendships with the largest possible number of states."[139]

Beck recognized the French version of the Four Power Pact as an im-

135. Comparison of drafts and final text in Jarausch, *Four Power Pact*, 230–41.

136. Beneš, *Boj o mír*, 714–67; comments in Noël to Paul-Boncour, 29 Apr., 10 May 1933, MAE, Z 864.1, Tchécoslovaquie 2569; briefing 11 May, KV, CPP.

137. See DDF, I, III:404, 472n., 555.

138. See Grzybowski to Beck, 24 Apr. 1933, AAN, MSZ 5504; compare Noël and Laroche to Paul-Boncour, 25, 27 Apr., MAE, Z 864.5 Tchécoslovaquie 2586; d'Arbonneau report, 5 Apr., SHA, EMA/2, Pologne 12.

139. Girsa's reports (for ex., 27 Apr. 1933, CPP) could only strengthen Beneš's reluctance to go beyond a vague eternal friendship pact. A draft was apparently prepared by Heidrich, but his account lacks clarity, especially about the sequel of events. Heidrich, *Canses*, 1:6. Citation from Beneš, 13 Feb. 1933 in Bláha, *Branná politika*, 152.

provement, but he continued to oppose the entire trend of France's policy. Laroche understood that it was a matter of principle and Warsaw would not budge.[140] As for a rapprochement with Prague, Beck avoided the subject of his visit with the Czechoslovak envoy, and in conversation with Laroche dwelt on the familiar Polish grievances against Czechoslovakia.[141] Warsaw seemed to be exploring other options.

On 2 May, the diplomatic world was surprised to learn of a conversation between Hitler and the Polish envoy, Alfred Wysocki, followed by a joint communiqué. According to it, the chancellor stated his intention of maintaining German policy toward Poland within the framework of the existing treaties, Piłsudski had extracted this statement from Berlin by use of a veiled threat accompanied by hints that Poland needed no intermediary to talk to Germany.[142] The Hitler–Wysocki interview, was, as Laroche later wrote, a Polish response to the Four Power Pact. To the revisionism of Rome, Warsaw was opposing its détente with Berlin.[143] Speaking from a position of greater strength, Beck now declared that had the pact been accepted in its original form "something would have had to change in the relations between Poland and France."[144] The minister was warning Paris not to take Poland for granted. Linked with a simultaneous rapprochement to Russia, Warsaw's diplomacy—"full of surprises," in Laroche's words—was aiming at the creation of its own system in East Central Europe.[145]

The French cautiously welcomed the Hitler–Wysocki communiqué as an indication, even if temporary, of a German-Polish détente.[146] François-Poncet ruminated about Hitler's real intentions: "Does he not try thus to destroy our alliance and draw Poland away from France, so as to defeat the separated states more easily?"[147] Beneš characterized the communiqué,

140. Laroche reports in DDF, I, III: 221–22, 280–83, 291; 24 Apr. 1933, MAE, Z 698.1, Pologne 2099. Compare Beck telegram, 21 Apr., HIA, Amb. Paryż, box 5. For Daladier's assurances that France would not accept a directory of powers, see Górecki to Beck, 25 Apr., SI, MSZ, A.11.49/F/3/22.

141. See Laroche to Paul-Boncour, 27 Apr. 1933, MAE, Z 864.5, Tchécoslovaquie 2586; Girsa report, 26 April, CPP.

142. On Hitler–Wysocki conversation and background, see Jędrzejewicz, *Lipski*, 71–90; compare DBFP, II, V:202, 218, Lipski–Bastianini conversation, 12 May 1933, AAN, Amb. Berlin, 794.

143. Laroche to Daladier, 6 Feb. 1934, DDF, I, V:642.

144. Interview, 7 May 1933, Beck, *Przemówienia*, 69.

145. Laroche to Paul-Boncour, 13 June 1933, DDF, I/III:706–708.

146. See DDF, I, III:415–16; d'Arbonneau report, 11 May 1933, SHA, EMA/2, Pologne 12; Chłapowski telegram 6 (?) May, HIA, Amb. Paryż, box 5; note, 3 May; AAN, Akta Świtalskiego, 71.

147. Cited in MS, OSS, Wysocki, III, 239; compare 193.

when speaking to Grzybowski, as a "happy tactical move," but did not exaggerate its value. Girsa described it as "a sensible act" that helped to clarify the situation. Apparently Prague did not regard it as conflicting with a Polish-Czechoslovak rapprochement, for Beneš reiterated his interest in seeing Beck, and suggested that the Pole's visit coincide with the forthcoming meeting of the Little Entente. In Geneva, Beneš continued to make pro-Polish statements to Raczyński.[148] The parting of the ways came only in late May.[149]

Trying to finalize the Four Power negotiations, the French government sought to overcome domestic opposition and that of the eastern allies. Once more, such terms as "the gravest offense against peace" and a treason of "our sure allies" would be flung by the opponents. According to Herriot, the pact would be "useless if it contained nothing or dangerous if it contained something."[150] Ybarnegaray warned Daladier: "Take care that they [the eastern allies] do not move away from us." He thought the term "little powers" inappropriate for states with a joint population of 75 million and armies of 800 thousand.[151]

Daladier rejected the accusation that France was willing to abandon its protegés, but was disinclined to debate the issue while Paris was negotiating with the great powers and the East European capitals. Repeated French attempts to persuade Warsaw to drop its opposition to the pact proved, however, futile. Warsaw could be moved neither by threats of losing the support of French public opinion nor by promises of notes reaffirming French engagements. As Paul-Boncour realized, it was a matter of confidence, and the Poles seemed to have none in Paris.[152] If Daladier and Paul-Boncour were annoyed with Poland, Mühlstein wrote, that was too bad; they had to understand that to maintain Franco-Polish relations on a normal level, the Polish viewpoint must be recognized.[153] The fact that not only Piłsudski, for whom the Four Power Pact was anathema and a new

148. See Grzybowski reports, 9, 23 May, and to Szembek, 20 May 1933, MSZ 5504 and 5505; also Raczyński, *Od Narcyza*, 69; compare Noël to Paul-Boncour, 14, 23 May 1933, MAE, Z 864.5, Tchécoslovaquie 2586.

149. By 23 May it became clear that Beck would not come. See above report of Noël.

150. See 24 May 1933 session, CAE/Ch.

151. 30 May 1933 session, J.O. Chambre, 2725–27.

152. See Paul-Boncour to Massigli, 23 May 1933, MAE, Z 864.10, Tchécoslovaquie 2602; Laroche to Paul-Boncour, 31 May, MAE, Z 698.1, Pologne 2099; correspondence in DDF, I, III:552–53, 575–85, 600–601; Beck–Laroche conversation, 25 May, AAN, MSZ 108. On Daladier's hopes that Warsaw would give in see Chłapowski telegram, 21 (22?) May, HIA, Amb. Paryż, box 5.

153. DTJS, I, 32–33; compare Chłapowski report, 17 June 1933, AAN, Amb. Berlin, 1549.

version of Locarno, but also Polish public opinion opposed the French policy made the application of any kind of pressure doubly difficult.[154]

The Little Entente was also defiant. In early May Titulescu was telling Paul-Boncour that if France forsook "her sacred mission of defending the smaller powers . . . we shall go ahead without her."[155] Beneš warned Paris in a personal note of "very grave complications" unless it were made clear that previous French engagements would in no way be violated. Also, France, Italy, and the Little Entente should reach agreement on Central Europe. France must not be torn between obligations to its allies and its collaboration with Rome. No equivocation was possible.[156] Paris decided then to send an explanatory note to the Little Entente: Under the Four Power Pact no discussions of territorial issues would be possible without a unanimous vote including the interested parties.[157] Paul-Boncour countered German and British objections to this further reduction of the significance of the pact by stressing the international détente it would bring, while Léger called the note a mere "interpretation of the bearing of the pact on the relations between France and her allies."[158] Cautioned by Paul-Boncour that should the Little Entente persist in its opposition, the Daladier cabinet would fall and be succeeded by a rightist ministry, Beneš persuaded his somewhat reluctant colleagues, meeting in Prague, to withdraw their objections to the pact. They did so in a communiqué published on 30 May.[159] The Poles did not change their position, and Grzybowski accepted neither Beneš's explanation nor the argument that the differences between Warsaw and Prague were merely tactical.[160]

The stance adopted by the Little Entente facilitated the French government's task during the 9 June debate. Daladier told the chamber that Po-

154. On Piłsudski, see Wysocki, *Tajemnice*, 177; compare DBFP, II, v:334–35; also Giurescu, "La Diplomatie," 96–97, and Bystrický and Deák, *Európa*, 336. On public opinion, see Rakowski, "Pierwsze reakcje polskie"; also Kuźmiński, "Wobec zagadnienia," 37–38.

155. Cited in R. Deutsch, "The Foreign Policy of Roumania and the Dynamics of Peace 1932–1936," *Revue Roumaine d'Histoire*, 5 (1966), 126. On French pressures, see DDF, I, III:555; Aloisi, *Journal*, 125–26; Carmi, *La Grande Bretagne*, 249.

156. Penciled note of Beneš for Paul-Boncour, probably 22 May 1933, MAE, P.A. Massigli 4; compare Beneš to ministry, 25 May, CD, NA, T120 1316/D 497 194–96.

157. DDF, I/III:578–579; note 7 June, MAE, Z 865.10, Tchécoslovaquie 2602.

158. See DBFP, II, v:281; ADAP, C, I/2:547, 563–64.

159. See Bystrický and Deák, *Európa*, 331; Čulaková, "Pakt Ctyř," 78–79; DDF, I, III:583–84, 594–97, 615–16; Kvaček, *Nad Evropou*, 32. The French explained that their note was necessary to gain the support of the Little Entente, without which the parliament would not endorse the pact. See Carmi, *La Grande Bretagne*, 249; DBFP, II, V:280–81.

160. Grzybowski to Beck, 1 June 1933, AAN, Amb. Berlin, 51; compare Tomaszewski and Valenta, "Polska," 705; briefing 13 July, KV, CPP.

land had received assurances that nothing in the pact would impair its dignity as a "great nation of Europe." If he did not convince critics such as Marin and Franklin-Bouillon, he gained last minute support from Herriot.[161] Without much enthusiasm, the chamber voted its approval. Krofta felt that while "we had to be satisfied with French assurances," one could hardly expect the pact to "bring us anything good."[162] Osuský believed that had a common front between the Little Entente and Poland been maintained, the pact would have been prevented. Beneš, on the other side, hoped that the accord would favor Franco-Italian cooperation in the Danubian area.[163]

Warsaw's bitterness permeated a communiqué and a verbal note to Laroche. No treaty modifications, unless affecting exclusively the interests of the four powers, would be binding on Poland.[164] In the press and in private there were references to the "cowardly capitulation" of the Little Entente and Beneš.[165] It is hard to understand how the Czechoslovak foreign minister—while telling the French that he found Polish attitude incomprehensible and deplorable—could still count on Beck coming to Prague, or how Girsa could believe that Warsaw would be forced to turn to Czechoslovakia.[166] The Poles suspected that Beneš's mention of the pact of friendship (in his 25 April speech) had been meant to embarrass them. Beneš's overture, the counselor of the Polish legation quipped, sounded like somebody saying: "If you do not want to talk to me, let us at least call each other by our first names."[167]

Grzybowski explained that the idea behind Beck's proposed visit had been to demonstrate a common front of the two countries; the stand of the Little Entente made such a demonstration pointless. As for a Polish-Czechoslovak rapprochement, many issues needed to be clarified first. Al-

161. 9 June debate in J.O. Chambre, 2819–44. Herriot told Chłapowski that he could no longer oppose the pact because he was not prepared, should the Daladier cabinet resign, to form a ministry himself. Chłapowski telegram of late May, HIA, Amb. Paryż, box 5. For criticism of Chłapowski meddling in French politics, Ibl report, 28 May, CD, NA, T120, 1316/D 496 944–46.

162. Briefing, 22 June 1933, KV, CPP; compare *L'Europe Centrale*, 10, 17, 24 June.

163. Chłapowski report, 13 June 1933, AAN, MSZ, z.2, w.36a, t.18 (old classification); compare DTJS, I, 34–38.

164. See Beck, *Przemówienia*, 70; Laroche dispatches, 9 June 1933, DDF, I, III: 692–93 and MAE, Z 698.1, Pologne 2099.

165. See DBFP, II, v:335; d'Arbonneau report, 28 June 1933, SHA, EMA/2, Pologne 12. Beck's contempt for Beneš in *Dernier rapport*, 41–42, 270, and Starzeński, *Trzy lata*, 80.

166. See Noël to Paul-Boncour, 31 May, 2, 3 June 1933, MAE, Z 864.10, Tchécoslovaquie 2602 and DDF, I, III:625–26. Girsa believed in Beck's visit until the end of May; see reports 29, 31 May 7, 9, 22 June, CPP.

167. Grzybowski to Beck, 28 June 1933, AAN, Amb. Berlin, 51.

though the envoy opined that Beneš wanted an accord devoid of all commitments, he advised, on tactical grounds, not to ignore this overture but
force Prague to be more specific by posing conditions: concessions for the
Polish minority; economic privileges; and coordinated policies toward the
minority treaty, disarmament, and the initialed Four Power Pact.[168] Warsaw did not follow this advice. Piłsudski said that Poland would never get
together with the Little Entente not only because of "this . . . Beneš" but
because it wanted to adhere to its own ideas and traditions.[169] The semiofficial *Polityka Narodów* accused Prague of seeing Poland only as a light-
ning rod drawing away German revisionism and allowing Czechoslovakia
to consolidate.[170]

As always, the French were upset by the deteriorating relations between
Warsaw and Prague. By and large Paris blamed the Poles, and Daladier
told the Czechs that Polish maneuvers over the Four Power Pact might
force France to abrogate the alliance.[171] It was only eighteen months later
that a Quai d'Orsay memorandum critically appraised Prague's Polish policy. Beneš, it said, "perceived too late the importance of the Polish factor";
when he offered Warsaw "a guarantee [?] pact," already "different possibilities presented themselves to Poland."[172]

Hopes Deceived

The emasculated Four Power Pact—"an elaborate nullity"—was meant to
create an international constellation improving France's position, and providing, in Paul-Boncour's words, "a new foundation of security strengthening that of Locarno."[173] Indeed, the accord was in some ways a logical
sequel to the Rhine pact, with Rome taking the place of Berlin. Effective
cooperation between France and Italy, especially in Central Europe, was
essential, and as a French writer put it: "Concluded on the banks of the
Tiber, it would be on the banks of the Danube that the pact would pass its
test."[174]

A stabilization of the Danubian region involved, as before, an agreement

168. Grzybowski to Szembek, 5 July 1933, AAN, MSZ 5505. Did Grzybowski receive
then a concrete proposal, as Beneš later claimed? His report does not say so. See Kozeński, *Czechosłowacja*, 61–62; compare Tomaszewski and Valenta, "Polska," 798.

169. Piłsudski's remarks, 20 July 1933, quoted in Wysocki, *Tajemnice*, 177.

170. See Lapter, *Pakt*, 188.

171. See Kozeński, *Czechosłowacja*, 61; Noël to Paul-Boncour, 23 June 1933, MAE,
Z 864.10, Tchécoslovaquie 2602, on his mediation attempts.

172. Note, 14 Nov. 1934 for foreign minister, DDF, I, VIII:97.

173. Respectively, Vansittart, *Mist Procession*, 454; Paul-Boncour, *Entre deux
guerres*, 2:345.

174. A. Musset cited in Jarausch, *Four Power Pact*, 178.

on the maintenance of Austria's political independence, an equilibrium superseding the two rival blocs, and regional economic cooperation. French and Italian interests converged with regard to the prohibition of Anschluss, except that for Rome some form of a union between Austria and Hungary under its aegis remained the best deterrent. Paul-Boncour's unwillingness to challenge this idea ran into sharp attacks by Pertinax in the press and a stubborn veto of the Little Entente.[175] Beneš's formula for Austria continued to be political neutralization guaranteed by France and Italy, and economic cooperation with the Little Entente assisted by Paris, Rome, and London. He believed that Paris ought to persuade Rome to affirm publicly its commitment to Austrian independence; this would give Mussolini an illusion of a dominant voice in Danubian affairs and help to estrange Italy and Germany. On his side, Beneš wished to keep the duce in a state of uncertainty about the stand of the Little Entente, which explains the latter's refusal to issue an anti-Anschluss declaration of its own.[176]

French pressure on Italy was not productive. Given their economic predominance in the Danubian area, the Italians wanted to have a free hand "to treat, when and how we would like to, with the Little Entente."[177] The ever-resourceful Beneš wished Paris to take the initiative, and by delaying the ratification of the Four Power Pact, make Italy accept a plan of cooperation he had devised. It aimed at a final agreement on a general statement against the Anschluss and an accord to protect Austrian neutrality (to be submitted for acceptance to Germany and then to Poland and Britain), and a nonaggression accord between Hungary (asked to renounce its territorial claims) and the Little Entente. France, Italy, and possibly Britain would guarantee this "political truce." In the economic sphere, Beneš proposed that the Little Entente strive for an agreement first with Hungary and then with Austria. Once these agreements were achieved—under the aegis of France and Italy—and extended to include special arrangements between the five Danubian states and Italy and Germany, Britain and Poland might then be asked for their approval.[178]

The Quai d'Orsay was dubious about the merits of this plan. By assuming a central role in the negotiations, France would run the risk of being

175. For Paul-Boncour's ideas and Puaux formula—defending Austrian independence, France "fights to maintain a system destined to assure its own security"—see DDF, I, III:828–30 and IV:478. Compare Chłapowski telegrams, 29 July, 9 Sept. 1933, HIA, Amb. Paryż, box 3. Also Beneš to ministry, 22 June, CD, NA, T120, 1316/D 497 198–99; and DDF, I, III:505–11, 721–25.

176. See Gajan, "Die Rolle," Kvaček, "Boj," 242–46. Compare DDF, I, III:835–36; DTJS, I, 34–38.

177. Aloisi, *Journal*, 136; compare Osuský reports, 22 June, 21 July 1933, CD, NA, T120, 1316/D 469 951–56.

178. See DDF, I, III:770–72, 802–805, 860–63; also Beneš telegram, 10 July 1933, CPP.

blamed by either side in case of failure. To start with political issues was to court defeat. Although Beneš's formula of political truce was judged "quite clever," Paris preferred to work for a general treaty of arbitration and conciliation or for a general pact of nonaggression. In the economic field, Beneš's idea of treating the Little Entente as a nucleus of Danubian cooperation might evoke suspicions of hegemonic designs. The Quai d'Orsay suggested therefore that the five states deal individually with each other, and a general intra-Danubian convention be followed by a separate convention of non-Danubian countries comprising France, Italy, Britain, Poland, and hopefully Germany. These powers would engage themselves to assist the Danubian economy, refrain from political meddling, and respect the territorial and political independence of the Danubian states. The proposed inclusion of Poland stemmed from the Quai d'Orsay's desire to compensate it for nonparticipation in the Four Power Pact and for possible economic inconveniences. The two conventions were perceived as the foundation of a vast system similar to Locarno, effectively countering the accusation that France "under the cover of security," aimed to assume a dominant role.[179]

The tendency to downplay the Little Entente and to enhance the position of Rome was noticeable. Jouvenel wanted to go even farther in conciliating Rome and urged that France recognize a special regime for Italy and the existence of two distinct groupings in the Danubian area. The Quai d'Orsay was more prudent. It agreed, however, that some satisfaction ought to be given to Italy, and advised the opening of direct talks between the Little Entente and Rome.[180]

Thus, to the existing three approaches—German (Anschluss), Italian (Austro-Hungarian union), and Czechoslovak (Little Entente plus Austria and Hungary)—Paris was responding by a proposal reminiscent of the old Tardieu Plan. The latter had foundered on Franco-Italian rivalry; now the chances of success seemed brighter.[181] But would a new version of the Tardieu Plan, giving semblance to Italy's dominant position, work? Rome was unlikely to exchange substance for illusions. Paul-Boncour seemed aware of this danger, hence his emphasis on the dominant place of Franco-Italian cooperation in the whole scheme and warnings to Prague to restrain its ambitions.[182] Naturally, the Czechs were uneasy. The French belief that an accord between Italy and Czechoslovakia was "obviously the key to the

179. Note by political director, 30 June 1933, MAE, P.A. Massigli 4.

180. See Jouvenel in DDF, I, III:788–81, 885–87, and comments on his suggestions, 30 June 1933, MAE, P.A. Massigli 4.

181. Paul-Boncour at 28 June 1933, session, CAE/Ch.

182. See DDF, I, III:860–63, 892–93, IV:246–48; Osuský report, 27 July 1933, CD, NA, T120, 1316/D 496 958–60.

entente between the countries of Central Europe," accompanied by expectations that Beneš would show an "open mind," sounded disquieting.[183] Beneš told the cabinet that Jouvenel was planning to "leave the leadership of Central European matters to Rome." The French seemed willing to pay for the Italian support against Germany by concessions in the Danubian area, but would the duce align himself unreservedly with Paris against Berlin?[184] Pressed by the French to engage in conversations with the Italians, Beneš said repeatedly that his visit to Rome would be fruitless unless there was near certainty of concluding a meaningful accord with Mussolini. Beneš and Osuský made it clear that they understood France's wish to act jointly with Italy, but they also recalled Czechoslovakia's unwavering loyalty to Paris. The Little Entente must not get the impression that France now sided with Italy rather than with its trusted friends.[185] Referring to the "great power position of the Little Entente," Krofta said that nothing could be done in Central Europe without it. He hoped that the notion that this region belonged to the nations that inhabited it was gaining recognition.[186] Beneš declared publicly that Czechoslovakia did not oppose Franco-Italian cooperation or the rapprochement of the five Danubian states, but it had its own views on the subject.[187]

In September, Paris and Rome defined their respective positions.[188] That of Italy was based on the advocacy of bilateral accords, preferential treatments for Austrian industrial products, and a privileged position for itself. Not only would Italian products receive preferences (on the grounds that Italy had a negative commercial balance), but Rome would participate in both intra-Danubian negotiations and those held simultaneously by the signatories of the Four Power Pact. Not surprisingly, the Italian memorandum was unfavorably received in Paris and Prague, although Beneš did not want to reject it, hoping instead to bring about its complete modification by negotiation.[189] Mussolini, however, was in no hurry to negotiate. Franco-Italian rapprochement was being stalemated, and Paul-Boncour worried about the "excessive distrust" of the Little Entente and its adverse

183. DDF, I, III:845–47, IV:207.

184. Beneš cited in Kvaček, "Boj," 244; compare Bystrický and Deák, *Európa*, 364–69.

185. DDF, I, IV:508–10; compare Jouvenel–Paul-Boncour–Massigli–Noël–Monicault correspondence, MAE, Z 864.10, Tchécoslovaquie 2569, 2602, 2604. Relevant material in DDF, I, III; DBFP, v, 447–48; 566–67; Šejnocha to ministry, 23 Aug. 1933, CD, NA, T120, 1316/D 497 127–28.

186. Briefing, 13 July 1933, KV, CPP.

187. 31 Sept. 1933, Beneš, *Boj o mír*, 799; compare briefing, 7 Sept., KV, CPP.

188. French and Italian memoranda dated 10 and 30 Sept. 1933.

189. See DDF, I, IV:363–64; also Gajanová, *ČSR*, 315.

effect on the future of the Four Power Pact.[190] At the Sinaia conference of the Little Entente in late September, Beneš emphasized that Italy must be forced to choose between Germany, which was clearly sabotaging the disarmament conference, and France and its allies. Only firmness, he said, could save Austria.[191]

Far from helping to resolve Danubian matters through Franco-Italian cooperation, the Four Power Pact had only introduced an element of irritation between Paris and Prague. As for Poland, Beck watched the events, trying to ascertain whether France was capable of reacting when French interests in the region were menaced. When queried by Laroche about Warsaw's seeming disinterest in the threat of Anschluss, the foreign minister replied that the Anschluss could only be stopped by French and Italian mobilization.[192] "We are ready to sell this Anschluss," Piłsudski told a Polish diplomat, "but we must get a good price for it." The marshal affirmed that Poland would always be ready to fulfill its obligations to France—the alliance being "one of the cornerstones of my policy"—but this applied only to German aggression directed against either of them. Otherwise Paris and Warsaw had "complete freedom of maneuver."[193]

Using this freedom, Polish diplomacy continued to cultivate Soviet Russia. Here, Piłsudski thought, he was dealing with "real and not paper" objectives.[194] Moscow, worried by Far Eastern problems and its exclusion from the Four Power Pact, was responsive. The Russians became staunch opponents of revision; words like the "corridor" disappeared from the Soviet press; a Soviet-Polish honeymoon set in and lasted through a good part of the year.[195] In April, Bogusław Miedziński, editor of *Gazeta Polska*, had gone to Moscow; in July, Karl Radek returned the visit. In the course of conversations, approved on the highest level, Miedziński sought to allay Soviet fears of a Polish-German war against Russia, which, he insisted, would place his country at Germany's mercy. Radek tried to reassure the Poles that the Rapallo policy was dead, and even proposed mil-

190. See Massigli to Léger, 7 Oct. 1933, MAE, P.A. Massigli 4. For Paul-Boncour remarks on Italy and laudatory about Beneš, see 8 Nov. session, CAE/Ch.

191. See DDF, 1, iv:416–17, 440–41, 509. Also Massigli to Léger, 6 Oct. 1933, MAE, P.A. Massigli 4, and Naggiar to Paul-Boncour, 9, 13, 30 Sept., MAE, Z 864.10, Tchécoslovaquie 2602. Compare briefings, 21 Sept., 12 Oct., KV, CPP.

192. See Gawroński, *Moja misja*, 42; also DDF, 1, iv:280–81.

193. See Wysocki, *Tajemnice*, 178–79. Compare *Gazeta Polska*, 18 July 1933 on Anschluss.

194. Wysocki, *Tajemnice*, 178.

195. Already in late Mar. Juliusz Łukasiewicz and Litvinov jointly criticized the Four Power Pact perceived as anti-Soviet. See Rakowski, "Polsko-radzieckie," 98–101. For Soviet-Polish rapprochement, see Zabiełło, *W Kręgu*, 135–41; Leczyk, *Polityka*, 303–28; Skrzypek, *Strategia*, 46–81; Mikhutina, *Sovetsko-polskie otnoshenia*, 93–126; Beck, *Dernier rapport*, 35–36.

itary cooperation. The Poles were not interested, arguing that they wished to be aligned with neither neighbor. Moreover, Piłsudski suspected, not without reason, that the Soviet Union wished to worsen Polish-German relations while retaining its own link to Berlin.[196] But Poland gladly signed on 3 July the Convention for the Definition of Aggressor with Russia and virtually all its European neighbors.

The growing intimacy between Poland and Russia evoked mixed feelings among the French and the Czechs. Girsa wondered what the Soviets could offer Poland. Although a stabilization of Eastern Europe was "most desirable for the cause of peace," the envoy observed, a Polish-led bloc comprising Russia's neighbors, particularly Romania, would have to be built on the wreckage of the Little Entente.[197] Was the rapprochement a bluff, the French wondered, for they had been told by the Soviets that a military convention was not possible? Or were contacts occuring between the two armies to be taken seriously? Laroche admitted that Poland's resolute stand in the matter of the Four Power Pact increased Warsaw's prestige in the area, but the question remained whether one could take at face value Beck's remarks that a Polish détente with Moscow and Berlin lay in the interest of the Franco-Polish alliance.[198] This détente, wrote General d'Arbonneau, "gives the Polish policy a certain independence allowing it to move away from our orbit." Yet, on military grounds a Soviet-Polish rapprochement would undoubtedly reinforce Poland the day when a European conflict would make it "take up arms on our side." Freed from eastern preoccupations, Poland could concentrate all its forces in the west. The assistance of Soviet war industry would be of capital importance.[199] The French chargé d'affaires concurred with this view, but he added that the Franco-Polish alliance seems to have become in Piłsudski's view a "kind of reinsurance" to be invoked only in grave circumstances.

Those French politicians who favored playing the Russian card—and Herriot was foremost among them—were aware of the need to handle the Polish aspect gingerly. During the ratification debate of the Franco-Soviet nonaggression treaty in mid-May 1933, several speakers had stressed that the document had been signed with full approval of Poland and the Little Entente.[200] Laroche had earlier rebuked his Soviet colleague, who sug-

196. See Miedziński, "Droga" and "Pakty wilanowskie." On Soviet endeavors to retain the German connection see DVP SSR, XVI, 133–34; ADAP, C, I/1:86, 138–43; I, II:443–45, 708–10; II, I:324–26. Compare Girsa report, 7 June 1933, CPP.

197. See DDF, I, III, 613–14.

198. See DDF, I, III:635–36, 782–85, 887–88, IV:4–5, 55–56, 60, 111–12, 134–35. For Laroche's uneasiness about too far-reaching Polish-Soviet involvement, see Erskine to Simon, 28 June 1933, FO 371 417 33.

199. Report, 25 July 1933, SHA, EMA/2, Pologne 12; also DDF, I, IV:152–53.

200. For the 16-18 May debate see J.O. Chambre, 2382–2440.

gested that the Soviet Union take Poland's place. The Russian wished to bury the Franco-Polish alliance all too soon, the ambassador remarked; French and Polish pacts with Russia were perfectly compatible.[201] When later in the year, Cot brought a proposal from Moscow for a security pact, Paul-Boncour argued that it would have to be reconciled with the existing alliances and preceded by Russia's entry into the League. Laroche warned that one must avoid anything that would arouse the suspicion in Warsaw that "we are seeking to substitute an entente with the USSR for our alliance with Poland." Reiterating the opinion that Moscow's rapprochement with Warsaw "singularly reinforces for us the value of the defensive alliance" with Poland, the ambassador recommended that the whole relationship with Russia be handled cautiously.[202]

The French Right and Center were generally hostile to any intimate collaboration with Russia. The radicals were split; the socialists found it hard to reconcile their pro-Soviet feelings with the abhorrence of military alliances. Weygand saw some merit in a policy that would drive a wedge between Germany and Russia, and he appreciated the possible military advantages but otherwise was reserved.[203] Léger was inclined to some form of a multilateral arrangement involving Moscow rather than to a direct Franco-Soviet alignment.[204] Welcoming the Convention for the Definition of the Aggressor, Paris did not wish to join it because it could affect France's leeway in determining its obligations, as affected by Locarno provisions.[205]

Daladier, as we know, was far more interested in a rapprochement with Berlin than with Moscow. According to Paul-Boncour, he was "obsessed" with this idea, and his informal overtures run parallel to François-Poncet's conversations with the Germans leaders.[206] Through Fernand de Brinon and Joachim von Ribbentrop, acting as principal intermediaries, the French premier and the Führer explored even the possibility of a secret encounter. Apparently Daladier withdrew at the last moment fearing an

201. Laroche to Paul-Boncour, 21 Feb. 1933, DDF, I, II:672–73.

202. See DDF, I, IV:476–77. The Poles were annoyed that Herriot visited Moscow without stopping in Poland, and Paul-Boncour allegedly agreed that this was unfortunate. See Beck telegrams, 26 Aug., 21 Sept. 1933, HIA, Amb. Paryż, box 3,5.

203. See Scott, *Alliance*, 104–15, 140–47; Bankwitz, *Weygand*, 249.

204. See note, 19 July 1933, DDF, I, IV:32–33.

205. See Paul-Boncour on 3 Nov. 1933, CAE/Ch; also DDF, I, III:877–79, IV:591. Compare Chłapowski to Beck, 26 July 1933, PI, Amb. Londyn, reel 47.

206. On Daladier's "obsession," see Paul-Boncour, 9 Mar. 1948, *Les Evénements survenus en France*, 3:790. The topic itself is treated by Duroselle, *Décadence*, 206–208; Weinberg, *Foreign Policy*, 170–72; Jäckel, *Frankreich in Hitlers Europa* (Tübingen, 1966), 26–27; Bloch, "La Place"; Brinon, *Mémoires*, 28–29, and rich documentation can be found in DDF, ADAP, and DBFP.

adverse reaction of Paul-Boncour and the parliament. The talks confirmed Berlin's interest in an entente with Paris, provided France loosened its links to the eastern allies and accepted the German viewpoint on limited armament. François-Poncet thought it would be useful to "clear the atmosphere" in a way it had been done by the Hitler–Wysocki encounter. The French government hesitated. When in late September the Germans raised again the idea of a frank exchange on all questions dividing France and Germany, Paul-Boncour was greatly tempted to resolve thus all the difficulties connected with the organization and maintenance of an unstable Western front in Geneva, but he felt it would be too dangerous to sacrifice it to an attempted direct entente with Berlin.[207]

On 20 September, Beck came to Paris. Seemingly this visit was his own initiative, although the French welcomed it as a visible sign of an improved Franco-Polish atmosphere, and an opportunity for dissipating misunderstandings over Poland's rapprochement to Russia and détente with Berlin. The Quai d'Orsay, however, thought that the importance of this détente should not be exaggerated. Laroche thought that even if Polish foreign policy required a certain vigilance, it was basically "wise and peaceful" and accorded with that of Paris. Paul-Boncour repeated this formula in an interview for the Polish news agency Iskra.[208]

The French government gave Beck a great reception, marred only by the absence of a cabinet member at the railroad station, but the result of the conversations was meager. Beck tried to raise the question of the 1921 military convention, presumably to make its working more precise, but Daladier ignored this overture. The final communiqué was rather platitudinous; *Gazeta Warszawska* on 23 September ironically compared it to some of the old Zaleski declarations.[209]

---

207. Paul-Boncour to Daladier, 29 Sept. 1933, DDF, I, IV:443–46.

208. See DDF, I, IV:280–81. For Iskra interview see Kuźmiński, *Polska*, 131. Osuský had been urging the French to make a pro-Polish gesture that would also be in Prague's interest. See dispatch, 27 July 1933, CD, NA, T120, 1316/D 496 598–60.

209. Beck received the grand cordon of the Legion d'Honneur, and the Parisian press devoted great attention to his visit. I found, however, no record of the conversations. Beck telegram, 21 Sept. 1933, HIA, Amb. Paryż, box 3, is laconic. Only a brief summary appears in the note of the political director, 15 Feb. 1934, MAE, Z 698.12, Pologne 2200. According to Léger dispatch to embassy in Moscow, 25 Sept. in MAE, Z 698.12, the French government had no concrete issues to discuss. Compare Tyrrell telegram, 22 Sept., FO 371 1723 HM 03877. Only Kuźmiński, *Polska*, 129, ascribed the visit to French initiative. Also, DDF, I, IV:527, and correspondence in MAE, Z 698.12, Pologne 2202, and SHA, EMA/2, Pologne 12. On the incident at the railroad station, see Paul-Boncour, *Entre deux guerres*, 3:535; Frankowski to Dębicki, 22 Sept. 1933, SI, MSZ, A.11.49/F/3, no.32. For Beck's overture to Daladier: mention in DTJS, I, 161; Herriot, *Jadis*, 2:423, and the more oblique references in Barthou at 9 May 1934 session, CAE/Ch. (Polish translation in Wandycz, "Barthou," 114) and in DDF, I, VI:347 where the footnote mistakenly links it to Col. Koeltz's visit.

As the disarmament conference reconvened on 9 October, the French tactics of dragging out the proceedings, in order to make an isolated Germany succumb to the pressures of a common front, received the endorsement of Beneš but not of Beck.[210] The Polish foreign minister continued to fear that as time went on France might be driven to purchase the support of other great powers by concessions, including a discussion of territorial issues. He also regarded the French-proposed armament controls as ineffective, and the militia-type armies as a threat to the Polish armed forces. Beck preferred the Versailles provisions, even if evaded, to a compromise system that France and Poland (but not Germany) would be obliged to observe.[211] News of Franco-Polish differences leaked out to the press, and Pertinax assailed his government for its willingness to sacrifice Polish interests. "French foreign policy," he wrote, "as defined by M. Daladier, is the policy of Sadova aggravated by the demolition of the French army." The journalist foretold a rupture between France and its allies. Although Beck and Paul-Boncour minimized their disagreement, its existence was undeniable.[212]

The French international position was difficult. Earlier hopes for an economic entente with the United States had been dashed, and Roosevelt's torpedoing of the London Economic Conference (12 June–27 July), as it was put at the time, was a blow. The British were sabotaging any French independent action in Geneva, making it clear once more that France could not expect any automatic aid in case of a conflict arising out of an East European crisis.[213] The common front was crumbling, and Hitler took no great risk when he announced on 14 October Germany's withdrawal from the disarmament conference and nine days later from the League of Nations.

Berlin's move, all other consequences aside, spelled the doom of the Four Power Pact, which had caused so much trouble for French diplomacy. None of the hopes placed in it was fulfilled. Franco-Italian cooperation in the Danubian area proved harder to achieve than anticipated, and it aroused the Little Entente's fears of an abdication of France's leadership. The injury the pact did to Polish-French relations was serious. The French ambassador in Moscow, Charles Alphand, wrote to Paul-Boncour that the

210. Beneš hoped that Germany would either see reason or suffer a diplomatic defeat, which could lead to Hitler's fall and the return of a German regime with which one could talk. See DBFP, II, v:675–77.

211. Beck's Geneva conversations, Sept. and Oct. 1933, AAN, MSZ 108.

212. See Pertinax in *L'Echo de Paris*, 9 (also 2 and 5) Oct. 1933; for Franco-Polish talks, DDF, I, IV:529–37, 550.

213. Commenting on the British position, Ambassador Corbin wrote to Paul-Boncour: "We have often asked ourselves how our [public] opinion would react if France were implicated in a conflict caused by a grave threat or an act of violence against one of our little allies"; DDF, I, IV:473.

pact represented "the first breach in the principle of equality of nations" and started a process of "disintegration of our alliances."[214] Could the damage be undone, or was it, as a prominent French historian wrote, "the moment to revise a policy based on ineffective alliances with weak countries, and base [France's] security on the entente of the great powers capable of containing Germany?"[215] Growing weaker and more dependent on other powers, France, wrote Ambassador Tyrrell, "lost some of her faith in the satellite system" and was "not anxious to strengthen it," but was trying instead to escape the existing obligations.[216] This could not be done openly, because, as Paul-Boncour put it, "no French statesman would ever think of reversing the by now traditional direction of our foreign policy" by loosening France's ties to East Central Europe. There were still voices like Franklin-Bouillon's urging that the French system be made to work. "Have you forgotten," the deputy said, "that counting Poland and the Little Entente, there are sixty million people in Central Europe resolved not to allow anyone to touch a single square meter of the frontiers established by the Treaties?"[217] France could neither renounce its system in favor of great powers' entente—indeed the system was meant to enhance France's power status—nor revitalize it. A vicious circle existed.

214. Alphand to Paul-Boncour, 5 Dec. 1933, DDF, I, v:171.

215. Duroselle, *Décadence*, 73.

216. Tyrrell to Simon, 7 June 1933, DBFP, II, v:331–32.

217. See 9 and 14 Nov. 1933 sessions, J.O. Chambre, 4039, 4103, 4113–115, 4117–119.

Chapter Ten

At Crossroads, The German Polish Declaration of Nonaggression

Alternatives

The German departure from Geneva stunned the French and delivered a rude blow to policies anchored on the League. Pierre Viénot, a veteran of Franco-German reconciliation and now a deputy, wrote to Paul-Boncour, Camile Chautemps, and Daladier that a new policy was needed but would be effective only if it took the form of a shock therapy administered to France and Germany.[1] The chances of devising and applying such policy were minimal in a country in a state of "absolute political helplessness."[2] Economically France was in deep trouble, with radicals and socialists split on possible remedies. The Daladier cabinet fell in late October; its successor, the Sarraut ministry, lasted less than a month, making room for an equally short-lived cabinet of Chautemps. A Daladier government returned in January 1934. The recurring changes hardly did more than reshuffle the ministerial posts. Disgusted with the weak chamber and cabinet switches, the extremists of Croix de Feu were taking to the streets. The Stavisky financial scandal cast further discredit on the radical leaders. People openly spoke of the bankruptcy of France—political, financial, and moral. The Third Republic was being "emptied of its spiritual content, its creative dynamism."[3]

The continued presence of Paul-Boncour and Daladier at the helm of diplomacy and defense provided some continuity, but the ministers could hardly speak with authority. Paul-Boncour was worried lest Germany's exit from Geneva invalidate Locarno ("a genuine guarantee"), which, in Simon's words was "a potent restraining influence" on France insofar as it precluded immediate involvement on behalf of the eastern allies.[4] Frank-

1. See DDF, 1, v:149–154.

2. Osuský to ministry, 25 Nov. 1933, CD, NA, T120, 1316/D 496 980–81.

3. Post-1945 Parliamentary Commission of Investigation cited in Bankwitz, *Weygand*, 196.

4. Simon to Inskip, 2 Nov. 1933, FO 800, 285. On Paul-Boncour, see DDF, 1, iv:608–609; also on 8 Nov. 1933, CAE/Ch.

lin-Bouillon had other worries. "How can one act effectively with our al-lies and friends," he asked, "if we do not present first of all a united front like all the great nations of the world?" The government, he exclaimed, represented "the same illusions, the same people, the same results, that is to say the same failure."[5]

In principle, Paris had several foreign policy options. It could continue to work, in cooperation with London and Rome, for a convention on the limitation of armaments in the hope that an isolated Germany would re-turn to the conference table. It could try a direct dialogue with Berlin. Or it could abandon the search for disarmament and adopt a firm line toward Berlin, backed by a seriously pursued Moscow connection. Military meas-ures were hardly a possibility. Weygand and Koeltz gave the British to understand that the reoccupation of the Rhine bridges would be an effec-tive way of stopping German rearmament. But, as before, they indicated that the French could do it only if assured of Britain's support. The Foreign Office comment was characteristic: no doubt an effective Franco-British alliance would eliminate the German danger, but British public opinion did not see it that way and would not stand for such an involvement. Ret-rospectively, Paul-Boncour wrote that France's duty in the autumn of 1933 was clear: Fortify the existing alliances and seek new friends, espe-cially Italy and Russia. But his policy at the time hardly reflected such clar-ity and unity of purpose.[6]

Paul-Boncour's policy was not only predicated on British support but also had to consider the socialists. Blum was arguing in favor of a reduc-tion of armaments with or without German participation; Jean Longuet spoke of a "universal conscience" that was asserting itself against Nazi Germany.[7] Critical references by Sarraut and Paul-Boncour to old-fash-ioned alliances (although accompanied by reassurances to the eastern al-lies) were calculated to gain the support of the Left.[8] The Czechoslovaks and the Poles were asked to adhere, at least for the time being, to the pos-itive French line in Geneva. Beck remained skeptical, and he also differed from the French in regarding Hitler's actions as both a tactical move and

5. See 14 Nov. 1933, session, J.O. Chambre, 4113 and 4130. This was the moment, said the president of army senatorial commission, to call on France "reveille toi!" 14 Nov. CA/Sén.

6. See Paul-Boncour, *Entre deux guerres*, 2:361. For analysis of French options, see Beneš to ministry and Osuský to Beneš, 16, 21 Oct., 5 Dec. 1933, CD, NA, T120 1316/ D 497 202–203; D 496 970; D 496 984; also DBFP, II, VI:4–5; Massigli to Léger, 13 Nov. MAE, P.A. Massigli 4. For the Franco-British military angle, see Col. Heywood reports, 21, 25 Oct., FO 371 16709 C 9390 and DBFP, II, V:732–35, Foreign Office minutes, FO 371 16709 Hm 0396. Compare DDB, III, 236, 361.

7. See 14 Nov. 1933 session, J.O. Chambre, 4111–13, 4127–28.

8. See Chłapowski report, 17 Nov. 1933, PI, Amb. Londyn, reel 46. Ministerial speeches 14 Nov. session, J.O. Chambre, 4100–4106, 4123–26.

a definite breach with the League international system. It would be a grave error to try to bring Germany back, he argued and Massigli concurred, through policies that would result in concessions.[9]

Warsaw's reaction to the German departure from Geneva had been swift. Army maneuvers were held, and Piłsudski after conferring with Beck and the chief of staff General Janusz Gąsiorowski, demanded a detailed report (including French data) on the state of German armaments. Informing Laroche of that request, Beck explained that it did not reflect nervousness but a determination to study seriously the consequences of Berlin's move. The French embassy asked Paris to respond positively, "insofar as possible," stressing that this was the first time that Piłsudski's military preoccupations were so clearly directed to the German issue and to cooperation with the French general staff.[10] Consequently, Colonel Koeltz arrived in Warsaw bringing French documentation, was received by Piłsudski, and was given in exchange some important German documents including mobilization plans. The evident Polish desire to strengthen military collaboration with Paris did not mean, however, as Laroche realized, that Warsaw intended necessarily to depart from its policy of détente with Germany.[11]

Piłsudski, however, took yet another step about which we have imprecise and somewhat confusing information. He ordered Ludwik Hieronim Morstin, a writer who had once served as a liaison officer with Marshal Foch and had good personal relations with General Weygand, to go to Paris and present two questions to the French government. One, if Germany attacked Poland along its borders would France respond with general mobilization? Two, would the French concentrate all their available forces on the Franco-German frontier? Morstin's questions, allegedly conveyed through Weygand to Paul-Boncour and the cabinet, were answered in the negative. Paris could only promise aid in arms and munitions, collaboration of the general staffs, and political support.[12]

Even if there are lingering doubts about the veracity of this story, it is obvious that the faltering Daladier cabinet (or its successor) would fear to be drawn into a conflict possibly provoked by Piłsudski. Rumors about preventive war were still current, and there may have been a connection

9. See DDF, I, IV:680–81, 721, 725–26; also Vaïsse, *Sécurité*, 526.

10. On Piłsudski's conference, 21 Oct. 1933, DTJS, I, 81–82; on military measures Zgórniak, "Sytuacja," 207–208; also DDF, I, VI:623–25, and d'Arbonneau reports, 23, 21 Oct., SHA, EMA/2, Pologne 12.

11. See DDF, I, IV:673; summary of Koeltz's report in Castellan, *Reich*, 475–76.

12. See Zaufall, "Misja." Jędrzejewicz dates it (in "Preventive War," 86) as prior to 5 Nov.; Rollet, *Deux mythes*, 243 questions the likelihood of the French cabinet deliberating on such a question and giving an answer to an unofficial emissary. Neither Vaïsse nor I could find any trace of the mission in the French archives, including Weygand's personal journal.

between such fears and Jean-Louis Faure's article on 29 October in *Revue Hebdomadaire* that told the Poles they had no right to ask France to make new sacrifices that could bring it down in ruin.[13]

German departure from Geneva produced an alarmist mood in Prague that the foreign ministry tried to calm. Beneš favored a wait-and-see attitude, but he also recognized the need to prepare for possible complications. One had to strengthen the ties between the Little Entente countries and even "try to achieve closer collaboration with Poland."[14] Masaryk and Beneš devoted great attention to the military preparedness of their country. True, military service had been shortened to fourteen months in 1932, but efforts were made to coordinate defense on a political-military level. A consultative military committee (Armádní poradní sbor) analogous to the French CSG was established and followed in October 1933 by a supreme state council of defense (Nejvyšší rada obrány statů). A major program of strengthening armed forces was initiated. In the spring of 1934 extraordinary credits were voted and the decision taken to construct fortifications along the German borders. The first tanks produced by Škoda came off the assembly line in 1933–34.[15] Masaryk and Beneš were saying that their past advocacy of pacifism stemmed largely from the need to gain time. The American ambassador in Berlin was struck by Beneš's remarks about the German threat to Czechoslovakia's territorial integrity; the minister seemed "ready to fight at the drop of a hat."[16]

Polish and Czechoslovak resolve contrasted with the mood in Paris. Even the firmness of the Right vis-à-vis Germany was confined to certain groups and individuals such as Poincaré, Marin, Tardieu, or Franklin-Bouillon. The républicains de gauche headed by Flandin stood for a dialogue with Germany; *Le Temps* was close to their views and so was the Comité des Forges. Even Weygand saw some merit in talking to the enemy.[17] Hence, Chłapowski did not cherish the prospect of a right-central cabinet.[18]

In a sense, as Osuský reported, one could not speak of policies of the

13. See S. R. report, 4 Jan. 1934, SHA, EMA/2, Pologne 37. Faure's article cited in Vaïsse, *Sécurité*, 474.

14. Beneš to ministry, 16 Oct. 1933, CD, NA, T120, 1316/D 497 202–203; compare briefing, 19 Oct., and Beneš–Eden conversation, DBFP, II, IV:113–16.

15. See Faucher reports, 19 Apr., 13 Dec. 1932, SHA, EMA/2, Tchécoslovaquie 2 and 3; also DDF, I, v:181–92; and Beneš's lectures published as *Democratická armáda*, and Bláha, *Branná politika*. See Ressel, "Mnichov," 302–58; Sander, "Přehled," 359–404; Novotný, "Několik," 1046–77.

16. Entry, 1 Dec. 1933, *Diary*. Compare DDF, I, VI:437–38, 502–503; Noël report, 26 Nov. 1933, MAE, Z 864.1, Tchécoslovaquie 2569.

17. Höhne, "Die Aussenpolitische," 212–34.

18. Chłapowski report, 27 Oct. 1933, PI, Amb. Londyn, reel 46.

Left and the Right in France, but rather of a pro-Russian and a pro-German camp. Chłapowski wrote that while Daladier wanted to talk to Hitler, Herriot was trying to get Paul-Boncour's support for the "completely fantastic idea of a Russian alliance."[19] The idea, of course, was not so fantastic. The Franco-Russian exchanges, surveyed in the preceding chapter, culminated in the 31 October meeting between Paul-Boncour and Litvinov and their discussions about completing the nonaggression pact by a mutual-aid convention. The Frenchman saw the main advantage of a link with Russia in completing and strengthening the "alliance de revers" to use the traditional term.[20] This aspect also appealed to the military leaders.

Soviet-French conversations were conducted in strict secrecy, broken only when the French told Beneš, in mid-November, about their main thrust. The Poles learned solely that the ongoing commercial negotiations were the first step toward a rapprochement between Paris and Moscow. Chłapowski wrote that Soviet propaganda was spreading the earlier-mentioned view that a weak Poland was insufficient as a French ally in the east and that Russia was needed as an element of balance in Europe.[21] The political director's office at the Quai d'Orsay labored the point that Poland could assist France much more effectively if relieved of preoccupations on the Russian side. In turn, French obligations could only be fulfilled if supplies to Poland could be sent through a Russian harbor. All this would enhance Poland's value as an ally of France, and the Quai d'Orsay contemplated the possibility of a tripartite economic agreement with provisions for transit facilities.[22] In mid-December Paul-Boncour thought that ascertaining Polish views on the idea of "welding" Poland and Russia would be advisable, but seemingly nothing was done. Probably Paris feared Warsaw's objections that could complicate the Franco-Russian exchanges. As for Beneš, there were no doubts. Czechoslovak leaders told Cot during his visit in Prague that "finally France had realized that its Slav policy could only be fulfilled in Moscow."[23]

Deliberating over Soviet proposals of bilateral collaboration within a wider security scheme, Paris came to the following conclusions: a bilateral mutual assistance pact was out of the question in view of French commitments under Locarno; Soviet entry into the League was indispensable, for only then could USSR assume genuine obligations; a Franco-Soviet ar-

---

19. Respectively, reports of Osuský, 25 Nov. 1933, CD, NA, T120, 1316/D 496 980–81, and Chłapowski, 1 Dec., PI, Amb. Londyn, reel 47.

20. See Paul-Boncour, *Entre deux guerres*, 2:361–62.

21. Chłapowski report, 17 Nov. 1933, PI, Amb. Londyn, reel 47.

22. See DDF, I, V:45–48, 234–36, 271–74.

23. Cot on 13 Dec. 1933, CAE/Ch. Compare Kvaček, *Nad Evropou*, 71; DaM, II, 631–32.

rangement would have to be part of a larger scheme, the exact model of which still had to be devised.[24] A rapprochement with the Soviet Union appeared as a useful means of pressure on Germany. As Beneš expressed it, France "did not expect from the current rapprochement with Soviet Russia an alliance but a separation of Russia from Germany." And Ambassador Alphand wrote that the formula ought to be "if Berlin, so much more Moscow." He also shared François-Poncet's notion of "a network of counterassurances."[25]

Hitler had coupled his announcement of leaving Geneva with direct overtures to Paris, and Paul-Boncour wondered whether one should try some concessions to bring Germany back to the conference and the League. Opining that Berlin wanted to enlarge the scope of the disarmament debate by feelers to France, Poland, and Czechoslovakia, François-Poncet thought that Germany might be asked to provide a quid pro quo in the form of an Eastern Locarno. He took it for granted that the negotiations would be handled by Paris, but his soundings in Berlin did not meet with a favorable reception.[26] Paul-Boncour also insisted that the issue of German armaments was not a Franco-German but an international concern. A rapprochement between Paris and Berlin could only be contemplated if it accorded with France's international obligations and special friendships. As the note of the Quai d'Orsay legal adviser expressed it: "A Franco-German conversation is inconceivable unless Germany provides proofs and guarantees of nonrearmament."[27]

The Auswärtiges Amt estimated that Paris was uncertain what to do. It could strive for an understanding that included Eastern Locarno concepts, or try to isolate Germany and even prepare together with its eastern "satellites," for a showdown. In this situation, Germany could procrastinate in matters of security guarantees and await the clarification of French demands concerning rearmament.[28] The Czechoslovak diplomats thought that Hitler sought "to strengthen pacifist trends in France and separate France from its allies," but they believed that Daladier was fully aware of these dangers and would counter them effectively. As for a Berlin plan to

24. See DVP SSSR, XVI, 684–85, 772–74; DDF, I, v:535–42. Also Radice, *Appeasement*, 20; for a Soviet perspective, see the relevant sections of Borisov, *Sovetsko-frantsuskie otnosheniia*.

25. Beneš cited in Kvaček, *Nad Evropou*, 71; Alphand in DDF, I, v:312–13.

26. See Phipps to Simon, 21 Nov. 1933 and Foreign Office minutes, DBFP, II, VI:90–91 and FO 371 167 C 10268. Also DDF, I, IV:699–701; compare Paul-Boncour on 8 Nov., CAE/Ch. Also ADAP, C, II/1:94–96, 105–109.

27. See DDF, I/IV:717–18, 734.

28. See ADAP, C, II/1:111–18.

propose nonaggression pacts to Poland and Czechoslovakia, that news could be a "trial balloon."[29]

On 2 November, a Baltic German, Wiegand von Hohen Aesten, representing allegedly high Nazi circles, approached the Czechoslovak envoy in Berlin to learn how Prague would react to a proposal of a nonaggression pact. Vojtěch Mastný cautiously replied that this was a matter for regular diplomatic exchanges. As for his own private view, one had to bear in mind that Czechoslovakia was a member of the Little Entente, had a special relationship with France, and was bound to consider Poland. Hence, a system of nonaggression pacts ought to embrace all three. The envoy proceeded to inform the French ambassador and reported the conversation personally to Beneš and Krofta on 6 November. The information was also passed to Warsaw but, owing to a technical error, did not immediately reach the top foreign ministry officials. Beneš viewed the German move as "officious soundings," and the French regarded the initiative as strictly unofficial in view of Hohen Aesten's dubious credentials. A week later, the content of the Mastný–Hohen Aesten conversation was leaked out to the *Daily Herald*, which magnified its nature by writing of a German offer of a nonaggression pact to Czechoslovakia that Beneš would consider only if the Little Entente and Poland were included and Paris consulted.

The Hohen Aesten initiative surprised and annoyed the Auswärtiges Amt. Mastný was told at the Wilhelmstrasse on 15 November that in the absence of any controversy between Germany and Czechoslovakia, a nonaggression pact would be superfluous. When the Baltic nobleman continued to pursue, in a cloak-and-dagger fashion, the Czechoslovak envoy, he was disavowed by German authorities and then arrested.[30] The episode was devoid of deeper significance, except that it allowed Beneš to boast of his loyalty to France and the correctness of his behavior vis-à-vis Poland. In fact, Beneš asserted later that when Hitler discovered he could achieve nothing in Prague, he turned to Warsaw.[31] This interpretation, however, is not tenable.

In early November, Beneš was anxious to learn if Poland was also the object of German advances, and French diplomacy attempted to evaluate the meaning and the possible consequences of German eastern initiatives

29. Briefing, 19 Oct. 1933, KV, CPP. Compare Phipps telegram, 17 Oct., FO 371 16729 Hm 03977.

30. The above is based on: Mastný to Beneš, 29 Nov. and to Krofta, 13 Dec. 1933, ANM, Mastný, dodatky, sv.6; briefings, 16, 23 Nov., 1 Dec., KV, CPP; Grzybowski report, 24 Nov., AAN, MSZ 5504; DDF, I, IV:693–94,707; Noël to Paul-Boncour, 29 Nov., 22 Dec., MAE, Z 864.1, Tchécoslovaquie 2567; note of S.R., 7 Nov., SHA, EMA/ 2, Tchécoslovaquie 14; ADAP, C, II/1:123–25, 144–45, II, II:537. The best analysis is in Kvaček and Vinš, "K sondážím," 885–87.

31. See DBFP, II, VI:113–16, and Beneš's letter, 20 Apr. 1944, in Namier, *Europe in Decay*, 281.

for the Paris-Berlin relationship.[32] Beck, when questioned by Laroche about a German offer of a nonaggression pact to Poland, replied that should such a proposal materialize it would be carefully studied to see if it was not a simple maneuver to break the Franco-Polish front, as Hitler's overtures to France seemed to be. The Poles would not consent to territorial concessions, a weakening of previous engagements, or a discussion of anything touching on the alliance with France.[33]

The state of German-Polish relations, Danzig included, appeared more satisfactory in the autumn of 1933 than in the preceding years. Speaking to Neurath and the propaganda minister Joseph Goebbels in Geneva, Beck stressed the usefulness of direct contacts, and his interlocutors assented. François-Poncet explained that Hitler's prudent line toward Poland was affected by his belief that Warsaw was capable of a coup (like in Westerplatte) directed against East Prussia or Berlin.[34] The Polish foreign ministry pointed out that the present Nazi regime—in which non-Prussians predominated—seemed more interested in south and west Europe, and it recognized Poland's will power and ability to resist. The decisive factor, however, in Berlin's foreign policy was the preoccupation with armaments. Should Warsaw take a moderate view on that issue, a further détente would be facilitated. Such development was likely, because a "ring of anti-German feelings" existed in Europe, and German efforts to escape this encirclement were probable. The ministry concluded that Poland should not adopt a negative attitude toward Hitler but rather watch that his regime does not become specifically anti-Polish. As Premier Janusz Jędrzejewicz publicly affirmed, Poland would respond to a policy of normalization based on the status quo.[35]

Two days after this statement, on 5 November, Piłsudski asked Józef Lipski, recently named to the Berlin post, for an analysis of the situation. The marshal seized on the notion that the Nazi regime did not identify with the Prussian Junkers, and chided Beck for underestimating this fact. He instructed Lipski to tell the chancellor that Piłsudski had not been impressed by the international uproar that had accompanied Hitler's rise to power. The envoy was to stress that Poland's security rested on two elements: direct relations with the powers and use of the League as a backup. German departure from Geneva deprived Poland of the second element, and Lipski using a subtle threat—for Piłsudski did not wish to

32. See DDF, I, IV:707 and DBFP, II, VI:14. Compare Phipps and Tyrrell to Simon, 7, 8 Nov. 1933, FO 371 16729 C 9732.

33. Laroche to Paul-Boncour, 2 Nov. 1933, DDF, I, IV:680–81.

34. See DDF, I, IV:268; compare Girsa dispatch, 12 Oct. 1933, CPP; also Wojciechowski, *Stosunki*, 68–72.

35. Circular in DTJS, I, 82–84; compare Beck, *Dernier rapport*, 29–33. Jędrzejewicz's statement, 3 Nov. 1933, Sprawozdania stenograficzne sejmu, 14.

"strain the atmosphere between the two states by reinforcing Poland's defense measures"—was to ask how Berlin could "compensate" Poland. Should Hitler offer a nonaggression pact, Piłsudski would consider it seriously. The marshal ended the conversation by saying that if the envoy succeeded, Beck would have a problem (presumably taking care of the diplomatic repercussions), but if he failed, Piłsudski as commander-in-chief "would be in trouble."[36]

News about Lipski's presence in Warsaw and of the subsequent trip by Ambassador von Moltke to Berlin made Laroche contact Beck and try to reappraise the situation. He rightly surmised that Warsaw would not ignore German advances but use them to strengthen its position. But what advantages could Germany derive from a nonaggression accord? Unlike Beck, who tended to believe that Berlin's main motive was to show that one could substitute a new international system for that of the League, Laroche opined that Germany's principal objective was to divide France, Britain, Poland, and Czechoslovakia as well as to manifest Hitler's peaceful intentions.[37]

While Laroche was able to obtain some information from Beck, the efforts of the Czechoslovak envoy to engage in conversations with the Poles proved vain. Beck did not comment when Girsa mentioned Beneš's stand on a possible German offer of a nonaggression pact. Asked whether Poland had been also approached he said no, and refused to speculate about the future. Girsa was upset. One could not expect anything from the Poles, he wrote to Prague. Clearly Warsaw was awaiting a move by Berlin, and as for the possibility of a Czechoslovak-Polish alliance, it was "evident that Poland would only enter it on conditions that would be very onerous for us."[38] Indeed, Warsaw's desire and ability to act on its own was stressed by Beck in his speech broadcast on 13 November. It contained an allusion to brilliant statesmen whose standing did not reflect the actual power of their countries. Laroche understood this remark to be aimed at Beneš.[39] Weighing at this moment the pros and cons of its own talks with Berlin, Paris was very anxious lest a separate and independent Polish action complicate the tasks of French diplomacy.

Hitler received Lipski on 15 November, and it is unlikely that the delay stemmed from a desire to clarify first the Czechoslovak position.[40] Largely monopolizing the conversation, the chancellor disclaimed any aggressive

36. See Jędrzejewicz, Lipski, 94–98; DTJS, I, 84–85; Lapter, Pakt, 270–71.

37. Laroche to Paul-Boncour, 10, 14 Nov. 1933, DDF, I, IV:745–46, V:19–21.

38. Girsa report, 14 Nov. 1933, CPP.

39. Speech in Beck, Przemówienia, 79–83; compare Laroche to Paul-Boncour, 27 Nov. 1933, MAE, Z 864.5, Tchécoslovaquie 2586.

40. See Tomaszewski and Valenta, "Polska," 79–83. It seems more likely that the delay was caused by the Reichstag elections.

designs against Poland or France. War, he said, ought to be excluded as a means of settling differences. When Lipski suggested the publication of an official communiqué embodying this statement, Hitler agreed.

The Hitler–Lipski communiqué perplexed Polish public opinion. The Right warned against German tactics of separating Poland from France; the socialist papers sounded uneasy. Following Beck's instructions, Polish diplomats were to interpret the communiqué as "filling through direct means the gap created by Germany's departure from the League of Nations," and to deny the existence of further negotiations.[41] To Laroche who came to seek clarifications after a telephone call from Paul-Boncour, Beck explained that the Poles would not have entered the road of direct talks with Berlin had they not been told by Hitler that he wished to pursue a peaceful policy toward France. They discussed nothing bearing on the limitation of armaments. Laroche thought that Warsaw may have feared to be overtaken by French or Czechoslovak talks with Berlin and wanted to stress its ability to negotiate directly. It wished to normalize its relations with Germany, but not at the expense of the Polish-Soviet détente or the Franco-Polish alliance. Asked if a written nonaggression agreement was contemplated, Beck thought that this was premature.[42] Lipski admitted, however, to François-Poncet and Mastný that the possibility of a subsequent accord on the exclusion of force had been mentioned by Hitler, but it was too early to contemplate it.[43]

French diplomacy found the Polish move annoying, partly because Paris had not been extensively consulted, partly because the initiative diverged from the general line of Paris. The legal adviser of the Quai d'Orsay wondered if the communiqué might not mean that Polish obligations under articles 10, 16, and 17 of the Covenant, as well as those under the Franco-Polish alliance of 1925, would be affected.[44] Léger told Osuský that insofar as France had not been able to obtain a German guarantee for Poland's border, and had always counseled Warsaw to reach a direct agreement with Berlin, one ought to welcome the communiqué. At the same time, the communiqué was disappointing because of its failure to touch on the territorial issue. The Poles seemingly wished to strengthen their diplomatic

41. See DTJS, I, 85–87; Beck's statement, 16 Nov. 1933 in Beck, *Przemówienia*, 84; compare ADAP, C, II/1:126–27. Also Beck's telegrams, 16, 19 Nov., HIA, Amb. Paryż, box 5; the governmental *Gazeta Polska* spoke of the filling of the gap of Locarno. Compare *Gazeta Warszawska*, 17, 18, 19 Nov.; *Robotnik*, 30 Nov.

42. See DDF, I, v:27–29, 37–39. Compare Cudahy to Secretary of State, 18 Nov. 1933, SDNA, 760C 62/214.

43. See DDF, I, v:32–34; Mastný to Beneš, 29 Nov. 1933, ANM, Mastný, dodatky, sv.6. Compare Kvaček, *Nad Evropou*, 77.

44. Note, 17 Nov. 1933, DDF, I, v:41; compare DBFP, II, VI:128–33.

position and enhance their prestige.[45] François-Poncet was more outspoken as well as resentful of Lipski's departure from Wysocki's habit of consulting the French ambassador. In his view, Germany attempted to drive a
wedge between Poland and France, and Hitler's objectives could only be
achieved at the expense of Russia and the Baltic states. François-Poncet
observed that either the German-Polish détente would progress and the
"corridor" cease to be a threat to peace—in which case France's burden
would be alleviated—or circumstances would remain unchanged, and the
Poles would learn how unjust had been their criticism of France. The
November communiqué, he concluded, "would liberate us, if not of our
scruples, at least of our illusions."[46] Massigli, while more understanding
toward the Poles, thought that Germany was using the communiqué to
place France in an awkward position.[47]

Reporting on French public opinion, Mühlstein commented that "dissatisfaction was general, it was only expressed in different forms." It
seemed inconceivable that Poland would talk with Germany without the
participation, or at least the approval, of Paris. The phrase "la Pologne
nous lache" became current. The pro-German *Volonté* attacked Warsaw
because it was complicating French attempts at rapprochement with Berlin. Pfeiffer wrote in *Notre Temps* on 18 November that German-Polish
détente was rooted in common aggressive designs on Russia. "The policy
of Colonel Beck," he concluded, frees "French diplomacy from a heavy
mortgage." The Poles countered by recalling instances when France had
acted without consulting its ally; they wanted continued collaboration
with France but "the era of vassalage was ended once and for all."[48]

The Czechoslovak foreign ministry adopted the line that Prague welcomed the Hitler–Lipski communiqué, for Poland would certainly not undertake any obligations that could adversely affect its alliances and friendships.[49] The Czernin Palace cultivated the impression that the country
needed no similar agreement with Germany. Warsaw turned to negotiations with Berlin because of its worry over the "corridor," Beneš told Anthony Eden, then undersecretary of State at the Foreign Office. The Czechoslovak minister "did not conceal his disapproval" of the Polish course,
and he tried to find out from the French whether the Berlin communiqué

45. Osuský report, 21 Nov. 1933, CD, NA, T120, 1316/D 496 778–79.

46. See DDF, I, v:80–85; compare Berber, *Europäische Politik*, 26, and DBFP, II,
VI:90, 124–25.

47. Raczyński report, 21 Nov. 1933, PI, Amb. Londyn, reel 46.

48. See DTJS, I, 91–93; compare Raczyński and Chłapowski reports, 20, 25 Nov., 1
Dec. 1933, PI, Amb. Londyn, reel 46 and 47. Also DBFP, II, VI:261–63; briefing 23
Nov., KV, CPP.

49. See Noël to Paul-Boncour, 16, 18 Nov. 1933, MAE, Z 864.1, Tchécoslovaquie
2569. Compare *Hospodářská Politika*, 25 Nov. 1933.

had any bearing on the Austrian issue. Laroche was inclined to accept Beck's word that the Anschluss had not been discussed. Fantastic rumors of German-Polish plans to conquer jointly the Soviet Ukraine were groundless. Encouraged somewhat by Hitler's remark to François-Poncet that Germany would be willing to sign nonaggression treaties with all its neighbors, Beneš reverted to his usual optimism. By late December, he told the cabinet that the Hitler–Lipski communiqué was "a tactical episode," already clarified, and Poland was likely to return to a policy of alliance with France.[50]

Perhaps the most perceptive appraisal of Polish motivation came from the Soviet envoy in Warsaw, Vladimir Antonov-Ovseienko. Poland, he wrote, had always believed that there would be no common anti-German front; hence, Poland rather than Germany could find itself isolated. If preventive war was out of the question, one had to gain time. As a prominent Pole told Antonov-Ovseienko: "You will be in all the combinations. But we?" The envoy inclined to share the Polish viewpoint that Paris was moving toward bilateral negotiations with Berlin of which Poland could well bear the cost.[51]

The marshal, who felt that the communiqué did "not give [us] much," now favored a certain reserve vis-à-vis Berlin. Was this purely tactical or did he intend to exploit the communiqué for the purpose of a rapprochement with France and Russia? He deemed the former easier and decided to talk confidentially (as soldier to soldier) to General d'Arbonneau. He remarked that if Daladier—then minister of war to whom the military attaché would report—was "a man of honor," secrecy would be observed in Paris. Thus, although Piłsudski did not intend to subordinate any future moves toward Germany to the dictates of Paris, he took the French angle most seriously into consideration.[52]

Shortly before the conversation with d'Arbonneau, the marshal singled out Laroche and the Romanian envoy at a reception, as if to stress their special position as allies.[53] Talking to the French military attaché on 24 November Piłsudski went over familiar ground, explaining Poland's reasons for clarifying the situation with Berlin. He assured d'Arbonneau that the chancellor accepted Poland as it was, with its existing borders. The Germans had hinted that the Hitler–Lipski talk could eventually lead to a

50. See Laroche and Noël dispatches in DDF, 1, v:126–30, 134–35, 197–98; also briefing, 23 Nov., KV and Girsa report, 21 Nov., CPP; Kvaček, *Nad Evropou*, 77. Eden–Beneš conversation in DBFP, II, vi:113–16. Compare Mastný to Beneš, 29 Nov. 1933, ANM, Mastný, dodatky, sv.6.

51. Antonov-Ovseienko to Stomonyakov, 27 Nov. 1933, DIM, vi, 122.

52. For Piłsudski's remarks, 20 Nov. 1933, Jędrzejewicz, *Lipski*, 100. An interesting analysis appears in Zacharias, *Polska*, 98–99.

53. Laroche to Paul-Boncour, 22 Nov. 1933, MAE, Z 698.1, Pologne 2099.

treaty, but the Poles did not wish to encourage them. Neither side had mentioned France. The marshal answered affirmatively d'Arbonneau's question whether a détente with Germany would facilitate the settlement of economic and "moral" differences between the two countries. He evaded a further query about the real value of a future pact if it did not carry German recognition of Polish frontiers. Asked whether he considered a détente as a sufficient reason to cut the size of Polish armed forces, Piłsudski replied that "we cannot diminish our army by a single man." As for the personal element, the marshal felt that Hitler, being a man of the people and not a Prussian, was the most likely person to change the mentality of his nation. He was also flexible, although Piłsudski did not say that he could be trusted. The marshal believed, however, that internal difficulties of the Nazi regime would persist. Personally, he wished Hitler to last as long as possible.

Piłsudski's manner of expressing his ideas, particularly in French, was not always lucid, and d'Arbonneau sought further clarifications. General Gąsiorowski explained that Piłsudski did not believe Germany capable at this point of making war on Poland, a view d'Arbonneau deemed over-optimistic. The attaché also wondered how a man so distrustful as Piłsudski could attach so much weight to Hitler's assurances. Perhaps he wanted to believe because he had no desire to wage war against Germany. D'Arbonneau was struck by the fact that Piłsudski had made only one passing reference to France during their entire conversation. Gąsiorowski's explanation—that the marshal did not mean to be disagreeable, but simply felt that there could be no question of changing anything in Franco–Polish relations—sounded lame.[54] Surely Piłsudski had previously said to Beck and Szembek that he would tell the military attaché that "we wish to know what France really wants," and that "further talks with the Germans would depend on the answer."[55] Yet he said no such thing to d'Arbonneau. What made him change his mind? In the absence of such exchanges, the conversation brought no new elements. It certainly did not modify the French view that the communiqué did not provide a major advance to the cause of peace of confidence in Europe, even though it brought some respite to Poland. There was much ado about little, and one should be careful not to be tricked.[56]

Three days after the Piłsudski–d'Arbonneau talk, Germany proposed a written declaration on nonaggression in order to find out how far Poland would go. The Germans insisted that détente with Warsaw would pave the way for an understanding with Paris, but Lipski sensed the tendency to

54. D'Arbonneau report and Laroche comments, 28 Nov. 1933, DDF, 1, v:116–21.

55. See Jędrzejewicz, *Lipski*, 100.

56. See d'Arbonneau report, 23 Nov. 1933, SHA, EMA/2, Pologne 12; DDF, 1, v:119n.

separate Poland from France and undermine the French system. The Poles began to play for time, and three weeks elapsed between German overtures and Lipski's resumption of negotiations on 16 December. The argument that Warsaw was awaiting a French reaction to the Piłsudski–d'Arbonneau conversation is unconvincing for the talk did not call for an answer.[57] True, the Poles did wish to discuss a coordination of the diplomatic line with Paris. Warsaw was only trying "to catch up with France in the domain of relations with Germany," Mühlstein told Massigli. For years the German-Polish controversy was described as a liability to France; why were the French so unhappy now that a détente had intervened? When Massigli remarked that Warsaw's tactics were facilitating Hitler's plans, the Polish diplomat asked whether the French would not have taken up conversations with Hitler if there had been no Hitler–Lipski encounter? "If France wanted to conduct a policy coordinated with Poland and corresponding to the spirit of our alliance . . . [France] would meet with no reservations on our part. It is not we who had loosened the Polish-French alliance. For years we have drawn [your] attention to the necessity of a closer and better coordination of the activities of both governments, but unfortunately we had not found genuine understanding. Even now it was not too late: let the French government show us that it understands the need for close collaboration with Poland, and we shall respond with the greatest willingness. But such initiative must come from the French side."[58] In another conversation, Mühlstein seized on Laval's remark that Poland was becoming "more difficult and less docile" to point out that the French still thought of his country as a client. Laval had to admit that the responsibility for an unsatisfactory state of Franco-Polish relations was mutual.[59]

Similarly, Laroche, trying to explain Polish preoccupation with the solidity of the French alliance, commented: "So much has been written and said in France for several years, in certain newspapers and in certain circles, that we would not fight for the corridor, that people here could not turn a deaf ear." He appealed to Paris: "As long as we regard the alliance with Poland a necessary guarantee of our security and of general peace, we must convey to this country a very clear sentiment that we are on its side."[60]

A dramatic gesture was needed. Would a visit by Paul-Boncour, which the Poles had been encouraging since October, constitute a visible sign of French interest in Poland? Mentioning the visit to Laroche on 17 Novem-

57. For the argument, see Szembek, "Tentatives d'appaisement et inévitable conflit," SI, Papiery Jana Szembeka

58. 7 Dec. 1933 conversation, DTJS, I, 96–99.

59. Chłapowski report, 9 Dec. 1933, PI, Amb. Londyn, reel 47.

60. DDF, I, V:220–28; compare d'Arbonneau report, 21 Dec. 1933, SHA, EMA/2, Pologne 12.

ber, Beck used the words "particularly desirable and opportune in the present circumstances." Mühlstein told the influential Elie Bois of the *Petit Parisien* that such a trip would be most important because "further non-coordination of tactics between the two governments could adversely affect French interests." If France wanted to talk to Hitler without being isolated, it ought to consult with Warsaw.[61] Paul-Boncour apparently failed to appreciate the urgency of Polish requests. True, the tense domestic situation and the difficult disarmament negotiations claimed his attention; a vaguely favorable response to Polish overtures resulted only in further delays. By the end of December, Paris decided to postpone the projected trip indefinitely; the Poles were greatly disappointed. No common strategy vis-à-vis Berlin emerged. Laroche was being generally informed that the Germans were making some proposals, and he received a promise to be kept posted should any negotiations develop.[62] In Paris, Mühlstein made an effort to talk to Daladier, who, according to Osuský, had been so annoyed with Poland that he would have gladly denounced the alliance. Daladier allegedly thought that France should get close enough to Germany to grant it virtually a free hand against Russia.[63] Mühlstein's appraisal was calmer. He considered that one should not dramatize Daladier's interest in a dialogue with Berlin. Even if he became premier again—which he did on 30 January 1934—such a dialogue would lead nowhere and present no dangers from the Polish viewpoint.[64]

Czechoslovak diplomacy was more concerned with Franco-German exchanges. Although Beneš assured Eden that he had nothing against them, he followed them closely. Osuský reported about alleged overtures made by an emissary of Papen and the leaders of heavy industry for a Franco-German alliance in exchange for France's consent to German fortifications along Czechoslovak and Polish borders. A Czechoslovak attempt to have *Petit Parisien* publish secret directives of the Auswärtiges Amt pertaining to close French-German collaboration failed, as Daladier personally intervened to prevent the publication. Beneš told his collaborators that German propaganda, backed by financial means, was making every effort to gain favor with the French press. Having struggled for fifteen years to defend

61. See Komarnicki conversation, 7 Oct. 1933, AAN, MSZ 108; Mühlstein in DTJS, I, 91–96; Chłapowski reports, I, 9 Dec., PI, Amb. Londyn, reel 47 and AAN, Amb. Berlin, 81. Also DDF, I, v:201.

62. See Laroche to Paul-Boncour, 12, 23, 28, 29 Dec. 1933, MAE, Z 698.12, Pologne 2200 and 2198, and to Léger [?] 13 Dec., 2202; also DDF, I, v:134, 379–81. Chłapowski report, 28 Dec., AAN, z.4, w.3, t.13 (old classification); Girsa dispatch, 28 Nov. For analysis Wojciechowski, *Stosunki*, 85–95.

63. Osuský report, 25 Nov. 1933, CD, NA, T120, 1316/D 496 980–81.

64. Mühlstein to Dębicki, 9 Dec. 1933, SI, MSZ, A.11.49/F/3.

the peace treaties and then being forced to make concessions, the French were getting tired.[65]

According to the Quai d'Orsay, Franco-German talks could bear on specific bilateral issues (the Saar) as well as on disarmament and security. Germany was mainly interested in the first two categories; for the French the matter of security claimed precedence. It was felt that if Berlin rejected the French position on disarmament, Paris ought to make use of its rights under the treaties.[66] As Hitler was multiplying his pacific pronouncements, the views in Paris on the merits of talks with Berlin were still divided. There were fears that unwillingness to be conciliatory would alienate London. Time, as François-Poncet remarked, was not working in France's favor. The military attaché in Berlin, General Gaston Renondeau, wrote to Daladier that one ought to build a dam against German unlimited rearmament; otherwise France would have to face a conflict later rather than now "when the balance of our forces was still tilted to our advantage."[67] A rightist deputy pleaded to break off the talks with Berlin and "group around France the only alliances that count: Poland and the Little Entente."[68] The government did not seem to regard it as a realistic policy option.

An Intermezzo

On 14 December, Beneš came on a three-day visit to Paris as a spokesman not only for Czechoslovakia but for the entire Little Entente. His objective was to strengthen France as the leader of the eastern system and dissipate French fears of diplomatic isolation.[69] Georges Bonnet wrote later that Beneš aimed to destroy the possibility of a Franco-German arrangement, which is only partly accurate.[70] The minister did not hide his doubts about the usefulness of a Paris-Berlin dialogue but asked for little more than to be kept informed.[71] Czechoslovakia continued to oppose German rearmament as well as to approve, for tactical reasons, a policy of submitting

65. Osuský reports, 15, 20, 25 Nov. 1933, CD, NA, T120, 1316/D 496 975 and 977 and 980–81. Briefing, 1 Dec., KV, CPP; compare Ripka's article in *Lidové Noviny* 10 Dec., with the phrase: "if France were to desert its eastern allies, especially the Little Entente, she would desert itself."

66. Notes, 11, 13 Dec. 1933, DDF, I, v:204–208, 233–34.

67. Renondeau to Daladier, 13 Dec. 1933, DDF, I, v:250.

68. Ybarnegaray, 6 Dec. 1933, CAE/Ch.

69. See Benton to Secretary of State, 21 Dec. 1933, SDNA, 840.00/397; Chłapowski report, 20 Dec., AAN, Amb. Berlin, 81. Tyrrell in his report noted a certain reserve of the French official circles, see DBFP, II, VI:206.

70. Bonnet, *Quai d'Orsay*, 129.

71. See Kvaček, "Jednání," 8.

a positive program, although Beneš had no concrete ideas about its nature. Nor did he have a ready answer when Paul-Boncour broached the old notion of invoking article 213 concerning League investigations in Germany and asked what could be done if Berlin refused to go along. Both statesmen seemed to agree that nonaggression pacts with Germany could be meaningful only if concluded, as part of a larger scheme, under the aegis of the League. Despite some differences on Austria, Beneš was willing to cooperate with France in the Danubian area and to avoid impeding an understanding with Rome. He was working for a normalization of relations between the Little Entente and Russia.[72]

Beneš summed up optimistically the results of his Paris trip, speaking of the full identity of views between Czechoslovakia and France on Germany. Daladier struck a similarly sanguine note when he affirmed that France was ready for all the contingencies; rapprochement with the USSR was making progress and mistrust toward Poland abating. "In general, one can state that . . . the period of hesitations was over, and even if the present cabinet fell this would not affect [French] determination."[73]

During his visit, the Czechoslovak foreign minister had a talk with the Polish ambassador. Recalling his loyal stand toward German overtures to Prague, Beneš said that if it came to such a calamity as a war between Germany on the one side and France and Poland on the other, Czechoslovakia would join its friends with all its forces. Beneš wished Chłapowski to know that "he was ready, at any moment, even tomorrow, to open appropriate talks with the Polish government in order to give a constant and unchangeable form to our relations."[74]

To appreciate fully these advances, we need to place them in the context of Czechoslovak-Polish developments that occurred in the preceding two months. Krofta noted that the Poles had asked General Weygand during his visit to Czechoslovakia from 27 September to 4 October to urge more extensive contact between the two armies.[75] Indeed, the top echelons of the Polish military did not conceal their mistrust of Germany, stressed loyalty to France, and showed interest in closer ties with Czechoslovakia as illustrated by a new communication from General Gąsiorowski to General Syrový. The chief of Masaryk's military chancellery, General Silvestr Bláha, insisted on his side that without strategic cooperation with Poland

72. See DDF, 1, v:268–70; compare 432–33, DBFP, II, VI:156. Also Kvaček, *Nad Evropou*, 61.

73. Pavlů to missions, 23 or 25 Dec. 1933, CPP; also CD, NA, T120, 1316/D 497 114.

74. Chłapowski reports, 16, 20 Dec. 1933, AAN, Amb. Berlin, 81.

75. Briefing, 12 Oct. 1933, KV, CPP. On Weygand's visit, apparently undertaken to improve Czechoslovak morale, see Faucher to Daladier, 5 Oct., SHA, EMA/2, Tchécoslovaquie 3, and Noël, *Guerre*, 56n.

"Czechoslovakia could not develop any operational plans."[76] Under the pressure of the general staff, Beneš was giving more serious thought to some form of a military agreement, but he wanted it to be preceded by a political accord (the perpetual friendship pact?).[77] An encounter with Beck in Geneva on 2 September was inconsequential, but four weeks later, Beneš publicly praised Poland and spoke of an evolution toward better and more intimate collaboration between the two countries.[78] Shortly thereafter a Polish periodical reflecting the views of the foreign affairs ministry printed a critical, and probably inspired, article about Czechoslovakia that drew freely on the arguments of Beneš's rightists critics in describing his policies: exclusive reliance on France, rejection of war as an instrument of diplomacy, and the treatment of Poland as a lightening rod attracting German strikes. The article concluded that Czechoslovakia was surveying "the ruins of its own conceptions."

Girsa ascribed the article to a persisting annoyance with Beneš's diplomacy combined with some sympathy for the Czechoslovak Right. The Poles were seeking to gain over Slovak autonomists, fan Polish discontent in Teschen, and discredit Beneš's alleged germanophilia. Warsaw was also affected by the endemic pro-Hungarian leanings, and the expectation that Anschluss would so weaken Czechoslovakia as to place it as Poland's mercy. A reply by Hubert Ripka, a publicist close to Beneš, sought to refute Polish assertions. It concluded that "our faith in France is not shaken," and that Masaryk's dictum that Czechoslovak and Polish independence was mutually interdependent was still valid. So was a desire for cooperation with Warsaw, "in order to arrive at a sincere alliance between our two countries."[79]

Beneš's complaint that "it takes two to get married"[80] was appreciated by the French diplomats. But they also pointed out that just as Czechoslovakia had not wanted in the past to be tied to a more exposed country, so

76. On Polish army interest in collaboration, see Grzybowski report, 24 Nov. 1933, AAN, MSZ 5504; Laroche and Noël to Paul-Boncour, 2, 7, 9 Dec., MAE, Z 864.10, Tchécoslovaquie 2604 and Z 864.5, Tchécoslovaquie 2586; Girsa reports, 2, 7 Dec., CPP and 15 Jan. 1934 in Berber, *Europäische Politik*, 29. On Gen. Fajfr's (head of aviation in ministry of national defense) visit to Poland, see Faucher report, 28 Nov., SHA, EMA/2, Tchécoslovaquie 3. Bláha cited in Grzybowski's letter, 11 Dec., AAN, MSZ 5505. See also Tomaszewski and Valenta, "Polska," 711–12.

77. See Bułhak, "Z Dziejów stosunków 1927–1936," 126–27; Zgórniak, "Sytuacja międzynarodowa Czechosłowacji," 17–18; *Češi a Poláci*, 2:547. Compare DDF, 1, III:488–89. For rightist criticism, see Gajanová, *Dvojí*, 94.

78. Beneš, *Boj o mír*, 786–87.

79. Ripka's reply to S. Adamski's article in *Polityka Narodów* 7 (1933) 88–94 appeared in *Lidové Noviny*, 14 Oct. 1933; Girsa's comments and analysis, 12, 14 Oct., CPP.

80. See Noël to Paul-Boncour, 18 Oct. 1933, MAE, Z 864.5, Tchécoslovaquie 2586.

Warsaw, considering that the course of international events had justified its stand, viewed with equanimity the possibility of Anschluss. In brief, both governments were equally to blame for the handling of the German menace.[81]

Girsa criticized the illusions of the Czech rightists, the Slovaks, and to some extent the agrarians about Poland, but he too regarded a situation in which military collaboration contrasted with political reserve as highly anomalous. He urged that Poland explain its political program so "that we would know where we stand."[82] Seeking to achieve that, and non-plussed by the Hitler–Lipski communiqué, Beneš expounded in late November that the Czechoslovak view of the international situation to the Polish delegate in Geneva. He stressed that France had to rely on the Little Entente and Poland, and were Paris to seek a new combination he (Beneš) would denounce the alliance. Krofta made similar remarks to Grzybowski, who now came to the conclusion that if approached by the Poles the Czechs would respond by a formal proposal of an alliance rather than a mere pact of friendship. Grzybowski recognized that such an alliance would make perfect sense on military grounds but would be of questionable value in view of the divergent foreign policies of the two states. It would be a different matter if Czechoslovakia accepted Poland's lead even in opposing French wishes.[83]

Beneš's confidences to Chłapowski in Paris and the conversation between Girsa and Beck just before Christmas must be viewed against this background.[84] The Czechoslovak envoy, still resentful of Beck for not having confided in him about the Hitler–Lipski encounter, was greatly surprised by the foreign minister's attitude. Beck kept him for two hours surveying the main lines of Polish foreign policy. This was the first such intimate audience, and Girsa not unnaturally attached great importance to it. Beck explained that the relationship with Russia had become satisfactory and Warsaw intended to strengthen it. As for the Wysocki and Lipski talks with Hitler, the Poles believed that the chancellor, not being a Prussian, was desirous to normalize relations with Poland. The Polish-German issue had been generally considered a threat to general peace; Warsaw's

---

81. Note, 24 Oct. 1933, MAE, Z 864.5, Tchécoslovaquie 2586.

82. Girsa's listing of Czechoslovak grievances (disloyal behavior at the time of the Hitler–Lipski communiqué, silence at the proposal to award the order of White Lion to Piłsudski and Mościcki, absence of reaction to Beneš's overture) dispatches 16, 17, 21, 24 Nov. 1933, CPP. On the agrarians' pro-Polish views see 11 Dec., note, AAN, MSZ 5504 and Noël to Paul-Boncour, 30 Oct., MAE, Z 864.10, Tchécoslovaquie 2586.

83. Respectively, Raczyński report, 22 Nov. 1933, and Grzybowski to Schaetzel, 11 Dec., AAN, MSZ 5504 and 5505.

84. Girsa report in Kozeński, *Czechosłowacja*, 72; also Tomaszewski and Valenta, "Polska," 713. Compare Girsa's account to Laroche forwarded to Paul-Boncour, 8 Jan. 1934, MAE, Z 864.5, Tchécoslovaquie 2586.

ambition was to eliminate this handicap. Détente was a fact, but only the future could show its real dimensions. Rumors about territorial exchanges including compensation for Poland in the Ukraine were pure fantasy.[85] The alliance with France remained an essential and unchangeable factor in Warsaw's policy; all Poland wanted was to reconcile it with a certain freedom of movement befitting a great power. Poland also wished to remain attached to the League, provided it upheld the principle of equality of all members and opposed the attempts toward a great powers' hegemony. Similarly, Poland energetically opposed revisionism, although Beck made no specific references to Anschluss, the Balkans, or the Little Entente.

Girsa considered these statements as the first real attempt to improve the Czechoslovak-Polish relations in the *political* sphere. Beneš also seemed impressed, and decided to put aside his amour propre by making yet another offer to Warsaw. He assumed, as already mentioned, that Poland was returning to a pro-French line. True, Mastný reported from Berlin that Lipski was preparing something, but he also wrote that Bülow had dismissed a written accord with Poland as "a papier de plus."[86] The Czernin Palace believed that although the Poles might be interested in a non-aggression pact with Germany, its realization was "problematic." Doubts about Polish loyalty persisted.[87]

Beneš empowered Girsa to "offer formally to Poland a pact of friendship possibly completed by organized military collaboration" (l'organisation de la collaboration militaire eventuelle). As the envoy told Laroche, "we are proposing a defensive alliance based on the pacific principles of our foreign policy," a somewhat ambiguous formula. Returning from Prague, where he went for Christmas, the Czechoslovak envoy announced that he was the carrier of a message from Beneš and was immediately (8 January?) received by Beck. He accompanied the offer with a statement on Czechoslovak views on the international situation, reciprocating the Polish confidences. Prague, he said, was firmly attached to the League and to France, with whom it was in full accord on how to strive for the preservation of peace. If France and Poland were attacked by Germany, Czechoslovakia would aid them with all its forces. A bloc composed of France, the Little Entente, and Poland was the best guarantor of peace provided it remained unaffected by internal splits. Beck responded that he needed time to reflect on the Czechoslovak offer, and Girsa understood that this meant consulting Piłsudski. The answer would be given to Beneš in Geneva, but

85. A few days earlier Piłsudski told Herman Rauschning: "Poland would never under any circumstances respond to any German attempts to turn Polish efforts toward the Russian Ukraine," cited in Weinberg, *Foreign Policy*, 72.

86. Mastný report, 14 Dec. 1933, ANM, Mastný, dodatky, sv.6.

87. Noël to Paul-Boncour 29 Dec. 1933, MAE, Z 864.10, Tchécoslovaquie 2604.

should a decision be taken earlier, Girsa would be asked to transmit it to Prague.[88]

The importance of Beneš's proposal consisted in the possible addition of formalized military collaboration to a friendship pact, which Beneš was ready to discuss further on a visit to Warsaw. Underestimating the likelihood of a German-Polish declaration of nonaggression, he apparently did not think it necessary to win over Warsaw at all cost—that is, by accommodating Czechoslovak foreign policy to that of Poland. Was Beck's original overture a tactical maneuver? The chronology is important. Two days before the first Beck–Girsa conversation Lipski had resumed talks with Neurath, but a Polish counterproject to a German proposal was not ready until 28 December. If Beck's mind was already set, Piłsudski gave his approval only on 9 January. It is likely that Warsaw was still undecided what course to take and was checking how far Czechoslovakia would be willing to go in its cooperation with Poland. Beneš's proposal must have been judged insufficiently attractive to change the course, and Girsa was not summoned again to the Brühl Palace. Laroche, who tried to elicit Beck's views on the subject of Czechoslovak-Polish relations, met with evasions.[89]

What were the Poles after? Warsaw's main preoccupation at this point was with possible French concessions to Germany in the matter of disarmament and security. Possibly Poland tried to gain Prague to stiffen the stand of Paris or even jointly to oppose and restrain French policies. Talking to the British, Beck discretely criticized London's policy of pushing France toward an accord with Berlin, which would affect many other states beside France. He contrasted it with a possible German-Polish agreement that would concern only the two countries.[90]

On 1 January 1934, the French presented a memorandum to Berlin that expressed the willingness to examine proposals tending to promote peace and international collaboration. The memorandum, resulting from diverse pressures at home, was conciliatory in form but still unacceptable to Germany. The Poles were glad to see Berlin reject it, which made Paul-Boncour—who consistently failed to understand Polish policy toward disarmament—express the hope that Poland would at least not oppose the French line in Geneva. On his side, Beck hoped to elucidate matters in further conversations with the French foreign minister.[91] Noting the nervousness surrounding German-Polish détente, Beck stated publicly that the

---

88. Laroche to Paul-Boncour, 9 Jan. 1934, MAE, Z 864.5, Tchécoslovaquie 2386.

89. See DDF, 1, v:431, 456, and Laroche dispatch, 14 Jan. 1933, MAE, Z 698.1, Pologne 2100.

90. See DDF, 1, v:379–81; Erskine dispatch, 7 Jan. 1934, FO 371 17744 C 153.

91. DDF, 1, v:440–43; Laroche to Paul-Boncour, 12 Jan. 1934, MAE, Z 698.12, Pologne 2198.

relations between France and Poland continued to be based on the 1921 alliance. There was no need "to change a single word in these documents."[92] At this point, the Polish foreign minister was already determined to accept the German proposal for nonaggression, "even if," as he told the British ambassador Sir William Erskine, "France rejected [a]similar proposal but they [the Poles] would see to it that such a pact did not affect [the] French alliance."[93]

Paris did not seem to realize the gravity of the situation. Several rightist senators expressed their usual concern with foreign policy in general and the eastern allies in particular who "represented the surest security" France had. One must help Poland ("worried if not discontented") and the Little Entente to improve their armaments. Paul-Boncour protested against the "myth" according to which French ties with the eastern countries were weakening; on the contrary, they were "solid and more alive than ever." France was also seeking other friends, notably Italy and Russia, but not reverting to a policy of blocs or old-type alliances. Before France would be obliged to turn to armaments every other means of negotiations must be exhausted.[94]

On the eve of Beck's departure for Geneva, Laroche conveyed to him Paul-Boncour's desire to visit Poland sometime in February 1934. This information could no longer have any impact on the proceeding German-Polish exchanges. Beck mentioned the latter, possibly in a casual manner, to the French foreign minister in Geneva, suggesting that Laroche, who was then in Paris, return to Warsaw. Paul-Boncour passed this message to the ambassador orally on 25 January, on the eve of the signing of the German-Polish declaration.[95]

The Beck–Beneš conversation in Geneva on 20 January, which was to bring the Polish answer to the Czechoslovak offer, was bound to be inconclusive. A good deal of time was spent on developing the points that had been made in previous exchanges. Still, Beck seemed eager to talk to Beneš, and the latter remarked that he displayed a greater courtesy and goodwill than on earlier occasions. Beck reiterated that the relationships to Russia, Germany, and the Baltic states were the three vital questions and drew Beneš's attention to the fact that both the great neighbors of Poland were outside the League. The powers that sought cooperation outside of Geneva (i.e., the Four Power Pact) were weakening it even more. Warsaw, having achieved a good relationship with the USSR, was in the process of settling

92. Interview for *Excelsior*, 6 Jan. 1934, Beck, *Przemówienia*, 89–93.

93. Erskine to Foreign Office, 7 Jan. 1934, FO 371 17744 C 153.

94. Ambruster and Millerand, 12 Jan.; Lémery, Paul-Boncour, Jouvenel, 16 Jan. 1934, J.O. Sénat, 18–25, 37–42, 44–50.

95. Laroche, *Pologne*, 146–47.

the German problem, and although it knew that Germany was dangerous and could not be trusted, conversations with Nazi Germany proved easier than with the Weimar republic. Poland's relations with France would remain unchanged; in the Baltic area the goal was to achieve a balance with other powers. In comparison, Polish interests elsewhere were secondary, but Poland was now freer to turn to the region south of the Carpathians, largely neglected thus far, that comprised nations with whom it had common interests. There was the alliance with Romania that remained valuable; it would be necessary to resolve all questions touching on the Polish relationship to Czechoslovakia.

In turn, Beneš characterized his diplomacy as being determined by the Geneva policy and the existing alliances, the two being interconnected. Czechoslovakia stood close to France, and although it had no controversies with Germany it would be on the French side in case of a Franco-German clash. Unlike Poland, Prague treated Central Europe as a very important area. Because of the Little Entente it had no fear of Hungary, but Austria remained a burning issue. The great powers understood, however, that this was an all-European problem that would have to be dealt with as such. As for Czechoslovak-Polish relations, Beneš emphasized the continuity of Prague's policy, and complained of perennial Polish noninvolvement with his country. Their relations could be envisaged in three variants: unchanged (correct but characterized by some indifference, imprecision, and periodic friction); clarified (achieved by the elimination of misunderstandings, which was important because the year 1934 would be "une année tournante"); or improved (based on a pact of friendship).

Beneš said he could live with either of the three situations. He intimated that he favored a pact of friendship for which everything was prepared. He would like to reach a settlement also "for personal reasons, because he had resolved all other questions" affecting his country. He was not influenced merely by the current state of German affairs, but he did feel that "the development of the situation in Germany created a favorable atmosphere at home, so that nothing now stood in the way of a definite clarification of Czechoslovak-Polish relations—neither our Germans nor the views of our political parties toward your regime."[96]

The Czechoslovak foreign minister alluded to general staff collaboration but did not speak of a military alliance sensu stricto, and Beck did not press him. Beneš later told Noël that he was not at all keen on a "military accord with Marshal Piłsudski" (*je n'y tiens nullement*) and much pre-

96. The date of 19 Jan. given by some sources is erroneous. Czechoslovak note of the conversation, 20 Jan. 1934 in Polish translation, Balcerak, "Legenda," 201–206. Compare Beneš's account in Noël to Paul-Boncour, 31 Jan., MAE, Z 684.5, Tchécoslovaquie 2586; also briefing, 25 Jan., KV, CPP.

ferred "unofficial cooperation" on the staff level.[97] Although he said it after the signature of the German-Polish declaration, and may have been making *bonne mine au mouvais jeu*, it probably reflected his view all along. At least one of Beneš's objectives was to gain an alibi, so that if Czechoslovak-Polish relations did not improve, it would be evident that "this is not our fault."

Regarding the current state of German-Polish negotiations, Beneš informed the missions that he had learned of the German offer of a non-aggression declaration to Poland during the Christmas of 1933 but did not mention it to Beck.[98] Beneš contradicted this statement in a letter to the British historian Lewis Namier written during World War II and in a remark made to the German emissary to Prague Albrecht Haushoffer in 1936. He wrote that he had asked Beck "directly whether he was negotiating with Berlin. He denied everything categorically."[99] Speaking to Haushoffer, Beneš provided another version, maintaining that he knew about the pact because "Beck told me everything."[100]

During the Geneva encounter, Beck fenced as well as Beneš. If he showed an eagerness to explain Polish policy, this was mainly to keep the lines of communication with Prague open. The interpretation that Beck wished to say more but was stopped by Beneš's remark that Czechoslovakia did not feel endangered by Germany is not very convincing. Nor is it plausible to see in Beck's reference to Polish interests south of the Carpathians an overture for closer cooperation with Prague.[101] The Polish foreign minister later wrote that he wanted Beneš to know that the Poles were aware of his real attitude, which sounds a bit nebulous. He also dwelt on his critical observations about the Czechoslovak treatment of the Polish minority, which may have been at best of marginal importance in the conversation.[102]

The Geneva encounter showed once again that the ways of Polish and Czechoslovak diplomacy were virtually irreconcilable. Their uneasy relationship was likely to develop only in one direction by becoming more strained and antagonistic.

97. Noël to Daladier, 31 Jan. 1934, DDF, I, v:575.

98. Circular, 28 Jan. 1934 (mentioning Girsa 19 Jan. report), CPP. Printed with some omissions in Beneš, *Memoirs*, 44–46. The relevant words are: "not one word was said about negotiating or signing the declaration." Compare Grzybowski report, 29 Jan., AAN, MSZ, 5504.

99. Namier, *Europe in Decay*, 288.

100. Cited in Pułaski, *Stosunki*, 140, based on Haushoffer report.

101. Balcerak, "Legenda," and criticism by Tomaszewski and Valenta, "Polska," 715–16.

102. Beck, *Dernier rapport*, 51–52.

The Declaration of 26 January 1934

The German-Polish declaration on the nonuse of force—more commonly if less accurately called a nonaggression pact—satisfied the Poles on what they regarded as the essential points: explicit maintenance of all of previous international obligations; a reference to the Kellogg–Briand pact but not to Locarno; and a clause forbidding interference in domestic (i.e., national minority) issues. The document, given its effect on international relations, met with a good deal of criticism then and later. Among French historians, Maurice Baumont, criticizing Polish "blind naïveté" tinged with "arrogance," opined that Poland had become an "annex to German policy." J. B. Duroselle spoke of Warsaw's "little game" with a "potential adversary whose bad faith was evident, under the pretext of turning the thunder away from it." For Bariéty and Bloch the net effect of the declaration was that France "had lost its principal ally in Eastern Europe"; Vaïsse called the pact "the end of the Franco-Polish alliance." According to Neré, Poland had made a choice between its two neighbors. Gerhard Weinberg as well as Kvaček and Olivová stressed that the pact enabled Nazi Germany to overcome its isolation and break the ring of French alliances around it, and facilitated its Drang nach Osten. The "deliberate secrecy" with which the Poles surrounded the negotiations had contributed to this nefarious result.[103] A prominent historian of Nazi foreign policy judged the declaration "an extraordinary political success of Hitler," which the traditional conservative circles viewed with horror as implying the abandonment of revisionism vis-à-vis Poland.[104]

Seen from the contemporary London perspective, the importance of the declaration lay not so much in what it said but in what it implied. Protected by Locarno in the west, Hitler took a great risk and paid a high price to "rid himself of the danger of a preventive war on his eastern frontier." Claiming to have made a telling contribution to European security, he could argue that Paris may no longer justify its opposition to a reduction of armaments by citing the endangered Poland. One could assume that Hitler had in mind an anti-Soviet policy based on cooperation between Berlin and Warsaw, but it was uncertain whether Poland would consent to play "so dangerous a game with so dangerous a partner." But Poland might find it difficult in the long run to resist constant German pressure.[105]

103. Baumont, *Origins*, 90; Duroselle, *Décadence*, 101; Bariéty and Bloch, "Une Tentative," 463; Vaïsse, *Sécurité*, 476; Neré, *Foreign Policy*, 141; Weinberg, *Foreign Policy*, 73; Olivová and Kvaček, *Dějiny Československa*, 193. Compare Lapter, *Pakt*; Gasiorowski, "German-Polish Nonaggression Pact," Cienciala, "Significance."

104. Jacobsen, *Locarno*, 404.

105. Sargent's minutes on Phipps report, 27 Jan. 1934, FO 371 17744 C 676.

Beck saw the situation in a somewhat similar but not an identical fashion. Hitler sought to overcome Germany's isolation and to weaken the French alliance system. He subscribed to a bilateral rather than multilateral approach to international relations. Allegedly critical of the historic Prussian pro-Russian policies, he initiated a "radical turn" for the better in German-Polish relations. In that sense the declaration transcended "usual neighborly relations."[106] Polish diplomacy did not seem to worry unduly about Hitler's hopes of associating Warsaw in a common drive against the USSR. It was only four years later that Szembek, wondering about this element as the main motive behind the declaration, commented that if this were so then "the whole policy of good neighborhood, stemming from the 1934 agreement," was "a fiction."[107]

Piłsudski's motives and his appraisal of the declaration emerge from the remarks at a meeting with the president, Beck, and several former premiers on 7 March. Piłsudski recalled that since the end of the war Poland had been regarded as the "center of troubles." The alliance with France "did not bring sufficient strength, and it was necessary to make sacrifices." Everyone exploited Poland's exposed position, and the Poles could only lick everyone's boots. While Russia agreed to establish peaceful relations, Germany remained hostile. Piłsudski recalled his initiative to demand some "guarantee of security" from Berlin, and how Hitler seized this opportunity, acting against the Prussian tradition. This psychological change in Germany was more important than written agreements. Through the declaration, Poland achieved a position it had never had before and accomplished a most difficult thing—namely, conclusion of pacts with Russia and Germany without any additional commitments on the Polish side. Because Germany and Russia were quarreling, it was essential not to engage Poland to support one side against the other. As for the alliances, they had to be maintained as counterweight, but Poland need no longer pay for them with sacrifices. Piłsudski warned that these good relations with Germany "may last perhaps for four more years"—the declaration was valid for ten—but he could not guarantee a longer period. Piłsudski ruminated that it would be difficult to maintain the existing state of affairs after his death, for he had a special knack for initiating delays or changes when they became necessary.[108]

Obviously, the marshal was well aware of the precariousness of the balance between Germany and Russia. As he put it a few months later: "We

106. See Beck to ministry, 17 Jan. 1933, DTJS, I, 131; Jędrzejewicz, *Lipski*, 122–23; Kennard dispatch, 4 Feb. 1935, Fo 371 18846 Hm 04023; Beck's speech in Beck, *Przemówienia*, 96–100.

107. Szembek–Grzybowski conversation, 10 Dec. 1938, DTJS, IV, 380.

108. Full text in Wandycz, "Wypowiedzi." Inadequate summary in Beck, *Dernier rapport*, 61–63. For Beck echoing Piłsudski that one could not count on ten years of truce, see Kennard dispatch 4 Feb. 1925, FO 371 18896 Hm 04023.

are sitting on two stools that cannot last long. We must know which one we shall fall off first and when."[109] In early April, he asked a selected group of generals and colonels (plus Beck and Szembek) to ponder this question and report in writing. The majority thought Germany represented the greater threat, but those who put Russia first comprised such leading generals as Sosnkowski, Rydz-Śmigły, Kasprzycki, and Gąsiorowski. Beck and Szembek considered Russia more dangerous in the short run but thought the situation would change in about three to four years. Piłsudski himself inclined to view Russia as more threatening, and he opined that while Poland was likely to confront Germany in the company of other states, it might have to face Russia alone.[110]

The official interpretation of the declaration was provided by Beck and Radziwiłł (as chairman of the foreign affairs commission). Disclaiming naïveté and denying unwillingness to continue cooperation with the League, despite its inability to resolve major international problems, they stressed that the Franco-Polish alliance was in no way affected. The declaration "concerned exclusively matters involving the two states." France and Romania had been informed beforehand of the negotiations leading to the signature. Polish diplomats abroad were enjoined to underline very strongly that it was useless to seek any hidden objectives beyond those spelled out in the text.[111]

At Brühl Palace there was elation over the greater freedom of diplomatic maneuver, although Lipski was repeating "pourvu que ça dure."[112] Such former heads of foreign ministry as Kajetan Morawski and Zaleski welcomed the declaration as a very important tactical gain.[113] The opposition, although recognizing the usefulness of the document, appealed for vigilance and was worried about a possible estrangement with France. The conservative publicist, Stanisław Cat-Mackiewicz, opined that if the event were to increase tension between France and Germany, it would not be a bad thing from the Polish viewpoint.[114]

Paris saw the declaration as a blow not only to its foreign policy but also

---

109. Noted by General Fabrycy, DTJS, I, 155.

110. See DTJS, I, 153–54; analysis in Bułhak, "W Sprawie oceny," 370–72.

111. See DTJS, I, 134; Beck, *Przemówienia*, 96–100; Radziwiłł speech reported by Laroche to Barthou, 21 Feb. 1934, MAE, Z 698.1, Pologne 2100.

112. Schimitzek, *Drogi*, 368.

113. See Kajetan Morawski, *Wczoraj* (London, 1967), 217; Wandycz, *Zaleski*, 131.

114. *Gazeta Warszawska*, 28 Jan., 8 Feb., 13, 15 Apr. 1934; *Robotnik*, 3, 8, 20 Feb. Debates, 5–6 Feb., 13 Mar., Sprawozdania stenograficzne, sejmu 22–23, 52–60, 62–68, 79, 88, 92. Compare Faryś, *Koncepcje*, 284, 310, 368; Ziaja, *PPS*, 216–22; On Mackiewicz, see Micewski, *W Cieniu*, 145 and Jerzy Jaruzelski, *Mackiewicz i konserwatyści* (Warszawa, 1976), 145. Laroche comments in dispatches, 6, 7 Feb., 195, MAE, Z 698.1, Pologne 2100.

to its prestige. The announcement had come as a surprise, and the text was not officially shown.[115] The Quai d'Orsay tried hard to conceal its vexation; Paul-Boncour endeavored to save face through a public statement cleared with the Poles. "France," it said, "had been kept very fully and very amicably au courant of the talks which resulted in a solution that I regard as happy for Poland and for peace." The minister expressed satisfaction that the pact settled peaceably the neighborly relations between Poland and Germany, while expressly maintaining the validity of all previous Polish engagements, including the alliance with France, the Polish-German arbitration treaty signed in Locarno, and the obligations under the Covenant.[116]

Few people in the know were deceived by these assurances and by French attempts to behave as if nothing had happened. François-Poncet, who took Lipski's silence during the negotiations as a personal insult, excluded the envoy from friendly gatherings of allied diplomats. "Lipski est un cochon," he told his British colleague; the Romanian minister echoed that Poland was guilty of bigamy.[117] The French ambassador conceived of a German-Polish pact as acceptable only if concluded under the auspices of the League and "more particularly with the agreement and participation of France."[118]

French diplomacy scrutinized the text looking for objectionable or ambiguous wording, and came up with several questions. Could Poland remain true to the League if a third party's intervention in German-Polish relations was excluded? Did the declaration abrogate the 1925 German-Polish arbitration treaty, and, if so, did the Franco-Polish treaty of that year remain valid? Could force be legitimately used in a controversy over national minorities? A situation arose in which it would be useful "to examine if our political and military accords with Poland should not be clarified." A note from the army quarters, while opining that Warsaw probably wanted to gain time and improve its military potential, underlined Berlin's likely intention to use the declaration to sow doubts in France about the value of the Polish alliance as well as to prevent Czechoslovak-Polish cooperation. Berlin might even seek to gain Poland's neutrality in case of Anschluss or expansion directed at Czechoslovakia. Laroche con-

115. The French embassy had no communications from 21 Dec. to 26 Jan., See DDF, I, VII:907–10.

116. See *Le Temps*, 28 Jan. 1934; DTJS, I, 133; Laroche, *Pologne* and in DDF, I, V:642–43. Compare DBFP, II, VI:349, 357–60; DVP SSSR, XVII, 99–100; Cudahy to Secretary of State, 24 Feb. 1934, SDNA, 760C.6212/24.

117. Phipps to Sargent, 6 Feb. 1934, FO 371 1774 C 871; compare François-Poncet dispatches, DDF, I, V:542–43, 621–25, 822–24. In the last he said that as a person Lipski was "charming, courteous, and well-disposed toward France."

118. François-Poncet, *Souvenirs*, 164.

curred that the Germans could exploit the declaration to undermine French confidence in Poland. This approach would replace the old line of Poland being a danger to peace and a liability to France.[119]

Laroche wondered if the Poles were sophisticated enough politically to appreciate all these consequences; they had difficulties in understanding Western mentality and the complexity of European politics. They might have seized the opportunity of a deal with Berlin without thinking too much about long-range repercussions. On the other hand, in view of their exposed position, they might not really be able to adopt long-range perspectives.[120]

Telling Laroche not to look for things that were not in the text, Piłsudski assured him that Polish freedom of action toward Austria, Russia, and the Baltic countries remained unchanged. Poland was also free to act should disarmament talks fail and France take a firm stand, invoking perhaps article 213 of Versailles. Piłsudski resorted to heavy irony when speaking of French firmness. It was precisely because he doubted it that he had signed the declaration. He had wanted to prolong the conversations with the Germans but accelerated them because of François-Poncet's talks with Berlin. This was a half-truth, but the marshal was sincere when he asserted that if Germany had accepted the French disarmament memorandum of 1 January, the bases of Versailles would have been sapped. Laroche countered by saying that while Poland had every right to settle its relations with Germany, and a détente was desirable, the "operation of our alliances and our efforts for the organization of security" must not be harmed thereby.[121] The French would return to this issue again and again.

General d'Arbonneau believed that the declaration, although not adding anything strikingly new to the Hitler–Lipski communiqué, represented a high point in the evolution of Polish thinking about France. Piłsudski began to view the alliance with "a slight condescension of one who thinks he can give more than he receives," even though he had no intention of abandoning military cooperation. In fact, the reception of French intelligence officers led by a Major Schlesser was warmer than in the past. The French noted "frank and loyal" Polish offers of "perfect collaboration."[122] French public opinion, however, was not appeased. Uniformly critical of the January declaration, the press circulated rumors about secret clauses. Had France not been then in the midst of a domestic crisis, the adverse coverage of the German-Polish accord would have been much wider.[123]

119. See respectively, DDF, 1, v:542–43, 560–61, 610–11, 737–40, 891–92.

120. Laroche dispatches, 6 Feb., 7 Mar. 1934, DDF, 1, v:641–44, 891.

121. Laroche to Paul-Boncour, 29 Jan. 1934, DDF, 1, v:552–55.

122. See SHA, EMA/2, Pologne 43; also Castellan, *Reich*, 427–77. Compare d'Arbonneau reports, 14 Feb., 3 Apr. 1934, SHA, EMA/2, Pologne 12.

123. See Kuźmiński, *Polska*, 148–50.

François-Poncet contrasted Polish secretive behavior—a sign of guilty conscience—with the loyalty of the Czechs.[124] The latter, upset by the January declaration, did their best not to show it and even made some positive comments initially. The *Prager Presse* deemed the pact advantageous for Poland and Czechoslovakia, provided it had no ulterior motives. Subsequently (29 January) it surmised that Germany wanted to obtain a free hand in the southeast. *České Slovo* (27 January) viewed the declaration as a completion of Locarno and thought that it removed the immediate cause of a European conflict. The next day, the paper qualified its assessment by noting that Germany had broken out of her isolation and could concentrate on Austria, and on 30 January, it critically analyzed the declaration's impact on Poland, Germany, and Czechoslovakia. Was the Czernin Palace influencing the commentaries? Within a short time the tenor of the whole press—Slovak autonomists and the extreme Right excepted—became strongly negative.[125]

Beneš was obviously annoyed that he had not been forewarned by Beck or Paul-Boncour in Geneva.[126] Summoning Grzybowski he wanted to know if Poland had assured Germany of its disinterest in Austria and promised not to conclude a military accord with Czechoslovakia. Grzybowski thought it most unlikely, and he explained the background and the intent of the declaration in the already-familiar terms. Beneš commented that the Poles would actually be helping Hitler to reverse the Stresemann priorities on the "corridor" and Anschluss. The declaration could push France toward an agreement with Berlin, which surely would be unacceptable to Warsaw. The declaration was a blow to European politics, because Germany could now rearm without any restraints. The entire French system was undermined, and time was operating in favor of Germany, not of France and its allies. The minister uttered a veiled threat, namely that he would no longer be morally bound against making diplomatic moves behind Warsaw's back. He was still prepared, however, to implement any of the three variants in Czechoslovak-Polish relations he had mentioned to Beck. Grzybowski wrote that he had never yet seen Beneš so depressed, worried and disoriented. The German-Polish declaration had filled him with great anxiety, and he evidently wished to salvage at least the appearance of good relations with Warsaw.[127]

124. François-Poncet to Daladier, 4 Feb. 1934, DDF, I, v:622.

125. Press surveys in trimestrial reports, SHA, EMA/2, Tchécoslovaquie 9. Compare Grzybowski reports in Łossowski, "Stosunki," 140.

126. See DDF, I, v:545–46; Gen. Faucher's letter, 29 Jan. 1934, SHA, EMA/2, Tchécoslovaquie 3; briefing, 1 Feb., KV, CPP.

127. Grzybowski report, 29 Jan. 1934, AAN, MSZ 5504; Beneš, *Paměti*, 16–17; DDF, I, v:551–52. Beneš's "usual optimistic tone was lacking," reported Benton to Secretary of State, 1 Feb. SDNA, 840.00/398.

Beneš devoted an entire circular telegram to an analysis of the German-Polish declaration.[128] He sounded more optimistic that he actually was, when opining that Germany's greater freedom of action toward Austria was no cause for concern. He anticipated Berlin's overtures to Prague, which would not be heeded without consulting Paris. The near future would show to what extent the January declaration was a mistake, and he warned representatives abroad not to be misled by the press or official statements. The official attitude toward the document was as follows: If Warsaw really thought it would last for ten years it was mistaken for the exclusion of territorial issues contained germs of conflict. "In spite of this it represents a temporary lull from which we can also profit. The declaration will, at least morally, hinder revisionist undertakings. Besides, Poland was gaining time through the agreement, and the remaining [countries], including us, can gain respite at least to the same degree as the Poles. As for Poland's attitude toward us, we need have no fears. . . ." [this passage was deleted from the printed text]. The advantages for Germany consisted in overcoming the threat of isolation, gaining time to grow stronger (which it could do more effectively than Poland), indirectly strengthening the anti-Geneva line, and exploiting this seeming proof of pacific intentions against France. Beneš questioned Warsaw's assumption that the great powers would fail to reach agreement on disarmament. Czechoslovak policy, he concluded, remained unchanged, and Prague continued its endeavors for rapprochement with Warsaw, which entailed a pact of friendship. Commenting on this point, Krofta was closer to the truth when he said that in fact Czechoslovak policy toward Poland was affected, for hitherto Prague had been able to count on Polish military cooperation.[129]

D'Arbonneau contested the view that the change in the military configuration stemmed from German pressure on Poland. Berlin did not need to demand any promises from Warsaw, "as my Czech colleague would like to think," for "only the imminence of a real threat could bring" Poland and Czechoslovakia "closer together. As the danger becomes more remote so does all intention of a rapprochement."[130] The French rejected the assumption that Poland could become an ally of Germany, but if Poland remained neutral, the Czechoslovak military position, if not hopeless, would be extremely grave. An encircled Czechoslovakia could only be saved by external intervention (French, Russian, or Italian): Hungarian

128. 28 Jan. 1934, CPP. Printed with omissions in Beneš, *Paměti*, 17–21 and *Memoirs*, 44–46, where the translation is not always exact.

129. Briefing, 1 Feb. 1934, KV, CPP.

130. D'Arbonneau report, 7 Feb. 1934, SHA, EMA/2, Pologne 12. Jan Masaryk mentioned Beneš's belief that Hitler had actually asked the Poles to promise not to sign a pact with Czechoslovakia but they refused. See DVP SSSR, XVII, 115.

help might have to be purchased at the price of heavy concessions.[131] The feeling that Czechoslovakia, deprived of Polish assistance, would face a desperate situation must have been fairly widespread, because Masaryk had to be brutally outspoken in a small gathering: "A people that really wants to fight," he asserted, "cannot perish."[132]

Meanwhile Czechoslovak-Polish military contacts continued; conferences were duly held on 8–10 February and on 28–31 August. Generals Syrový and Ludvik Krejči (chief of staff) attended a celebration of Piłsudski's birthday, at which General Bláha extolled cooperation between the two armies.[133] This praise contrasted with the harsh words Beneš used when speaking to Soviet and British diplomats about the Poles. The Poles had long tried to direct German expansion toward the southeast, while unjustifiably suspecting Czechoslovakia of doing the same in the north. Poland had always been a useless country, and it lay in Polish character to stab friends in the back. Only the Poles could take seriously this ridiculous pact with Germany. If they got in trouble, they would only get what they deserved. The British envoy, Sir Joseph Addison, wondered whether he "was merely dreaming" of talking with the foreign minister of Czechoslovakia rather than with "Dr. Goebbels or General Goering."[134]

Beneš's anger grew in conjunction with a regular anti-Czech campaign in Poland, which he associated with the declaration of nonaggression. Beck pointedly excluded Girsa when he invited diplomats to hear an explanation of the meaning of the January accord.[135] The Polish governmental press, seconded by *Ilustrowany Kurjer Codzienny* and the conservative *Czas*, denounced the government in Prague and the Czechs for their alleged mistreatment of Poles in Teschen. The tone of these articles was often crude and insulting; public demonstrations added fuel to the heated atmosphere. The campaign reached its high point in early February and March, and then flared up again in June. Czechoslovak-Polish press agreement was one of its victims, as well as individual Czechs and Poles expelled from the two countries. To the Czechs and the French, it all looked like a series of calculated Polish provocations exploiting the smallest Czechoslovak transgression for some hidden political purpose.[136]

131. See note, DDF, I, v:738–40; compare DBFP, II, VI:563.

132. Cited in Noël to Barthou, 18 May 1934, DDF, I, VI:503.

133. See Bułhak, "Z Dziejów 1927–1936," 133–36; compare Col. Czerwiński's analysis, 4 May 1934, AAN, MSZ 5504. For ceremony, Agence Havas, 19 Mar.

134. Addison to Simon, 3 Feb. 1934, FO 371 18517 W 1510/1/98. Also DaM, II, 459–64.

135. Laroche to Daladier, 2 Feb. 1934, MAE, Z 864.5, Tchécoslovaquie 2586.

136. See Kozeński, *Czechosłowacja*, 81–89, 130–36; *Češi a Poláci*, 2:551–54; press cuttings in MZV-VA 478.1250; Noël reports in MAE, Z 864.5, Tchécoslovaquie 2586.

The national democratic, Christian democratic, populist, and socialist press in Poland voiced its concern. What had suddenly changed for the worse in the position of the Polish minority in Czechoslovakia? Naturally, the Poles in Teschen had to be protected and their grievances redressed, but the whole issue must be treated in reference to complex international problems. Why concentrate all the fire on the Czechs? Cui bono? asked *Kurjer Warszawski.*[137]

Polish governmental circles denied that the press campaign was "the first direct consequence of the Polish-German declaration."[138] Yet, a connection between the two indubitably existed. The declaration gave the Poles a feeling of self-confidence and elation. As the British put it somewhat crudely, at last Poland could "afford the luxury of a brawl with her less powerful and well-hated neighbour."[139] While the foreign service had been fanning the Polish irredentist flame for some time, the new consul in Moravská Ostrava, Leon Malhomme, began to do it more brazenly. Even the army organ *Polska Zbrojna* (6 April 1934) displayed a certain malice over the weakening of the Czechoslovak position as compared with Poland's. In a memorandum on "Czechoslovakia in 1933," Grzybowski opined that Beneš by following Briandism had shown lack of political realism, and the advent of Hitler invalidated the three basic premises of Prague's foreign policy: Czechoslovakia was an indispensable element of postwar Europe, furthered its objectives through international institutions, and relied on a policy of alliances. Prague had to reorient its course and oscillate between France and Poland. At this point, Warsaw's coolness left Paris as the only alternative, but Grzybowski judged that for military and economic reasons Czechoslovakia's gravitation toward Poland would have to increase. Warsaw should not encourage this process prematurely but wait until it could dictate the conditions of a rapprochement.[140] A contemporary document drafted at Brühl Palace, after stressing that "we can only exist as a power," argued that Poland must achieve leadership in the region. Because Czechoslovakia proved not to be a possible partner, its elimination from the diplomatic game would be beneficial.[141]

If the above notions accurately reflected the trend of Polish diplomacy,

---

Also pamphlet *Sytuacja ludności polskiej w Czecho-Słowacji: memorjał polskich stronnictw politycznych w Czecho-Słowacji* (Warszawa, 1934).

137. See *Kurjer Warszawski*, 18 Mar. 1934, *Gazeta Warszawska*, 20 Mar., 12, 17 Apr., 4 July; *Robotnik*, 24, 29 Mar.; *Piast*, 1 Apr.; numerous articles in *Polonia* throughout Mar. Compare d'Arbonneau report, 3 Apr., SHA, EMA/2, Pologne.

138. Kvaček, *Nad Evropou*, 77–78; compare Káňa and Pavelka, *Těšínsko*, 41.

139. Annual report 1934, Poland, FO 371 18887 C 85.

140. Grzybowski to Beck, 14 Mar. 1934, AAN, Amb. Berlin, 52.

141. Summary of unsigned draft (Feb. or March 1934?) and comments in Tomaszewski, "Miejsce Polski," 186–90.

the pressure on Prague and an increased interest in Slovakia become much more understandable. Grzybowski had already recommended in December 1933 that the Slovaks be taken more seriously. The Hlinka populist (ľudák) party had taken in early 1933 a more determined stand, demanding not only autonomy but a transformation of the republic into a federation. If Rev. Andrej Hlinka himself appeared conceited, ambitious, and too prudent to throw his political lot unreservedly with Poland, the rising Slovak leaders, notably Karol Sidor, were strongly polonophile and deserved to be supported. In July 1934, Hlinka wished for the Slovaks to become a "golden bridge" between Czechs and Poles; on several occasions the *Slovák* called for a pro-Polish course and criticized Beneš's policy.[142]

The anti-Czech campaign, all its emotional aspects notwithstanding, may be seen then as an attempt to "soften" Prague and to prepare the Polish public opinion for political changes. The older concept of pressuring Czechoslovakia and the Little Entente through Romania was making room for policies of confrontation. Whether the final goal was to force Prague to cooperate with Warsaw on Polish terms or to eliminate it as a political factor was probably not yet decided. Thus, the Czechs oversimplified the issue when they argued that Polish attempts to weaken Czechoslovakia (which facilitated Germany's role in the Danubian region) was a quid pro quo for Berlin's respect of the "corridor."[143]

Insofar as the declaration of nonaggression was the culmination of a policy of balance, it naturally mattered that the equilibrium also be maintained on the eastern, Soviet side. Seeking to dispel Russian anxiety over the November Hitler–Lipski communiqué, the Poles had expressed interest in a common effort to strengthen security in the Baltic region. Litvinov promptly proposed a formal agreement; Warsaw hesitated. A rapprochement in this area could solidify Soviet-Polish relations and drive another wedge between the USSR and Germany, but it could also be a trap to confine Poland's freedom of maneuver and be seen in Berlin as an inimical act. Besides, the countries concerned, especially Finland, opposed outside guarantees, and Warsaw did not wish to compromise its position.[144]

142. See consular reports from Bratislava, notably 26 Apr. 1933, AAN, Pos. Praga, 38. Also Noël to Barthou, 11 July, 1 Sept. 1934, MAE, Z 864.5, Tchécoslovaquie 2587. On Slovak-Polish relations in addition to earlier-mentioned works: Alena Bartlová, "Slovensko-poľske vztáhy v rokoch 1919–1938," *Historický Časopis*, 20 (1972) and her "Przyczynek," and the more directly relevant Batowski, "Z poľsko-slovenských." Also Kozeński, *Czechosłowacja*, 190–85; for background Karol Sidor, *Andrej Hlinka, 1864–1926* (Bratislava, 1934).

143. See Hubert Ripka in *Lidové Noviny*, 17 Aug. 1934; compare Noël to Barthou, 17 Aug., MAE, Z 864.5, Tchécoslovaquie 2587.

144. On this complex issue, see Jędrzejewicz, *Lipski*, 131–34; Leczyk, *Polityka*, 342–46; Skrzypek, *Strategia*, 103–109; Budurowycz, *Polish-Soviet Relations*, 40; Zacharias, *Polska*, 113–19; Gregorowicz, *Polsko-radzieckie stosunki*, 144–66; Fabry, *Die Sowje-*

The signing of the January declaration met with Soviet reservations.[145] The Russian diplomacy reiterated its desire to see Beck in Moscow, possibly having in mind some political agreement, perhaps an alliance, as a "guarantee of our unchanged negative attitude toward Hitlerite Germany."[146] The Polish foreign minister wanted also to go in order to demonstrate publicly that the Berlin declaration was not contrary to Soviet-Polish détente. He was determined, however, to treat with "utmost circumspection" any Soviet political proposals that "without bringing us real Russian support could complicate our relations with other powers."[147] Beck suspected the French of having "intentionally represented to Poland that the Soviet Government was much more irritated by, and suspicious of, Polish policy with regard to Germany that was in fact the case."[148] The lavish reception in Moscow only confirmed his view. Beck's belief, however, that the visit was a great political success was not borne out by facts.[149]

The conversations between 13 and 15 February showed that Litvinov was not convinced by Beck's analysis of the German situation. He particularly doubted whether the decline of Prussian ascendancy and the internal difficulties of the Reich were cause for optimism. He shared neither Beck's view that Hitler did not want war, nor the Pole's preference for bilateralism. The commissar thought that Beck's attitude closed the way for exploring the possibilities of a Soviet-Polish political or military entente directed against Germany. He did not think that a secret German-Polish agreement existed but did not rule out its appearance in the future. Litvinov concluded that Poland wished to obscure its new policy by stressing good relations with Russia.[150] Such tactics temporarily suited Moscow.

Apart from a subsequent prolongation of the nonaggression treaty and the elevation of respective legations to embassy rank in April, the Moscow talks produced no results. Beck had not succeeded in convincing the Russians of the merits of Warsaw's policy of balance or in allaying their perennial mistrust of Poland.

---

tunion, 41–43. Also DDF, I, v:62–63, 111–12, 399–400; DiM, VI, 136, 147; Beck-Antonov Ovseienko conversations, 20, 23 Nov. 1933, AAN, MSZ 108.

145. See *Izvestia* and *Pravda*, 29 Jan. 1934, and comments by Chilston to Simon, 29 Jan. and J.V.A. McMurray to Secretary of State, 20 Mar., respectively FO 371 17744 and SDNA 760C.6212/33. Compare Smetana report, 1 Feb., CPP.

146. Łukasiewicz cited in Leczyk, *Polityka*, 349–50.

147. Beck, *Dernier rapport*, 37. Compare Matuszewski in *Gazeta Polska*, 12 Feb. 1934.

148. Beck's remarks to Władysław Besterman in Cudahy to Secretary of State, 20 Feb. 1934, SDNA, 760C.61/670.

149. See DDF, I, v:783–85.

150. See DiM, VI, 185–92; compare DDF, I, v:826–29, 834–35; also Girsa report, 27 Feb. 1934, CPP.

The German-Polish declaration was an important event, and it was use-less to pretend that the situation could ever be the same as before 26 January. Poland embarked on a voyage that was likely to be perilous in the long run, although at this juncture the declaration appeared to be a great success. British congratulations were an accolade to which the Poles had not been accustomed. Embassies in both Moscow and Berlin testified to Poland's increased prestige and its status as an almost great power. It was unlikely that London or Rome would ever again exclude Warsaw from such combinations as the Four Power Pact.

The declaration left the Franco-Polish alliance legally intact, but under a cloud similar in some ways to the shadow cast by Locarno. When asked whether the declaration might not undermine "the effective force" of an understanding with France, Beck replied that the defensive alliance be-tween the two countries had already been modified in 1925.[151] The Polish-German agreement, Jouvenel wrote, was "logically included in the accords of Locarno"; Soutou has opined that the declaration "should not have been a surprise for Paris."[152] Krofta, writing as a historian rather than a politician, estimated that "the absence of will on the part of the Western powers to oppose, together with Poland, energetically the dynamics of the new Germany probably contributed most" to the Berlin accord.[153] It was not so much that the declaration destroyed an anti-Nazi front, for none in effect existed, but it affected future efforts to construct one. Concentrating on developing their own system, based on bilateral relations with their big neighbors, the Poles began to distance themselves from the French system. Could alliances and balance coexist in the long run? Would not the policy of balance become "a more difficult gymnastic feat" than anticipated. As a Foreign Office comment put it, even Britain, which "more than any other European State [had] the qualifications necessary for this difficult policy," was bound largely to abandon it, and "where Great Britain has failed it is not likely that Poland will succeed."[154] A test was to come soon as the new foreign minister of France, Louis Barthou, began a major diplomatic coun-teroffensive in the spring of 1934.

151. Cudahy to Secretary of State, 29 Jan. 1934, SDNA, 760C.6212/14.

152. Jouvenel, *D'une Guerre*, 1:399; Soutou, "L'Alliance," 347.

153. Krofta, *Z Dob*, 100.

154. Sargent's minute, 11 Sept. 1934, with Vansittart's annotation "very true," DBFP, II, VII:734–35, XII:119, n. 3.

Chapter Eleven

Louis Barthou and His Diplomacy

Beginnings

The German-Polish Declaration was barely ten days old when the domestic crisis in France reached its climax. On 6 February, a veritable battle raged on Place de la Concorde. Thousands were wounded, and the nation was on the brink of civil war. The impression these events created in Poland was catastrophic for the French prestige.[1] Krofta saw a certain analogy between the developments in France and those in Italy and Germany that had preceded the rise of Mussolini and Hitler, but he hoped that the country would recover its balance.[2] Foreign commentators spoke of the need for a drastic change. Was the constitution of a cabinet of national union on 9 February, under the presidency of Gaston Doumergue a herald of such a change or a palliative?

The new government, including six former premiers and five ex-foreign ministers ranging from Tardieu to Herriot, looked impressive. Louis Barthou was at the Quai d'Orsay, and Pétain served as minister of war. The septuagenerian Barthou was perhaps the last of the great political figures of the Clemenceau and Poincaré generation. Once close to Poincaré, he was a more adroit negotiator. Critical of Briand's German policies, he nevertheless maintained good personal relations with that statesman. A Gascon, subtle and imaginative, a noted writer and orator, endowed with personal charm and a dry sense of humor, Barthou was a pragmatist rather than a doctrinnaire. Disliked by both the extreme Left and Right, he projected the image of a solid republican, liberal and patriotic.[3]

Barthou perceived in the international situation certain similarities to the state of affairs in 1914. The disarmament debate had reached an impasse, and throughout February and March, Paris traded memoranda with

1. Laroche, *Pologne*, 152; compare Noël to Barthou, 18 Apr. 1934, MAE, Z 864.5 Tchécoslovaquie 2587.

2. Briefing, 8 Feb. 1934, KV, CPP.

3. See characterization by Baumont, *Origins*, 83–84; Duroselle, *Décadence*, 88–92.

Berlin seeking simultaneously to persuade London to undertake concrete engagements. The French believed, as Barthou put it, that "only a Franco-British entente was capable, in the existing conditions, to save liberty."[4] Should Paris accept vague British assurances and a convention on arms limitation that could possibly act as a brake on Germany, or adopt a negative stance, risking estrangement with London and unlimited German rearming? François-Poncet and the military attaché in Berlin advised the former course, and the commission on foreign affairs also favored a convention. Barthou hesitated.[5]

Doumergue, supported by Tardieu and Herriot, opposed any policy that could legalize German rearmament. The general staff, while opposed to cuts in the defense budget, concluded that an enforceable convention replacing Versailles had undoubted merits, although from a strictly military viewpoint it was preferable to retain freedom of action. Such freedom "would allow us to establish, together with our allies, a 'plan of defense of Europe,' the preventive efficacy of which would be known." Weygand believed that it would be impossible for France to sign a convention that officially recognized "German clandestine rearmament." East European aspects were also considered. Because British aid would come after a considerable delay, "only Poland could bring us effective assistance initially" Gamelin argued. Czechoslovakia could resist a German offensive but would need to be assisted by the Little Entente and Poland. Weygand thought that the moment was particularly favorable to redress French foreign policy and do something about the general concern for the fate of Central Europe.[6]

The argument that an effective convention would do more harm than good, morally and from the point of view of enlarging the French alliance system, seemed to gain the upper hand. In early April, the commission of studies of CSDN concluded that controls would be ineffective. A special commission co-chaired by Herriot and Tardieu opined that reductions of French forces were unacceptable. It was better to run the risk of German rearmament. On 16 April, Doumergue produced the draft of a statement that, when adopted the following day by the cabinet, became the famous note that contained the key phrase: "France must put in the first place of its preoccupation the conditions of its own security." Barthou went along

4. See DDF, I, v:741–42.

5. See DDF, I, v:598–600, 812, 829–32, 869–71; VI:725, 735; also ADAP, C, II/2:568–59, 632, 735; sessions 2, 14 Mar. 1934, CAE/Ch; Herriot, *Jadis*, 2:395–96; François-Poncet, *Souvenirs*, 168–75.

6. In Jan. and Feb., Weygand repeated that "it was only in its strength that France could find support for a policy of dignity, calm, moderation and pacifism"; cited in Minart, *Le Drame*, 69. On army reduction debates, see Bankwitz, *Weygand*, 104–106; Gamelin, *Servir*, 2:98–100; 14 Feb. 1934 session, CA/Ch. Documentation in DDF, I, v:875–83, 903, 939–43.

with this formula, possibly converted by Doumergue or swayed by the belief in the need of maintaining a continuity in French policy.[7]

The 17 April note, MacDonald remarked, made sense only if the French "were decided to oppose German rearmament by force."[8] But this was hardly the case. Weygand still insisted on the merits of a defensive strategy, and arguments in favor of creating a highly mobile professional corps—spelled out in Colonel de Gaulle's book *Vers l'armée de métier*—gained no support either among the military or the politicians, few exceptions apart.[9] Thus, the note was not followed by any changes in French military doctrine; in fact, armament credits were lowered and no coherent plan of industrial mobilization was adopted.[10]

Politically, the note expressed a policy—which was not that of the Quai d'Orsay—stemming from exasperation with Germany and annoyance with Britain.[11] Doumergue may well have treated it as a first step toward a Franco-Italian-British agreement that would isolate Germany and force it to seek some accommodation with the Western powers, but if this was so, he overestimated the will of his country. The French secretary general of the League saw matters realistically: "We are at crossroads," he wrote. Germany was moving ahead and Italy was reconstructing its Central European policy in order to limit German influences. Poland hastened to choose "an autonomist and realist" course. "As for us, after ten years when we allowed the world to consider the Treaty of Versailles a subject of revision, one asks oneself if we are not going to proclaim solemnly our respect [for the Treaty] but naturally take no measures to exact it." If "we cannot either defend the rules of the past or attempt to protect Europe by new means, we are risking to arrive at a situation that is dangerous and obscure." To pursue a pacific policy, France had to fulfill two conditions: "to be strong and know what [it] wants."[12] And Pertinax commented: "in the final analysis we return always to the same dilemma in foreign policy: we must choose between our own forces and an uncertain international action."[13]

---

7. Text in DDF, I, VI:270–72. The authoritative analysis in Vaïsse, *Sécurité*, 541–73. Varying interpretations in François-Poncet, *Souvenirs*, 178; Herriot, *Jadis*, 2:410; Baumont, *Origins*, 96; Scott, *Alliance*, 159–60; Bonnet, *Quai d'Orsay*, 129–30; Duroselle, *Décadence*, 95–98; Soulié, *Herriot*, 441; Young, *In Command of France*, 52–58.

8. DDF, I, VI:322; compare 249–354.

9. Weygand's views in DBFP, II, VI:683–85. See de Gaulle, *Mémoires*, 1:7. Czech comments on de Gaulle's earlier article appear in *Národní Politika* and *Národní Listy*, respectively 14 and 16 June 1934.

10. See d'Hoop, "La Politique française," 2–8.

11. Vaïsse, *Sécurité*, 578–79.

12. Avenol to Massigli, 19 Mar. 1934, MAE, P.A. Massigli 6.

13. *L'Echo de Paris*, 18 Apr. 1934.

The sequel of the 17 April note was a French diplomatic counter-offensive, which harked back to Briand's old concepts of an Eastern Locarno, and to Paul-Boncour's attempts to develop the system of alliances by involving Italy and the Soviet Union and by tightening the bonds with the Little Entente and Poland. Barthou gave a somewhat different twist to this approach. Conscious of the difficulties that a rapprochement with Rome and Moscow entailed for the eastern allies, he moved cautiously with regard to the former and devoted special interest to the latter.[14]

The situation in Southeastern and East Central Europe was volatile. The formation of the Balkan Entente on 9 February 1934—comprising Yugoslavia, Romania, Greece, and Turkey—may have reinforced the antirevisionist forces, but it also drew the four countries deeper into purely Balkan affairs. Paris had deliberately stayed aloof, but it was interested in the military implications, particularly the perennial question of war transit through Saloniki.[15] Desirous to be more intimately associated in the military affairs of the Little Entente, the French sent General Victor Pétin in April to Romania for a thorough briefing. After his visit, Beneš agreed with Titulescu that a French delegate would henceforth always participate in meetings of the Little Entente general staffs.[16]

Plans for the Danubian economic cooperation remained as nebulous as ever.[17] In late January, the Czechoslovak government adhered to the 1932 protocol providing a loan to Vienna, and Beneš kept arguing that the Anschluss was an all-European problem in which the great powers ought to take the lead. Actually, Austria was coming closer to Italy, and Chancellor Engelbert Dollfuss's bloody showdown with the socialists on 12–14 February strengthened this trend as well as the authoritarian character of the Vienna regime. This was a blow to Czechoslovakia and to a lesser degree to France. The repugnance of the Little Entente to discuss economic problems separately and directly with Austria and Hungary increased. Barthou felt that Italy's neglect to concert with France and Britain while working out a tripe arrangement with Budapest and Vienna justified French reservations about Rome's policy in East Central Europe. A Franco-Italian reapprochement could bear fruits only if Italy reassured the Little Entente

14. A trend toward revitalizing the eastern alliances was noticed by the British. See DBFP, II, VI:683; compare Jędrzejewicz, *Lipski*, 144.

15. See DDF, I, V:896; correspondence and notes, including "Transit par Salonique," 20 Mar. 1934, MAE, Z 864.10, Tchécoslovaquie 2604. Also SHA, EMA/2, Pologne 21.

16. See d'Ormesson report, 17 Mar. 1934, MAE, Z 864.10, Tchécoslovaquie 2604; Pétin's report in DDF, I, VI:176–81. On Beneš–Titulescu meeting, DaM, II, 656–57.

17. See Noël reports, 8, 10, 18 Jan. 1934, MAE, Z 864.10, Tchécoslovaquie 2603; compare 11 Jan. briefing, KV, CPP. On the Little Entente's Zagreb meeting, 22 Jan. See Kvaček, *Nad Evropou*, 61, and "Boj," 247; Beneš's circular, DaM, II, 643–44.

and exerted its influence in favor of regional cooperation on the Austrians and the Hungarians.

Simultaneously Barthou tried to explain to the Little Entente that while France would watch over the interests of its friends, it could not openly counter Rome's moves. Prague must not operate on the assumption that an Italo-Austro-Hungarian grouping would not be viable, nor must it try to oppose the Little Entente to the nascent Rome-led bloc.[18] Beneš was reassuring the French that he understood their position and was willing to cooperate; he made conciliatory statements to Alberto Theodoli, the Italian president of the League's Mandates Commission. But he remained opposed to Italian control of Austria, to an Austro-Hungarian union, and to the Danubian confederation.[19]

There was a good deal of déjà vu and ambivalence in all of this. Warsaw wondered whether Paris was playing a double game by seeking to involve Rome in the defense of Austria—even if the Little Entente were to pay some of the costs—or was simply oscillating between a pro-Italian and a pro-Little Entente line.[20] Krofta voiced similar doubts and appeared critical of what he perceived to be a French policy of demanding sacrifices from Prague, Belgrade, and Bucharest.[21] No wonder that Beneš appeared, as Theodoli put it, "at a loss as to what policy to pursue. The predictions which he had made to me and to others a year ago concerning events in Germany have proved completely inaccurate." The British envoy similarly commented on "confusion, nerviousness and anxiety" among the governmental circles in Prague.[22]

The signing of the Italo-Austro-Hungarian protocols on consultation and increased economic collaboration on 17 March 1934 in Rome signified that Mussolini decided to act openly as the protector of Austria and as head of a grouping rival to the Little Entente. His strongly revisionist speech added to the existing concern.[23] Although Beneš shared with the French his disbelief that the Rome protocols meant a real change in the situation, he responded with a major speech on 21 March. Reserving judgement on the Italian move, he recalled that Masaryk's and his own opposition to the Anschluss had been influenced by and conformed to the

18. See DDF, I, v:840–42, 845–49.

19. See Beneš to mission, 18 Feb. 1934, CPP. For Beneš's statement that he had French assurance that an Italo-Austro-Hungarian bloc would be prevented, see Kvaček, "Boj," 248; compare DDF, I, v:863–68.

20. See Gawroński, *Moja misja*, 143–47; also his report, 14 Mar. 1934, AAN, MSZ, Z.4,w.3, t.13 (old classification). Compare DDF, I, v:573–96.

21. Briefing, 15 Mar. 1934, KV, CPP.

22. Drummond report, 10 Mar. 1934, FO 371 18383 R 1643/1643/12; also DBFP, II, VI:514–18.

23. See DBFP, II, VI:564–67; compare DDF, I, VI:60–62, 70–71.

stand taken by Italy, France, and Britain toward the end of World War I. By insisting again that the Anschluss was a European issue, he was warning that Prague would not be prepared to pay an exorbitant price for the prevention of a German-Austrian union. Such an attitude evoked some surprise in Paris.[24]

In these circumstances, Barthou was unwilling to force the pace of a reapprochement with Rome.[25] A similar circumspection characterized his policy toward the USSR. The Quai d'Orsay had been considering Soviet proposals for a Franco-Russian alignment within a larger grouping at the turn of 1933–34, but conversations came to a halt. Regarding Léger as being "too soft with the Russians," Barthou was unprepared to move decisively toward a rapprochement with Moscow.[26] One reason (if not the main reason) for his caution was the Polish angle. The foreign minister wished to explore the unhappy state of Franco-Polish relations, and he quickly resorted to personal diplomacy. On 19 February, he outlined to Chłapowski the French objectives with regard to disarmament, the League, and Austria, and recalling his acquaintance with Piłsudski he voiced worries about Poland's German policy. The ambassador reminded Barthou of instances when Paris had neglected to consult Warsaw; the minister stressed his own past opposition to the Four Power Pact. In answer to Barthou's question what could improve the relations, Chłapowski mentioned a visit to Warsaw. Both the minister and Premier Doumergue, who pointed out that Barthou's presence at the Quai d'Orsay was "a guarantee of the best possible collaboration" with Poland, were interested.[27]

On 6 March, Beck officially invited Barthou to come to Poland, and a few days later the foreign minister accepted the invitation. A good part of March and early April was spent on extensive preparations, which included Franco-Polish exchanges. Barthou hoped to eliminate misunderstandings between the two countries and wanted assurances that Warsaw would continue to honor its obligations; he knew that Beneš, for one, believed that Piłsudski and Beck could not be fully trusted.[28] Barthou planned to question Piłsudski himself about the nature of the nonaggres-

24. For the speech, see Beneš, *Problem of Central Europe*. Replies to questions, 23 Mar. 1934 in Agence Havas communiqué; see also briefing, 29 Mar., KV, CPP; compare François-Poncet to Barthou, 29 Mar., MAE, Z 864.1, Tchécoslovaquie 2569; comments in Gajanová, *ČSR*, 319–20; Kvaček, *Nad Evropou*, 63.

25. See DDF, I, VI:98–101, 219, 302–303, 378–80,

26. See Cameron, "Léger," 385; Barthou's views at cabinet meetings, 20 Feb., 8, 9 Mar., 10 Apr. 1934 in Herriot, *Jadis*, 2:389, 391, 395–96, 403, 501. See also DDF, I, V:606, 863 and VI:213–15; compare DVP SSSR, XVII, 165–66, 220–21.

27. Chłapowski telegrams, 19, 20, 24 Feb., and Beck and Szembek telegrams, 21, 27 Feb. 1934, HIA, Amb. Paryż, resp. box 3 and 5.

28. See Barthou, 4 Mar. 1934 session, CAE/Ch.

sion declaration, raise the issue of the military convention, and talk about economic problems. He expected to be questioned in turn about ways to "restore . . . mutual confidence to Franco-Polish relations."[29]

The French regarded the alliance, Laroche made it clear, as involving more than a mere application of *casus foederis*; it should be a "constant entente" that implied concordance of diplomatic efforts. For a long time, the ambassador wrote to Barthou, the Poles had been worried by the revisionist campaign in France, and the representation of their country as an obstacle to Franco-German reconciliation. Statements by some public figures in France that France would not fight for Poland did not pass unnoticed. Laroche dwelt on Polish lack of appreciation of Locarno and incomprehension of the Anglo-Saxon aspect of French policy. He explained the Polish stand on disarmament, the attitude toward the League and toward the Little Entente (permeated by some jealously), and the importance of the prestige factor. Warsaw counted on internal difficulties in Germany and Russia to provide a longer period of respite than it was generally assumed. In sum, Poland wanted "to make a great power policy and, while proclaiming its fidelity to alliances, demonstrate that they should include liberty of movement compatible with its dignity." The question was how far did the Poles intend to go, and the ambassador recommended the use of firm language. A strengthening of military cooperation would be well received in Warsaw, but it must have as counterpart a political consolidation of the alliance.[30]

Barthou listened in turn to Chłapowski's deputy Mühlstein, who on Piłsudski's orders, explained Polish views on disarmament including the observation that France's precarious position was due to constant concessions to Germany. Barthou assured the counselor that although his country would not respond militarily to German rearmament, it would not "legalize" it. Mühlstein quipped that the Poles believed that illegal guns were just as effective as legal weapons. During the talks, the foreign minister touched on the bad state of Czechoslovak-Polish relations, but when Mühlstein failed to respond, he did not pursue the subject.[31]

Barthou was well informed about the ongoing Czechoslovak-Polish disputes, which the Parisian press deplored.[32] Beneš kept complaining to Noël

29. Chłapowski telegram, 13 Mar. 1934, HIA, Amb. Paryż, box 3; DTJS, I, 148–49.

30. Barthou–Laroche exchanges, DDF, I, V:922, 937–39, VI:13–16.

31. See Mühlstein telegrams, 19, 20 Mar. 1934, HIA, Amb. Paryż, box 3; DTJS, I, 150–51. Also Mühlstein, "Świadectwo," 127–32. Compare, DDF, I, VI:58–59, Ministry to Laroche, 21 Mar., MAE, Z 698.12, Pologne 2200.

32. See DDF, I, VI:34–35, 182–84, 218n.; Laroche, Noël and Barthou dispatches in Mar., MAE, Z 864.5, Tchécoslovaquie 2586 and 2587 and MAE, Z 698.12, Pologne 2200. Compare Benton to Secretary of State, 5 Apr. 1934, SDNA, 760C.60F/141. The signing of a Czechoslovak-Polish commercial agreement on 10 Feb. marked no change in their relationship.

that his advances to Warsaw had been ignored, and he inspired or even wrote himself articles contesting Polish grievances. He told Massigli that the very existence of the Little Entente was at stake, because its disappearance would facilitate Polish policy "tending to deflect German expansion toward the Danubian basin." Barthou should make the Poles realize that by trying to weaken France's friends in this region, "Poland was acting contrary if not to the letter, at least to the spirit of the Franco-Polish alliance." Massigli noted the importance that Beneš attached to the mediatory action of Barthou in Warsaw.[33]

At the Quai d'Orsay's request, Laroche summarized the main causes of Polish antagonism toward Czechoslovakia, stressing its historic origins, the Ukrainian and Russian angles, and a certain jealousy of Beneš. He emphasized Warsaw's preoccupation with prestige, Poland having smarted for many years under the criticism of the "corridor" and the handling of national minorities. Beneš, whose ex cathedra pronouncements had for a long time annoyed the Poles, was a good target for attacks; Czechoslovakia was used as a scapegoat. Laroche found it deplorable that Poland "pour se grandir" decided to treat "a friendly nation and a natural ally" in such a cavalier fashion.[34] No wonder that Barthou decided to add to his Warsaw visit (22–25 April) also a trip to Prague (26–28 April).

The news of what was to be the first visit by a French foreign minister was naturally greeted with great satisfaction by the Polish press. According to governmental journals, it signified the recognition of Poland's importance in the world. Using flattery, *Le Temps* wrote that Poland, "a vigorous and united state, based on one of the best armies in Europe," wished to be treated as a great power; the rightist press eagerly picked up the theme.[35]

Position papers prepared for Barthou covered a wide range of subjects. A note entitled "Poland and the League of Nations" argued that Warsaw ought to pay greater attention to this "linchpin of the present system of security in Europe." The League acted as a brake on imprudent Polish actions; and even if Poland's representative in Geneva did not always extend the helping hand one could expect from a member of the "clientèle," his presence was advantageous for France.[36] Pointing out that the new Polish diplomatic course was inspired by methods that signified a departure from

---

33. See Massigli and Noël to Barthou, respectively, 12, 17 and 26 Apr. 1934, MAE, Z 864.5 Tchécoslovaquie 2587.

34. See Laroche report in DDF, I, VI:64–65, also 137–39. 4 Apr. 1934 dispatch, MAE, Z 864.5, Tchécoslovaquie 2587.

35. *Gazeta Warszawska*, 16 Mar., 11, 20 Apr. 1934; *Le Temps*, 10 Apr.; on governmental press, see Laroche and Bressy reports, 4, 12, 13 Apr., MAE, Z 698.12, Pologne 2200.

36. Note of Service français de la SdN, 22 Mar. 1934, MAE, P.A. Massigli 4.

the policy of collaboration and solidarity with France, another note underlined the need to update the alliance. The military convention needed to
be amended by accords that, in the hypothesis of a Soviet-Czechoslovak-
Polish rapprochement, would allow Poland to obtain strategic materials
from its neighbors rather than from the geographically remote France. In
view of the evolution of Soviet policy, the advisability of a regional accord
in Eastern Europe was explicitly mentioned.[37]

Ideas on an Eastern Pact were presented in a separate explanatory note
of 30 March, which suggested that Warsaw could best remove doubts
about its nonaggression declaration and manifest its attachment to a policy of international solidarity by adhering in principle to a regional pact of
mutual assistance. Given their old criticism of the Locarno "gap," the
Poles might find it awkward to reject a scheme that would bring them the
help of the USSR and Czechoslovakia. Such an East European combination must not appear to be directed against a third party, and indeed German participation could make it somewhat complementary to Locarno. Its
members—Poland, the USSR, Germany, Czechoslovakia, and the Baltic
states—would engage themselves to assist a neighbor attacked by another
signatory. In the absence of a Russo-German border, Soviet assistance
would be extended to Germany and vice versa if either was attacked by
Poland. Here was one of the earliest French formulations of the future
Eastern Pact.[38]

The French government, another note said, "should aim at bringing Poland to the notion of European solidarity, and specifically toward a détente
in the relations between Poland and Czechoslovakia."[39] A special survey
of these relations recalled that Czechoslovakia "had always regarded Poland as a fragile state, undermined by internal dissensions, and destined
one day to succumb to joint attacks by the Germans and the Russians."
Consequently, Prague "did not wish to tie its fate to such uncertain destiny." Although past efforts to improve Czech-Polish relations produced
solely reciprocal complaints, a reconciliation of the two countries should
be "one of the first objectives" of French policy. Were it to prove impossible at this point, one ought to create at least a more favorable "climate."[40] In a related note, the Quai d'Orsay examined Poland's attitude
toward the Anschluss and concluded that irrespective of whether there existed any German-Polish understanding in its respect, France could hardly
count on Poland to check Nazi plans in Central Europe.[41]

37. See DDF, I, VI:40–46, 97–98.

38. See DDF, I, VI:133–35.

39. See project, 19 Mar. 1934, MAE, Z 698.1, Pologne 2100.

40. Note for minister, 31 Mar. and note for minister's cabinet, 27 Mar. 1934, MAE,
Z 698.12, Pologne 2200, and Z 864.5, Tchécoslovaquie 2586.

41. Note for minister, 31 Mar. 1934, MAE, Z 698.12, Pologne 2200. Hoffinger in

Franco-Polish economic relations were examined in a separate document, which stated, after mentioning Polish complaints about the lack of financial assistance, that France had extended over 2,316 milliard francs to the Poles. France, however, was not in a position to grant any more money, especially because the Polish attitude toward French investors had antagonized bankers and industrialists. The note spoke of the attacks against the directors of Żyrardów, sequestration orders, and a bitter campaign waged by Polish press.[42] All of this seemed to be linked with a general trend in Poland toward state intervention. Commercial negotiations, rendered necessary by a new Polish tariff and French policy of contingents, had been suspended in late December 1933. Suffering from an unfavorable balance of payments with France, the Poles strove to improve their commercial balance, which ran counter to the interests of French farmers and industrialists. The note observed that French agricultural quotas hurt the Polish economy. In turn, because the French industry needed Polish orders, some pressure had been exerted on Warsaw to have submarines built in French shipyards.[43]

This last item illustrated the connection between economic and military matters. D'Arbonneau had tried to interest Schneider in Polish orders for antiaircraft guns, but had "run into a wall."[44] Schneider's default on the financing of the Silesian railroad had adverse strategic connotations. Polish interest in the delivery of modern French tanks, "which we have always refused to show to them," was not satisfied.[45] The result was a good deal of bad blood.

The Quai d'Orsay, considering the perennial issue of arms delivery to Poland, thought of pushing the country toward a transportation agreement with the USSR. France could build certain types of armaments in Russia (tanks and planes), which could be then ceded to the Poles, thus bypassing a likely Polish refusal to accept direct Soviet aid. This plan would necessitate changes in the 1921 military convention, and the Quai d'Orsay wanted to get rid of article 2 (on French aid to Poland if attacked by the USSR) as incompatible with the planned Franco-Polish-Russian

---

report to Schuschnigg, 27 Aug. 1934 (intercept), SHA, EMA/2, Pologne 37 correctly observed that Poland's disinterest in Austria was not the result but one of the causes of the German-Polish rapprochement.

42. See Landau and Tomaszewski, *Sprawa*, 182–216.

43. See DDF, I, VI:139–44. On economic-military problems see Laroche to Barthou, 15 Mar. 1934, MAE, Z 698.12, Pologne 2198; D'Arbonneau reports, Nov. 1932–Feb. 1934, SHA, EMA/2, Pologne 12; compare Cudahy to Secretary of State, 13 Apr. 1934, SDNA, 860C.655/13. For the vast Polish documentation, see AAN, MSZ 3885 and 3888.

44. D'Arbonneau report, 25 May 1933, SHA, EMA/2, Pologne 12. The attaché noted Polish interest in motorization and armor, theoretical because of lack of funds.

45. Note of the second bureau, 22 Mar. 1934, SHA, EMA/2, Pologne 19.

agreement. Barthou, however, was not to raise these questions in Warsaw but merely indicate the thinking of Paris in preparation for future Franco-Polish talks between the military.[46]

The general staff regarded an explication on the German-Polish declaration as "salutary," but was more doubtful about the other issues. Suggestions of aid via Russia could give the impression of France wishing to "patronize" Warsaw and would be resented. One could do no more than try to find out to what extent Piłsudski intended to develop Polish-Soviet collaboration and use it against Germany. Massive aid to Poland could be considered by going back to the 1929–31 Polish requests for 1.5 milliard francs in credits that had lapsed. As for the needed revision of the military convention, this proposition was delicate. The Poles must not think that "France was seeking a way to free itself from the alliance and to abandon Poland." If one discarded some dated clauses, crossed out references to Soviet Russia and Germany, and eliminated the obligation to deliver aid to Polish ports, a "new military convention would contain many lacunae as compared with the old."[47]

The Quai d'Orsay recommended raising questions for the Warsaw conversations rather than presenting problems and formulated the following list: Did the German-Polish arbitration treaty remain valid? Would it be helpful to update the military convention? How could the difficulties of the French enterprises be resolved? Would Poland, who had regretted the absence of an Eastern Locarno, find a mutual assistance accord with Czechoslovakia or even the USSR useful? What appeasements could be given to the Baltic states? Finally, how did Poland intend to demonstrate its attachment to international collaboration and to the League? Was it prepared to adopt the same attitude as France toward Danubian economic cooperation? Was it ready to support the entry of Soviet Russia into the League? In the memorandum handed to the Polish ambassador on 13 April, these questions—with a notable absence of any reference to Czechoslovakia—appeared under three headings: general policy matters concerning both countries directly; those concerning them indirectly; and special issues (with one item, French enterprises in Poland). Barthou's annotations indicated that he wished to emphasize the validity of the 1921 and 1925 treaties; to raise economic issues, notably the order for submarines; and to discuss air and press accords.[48]

46. See Bargeton–Gen. Loizeau conversation, 22 Mar. 1934, SHA, EMA/2, Pologne 43. Compare note on Polish-Soviet and Polish-Baltic relations, 31 Mar., MAE, Z 698.12, Pologne 2200, which having surveyed the 1932–34 developments concluded that a malaise was evident, and that the Polish-Lithuanian difficulties remained acute. See also DDF, I, VI:306–307.

47. Note 27 Mar. 1934, SHA, EMA/2, Pologne 19.

48. Respectively, 26 Mar. 1934 note, MAE, Z 698.1, Pologne 2100, and aide-mé-

The omission of Czechoslovakia resulted from French desire to avoid controversy, and Chłapowski appreciated Barthou's discretion. There was another exclusion, namely of the disarmament question, because at this moment, the French were on the eve of adopting the 17 April note. Noticing it immediately, Beck expressed fear that France might contemplate new concessions. Laroche recommended that Barthou personally discuss the issue, which the Poles felt so strongly about that Beck had even intimated that should disarmament clauses be revised, so could the provisions regarding protection of national minorities.[49] After the French note of 17 April, the Poles (and the Czechoslovaks) wanted to know what would happen if Germany continued to rearm. Would France close its eyes or oppose Germany and by what means?[50]

Beck's acceptance of the proposed agenda was received with satisfaction by Barthou.[51] Yet if the Poles attached great hopes to the foreign minister's visit, the French position papers brought into relief the different perceptions by Paris and Warsaw of international problems and Franco-Polish cooperation. Was it possible to narrow these differences?

In Warsaw and Prague

On Sunday, 22 April, Louis Barthou arrived in Warsaw. Beck was not at the station to greet him, having reproduced exactly the protocol of his own reception in Paris in September 1933. Meant to accentuate the equality of status between France and Poland, this discourtesy toward the old French statesman was immediately noticed by the diplomats and the press.[52] Barthou was unperturbed, even though the reception in his honor began in a somewhat cold atmosphere. The first jarring note slowly faded as Beck in his welcoming speech stressed the Franco-Polish alliance as one of the "strongest, most vital and durable factors of international politics," and presented Barthou as the architect of the 1921 treaty of alliance.[53]

The next day, the French foreign minister held an hour-and-a-half-long

moire, 13 Apr., DDF, 1, VI:217–18, also DTJS, I, 152–53. Barthou reaffirmed that as an old friend of Poland he appreciated its great power position. See telegram of Chłapowski, 14 Apr., HIA, Amb. Paryż, box 3.

49. See DDF, I, v:885–88, VI:269–70. The French regarded such Polish notions dangerous, for they could open the gates of revisionism, territorial revision included. See Massigli to Barthou, 12 Apr. 1934, MAE, Z 864.5, Tchécoslovaquie 2587.

50. See DDF, I, VI:289–90; compare Herriot, *Jadis*, 2:420.

51. Chłapowski telegram, 20 Apr. 1934, HIA, Amb. Paryż, box 3.

52. See Laroche, *Pologne*, 155; Fiala, *Soudobé Polsko*, 275; Beck, *Dernier rapport*, 58. American and British accounts in Cudahy to Secretary of State, 26 Apr. 1934, SDNA, 751.60C/46 and DBFP, II, VI:669–70 and 688–89. Barthou's virtually dismissed the incident in an "off the record" answer, at the 9 May 1934 session, CAE/Ch.

53. Text in Beck, *Przemówienia*, 110–11.

conversation with Piłsudski; Beck said he had never seen the marshal show so much friendship to a foreign visitor.[54] Barthou found Piłsudski "neither aged nor tired"; his memory was "impeccable and his intelligence very lucid." He expressed himself with a "good deal of force and logic."[55] Both statesmen began by recalling Piłsudski's visit to Paris in 1921 and the signing of the alliance. In his explication of the main issues of Poland's foreign policy, namely the relations with the two neighbors—those with Britain and Italy were but of secondary importance—the marshal emphasized that he made no commitment either to Germany or Russia. Poland's alliances, and he reiterated his fidelity to them, were in no way affected. In answer to Barthou's question, Piłsudski said that the Germans had not tried to introduce any political postulates into the conversations, although he himself had expected them to do so. He emphatically denied rumors about an exchange of personal letters with Hitler; if a meeting with the Führer were proposed, the marshal would not favor it.[56] He thought, however, that collaboration with Germany was likely to develop; he believed in the usefulness of a bilateral approach to international relations. The marshal interjected here some bitingly critical remarks about the League, claiming it would die of anemia unless it reformed itself.

The Polish leader delivered a scathing critique, although couched in a friendly fashion, of the French policy toward disarmament. "You will give in again," he told Barthou, and when the latter protested, assuring Piłsudski that the decisions taken by the French government were definitive and firm, the marshal replied that if Barthou would not give in, his successor would.

Piłsudski did not wish to be drawn into an argument about problems connected with the Franco-Polish alliance, and when Barthou asked, "Do you have something to reproach us?" he referred him to Beck. Asked whether he would consider the possibility of adapting the military convention to current needs, the marshal cautiously replied that he would but would not take the initiative. Beck later explained to Barthou that Piłsudski referred here to Beck's vain attempt to raise the matter with Daladier in September 1933. The Poles did not want to be snubbed again. Barthou, suggesting staff talks, used deliberately the expression "conversation of technical nature" to imply that political aspects would be excluded. Piłsudski assented to a mission by General Pétin for the purpose of further talks. The general, Barthou stressed, was no friend of Weygand but enjoyed the confidence of Marshal Pétain to whom he would directly report.

The French foreign minister handled gingerly the Russian question, lis-

---

54. Laroche to ministry, 24 Apr. 1934, DDF, 1, VI:333.

55. Barthou at 9 May 1934 session, CAE/Ch.

56. Barthou passed this information to Litvinov. See DDF, 1, VI:498.

tening to Piłsudski's expressions of skepticism concerning the domestic recovery of the Soviet Union and lack of faith in its stability. The marshal did not believe that the Soviet Union was likely to enter the League or could be counted upon internationally. Rapallo was too recent an experience. General d'Arbonneau interpreted these remarks as meaning that the Russian front, militarily at least, would continue to claim the marshal's attention, and if we recall Piłsudski's earlier-mentioned belief that Russia was more dangerous than Germany, this was an accurate estimate.[57]

The cordial nature of the Piłsudski–Barthou conversation and Beck's subsequent efforts to show greater warmth to the French statesman during their joint trip to Cracow, allowed further confidential talks. Barthou obtained additional clarifications of the German-Polish relationship, of Poland's free hand vis-à-vis its neighbors, and of the attitude toward disarmament. The issue of the stillborn Soviet-Polish guarantee for the Baltic states was lightly touched upon, as was the general question of Soviet-Polish relations. Barthou advocated a speedy signature of the prolonged nonaggression treaty (which occurred a few days later) but, mindful of Piłsudski's suspicious stance toward Moscow and of his preference for bilateral agreements, did not mention the concept of an Eastern Pact. The Frenchman did not want to spoil the genial atmosphere he had worked hard to create.[58] It is also possible that Barthou's own thinking on the subject was not yet fully clarified.

Profiting from the growing intimacy with Beck, Barthou asked for permission to speak about the Czechoslovak-Polish question and to express his concern. In reply Beck spoke of the infringements of the rights of the Polish minority in Czechoslovakia, although he deemed it a matter of local significance. He authorized Barthou to repeat this to Beneš. He spoke as Laroche put it, with "more force than sincerity."[59] Another touchy matter, the Franco-Polish economic difficulties occupied relatively little place in the exchanges. Barthou did not wish to appear as an advocate of French private interests. Sensing Beck's skepticism about the good will of the French capitalists in Poland, he promised to work for an accommodation, all the while insisting that the French not be discriminated against. As for the Danubian area, he encouraged the Poles to improve relations with Bucharest.

The visit, which began with a sour note, seemed to end as Barthou's

57. Account of this conversation and of subsequent Barthou–Beck talks based on DTJS, I, 156–63; DDF, I, VI:333–35, 345–48, 637–38; d'Arbonneau report, 2 May 1934, SHA, EMA/2, Pologne 12; Barthou on 9 May, CAE/Ch, in Polish translation Wandycz, "Barthou"; Beck, *Dernier rapport*, 58–59; Herriot, *Jadis*, 2:422–23; Laroche, *Pologne*, 159–60, 166.

58. See DVP SSSR, XVII, 795n.; ADAP, C II/2:862–28; Skrzypek, *Strategia*, 136–37.

59. Laroche, *Pologne*, 160.

personal triumph. Not only did Polish crowds incessantly acclaim the old Frenchman but the final interviews by both foreign ministers were couched in most cordial terms. Beck described the moments spent with "such a prominent statesman as Barthou as the most important of my political career." Barthou spoke of friendship that nothing could destroy. The alliance, all minor misunderstandings apart, was "as indestructible today as it had been in 1921." Poland was "a great power," and its alliance with France did not signify dependence on Paris. If the German-Polish pact contributed toward peace so much the better, but in no case would it affect Franco-Polish relations.[60]

Before assessing the political results of the Warsaw visit, Barthou's trip to Prague needs to be briefly surveyed. There were no specific problems that required discussion with the possible exception of Prague's continued preference for a neutralization of Austria. The position paper was mainly informative, although a note on Czechoslovak position on disarmament contained some general evaluations of Beneš's diplomacy.[61] Czechoslovakia was "the surest and the most active supporter of French policy" whose loyalty as an ally had never wavered, although a distinction had to be made between Beneš's personal role and Prague's actions. Beneš had always exerted "an excellent influence" on his country's policy. Unlike the Poles, who had created difficulties for France in the realm of disarmament, Beneš constantly asked for detailed explanations in order to be able better to defend the French thesis. His influence on the Little Entente was beneficial. Since Hitler's advent to power, the hypothesis of a conflict with Germany appeared much less theoretical than before, and Czechoslovakia was taking defensive measures.

Such unqualified praise was indicative of the Quai d'Orsay's view of Beneš as *the* French ally in East Central Europe. His reputation as a man of the Left did not interfere with the good rapport he established with the rightist government of Doumergue, which at one point he called "a great blessing."[62] During long conversations in Paris on 15–16 February, he seemingly reinforced this personal relationship. Commenting on Barthou's visit, the press organ of the Czechoslovak foreign ministry spoke of French national revival and an overhaul of the country's internal and external policies. The foreign minister's stay in Prague was to be a manifestation of friendship and intimacy, providing an opportunity for a comparison of

60. See Beck, *Przemówienia*, 112; Agence Havas, 26 Apr. 1934, and *L'Echo de Paris* 24 Apr. with final communiqué.

61. Respectively, note, 16 Apr. 1934, DDF, I, VI:252–58, and 19 Apr. note of the Service français de la SdN, MAE, Z 698.12, Pologne 2200.

62. Beneš to Herriot, 17 Apr. 1934, see Herriot, *Jadis*, 2:411–12.

notes on international developments by "very old personal friends," to use Barthou's words.[63]

Public pronouncements of the two foreign ministers immediately reached a high pitch of amity and closeness. At the state dinner in the Hrad, Beneš declared that he had never experienced any indication of French "hegemony or overlordship." Speaking for the Little Entente, he affirmed that "our nations are and want to be your younger sisters" in Central Europe. To France belonged "a great mission of peace and stability" without which "today's Europe, divided and tortured, would be lost."[64] Echoing these sentiments *Lidové Noviny* wrote on 28 April that France could never be too great and too powerful as far as the Czechs were concerned.

Barthou held three conversations with Beneš, but it is not clear whether Masaryk, whom Barthou had know since 1920, participated in all or any of them.[65] As expected the French foreign minister singled out Austria for discussions, and Beneš stressed that only loyal entente between Paris, Prague, and Rome could in the long run save Austria and Hungary. Some concessions to Italy were acceptable, but only within limits agreed with Yugoslavia. The Czechoslovak minister reiterated his opposition to a Habsburg restoration, but otherwise was flexible in his approach and confident in French leadership. Later, Barthou would describe the Prague talks as easy and resulting in full agreement.[66]

Both statemen touched on the Polish issue, but made few references to it in public. Barthou tried to allay Czechoslovak fears about Warsaw's alleged commitments concerning Austria; he told the press that the German-Polish declaration in no way affected the friendship between France and Poland.[67] Barthou's entourage and the French journalists were less reserved and let it be known that Paris realized that the Poles would adhere to the alliance only as long as it suited them. The Polish legation suspected that the Czechs sought to make Barthou suspicious of Poland and its foreign policy[68] and were probably right, if we bear in mind Krofta's and especially Beneš's current interpretations of Polish moves. Krofta surmised that the anti-Czechoslovak campaign in Poland might be part of a three-

63. Barthou on 9 May 1934, CAE/Ch; compare Beneš circular, 3 May 1934, CPP. *Zahraniční Politika* article, 13, 5/6 (1934), 318.

64. Speech and statement for Havas Agency, 26, 28 Apr. 1934, MZV-VA, 190.494.

65. Communiqués, 26, 27, 28 Apr. 1934, MZV-VA, 190.494.

66. 9 May 1934, CAE/Ch; DDF, I, VI:639–40; compare Beneš's circular, 3 May CPP.

67. See *Polityka Narodów*, 3 (1934), 471; compare Kiernik to Paderewski, 5 May 1934, *Archiwum Polityczne Ignacego Paderewskiego*, III, 238.

68. Benton to Secretary of State, 30 Apr. 1934, SDNA, 751.60C/45; also Grzybowski report, 28 Apr., AAN, Z.4,w.3, t.17 (old classification).

stage plan of achieving, first, equality for the Polish minority; second, an occupation of Teschen; and third, eventual border revision that would link Poland with Hungary.[69] Beneš, in a circular to missions, saw Polish behavior toward France and Czechoslovakia as indicative of Warsaw's search for a new course, based on the following appraisal of the situation: French power was on the decline domestically and internationally, and correspondingly Poland's importance in Europe was increasing. This correlation will be appreciated more if Poland's independence is stressed. The Anschluss was a foregone conclusion, and because it would lessen German pressure in the east, opposition to it did not lay in the Polish interest. The League of Nations was growing weaker, which to some extent was advantageous for Poland, providing an opportunity for emancipation from minority obligations. Warsaw was interested in the perpetuation of both Nazi and Soviet regimes, for their abnormality gave Poland a better position and increased its relative might. Democracy being in the throes of a crisis was unlikely to survive in France and Czechoslovakia. Because the latter was doomed, there was no reason to provide protection.

Beneš rejected all this reasoning. France would recover and maintain its standing; German gains of some rearmament concessions would only bring France, Britain, and Italy closer together. Hitler would face increasing domestic difficulties, and he had already lost his chance of affecting the Anschluss. The League of Nations would be strengthened by the Soviet entry; democracy would adapt itself to new conditions. Beneš judged Polish foreign policy as not only based on wrong assumptions but also being double-faced.[70] His appraisal, which missed the importance of Piłsudski's concept of balance, was colored by some wishful thinking, but it corresponded largely to French estimations. This was also true for the nascent concept of the Eastern Pact, which Beneš not only favored but claimed to have participated in shaping.[71]

One does not know whether Beneš shared these views with Barthou in Prague, but they were familiar to the French. The foreign minister alluded to some of them in conversations with Noël. Moreover, the above circular itself, although without its author's name, came into the possession of the Quai d'Orsay during Barthou's visit.[72]

The visit boosted the Czechoslovak morale, which was one of its objectives, and strengthened the position of Beneš and Masaryk. Presidential

69. Briefing, 29 Mar. 1934, KV, CPP.

70. Beneš to missions, 18 or 19 Apr. 1934, CPP. For a Polish translation of the document dated 18 Apr., see Balcerak, "Pogląd Beneša," 179–82. Excerpts in Berber, *Europäische Politik*, 22–23. Compare Beneš–Titulescu conversation, 11 Apr., DaM, II, 657.

71. He told this to the cabinet on 20 Apr. 1934. See Kvaček, *Nad Evropou*, 81.

72. See Noël to Barthou, 18 Apr. 1934, MAE, Z 864.5, Tchécoslovaquie 2587. Circular received via Copenhagen, 27 Apr., MAE, Z 698.1, Pologne 2100.

elections were to be held in May, and French references to continuity at the Hrad and the Czernin Palace being a trump card of the reborn state, must be understood in this context.[73] When Barthou called Beneš "my dear friend" and referred to his "exceptional gifts," which "have made you one of the chiefs of European diplomacy," this was precious to the minister, more vulnerable to domestic opposition since the death in December 1933 of Švehla. Although no political friend of Beneš, Švehla had been a stabilizing factor in Czechoslovak politics. As for the Paris-Prague relationship, there was, in Barthou's words, "more than friendship, even more than alliance; there was fraternity."[74]

Indeed the existing shadows, mainly in the economic sphere, appeared minor. Paris was annoyed by the devaluation of the crown effected under the agrarians' pressure. On the Czechoslovak side there were complaints about the "deplorable" state of commercial relations with France, characterized by a negative balance.[75] Beneš did present Barthou with a special memorandum on the subject, and Noël, although opining that Prague did not fully appreciate French difficulties, recommended that some satisfaction be given to it.[76] The minister of commerce, Lucien Lamoureux, while assuring the foreign affairs commission that he pursued "a purely commercial and egoist policy," also opined that concessions "in special cases" had to be made.[77] Yet, negotiations did not proceed smoothly, and Beneš complained that the intransigence of Paris was exploited by critics at home who accused him of subservience toward France. Noël worried lest the "bad example" of Poland prove contagious, but he did not overestimate the degree of dissatisfaction in Prague.[78] Czechoslavak-French relations were secure enough.

By contrast, Barthou's visit to Poland had been his personal success rather than that of French foreign policy. His trip brought no improvement in the Warsaw-Prague relationship, even though the intensity of the anti-Czechoslovak campaign abated somewhat.[79] Talking to Chłapowski, the cabinet, and the parliamentary bodies, Barthou emphasized the "grandeur and the national force of Poland," and admitted that France had

---

73. See *Zahraniční Politika*, 12, 5/6 (1934), 319.

74. See Agence Havas, 28 Apr. 1934, MZV-VA, 190.494. For a caustic appraisal of Barthou's visit see Noël, *Tchécoslovaquie*, 164–67.

75. See Olšovský, *Světový obchod*, 260, 267; *Lidové Listy*, 27 May 1934; briefing, 15 Feb., KV, CPP; Noël to Barthou, 10 Feb. 1934, DDF, I, VI:664–65.

76. See DDF, I, VI:732–35; also *Le Temps*, 3 May 1934.

77. 30 May 1934, session, CAE/Ch.

78. See DDF, I, VII:658–64. Also Noël to Barthou, 17 Sept. 1934, MAE, Z 864.1, Tchécoslovaquie 2569.

79. See Kodeński, *Czechosłowacja*, 140–46; compare 3 May 1934 briefing, KV, CPP; also Girsa report, 26 Apr., CPP; compare Kvaček, *Nad Evropou*, 80.

erred in the past as a father does when he tries to impose "too oppressive a tutelage" on a grown-up child. One could not deny that Poland could be difficult, but it was a power and had to be treated accordingly. He intimated that he had succeeded in winning over Beck but was not more precise than that. Herriot's assessment of the discussions was that Barthou had one more statesman in Europe whom he could call "my dear friend."[80] *Journal des Débats* opined on 26 April that only the beginnings were made: "the essential remains to be accomplished."

For Beck the most important outcome of the talks was Barthou's acceptance of the main lines of Polish diplomacy, and the avoidance of anything that could be understood as "a desire to influence our policy, or an attempt to use us for furthering the objectives of French policy."[81] In fact both he and Piłsudski were disappointed with Barthou's failure to propose a scheme for a political, military, and economic revitalization of the alliance. Poland, hoping to have placed itself through the declaration with Germany in the position of a partner rather than a supplicant or a liability to France, expected a return to the pre-1924 nature of the alliance with France. Instead, Barthou flattered the Poles but proposed only a revision of the military convention.[82]

The choice of General Pétin, whom Beck called "a sort of a French military agent for Eastern Europe," aroused Polish irritation. The last thing the Poles wanted was to be treated as an element of French "combinations" in the region.[83] Bowing to Polish demands for a higher ranking officer, Paris decided to send the former chief of the general staff, General Debeney, whom Piłsudski knew and appreciated. Debeney had already been virtually entrusted with the task of coordinating military missions in East Central Europe, especially in the Little Entente states, and of creating bases for interallied cooperation in case of a general conflict.[84] His visit to Poland in late June, however, took place under inauspicious circumstances. Polish hopes for "grand-scale negotiations" over economic issues, half-promised by Barthou, were deceived. The French were willing to contemplate neither a flow of new capital, with profits reinvested, nor a change in the commercial balance. They tied some compensatory measures to the submarines contracts, and each side accused the other of black-

---

80. See DTJS, I, 159–63; Herriot, *Jadis*, 2:424; 9 May 1934 session, CAE/Ch.

81. Beck to missions, 28 Apr. 1934, HIA, Amb. Paryż, box 5.

82. Laroche realized it clearly; See DDF, I, IX:343–47; also *Pologne*, 200.

83. See Beck, *Dernier rapport*, 60; on Polish objections to Pétin and the confusion with Pétain, see d'Arbonneau reports, May 1934, SHA, EMA/2, Pologne 12.

84. See note for Debeney, 14 Mar. 1934 approved by Pétain, SHA, EMA/3 7 N 3446/1. Gen. Maurin criticized this choice, regarding Debeney as a "conceited and cold man" whose past relations with the Polish general staff were not good. See Chłapowski report, 14 Jan. 1935, AAN, MSZ 3802.

mail.[85] To make matters worse, on 25 June, when Debeney held his first conversation with Piłsudski, Laroche submitted the proposal that Poland adhere to the projected Eastern Pact. This proposal, as the general's aide remarked "could have hardly contributed toward creating a favorable atmosphere."[86]

Paris aimed at having the 1921 convention "modified or at least readjusted," so that only military arrangements "of execution," applicable to operations against Germany and fairly general in nature, be included.[87] These were to be updated periodically by modifications in military, naval, and air annexes to the agreement. Mutual obligations were to be defined concerning military effort in proportion to the respective populations; and mobilization, concentration, intervention, and the timetable of execution, as well as the minimum of forces to be used. Military liaison missions would be constituted; France would do its best to facilitate the dispatch of war materials that Poland could neither produce nor obtain from allied or neutral countries to a "good port." Should Poland ask for assistance in the production of armaments, efforts would be made to promote (for the sake of unification) models used in France. General staffs would cooperate continuously, by exchanging intelligence data on Germany, studying lines of communication and the possibilities of French aid, working out the previously mentioned annexes, and checking efforts made for the execution of the convention. Exchange of officers on instruction was contemplated.

General Debeney was to remain in close contact with the embassy, which, however, had not been forewarned and could not "define the exact character" of his mission.[88] He was not to negotiate, but prepare the ground by conversations with Piłsudski. It was essential to persuade the latter that France, seeking to "adjust" the convention, "was in no way seeking to reduce its obligations of an ally," and wanted to assume only such duties "that it would be certain of being able to fulfill." This line was hardly new. Debeney was reminded that France could not envisage any financial aid to Poland, and thus had nothing at his disposal.

Did Barthou really believe that, having obtained Piłsudski's grudging assent to technical conversations, he could win his agreement to a genuine revision of the convention? Even the francophile General Sikorski had told

85. See Lamoureux at 30 May 1934 session, CAE/Ch; Stebelski to Dębicki, 16 May, Beck to Chłapowski, 22 May, 17 June, Chłapowski report, 22 June; AAN, MSZ 3888. Also documentation in AAN, MSZ 3886. Poland was paying France annually eighty-five million francs in interest and amortization of loans.

86. Report of Commandant Mery, 6 July 1934, SHA, EMA/2, Pologne 19. Barthou later admitted that the timing of the Debeney mission was bad. See DVP SSSR, XVII, 459.

87. See Quai d'Orsay to war ministry, 4 June; aide-mémoire for General Debeney, 12 June 1934, SHA, EMA/2, Pologne 19 and documentation in Pologne 43.

88. See DDF, 1, IV:782–84; Mery report, 6 July 1934, SHA, EMA/2, Pologne 19.

Debeney that if he were in Piłsudski's place he would not accept it.[89] Indeed, although Debeney was received with all the military honors, his interview with Piłsudski was a failure. The Polish leader drew a clear distinction between purely military and political arrangements: the former should be dealt with only by the army, the latter by Beck. It was obvious to Laroche that the proposed modifications "constituted really an interpretation of the treaty itself."[90] Not surprisingly, Piłsudski reminded the general that this question had been raised in the past and did not and could not produce any positive results. In their second conversation, the perplexed Debeney tried to explain that he came to talk precisely about military issues. He invoked the authority of Pétain. In response, Piłsudski launched into an unrelated monologue, making it obvious that he had no intention of discussing issues raised by Debeney. D'Arbonneau later wrote that the mission provoked the marshal's distrust.[91] As Laroche more accurately noted, Piłsudski was "profoundly disenchanted" by Debeney's visit, which made him lose the remaining illusions about the object of Barthou's trip and about the foreign policy of the Doumergue cabinet.[92] Szembek told a colleague that Piłsudski "was so indignant against the French, as he had not been for a long time."[93]

The Eastern Pact

On the eve of his departure to Warsaw, Barthou had resumed talks with Ambassador Dovgalevsky. They were to continue in deepest secrecy, but the Russians quickly complained about leaks to Osuský, Beneš, and Titulescu. Litvinov was also warning Paris about the untrustworthiness of Polish foreign policy. Was he trying to counter an anticipated negative reaction by Poland to the Eastern Pact?[94]

On 29 April, the day Barthou was leaving Prague, Léger outlined the ideas on the pact to the Soviet representative.[95] They corresponded roughly to those already mentioned in the 30 March note. The Russians were surprised both by the proposed membership of Germany and the absence of France in the regional pact. Barthou told Litvinov during their

89. See Ciałowicz, *Polsko-francuski sojusz*, 205; compare DVP SSSR, XVII, 340.

90. Laroche, *Pologne*, 166–67.

91. D'Arbonneau report, 22 Aug. 1934, SHA, EMA/2, Pologne 12.

92. Laroche, *Pologne*, 200.

93. See MS, OSS, Wysocki, III, 258. For a view that the Poles were incensed by what appeared a tendency to subordinate the Polish general staff to Paris, see Cudahy to Secretary of State, 5 July 1934, SDNA, 751.60C/54.

94. See DVP SSSR, XVII, 295–98; DDF, I, VI:340–42; Gregorowicz, *Polsko-radzieckie stosunki*, 188–89.

95. See DDF, I, VI:376–78; DVP SSSR, XVII, 309–11.

Geneva encounter on 18 May that Paris could not be associated in guarantees in the Baltic area; when asked if the pact could hold even if Germany refused to join, Barthou replied with a qualified yes. The invitation to Berlin thus appeared largely tactical. The commissar, who doubted that Warsaw really retained a free hand, inquired about the chances of Polish acceptance of the pact. Were the Poles informed of Soviet-French exchanges? Barthou admitted that he had not said much on the subject while in Warsaw. The Poles "know that we are talking and in what sense," but they were not given precise information. Even the French cabinet would be informed only when a project became ready for submission.[96]

Was Barthou seeking at this point a Franco-Soviet accord on mutual assistance, the Eastern Pact being merely a pretext to achieve it?[97] Even though he told the commissar that the cabinet wanted friendship with Russia "going as far as a military alliance,"[98] a bilateral alliance and the pact were not seen as an either-or-proposition. Paris was after a multilateral pact—acceptable to Britain and Italy and in keeping with the tradition of French diplomacy—within which a special Franco-Russian relationship could be established.[99] From the military viewpoint, the pact could strengthen France by shifting some of the burdens on the USSR without the necessity of new budgetary outlays.

Barthou told the cabinet that he favored Soviet entry into the League but admitted that Soviet leaders were still divided on that issue. In general his approach was much more cautious than that of Herriot.[100] His major speech on foreign policy on 25 May, enthusiastically received by the chamber, contained virtually no references to the Eastern Pact. It mentioned only the USSR in connection with the League and the prolongation of the nonaggression pact with Poland, for which he claimed some credit to the annoyance of Warsaw.[101] The parliamentary success strengthened his hand in the negotiations with the Russians, and on 4 June an agreement was reached on the nature of the Eastern Pact. It would consist of a regional mutual assistance pact (from which the clause about aid being limited to a

96. See DDF, I, VI:496–502; compare DBFP, II, VI:707–708, 719–720. For Barthou's fear of leaks from the cabinet, see DVP, SSSR, XVII, 312–13.

97. This seems to be Duroselle's view in *Décadence*, 534; compare Radice, *Appeasement*, 92–94.

98. Litvinov to Nardomindel, 19 May 1934, DVP SSSR, XVII, 798, n. 156.

99. In British opinion "the scheme for an Eastern Pact was first and foremost a French device for converting the Soviet proposal for a bilateral agreement into something no less useful to France, but more acceptable to world opinion, as being in harmony with the principles of security advocated by the League." Annual report 1934, Poland, FO 371 18887 C 85. Compare with Barthou's formulation in DDF, I, VI:771–72.

100. See Herriot, *Jadis*, 2:432.

101. Speech and relevant interpellations, J.O. Chambre, 1250–62.

neighbor was eliminated); a Franco-Soviet guarantee pact (based on articles 15, paragraph 7, and 16 of the Covenant); and a general treaty signed by all participants. Under this scheme France would be the guarantor of the regional pact, while Russia assumed obligations toward France as if it were a signatory of Locarno.[102]

The French cabinet approved the plan on 5 June; Laval, who favored an accord with Germany, was the only opponent. Barthou still displayed a certain reserve toward a full-fledged Franco-Soviet alliance,[103] which probably stemmed from consideration of Britain, Italy, and Poland. Well aware of Warsaw's crucial position in the proposed scheme, Barthou—who had already talked with Raczyński in Geneva—instructed Laroche to acquaint Beck with the elements of the mid-May conversation with Litvinov. Calling Polish attention to the preliminary and confidential nature of the exchanges, the ambassador pointed out that Poland's participation would make the system an equivalent of an Eastern Locarno and correspond to the Polish policy of balance—a rather strained interpretation. Beck promised to consider the matter, but raised immediately two questions: How could the pact (presumably tied to the League) work since neither Germany nor Russia were members? Should not Romania be included?[104]

The Poles were clearly unenthusiastic. Already in late April, Beck had been telling the Romanian envoy that Poland considered its alliance with France as satisfying its need for security and was not keen on a scheme that would include Germany and Russia.[105] Talking to Barthou on 4 June, Beck was reserved and suspicious. He did not object "in principle" and did not wish to interfere with the French policy, but Warsaw had worked hard to establish an equilibrium in Eastern Europe and wanted to maintain it. The pact would be unthinkable without Germany, and there was no reason to exclude Romania. Beck expressed reservations about including Lithuania with which Poland had no diplomatic relations.[106] On his way back to Warsaw, the foreign minister stopped in Berlin where the matter of the Eastern Pact came up in a conversation with Foreign Minister von Neurath. The French suspected Beck of trying to prejudice Germany against the project, which was not absolutely correct, for although in the months to come Warsaw and Berlin shared a negative attitude, Beck did

102. Text in DDF, I, VI:602–604, 655–56.

103. See Herriot, *Jadis*, 2:437; compare Scott, *Alliance*, 171–72.

104. See DDF, I, VI:513–14, 517–18. Compare Léger's comments in Chłapowski telegram, 26 May 1934, HIA, Amb.Paryż, box 3; also Kuźmiński, *Polska*, 178–81, and Jurkiewicz, *Pakt wschodni*, 139.

105. Laroche to ministry, 28 Apr. 1934, DDF, I, VI:374.

106. For Beck–Barthou conversation, see DTJS, I, 165–66; Beck, *Dernier rapport*, 74–75; DDF, I, VI:645–46.

not want to coordinate his policies with Germany fearing an increased dependence on the latter. Beck spoke to Laroche of German hostility to the pact and enlarged on his own reservations. Czechoslovak participation, for instance, would involve Poland in Danubian problems that it wanted to avoid. The whole composition of the regional pact made little sense; while France wanted to consolidate peace, Russia sought to isolate Germany.[107]

Obviously, Soviet goals differed from the French. Litvinov contemplated entering the League only in order to come closer to Paris, and to cover the European flank in case of a showdown with Japan. The Russians may still have preferred a return to a policy of collaboration with Germany and had doubts about France. Litvinov, however, was reaching the conclusion that matters had gone too far to imagine that Paris was just playing a vast diplomatic game.[108]

A Franco-Soviet partnership appeared highly desirable to Prague, which wished to complement it by its own ties with Moscow. Profiting from a reshuffling of the cabinet and the Little Entente's pronouncement in favor of a de jure recognition of the Soviet Union, Beneš, followed by Bucharest, announced on 9 June the establishment of diplomatic relations with the USSR. He told Litvinov that his country wanted to be as intimate with the Soviet Union as it was with France, and the commissar treated these assurances seriously.[109] The Czechoslovak foreign minister thought that the Eastern Pact would produce a new balance and a new constellation in Europe. German and Polish hands would be tied, and the two countries would find it difficult to avoid participation.[110] Associated with Russia, France would no longer have to face alone the two arbiters—Britain and Italy—who pushed France toward concessions. The pact would prevent other powers from using a Russo-Japanese conflict to pursue their anti-Soviet designs, which could result in a general conflagration. The possibilities of Czechoslovak diplomacy would be enhanced.

107. For this paragraph, DDF, I, VI:620–21, 700–703; ADAP, C II/2:860–62, 866–68; compare Weinberg, *Foreign Policy*, 183.

108. See DDF, I, VI:602, 668–70, 698–99, 755–57; DBFP, II, VI:875–77, 881–82; DVP SSSR, XVII, 400–401, 412–13; Osuský report, 15 June 1934, CPP; Bullitt to Secretary of State, 16 June, SDNA, 740.0011, Mutual Guarantee/3, Eastern Locarno; and to Moore, 6 Oct. in Bullitt, *Correspondence*, 98. Compare Fabry, *Die Sowjetunion*, 45–46; Scott, *Alliance*, 198–99; Kzál, *Spojenectví*, 36; Girardet, "Litvinov," 103–35. From a wider perspective, see Tucker, "The Emergence"; and for the divergence in their interpretations, see Jiři Hochman, *The Soviet Union and the Failure of Collective Security* (Ithaca, 1984), and Jonathan Haslam, *The Soviet Union and the Struggle for Collective Security in Europe 1933–1939* (London, 1984).

109. See DVP SSSR, XVII, 378–79, 417–19.

110. Briefings, 7, 16 June 1934, KV, CPP.

Strangely enough Beneš attempted to influence Warsaw in favor of the Eastern Pact, although such a demarche could only irritate the Poles and produce an opposite effect to the one intended. A similar representation in Berlin evoked Neurath's sarcasm. Optimistically, the foreign minister believed not only that the pact was "likely," but also that Hitler's days were "numbered," A more conservative regime that might succeed him would be more prone to enter, by means of the pact, into direct conversation with Paris and conclude a disarmament convention.[111] Beneš's optimism was affected by a belief in solid support by Paris and Moscow. The Russians, Krofta told Noël, "treat us now as allies and keep us informed of all their diplomatic actions."[112] If Beneš's speech on 2 July contained some sober notes, it emphasized that the pact would not alter French policy in the region. France "would not abandon its friends" just "as the Central European friends of France would not abandon it."[113] Indeed, a few days before Debeney arrived in Warsaw on his thankless errand, Barthou experienced an enthusiastic reception in Bucharest and Belgrade.[114] The French strove to reassert their position in the Danubian area undermined by German economic expansion.[115] "Only the force of France," wrote the envoy from Budapest, "can tighten the [eastern] alliances and make Germany stop and think."[116] Paris wished also to act as mediator between Yugoslavia and Rome, and to strengthen Titulescu's hand vis-à-vis Hungarian revisionism.

French efforts to integrate the strategies of the Little Entente under the aegis of Paris led in July to staff talks between generals Gamelin and Lucien Loizeau and their Czechoslovak colleagues, Krejči and Karel Husárek. The Czechoslovaks wanted France to convince the Romanian general staff that in view of Czechoslovakia's concentration on Germany, it would be up to the other two partners of the Little Entente to deal with Hungary. Bucharest should also be persuaded that a Russian attack, particularly if the Eastern Pact was achieved, was improbable. Gamelin and Loizeau con-

111. See Beneš to missions, 17 June; briefing, 21 June, KV, CPP; Mastný report, 14 July 1934, AAN, Mastný. Compare DDF, I, VI:779–80, 784–85, 801–803, 842; also Benton to Secretary of State, 27 June, 18 July, SDNA, 862.00/3306 and 740.0011, Mutual Guarantee/6 and 22, Eastern Locarno. See also Jurkiewicz, *Pakt Wschodni*, 64; Kzál, *Spojenectví*, 38; Kvaček, "Situation," 223, and *Nad Evropou*, 87–88; Lipski report, 24 March, AAN, Pos. Praga, 12.

112. See DDF, I, VI:822.

113. Speech in Těsnopisecké zprávy, poslanecká sněmovna, 389 schůze, 5–17; discussion, 3 July 1934, 340 schůze, 4–56.

114. See Balcerak, "Wizyty"; see also Barthou's comment, 6 July 1934, CAE/Ch.

115. Berlin was wooing Bucharest and on 1 May signed an economic treaty with Belgrade. The German-Hungarian treaty of 21 Feb. 1934 was in a sense more important economically than the Rome Protocols. See Kaiser, *Economic Diplomacy*, 74–79.

116. Vienne to Barthou, 6 June 1934, DDF, I, VI:631–34.

tinued to insist that Bohemia be used as a pivot of a maneuver against Germany; this plan called for resistance along the Silesian and Austrian borders, which were to be fortified, until French forces could arrive on the right bank of the Rhine.[117] In late September, Gamelin came on a two-week visit to Czechoslovakia. He assisted at army maneuvers and held conversations with members of the government. French-Czechoslovak brotherhood in arms was confirmed.[118]

In late June, the French formally submitted a memorandum on the Eastern Pact, and on 9–10 July Barthou went to London to gain the British endorsement and a promise of promoting it in Warsaw and Rome. He argued that the scheme was not meant to replace the entente with Britain by that with Russia. Paris had resisted Soviet overtures for an alliance but might be forced into it—to prevent a German-Soviet alignment—should the Eastern Pact fall through. The British attempted to link their support with a formula on limited German rearmament and thought they were successful, but Barthou subsequently contested this point by asserting that he had only agreed to consider—*after* the signature of the pact by all prospective members—the question of armaments limitation. He did agree, however, that the system of mutual guarantees between France and Russia be extended to Germany through a tripartite accord.[119]

At this point, Barthou and Beneš reached the conclusion that if the pact fell through in its original form, a Franco-Soviet-Czechoslovak alliance would have to come into being,[120] although the latter arrangement was not preferred. A policy of alliances was opposed by French communists, but not the pact that they saw as a Soviet initiative. The views of the socialists and of such radical leaders as Herriot, Yvon Delbos, Bonnet, and Cot were somewhat similar; Paul-Boncour, however, was torn between conflicting ideas. The moderate Right advocated rapprochement with Moscow but not an alliance. Louis Marin and Tardieu opposed both. Pertinax favored even an alliance but as means of strengthening the eastern allies. Pétain, Gamelin, and Denain, while appreciative of Soviet military power, were skeptical of the Red Army's offensive capabilities. They favored an alliance but not a military convention. Weygand's attitude appeared ambiguous. Fear of Bolshevism accounted for the hostility of the

117. Conversations, 11 July 1934, SHA, EMA/3 7 n 3446/2; Cabinet de Ministre de la Guerre, Tchécoslovaquie 5 N 579/6.

118. On Gamelin's visit, DDF, I, VII:635–36.

119. See DBFP, II, V:769–70, 776–78, 785–87, 801–803; DDF, I, V:940–44, VII:954–65; FRUS 1934, I, 494–95; DVP SSSR, XVII, 489; also Radice, *Appeasement*, 69–74; Scott, *Alliance*, 179–83.

120. See Bullitt telegram, 20 July 1934, SDNA, 740.0011, Mutual Guarantee/15, Eastern Locarno; Barthou intimated this on 6 July, CAE/Ch, and Beneš said it explicitly in early Aug., DDF, I, VII:154.

extreme Right, *L'Action Française* calling collaboration with the USSR "insanity."[121]

The Eastern Pact was to some extent a "psychological means to operate a profound change that Barthou wanted to bring into French policy."[122] It was to restore a dynamic quality, or as the Germans saw it "extend and strengthen France's position of hegemony in Europe."[123] Although this hegemony would be shared with Russia—on which certain French prerogative in Eastern Europe would by necessity devolve—and with Italy in the Danubian basin, it would enable Paris to collaborate on an equal footing with London and treat, from a position of strength, with Berlin.

A realization of the pact hinged on the Poles, whom Barthou tried to cajole and browbeat into following the French lead. Warsaw could hardly admit openly its real objections, for—as a British diplomat in Warsaw rightly saw—the Eastern Pact "run counter to the foreign and military policy of Poland" from "almost every point of view."[124] Beck regarded it as a combination designed to guarantee France's position in the east, and a "form of a big concern, this time Russo-French, to push Poland down."[125] This view accorded with Piłsudski's distinction between the indispensable Franco-Polish bilateral alliance and "the French system in Eastern Europe oriented toward Prague," which he disliked.[126] Barthou's scheme ran counter to Polish efforts to promote their own regional system from the Baltic to Romania; if Beck raised the question of Romanian participation in the Eastern Pact, it was not simply to complicate the negotiations. Titulescu's subsequent efforts to have his country included—which made Paris and Moscow accuse him of being Poland's dupe—as well as his proposals of a tripartite Soviet-Polish-Romanian guarantee pact produced no result (even though Moscow played with it later).[127] In turn, Beck's trip to the Baltic countries in July proved inconclusive.

121. *Le Journal*, *Matin*, and *Journal des Débats* argued that rapprochement with Russia would reinforce international communism, push East Central Europe into German arms, and drag France into a European conflict. See Duroselle, *Décadence*, 113–20; Höhne, *Die Aussenpolitische*, 209, 215–16; Scott, *Alliance*, 195–98; Micaud, *French Right*, 34–35; Gamelin, *Servir*, 2:132–34.

122. Duroselle, "Barthou," 545.

123. Neurath circular, 17 July 1934, ADAP, C, III/1:171–77.

124. Annual report 1934, Poland, FO 371 18887 C 87.

125. 2 July 1934 conference attended by premier Kozłowski, Beck, Sławek, Prystor, and Świtalski. PI, MS, Dziennik Świtalskiego, copy.

126. See Beck, *Dernier rapport*, 21, 73. On the growing gap between the policies of Poland and the Little Entente, see Noël to Barthou, 4 July 1934, MAE, Z 864.5, Tchécoslovaquie 2587.

127. On the Romanian angle, see Skrzypek, "Zagadnienie rumuńskie," 198–200; Teichman, "Titulescu," 673; Zieliński, "Stosunki"; Iordache, *La Petite Entente*, 220–21.

The Poles realized then that to accept the Eastern Pact meant renouncing their own security projects and becoming resigned to Franco-Soviet hegemony. The British saw that also: "Poland's role and prestige, as France's principal ally, would inevitably diminish, and the prominent place she occupied . . . would sooner or later be transferred to Russia."[128] The proposed pact ran counter to both Piłsudski's "canons" of alliances and balance. To rely on one mighty neighbor against the other meant, everything else apart, loss of freedom of decision.[129] Moreover, in the unlikely case of German adhesion, Berlin's price for it would be concessions in the realm of rearmament.[130] Should either Germany or Russia violate the pact, Poland would be obligated to allow the passage of troops through its territory, becoming a battlefield in a war that might not concern it directly. Even if the Poles themselves became victims of aggression, they did not want to be defended by Russia against Germany or vice versa; the memory of partitions was too fresh.[131] In these conditions, Polish diplomacy had to continue its own course and sabotage the Eastern Pact (with all the risks this entailed), for the other alternative, of becoming subordinate to a Franco-Soviet regime, was unacceptable not only to Piłsudski and Beck, but even to the francophile national democrats who had long advocated a return of Russia to European councils.[132] As the British Ambassador Sir Howard Kennard wrote retrospectively, the Eastern Pact was a scheme that "in its original form no Polish government could have subscribed to."[133]

The long story of French demarches and representations in Warsaw to gain Poland's assent to the pact was characterized by lack of candor on both sides. Beck's tactics consisted in raising difficulties. He insisted on the inclusion of Romania and the exclusion of Lithuania and Czechoslovakia. Later he accused the French of accepting the link between the pact and the authorization of German rearmament. Realizing that Polish objectives stemmed from the fear of Russia replacing Poland as France's main ally, the French tried to dispel these anxieties. Laroche advised caution lest the

---

128. Annual report 1934, Poland, FO 371 18887 C 87.

129. See Raczyński, *Od Narcyza*, 80; Komarnicki, *Piłsudski*, 76; Cat-Mackiewicz's article cited in Crosby to Secretary of State, 23 Aug. 1934, SDNA, 740.0011, Mutual Guarantee/43, Eastern Locarno. Compare Władysław Grabski, *Idea Polski* (Warszawa, 1935), 40.

130. British and Italian appraisals in DBFP, II, VI:898–901; DDF, I, VII:226. Compare Zacharias, *Polska*, 172–73.

131. See Łepkowski's argument to that effect in DDF, I, VII:751.

132. See *Gazeta Warszawska*, 17, 18, 28 July, 2, 7, 17 Aug. 1934. Compare Budurowycz, *Polish-Soviet Relations*, 58; Beck on 2 July, AAN, Akta Switalskiego, 71; DTJS, I, 167–69; Erskine report cited in Radice, *Appeasement*, 59.

133. Kennard to Hoare, 15 Dec. 1935, FO 371 18896 Hm 04023.

Poles be driven into German arms. A growing feeling of exasperation permeated the Barthou–Laroche correspondence, replete with comments on Polish "policy of sacred egoism" and sarcastic reference to Poland as "a great power."[134]

Laroche wondered if the Polish government was fanning the smouldering Żyrardów controversy to excite public opinion against France. Prominent Poles were recalling old grievances and complaining about current practices.[135] Pertinax's article "A Secret German-Polish Accord" in *L'Echo de Paris* (24 August) asserted that commercial negotiations between Warsaw and Berlin were aiming at an agreement to provide Polish raw materials to Germany in case of war. Such an agreement would mean a "rupture of the French-Polish alliance" and repudiation of Poland's obligation under the Covenant. Although the next day a Polish denial was printed, the paper commented that if the Poles wished to prove the inaccuracy of such charges, they should cease their press attacks and adhere to the Eastern Pact. It is significant that even the Quai d'Orsay—which had tried to prevent the publication of Pertinax's article—thought at first that the accusation may be true. So did Laroche. The British regarded such allegations as an "absurdity."[136]

The criticism of Polish diplomacy occupied a prominent place in *L'Oeuvre, La République, L'Ere Nouvelle,* and the *Populaire. Journal des Débats* (8, 14 August; 27 October), while opposing the "mirages" of the Eastern Pact, regretted that it provided Warsaw with a pretext to play a game that did not correspond to the spirit of the Franco-Polish alliance.[137] Polish governmental papers responded angrily. *Gazeta Polska* accused the French press of spreading falsehoods and engaging in innuendos. *Kurjer Poranny,* after recalling that nothing remained of the policies of Briand and Paul-Boncour, asked what would remain of those of Louis Barthou. Poland could not follow "the tortuous path" of French diplomacy. Na-

134. Numerous dispatches between 21 June and 20 Aug. 1934 in DDF, I, VI and VII; British comments, DBFP, II, VI:782–84, 839–40, 858–61, 885–86, 892–95, and XII:3, 27. Also note on Beck–Laroche conversation, 5 July; Beck telegram, 14 July; Lipski to Beck, 13 July; HIA, Amb. Paryż, box 5 and 8, and Jędrzejewicz, *Lipski,* 148–50. Compare Bullitt and Cudahy to Secretary of State, 27 July and 1 Aug., respectively FRUS 1934, I, 504 and SDNA, 740.0011 Mutual Guarantee/32, Eastern Locarno.

135. See notes from Quai d'Orsay to Laroche, 20, 22 Aug. 1934, MAE, Z 698.12, Pologne 2198; also DDF, I, VII:205–207, 228–29. Compare Chłapowski telegram, 22 Aug, HIA, Amb. Paryż, box 5.

136. See DBFP, II, XII:50; compare 48. For Polish reaction, see *Gazeta Warszawska,* 26 Aug. 1934, and *Polityka Narodów,* 4 (1934).

137. On press and the irresponsibility of some French papers, Cudahy and Bullitt to Secretary of State, 31 Aug. 1934, SDNA, 7400.0011, Mutual Guarantee/48 and 53, Eastern Locarno; also reports by Laroche, 2, 5, 7 Sept., MAE, Z 698.12, Pologne 2199 and dispatches in 2198.

tional party press organs, although critical of the style of Polish diplomacy and the tone used by the governmental papers, opined that attacks in French journals only profitted Germany.[138] The atmosphere was becoming so unpleasant that Barthou assured Laroche that he would not leave him long in Warsaw, "this hornets' nest."[139]

Polish diplomacy was painfully aware that the French believed in a co-ordination between Warsaw's line and that of Berlin.[140] There was little it could do to change this image, especially because it strove to improve bi-lateral relations with Germany. Commercial agreements, Goebbels's visit to Poland, and the elevation on 1 November of legations to embassies testified to it. Paris took little comfort from numerous indications of mutual German-Polish reserve, Chłapowski's assurances that all Poland would oppose a real connection with Berlin, or General Kazimierz Fabrycy's view that it was "ridiculous and absurd" to imagine a Polish-German alliance. Assertions that Warsaw's main objective was "to keep Germany and Russia distrustful and apart" did not help either.[141] Laroche felt that Poland could have given its adherence in principle and then discussed problems connected with the Eastern Pact; what was lacking was "the sentiment of friendship for France."[142] Doumergue opined that Poland was "no longer our friend."[143] The French ambassador in Moscow commented that if the Eastern Pact destroyed Poland's concept of balance and relegated her to a secondary position in the eastern system, it would be one of the happier results of "the present policy of our country vis-à-vis the USSR." As long as Poland was *the* principal ally it could get from France "all it wanted without even giving to our industry and our commerce the satisfaction they had the right to expect."[144]

---

138. See *Gazeta Polska, Kurjer Poranny*, 2, 3 Sept. 1934. For Beck's somewhat contemptuous remarks about French newspapers, Cudahy to Secretary of State, 5 Sept., SDNA, 740.0011, Mutual Guarantee/54, Eastern Locarno. The tone of the governmental press made the British observe that the Poles were "suffering from swollen head." See Perowne's minutes on Aveling to Simon, 10 Sept., FO 371 17794 Hm 04002. For national democratic press, see *Gazeta Warszawska*, 5, 11, 16 Sept.; *Dziennik Poznański*, 31 Aug.

139. Laroche, *Pologne*, 180.

140. See Raczyński note, 27 Aug. 1934, SI, Komarnicki Collection, 37/3.

141. For the subject, see the many dispatches in DDF, I, VI and VII. Compare Beck telegram 14 June 1934, HIA, Amb.Paryż, box 5; Lipski to Beck, 27 Aug., Jędrzejewicz, *Lipski*, 153–57; compare Weinberg, *Foreign Policy*, 186. Fabrycy's remark cited in Cudahy to Secretary of State, 4 Oct., SDNA, 760C.62/252.

142. See DDF, I, VII:351–52, also 236–39.

143. At cabinet meeting, 22 Sept. 1934, Herriot, *Jadis*, 2:453. For Beck's endeavors to minimize Franco-Polish differences; see Cudahy to Secretary of State, 9 Oct., and Erskine dispatch, 8 Oct. SDNA, 751.60C./58, and FO 371 17794 Hm 04002.

144. Alphand to Barthou, 26 Sept. 1934, MAE, Z 698.1, Pologne 2100.

Beck was playing for time. A cartoon in a Polish satirical journal showed Barthou in a captain's uniform on board a ship called "Eastern Locarno" and Beck, standing on a desert island with two life preservers inscribed: "nonaggression declaration with Germany" and "nonaggression treaty with the USSR." Barthou calls out, "It is safer aboard," and Beck replies, "I will wait."[145] An American diplomat could think of no other word to characterize French feeling toward Poland than "disgust."[146] On the Polish side, Premier Leon Kozłowski repeated the phrase that the Poles were France's allies, but "will not be slaves nor will we be sold out."[147]

Moscow's willingness to join the League of Nations made Paris nervous about the Polish reaction. Beck raised no objections provided Russia expressly assured the Poles that it would honor all its obligations as a member and reaffirm the Treaty of Riga articles on noninterference in domestic affairs. Parallel Polish-Russian and French-Russian negotiations ensued, crowned at the last moment by Soviet acceptance of Warsaw's demands. On 8 September, French and Polish governments exchanged notes concerning Russian commitments; two days later a Soviet-Polish exchange of notes followed. All this did not bring Warsaw and Paris any closer to one another. Beck speaking with Barthou on 7 September did not depart from his previously stated reservations, which, according to Barthou, would void the Eastern Pact of any content. The Frenchman uttered a veiled threat: France might have to sign a bilateral accord with Russia. Beck replied that this was France's affair.[148]

On 10 September, Germany officially stated its negative position toward the Eastern Pact; seventeen days later a Polish memorandum made it clear, without slamming the door to further negotiations, that Warsaw could not join the pact under present circumstances.[149] French annoyance with the Polish stand was compounded by Beck's unexpected announcement in Geneva on 13 September that as long as the regime of national minority protection was not generalized, Poland would refuse to cooperate with international organs entrusted with it. The statement, although related to the Soviet entry into the League, was meant to demonstrate Poland's inde-

---

145. Cartoon in *Mucha*, reproduced in Ziaja, *PPS*, 237.

146. Einstein's private letter to Secretary of State, 28 Sept. 1934, SDNA, 840.00/383 1/2.

147. Cited in Cannistraro and Wynot, "Polish Foreign Policy," 79–81.

148. See DDF, I, VII:390–92 and DTJS, I, 170–71. Beck told Eden that Poland was "not prepared to sacrifice these good relations [with Germany and Russia] for an uncertain gain." See DBFP, II, VII:734–35. Compare Komarnicki–Jean Paul-Boncour conversation, DTJS, I, 174–76. Potocki remarked that if a Franco-Soviet entente materialized instead of the pact, Poland would have to make "bonne mine au mouvais jeu." Cited in Jurkiewicz, *Pakt wschodni*, 84.

149. Memorandum, 27 Sept. 1934, DDF, I, VII:590–92; DTJS, I, 178–81. Beck's comments in telegram, 4 Oct., HIA, Amb. Paryż, box 5.

pendence in international life.[150] The returning Beck received a hero's welcome in Poland; the jubilation was not restricted to governmental circles.

French diplomats spoke of a serious tactical error on Warsaw's part, and the press went farther. "The Treaty of Versailles is torn to pieces," *Le Quotiden* entitled its lead article on 14 September. Recalling all that had been done for Poland, Elie Bois wrote in *Petit Parisien* (27 September) that this was how Warsaw was repaying France. Buré accused Beck in *L'Ordre* (15, 21 September) of hatred for France. By destroying the minority treaty, Warsaw was working "pour le roi de Prusse." And he added: "our country has pardoned everything till now, but its patience is wearing thin." The Polish government press hotly responded.

General d'Arbonneau commented on the "sickly exaltation" of Polish public opinion that "likes to get drunk periodically with the 'great power elixir' served it by the government."[151] The chargé d'affaires, analyzing the "permanent causes, largely of psychological nature" that accounted for the Polish-French crisis, stressed the xenophobia of the regime, personal characteristics of Piłsudski and Beck, and the overoptimistic appraisal of the two neighbors. France seemed corrupt, degenerate, and unable to overcome its own malady. The Eastern Pact initiative was a move in which Poland could become the object of "horse trading."[152]

Beck assumed that Barthou, having achieved his object of bringing Russia to the League, would now work for further rapprochement with Moscow. As long as the present Franco-Russian flirtation continued, Beck told the British ambassador, Polish relations with France were "unlikely to resume their cordiality."[153]

Czechoslovak-Soviet rapprochement ran parallel to that between Paris and Moscow. Beneš conferred with Litvinov and positively responded to the idea of a nonaggression pact, provided it was signed by all members of the projected Eastern Pact and treated as a step toward close tripartite Franco-Soviet-Czechoslovak cooperation. The French were pleased with the foreign minister's handling of the Russian question and grateful for his efforts to encourage the USSR to join the League.[154] Were it only possible to close the Prague-Warsaw gap.

150. For the background and synthesis see Michowicz, *Walka dyplomacji polskiej*. Also, Raczyński, *Od Narcyza*, 71–79; Noël to Barthou, 18 Apr. 1934 and Payart to Barthou, 18 June, MAE Z 864.5, Tchécoslovaquie 2587 and Z 698.13, Pologne 2195. Compare DDF, I, VII:359–60.

151. D'Arbonneau report, 3 Oct. 1934, SHA, EMA/2, Pologne 12. Compare 19 Sept. report.

152. Bressy to Barthou, 3 Oct. 1934, DDF, I, VII:561–67.

153. Cited in Radice, *Appeasement*, 92.

154. Correspondence in DDF, I, VII:336–89, 499, 644; also chargé to Secretary of State, 7 Sept. 1934, SDNA, 740.0011, Mutual Guarantee/53, Eastern Locarno.

During General Gamelin's visit in September the Czechoslovak command and the defense minister, Bohumír Bradáč, publicly displayed pro-Polish sentiments. This happened to coincide, however, with war games held by Piłsudski at Moszczenica, the theme of one of them being a military seizure of the contested area in Teschen in the event of Czechoslovakia's disintegration or capitulation to Germany. The Czechs associated this war game with the alleged plans of Polish-Hungarian cooperation directed against their country and were seriously disturbed.[155] The assassination of Poland's interior minister, Bronisław Pieracki, by a Ukrainian nationalist in June led in turn to Polish accusations of Prague for harboring the Ukrainian emigration. In the course of sharp press polemics the *Ilustrowany Kurjer Codzienny* wrote that in 1933 Poland had proposed a military alliance to Prague that the latter turned down. *Prager Presse* and *České Slovo* rejoined that this charge was untrue. Eventually, Beneš's private and public efforts—which even Beck had to acknowledge—temporarily helped to ease the tension, but no real improvement was in sight.[156]

Beneš could hardly approve of the Polish action in Geneva. He explained to Raczyński that his own past demands for the generalization of the minorities' protection were being made for tactical purposes. But Beck's move had weakened the League. Poland's policy of balance, he opined, could lead to a collapse of the Franco-Polish alliance, and if Paris broke with Warsaw and entered the road of cooperation with Berlin, Prague would follow its lead. As long as the alliance existed, however, Czechoslovakia was on Poland's side.[157]

Beneš seemed to believe, or pretended to, that German southward expansion would stop and the offensive against Poland resume. Such views were colored by wishful thinking. True, Hitler had not succeeded in winning over Mussolini at their June encounter in Venice, and the murder of the duce's Austrian protegé, Chancellor Dollfuss by local Nazis incensed Rome. Still, Mussolini continued to regard Czechoslovakia as a mosaic of nationalities that could not survive. Beneš himself heard rumors that Hitler was seriously envisaging an attack on Austria and France, counting on Poland to stay neutral and Yugoslavia to keep Italy in check.[158]

155. See Bułhak, "Z Dziejów 1927–1936," 136–37; Polish military attaché report, 3 (?) Oct. 1934, AAN, MSZ 5424. For Bradáč's remarks, Noël to Barthou, 16 Sept. 1934, MAE, Z 864.5, Tchécoslovaquie 2587, and *České Slovo*, 11 Sept. On Moszczenica, Jędrzejewicz, *Kronika*, 2:490–91, and compare DDF, I, VII:570–71; d'Arbonneau report 3 Oct., SHA, EMA/2, Pologne 12.

156. See Kozeński, *Czechosłowacja*, 117–25; Noël and Laroche to Barthou, 26, 30 June, 2, 4, 5, 21 July 1934, MAE, Z 864.5, Tchécoslovaquie 2569 and 2587.

157. Beneš–Raczyński conversation, 16 Sept. 1934, SI, Komarnicki Collection 37/3. Krofta minimized the significance of Beck's move; see 20 Sept. briefing, CPP. On Beneš's views, see DDF, I, VII:461.

158. See Kvaček, "Boj," 251. Noël to Massigli, 3 Oct. 1934, MAE, P.A. Massigli 6. A

Around 20 September, the utterance of the Polish envoy Grzybowski seemed to have become more conciliatory. Warsaw, he said, was satisfied that Prague had properly handled the Ukrainian issue. Poland had no intention of leaving Geneva or siding with Germany. Were the Poles trying to be reassuring on the eve of their virtual rejection of the Eastern Pact, or did they, as Krofta and Noël speculated, experience a feeling of isolation?[159] Beneš, who had been willing to find a formula that would not involve Polish obligations to Czechoslovakia under the Eastern Pact, and so remove Polish objections to it was bitter about Poland's negative stand.[160] If Girsa regarded Piłsudski as "too astute" to bring his country too close to Germany, many Czechoslovak papers took seriously the earlier-mentioned allegations of a secret German-Polish deal as described in *L'Echo de Paris*.[161] Some Czechoslovak circles believed that the marshal, who had "never concealed his dislike for a democratic form of government," secretly sympathized "with Nazi methods." By fanning the distrust of Polish leaders, Soviet Russia was contributing to a further poisoning of the Czechoslovak-Polish atmosphere.[162]

The efforts by Paris and Prague to salvage the Eastern Pact receded temporarily into the background as Barthou turned to the issue of a Mediterranean or Danubian accord (or a combination of the two) that was to constitute the southern wing of his "great design." Such a vast scheme, meant to replace the tripartite Franco-Italian-Yugoslav project opposed by Mussolini, had been in an embryonic stage already in mid-June.[163] The duce's resolute stand after Dollfuss's assassination heightened French interest in closer collaboration with Rome, even though Barthou still displayed caution. The French Right pressed for a rapprochement in the belief that France and Italy could jointly make the Rhine and the Danube effective ramparts against German expansion.[164] By mid-September, Barthou became inclined to examine more seriously the modalities of Franco-Italian cooperation in the frame of a Danubian organization. His assurances that he would not consent to sacrifices by the Little Entente apparently

few months later Hitler was telling Gömbös "I shall utterly crush France"; Weinberg, *Foreign Policy*, 114.

159. See briefing, 20 Sept. 1934, KV, CPP; Noël to Barthou, 20 Sept., MAE, Z 864.5, Tchécoslovaquie 2857; Benton to Secretary of State 20 Sept., SDNA, 740.0011, Mutual Guarantee/60, Eastern Locarno.

160. See Noël to Barthou, 29 Sept., 4 Oct. 1934, MAE, Z 864.5, Tchécoslovaquie 2587 and DDF, I, vii:661–63. Compare 24 Sept. and 4 Oct. briefings, KV, CPP.

161. Trimestrial survey of Czechoslovak press, 1 Oct. 1934, SHA, EMA/2, Tchécoslovaquie 9; also briefing, 13 Sept., KV, CPP.

162. See, respectively, chargé to Secretary of State, 5 Sept. 1934, SDNA, 760C. 60F.151 and DDF, I, vii:573–74.

163. Clerk to Simon, 15 June 1934, DBFP, II, vi:759–60.

164. See DDF, I, vi:705–706, 709–11; also Höhne, *Die Aussenpolitische*, 223.

diminished the anxiety of their ministers who, meeting in Geneva, came out in favor of a Rome-Paris rapprochement. King Alexander of Yugoslavia appeared more skeptical. It was largely to convince him that the French invited the king on a state visit to France. In the course of his stay an accord on common policy was to intervene. Barthou planned a subsequent trip to Rome, aiming to resolve bilateral differences and bring about a modus vivendi between Italy and Yugoslavia. We will never know how successful he would have been, for on 9 October, shortly after Alexander's arrival at Marseilles, the king succumbed to an assassin's bullets. Barthou, grieviously wounded, bled to death.

This tragic event was heavy with consequences for France and Europe. Barthou had succeeded in restoring to French diplomacy a certain drive and prestige that had been sorely lacking. Of course, his efforts were not uniformly successful. The Eastern Pact proposal brought Paris into a collision course with Warsaw, which Barthou's personal diplomacy could only obfuscate. The degree of Polish bitterness could be gauged from the fact that the government failed to offer condolences to the French embassy on the minister's death.[165] By contrast, Czechoslovakia responded to the news from Marseilles by decreeing three days of national mourning.[166]

Barthou's demise left much unfinished business. Promoting the Eastern Pact seemed futile, but could a formula be still devised to preserve some of its essence? Was the projected Danubian Pact its competitor or a complementary device? Could the eventual alignments with Russia and Italy form the elements of a still wider combination, including even London and Berlin? And how would the eastern alliances fare in all these possibilities? How Barthou would have played his hand in the long run is hard to say, but his successor was left with cards that could be dealt in several different ways.

165. An oversight is hard to imagine, for condolences were extended to the Yugoslav legation. The French chargé d'affaires bitterly commented that Barthou had not only been a signatory of the 1921 alliance but also the bearer of Poland's highest order of the White Eagle. Bressy thought that the incident was symptomatic of Piłsudski's state of mind. See DDF, I, VIII:725.

166. See Havas correspondence, 15 Oct. 1934, MZV-VA, 190.949. Compare DDF, I, VIII:240n.

Chapter Twelve

Fronts or Façades?

Laval's First Steps

Barthou's succession went to Pierre Laval who continued, after the fall of Doumergue's cabinet in November, as foreign minister in the government of Pierre-Etienne Flandin. Laval's appearance and certain vulgarity of manner made many contemporaries liken him to a Levantine salesman. To a ranking British diplomat he epitomized the tricky, unscrupulous, and corrupt French politician.[1] A strong personality, more shrewd than knowledgeable, Laval was a pragmatist, even an opportunist, who regarded Briand and Caillaux as his political mentors. The stigma of his collaboration with Nazi Germany during the Vichy period, transferred retroactively to his activities in the mid-1930s, blackened his image as France's foreign minister to an extent that does not appear warranted.[2]

The domestic situation Laval inherited was characterized by political and economic strains. Doumergue's vain efforts to strengthen the executive finally led to his fall, and the radicals who had largely engineered it reentered the Flandin government, whose composition did not appreciably differ from that of its predecessor. Premier Flandin was cartooned as a stork standing on one leg and wondering: "sur la droite ou sur la gauche?"[3] A "neo-opportunistic" trend (to borrow Duroselle's term) prevailed, and Laval with his involvement with the Parisian press and various rightist and leftist pressure groups suited this trend well.

Laval's diplomacy sought to combine the Briandist approach to Germany with the external trappings of firmer policies associated with Barthou. If a real dialogue with Berlin was not possible, hopes for détente

1. "Laval reeked of *la pourriture*," commented Vansittart, *Lessons*, 38.

2. See Warner, *Laval*, 24–26; Baumont, *Origins*, 100–104; Duroselle, *Décadence*, 125; Adamthwaite, *France*, 32; Robert O. Paxton, *Vichy France: Old Guard and New Order 1940–1944* (New York, 1972), 27; Paul-Boncour, *Entre deux guerres*, 3:2. For a contemporary portrait by Hoesch, see ADAP, C, III/1:477–81. According to Flandin, *Politique*, 166, Laval "differed from Briand only with respect to means."

3. Cited in Reynaud, *Mémoires*, 1:380.

were. If Laval was more suspicious of London than his predecessors, he could not ignore Britain. Rapprochement with Italy and talks on the Danubian Pact took precedence over cooperation with Russia and discussions of the Eastern Pact. The foreign minister was willing to dilute the proposed Eastern Pact in the hope of overcoming German and Polish opposition, and avoiding a tête-à-tête with Moscow. Laval's final objective was to entangle the major powers and lesser allies in a network of accords, pacts, and fronts constituting a complex security system that would prevent a direct threat to France. Was "a consolidation and a revision of the French position with regard to Poland, the Little Entente, and more generally Central Europe" implied in the above? Flandin later asserted that it was.[4]

In explaining the main lines of his policy, Laval tried to reassure the parliament that the entente with Rome would be subordinated to that between Italy and the Little Entente, especially Yugoslavia. Poland, he hoped, would accept a modified Eastern Pact. He evaded, however, the question whether France would sign an accord with Russia should the pact flounder on the rocks of German and Polish opposition.[5] His remarks were generally well received. True, Franklin-Bouillon criticized past mistakes, warned against Nazi Germany, and rejected the idea of direct talks as well as the legalization of German rearmament. He demanded the strengthening of France, particularly in the military field.[6] Other deputies insisted that only a complete entente with Russia would stabilize Europe. All this was hardly novel. The debate was marked by just one departure from the tradition: all the usual references to Poland were missing, a fact that reflected the strain between Warsaw and Paris.[7]

The unfortunate timing of the Hungarian premier Gyula Gömbös's visit to Warsaw—coinciding with King Alexander's funeral—led to speculations about Hungarian-Polish-German alignment. Although Laroche perceived the relative unimportance of Gömbös's trip, suspicions increased as Warsaw showed itself friendly to Hungary while the latter was being censored in Geneva over the Barthou–Alexander murder.[8] "It would be absurd and even ridiculous to speak still, at this moment, of a Franco-Polish

---

4. Flandin, *Politique*, 170.

5. Sessions, 15 and 30 Nov. 1934, respect. CAE/Ch and J.O. Chambre, 2834–35.

6. See 30 Nov. 1934 session, J.O. Chambre, 2838, 1842–43.

7. 1 Dec. 1934, session, J.O. Chambre, 2861. For Poles noting it, see Laroche to Laval, 5 Dec. 1934, MAE, Z 698.12, Pologne 2199.

8. On the Gömbös visit and the Geneva debates, see Juhász, *Foreign Policy*, 118; Fiala, *Soudobé Polsko*, 180, 280–81; Gawroński, *Moja misja*, 221; Günther, *Pióropusz i Szpada*, 137–38; Kuźmiński, *Polska*, 205–206; Bennett Kovrig, "Mediation; DDF, I, VII:856–58, VIII:222–24, and numerous reports in MAE, Z 698.1, Pologne 2100; Z 698.10, Tchécoslovaquie 2604; SHA, EMA/2, Pologne 12. Compare speeches of 7 and 10 Dec. in Beneš, *Le Sens*.

alliance that exists on paper but no longer in fact," wrote *Journal des Débats* on 27 October. *La Revue Hebdomadaire* spoke of "the Polish enigma" (3 November); *Le Temps* expressed concern and amazement (16 October) over Polish external policy.

The Quai d'Orsay traced the growing estrangement to Beck's nomination in 1932 through Hitler's ascent and the Four Power Pact.[9] Although the French took some comfort in the criticism of Beck by the opposition and even by some government circles, Laroche did not entirely subscribe to the theory that an improvement in Franco-Polish relations was impossible as long as Beck remained in charge. Piłsudski, growing ever more despotic, was probably issuing directives that no one dared to modify. Laroche recommended firmness but warned against questioning the value of the French-Polish alliance that only would push Warsaw into German arms. The alliance mattered and should be adjusted; the stronger France was, the less would the Poles be tempted to seek counter-assurances elsewhere. President Mościcki, "all the high personalities," and diplomats like Lipski wanted to maintain the alliances.[10] General Louis Faury, the former commander of the Polish Higher War College, after visiting Poland in November concluded that the damage done was "not too great," and the army as well as the population remained francophile.[11] In fact, it was the French high command that showed a good deal of reticence. General Gamelin thought that it would suffice "to maintain the façade" of collaboration between the intelligence services; he ordered that Colonel Józef Englicht of the Polish second bureau be shown no important documents while in Paris.[12]

It fell to a ranking Piłsudskiite and a reputed francophile, General Roman Górecki, to open a dialogue with the French. As president of the Polish section of allied veterans association (Fédération Interalliée des anciens combatants, or FIDAC), he addressed in mid-November an open letter to the former French comrades in arms. The letter was obviously cleared or even written with the help of foreign ministry; perhaps Beck himself had a hand in it.[13] General Faury wondered if this unorthodox

9. Note of direction politique, 2 Nov. 1934, MAE, Z 698.12, Pologne 2199.

10. See DDF, I, VII:868–71; also François-Poncet report, 13 Jan. 1935, MAE, Z 698.12, Pologne 2199. For attacks on Beck see Sprawozdania stenograficzne sejmu, 11 Dec. 1934, 25–27; *Gazeta Warszawska*, 21 Oct. and 23 Nov.; *Robotnik*, 24 Nov. also DDF, I, VIII:370–72. Piłsudski, feeling increasingly pessimistic about French military capabilities, told a Warsaw lawyer: "France will not win this war [with Germany]"; see Jędrzejewicz, *Kronika*, 2:495.

11. See DDF, I, VII:916, VIII:81–82; d'Arbonneau reports, 14 Nov. 20, 26 Dec. 1934, SHA, EMA/2, Pologne 12.

12. Koeltz to d'Arbonneau, 23 Oct. 1934, SHA, EMA/2, Pologne 12.

13. Reports of d'Arbonneau and Laroche, 14, 22 Nov. 1934, respectively SHA, EMA/2, Pologne 12, and MAE, Z 698.12, Pologne 2199.

gambit was chosen to avoid a possible loss of face; the Quai d'Orsay called it a "maneuver," but it could not be ignored.[14]

Górecki, having asserted his unshakable faith in the Franco-Polish alliance and calling on the veterans to dissipate the existing misunderstandings, proceeded to list Polish grievances. They included the absence of a Polish state loan on the French market; insufficient credits, most of which had to be spent on purchases in France; and unsatisfactory operations of French private capital in Poland. These grievances, as well as the unfavorable Polish trade balance and the bad treatment of Polish workers in France, suggested that Paris was hardly making a sustained effort to assist its ally economically. In the political sphere, Locarno and its consequences weighed heavily on their relationship. Paris behaved as if it "regarded the alliance indispensable for Poland but facultative for France." It paid scant attention to its ally's interests in the evacuation of the Rhineland, the Gleichberechtigung declaration of December 1932, the Four Power Pact, or in pressuring Poland to hasten its nonaggression treaty with the USSR. But if the Poles had cause to complain, they hoped that the damage could be repaired. They did want to collaborate, but not to play the role of a satellite or client.[15]

The reply by the chairman of the French veterans (prepared in cooperation with the Quai d'Orsay and the association of French industrialists in Poland) appeared on 10 January 1935 in *L'Oeuvre*.[16] It acknowledged the justified Polish pride over their achievements but questioned their oversensitivity. It claimed that Poland had not always kept France informed of its policy. Some Polish complaints appeared contradictory; French capital was simultaneously sought after and discriminated against. Górecki's interpretation of Locarno, the Four Power Pact, and the Soviet-Polish negotiations was disputed. Paris did not reproach Poland the conclusion of the pact with Germany; it only questioned some of its consequences. Having denied the validity of Polish grievances, the letter stated that "France had never departed from practices based on sincerity and trust, which one expects between allies." Warsaw had to realize, however, that while Poland could behave like an architect who builds in an open space, the French were encumbered by various constraints. They had to respect many structures, among which the alliance was considered a most valuable factor in a policy of peace.

The Górecki letter, meant to clear the air and appeal directly to French public opinion, was not a success. Nor was a much less publicized inter-

14. Note and commentary, 6, 10 Dec. 1934, MAE, Z 698.12, Pologne 2199; compare session, 21 Nov., CAE/Ch.

15. Excerpts in DTJS, 1, 182–86. Original in French (thirty-two pages) attached to minutes of 21 Nov. 1934 session, CAE/Ch; printed in *Revue Hebdomadaire*, 22 Dec.

16. For documentation see MAE, Z 698.12, Pologne 2199.

view by Radziwiłł. A diplomat commented: "the Poles may be tiresomely self-confident but I think they are justified in claiming that the French misunderstand them."[17] Even worse, some French actions went beyond misunderstanding. In March 1935, *Le Bourbonnais Républicain* (owned by former minister L. Lamoureux, a friend of Marcel Boussac) printed a purported text of a secret German-Polish pact of 25 February 1934, according to which the signatories bound themselves to closest political collaboration and even joint military action in case one of them was victim of aggression. *La République* reprinted the "document" on 18 April.[18]

Regarding press polemics as harmful, Laval thought that if Poland owed a good deal to France the French had a tendency to remind the Poles of it rather too often. He proposed to make Poland cultivate the same policy toward France "that I intend to practice vis-à-vis" Poland.[19] The Poles, having on the whole welcomed Laval at the Quai d'Orsay, thought they detected signs, already before Barthou's death, of a slackening in the promotion of the Eastern Pact.[20] Now they hoped that Laval would drop it altogether. Chłapowski characterized him as more interested in a détente with Berlin than in further rapprochement with Moscow, and seemingly desirous to improve Franco-Polish relations. Mühlstein wrote that Warsaw might not fully realize the extent of anti-Polish feelings released by its diplomacy. The popular opinion in France was that the Poles had abandoned the alliance and gone over to the German side. The counselor did not advise, however, any drastic policy changes, for should Poland in its search for French amity worsen its position in Berlin, the Polish cause in Paris would hardly be helped. Chłapowski suggested concessions in the Żyrardów affair and regarding commercial orders placed in France.[21]

The Quai d'Orsay had refused to treat the Polish memorandum of 27 September as amounting to a rejection of the Eastern Pact. Laval hoped that by satisfying Polish objections about Lithuania and Czechoslovakia, and by working out a formula on German armaments, he could entice Warsaw into collaboration. Beck responded that the Eastern Pact was not a well-chosen terrain for the improvement of French-Polish relations. The British were warning Laroche not to press the Poles too hard: a Franco-

17. Minute on Erskine 13 Dec. 1934 dispatch, FO 371 17794 C 8652; for Radziwiłł interview, see Radice, Appeasement, 104.

18. Noël claims in *Polonia*, 101, 168, that Boussac was the instigator. The Polish embassy ignored these "revelations"; however, it cut subsidies to some papers.

19. Sessions, 15 Nov. 1934, CAE/Ch.

20. See DTJS, I, 174; Skrzypek, *Strategia*, 178. Compare Erskine telegram, 8 Oct. 1934, FO 371 17794 Hm 04002.

21. Beck–Chłapowski exchange, 26 Oct. 1934, HIA, Amb. Paryż, box 5 and AAN, Pos. Praga, 8; Mühlstein to Dębicki, 2, 7 Nov., SI, Komarnicki Collection, kol.37/3 and DTJS, I, 181–82. Also DDF, I, VII:847–50; Laroche, *Pologne*, 184.

Soviet alliance would not compensate Paris for the loss of Poland. Ambassador Laroche's argument that the Eastern Pact had been originally conceived precisely to reconcile the Polish alliance with a rapprochement with Moscow sounded unconvincing. London believed that the French saw the pact mainly as a compensation for rearmament concessions that would eventually be made.[22]

Beck, while professing a desire to talk to Laval, failed to appear in Geneva, leaving his delegate to reiterate Polish objections. This had a chilling effect on French governmental circles.[23] Persevering, the Quai d'Orsay virtually accepted all Polish reservations in a note of 23 November; it even agreed to an explicit reference in the pact to the German-Polish declaration.[24] The ministry suggested the following timetable of negotiations of the Eastern Pact. Once Warsaw admitted that its objections had been met, Paris should offer Germany a collective pact of nonaggression and consultation, *without* a mutual assistance clause. Such a pact would still be acceptable to Litvinov because it would provide a basis for a Franco-Soviet accord on mutual aid. Having obtained the general consent of Berlin, the French would turn again to Poland to persuade it to accept a diluted version of the pact. Only at this stage would comprehensive Franco-German conversations intervene. The entire operation was to be carried unhurriedly, the final negotiations following a settlement in the Saar.[25]

The slow pace (which Beck had taken for granted) suddenly changed, and Laroche demanded a prompt conclusion of discussions. The earlier signals were explained away as a "misunderstanding" much to Polish surprise. The volte-face was due to strong Soviet pressure, seconded by the Little Entente, on Laval to mark progress in the Franco-Soviet rapprochement.[26]

French soundings in Berlin, Laval's contacts with Ribbentrop, and visits by prominent Frenchmen in Germany aroused misgivings. The great

22. See Chłapowski telegram, 1 Nov. 1934, HIA, Amb. Paryż, box 5, and Beck to missions, 3 Nov., SI, Amb. Londyn, A.12.52/13; and to embassy in Paris, 7 Nov., AAN, MSZ 55. Also DDF, I, VIII:52, 158–61.

23. See Beck telegram, 19 Nov. 1934, AAN, MSZ 55. Also DBFP, II, XII:227; Massigli and Laroche to Laval, 20, 22 Nov., 11 Dec., MAE, Z 698.12, Pologne 2199 and DDF, I, VIII:345–46. Also Laroche, *Pologne*, 186; Herriot, *Jadis*, 2:488.

24. DDF, I, VIII:200–203; comment and summary in Kuźmiński, *Polska*, 219, Pułaski, *Stosunki*, 97, and Wojciechowski, *Stosunki*, 154 who argues that Paris strove to obtain a confirmation from Warsaw that the declaration would not diminish Polish obligations toward France if Poland joined the Eastern Pact.

25. See DDF, I, VII:900–902; DBFP, II, XII:216.

26. See Beck and Chłapowski telegrams, 19, 23 Nov. 1934, AAN, MSZ 55, and HIA, Amb. Paryż, box 5; also DDF, I, VIII:15–16, 235–37; minutes on Erskine dispatch, 2 Dec., FO 371 17794 Hm 04002; Palairet and Erskine to Simon, 8, 21 Nov., FO 371 17794 C 7622.

French industrialist François de Wendel wrote: "Laval wants to outsmart the Germans, but he will be duped by them."[27] Hitler took conciliatory gestures for a sign of weakness stemming from a belated realization that France had missed the opportunity of a preventive war.[28] Even if Laval saw a rapprochement within a broader collective framework, apprehension was aroused in Prague and serious reflection in Poland.[29] As for Moscow, Ambassador Alphand opined that if it felt a real threat of a Franco-German alignment it "would not hesitate to overtake France and respond to German overtures" itself.[30]

On 5 December, Litvinov extracted from Laval a formal French engagement in the form of a joint protocol that stated that neither signatory would enter into negotiations—aiming at the conclusion of bilateral or multilateral accords contrary to the spirit of the Eastern Pact—with future members of it. Each side would inform the other if it became the recipient of such proposals; both affirmed their determination to work for the pact. If the protocol restricted Laval's freedom of maneuver, the agreement not to abandon efforts for the Eastern Pact, except by mutual consent, allowed him to promote slowly different variants while delaying the conclusion of a genuine treaty with Moscow.[31]

The French acquainted Warsaw with the protocol, which pleased Beck, especially in view of circulating rumors of a French alliance with the USSR or Germany, but this courtesy did not change his attitude.[32] To the American Ambassador John Cudahy he described the projected pact as a "building with a beautiful façade" with "nothing behind the façade." To avoid, however, a purely negative position, Beck proposed a formula acceptable to Laval: Poland gave its "adhesion de principe" not to the pact itself, but to the "enterprise diplomatique au cours de négociation." Warsaw would not object to further negotiations while making its acceptance of the final outcome dependent on German participation and the right phrasing of the document.[33] Beck's stand may have been influenced by Chłapowski's report that, although Laval would not abandon the path leading to an alli-

27. Entry, 24 Nov. 1934 in Jeanneney, 543.

28. Hitler on 4 Dec. 1934, ADAP, C, III/2:688.

29. See Kvaček, "Jednání," 27; *Nad Evropou*, 100–101; Kuźmiński, *Polska*, 207–210.

30. See DDF, I, VIII:67–69. Compare I, VII:753–58, 785, 789–90.

31. Text, DDF, I, VIII: 319, also X:509–10. Compare ADAP, C, III/2:708–709; Scott, *Alliance*, 212; Ádám, "Les Pays," 16; Ormos, "Sur les causes," 28; Kvaček, "Jednání," 26.

32. See DDF, I, VII:223–31, 233–34, 319.

33. See Beck circulars, 6, 16 Dec. 1934, AAN, MSZ 55; MS, OSS, Wysocki, III, 371–73; FRUS 1934, I, 522–23; Jędrzejewicz, *Lipski*, 157–62; DTJS, I, 200. For French pressures, see DDF, I, VIII:378, 411–12, 436–37.

ance with Russia, he was reluctant to finalize the deal. Moreover, whereas the original Eastern Pact had been a screen for negotiations with the USSR, in Laval's hands it became a screen for a rapprochement with Berlin. A Polish general placet would permit Paris to continue further exchanges.[34] As for German rearmament, Laval was willing to discuss it with Germany but not before the Eastern and Danubian pacts were well advanced.[35] The Poles were told again that although there was no formal link between Germany's adhesion to the Eastern Pact and a legalization of its armaments, a certain de facto connection could not be denied.[36]

During conversations in Geneva (16 and 19 January) Beck repeated the objections to the Eastern Pact and recalled Piłsudski's statements to Barthou that Poland's policy could never become dependent on Moscow or Berlin. Laval tried to persuade his colleague that France had no vested interests in Eastern Europe outside of Poland and kept calling the latter a great power. Beck replied that Poland was not that, but in the region meant to remain its own master. Laval later told Beneš that he confronted the Pole with a brutal question, whether Warsaw was going with Berlin or Paris. One does not find this statement in the records, nor is it likely that Laval warned Beck of the heavy responsibility Poland would incur if it sabotaged the pact. In fact, Beck seemed confirmed in his view that Laval was mainly interested in a détente with Berlin, and his advocacy of the Eastern Pact stemmed from Czechoslovak and Soviet pressures. Although the conversation ended with mutual professions of amity, it satisfied neither side.[37]

Prague, which acceded to the Laval–Litvinov December protocol, had hoped ever since Barthou's death that his policies would be continued. Attending Barthou's funeral, Beneš lost no time seeking to obtain a clear picture of Laval's diplomacy, and expounding his own views to Doumergue, Laval, Léger, and the military leaders. Learning that Paris would slow down the tempo of its rapprochement with Russia, he feared that Germany would try to exploit it by creating havoc in Central Europe, isolating Russia, and imposing what would amount to a most disadvantageous compromise on rearmament. Beneš repeated his well-known views on the Italo-Yugoslav angle, the Anschluss, and the Habsburg restoration.

---

34. Chłapowski reports, 8, 31 Dec. 1934, AAN, Amb. Berlin, 83 and 84. For Laval's stress on conciliations with Germany, see DBFP, II, XII:228.

35. See Franco-British conversations, 22 Dec. 1934, DBFP, II, XII:342–56.

36. See conversation with Bargeton, 15 Jan. 1935, DTJS, I, 469–70.

37. See DDF, I, IX:77–78, 89–90, also VIII:637–38, IX:31–32; Herriot, *Jadis*, 2:495–96. Compare Beck telegrams, 19, 24 Jan. 1935, SI, Amb. Londyn, A.12. 52/13, and AAN, MSZ 55; Chłapowski telegram, 25 Jan., AAN, MSZ 3768. Also, Beneš–Laval conversation, 17 Jan., ANM, Mastný, 12.028.33. Laval's statement that he would sign the Eastern Pact irrespective of Poland and Germany does not appear in the Polish account.

He continued to advocate Franco-British entente in Geneva and a careful handling of Russia so that it would not turn to Germany. As for Poland, he saw it as a problem for Laval's Russian policy, just as it had been a complication for Briand's policy toward Germany. As always, Beneš criticized Poland's great-power aspiration and its mistaken belief in the equilibrium between Russia and Germany. Piłsudski, having been "formed by Austria" and having fought on the Central Powers' side, naturally inclined toward Germany; and Beck was full of tricks. But if the Poles could hardly be trusted, and the evolution of their policy could adversely affect the balance of power, the Polish alliance was necessary (and also valuable for Prague) as long as Russia did not offer the certainty of becoming Poland's replacement.[38]

In his parliamentary speech of 6 November, Beneš prophesied that the next twelve to eighteen months were likely to be decisive for the destiny of Europe.[39] He worried lest a Franco-German rapprochement fail to provide all the necessary safeguards and tried to make the French believe that if it were in the offing Prague would join in or even "overtake us [the French] a little."[40] In this regard, Beneš was bluffing, for Hitler's adverse views of Czechoslovakia were well known: a nest of Jewish-emigré intrigues and an "ulcer" that had to be eliminated.[41] Military preparedness continued to enjoy high priority in the country. By December 1934 the military service was extended to two years.[42] If the Czechoslovak general staff was pondering the question of whether French military effort was comensurate to France's allied obligations, it refrained from voicing criticism, although General Faucher felt that it would not have been misplaced. Faucher himself was worried about "our real plans" of aid that the defense-oriented French high command had vis-à-vis East Central Europe.[43] As a more outspoken Czechoslovak general told the British military attaché confidentially, the situation was bad, for "France could not give Czechoslovakia security and Poland was hostile."[44]

38. See Laval–Beneš conversation, 16 Oct., 1934, DDF, I, VII:753–58; compare DBFP, II, XII:163; 11 Oct. briefing, KV, CPP; Kvaček, *Nad Evropou*, 96; *O Československé zahraniční politice*, 242; Olivová, "Československo-sovětská," 483.

39. Beneš, *Vers un regroupement*, 21, 32; For his worries about the domestic situation in France, see 25 Oct. 1934 session, KV, CPP.

40. Noël to Laval, 8 Nov. 1934, DDF, I, VIII:61–62.

41. Hitler's pronouncements in Mastný to Beneš, 27 Jan. 1935, ANM, Mastný, dodátky, sv.11. Compare DDF, I, IX:188–89, 269–73. Also 31 Jan. briefing, KV, CPP.

42. See Faucher reports and other documentation in SHA, EMA/2, Tchécoslovaquie 3 and 6; compare Col. Daly report, 8 Dec. 1934, FO 371 18384 R 7103; Dobrý, *Hospodářska krize*, 103; Wright to Secretary of State, 18 Oct. 1935, SDNA, 860F. 20/2.

43. Faucher to war minister, 30 Oct. 1934, SHA, EMA/2, Tchécoslovaquie 3.

44. Gen. Šnejdarek in Addison to Simon, 16 Feb. 1935, FO 371 19494 R 1115.

The Russians kept aggravating Czechoslovak-Polish difficulties by pass-ing rumors about a German-Polish military threat to Prague. Neither the French nor the Czechoslovak intelligence found anything to corroborate these stories. The visit of Colonel Englicht in early 1935 went smoothly. Czechoslovak army circles still assumed that Poland would remain neutral in case of a limited Czechoslovak-German conflict.[45] Beck's diplomacy, however, continued to preoccupy Czernin Palace, as evidenced by Beneš's remarks to Laval and references in public speeches.[46] Once again Krofta confessed his incomprehension of Warsaw's diplomacy, which was leading Poland into international isolation. Both he and Girsa insisted on Piłsudski's and his followers' special enmity toward Czechoslovakia.[47]

On 20 and 21 November, *Národní Politika* published two lengthy anonymous articles on "Czechoslovakia and Poland" subsequently printed as a pamphlet. Containing a survey of their relations since 1918 the text purported to seek the truth, an indispensable basis for an under-standing that Czechoslovakia, although deeply hurt by Polish policies, was still willing to pursue. The author was obviously a high official; actually, as the French discovered, it was Beneš himself. His authorship had never been publicly acknowledged or denied.[48] The pamphlet produced a stir in Czechoslovakia and was viewed in Poland as a semi-official statement and an overture. Opposition papers like *Polonia* and *Kurjer Warszawski* wel-comed it; the conservative *Słowo Wileńskie* debated it; the army's *Polska Zbrojna* termed it an odd way of seeking understanding.[49]

As with the Górecki letter, the enunciation failed to pierce the clouds between Prague and Warsaw. Girsa believed that the Poles might be will-ing to cooperate only at the price of territorial revision and changes in Prague's minorities policy.[50] Beneš's hopes for a talk with Beck were dashed by the Pole's absence from Geneva. Once more the Czechoslovak foreign minister wished for French intervention, and Noël concurred: a prolongation of "the tension between our two allies would provide Po-land with means to counter indirectly again our policy and harm our au-thority in Central Europe," he wrote.[51]

45. See DDF, I, VII:937 and Noël to Laval, 12 Nov. 1934, SHA, EMA/2, Tchécoslo-vaquie 12. On Englicht's visit, see rapport of d'Arbonneau, 6 Feb. 1935, SHA, EMA/2, Pologne 12. Also briefing, 25 Oct. 1934, KV, CPP.

46. See Beneš, *Vers un regroupement*, 18–19, 24–25.

47. See briefings, 11, 25 Oct., 22, Nov., 20 Dec. 1934, KV, CPP.

48. On Beneš's authorship of *Československo a Polsko* (Praha, 1934), see Noël to Laval, 21, 24, 30 Nov. 1934, MAE, Z 864.5, Tchécoslovaquie 2569.

49. Press cuttings in MZV-VA, 478.1250.

50. Girsa report in Berber, *Europäische Politik*, 37–38; compare Kozeński, *Cze-chosłowacja*, 155–59.

51. Noël to Laval, 30 Nov. 1934, MAE, Z 864.5, Tchécoslovaquie 2587.

What could be done? Laval, informing Warsaw of the Czechoslovak access to the 5 December protocol, stressed that this had no anti-Polish edge. Beneš told Grzybowski of his intention to renew the offer of a friendship pact.[52] Because there was no indication that Warsaw would respond, it must have been for the record only. Grzybowski explained to Krofta that while Poland had no engagements vis-à-vis Berlin affecting its policy toward Paris and Prague, it wished to remain allied to but not dependent on France. Poland's relationship to the French could have no impact on its policy toward Czechoslovakia. Noël commented that such an inherently contradictory statement could only be the product of Slav mentality. He repeated that Poland, by deepening each day the division that separated it from Czechoslovakia, was continuing to create difficulties for France.[53]

Toward the Stresa Front

Franco-Italian entente had constituted the second segment of Barthou's "grand design," and the Italians welcomed Laval in the belief that he would pursue it energetically. Paris realized, however, that the Yugoslav problem remained acute, and one could fear that any equivocation could result in France being deserted by the Little Entente just as it had been "deserted" by Poland.[54] Beneš's insistence on assurances against a Habsburg restoration had also to be taken into account. These considerations were delaying Laval's journey to Rome, not to mention the inquiry—likely to be embarrassing for Italy—in Geneva on the international background of Alexander's assassination.

At the League, France made every effort to avoid a Yugoslav-Italian showdown and, by obfuscating the issues and directing some of the fire against the less-involved Hungary, helped to stage a rather unedifying spectacle. Eventually, France succeeded in preventing the Marseille tragedy from destroying the chances of a rapprochement with Rome, but hard bargaining still lay ahead. By January, Paris compromised on a promise of equal participation of the Danubian states in making a guarantee to Austria and failed to exact iron-clad commitments regarding Yugoslavia.[55] The Danubian Pact, as planned, would comprise Austria and its neighbors (including Italy and Germany); France, Poland, and Romania were free to accede to it. Poland's participation was Mussolini's condition for the

---

52. See DDF, I, VIII:260, 373, 463, also Noël to Laval, 10 Dec. 1934, MAE, Z 864.5, Tchécoslovaquie 2587. Compare Kvaček, "Jednání," 27; Král, *Spojenectví*, 45.

53. Noël to Laval, 8 Dec. 1934, MAE, Z 864.5, Tchécoslovaquie 2587; compare briefing, 6 Dec., KV, CPP.

54. Capt.Decoux in DDF, I, VIII:337; compare VII:938–39, VIII:1.

55. See Ormos, "Sur les causes," 39–44; Duroselle, *Décadence*, 130–32; Herriot, *Jadis*, 2:492, Höhne, *Die Aussenpolitische*, 224; Aloisi, *Journal*, 237–38.

acceptance of Romania, and Laval's reluctance spoke volumes for the French distrust of Warsaw. Beneš had actually hoped that the Danubian grouping would in effect "isolate Poland and force her to modify seriously her policy."[56]

On 4 January 1935 Laval journeyed to Rome where three days later he signed several accords and protocols, including the controversial Ethiopian "deal."[57] Did Mussolini pretend to engage himself on the French side in Europe to have a free hand in Africa? Did Laval treat the rapprochement with Italy as a means of strengthening his position in subsequent negotiations with Germany? Possibly, but Laval mainly saw the Danubian Pact as a web enmeshing Germany in the south, just as the Eastern Pact would entangle it in the east.[58]

A protocol recognizing the principle of Gleichberechtigung provided for consultation between France and Italy in case Germany unilaterally abolished the disarmament clauses of Versailles. A procès-verbal (relating to Austria) which constituted the basis of the Danubian Pact, recommended to future signatories the conclusion of a convention within the frame of the League stipulating respect of territorial integrity and noninterference in domestic affairs. The signatories could also conclude more far-reaching accords among themselves. In the transition period—before the grouping materialized—France and Italy would consult with each other and with Austria in case of a threat to its independence and integrity.

A presence of Germany in a collective Danubian system, guaranteed by Rome and Paris, appeared an attractive prospect to the French Right and to those in heavy industry. Those favoring a connection with Russia feared that it might eclipse the Eastern Pact negotiations. When Premier Flandin spoke of France's mission of pacifying Europe through the two schemes and creating "invincible solidarity" against aggression, Osuský rightly pointed out that the Danubian Pact would create a feeling of false security, being in reality only a procedure for consultation. French and Italian objectives were not identical, and Germany with its economic leverage over Yugoslavia and Romania, intended to use future talks to undermine the whole scheme. The Hungarians, preferring a German-Austrian-Hungarian-

56. See DDF, I, VIII:519–20, and on invitation of Poland, 464–65, 494–95, 544–45, 553. Compare Roberts to Southern Department, 17 Jan. 1935, FO 371 19497 R 377. Also, DTJS, I, 197–98, 201. Wysocki pointed out to Mussolini the cardinal importance of the Franco-Polish alliance lest the duce mistakenly count Poland as part of a German bloc. See MS, OSS, Wysocki, III, 319.

57. All texts in DDF, I, VIII:603–10.

58. Compare views of Baumont, *Origins*, 126–30; Noël, *Illusions*, 161; and Ormos, "Sur les causes," 51 who argues that while under the Four Power Pact Poland was to be the object of revision and Austria saved, now the roles were reversed. See also Aloisi, *Journal*, 239–47, 255.

Polish alignment, were bent on sabotaging the negotiations. In fact, only Vienna seemed genuinely interested.[59]

The Little Entente did not endorse unequivocally the Laval–Mussolini accord. Belgrade felt that the French had disregarded its interests; Beneš and Titulescu feared that Paris may now neglect if not drop the Eastern Pact. Russia worried lest Germany, dammed in on the Austrian side, direct its expansion due east.[60] As always, Beneš sought to influence French policy by working within its frame rather than challenging it. At the Ljubljana meeting of the Little Entente on 11 January, he prevailed on his colleagues to acknowledge that no vital interests of theirs had been sacrificed. Arguing that France had been able to conclude an accord with Italy precisely because of its rapprochement with Russia, which enhanced France's international standing, Beneš induced the Little Entente to pressure Paris to proceed with the Eastern Pact. Should it prove impossible to achieve, one should work for a Franco-Soviet-Czechoslovak treaty. The elaboration of the Danubian Pact should come next, to be followed by a ratification of the Franco-Italian colonial agreement and finally by a Franco-German agreement.[61]

In Geneva, Laval promised the three Little Entente leaders to increase his efforts to achieve the Eastern Pact, even if Germany and Poland refused to participate. In conversations with the French, Russians, Italians, and British, Beneš promoted his idea of interdependence between the two pacts and the rearmament issue; he insisted that the Danubian organization be based more squarely on Franco-Italian-Little Entente collaboration than on a Paris-Rome axis. He hoped for an eventual emergence of a nucleus composed of France, Russia, Czechoslovakia, and Yugoslavia around which the others would gather. Laval praised Beneš as the only rational statesman whom he could trust; the Czechoslovak minister felt that Laval behaved loyally although he was still hesitant. If the Eastern Pact failed, should Paris contemplate a military alliance with Russia? Should it engage in direct talks with Berlin? Or perhaps talks to restore the Polish alliance to a central place in the eastern policy schemes?[62]

59. See Höhne, *Die Aussenpolitische*, 217–25; Ormos, "Sur les causes," 45–46, 52; Deák, "Die Kleine Entente," 136. Also Pułaski, "Projekty," 218–19; Herriot, *Jadis*, 2:492–94. Speech, 10 Mar. 1935 in Flandin, *Discours: Le Ministère Flandin, novembre 1934–mai 1935* (Paris, 1937), 171. Ádám, "Les Pays," 3, 6, 13–14, 17–18.

60. See DDF, I, VIII:599–600, 631–632, IX:18, 37; DBFP, II, XII:366–37; DTJS, I, 462–64. Beneš–Litvinov conversation (Záznam) 14 Jan. 1935 in ANM, Mastný 12.026–027. Compare Král, *Spojenectví*, 47.

61. See procès-verbal, 11 Jan. 1935, MAE, P.A. Massigli 4, and the more detailed Záznam o rozhovorech Min. dr.Beneše při mimořádné konferencí Stále Rady Malé Dohody, 11 Jan., ANM, Mastný, 12.009–014. Also DDF, I, IX:72–73.

62. Record (Záznam) of Beneš's conversations with Laval, Aloisi, Eden, Massigli, etc. 12–20 Jan. 1934, ANM, Mastný, 12.015–033 and 050–055; also DBFP, II, XII:414–

The Little Entente had been urging Laval to force Warsaw to go along with the Eastern Pact. It suspected that Beck's interest in the Danubian scheme stemmed from the hope to relegate the former pact to oblivion. Indeed, after the Laval–Mussolini accords, Warsaw had concluded that the Danubian scheme seemed "much more sensible" than the Eastern Pact. If Budapest was willing to join, Warsaw's adhesion would not be impossible.[63] The reasons were clear. Poland had long favored a Franco-Italian rapprochement. The Danubian Pact was not likely to strain relations between Poland and Germany, especially because Laval—in Beck's words—"exhibited the most conciliatory attitude toward Germany of any French foreign minister within his acquaintance."[64] It was convenient for Warsaw to be able to identify itself with Paris on a major issue. Warsaw, which had declared itself unwilling to assume any obligations to Czechoslovakia under the Eastern Pact, had no qualms in this case provided Hungary was a member and the Danubian Pact contained no obligatory clause of mutual assistance. Thus, Beneš's suspicion that the Poles secretly advised Hungary not to join was incorrect. Polish diplomacy refrained from any pressures, promising Budapest only not to participate should the Hungarians decide to reject the pact. From Warsaw's viewpoint, Hungary's presence had the advantage of altering the existing balance in the Danubian basin.[65]

Beck's speech on 1 February, which contained only guarded and banal references to the French alliance and to Czechoslovakia, worried Paris and Prague. His assertions that the main lines of Polish diplomacy remained unchanged met with skepticism.[66] Beck's statement on the first anniversary of the German-Polish declaration on nonaggression, contrasting this clear and precise accord with nebulous projects—which sounded like an allusion to the Eastern Pact—was hardly reassuring.[67] Hermann Goering's visit to Poland on 27–31 January only added to the existing anxieties.

15; DDF, I, IX:107–108, 302–304, 381–82; Olivová, "Československo-sovetská," 486–87.

63. See DDF, I, VIII:637–38, IX:31–32; Kuźmiński, *Polska*, 221. Also DTJS, I, 197, and 4 Jan. 1935 telegrams, HIA, Amb. Paryż, box 5.

64. See Cudahy to Secretary of State, 11 Jan. 1935, also 22 Mar., FRUS 1935, I, 171–72 and 207; DTJS, I, 446–69, DDF, I, IX:64–65, 77–78, 294–96; Beck telegram, 24 Jan., AAN, MSZ 55; Gawroński, *Moja misja*, 247.

65. See DDF, I, IX:251; DTJS, I, 471–73; MS, OSS, Wysocki, III, 337; T. Brzeziński's retrospective note on the Danubian Pact, 30 Aug. 1935, AAN, MSZ 32600. Compare, 17 Jan. briefing, KV, CPP.

66. Speech, reply, and discussion in Beck, *Przemówienia*, 142, 150–52; *Kurjer Warszawski*, *Gazeta Warszawska*, 2 Feb. 1935; sejm's criticism in Sprawozdania stenograficzne sejmu, 1 Mar., LXXIII/55-63. Appraisals in Laroche, François-Poncet and Alphand to Laval, 1, 2, 4, 6, 10 Feb., MAE, Z 698.1, Pologne 2100; Monicault to Laval, 2 Feb., Z 864.5, Tchécoslovaquie 2587; d'Arbonneau report, 6 Feb., SHA, EMA/2, Pologne 12.

67. Beck, *Przemówienia*, 141.

The Prussian premier came ostensibly to hunt in the Białowieża forest, but the secrecy surrounding his trip seemed ominous.[68] Talking informally to his fellow hunters, generals Sosnkowski and Fabrycy, Goering virtually proposed an anti-Soviet alliance. When received by Piłsudski on 31 January, Goering disregarded Lipski's warnings and spoke emphatically about German enmity to Russia. The marshal "froze" and curtly responded that Poland needed peace on its eastern borders. By contrast, he echoed Goering's critical remarks about Czechoslovakia.[69] Despite Polish assurances to Laroche that neither German armaments nor the Eastern Pact had figured in the conversations, Goering did reiterate Berlin's opposition to the latter. As for his advances, Laroche learned indirectly that some had been made but not taken up by the Poles. Girsa heard the same story, but he was convinced that both governments had reached an oral agreement to cooperate on all international issues.[70] Laroche's attempts to point out to the Poles the disturbing character of the visit were met with a reply that the French constantly misunderstood the nature of Warsaw's foreign policy. Privately, Undersecretary Szembek worried that France might denounce the alliance, and he counseled Beck to go to Paris to calm French fears. The minister disagreed: a denunciation of the alliance, he said, would be suicidal for France and could be ruled out.[71]

Goering's visit almost coincided with the journey of Flandin, Laval, and Léger to London. The French had virtually admitted that their 17 April 1934 formula on security had become an empty phrase. They were willing to compromise on their former demand that the German adhesion to the two pacts *precede* a resolution of the rearmament issue. They strove to obtain British backing for the policy of pacts, and the Foreign Office, trying to discourage a Franco-Soviet alliance, was inclined to assist, without conveying the impression of seeking to impose the Eastern Pact on Germany.

The 3 February communiqué that concluded the London talks sounded like a compromise, but the French made the greater concessions in discus-

68. French attempts to learn something were largely unsuccessful. After the visit, Laroche was told that Goering solemnly confirmed the validity of the nonaggression policy. See DDF, I, IX:240, 254–55. Compare d'Arbonneau report, 6 Feb. 1935, SHA, EMA/2, Pologne 12.

69. See Jędrzejewicz, *Kronika*, 2:498–99; DTJS, I, 223–25, 230–31.

70. Compare Girsa report, 4 Mar. 1935, CCP, and DDF, I, IX:294–96. Also see 104, 106–107, 123–24, 141, 173–74, 202–203, and DTJS, I, 216–18, 220–23.

71. See DTJS, I, 223. The Poles did attach weight to Goering's assurances that Hitler personally stood behind the policy of détente. They may have been unaware of or underestimated Hitler's private remarks about the possibility of an exchange of the "corridor" for lands in the east (see Mastný to Beneš, 27 Jan. 1935, ANM, Mastný, Dodátky, sv.11) or building a highway linking Germany with East Prussia (Lothian to Simon, 30 Jan., FO 800 290).

sions concerning the pacts and rearmaments. The proposal of an "Air Locarno" limited to Western-Europe, which was a British gesture to France, did not redress the scales. Prague was upset, and if Beneš expressed pleasure over British endorsement of French policies, he reiterated his concern over the handling of the disarmament issue.[72] Polish dissatisfaction was evident. Warsaw could argue that its endeavors to facilitate French policy had not been made in order to be asked now to approve an increase of German forces. Germany's presence in the Eastern Pact could not only pose a potential danger of a great-power consortium but also lessen the value of the German-Polish nonaggression declaration in Berlin's eyes.[73] After asking Laroche to congratulate Laval on securing British collaboration, Beck remarked ironically that he was not surprised by French concessions, which Piłsudski had predicted in his conversation with Barthou. He thought it worth mentioning that the Air Locarno proposal was made without consulting Poland, as the French were constantly accusing Warsaw of failing to consult Paris. Beck also asked how did the French propose to resolve the issue of rearmament. Poland would respect the provisions of Versailles but only to the same extent as the great powers.[74]

As a result of the London meeting, the British assumed the role of unofficial mediators. Prime Minister Simon and Eden (now Lord Privy Seal) were to go to Berlin; Eden proceeding thereafter to Moscow, Warsaw, and Prague. Hitler, however, showed interest only in the air pact and hinted to the Poles that he would like to see them included. He cleverly intimated thus that he was more concerned with Warsaw's interests than were the French.[75] In mid-March, Laval declared his intention of pursuing both the Danubian and the Eastern Pact, but chances of progress were slight. No date could be set for a conference of the future participants of the Danubian group.[76] As for the Eastern Pact, the British suggested a further emasculation, namely basing it on the existing bilateral nonaggression treaties in Eastern Europe, so as to make the pact more attractive to Germany and

72. For Czechoslovak views, see DDF, I, IX:242, 284; 7 Feb. 1935 briefing, KV, CPP. For London meeting and its background, outside of rich documentation in DDF and DBFP, see Clerk to Simon, 18 Jan., FO 800 290; sessions of CSG, 15 Jan. SHA, CSG, 50; also Massigli to Léger, 10, 13 Jan., and notes 24 and 26 Jan., MAE, P.A. Massigli 6. Laval's remarks 13 Feb., CAE/Ch.

73. Wojciechowski, *Stosunki*, 155–56; 23 Jan. 1935 note, MAE, P.A. Massigli 5.

74. See DTJS, I, 477–78; compare 232–33 and Beck telegrams, 8 Feb. 1935, HIA, Amb. Paryż, box 5; Laroche in DDF, I, IX:266–68 and 17 Feb., MAE, Z 698.1, Pologne 2101. Also DBFP, II, XII:507.

75. See Wojciechowski, *Stosunki*, 162–64; Jędrzejewicz, *Lipski*, 165–68, 171–75; compare 18 Feb. 1935 note, DDF, I, IX:369–71.

76. See Ormos, "Sur les causes," 45–63, 72–77; and Monicault dispatches from mid-Feb. to early Apr. 1935 in DDF, I, IX. For analysis of issues to be raised at a conference, note 30 Apr., MAE, P.A. Massigli 4.

Poland.[77] The Quai d'Orsay still hoped that neither of them would want to assume the responsibility of formally rejecting it. Should this happen, the alternative would be a collective Franco-Russian-Czechoslovak-Romanian accord, and failing even that, a Franco-Russian treaty was seen as a "last resource."[78]

In the shifting international scene, Czechoslovak-Polish animosity remained a grim constant. Again Laval urged the Poles to improve their relationship with Prague, for the Czechs felt that Warsaw was deliberately fanning the flames and behaving in a provocative fashion.[79] Invoking a book, then published in Poland, that advocated reducing Czechoslovakia to its ethnic borders, the Czernin Palace thought that such views were not far different from those of Grzybowski and his superiors.[80] The Czechoslovak military attaché sent warnings that Polish public opinion was being influenced by the argument that a seizure of Teschen would be a justified retribution for the Czech action in 1919. Several diplomats assumed that Warsaw was keeping the issue of the Poles in Teschen alive and acute, partly as a means of pressure, but partly with an eye to a future recovery of the area.[81]

While the Polish counselor in Prague reproached Krofta for blindly following France instead of trying a more independent line like Poland, the Czech retorted that the French were "criticizing Laval for conducting a Czechoslovak and not a French foreign policy."[82] *L'Europe Centrale* maintained that Beck changed only the style and the rhythm of Polish diplomacy, which was determined by a search for a great-power status, grievances against unreliable friends (France and Czechoslovakia), delaying actions on the German side, and hostility toward the USSR.[83] Krofta

77. See DBFP, II, XII:468, 535–37, 550–51.

78. See DDF, I, IX:145–47, also 190–91. According to Avenol, neither Léger nor Massigli favored a bilateral Franco-Soviet accord. See also DBFP, II, XII:520; FRUS 1935, I, 195.

79. Laval told Wysocki in Rome "you must reach an agreement with the Czechs"; MS, OSS, Wysocki, III, 327. For current squabbles, see documentation in AAN, MSZ 5506; Laroche to Laval, 22 Jan., 17 Feb. 1935, MAE, Z 864.5, Tchécoslovaquie 2578. Also briefing, 24 Jan. KV, CPP.

80. *System polityczny Europy a Polska* (Warsaw, 1935) by the maverick Władysław Studnicki. Comments in Kozeński, *Czechosłowacja*, 163–64; *Češi a Poláci*, 2:561. Also 21 Feb. 1935 briefing, KV, CPP.

81. See Laroche and Bressy to Laval, 30 Jan., 18 Sept. 1935, MAE, Z 864.5, Tchécoslovaquie 2587. Minutes on Kennard to Hoare, 22 Nov., FO 371 19494 R 6977. See also Szklarska-Lohmannowa, "Z Raportów dyplomatów," 195; DTJS, I, 196–97. For broader context, see Ort, "Dvacáté výročí," 387. For criticism of the anti-Czechoslovak course in sejm, see 6 Feb. debate Sprawozdania stenograficzne sejmu, 21–23, 34.

82. Briefing, 28 Feb. 1935, KV, CPP.

83. On 2 Feb. 1935. See Monicault dispatch, 5 Feb., MAE, Z 698.1, Pologne 2100.

speculated about three possible developments. One, Poland, having partly weakened Russia, would intensify the anti-Czech line and demand Teschen if not more. Two, having met with lack of success, Poland would enter the road of collapse, which would force Czechoslovakia to rely exclusively on Russia, a prospect Krofta did not cherish. In case of an international conflagration Russia would pull through, but would Czechoslovakia? The third, most desirable variant would be Warsaw's return to its old policies.[84] This seemed unlikely, and Beneš castigated the Poles who based their policy on "misguided and disproved assumptions," such as that the League would prove ineffective; Russia would come to blows with Japan; France and Italy would show themselves unable to reach agreement; and, the "most mistaken assumption of all," that "France would be enfeebled."[85]

As sympathetic as they were toward Prague, French diplomats wrote on occasion that the Czechoslovak government did not show much adroitness in handling Warsaw. Either it was publicly admonishing the Poles or extending a hand they did not wish to grasp. The French did their best to dissuade Beneš from offering once more a treaty of friendship to Poland, a move clearly calculated to embarrass Warsaw.[86] Beneš's method of trying to pressure the Poles through the great powers caused irritation. In March, for instance, the Czechoslovak foreign minister was urging Laval to make Eden demonstrate his disapproval of the Polish policy toward Czechoslovakia as contrary to Franco-British actions aimed at pacifying Europe.[87]

Seeking to analyze the Polish policy for Paris's sake, Laroche referred to Beck's diplomacy as "shifty," but warned against treating Piłsudski as either a germanophile or germanophobe. His hopes for a reinforcement of the alliance with France had been deceived by Barthou. His policy of balance might be tipping toward Germany—for what appeared at first a truce and a lesson to the French was becoming a fixture of Warsaw's diplomacy—but Piłsudski's opposition to the Eastern Pact was fundamental. If Poland were attacked by Germany, he might resign himself to a Russian alliance, but not beforehand. Even the pro-French Sosnkowski was distrustful of a Russian connection, which he saw as harmful to the Warsaw-Paris relationship.[88] Indeed, Polish mistrust was easily aroused. When Massigli remarked that the Franco-Polish alliance was after all dependent

---

84. Briefing, 7 Feb. 1935, KV, CPP.

85. J. B. Wright to Secretary of State, 28 Jan. 1935, SDNA, 840.00/419.

86. See Noël and Laroche to Laval, 7, 14, 22 Jan. 1935, MAE, Z 864.5, Tchécoslovaquie 2581; DDF, I, VIII:677–79.

87. See Grzybowski report, 14 Mar. 1935, AAN, Amb. Berlin, 53, and Monicault to Laval, 9 Mar., MAE, Z 864.5, Tchécoslovaquie 2587.

88. See DDF, I, IX:70–72, 266–68, 325–29, 343–47. Compare discussions at Groupe Parlementaire Franco-Polonais, 7 Feb., 28 Mar. 1935, AAN, MSZ 3768.

on the League, Mühlstein responded that if this was the official interpretation it would mean that France was throwing the alliance overboard.[89]

In late February, the Quai d'Orsay worked out a project of the Eastern Pact confined to nonaggression and consultation (mutual assistance was optional).[90] The Russian ambassador protested that this constituted a violation of the Laval-Litvinov protocol, but Paris disregarded the protest wishing to gauge German and Polish reactions. This was the last desparate effort "to avoid a Franco-Russian agreement except as part of a homogeneous regional arrangement."[91] It did not work. To Beck the pact was a screen for strengthening Soviet influence in Central and Eastern Europe.[92] As for Germany, its victory in the Saar plebiscite on 1 March only made it more intransigent.

At this point, as the country was approaching the "lean years," the issue of French military security came into the limelight with a decision to reintroduce the two year military service. Except for the Maginot Line, the military build-up was being delayed by France's limited industrial capacity, political ambivalence, and financial problems.[93] In January 1935, General Gamelin had replaced Weygand, uniting in his hands the functions of chief of the general staff, vice president of CSG, and inspector general (commander-in-chief designate). Gamelin lacked his predecessor's impetuous drive and relied on diplomacy in dealing with the government, which made him more accommodating.[94] Neither he nor any other army chief advocated drastic changes in organization or military doctrine. De Gaulle's idea of a highly mobile professional armed corps, advocated then by Reynaud in the chamber, ran into an overwhelming opposition on political, military, and ideological grounds. Rejecting the very notion of aggressive strategy, the minister of war Louis Maurin exclaimed: "How can anyone believe that we shall think again of an offensive when we have spent milliards in order to construct a fortified barrier? Would we be mad enough to advance beyond this barrier on some unpredictable venture?"[95]

89. Mühlstein report, 8 Mar. 1935, and Chłapowski to Beck, 22 Feb., respectively AAN, MSZ 3802 and 3897.

90. 27 Feb. 1935, DDF, I, IX:447–51.

91. Laval cited by Clerk, also Simon–Laval conversations, DBFP, II, XII:581–82, 590–94.

92. See Cudahy to Secretary of State, 8 Mar. 1935, SDNA, 740.0011 Mutual Guarantee/112 Eastern Locarno. Also Wojciechowski, *Stosunki*, 168; briefing 14 Mar., KV, CPP.

93. See Dutailly, "Programmes," 105–27; Le Goyet, *Mystère*, 71. Between 1931 and 1935 seven infantry divisions were motorized but only one light mechanized division created.

94. See Dutailly, *Problèmes*, 18.

95. Cited among others by Reynaud; see *Au Coeur de la mêlée 1930–1945* (Paris,

The debate in the chamber preceded by one day Hitler's announcement on 16 March of military conscription and the creation of a 600,000 strong army. This open violation of part 5 of Versailles sounded like a slap in the face of Western politicians trying to work out a formula to legalize German rearmament. All that the French cabinet could do on 20 March was to appeal to the League of Nations under the least forceful article 11. Lucien Romier jeered in *Le Figaro* on 31 March: "For some years French policy resembles a choir singer who can no longer sing solo." The government's only concern was to be able to tell the public: "more than ever attached to the principle of international collaboration we have just been kicked in the company of several friends."

The Haut Comité Militaire (organized in 1932 and attached to the president of the council of ministers) noted on 22 March that in view of long-range German preponderance and the necessarily delayed aid from Italy and Russia, the only real assistance could come from Britain. Czechoslovakia was paralyzed by its neighbors, Poland included.[96] Could the French army respond forcefully to a German violation of Austria or an occupation of the Rhineland? Laval asked the Comité two weeks later. Gamelin was evasive. An offensive action would only be possible in a later stage of the conflict. It would be advantageous if war began in Central Europe, so that the French army would face an enemy whose main forces were engaged elsewhere.[97] No wonder that d'Arbonneau was anxious about Poland's place in this strategy.[98] General Maurin asserted on 23 March that the alliance with Warsaw was still valid, but Polish policies could endanger both countries. The second bureau expressed doubts that Poland would furnish immediate help in the case of German aggression against France. Interstaff collaboration had deteriorated, and it would be further complicated if France signed an alliance with the USSR.[99]

Laval sought to ascertain Poland's reaction to German conscription.

1951), 149–57. Also Le Goyet, *Mystère*, 59–87; Tournoux, *Haut commandement*, 220–38; Bankwitz, *Weygand*, 107–14; Frankenstein, "Réarmement français," 4–6, and Frankenstein's exhaustive *Le Prix de réarmement 1935–1939* (Paris, 1982), with its most useful graphs in chapter 1. Also Feller, *Le Dossier*, 206–19; Duroselle, *Décadence*, 251–66; Herriot, *Jadis*, 2:513–14, 517–20. For the 15 Mar. debate, see Blum and Reynaud, J.O. Chambre, 1022–27, 1040–42.

96. See DDF, 1, ix:686–91; Duroselle, *Décadence*, 135–36.

97. See Le Goyet, *Mystère*, 116–17, and Dutailly, *Problèmes*, 42. Gamelin's strategy was reflected in the "mis au point" of plan D, based on the notion that France could not attack until the bulk of German forces was engaged by the allies, the "espace de maneuvre" being abroad and not on French soil.

98. See especially his long note, 11 Apr. 1935, SHA, EMA/2, Pologne 12.

99. See Chłapowski to Beck, 25 Mar. 1935, AAN, MSZ 3802. For greater French than Polish reserve toward collaboration, see d'Arbonneau reports, 20 Mar., 3 Apr., 29 May, and note of the deuxième bureau, 15 May, SHA, EMA/2, Pologne 12 and 17. Also Dutailly, *Problèmes*, 43.

Beck told Laroche that the matter was grave and he was willing to study French suggestions. But Laroche had none to make, and Warsaw, which seemingly expected Paris to propose closer collaboration or even invoke the alliance (to which Beck would have been receptive), adopted an evasive position.[100] When it became obvious that the French would not go beyond an appeal to the League, Lipski limited himself to an expression of concern in Berlin about the consequences of Hitler's move. Beck was quite convinced that Germany would not back down; hence, empty protests made little sense.[101] The Polish foreign minister performed a balancing act in Geneva on 17 April. He first criticized various collective security initiatives, which infuriated the French, and then voted to censure Germany, to the amazement of friends and foes alike.[102]

Hitler's move had aroused emotions in Prague, where voices were heard that with Poland so close to Germany, Czechoslovakia was completely outflanked.[103] Beneš himself thought that the Führer's announcement was merely an admission of the existing state of affairs. He recommended concerted action by the three Western powers in Geneva, which Czechoslovakia, foregoing any initiatives of its own, would join. Hoping for Western consolidation, Beneš foresaw an evolution from a "fictitious preponderance of the French bloc" to a real front. An armed conflict he deemed unlikely in the near future, although a struggle for Austria, Memel, and Danzig would go on as Hitler continued with his agenda.[104]

Beneš's predictions seemed overoptimistic. Britain protested against the breach of Versailles but did not cancel Sir John Simon's visit to Berlin. To molify the French, Anthony Eden came to Paris for talks with Laval and Suvich, Italy's deputy foreign minister, on 23 March.[105] It proved neces-

100. See DDF, I, IX:597, 617–18; Beck's comments, DTJS, I, 246–47; compare DBFP, II, XII:673–74; FRUS 1935, I, 217–22. Warsaw's readiness to fulfill its obligations confirmed by Wysocki (invoking Beck) and President Mościcki: Chambrun and Laroche to Laval, 31 Mar., 10 Apr. 1935, MAE, Z 698.1, Pologne 2101.

101. See DDF, I, X:2–3, 6, 26–27; DTJS, I, 243–46, 248–49; Beck telegram, 23 Mar. 1935, HIA, Amb. Paryż, box 4; Jędrzejewicz, *Lipski*, 179–82; compare FRUS 1935, I, 205–208 and DBFP, II, XII:747–50. An Austrian diplomat opined that Poland like Britain was "sitting on the fence" but if London were to organize a bloc Poland would slowly detach herself from Germany and join it. Hoffinger to Chancellor, 13 Apr. 1935 (intercept), SHA, EMA/2 Pologne 37.

102. See *Polityka Narodów*, 5 (1935), 607–608; Beck telegrams, 16, 17 Apr. 1935, SI, Amb. Londyn, A.12.52/13 and DTJS, I, 271–72, 496–99. Also DDF, I, X:343, 350, 369–70, 413–14, 449–51, 461–63; ADAP, C, IV/1:72; Aloisi, 267; *Journal*, Jędrzejewicz, *Lipski*, 188–91; Girsa report, 29 Apr., CPP.

103. See Pułaski, *Stosunki*, 113–14.

104. Beneš to missions, 21 Mar. 1935; briefing, 22 Mar., KV, CPP; compare Wright to Secretary of State, 25 Mar., SDNA, 862.20/920; DDF, I, IX:612–13, 639, 669–70; DaM, III, 62; Kvaček, *Nad Evropou*, 112.

105. See Simon to the King and Laval, 18, 22 Mar. 1935, FO 800 290.

sary to display at least a token solidarity of the three powers, and a communiqué announced an Anglo-French-Italian conference to be held in Stresa. In the course of the discussions of the Danubian and Eastern pacts, Suvich commented on the real problem that a passage of Soviet troops would present for Poland, Laval, who agreed, under Russian pressure, to visit Moscow, now expressed an interest in direct talks with the Poles. Beck responded by inviting him to stop in Warsaw.[106]

Simon's and Eden's encounter with Hitler on 25–26 March revealed that the chancellor would not compromise on army figures. The only collective pact he might consider would have to exclude even facultative mutual-assistance agreements among its members. This position was unacceptable to Paris and Rome; Laval seems to have concluded that the time for seeking a general settlement was gone.[107] Perhaps a formula could still be found to make the Eastern Pact acceptable in Warsaw? The Russians counted on British pressure. "Your success in Warsaw," Litvinov allegedly told Eden, "will also be ours." The British, however, saw the trip as mainly a fact-finding mission.[108]

On 2 and 3 April, Eden was received by Piłsudski and held conversations with Beck. The marshal was ill and almost incoherent. Beck, on the other hand, made it crystal clear that Poland would not jeopardize its position, stabilized by the two nonaggression accords with the big neighbors. He was favorable to the Danubian Pact and, regarding armament limitations, repeated that concrete agreements made more sense than grandiose projects.[109] The Poles obviously attached great importance to Eden's visit. Beck who believed in Piłsudski's dictum that "the road to Paris led through London" found his conversations with Eden useful and the man himself understanding. He allegedly told the Romanian envoy that had Eden proposed a British-French-Italian assistance pact with military clauses

106. Notes, 22 Mar. and on 23 Mar. meeting, MAE, P.A. Massigli 5. Compare DBFP, II, XII:693–97; DDF, I, X:28–32, 56–57, 73–75, 123–24. For Mussolini's interest in inviting Poland to Stresa, see Girsa report, 30 Mar., CPP, and Laroche to Laval, 28 Mar., MAE, Z 698.1, Pologne 2101. Also Beck–Chłapowski exchange of telegrams, 1, 2 Apr., AAN, MSZ 3768.

107. See Clerk to Simon, 5 Apr. 1935, DBFP, II, XII:834–35; Hildebrand, *Foreign Policy*, 35–36.

108. See DDF, I, X:132. Compare Avon, *Dictators* 160–68. Simon wrote that if the French thought that the Eden trips were to be undertaken with the purpose of propagandizing the Eastern Pact and blackmailing these governments into cooperation, they were completely off the mark. See DBFP, II, XII:585. On Laroche's constant efforts see DDF, I, X:73–75.

109. See Avon, *Dictators*, 181–91; Nowak-Kiełbikowa, "Eden"; Zacharias, *Polska*, 375–77; Bullitt, *Correspondence*, 104; DBFP, II, III:803–10, 846; DTJS, I, 255–58, 260: notes, 2–3 Apr. 1935, AAN, MSZ 396; Beck telegram, 7 Apr., HIA, Amb. Paryż, box 5; Beck, *Dernier rapport*, 87–91; Schimitzek, *Drogi*, 379; DDF, I, X:138–39, 155–56, 167, FRUS 1935, I, 222–23.

directed against Germany, and asked Poland to join it, he might have been forced to accept.[110]

On 4 April, Eden had a long conversation in Prague with Beneš, who regarded the Danubian Pact as "indispensable" and felt it was progressing. He was less optimistic about the Eastern Pact. If Berlin and Warsaw refused to adhere, one could contemplate either a Franco-Soviet-Czechoslovak alliance open to others; a general pact under the League, including France, Russia, the Baltic states, Czechoslovakia, and Romania; or the pact in its original version without Poland and Germany with the characteristics of an alliance. Well aware of the British position, Beneš stressed that he would rather avoid an alliance with the USSR. He argued, however, that Russia be brought "in a friendly fashion" into Europe, because if it remained isolated it might be tempted to try either an accord with Germany or world revolution. The West dare not take such a chance. Beneš described his past misunderstandings with Italy as a by-product of bad Franco-Italian relations. Similarly, Prague's attitude toward Berlin was affected by Franco-German and Polish-German problems, for Czechoslovakia itself "had no conflicts with Germany and would not have them in the future." He had always advised Paris to reach an accord with Berlin; if left to a tête-à-tête with the Germans, he would do the same. Cleverly contrasting the Czechoslovak situation with that of Poland, he ascribed Polish fears of the Eastern Pact—seen as a smokescreen for a Franco-Soviet-Czechoslovak alliance—to Poland's difficult geopolitical situation. He thought, however, that Warsaw's search for assurances could be satisfied by the pact. It was because of Poland, Beneš repeated twice, that Germany was reluctant to adhere to the Eastern Pact. Dwelling on Warsaw's worries that Russia on reentering Europe would relegate Poland to a secondary role, Beneš hinted that Poland was a liability for the powers. Perhaps a change in the domestic power structure would bring some improvement. Eden subsequently commented that Beneš was "perhaps a little too dexterous" during these conversations.[111]

Eden's impressions from Eastern Europe had seemingly little impact on the British delegation as it joined the French and the Italians in Isola Bella near Stresa. The conference, held on 11–14 April, appeared to display a unanimity of views, as the three powers agreed on a common line vis-à-vis limitations of armaments and condemned German unilateral infractions. They envisaged a study of Austrian, Hungarian, and Bulgarian desire for

110. Cudahy to Secretary of State, 4 Apr. 1935 FRUS 1935, I, 217–19.

111. Avon, *Dictators*, 192. For talks see note, 14 Apr. 1935, ANM, Mastný, 12.059–074; DBFP, II, XII:812–17; DDF, I, X:169; FRUS 1935, I, 225–27, and Wright to Secretary of State, 9 Apr., SDNA, 862.20/948. For Beneš and Krofta on Polish diplomacy, see Marek report (intercept), May 2, SHA, EMA/2, Tchécoslovaquie 14. Eden avoided the topic of Czechoslovak-Polish relations both in Warsaw and Prague.

revision of disarmament clauses within a frame of general and regional guarantees of security. Reaffirming their declarations on Austrian independence and integrity, they recommended calling a conference to work out the Danubian Pact. The British and the Italians restated their obligation as guarantors of Locarno.[112]

The so-called Stresa Front was more formidable on paper than in reality. Paris had not obtained binding commitments from Britian in case of German treaty violations, particularly with regard to Austria and the Rhineland. The British viewed cooperation with Italy and France as a stop-gap arrangement before one could better gauge German intentions.[113] There was some feeling in the British Foreign Office that, as far as East Central Europe was concerned, one should dispense with all quasi-commitments and honestly admit that Britain would not go to war over an upheaval in that part of Europe.[114]

Neither the French nor the Italians wished to make Stresa too pointedly anti-German—hopes for a rapprochement with Berlin restrained Laval's interest in an alliance with Rome—but wanted to approach the German problem from a position of strength. Still, already after Laval's January visit to Rome, the Italian high command had begun to press Paris for the conclusion of a military convention. After Stresa an air agreement was negotiated, and in late June talks between Gamelin and Marshal Pietro Badoglio established the foundations for military cooperation in wartime. Notably, a French expeditionary force in Italy would act as a liaison with Yugoslav and Czechoslovak armies, and some Italian air squadrons might be based in Czechoslovakia. General Gamelin kept the chiefs of staff of the Little Entente informed, and reported that Beneš and General Syrový attached particular importance to the presence of a French corps operating on the right flank of the Italian army. Such an arrangement would promise the quickest assistance to Czechoslovakia.[115]

Although worried by the possibility of Hungarian and Bulgarian rear-

112. See DBFP, ii, xii:862–914; DDF, i, x:255–66, 276–88, 295–310, 314–16; also Noël, *Illusions*, 177–81. See also Rostow, *Anglo-French Relations*, 143.

113. See Vansittart to Clerk, 18 Nov. 1935, FO 371 18811 C 7837. Also Flandin, *Politique*, 173–74; Noël, *Illusions*, 78; Aloisi, *Journal*, 264; DDF, i, x:142–44, 157–58, 192. Position paper, 9 Apr., MAE, P.A. Massigli 5; compare DBFP, ii, xii:834–38; Chłapowski telegram, 9 Apr., HIA, Amb. Paryż, box 5; Rostow, *Anglo-French Relations*, 146.

114. See E. H. Carr memorandum, 30 Mar. 1935, FO 371 19498 R 2201.

115. See voluminous correspondence in DDF, i, viii, ix, and x. On the military convention talks, Gamelin to Fabry, 4 June 1935, SHA, EMA/3, 7 N 3446/1 and DDF, i, xi:282–84, Gamelin, *Servir*, 2:163–73; Le Goyet, *Mystère*, 104–106; Noël, *Illusions*, 93–98, 183–87, 201–203; Flandin, *Politique*, 172–73; Young, "Soldiers and Diplomats: The French Embassy and Franco-Italian Relations 1935–1936," *The Journal of Strategic Studies*, 7 (Mar. 1984), 76–82.

mament, Beneš and Krofta viewed Stresa as indicative of a definite and welcome change of Italian policy toward France and the Danubian region. In Beneš's thinking the necessary sequel to Stresa was a speedy conclusion of accords with Russia, which would result in the emergence of a "great security bloc."[116] By contrast, Beck, irritated that Poland had not been associated with the conference, viewed Stresa as an attempt to return to a great powers consortium. He was also skeptical about the alleged solidarity of the three, for "each of the powers only thinks how to reach a separate accord with Germany."[117] The immediate future showed that his estimate was more realistic than that of Beneš.

Paris, Moscow, Prague

Pressed by the Russians, Laval had promised them and the Little Entente that irrespective of what transpired at Stresa, he would sign a pact with the USSR by 1 May. The French sought to avoid a military alliance involving automatic aid and a strict definition of aggression, which made the Russians dubious about French intentions. Moreover, the French cabinet was divided.[118] An American diplomat commented: "There will be some sort of a pact, but its effect had already been largely negativated by the insincerity which inspires the policy of both the High Contracting Parties."[119]

The French general staff, fully conscious that Russian help to France and Czechoslovakia would be determined by the Polish attitude, considered three hypotheses: Poland allied with France, neutral, or allied with Germany. In the first two cases, it was unlikely that the Poles would permit the Red Army to operate on their soil, accepting at best material aid from the USSR. In the third case, Russia could force its way into Poland.[120] The deuxième bureau worried that even if the treaty with Russia were theoret-

116. See briefing, 18 Apr. 1935, KV, CPP, also Kvaček, *Nad Evropou*, 165–66; compare DDF, I, X:222–23, 320, 328–29, 359; Aloisi, *Journal*, 266–67.

117. Sierpowski, *Stosunki*, 408; Gawroński, *Moja misja*, 267–68; FRUS 1935, I, 271–22; DDF, I, X:274.

118. See DaM, III, 102; Kvaček, *Nad Evropou*, 122–23; Prasolov, "Československo-sovětská smlouva," 72, 124–25; Herriot, *Jadis*, 2:523–25; on Georges Bonnet's view, see Mühlstein report, 8 Mar. 1935, AAN, MSZ 3961. For Flandin's claim that he saved the Franco-Russian entente from the wreckage of the Eastern Pact, see his *Politique*, 159. Documentation in DDF, I, X; Scott, *Alliance*, 240–46. Tukhachevsky argued in *Pravda* on 31 Mar., that France was directly endangered by Germany and no longer capable of resistance. See Degras, *Soviet Documents* 3:124–26.

119. Wiley to Kelley, 30 Apr. 1935, FDR, Wiley Papers, box 1. Stalin told de Gaulle during World War II that in 1935 "We Russians did not trust the French either"; see Kvaček, *Nad Evropou*, 128.

120. Note, 8 Apr. 1935 sent by Maurin to Laval, DDF, I, X:227–29.

ically compatible with the Polish alliance, the "benefits that we can still draw" from the latter must not be diminished. In the final analysis, Polish help would depend on Warsaw's good will. It was most desirable to remove the threat of a new Rapallo, but one could not dismiss the risk of pushing Warsaw toward Berlin. Recalling history and stressing ideology, the second bureau showed great distrust of the Soviets, and on political and military grounds gave priority to a Polish alliance. The Russian alignment ought to complement it, with "full consent of the government in Warsaw." Its "preventive capacity" depended in any case on Poland being part of the anti-German bloc. Failing that, France would do better to base its defensive system on Britain, Italy, Belgium, and Czechoslovakia. Thus, the bureau's note opposed a strictly military alliance with Moscow, and advocated a free hand toward it.[121]

D'Arbonneau reasoned along similar lines. He insisted on a clarification of the military convention in case of a German aggression in the east and, underlining the continuous Polish military effort, believed it crucial that all possible material assistance be extended to Poland.[122] Laroche spoke of the "double assistance"—a strategic location and an excellent army—that Poland could furnish to France. To prevent Warsaw from becoming an instrument of Germany, Paris should dispel Polish fears of becoming involved in a Russo-German conflict, allowing it to determine the type of assistance from Russia, applying the principle of reciprocity, clarifying the working of the alliance if France attacked Germany (coming to the aid of a country invaded by the Germans), providing Poland with military credits and equipment, and, finally, reassuring Warsaw that the Franco-Soviet treaty would in no way diminish the value of the Polish alliance.[123]

The French were clearly trying to regain Poland's confidence. The Quai d'Orsay kept the Poles informed of the negotiations with Russia and occasionally consulted them. Already in December 1934 d'Arbonneau told the chief of the Polish general staff that French expectations of Soviet aid were, in a sense, of a "negative nature"—that is, denying this aid to Germany.[124] In late March, Laval let Beck know that Paris would bring no precisions to Franco-Russian relations without giving the Polish foreign minister an opportunity to reexamine the situation. Affecting a tone of nonchalance, Beck opined that if France wished to make an alliance with the USSR, that was France's business. It was also France's job to see that the new alliance was compatible with the Franco-Polish alliance. In reality,

---

121. Note, 24 Apr. 1935, DDF, 1, X:401–403, Also see Scott, *Alliance*, 266; Duroselle, *Décadence*, 140–41.

122. D'Arbonneau notes, 11 Apr., 1 May 1935, SHA, EMA/2, Pologne 12.

123. Laroche to Laval, 11 Apr. 1935, MAE, P.A. Noël 200.

124. D'Arbonneau report, 20 Dec. 1934, SHA, EMA/2, Pologne 12.

however, Beck was worried.[125] After the French approval of the final text on 30 April, Chłapowski was shown the document and told again that nothing would be changed in the Franco-Polish alliance. If Russia attacked Poland, the French still considered themselves bound by the treaty of 1921.[126]

The Czechoslovak position was naturally different from that of Poland, and already in September 1934 Litvinov and Beneš had outlined a program of economic and financial collaboration leading eventually to a "traité d'amitié."[127] In early April 1935, Krofta went to Paris to monitor Franco-Russian negotiations so as to align Czechoslovak policy with that of France.[128] On his side Beneš sought to ascertain whether, under the terms of the Franco-Polish alliance, Warsaw was entitled to remain neutral in case of a Franco-German war arising out of a German attack on Russia, Austria, or Czechoslovakia; and whether it would be guilty of breach if it turned against Prague? The Czechoslovak government said it was ready to define its obligations as an ally of France by engaging itself not to resort to any anti-Polish measures should Poland be attacked by Germany. Beneš stated emphatically that he would not undertake any obligations toward Russia beyond those to be assumed by France. He was prepared to state this in a formal letter to Laval, the project of which he submitted.[129]

The Quai d'Orsay informed Laval that Poland could remain neutral in the case mentioned by Beneš provided France itself was not the subject of attack or the victim of a violation in the Rhineland. Although there was nothing in the alliance forbidding Poland to act against Czechoslovakia, such action would be hard to reconcile with provisions about concerting and coordinating French and Polish efforts. Further assurances could be sought directly from the Poles, although the ministry was doubtful about doing so.[130]

The Franco-Soviet treaty signed on 2 May fell short of a full-fledged alliance. French aid was made dependent on the League and Locarno; if

---

125. See DDF, I, x:56–57, 73–75, 99–100.

126. See DTJS, I, 502–503; Chłapowski telegrams, 9, 27, 28, 30 Apr., 4 May 1925, HIA, Amb. Paryż, box 5. Also Laroche to Laval, 1 May, MAE, Z 698.12, Pologne 2199. The Foreign Office was puzzled to learn about the French position because Briand had twice assured Chamberlain that France had no obligation to assist Poland if attacked by the USSR. The Quai d'Orsay in reply referred the British to article 3 of the Franco-Polish 1921 alliance, which spoke of signatories concerting in view of defense of their territory. In reality, it was the military convention (article 2) that was specific about French aid, but naturally the French did not reveal this fact to the British. See DBFP, II, XIII:280, 372, 395–96. Also Appendix III.

127. See Olivová, "Československo-sovětská," 485–86.

128. Kvaček, *Nad Evropou*, 124; compare briefing 11 Apr. 1935, KV, CPP.

129. See DDF, I, x:360–62; also briefing, 25 Apr. 1935, DaM, III, 104.

130. See note, 9 May 1935, DDF, I, x:517–18.

Britain or Italy declared that German aggression against Russia had been provoked, France would not be obliged to act. The pact, as Laval put it, was "to prevent war and not to make it."[131] Article 4 of the Protocole de Signature—invoking the search for the Eastern Pact and specifically a mutual-assistance treaty between France, Russia, and Germany—placed the document within this broader context. Paris, Moscow, and Prague were still careful not to burn bridges to Germany.[132]

In France, the radicals and a part of the Right approved the treaty either enthusiastically or as an unpleasant necessity. The socialists were less eager; the communists were bewildered. The extreme Right loudly voiced its disapproval. Paul-Boncour later wrote that the treaty should have been further delayed because of the Polish attitude. By signing the document, France "deprived itself of means of pressure on Russia as well as on our allies."[133]

Prager Presse hailed 2 May as a "historical date" and a "victory for peace." Beneš immediately declared his willingness to initial a text as close as possible to the Franco-Soviet wording. He sought a formula that would link Czechoslovakia more firmly to the Locarno system—this appeared a little contrived to Krofta—and reassure Warsaw that the Czechoslovak-Soviet treaty would not be operative against Poland. Romania and Yugoslavia had insisted on this point, and as Beneš told the Soviet envoy Sergei Alexandrovsky there was no sense in providing Warsaw with anti-Czechoslovak arguments, although he himself neither feared nor needed Poland.[134]

Both Prague and Moscow were interested in a speedy conclusion of negotiations.[135] Beneš proposed that Czechoslovak assistance to Russia and vice versa be made dependent on France coming to the aid of either country. Because French help to the USSR was circumscribed by Locarno provisions, Beneš could later tell Laval that he had tied the treaty with the Soviets "to the Franco-Russian pact and to Locarno, so that England

131. At 19 June 1935 session, CAE/Ch.

132. See DDF, I, x:504–506. Compare Gregorowicz, *Polsko-radzieckie stosunki,* 263–64; Scott, *Alliance,* 246–75

133. *Entre deux guerres,* 2:374.

134. Beneš received a telephone call from Laval half an hour before the signing of the French-Soviet text. See Prasolov, *Československo-sovětská smlouva,* 81; DDF, I, x:476–77; Monicault to Laval, 15 May 1935, MAE, Z 864.1, Tchécoslovaquie 2569; also DaM, III, 114–16, 121. For a later statement by Beneš that he did not want to commit himself too far to Russia so as not to compromise future Czechoslovak-Polish cooperation, see Witos, *Moja tułaczka,* 243.

135. Prague wanted to have the treaty signed before the 19 May elections. See Prasolov, "Československo-sovětska smlouva," 99, also 91–93; Olivová, "Československo-sovětská," 944–45.

would be in it."[136] This meant that Czechoslovak obligations were more restricted than Russian obligations, and, as Beneš put it, Czechoslovakia would act not when France would be obliged to intervene but when it actually did intervene.[137] The principle of preliminary French assistance also suited Moscow, however, insofar as it did not wish to have to help Prague, with France standing aloof, especially over an issue like the Anschluss.[138] Czechoslovakia saw itself as "a bridge between East and West"—perhaps the earliest use of this famous phrase—and the second link in the future security chain.[139] Stressing the latter, Beneš told the German envoy that he would never allow his country to become "a vassal" of Russia.[140]

The Czechoslovak-Soviet treaty was signed on 16 May, and the instruments of ratification exchanged during Beneš's visit to Moscow in early June. The foreign minister agreed to convey to Laval the Russian feeling of urgency about the ratification of the Franco-Soviet pact; both sides affirmed their interest in a larger security scheme to which Poland and Germany could be attracted.[141] Beneš's query how the Soviet Union, separated by Poland and Romania from Czechoslovakia, envisaged aid to his country, was answered by the war commissar Kliment Voroshilov. The Red Army, he said, would not hesitate to cross foreign territory whether an agreement to that effect existed or not.[142] Although the Czechoslovak side did not rule out a future convention, Beneš and Litvinov concurred to proceed gradually in the field of military cooperation. Beneš later claimed that Stalin had offered him a guarantee against Poland, which he declined on the grounds that Poland was allied to France and Romania.[143]

136. Cited in Prasolov, "Československo-sovětska smlouva," 108.

137. See Kvaček, *Nad Evropou*, 130.

138. See Olivová, "Československo-sovětská," 493; DaM, II, 120–23.

139. *České Slovo* cited in Kalvoda, *Czechoslovakia's Role*, 77. On the treaty's conformity with French policy, see DDF, I, X:547, 557; also Kvaček, "Jednání," 43; briefing, 16 May 1935, KV, CPP. For Beneš's remarks on 5 Nov. on Czechoslovakia's international standing, see Beneš, *Struggle*, 58.

140. See dispatches in ADAP, C IV/I:159–60, 242–43.

141. For Beneš's emphasis on this theme, see DDF, I, XI:126–27. On economic aspects, see Sládek, *Hospodářské vztahy*, also O *Československé zahraniční politice*, 257–58, 268.

142. On the possibility of a Soviet-Romanian accord permitting the passage of the Red Army, see briefing, 13 June 1935, KV, CPP; DDF, I, XI:71, 136–37; Kennard to Hoare, 15 Dec., FO 371 188896 Hm 04023; Wright to Secretary of State, 8 May, SDNA, 760.611/6. Also Kvaček, "K vztahům," 279–87; Bułhak, "Polska a Rumunia," 334–36; Teichman, "Titulescu," 676–80; Deák, "Kleine Entente," 145.

143. See Gen. Schweisguth report, 26 Aug. 1936, SHA, EMA/2, Tchécoslovaquie 3. Also Harry Hanak, "The Visit"; Kvaček, *Nad Evropou*, 131–32; Prasolov, "Československo-sovětska smlouva," 102–103, 111, 116; Olivová, "Československo-sovětská,"

The French press, except for papers generally hostile to Russia, hailed the pact and Beneš's visit to Moscow. In Warsaw, the reaction was negative. The Polish diplomacy had tried in March and April to dissuade Czechoslovakia from an entente with Russia seen as provocative to Berlin. The Polish army proposed a round of general staff talks, which Beneš considered inappropriate as long as political relations between Warsaw and Prague remained unclarified.[144] On 7 May, he informed Grzybowski about the forthcoming treaty, assuring the envoy that the negotiations were conducted in a manner not to injure Polish interests. After the signature, Beck instructed Grzybowski to make a demarche in Prague. The foreign minister characterized Beneš's explications as vague and indulged in ironic remarks about Czechoslovak foreign policy. Laroche commented that the Poles felt that the menace of German hegemony would be replaced by the no less dangerous Russian domination.[145] The Czechoslovak leaders on their side, recalling their vain efforts to settle their relations with Poland before signing anything with Moscow, implied that it was Warsaw's fault that they had to turn to Russia.[146]

The Czechoslovak-Soviet treaty marked the end of cooperation between military intelligence of Prague and Warsaw, much to the chagrin of the Czechoslovak army.[147] New levels of mutual antagonism were marked by the recall of Girsa in late May and of Grzybowski in October. Only chargé d'affaires, Jaromír Smutný and Marian Chodacki, remained respectively in Warsaw and Prague.

If the Czechoslovak-Soviet treaty annoyed the Poles, that between France and Russia "fit scandale à Varsovie."[148] Public opinion was anxious to know whether Paris planned large credits to Russia, and what military aid did it expect from the Red Army in view of the geographic configuration.[149] Appraisals by the Paris embassy, however, were not unduly pessimistic. Chłapowski, who regarded the treaty as bordering on "diplomatic jugglery," opined that because the old French system no longer sufficed, Paris was exploring diverse options: a closer alliance with Poland com-

---

405–406; briefings, 13, 27 June 1935, KV, CPP; Gen. Faucher to Maurin, 13, 28 Aug., SHA, EMA/2, Tchécoslovaquie 3, and DDF, I, XI:69–71.

144. See briefings, 11 Apr., 2 May 1935, KV, CPP; Berber, *Europäische Politik*, 47–48; Kvaček, *Nad Evropou*, 125; Gajanová, *ČSR*, 336.

145. See Laroche, *Pologne*, 195; *Češi a Poláci*, 2:561; DiM, VI, 300–302.

146. 5 Nov. 1935 speech, Beneš, *Struggle*; Pułaski, *Stosunki*, 102.

147. See Gen. Bláha's article in *La Pologne Littéraire*, 15 July 1935, the commemorative Piłsudski issue. Compare Bułhak, "Z Dziejów 1927–1936," 139–41; Szklarska-Lohmannowa, "Z Raportów," 105–106.

148. Noël, *L'Agression*, 89.

149. See d'Arbonneau report, 9 May 1935, SHA, EMA/2, Pologne 12; compare *Gazeta Warszawska*, 11 May, article by S[tanisław] K[ozicki].

bined with a neutralization of Russia; a policy of rapprochement with Germany; and moderate friendship with Russia accompanied by stronger ties with Warsaw and attempts at rapprochement with Berlin. He thought that Laval preferred this last variant.[150] Mühlstein thought that the pact was only significant in the sense that it eliminated the possibility of both Soviet-German and Franco-German understanding. It enhanced Poland's value in Berlin as well as in Paris where the Poles could more easily influence Franco-Russian moves.[151] Poland's attitude, according to Beck's instructions, was one of disinterest with a hint that the treaty diminished the chances of a wider multilateral accord. The signing of the Franco-Soviet pact "was not pleasant for us" but did not disturb the formal side of the alliance, even though possibilities of Franco-Polish cooperation would be weakened. The treaty did not remove the threat of a new Rapallo, for should opportunities for a Soviet-German rapprochement arise, the treaty would be "a mere scrap of paper."[152]

Laval's visit to Warsaw on 10–11 May, en route to Moscow, was interpreted by the Polish press as an indication of Poland's important place in France's eastern policy.[153] Mühlstein recommended extending a warm and "brotherly" welcome to Laval, enabling him to claim that he repaired the damage done by Barthou.[154] The advice was not heeded, and the French were disappointed by Beck's colorless speech. In the final communiqué banalities replaced a phrase about community of views on the Franco-Soviet treaty (the French idea) and the treaty having left the Franco-Polish alliance unaffected (the Polish proposal).[155]

Beck found Laval more "nuancé" than his predecessors, and the Frenchman thought Beck quite tractable. The conversations were cordial; Laval even spoke of a "new climate."[156] The main topics were the Franco-Soviet treaty, the Eastern and Danubian pacts, and the Czechoslovak-Polish relationship. The perennial question of Żyrardów and of Polish workers in

150. Chłapowski to Beck, 10 May 1935, AAN, MSZ 3691.

151. Szembek—Mühlstein conversation, 4 May 1935, DTJS, I, 280–81.

152. Beck's observations, 16 Feb. 1935 in MS, OSS, Wysocki, III, 2, 35; DTJS, II, 389–90; Cudahy to Secretary of State, 12 May, SDNA, 751.60C/74. Also Beck telegram, 5 May, HIA, Amb. Paryż, box 5. Compare DDF, I, x:497–98.

153. See, for instance, *Gazeta Warszawska*, 5 May 1935.

154. See DTJS, I, 281; Chambrun cited in MS, OSS, Wysocki, III, 369.

155. Laval's train was not brought to the central station and Laroche complained about discouragement of crowds and exclusion of opposition leaders from the reception. The communiqué followed more closely the French project; Laval's speech made some concessions to the Polish viewpoint. See Laroche, *Pologne*, 213, 216–18; for the radio speech, see Beck, *Przemówienia*, 161. Compare Łubieński–Rochat conversation, 11 May 1935, AAN, MSZ 55. Also Pertinax in *L'Echo de Paris*, 13 May.

156. See DTJS, I, 283–284; DBFP, II, XII:280; DDF, I, x:538.

France received only a cursory review. Beck showed little eagerness when asked to influence Hungary to be more positive toward the Danubian Pact. He sounded skeptical when Laval explained that the treaty with Russia was so devised as not to harm the Franco-Polish alliance. The Frenchman stressed that the Eastern Pact should not be viewed as anti-German or as an expression of a pro-Soviet policy. But the present German-Soviet antagonism could not be taken as an invariable factor; moreover, Germany was the "greatest menace to peace" and had to be neutralized and forced to collaborate. Laval recalled that in 1931 France could have reached an agreement with Germany, were it not for the Polish "corridor," the implication being that Poland should now stand by France. Beck agreed then on a position that the French described as "adhesion in principle," and that the Poles ammended as "no objection in principle."

Denying any intention of playing Beneš's ambassador, Laval transmitted the earlier-mentioned question that Beneš had addressed to Paris: Would Poland attack Czechoslovakia, should the latter be victim of German aggression and benefit from French aid? Beck bristled. He asked Laval to tell Beneš that he refused to answer such a question: "This is a categorical and official point of view of the Polish government." He later explained that he found such a query most surprising, for Poland had never attacked Czechoslovakia, while he could mention Czech inimical acts beginning with the forceful seizure of Teschen in 1919. Laval ventured an offer of mediation, but Beck brushed it aside.[157] It was obvious that Warsaw was not interested in improving relations with Prague. Tension was kept alive by press polemics, public manifestations, a campaign of Radio Katowice, and diplomatic incidents. True, Beck, considering that a disintegration of Czechoslovakia was not likely to occur in the near future, ordered a scaling down of "diversionary action" in Slovakia and Subcarpathian Ruthenia and curtailed too blatant an involvement of Polish diplomatic and consular officials.[158] Nonetheless, the crisis assumed again almost unparalleled dimensions in October, the conciliatory efforts of Poland's primate, Cardinal August Hlond, notwithstanding.[159]

157. See account in DTJS, I, 284–90, and a slightly different version in circular 23 May 1935, AAN, MSZ 3691. Compare Beck telegram, 12 May (misdated 10 May) DiM, VI, 299–300; Chłapowski–Laval conversation, 6 June, AAN, MSZ 3768; also DDF, I, x:538; DBFP, II, XIII:250–51, 255, 274.

158. See DTJS, I, 312, 316.

159. For the Apr. and May Czechoslovak-Polish tension, see DTJS, I, 264; Bułhak, "Stosunki 1927–1936," 138; press cuttings in MZV-VA, 478.1255 and 1256. A characteristic attack appears in *Gazeta Polska*, 26 May 1935. For the summer and autumn, see Czechoslovak legation report, 11 July, CPP; and Berber, *Europäische Politik*, 51–52; Monicault, Naggiar, Bressy, and Noël dispatches in MAE, Z 864.1, Tchécoslovaquie 2687; Z 864.5, Tchécoslovaquie 2587 and 2569. Compare Koženski, *Czechosłowacja*, 102–11 and, on Polish-Slovak cooperation, 195–97. On Hlond's visit to Prague to at-

Laval did not see Piłsudski, who was dying. In his lucid moments, the marshal spoke of the Frenchman's visit, which "haunted him." He kept repeating that nothing good could come of Laval's journey to Moscow. Summoning Beck to his bedside, Piłsudski told him to maintain as long as possible the present relationship with Berlin, but also preserve "at any price the alliance with France." If only Britain could be drawn into it, the marshal mused, recommending sustained efforts in that direction. At one point Piłsudski seemed to enjoin Beck to follow a wait-and-see policy.[160]

On 12 May, the marshal died, leaving, as d'Ormesson put it in *Le Figaro* on 14 May, a "psychological void" in Poland. Premier Walery Sławek reminded the ministers that Piłsudski "had in his hands the most important state problems" and that military and diplomatic matters in particular "had never been the object of discussion of the cabinet." Sławek thought of establishing some consultative organ headed by the president, and in fact a "regency" of sorts came into being, composed of Mościcki, General (shortly marshal) Edward Rydz-Śmigły as commander-in-chief, and Beck. Sławek himself lost his power bid by October.[161] Immediately after Piłsudski's death, Beck reaffirmed that he would maintain the present foreign policy course.[162] The French wondered about the possible impact of the president and Rydz-Śmigły, a reputed francophile. The general made some moves toward reviving Franco-Polish military collaboration, and in June he ordered a study of Germany based on the hypothesis of a Polish-German war in which Czechoslovakia remained neutral.[163] The French alliance, which according to the Belgian envoy would shortly become "merely a beautiful façade," was repeatedly described by the Poles as essential. Lipski even argued that it was perfectly compatible with an under-

---

tend the International Eucharistic Congress, see *Lidové Listy*, 4 July 1935. A good survey of the anti-Czech campaign can be found in Naggiar to Laval, 6 Nov. 1935, MAE, Z 864.5, Tchécoslovaquie 2587.

160. Jędrzejewicz, *Kronika*, 2:512; Beck, *Dernier rapport*, 92–93; DDF, I, x:578.

161. See cabinet session, 20 May 1935, AAN, PPRM, LXXVIII, 443–45. Beck instructed Szembek to refer in his absence important foreign policy matters to the president and Rydz-Śmigły. The president in turn inaugurated conferences on foreign policies; Sławek, Beck, and Rydz-Śmigły participated in the first, held on 23 May. See DTJS, I, 39 and 303.

162. Circular telegram cited in Wojciechowski, *Stosunki*, 195.

163. Beck proved able to cope with the opponents within the government circles and in the opposition. See Beck, *Dernier rapport*, 109–11. For a restatement of external policy direction, *Polityka Narodów*, 5 (1935), 671–72. Compare DDF, I, x:620–21, 689–90, XI:224–25; Noël dispatch, 20 May 1935, MAE, Z 698.1, Pologne 2101. On military problems see Ciałowicz, *Polsko-francuski sojusz*, 215; Roos, *Polen*, 230–31; *Polskie siły zbrojne w drugiej wojnie światowej* (London, 1951–62), 1:114–16. Also Laroche to Laval, 15 May, and d'Arbonneau reports, 15 May, 12 June, 10, 24 July, 7 Aug.; appraisal of Rydz-Śmigły by generals Moinvelle and Bernard, 14 May, SHA, EMA/2, Pologne 12 and 43.

standing with Germany, for Berlin viewed it as pulling France away from
Russia.[164] Piłsudski's funeral on 17–18 May brought Laval from Moscow
to Poland where he joined Marshal Pétain, heading a large delegation, and
a host of foreign dignitaries.[165] His Moscow talks had produced a consensus on the desirability of enticing Germany to join a collective pact, as well
as Laval's insincere assent to explore Franco-Soviet military cooperation.
The Russians stressed their mistrust of Poland, which Laval tried to diminish.[166] In Cracow, the Frenchman lost no opportunity for conversations
with Goering to whom he outlined his ideas of a multilateral pact (including Czechoslovakia) in which the German-French-Soviet accord would be
the main element.[167] The Laval–Goering talks weakened the importance
of the recent French treaty with the USSR, which appeared to Neurath as
a "detour" on the way to a new version of the Eastern Pact.[168]

Germany would not play. In his speech on 21 May, Hitler put the emphasis on bilateralism, which made Warsaw feel that it had been correct
in its own line toward Berlin.[169] The Führer's phrase suggesting incompatibility between Locarno and the Franco-Soviet pact appeared ominous to
the French diplomacy. Laval realized that Hitler's speech practically nul-
lified the chances of further negotiations over an Eastern Pact, but, supported by Prague, he continued his efforts.[170] They became seriously undermined on 18 June by the signing of the British-German naval
agreement—a virtual violation of the London declaration of 3 February
and a repudiation of Versailles. The Stresa Front was given a jolt; Hitler
deemed the event the happiest day of his life.[171] The reaction of the French

164. See DTJS, I, 307, 308, 348, 351, 531; compare DDB, III, 171.

165. The French delegation comprised generals Colson, Faury, Pujo, and Admiral De-
coux. Bullitt's observation that Pétain and Laval were "treated throughout as if they
were unwelcome cousins" (Bullitt, *Correspondence*, 123–24) is not borne out by other
sources. See Władysław J. Zaleski, "W 40 rocznicę zgonu: pogrzeb Józefa Piłsudskiego
w Krakowie," *Niepodległość*, 10 (1976). Laval's astonishment that Poland had a navy,
however, was reported by many.

166. DDF, I, x:575–77; DTJS, I, 297; Kuźmiński, *Polska*, 232; DBFP, II, XXII:255,
260; Bullitt, *Correspondence*, 126.

167. For Laval-Goering conversation see DDF, I, x:604–13; DTJS, I, 295–99, 300–
302; DBFP, II, XIII:271; Laval at 26 June 1935 session, CAE/Sén; Chłapowski telegram,
24 May, HIA, Amb.Paryż, box 5.

168. See Kvaček, *Nad Evropou*, 135; DTJS, I, 290, 209, compare 287. ADAP, C, IV/
1:349–50.

169. See Starzeński, *Trzy lata* 41; Kuźmiński, *Polska*, 235; *Polityka Narodów*, 5
(1935).

170. See DDF, I, XI:126–27.

171. See Watt, "Naval Agreement," and Bloch, "La Grande Bretagne face au réarmement allemand et l'accord naval de 1935," *Revue d'Histoire de le Deuxième Guerre
Mondiale*, 63 (1966) 41–68. On French shock and anger see Herriot, *Jadis*, 2:561–62;

eastern allies was restrained. Czechoslovak public opinion was worried, but Krofta described the happening as a surprise that he did not view as very dangerous.[172] Beck thought that the event was important and necessitated careful watching of British policy.[173]

Coming after the naval agreement, Beck's visit to Berlin on 2–4 July could hardly be welcome to the French, as indicated in *Le Temps* and *Journal des Débats* (4 and 6 July). Although Beck had informed Laval beforehand of this return visit, French and Czechoslovak diplomacies were alerted.[174] Conjectures about Beck's intentions and the content of his Berlin talks ranged from sober assessments to wild rumors about German-Polish military cooperation against Russia and a German-Polish-Hungarian front against Prague.[175] Actually, the Polish foreign minister wished mainly to dispel Berlin's concern about a possible change in Polish diplomatic course, and test German resolve to continue the détente at a time when friction arose in Danzig, this "barometer" of German-Polish relations. The French aspect played a considerable part in Beck's calculations. The next general election in France could place in power either the Moscow-oriented Popular Front (which might necessitate a rapprochement between Warsaw and Berlin) or a rightist government seeking a direct understanding with Germany.[176] Should the latter occur, Beck might, in Beneš's opinion, try to steal a march on the French or at least try to threaten Paris with the possibility.[177]

Beck deduced from his conversation with Hitler on 3 July that Berlin's line toward Warsaw had not changed. On his side he affirmed that Poland would not participate in any encirclement of Germany. When Hitler fulminated against Russia and described its pact with Czechoslovakia as a threat to peace, Beck recalled Polish objections to the Eastern Pact, but added that Warsaw wished to maintain its relationship to the USSR as

---

Chłapowski telegram, 20 June 1935, HIA, Amb. Paryż, box 5; Einstein to Secretary of State, 27 June, SDNA, 840.00/383 1/2; Laval's statement at the 26 June session, CAE/Sén.

172. Briefing, 27 June 1935, KV, CPP; also DDF, I, XI:165, 207–208.

173. See Beck telegram, 21 June 1935, HIA, Amb. Paryż, box 5; also DTJS, I, 321, 334–35; Chargé Nielsen to Secretary of State, 28 June SDNA, 826.34/176.

174. See Noël to Laval, 1 July 1935, DDF, I, XI:285–86.

175. See DDF, I, XI:305, 334–35, 403, 419–21, 483, 485–86; also Quai d'Orsay to war ministry, 12 July 1935, SHA, EMA/2, Pologne 43.

176. See Jędrzejewicz, *Lipski*, 201–202, 204–205; compare DTJS, I, 328–29, 345; DDF, I, XI:306–307.

177. "This is a maneuver which will not end well for Poland because two powerful [states] will always come to an agreement more quickly at the expense of the weaker." Beneš at the 3 June meeting of the executive committee of the national socialist party, cited in Prasolov, *Československo-sovětska smlouva*, 124. Also DDF, I, XI:295.

based on the nonaggression treaty. France, he remarked, was pacific and not anti-German; the Soviet-Czechoslovak pact was ineffective.[178]

In Beck's judgment Hitler had no interest at this point in a direct involvement with Paris. Polish diplomacy, while manifesting its loyalty to the French, could offer its good services in steering Paris toward a Franco-Polish-German alignment and away from the Soviet and Czechoslovak pacts. Chłapowski informed Laval that Beck had failed to detect any anti-French accents in Hitler's remarks, and hinted at such a triple combination. Laval replied that this would be a solution to Europe's problems, but Berlin must first show its good will by accepting a collective multilateral pact. Talking to the new French ambassador in Warsaw, Léon Noël, Beck warned that Germany would not be convinced by the argument that the Soviet pact was compatible with Locarno. Stressing Hitler's anti-Russian and anti-Czechoslovak stance, Beck added his own suspicions of Prague. He seemed convinced of the existence of secret accords that were making Czechoslovakia the advance post of the Red Army. It was too late, he said, to prevent Beneš from becoming Russia's vassal.[179]

The French clearly mistrusted Beck and were unwilling to be guided by his counsels. François-Poncet and Noël agreed that the minister brought nothing tangible from Berlin.[180] Still, Laval found himself locked in a position in which an Eastern Pact of some sort seemed the only means of pursuing a policy of rapprochement with Berlin—a real vicious circle.[181] Domestic problems were complicating the situation. The Flandin ministry, denied powers to carry out deflationary measures, fell on 31 May. On 7 June, Laval became premier while retaining the foreign ministry. Chłapowski called this new government "a product of fatigue and resignation."[182] The radicals were split; the Popular Front was on the rise. On the Bastille Day, Daladier and Cot marched alongside the socialist Blum and the communist Maurice Thorez under the banner "Labor, Freedom,

---

178. See Wojciechowski, *Stosunki*, 203–204; Beck, *Dernier rapport*, 97–103; DTJS, I, 330–32; Beck telegram, 6 July 1935, HIA, Amb. Paryż, box 5; Szembek note, July 11 SI, Amb. Londyn, A.12.52/14.

179. See DDF, I, XI:321, 377–78, 386–88, 407–408; compare Smutný report, 11 July 1935, CPP, Chłapowski to Beck, 26 July, AAN, MSZ 3768. The French and the Czechs believed that the Germans had attempted to wrest from Beck some commitments against Prague, but he evaded them. This is not mentioned in any Polish source. Although Noël became ambassador in the spring, Laroche stayed on in Warsaw during Laval's visit in view of his long experience in Poland.

180. See DDF, I, XI:317, 469–70. Compare retrospective Noël to Flandin, 31 March 1936, MAE, P.A. Noël 200. The French recognized that Beck's resolution of the Danzig crisis by a policy that combined firmness with moderation was a success for the foreign minister.

181. See Phipps to Hoare, June 24, 1933, DBFP, II, XIII:470.

182. Chłapowski to Beck, June 15, 1935, AAN, MSZ 3802.

and Peace." Beck believed that Laval's absorption with domestic problems would result in a further weakening of French international activity.[183]

During the summer and early autumn of 1935, Laval pursued the elusive goal of achieving an understanding with Germany. Asking that Berlin just discuss the current problems on the assumption that a collective pact might eventually be included in a final accord, Laval even expressed a wish "to dissolve the French system of alliances or the individual alliances in the Eastern Pact," thus depriving them "of all bias against Germany." The Germans did not view this proposal as realistic, as the French army would vigorously object to any such schemes. Berlin aimed at opposing the Franco-Soviet-Czechoslovak alignment by concentrating on the weakest state, Czechoslovakia, which Bülow called the Soviet aircraft carrier in the region.[184]

Indeed, Czechoslovakia was in a difficult domestic and international position. The question of successor to the ailing Masaryk became a burning issue, and the old president threw all his prestige behind Beneš. Yet, Beneš, even if elected, could not hope to equal Masaryk's standing. The emboldened rightist opposition led by Kramář set up a movement called National Unity (Národní Sjednocení), which cooperated with Hlinka's Slovak populists and found itself on the same side of the political barricade as the Sudetendeutsche Heimatspartei of Konrad Henlein. Assisted financially by Berlin, the Sudeten party was menacing, and Beneš, encouraged by the French, made vain efforts to have it outlawed. Its victory in the parliamentary elections of 19 May, making it the biggest party in the parliament after the agrarians, created consternation in Prague and serious concern in Paris.[185] Krofta commented on the dangerous repercussions in the field of external policy, for the declarations by the Sudeten Germans of their loyalty to the Republic could hardly be taken at face value.[186] The Polish min-

---

183. See DTJS, I, 321. Allegedly Beck was interested at this point in an invitation to Paris, but Noël ignored it. See Noël, *Polonia*, 134.

184. For Laval's sentiments, as cited, see ADAP, C, IV/1:608; compare 484–87; also DBFP, II, XIII:585–611, 625–30; DTJS, I, 304; Ormos, "Sur les causes," 74.

185. See numerous dispatches in DDF, IX, X, XI; also Monicault, Naggiar, and François-Poncet to Laval, 21 May, 20 July, 5 Nov. 1935, MAE, Z 864.1, Tchécoslovaquie 2569. Compare FRUS 1935, I, 284; Gawroński, *moja misja*, 280; Noël, *Tchécoslovaquie*, 115; Olivová, *Doomed Democracy*, 191–94; Gajanová, *Dvojí*, 111, 131. On National Unity, see Frantisek Xaver Hodac, *Deset úkolů Národního sjednocení* (Praha, 1935), and the most recent Vladimír Fic, *Národní sjednocení v politickém systému Československa 1930–1938* (Praha, 1983). On the Sudeten-German problems, the most detailed are works by César and Černý in Czech; Brügel in German and English; and Ronald M. Smelser, *The Sudeten Problem 1933–1938* (Middletown, Conn., 1975); Radomír Luža, *The Transfer of the Sudeten Germans: A Study of Czech-German Relations 1933–1962* (New York, 1964); Francesco Leoncini, *La Questione dei Sudeti 1919–1938* (Padova, 1976); Batowski, *Austria*.

186. Briefing, 23 May 1935, KV, CPP.

istry of foreign affairs saw Henlein's victory as "a severe blow to the centralist policy of Prague," likely to affect Czechoslovak diplomacy.[187]

Paris tried to bolster Prague. French diplomacy assisted Czechoslovakia in its negotiations with the Vatican.[188] In late June, General René Keller arrived in the country for a military conference, which resulted in the signing on 1 July of an air force convention. Annexes to it were added on 14 December 1935 and 1 July 1937. The convention stipulated that if France and Czechoslovakia were simultaneously at war with Germany, one French reconnaissance and one bomber group would be sent to Czechoslovakia to assist in military operations.[189] Such arrangements did not completely dispel Beneš's uneasiness concerning Laval's German policy. Having learned that Paris contemplated asking Berlin for a guarantee for Czechoslovakia, he wrote that the proper way was surely a parallel Paris-Berlin and Prague-Berlin negotiation. Any other approach might be misunderstood by Moscow, among others. Laval explained that Osuský was victim of a misunderstanding; France would never undertake anything that would not be in full accord with Czechoslovak interests. Besides, it did not intend to open any negotiations with Berlin at this point.[190]

With the Eastern Pact deadlocked, the Quai d'Orsay recommended in early June renewed negotiations about the Danubian Pact. The question of mutual aid would be shelved to avoid an a priori exclusion of Germany and new arguments with Rome.[191] Beneš did not like the idea. The Danubian Pact, he said, was meant to bring Italy into collaboration with France and the Little Entente so as to maintain the established order in Central Europe (Austria included). Only mutual assistance agreements could make this scheme real. The Little Entente was willing to pay the price, namely by tolerating Austrian, Hungarian, and Bulgarian rearmament. But if mutual assistance was excluded and partial Hungarian rearmament accepted, it would mean in effect that Italy and Hungary would have a free hand.[192]

Beneš wanted above all precise Italian commitments, for he dreaded

---

187. See DTJS, I, 302–303; Jędrzejewicz, *Lipski*, 192–99.

188. It was no accident that the French Cardinal Jean Verdier presided as Papal legate over the Eucharistic Congress in Prague.

189. Text in DDF, I, XI:288–91. Compare "L'Analyse des dispositions nous liant à la Tchécoslovaquie," 2 June 1938, and air ministry to Daladier, 7 Sept., SHA, Cabinet du Ministre, Tchécoslovaquie 5 N 579.6. Also Faucher report, 1 July 1935, SHA, EMA/2, Tchécoslovaquie 3; Marès "La Faillite," 52–53. The timing of the convention may have been connected with the contemplated Air Locarno (inapplicable to German-Italian conflict in Central Europe) and the earlier-mentioned Franco-Italian air talks. See DDF, I, X:459.

190. See DDF, I, XI:380–81, 404, 438.

191. See DDF, I, XI:59–68.

192. See Kvaček, "Boj," 255–56; Pułaski, "Projekty," 221–22. Compare Mühlstein to Beck, 16 Aug. 1935, AAN, MSZ 3892, and Laval remarks, 26 June, CAE/Sén.

Czechoslovakia's isolation in case his country, by bringing aid to Austria, would find itself in war with Germany. A Habsburg restoration was an equally overriding threat against which he wanted protection. It was imperative that Paris declare its full solidarity with the Little Entente on that issue.[193] French possibilities of furthering its Danubian policy, however, were hampered, as always, by lack of adequate economic leverage. Laval admitted that commercial relations with Yugoslavia and Romania were practically nil, and he deplored the "fierce egoism" of France.[194] Even in the case of Czechoslovakia, *Le Temps* admitted on 3 May that France could have been buying some of the products it purchased in Germany from its Czechoslovak ally. Czechoslovak papers spoke of "sacrifices without advantages."[195] Yet, when in mid-July, Laval decided to go ahead with a watered-down Danubian Pact, Beneš acquiesced. It was "better than nothing," he said, although he still insisted on a preliminary assurance of aid from France and Italy against the Germans.[196] As the Italo-Ethiopian crisis mounted, neither Rome nor Paris was willing to commit itself. The situation was paradoxical. Krofta summed it up by saying that "when M. Mussolini was against us, he was present in Europe; now that he is with us, he is in Africa." Czechoslovak hopes that the Anglo-French-Italian conference, held in mid-August, would restore the Stresa Front and save the Danubian Pact crumbled with the collapse of the talks involving the three powers.[197]

The balance sheet of the ten months of Laval's diplomacy was negative. All efforts notwithstanding, it proved impossible to use the Eastern Pact concept either to avoid a Franco-Russian tête-à-tête or to entangle Germany in cooperation. The unratified Franco-Soviet pact was, properly speaking, neither the first link of a multinational chain nor an alliance. The Stresa Front turned out to be a façade that the British-German naval agreement undermined and the Italian invasion of Ethiopia destroyed. Even a watered-down Danubian Pact offered no chance of realization. Franco-Polish alliance remained under a cloud, and domestic problems in Czechoslovakia and France boded ill for the future.

193. See numerous dispatches in DDF, XI. A political crisis in Yugoslavia, which led to Milan Stojadinović's assumption of premiership and the foreign ministry on 23 June, was most disquieting for Prague.

194. At 19 June 1935 session, CAE/Ch.

195. See *České Slovo*, 8 May, *Lidové Listy*, 17 Apr. 1935.

196. See DDF, I, XI:431–32, 455–57.

197. Krofta cited in DDF, I, XI:649. On Beneš's efforts to make the Little Entente meeting in Bled approve a Danubian Pact without mutual assistance clauses see, DDF, I, XII:150. For Beneš's views on the Italo-Ethiopian crisis, see DDF I, XII:1–2, 108–10.

Chapter Thirteen

The Test of 7 March

The Impact of the Ethiopian Crisis

The Italian invasion of Ethiopia on 3 October 1935 placed Paris in a most difficult position. Laval and the French cared little for the Ethiopians, but they could not ignore that Ethiopia was a member of the League of Nations. After all, the entire policy of France had been based on the League, including Locarno and "the agreements that bind us to our friends of Central Europe."[1] With Britain becoming an ardent champion of the League, the Ethiopian affair transformed itself into an Italo-British showdown. Paris was faced with the necessity to take sides, a calamity Laval tried to avoid at all cost.

French public opinion was divided, with the Left and part of the Center being predominently pro-British, the Right favoring Italy. The crisis, the socialist Jean Longuet argued, had ramifications for all the small states of Europe. In that sense the cause of Ethiopia was a common cause of them all.[2] French diplomacy attempted to extract binding engagements from Britain to make up for the worsening relations with Rome but was not prepared to abandon the latter. Nor was Laval ready to abandon his overtures to Berlin. The resulting ambiguity made him appear more devious than ever.[3] French endeavors to clarify British commitments under Locarno in the case of a conflict with Germany originating in East Central Europe naturally affected Czechoslovakia, which approached the crisis mainly from the viewpoint of possible repercussions on European relations.[4] Beneš, presiding at this point over the League Council, tried to refrain from openly anti-Italian manifestations while attempting to steer

1. See Laval telegram, DDF, 1, XI:358–59.

2. 23 Oct. 1935 session, CAE/Ch.

3. Extensive treatment in Rostow, *Anglo-French Relations*, 180–233; Gamelin's reflections in Le Goyet, *Mystère*, 109–13; also Young, "Soldiers and Diplomats: The French Embassy and Franco-Italian relations 1935–1936," *The Journal of Strategic Studies* 7 (March 1984) 83.

4. Krofta's views cited in Gajanová, *ČSR*, 341.

Laval toward rapprochement with London. If Czechoslovakia had to opt between collaboration with Britain and the alliance with Italy, it would unhesitatingly choose the former.[5]

Even before the Italian invasion, Beneš had attempted to act as an intermediary between the French and the British. He intimated to the Foreign Secretary Sir Samuel Hoare that Laval would accept a united front with Britain, provided London undertook to side with France in resisting aggression in East Central Europe. Talking to Laval, Beneš pointed out "an unexpected and unhoped for opportunity" to gain British involvement, which had eluded them for the past fifteen years.[6] The Frenchman voiced skepticism that, in this instance, was only partly justified. Hoare was willing to interpret Locarno so that Britain would provide immediate aid to France (after the League determined an act of aggression) and intervene without awaiting the verdict if the aggression was clearly unprovoked and required an instantaneous riposte. The Quai d'Orsay thought that such a position might justify Franco-British staff conversations. Under Hoare's proposal not only French security but indirectly that of France's eastern allies would be greatly increased.[7]

Laval, however, was not prepared for an alliance with Britain that could involve him in war with Italy. What is more, his interpretation of the *application* of article 16 of the Covenant, as having to result from a collective decision of the Council, alarmed Czechoslovak diplomacy. The distinction he made between the right of the League members to act, before a recommendation of the Council, and an automatic obligation (which he contested) appeared dangerous for the working of eastern alliances. Indeed, delegates of the Little and Balkan Ententes meeting in Geneva began to voice open criticism of Laval.[8] Beneš spoke bitterly to Count Carlo Sforza: "If only they [the French government] would tell me frankly that they are not sure to keep the engagement of their alliance with us," Prague could try to approach Berlin and save what could be saved of Czechoslovak independence. "But any allusion of mine to such possibility is met with a haughty assurance that France will always remain loyal to her word." If

---

5. See DBFP, II, XIV:530; Gajanová, *Dvojí*, 132–33; Kvaček, *Nad Evropou*, 176–77; 185–87; Beneš's conversation with Berger-Waldenegg, 7 Sept. 1935, ANM, Mastný, 12.075–76; compare briefings, 3, 17 Oct., 13 Nov., KV, CPP.

6. Beneš–Hoare conversations, 9, 11, Sept. 1935; Beneš–Laval, 9, 11, 12, 24 Sept., in ANM, Mastný, 12.075–095; compare briefing, 26 Sept., KV, CPP. Brief accounts in DBFP, II, XIV:620–21, 681–82; XV:116–17. Also note, 27 Aug., MAE, P.A. Massigli 1. Compare DDF, I, XII:413–14, 455–56, 656–58, XIII:23–24.

7. See DDF, I, XIII:367–70.

8. See DDF, I, XIII:89–91, 104. Compare Kvaček, *Nad Evropou*, 179–80, and Deák, "Siedmy marec," 326.

Sforza's recollections were accurate, it was indeed "a painful" avowal for Beneš to make.[9]

The British thought also that Laval "might deal lightly with the interests of the Allies of France" in East Central Europe.[10] Flandin said that France would not go to war on their behalf, about which Vansittart had always been "more than doubtful." In such circumstances, another British diplomat argued, "we should be well-advised to work for some weakening of the French eastern commitments."[11] In December, a Foreign Office memorandum examined three possible courses of action: alignment with France and encouragement of resistance of the Eastern states; pressure on France to make concessions to Germany; or a continuation of the present policy of muddling through. The author concluded that a policy of concessions seemed the only possible alternative.[12] All this boded ill for Beneš's hopes of gaining British support for the eastern alliances at the price of supporting London's stand toward Italy.

The story of the condemnation of Italian aggression by the League in early October, and of subsequent sanctions is too well known to be told here. Suffice it to say that the British championship of the League did not prevent discrete attempts to end the conflict. In turn, Laval's endeavors to keep all the irons in the fire disturbed Gamelin so deeply that he cried after a meeting of the Haut Comité Militaire. But his frustration found no other expression than a wait-and-see attitude.[13]

The temporary loss of Italy only increased Laval's interest in Berlin. Not since the days of Briand, Chłapowski reported, "were there so many voices [in France] speaking objectively or positively in favor of an understanding with Germany."[14] A revived Comité France-Allemagne, enjoying the sponsorship of the Quai d'Orsay, came to comprise the respective presidents of the Comité des Forges and Comité des Houillières as well as notable representatives of veterans associations, deputies, and journalists. Laval assured the German ambassador Roland Köster that he would not be dragged into any adventures by Russia. The French army, he said, should only be used "in defense of the French soil, and in no circumstances beyond France's frontiers."[15] While the ambassador believed that Laval was

9. Sforza, *Totalitarian War*, 32–33. Sforza dates the conversation Sept. 1936, but his other comments suggest that it took place in Oct. 1935.

10. Memorandum by Sargent and Wigram, 21 Nov. 1935, DBFP, II, xv:715.

11. For Flandin's views, see DBFP, II, xv:49–51; minutes by Paterson, Wigram and Vansittart, FO 371 18811 C 7110.

12. Memorandum by O. O'Malley, 1 Dec. 1935, FO 371.20437 W 5075.

13. Gamelin's own account is cited in Le Goyet, *Mystère*, 113.

14. Chłapowski report, 30 Nov. 1935, AAN, MSZ 3802.

15. See Warner, *Laval*, 110–11, 130–31; also ADAP, C, IV/2:812, 908. DDF, I, XXII:330–33.

sincere in wishing a rapprochement, his overtures were largely seen as dictated by tactics.[16] Similarly, François-Poncet's pleas, on 21 November, for rapprochement, combined with hints about the desirability of a Hitler–Laval meeting, could not shake the Führer's position that a policy of understanding between Paris and Berlin was incompatible with a Franco-Soviet pact. Expressing confidence in Laval personally, Hitler was adamant in his refusal of French overtures.[17]

Prague professed itself undisturbed by French wooing of Berlin. Beneš repeated to Laval his old line: Czechoslovakia never was nor would be an obstacle to Franco-German understanding. It had no conflict with Germany, and if Berlin regarded Czechoslovakia as a barrier to its eastern expansion, this matter was of general European concern, for such an expansion was intolerable from a European viewpoint. Beneš felt that if Germany was contained, it would abandon designs on Austria and resume its Polish-directed *Drang nach Osten*.[18] Yet there was some anxiety in Prague lest Laval go too far and create the impression of willingness to grant the Germans a free hand in East Central Europe. Beneš told Emile Naggiar (who had become envoy in Prague in June) that it was essential to maintain a united Franco-British-Russian-Little Entente front. One had to be prepared for a conflict with Germany while showing a desire to talk to Berlin. An understanding with Hitler was most unlikely and could be exploited by the latter for his own ends.[19]

Warsaw was somewhat annoyed not having been informed of the outcome of the François–Poncet conversation with Hitler on 21 November. Léger assured Chłapowski that the ambassador had merely acquainted Hitler with French ideas; had it been otherwise France's allies would have been notified.[20] The exchange was symptomatic for the current state of Franco-Polish relations, and it must be placed in the context of the Ethiopian crisis. To Beck, as to Beneš, the conflict as such was of no real interest, and Beck denied that it could constitute a precedent. Poland did not wish to find itself in conflict with either Rome or London, but it had to join in the unanimous condemnation of Italy at Geneva. For the most part Polish policy accorded with that of France, and Beck was genuinely worried lest Laval be overthrown and replaced by Herriot. Allegedly Laval asked his

16. See Köster report, 18 Nov. 1935, ADAP, C, IV/2:813.

17. See DDF, I, XIII:384–86, 388–93; ADAP, C, IV/2:831–33; DBFP, II, XV:531; Jędrzejewicz, *Lipski*, 233–34, 241–48; DTJS, I, 412–13, 452; II, 27–28.

18. See Beneš–Laval conversations, 9, 11, 12, 24 Sept. 1935, ANM, Mastný, 12.075–095.

19. See DDF, I, XII:642; Kvaček, "K vztahům," 277–78; Gajanová, *Dvojí*, 129–30; Král, *Spojenectví*, 96; DBFP, II, XV:300.

20. Chłapowski report, 23 Nov. 1935, AAN, Amb. Berlin, 85.

Polish colleague to act on occasion as an intermediary with Eden.[21] This convergence in Geneva did not mean a cordiality of relationship. The contrary was true, for Beck himself and political developments in Poland were viewed very critically by Paris and by Prague.

The leadership crisis, which reached a culminating point with the nomination of Marian Zyndram-Kościałkowski cabinet on 3 October, was seen as the president's attempt to eliminate Sławek and emasculate the "colonels' group." Beck remained in the new ministry only after protracted negotiations.[22] The French were generally pleased with Kościałkowski's government, an ascendancy of Rydz-Śmigły, and a certain weakening of Beck's position. The socialist press, for which Beck epitomized the "colonels' regime," heaped insults and injurious epithets on the minister. When on 26 October, Pertinax called Beck in *L'Echo de Paris* a "sworn enemy of France," even the Quai d'Orsay found the attack regrettable, and Laval informed Beck that he deplored it.[23] Some of the attacks were fed by the persisting rumors of a German-Polish-Hungarian alliance; others were probably inspired by Polish political adversaries, including emigrés. Opposition parties raised their voices against the foreign minister.[24] Governmental circles were worried and felt that counter-moves were needed to alleviate Beck's difficult position.[25] Would his resignation result in a basic change in Polish policy? Noël for one was not sure.[26]

Beneš had no such doubts and thought that only a replacement of Beck could bring about a new course. The generally pro-Polish *Národní Listy*

21. See Beck's instructions and related material in DTJS, I, 338–39, 357, 360, 364, 385, 532n, 538–41; II, 369; compare DBFP, II, XIV:580–81, 612–15; Komarnicki to Beck, 2 Aug., Beck telegram, 3 Oct. 1935, SI, Amb. Londyn, A.12.54/14; MS, OSS, Wysocki, II, 440; Jędrzejewicz, *Lipski*, 222–25; Beck, *Dernier rapport*, 85–86, 105–106; speech, 15 Jan. 1936 in *Przemówienia*, 191–98, 204–205; discussion in Archiwum Sejmowe, Diariusze posiedzeń komisji spraw zagranicznych sejmu, pol. 176.

22. On domestic developments, see Pobóg-Malinowski, *Najnowsza historia* 2:576–92; Polonsky, *Politics*, 391–412; Jędruszczak, *Ostatnie lata*; and Wynot, *Polish Politics*. Compare DDF, I, XIII:117–18, 125–27, 152–55.

23. For Warsaw protests, see telegrams between Szembek, Schaetzel, and Chłapowski, 19, 20, 21, 24 Sept. 1935, HIA, Amb.Paryż, box 5. Notes for Bargeton and Léger; Laval to Noël, 26 Oct. 1935, MAE, Z 698.1, Pologne 2101.

24. Generals Sikorski and J. Haller suspected Beck of being "bought" by Germany; Lieberman warned Blum about Beck's sinister designs. See Witos, *Moja tułaczka*, 241; Lieberman's letter, 24 Jan. 1936, PI, Weinstein Collection, xxv. On Christian democrats' and populists' criticisms, see Borkowski, "Stronnictwo ludowe," 165; also Żarnowski, *Polska Partia Socjalistyczna*, 116.

25. See 15 Nov. 1935 conversation with Mościcki, AAN, Akta Świtalskiego, 71.

26. See DDF, I, XII:640–41; compare Noël's reports, 24, 27, 28, 30 Oct. 1935, MAE, Z 698.1, Pologne 2102. Also d'Arbonneau report, 24 Oct., SHA, EMA/2, Pologne 12. Also, Berber, *Europäische Politik*, 52; briefing 20 Nov., KV, CPP.

contrasted the new Polish premier with the foreign minister to the detriment of the latter. *Přitomnost* (13 November) attacked nastily Beck *ad personam*. Only the *Slovák* tried to defend Warsaw and criticized the polonophobia of the Czech press.[27]

In these circumstances, the leading circles in Warsaw considered an improvement of relations with Paris as necessary. Although Szembek found it difficult to persuade Noël that the German-Polish pact was useful as a deterrent to a new Rapallo, he spared no pains to insist that the Franco-Polish alliance was very much alive.[28] The president of *Bank Polski*, Adam Koc, suggested overtures to Paris for funds to sustain the bank—an operation that Beck viewed as unrelated to politics, and Koc, invoking Rydz-Śmigły's authority, envisaged as a step toward improved relations. Despite Mühlstein's doubts about whether this was the right moment to ask France for money—"lately we let no occasion pass to annoy her"—Laval instructed the Banque de France to respond sympathetically. Koc's mission to Paris produced not only some credit but also encouraging talks with the minister of finance, Marcel Regnier, and promises of support from the great banker Edouard de Rothschild and the steel magnate François de Wendel. Chłapowski concluded that the time was propitious to open talks aimed at "a real amelioration of both economic and political relations."[29]

The atmosphere continued to improve. In November, several leaders of the French veterans association visited Warsaw. General Górecki, elected president of FIDAC in October, gave pro-French speeches of "exceptional warmth" in Strasbourg. The activity of the Association France-Pologne increased.[30] The independent socialist politician Anatole de Monzie, after a visit to Poland, blamed both the French and the Poles for the existing misunderstandings, and described Beck as "a great personality." France, he said, had no right to wage a Soviet policy without concerting it with Poland. As for Germany, he cited an exchange he had with a Pole in Warsaw. Being told that it was France who had always advocated a German-Polish settlement, Monzie riposted: "We asked you to talk with Germany

27. See Naggiar to Laval, 22 Nov. 1935, MAE, Z 864.5, Tchécoslovaquie 2587, For the assertions by a Romanian diplomat that Poland "has sold out to the Germans," and that some of the ministry officials were "in the employ of the Reich," see Cudahy to Secretary of State, 16 Oct., SDNA, 750C.71/62.

28. See DTJS, I, 372–73, 377–78; also note pour le ministre, 16 Oct. 1935, MAE, Z 698.12, Pologne 2199.

29. See DTJS, I, 543–46; compare 364, 385–93, 395–97, 411, 413, 547. Also Noël to Laval, 27 Nov. 1935, MAE, Z 698.12, Pologne 2199. For François-Poncet's comment that Poland begins to show signs of "breaking away from her policy of subservience to Germany," see DBFP, II, xv:288–89.

30. See Noël to Laval, 8, 23 Dec. 1935; also various notes, MAE, Z 698.1, Pologne 2101, 2199, 2198. D'Arbonneau report, 13 Nov., SHA, EMA/2, Pologne 12.

not to sleep with her." To which the Pole replied: "You do not sleep [with Germany] but you certainly make her bed." Monzie concluded that the Franco-Polish alliance was "certainly not comfortable," but one had to get used to that. It would also work in a crisis.[31]

Beck, urged once again by Szembek to go to Paris, considered that the contact with Laval in Geneva was sufficient. In the discussion each man quoted Piłsudski to strengthen his argument.[32] In addressing a select group of senators and deputies, Beck compared France to an aunt who did not appreciate the fact that her nephew (Poland) had become an adult and continued to treat him as a child. The greatly annoyed nephew reacted angrily, but having made his point was willing to attend again his aunt's birthday parties. "I would also like to go to them now," the foreign minister concluded amidst laughter.[33]

The situation was more serious than that. As seen from Paris, the Franco-Polish relations "were never worse," Mühlstein reported. The British were disinclined to blame the Poles, who "had and have considerable reason to feel doubtful about French support," for that state of affairs. On the whole London agreed with Ambassador Kennard that the government in Warsaw was behaving in a "statesmanlike way," and had "safeguarded Polish interests in a situation full of pitfalls and grave dangers."[34]

The Polish military continued their efforts to get armament credits in France. When General Władysław Bortnowski had visited Paris in July, he dwelt on the theme that Poland had plenty of manpower but not enough material, while in France the opposite was true.[35] D'Arbonneau stressed the cordiality of the reception of colonels Maurice Gauché and Roux (of the deuxième bureau and the Service de Renseignement, respectively). It showed "how true and sincere" were the sentiments of the Polish high command for France and its army. He argued in favor of Polish requests, and commented on Polish plans to develop the road network and push on with motorization. The changes in the command structure introduced by Rydz-Śmigły gained the military attaché's approval. He was also favorably impressed by General Kutrzeba's comments indicating that the hypothesis

31. See Chłapowski to Beck, 18 Nov. 1935, HIA, Amb. Paryż, box 5; conversations in Warsaw, 25–26 Nov., DTJS, I, 414–17 and Monzie and Gaston Martin (who accompanied him) remarks on 18 Dec., CAE/Ch. Also Kennard to Hoare, 4 Dec., FO 371 18899 C 8092.

32. See DTJS, I, 438–39; compare 336, 434, 450.

33. On 15 Jan. 1936, DTJS, II, 37; also 368–69.

34. Kennard to Collier, 6 Nov., and to Hoare, 16 Dec. 1935 with minutes, FO 371 18896 C 4578 and 18896 Hm 04023. Mühlstein's remarks in DTJS, I, 447–48; compare DDB, III, 420.

35. Report of Capt. Le Laquet on Bortnowski's visit, SHA, EMA/2, Pologne 43.

of war with Germany appeared central to Warsaw's military thinking. Yet Paris seemed cool, and the chief of staff, General Louis Colson, responded in a manner that was dry in tone and largely negative in content.[36]

There were, of course, technical difficulties. Monzie had rightly pointed out that when the Poles were told to increase their armaments, "a dance" followed in Paris involving the Quai d'Orsay, the war ministry, and the ministries of finance and of commerce, and the end result was that a third country was selling arms to Poland. But the political reasons were paramount. The French did not wish to enhance the position of Beck, whom Noël began to suspect of being capable of almost anything, even of letting the German army through Poland to attack Russia. So the French decided to drive a wedge between Beck and Rydz-Śmigły, and prompted by d'Arbonneau, Gamelin expressed a wish to meet personally with the new Polish commander-in-chief.[37] Acting in a somewhat similar vein, the French general, on learning that General Sosnkowski would represent his country at the funeral of King George V, suggested that he come to Paris for conversations. Beck promptly instructed the embassy not to give too much publicity to this private visit.[38] The foreign ministry provided Sosnkowski with a note surveying Franco-Polish relations that emphasized that the French were trying to tie a settlement of outstanding financial-commercial problems with Polish armament orders for their industry. Indeed, the negotiations conducted by Koc were running into difficulties. Marcel Boussac was allegedly sabotaging them, although Koc also blamed "anti-French complexes" in Warsaw.[39] As for Sosnkowski himself, who had al-

36. See d'Arbonneau reports, 2, 24, Oct., 13 Nov., 11, 19, 24 Dec., and the exchange of letters with Gen. Colson, 21 Oct., 6 Nov. 1935, SHA, EMA/2, Pologne 12. Also note on invitation of Rydz-Śmigły in Pologne 43; report May 1934–May 1936, Pologne 13. Compare DTJS, I, 435–36. The talk d'Arbonneau–Kutrzeba was undoubtedly related to the latter's study of German and Polish military potential. See Eugeniusz Kozłowski, "Studium Gen. Tadeusza Kutrzeby nad możliwościami wojennymi Niemiec i Polski," *Wojskowy Przegląd Historyczny*, 9, 3 (1964), 249–89.

37. See DDF, II, 1:90; Chłapowski telegram, 17 Jan. 1936, AAN, MSZ 3769; DTJS, II, 40. For d'Arbonneau's comments on Rydz-Śmigły, see 13 Feb. 1936 report, SHA, EMA/2, Pologne 13.

38. See Noël to Flandin, 26 Jan. 1936, MAE, P.A. Noël 200; appraisal of Sosnkowski in note, n.d., SHA, EMA/2, Pologne 43. Beck telegram, 29 Jan., HIA, Amb. Paryż, box 6; also Tadeusz Katelbach, "Piłsudski i Sosnkowski," *Zeszyty Historyczne*, 34 (1975), 42.

39. See note for Sosnkowski, 24 Jan. 1936, AAN, MSZ 3796. On the Franco-Polish financial negotiations, material in DTJS, II, 21, 32, 39, 44, 61, 77–78, 104; 105; DDF, II, 1:297; Compare MS, OSS, Wysocki, III, 2, 35; also Chłapowski report and Mühlstein telegram, 10 Jan., 11 Feb. 1936, AAN, MSZ 3796 and HIA. Amb. Paryż, box 5. Compare Noël to Flandin, 5, 8, 11 Feb., MAE, P.A. Noël 200. On Boussac's role, Noël, *Polonia*, 168.

ways wondered what really was Piłsudski's motive for the rapprochement with Germany, he concluded that the marshal's ultimate objective had been "to get France" on Poland's side.[40]

Sosnkowski's visit was preceded by d'Arbonneau's strong pleas for armament credits to Poland; they gave an impulse to a special note on the subject stating that the question had to be studied from the viewpoint of the "value of the Franco-Polish alliance" and the "repercussions on Soviet-French relations." Recapitulating French financial aid to Poland since the end of the war—aid he did not deem excessive—d'Arbonneau wrote that the Polish army would be "almost defenseless when faced with an attack of armored vehicles" unless something was done to assist it. Massive aid was not only crucial but must come "immediately while there is still time."[41]

Sosnkowski did not raise the issue of armament credits during his February talks with Pétain, Gamelin, Maurin, the minister of the navy François Piétri, and Paul-Boncour, allegedly because he feared to receive a negative answer. He was told about the French resolve in case of a showdown with Germany and, on his side, indulged in criticizing past French mistakes.[42] The conversations also touched on the Rhineland and French determination to defend its status.

The dragging controversy between Warsaw and Prague was apparently not discussed in Paris, although not only the French but the British ambassador as well regarded the anti-Czech stance as the "most perplexing and unsatisfactory aspect of Polish foreign policy."[43] Rejecting the Czechoslovak October offer to submit the controversy to international arbitration, Warsaw insisted that what was needed was a change of administrative practices and not a formal procedural inquiry.[44] There was some truth in it, for as d'Arbonneau wrote, "even if we judge by the opinions of the Frenchmen who had experienced the chicaneries of the Czechoslovak administration, the latter bears a share of the regretable conflict."[45] But

40. DTJS, II, 52.

41. D'Arbonneau report, 3 Feb. 1936; compare report 16 Jan. and telegram, 23 Jan., SHA, EMA/2, Pologne 13; also Gen. Geriodias to d'Arbonneau, 24 Jan., and note on Polish armaments, 29 Jan., SHA, EMA/2, Pologne 43.

42. See DTJS, II, 71; compare Łowczowski, "Przymierze," 46. Also d'Arbonneau reports, 5, 13 Feb. 1936, SHA, EMA/2, Pologne 13.

43. Kennard to Simon, 16 Dec. 1935, FO 371 18896 Hm 04023.

44. See Beck, *Przemówienia*, 201–202. The Czechoslovak note of 30 Oct.—in answer to the "ironic and hard" Polish note verbale of 11 Sept.—proposed to refer the dispute to Geneva or submit it to the arbitration process foreseen by the 1925 Polish-Czechoslovak treaty. Noël hoped that Rydz-Śmigły might overcome Beck's animosity toward Beneš. See DDF, I, XIII:83, 105–106, 307–12.

45. See d'Arbonneau report, 13 Nov. 1935, SHA, EMA/2, Pologne 12. The view of *České Slovo* (5 Dec.) that Czechoslovakia appeared to Warsaw as an obstacle to its

that was not the real issue. The provocative behavior of the Polish consul led to his expulsion from Czechoslovakia; Warsaw responded by expelling Czechoslovak consular officers. Any false move by the Czechoslovak administration was eagerly exploited on the Polish side. In the heated atmosphere, appeals for a rational solution—as in a memorandum of Czechoslovak professors to their Polish colleagues or in articles in *Polonia*—produced no effect. Beneš's speech of 5 November led to the usual critique by Kramář and demands by Sidor for a rapprochement with Poland and not with the USSR. Yet, as Rev. Hlinka told the Poles, even the Slovaks were not unanimous in their criticism of Beneš's diplomacy.[46]

Greatly perturbed, Szembek told Beck that he could not understand where it was all leading. Both the undersecretary and the chargé d'affaires in Prague privately agreed that one could not put all the blame on the Czechs. Chodacki, who had little liking for Beneš and his countrymen, reported that Czechoslovakia was not at all in a state of decay as its adversaries claimed.[47] Beck realized that greater restraint was needed, but he also said that each Czechoslovak "provocation" would be answered with double force. During a special meeting devoted to Czechoslovakia, he said that if "there were genuine fears [in Prague] of armed aggression by our side, this would complicate the situation immeasurably," for Beck had no plans of resorting to military means. As for the Polish high command, d'Arbonneau noted its conspicuous absence from the anti-Czechoslovak compaign.[48]

The fact that Noël came to Warsaw from his Prague post rendered him suspect to the Poles and limited his effectiveness as a mediator. He recognized that while some anti-Polish Czech moves were justified, they were also "inopportune and regretable." The Czechs, he felt, ought to keep their "sang froid." Naggiar counseled moderation to Beneš and Krofta, and tried to persuade them to appoint a new minister to Warsaw. French anxiety was reflected in articles of *Le Temps*, which wrote (23 October, 13 November) that Polish-Czechoslovak tension might result in similar tension between Prague and Berlin.

The Poles wondered if Prague had consulted Paris about the proposal to submit the dispute to Geneva. Beneš, they thought, would exploit such an internationalization of the controversy to justify a closer rapprochement

policy, hence the desire to "destroy this red wedge" in Central Europe, had some validity.

46. For Beneš's speech and discussion, 6–7 Nov. 1935, see Těsnopisecké zprávy, poslanecká sněmovna, 20–32. Wolff's speech. 8, 3–25 Nov. Compare Noël and Naggiar to Laval, 7, 8, 10, 12, 15 Nov. 1935, MAE, Z 864.5, Tchécoslovaquie 2587.

47. See DTJS, I, 380, 404, II, 62–63.

48. For the Rabka meeting, 12 Nov. 1935 see DTJS, I, 403; compare I, 383, 394. D'Arbonneau report, 24 Oct., SHA, EMA/2, Pologne 12. Also DDF, I, XIII:220–21, 333–34.

with Moscow. The Quai d'Orsay was evasive and Laval sought to defend the Czechoslovak viewpoint. The Polish embassy gained the impression that Paris had come to believe in the existence of Warsaw's secret plans of aggression against Czechoslovakia, possibly in collaboration with Germany and Hungary.[49] Beck assured the French and British ambassadors that if Prague had shown good will, a détente would have followed "because there is no serious international dispute between us."[50] This was the old (and baffling) line, and the Polish note to Prague of 21 November was hardly conciliatory. Studiously polite, it contained a historical presentation that even Krofta found "insolent." Beneš now came to the conclusion that even if Beck retired there would be no major change to Polish foreign policy, for Warsaw had compromised itself too much with Berlin for a sudden volte-face.[51]

Beneš's difficulties with Warsaw were compounded by continuing domestic and regional problems. The rightist opposition and the agrarians continued to attack his policies. The Little Entente showed strains. Milan Stojadinović's government in Belgrade did not inspire trust; a threat to Titulescu's position in Romania caused concern. Masaryk's resignation, made official in December 1935, forced Beneš to seek the support of the agrarians, particularly of Milan Hodža, for his candidacy. On 5 November, Hodža became prime minister and on 20 December took over the foreign ministry. Although he assured the missions abroad and the public at home of his adherence to the policy of collective security as practiced by Beneš, his utterances had novel accents.[52] The French naturally supported Beneš's bid for presidency; the Poles opposed it.[53] On 18 December, Beneš

49. See Chłapowski reports, 8, 15 Nov. 1935, AAN, MSZ 2768, and telegram 9 Nov., HIA, Amb. Paryż, box 5. A verbal agreement between the Hungarian envoy in Warsaw and the anti-Czech deputy director of the political department at Brühl Palace, Tadeusz Kobylański, to work for the restoration of a common Polish-Hungarian border hardly merits the importance Komjathy assigns to it in *Crises*. I am indebted for the translation of Komjathy's source (Andreás Hóry, *A Kulisszäk Mögött* [Wien, 1965], 21) to Eva Balogh.

50. Beck telegram, 17 Nov. 1935, HIA, Amb. Paryż, box 5; compare DDF, 1, XIII:333–34, 364.

51. See Naggiar and Noël dispatches, 26 Nov. 1935, MAE, Z 864.5, Tchécoslovaquie 2587; DDF, 1, XII:466–67, 473–74.

52. See Gajanová, *Dvojí*, 138–59, 167–68, 177; Olivová, *Doomed Democracy*, 195–96; Hodža's interview, *Le Temps*, 12 Nov. 1935; Naggiar to Laval, 13 Nov., 6, 20 Dec., MAE, Z 864.1, Tchécoslovaquie 2569; briefing 2 Jan. 1936, KV, CPP; Wright to Secretary of State, 7 Jan 1936, SDNA, 765.84/3498.

53. Szembek approved the proposal of the legation in Prague to engage in anti-Beneš activities not so much to prevent his election (which seemed a foregone conclusion) but to limit the extent of his triumph. See Grzybowski to Beck, 28, 30 Sept. 1935, AAN, MSZ 5447; Chodacki report, 10 Dec. 1935, MSZ, P.III, w.55, t.1 (old classification); Szembek–Beck conversation, DTJS, 1, 354.

was elected by 340 out of 440 votes, and Chodacki considered the replacement of an "infirm old man" by a vigorous politician in his early fifties a very important development. The new president would not only continue to control foreign policy but also gain ascendancy over the army and become an arbiter among the nationalities.[54] Indeed, the envoy in Berlin, while offering his congratulations, expressed the hope that just as Masaryk had been the "president-liberator," his successor would be the "president-unifier."[55]

While Beneš was consolidating his position, that of Laval began to weaken. The Anglo-French scheme of early December—the Hoare–Laval Plan—to hand over a sizable part of Ethiopia to the Italians was leaked out by the French press. The general public was shocked; Hoare had to resign and the days of Laval's leadership were numbered. In Czechoslovakia the plan was seen as a most dangerous precedent of carving up a weak country, a victim of aggression, in order to achieve a settlement among the powers. If Beneš did not manifest his feelings too openly, there was general disgust with Laval's behavior.[56] The reaction in Poland was also adverse. After all the talk about the Italian breach of the Covenant, *Kurjer Poranny* wrote ironically, one suddenly learned that the whole affair was merely "a colonial matter." Beck was angry that Paris had not consulted him beforehand—typical Polish "vanity" commented the chargé d'affaires in Warsaw.[57] Beck spoke contemptuously about the comportment of the League; as for Laval—described by the Polish delegate in Geneva as "false and lying"—he was "a little man."[58]

In the chamber of deputies, the handling of the Italo-Ethiopian war was singled out for criticism by Blum, Delbos, Reynaud, and others. A deputy objected to the multiplication of French commitments to East Central Europe, stressing instead the obligations to the League. Emotions ran high, but Laval's brilliantly clever defense of his foreign policy on 28 December won the applause of the chamber, particularly when he asserted that "as long as Franco-German rapprochement was not achieved there would be no guarantee of effective peace of Europe." Working with Britain one had to bring Germany within a framework of collective security, which, however, would not be achieved at the expense of East European states. He

54. Chodacki report, 8 Apr. 1936, AAN, MSZ 5448.

55. Mastný to Beneš, 24 Dec. 1935, ANM, Mastný notebook, 136–37. On Naggiar's satisfaction over Beneš's election, see DDF, I, XIII:632–33.

56. Naggiar reports in DDF, I, XIII:579, 679–80, 703–705. Compare Deák, "Siedmy marec," 325–26; Radimský to Mastný, 5 Jan. 1936, ANM, Mastný 8.735; also briefing, 12 Dec. 1935, KV, CPP.

57. Bressy to Laval, 17 Dec. 1935, MAE, Z 698.1, Pologne 2101. Compare Cudahy to Secretary of State, 27 Dec., and 3 Jan. 1936, SDNA, 765.84/3408 and 3505.

58. See DTJS, I, 408; Gawroński, *Moja misja*, 314–15; MS, OSS, Wysocki, III, 2, 33.

denied that the pact of 2 May could be considered "a military alliance between France and the Soviets."[59] Laval's oratory only delayed his eventual fall, which Chłapowski saw as a victory for pro-Soviet circles. Fearing his pro-German course, they decided to eliminate him.[60] Laval's defeat was greeted with satisfaction in Prague. The leftist and centrist press pointed out that during his term of office Franco-Czechoslovak friendship was at its lowest ebb. The fallen statesman was accused of having unduly favored Mussolini, neglected the Little Entente, and delayed the ratification of the treaty with the USSR.[61] Hopes were expressed that the new cabinet would embark on a different course.

Formed on 24 January 1936 the ministry of Albert Sarraut, with Flandin as foreign minister, was de facto a caretaker government until the spring elections. Sarraut was colorless and undecisive; Flandin lacked willpower. The cabinet, while ostensibly the last of the National Union ministries, was again internally paralyzed, for it comprised both friends and foes of the Popular Front. It was tragic that it fell to this "ministère d'attente," presiding over a deeply divided country, to face six weeks later one of the greatest challenges of interwar French history.

Hodža Plan and the Ratification of the Franco-Soviet Treaty

The new French cabinet had to resolve two major problems of foreign policy: finding a way out of the conflict with Mussolini and making a final decision on the long-delayed ratification of the Franco-Soviet Pact. Both had a direct bearing on the relations with East Central Europe and were to some extent related. A settlement in Danubian Europe involved the large question whether Italy's place as a guarantor would be taken by Russia, or whether the region should strenghten itself by its own efforts? Beneš and Titulescu inclined to the first solution. Hodža as foreign minister became the champion of the second.

Hodža, a long-time advocate of an agrarian Central Europe, believed that economically the key to regional cooperation lay in the liquidation of difficulties arising out of agricultural surpluses. If this was achieved, the capacity of Central European markets for industrial products would increase, benefiting Czechoslovakia and Austria. In a sense this view was a modified version of the agrarian bloc combined with elements of the Tardieu Plan, which aimed at a political consolidation of Central Europe without the interference of the great powers. It was the first such plan

---

59. 27 Dec. 1935 debates, J.O. Chambre, 2800–2826, 2845; Laval on 28 Dec. 2863–67.

60. Chłapowski report, 27 Jan. 1936, AAN, MSZ 3705; compare Herriot, *Jadis*, 2:623–24.

61. See reports of Polish legation in Prague, 3, 11 Feb. 1936, AAN, MSZ 5426.

officially originating from the Little Entente circles. Hodža wished to obtain Italian blessings for his scheme and to consult France; his hope was to reach eventually an accord with Germany. But he wanted the Central European bloc to act as a unit and deal with the powers on an equal footing.[62] Despite some inconsistencies within the scheme and the difficulties of achieving even purely economic goals, Hodža launched his project with energy and determination. Personal ambition and rivalry with Beneš contributed to his desire to score a point. He found support in those parliamentary circles critical of pro-Soviet policies, but the industrialists were cautious, and the communists belonged to the staunchest opponents. Beneš followed the minister's activity with distrust, possibly even sabotaging his efforts. A promotion of the plan required a rapprochement with Austria and Hungary, and on 17 January Chancellor Kurt von Schuschnigg visited Prague. His visible interest sufficed to put Budapest and also Belgrade on their guards.

The French supported a policy of closer Czechoslovak-Austrian collaboration. The funeral of King George V, attended by several East Central European statesmen who passed through Paris, provided the opportunity for talks in late January and early February. It was evident that "the German peril was on everybody's mind," and concern with Anschluss appeared real. There was, however, no unanimity of views on how to cope with the existing dangers. Flandin allegedly opposed Titulescu's notion of replacing Italian guarantees with those of Russia, for this would suggest encirclement of Germany. The Quai d'Orsay's interest in bringing Little Entente and Austria together did not necessarily imply an endorsement of the Hodža Plan. Asked by the French where Poland stood in all this, Chłapowski jokingly replied that his country had already once saved Vienna (in 1683), which only contributed to a strengthening of German power.[63]

Hodža arrived in Paris on 9 February and remained there for seven days.[64] A novice in diplomacy who had no confidants at Czernin Palace, he relied mostly on agrarian collaborators from the press section of the premier's office. This led to undue emphasis on publicity, which Hodža was ill-prepared to handle. It proved necessary to issue denials and to ex-

---

62. See Kvaček, "Hodžuv plán," 348–49; and his "Boj," 238; Sládek and Tomaszewski, "Próby integracji w latach trzydziestych," 397; Gajanova, *ČSR*, 347; Ádám, "Les pays," 22–23; Pułaski, "Projekty," 222–23; Ránki, *Economy*, 167–69; Kühl, *Föderationspläne*, 41. Also see Hodža's speeches in Hodža, *Články*, 12:364–65 and on 5 Dec. 1935, Těsnopisecké zprávy, poslanecká sněmovna, 13–29; comments in Naggiar to Laval, 6, Dec. MAE, Z 864.1, Tchécoslovaquie 2569. Also Hodža, *Le Problème*, and his *Federation*.

63. See note on Paris talks, DDF, II, 1:221–27; Chłapowski reports, 4, 6 Feb. 1936, AAN, MSZ 3769.

64. For the program of the visit see *Zahraniční Politika*, 15, 3 (1936), 130–31.

plain some remarks he made at interviews. French rightist papers, playing partisan politics, sought to underline the differences between Beneš and the Slovak Hodža. Conversations with Flandin seemingly did not go beyond generalities, although Hodža assumed that he had gained French approval of his plan.[65]

On 15 February, *Le Temps* published an interview with Hodža that said that Austria did not have to choose between Anschluss and Habsburg restoration, because there was a third way, leading to the formation of a vast Danubian bloc. While Germany could enter it some day, there must be no anterior bilateral treaties between Germany and the Danubian countries. As for the Franco-Soviet pact, it was an accord "of pure assurance against an aggression, but nothing else." Such plain speaking was unusual for the foreign minister of Czechoslovakia, and it provoked vexation in Rome and anger in Berlin.[66] The Hodža Plan, which obviously went counter to German concepts of Mitteleuropa, desperately needed British support, which it lacked, and some approval from Italy. But Mussolini was not encouraging, despite Czechoslovak assurances that the plan was not anti-Italian.[67] The Little Entente partners were uncooperative, for they had little genuine interest in Danubian cooperation that would exclude Germany. Stojadinović spoke with contempt of Hodža, this "muddlehead" (*brouillon*) whom he wished to see replaced by Krofta, who "at least had the merit of knowing his job." To all practical purposes the Hodža Plan dissolved in a nebulously phrased communiqué of the Little Entente.[68] On 28 February, Hodža himself stepped down as foreign minister while retaining the premiership. The next day Krofta took over the Czernin Palace; Beneš's grip of foreign policy was fully restored.

Warsaw's attitude toward the Hodža Plan was at first colored by the feeling that the Slovak Hodža, whose party organ *Venkov* had often promoted cooperation between Czechoslovakia and Poland, and who

65. Flandin's banal statement referred to the need for Central Europe to organize itself before the powers were to intervene in its affairs, and mentioned conversations with Little Entente statesmen, including Hodža, which raised some new hopes. See 12 Feb. 1936 session, CAE/Ch. For the visit see briefings, 13, 20 Feb., KV, CPP; Chodacki reports, 12, 13, 18 Feb., AAN, MSZ 5425; Puławski, "Projekty," 224; Kvaček, *Nad Evropou*, 188–89, and his "Boj," 261-62. For Chvalkovský's ironic remarks about Hodža's maladroitness and vanity, see MS, OSS, Wysocki, III, 2, 27–28.

66. See DDF, II, 1:101–104, 256, 335, 340-44, 611–12. Hodža's 22 Jan. 1936 statement to journalists, AAN, MSZ 5448; compare Zawisza report, 3 Mar., MSZ 3260. Also ADAP, C. IV/2:1072–75; Chambrun's view on Hodža's interview in MS, OSS, Wysocki, III, 2, 24.

67. See briefing, 30 Jan. 1936, KV, CPP; also DDF, II, 1:167; Kvaček, "Boj," 263–64, 361–62.

68. See DDF, II, 1:369. Also Kvaček, *Nad Evropou*, 199–203; Puławski, "Projekty," 224–25. Hodža's later efforts to revive his plans transcend chronologically this study.

sounded pro-Polish himself, was much preferable to Beneš. In an interview for *Le Temps* (12 November), he had mentioned that a Central European organization ought to extend to Poland, and if Poland found it useful, even to the Baltic countries. Shortly after becoming foreign minister, Hodža received a message from Beck (through an Austrian intermediary) expressing the wish that Hodža would work for a détente with Poland. Beck welcomed the signs of a Czechoslovak-Austrian rapprochement, and hoped that this might attract the Hungarians. A regional grouping supported by France and Italy could become an important element of European peace.[69]

Poland's initial friendly reaction to Hodža and his ideas found no real reflection, save a limited détente in mid-January, in the general Czechoslovak-Polish relationship. Beck's references to Prague in his speech of 15 January did not depart from the usual critical vein.[70] Czechoslovakia hoped to improve matters by naming a ranking Slovak politician, Juraj Slávik, as the new envoy in Warsaw, but his first impressions were discouraging. Beck and Szembek studiously avoided talking politics, and the deputy director of the political department, Tadeusz Kobylański, sounded unfriendly. Slávik's advocacy of the Hodža Plan, presented as an effort to create an independent zone between Germany and Russia (conforming to Polish objectives), met with a rejoinder that burdened with the legacy of the Czechoslovak-Soviet pact, the plan could not lead toward a full emancipation of the region. Moreover, by provoking adverse German and Italian reactions, it stood little chance of realization.[71]

Warsaw's growing opposition to the Hodža Plan did not stem so much from the feeling that it endangered Poland's own projects for the region; consideration for Rome was a greater concern.[72] Beck spoke disdainfully about countries south of the Carpathians, "which had been unable to work out an independent foreign policy" and became a French sphere of influence. Poland "never wanted to be included in this group of balkanized states" and that was why it "moved toward emancipation." The Little Entente was an odd alignment that Poland viewed skeptically. "Only Italian ideas of a Danubian pact, based on mutual respect between these states,

---

69. See DDF, I, XIII:636. Compare Gawroński to Beck, 18 Dec. 1935, in which he passes the information that Hodža prefers Poland to Russia, AAN, MSZ 5425.

70. Chodacki report, 14 Jan. 1936, AAN, MSZ, Z.4, w.5, t.33 (old classification). Also Kozeński, *Czechosłowacja*, 111–12; discussion in foreign affairs commission, Archiwum Sejmowe, Diariusze posiedzeń komisji spraw zagranicznych sejmu, pol. 176.

71. See DTJS, II, 93, 95; Slávik–Kobylański conversation, 25 Feb. 1936, AAN, MSZ, P.III, w.68, t.3 (old classification). President Mościcki, however, reciprocated Slávik's warm remarks at the presentation of letters of accreditation, *Lidové Noviny*, 29 Feb. 1936.

72. The motive of rivalry is stressed by Kvaček, *Nad Evropou*, 207. For Beck's hesitations whether Warsaw should promote something akin to the Hodža Plan, see Gawroński, *Moja misja*, 316.

allowed Poland to interest itself in this region, which is so close to the area of our immediate interests."[73] Thus, Beck's attitude toward the Hodža Plan depended primarily on Mussolini's position, and it was not immediately apparent how the duce would react.[74] Once it became evident that the plan was failing and that the duce would not respond to Warsaw's hints about organizing a Danubian grouping under Rome's aegis—in which Poland might have been willing to participate—criticism of the Hodža Plan multiplied.[75]

Warsaw's stance toward Prague hardened. William Bullitt gathered from Beck that "Poland would offer no resistance, either physical or diplomatic, to a German attack on Czechoslovakia." The American diplomat had the impression that the minister would be glad "to see Germany control Austria and Bohemia, and to see Hungary walk off with Slovakia, while Poland got 'frontier rectifications' in the Teschen district."[76] This tougher line of Polish diplomacy was probably related to the opposite positions taken by Warsaw and Prague on the ratification of the French-Soviet treaty. For Czechoslovakia a speedy ratification was essential not only because it would activate the Czechoslovak-Soviet treaty, but also because it could complete the system by a possible inclusion of Bucharest. As for Warsaw, Beneš told Laval that "France could conduct its Russian policy vis-à-vis Poland only in accord with us; we are the link (*trait-d'union*)."[77] By contrast, although Poland could not oppose the ratification too openly in view of the previously mentioned military and financial talks with the French, it viewed it as most undesirable.

By deciding to submit the Franco-Soviet pact to the parliament for ratification—which may not have been indispensable on constitutional grounds—and by awaiting the proper moment, Laval delayed it by some nine months. He used this transition period to reassure Berlin but could not extend the delay indefinitely. He "wriggled like a devil in holy water,"[78] but finally decided, around 8 January, to proceed. Meanwhile, French public opinion had become increasingly divided over the merits of

73. See DTJS, II, 369–70.

74. Szembek felt that a Berlin-Budapest-Belgrade combination was preferable to a Paris-Prague (and possibly Rome) alignment. See DTJS, II, 47, 90–91. 103.

75. Chodacki report, 9 Mar. 1936, AAN, MSZ 5425; also *Polityka Narodów*, 7 (1936) 430; for Polish hints to Italy see MS, OSS, Wysocki, III, 2, 9; also Sládek and Tomaszewski, "Próby integracji w latach trzydziestych," 397.

76. Bullitt to Roosevelt, 22 Feb. 1936, Bullitt, *Correspondence*, 145; for tougher line, see DTJS, II, 49, 96–97, 103.

77. See Gajanová, *Dvojí*, 117–18; Kvaček, *Nad Evropou*, 143–49. For Beneš's arguments for speedy evacuation to Laval, AAN, Mastný, 12.089–095.

78. Phipps in DBFP, II, xv:531. Compare DBFP, II, xv:537, 548; also DTJS, II, 67–68.

the Russian connection. With the conclusion of the Popular Front electoral pact in January, the Right began to fear that a Franco-Soviet treaty might become a genuine alliance in the hands of a leftist government. If in early 1935 the majority of the Right had accepted the link to Moscow as a necessary contribution to security, a few months later only the more traditional nationalists (like Reynaud, Ernest Pezet, Pertinax, or Buré) continued to regard Germany as the greater menace. Such rightists as Louis Marin or Henri de Kérillis found it hard to choose between "the danger of Hitler and the danger of Stalin," and they worried lest the Soviet alliance drag France into war.[79]

In the course of discussions in the foreign affairs commission and the chamber, French freedom to determine the aggressor and the absence of provisions for automatic aid (as well as the subordination of the treaty to the machinery of Locarno) received strong emphasis. A concern that the treaty not appear too pointedly anti-German or disadvantageous to Poland was visible in the debates. The Polish embassy noted it with satisfaction.[80] The French army also tried to dispel Polish worries, reassuring Sosnkowski during his Paris visit that the pact was "mainly preventive" and would bring Poland a benevolent Soviet neutrality.[81] When Gamelin told Chłapowski that the objective was the "elimination of undesirable surprises from the Soviet side," something "that also lay in Poland's interest," the general seemed skeptical about real assistance by the Red Army.[82] The French military were less optimistic in private about the convergence of Polish and Soviet interests. A note listing the dangers stemming from the treaty included the risk of alienating Poland ("Polish military alliance appears incompatible with a Russian military alliance") and of provoking a German reaction likely to take the form of the reoccupation of the Rhineland.[83]

Watching the developments, Beck sought to dissipate the persisting worries in Poland that the nonaggression declaration with Germany had adversely affected the Paris-Warsaw relationship. Answering a prearranged question in the foreign affairs commission, Beck pointed out that since

79. See Scott, *Alliance,* 263–65; Micaud, *French Right,* 68–74.

80. 27 Nov. 1935 session, CAE/Ch; 11 Jan. 1936, J.O. Chambre, 349–59; also Chłapowski report, 10 Jan., AAN, MSZ, P.II, w.102, t.1 (old classification).

81. D'Arbonneau report, 16 Jan. 1936, SHA, EMA/2, Pologne 13.

82. Chłapowski telegram, 17 Jan. 1936, AAN, MSZ 3769. Gen. Colson allegedly made sure that neither Gamelin nor the minister of war would see Gen. Loizeau's report of 6 Oct. 1935, which contained the phrase: "the assistance to Central Europe by the Red army, retaining important German forces and giving a hand to Czechoslovakia, represents one of the essential factors of maneuver in case of a general conflict in Europe to which Poland cannot remain indifferent for long whether it likes it or not." Cited in Dutailly, *Problèmes,* 46.

83. See 27 Jan. 1936 analytical note, DDF, II, 1:152–54.

1934 two French foreign ministers had visited Poland, whereas none had come before; surely this meant an increase of Poland's value in French eyes. Noël and the Polish opposition were not impressed.[84] A day later, on 17 January, *Le Temps* wrote that the value of the alliance could only be measured by "the spirit in which it was practiced."

Doubts about this spirit were mutual. The Poles were upset by rumors that Paris contemplated huge credits to Russia. The French were suspicious of Beck's interrupting his return journey from Geneva with a stop in Berlin on 25 January. Although its main purpose was to settle a controversy over German default in payments for the railroad traffic across the "corridor," Beck's reserve about the political aspect of the talks worried Noël. Beck did say, however, that Germany, annoyed with the Franco-Russian rapprochement, might energetically respond to it.[85]

Flandin's criticism of Poland for not assisting French efforts to organize collective security angered Beck, who recalled Barthou's and Laval's assurances that the Franco-Soviet pact would impose no new obligations on Poland. He asked for a reconfirmation of this position, adding that Poland viewed negatively not only the political but also the financial consequences of France's Russian policy. After Vyacheslav Molotov, then chairman of the Council of the People's Commissars, made a speech on strengthening militarily the Soviet Union's western borders, the Poles alleged that Soviet armaments directed against them would be realized with French money. Flandin reiterated past assurances and denied that the pact would entail any financial or military orders.[86] Beck was not mollified. Airing privately his views on the Franco-Soviet treaty, he said that naturally it would weaken the "*possibility* of political collaboration with Paris; a *possibility*, for real cooperation never existed." The minister dismissed the argument, constantly used by the French, that the pact would prevent a return to Rapallo. Should conditions change, he said, the treaty would be of no consequence.[87]

Meanwhile in Paris, the ratification process was in full swing. On 12 February, Flandin answered questions in the foreign affairs commission how the pact would contribute to France's security. He admitted that it would merely accelerate the working of the machinery of the League. Be-

---

84. Discussion, 16 Jan. 1936, Archiwum Sejmowe, Diariusze, pol.176; also see DTJS, I, 454. For criticism *Robotnik*, 17, 22, 23 Jan.; *Kurjer Warszawski*, 16 Jan. Also Noël to Laval, 15, 17, 22 Jan., MAE, P.A. Noël 200, and DDF, II, 1:255.

85. See Cudahy to Secretary of State, 30 Jan. 1936, SDNA, 760C.62/310; DDF, II, 1:173–74; on rumored loan to Russia, d'Abbonneau report, 16 Jan., SHA, EMA/2, Pologne 13.

86. Exchange of Chłapowski–Beck telegrams, 4, 10 Feb. 1936, AAN, MSZ 3769, and 17 Feb., AAN, MSZ, P.II, w.101, t.2 (old classification). Compare DTJS, II, 96–97; DDF, II, 1:182.

87. Remarks on 15 Feb. 1936, DTJS, II, 390.

cause the ideal solution—a Franco-German reconciliation—proved impossible, one had to choose the second best. The minister seemingly agreed with a point made by one of the deputies, namely that the pact "brings relief to us through sharing our responsibilities" in East Central Europe with Russia.[88]

It would be superfluous to recount here all the arguments for and against the treaty made in the parliamentary debate, which lasted from 13 to 27 February. Critics dwelt on the inefficacy of alignment with a power that, having no common border with Germany, could hardly help France in wartime. They pointed to the difference between this treaty and those with Poland and Czechoslovakia.[89] Polish opposition to the pact and the passage of Soviet troops was also mentioned. Flandin responded that the treaty, not being a military alliance, was not so much affected by geography, but he also intimated that Warsaw might later change its mind. The pact, he stressed, had the support of the Little Entente.[90] Herriot remarked that France could not practice a policy of sacred egoism, hiding behind its fortifications. Already a guarantor of Romania, Czechoslovakia, Yugoslavia, and Poland, it could not disinterest itself from East Central Europe. But how could France shoulder these responsibilities without Russia's help? he asked rhetorically. Cot echoed Herriot by stating that the alliance with the USSR enhanced the value (*valorise*) of the French position in that region.[91]

Marshal Pétain was hostile to the ratification. Also, a circulating note of Weygand's asserted that the general had not been consulted as an army inspector (which was not quite exact) and as a private citizen he opposed the treaty. Another note emanating from the army circles warned that the Reich would regard the ratification as a breach of Locarno. Should the Locarno pact become void, France would lose its "last guarantee of security."[92]

As the debate continued, Flandin had another important conversation with Chłapowski on 17 February. In view of the fact that the relations with Poland "were not normal," the minister said, Paris had no certainty that Poland would defend Czechoslovakia or even remain neutral if the latter were attacked by Germany. Nor was it clear that, in the event of a German remilitarization of the Rhineland and French general mobilization, Poland

---

88. 12 Feb. 1936 session, CAE/Ch.

89. Montigny on 13 Feb. 1936, J.O. Chambre, 381–84.

90. 25 Feb. 1936 session, J.O. Chambre, 578–84. Vansittart commented: "It is doubtful whether any French politician, still less any French soldier, really expected military advantages from this treaty," DBFP, II, xv:780.

91. Herriot on 20 Feb., Cot on 27 Feb. 1936, J.O. Chambre, 492–99, 627–28.

92. See Bankwitz, *Weygand*, 249, 258; DDF, II, I:322–23. Compare Cairns, "March 7, 1936," 177.

would act in solidarity with France. Chłapowski replied evasively that it was up to Prague to improve relations with Poland; besides, he heard of no German plans of aggression against Czechoslovakia. He had, however, a distinct feeling, which he shared with Warsaw, that the French government really sought to "reach the heart of the matter" of the Franco-Polish relationship. Once, the French had tried to bully Poland, later they pretended they could do without it, but "now, facing a ripening threat," they seemingly looked for a genuine contact. The Sarraut cabinet did not believe in the possibility of an understanding with Germany, and it began to concentrate on defensive measures, military and diplomatic. The ambassador thought that in the long run Warsaw could not continue its present tactics of speaking in generalities and avoiding concrete conversations on the "practical application of the alliance in case of German aggression." Armament credits could hardly be obtained in France without an exhaustive discussion of the respective stands vis-à-vis major international issues."[93]

Beck did not share Chłapowski's conclusion. He told Szembek, who also favored substantive talks with the French, that apart from finding Flandin's attitude "insolent," it was "better not to speak in peacetime about what would happen in times of war."[94] The diplomatic world found Beck's posture puzzling. The American ambassador called Poland "the great enigma of Europe at the present time," especially "because of the baffling personality of Beck."[95] Did Warsaw have any secret agreements with Berlin directed against Russia? Sarraut and even Massigli seemed to take seriously such a possibility. Every new German-Polish contact tended to increase nervousness in Paris. On the day following the Flandin–Chłapowski conversation, Beck entertained Goering, who came for another of his hunting trips to Poland. Speaking in Hitler's name, the Nazi dignitary once more proffered assurances of friendship. Both he and his entourage dropped unmistakable hints about German-Polish collaboration against Russia. Goering also made it clear that the ratification of the Franco-Soviet pact would be viewed in Berlin as a violation of Locarno.[96] Beck, who had not informed the French of the Goering visit beforehand, now shared with Noël his firm belief that "any initiative directed against them [the Germans] would meet with a very strong reaction of Berlin." When Noël observed that France would not accept a unilateral repudiation of treaty provisions, Beck made no comment.[97]

93. Chłapowski to Beck, 21 Feb. 1936, DTJS, ii, 392–96.

94. 26 Feb. 1936, DTJS, ii, 94.

95. H. Wilson to Secretary of State, 27 Jan. 1936, FRUS 1936, i, 186.

96. See DTJS, ii, 83–84, 92–93.

97. See DTJS, ii, 81, 95; Noël to Flandin, 24, 25 Feb. 1936, DDF, ii, 1:315–16 and MAE, P.A. Noël 200.

On 27 February, the French chamber of deputies ratified the treaty with the USSR by 353 votes against 164. Beneš offered his congratulations, regretting only that the ratification had not taken place earlier, which would have eliminated some of the intrigues, and repeated that Czechoslovak relations with Moscow would be modeled in every respect on those that France decided to establish with the Soviet Union. He simultaneously told the German envoy that Prague could have had a military treaty with Russia but rejected it.[98] The Polish press reacted with restraint. D'Arbonneau wondered if the absence of bad humor might have been due to reassurances offered not only to Sosnkowski but also to Zaleski, who had visited Paris as a private individual. As for Beck, he decided to consult Rydz-Śmigły before issuing instruction to Chłapowski regarding Flandin's overture. After all, one could hardly ignore the views of the Polish high command, as exemplified by the remark of the recently deceased chief of staff, General Julian Stachiewicz, that if Germany attacked France, Poland would immediately attack Germany.[99]

Berlin did not give much time to France and its allies. Its response to the ratification of the Franco-Soviet treaty was swift and brutal. Five days after the event, orders were issued for the reoccupation of the Rhineland. On 7 March, German troops marched in, while Hitler officially denounced Locarno. The die was cast, and France's determination was put to a severe test.

***

Remilitarization of the Rhineland

Hitler's move took France by surprise, yet hardly ever had a government had such clear advance notice and so much time to prepare its riposte.[100] A German violation of the demilitarized Rhineland, being a breach of articles 42 and 43 of Versailles, constituted a "hostile act" calculated "to disturb the peace of the world." The Locarno signatories were bound, under article 4, to assist the victimized party immediately after the League's verdict. In case of "flagrant violation"—that is, if the victim claimed the existence of a threat to itself requiring instantaneous reaction—the Locarno powers were bound to bring assistance at once. While calling on Britain, Italy, and Belgium, Paris was presumably free to take simultane-

98. See DDF, II, 1:360; ADAP, C, IV/2:1156.

99. See Noël to Flandin, 26, 28 Feb. 1936, MAE, P.A. Noël 200, and 2 Mar., DDF, II, 1:376–77; compare d'Arbonneau report, 4 Mar., SHA, EMA/2, Pologne 13; also DTJS, II, 102–103. On Zaleski's trip, MS, OSS, Wysocki, III, 2, 45.

100. On 11 Mar., deputy Alexandre Varenne asked how the government could have been surprised "by an event foreseen for so long?" (CAE/Ch). François-Poncet wrote later that one had all the leisure to get ready (*Souvenirs*, 252). Reynaud echoed: "We had time to examine all the hypotheses, to draw up our plan, to hasten our preparations" (*In the Thick*, 123).

ous measures of defense. To make the system workable it was essential, however, that the Locarno guarantors, especially Britain, be willing to assume, in advance, concrete obligations. But their attitude was likely to depend on the precise nature of measures contemplated by France itself.

The French had brought up the matter with Eden and Suvich during the meeting of 23 March 1935, and again in Stresa on 12 April.[101] Flandin intimated that should a German violation occur, he would ask the government to authorize a mobilization. The British cabinet, considering the Rhineland status as not vital from Britain's standpoint, rejected a Foreign Office suggestion to warn Berlin formally against any rash moves. Besides, by the autumn, Vansittart came to believe that France, being "too rotten to honor her bond," would not go beyond mere protests.[102]

While François-Poncet virtually accused the Germans of looking for a pretext to reoccupy the Rhineland, and foreign diplomats reported from Paris that the French would respond with a general mobilization, the Quai d'Orsay was suggesting a discussion of precautionary measures with the British.[103] Perhaps one could tie in Franco-British military talks—concerned with the possibility of war with Italy—with a Rhineland operation. Once the Germans occupied the Rhineland, Léger said, the only response could be an appeal to the League, and because the League would be bound to find Germany guilty, military action would follow. Otherwise, it would be the end of Locarno. The Belgian ambassador warned Léger against a policy of bluff; if France itself proved unable to resort to force, it was better to do nothing. The secretary general concurred; the matter had to be examined by the French high command.[104]

The attitude of the army was obviously crucial. Allegedly, the war minister Maurin did discuss with Gamelin a riposte to the occupation of the Rhineland that entailed, after a general mobilization, an advance in the direction of Frankfurt and toward Liege, but the minister did not believe in limited operations, and feared the outcry that the term "offensive" would provoke.[105] A note presented by the general staff to the Haut Comité Militaire on 18 January 1936 emphasized a growing military dis-

101. See note for the minister, 2 Apr. 1935, MAE, P.A. Massigli 1; also DDF, 1, x:277.

102. Cited in Emmerson, *Rhineland Crisis*, 61.

103. See Duroselle, *Décadence*, 158; Weinberg, *Foreign Policy*, 241, 279; Herriot, *Jadis*, 2:501, 635; DBFP, 11, XIII:625–30, XV:289, 531; also Clerk and Eden to Foreign Office, 8, 20 Jan. 1936, FO 371 19883 C 157 and C 186, C 435. DDB, III, 449. Ample documentation appears in DDF, II, I. Reports by Gen. Renondeau and Consul Dobler clearly indicate their belief that the reoccupation was imminent.

104. See Kerchove to van Zeeland, 30 Jan. 1936, DDB, IV, 63–67.

105. See Tournoux, *Haut commandement*, 250–51. There had been, however, some loose talk at the general staff about the offensive value of the French army, as reported by Col. Heywood. See DBFP, II, XIII:625–30.

parity between France and Germany, and asked for increased funding. During the discussion Gamelin remarked that the intervention of the Polish army on the French side would be invaluable. The minister of war concurred: the only powers with whom resistance against German aggression could be organized were Britain and Poland.[106] But Gamelin had no plan to meet a German thrust by force, and General Colson envisaged only such precautionary measures as a reinforcement of the "front continu" in the fortified regions and the augmentation of mobile reserves. Nothing was said about their possible use.[107]

After the formation of the Sarraut–Flandin cabinet in January 1936, there began a "dialogue of the deaf"—to use Neré's apt phrase—between the government and the army. The Quai d'Orsay urged the war ministry to propose measures to be used as basis for negotiations with London. It expressed its belief that, if a flagrant violation occurred, Paris would not be obliged to delay military steps in order to await the decision of the Council of the League—nor would Britain and Italy. But France could not undertake any military operations, except when attacked, until assured of identity of views with London. Flandin approved this viewpoint, stressing that one must "avoid appearing as an aggressor."[108] In early February, Maurin speaking for the army mentioned the previously cited precautionary measures. Flandin regarded them as "incomplete," and asked for more concrete plans. Maurin was evasive. It was clear that neither the war minister nor the high command would envisage any military operations without the cooperation of Britain.[109] A vicious circle was created. Flandin was trying to convince London to go along with Paris, but without being able to say precisely what the French army was planning to do. Eden, foreign secretary since December 1935, suspected Paris of seeking an excuse not to oppose Germany by force, and being prepared to trade a capitulation in the Rhineland for additional security from London. A remilitarization, Eden reasoned, was "likely to lead to far-reaching repercussions of a kind that will further weaken France's influence in Eastern and Central Europe, leaving a gap which may eventually be filled either by Germany or by Russia."[110] The foreign secretary believed in the need of bargaining with Berlin

106. See DDF, II, I:109–11, 116–30.

107. See Le Goyet, *Mystère*, 118; Dutailly, *Problèmes*, 142; Defrasne, "L'Evenement," 257.

108. See DDF, II, I:174–76, 202–207, 218, 221.

109. See DDF, II, I:245–48, 290–95, 299–302, 317–18. The precautionary measures included such steps as: a simple alert with troops taking position on the Maginot Line; reinforced, with local reserves added; accompanied by call of "disponibles"; or "couverture" with three classes of "disponibles" and reserves.

110. Eden's memo drafted by Sargent, 14 Feb. 1936, DBFP II, XV:658.

to get a quid pro quo for a voluntary acceptance of German demands on the Rhine.

The French government was unlikely to share this point of view, and there was no progress in the Franco-British conversation, as there was none in the Flandin–Maurin dialogue. Finally, on 27 February, the French cabinet decided that in case of a German violation of the Rhineland, France would act only in agreement with the Locarno powers, and establish contact with the latter for the purpose of a concerted action. Awaiting the decision of the guarantors, however, the French government reserved the right to take all preparatory measures, including those of military character, to implement the collective action that presumably would be decided by the League and the Locarno signatories. Flandin defined these measures as stopping short of a general mobilization. The British were duly informed of this position on 3 March.[111]

Thus, the stage was set for the event of 7 March, before a single German soldier set foot in the Rhineland. The French government made itself London's prisoner in a political sense, and the high command, holding an exaggerated belief in German superiority (despite fairly accurate data supplied by intelligence), refused to devise offensive operational plans without the assurance of British support. All this reflected the prevailing atmosphere in France—the "pacifist depression" as the Greek envoy, Nicholas Politis called it. "A people that practiced such policy," he said, "ought no longer pretend to the name of a great power."[112]

By a supreme irony of history, the two French allies in East Central Europe, whose help against Germany could have been of the greatest value, had been excluded from Locarno and were thus not strictly bound to assist France. Their obligations under the alliance treaties and the Covenant were open to divergent legal interpretations. Czechoslovakia and Poland realized, of course, what was at stake here, and that Paris was facing a supreme test. As Alfred Fabre-Luce wrote in *L'Europe Nouvelle* (25 January), the nature of the French riposte in the Rhineland would provide the answer to how France would respond to aggression in Eastern Europe. If Paris did not react militarily to a threat on its own frontiers, one could hardly expect it to counter a German breach of Versailles in the east.

Prague was worried. Krofta listened most attentively to Naggiar's assurances that his country would not accept any unilateral violations of the treaty. Beneš thought that Germany ought to be made fully aware that a coup would provoke immediate French and British reaction. He stressed that before Germany launched an aggression in the east it would need to

---

111. See DDB, IV, 76–83, 85–88; DDF, II, 1:273–76, 339, 397; DBFP, II, XV:564–65, 572–75, 610–12. Also Flandin, *Politique*, 193–97; Emmerson, *Rhineland Crisis*, 61–71; Cairns, "March 7, 1936," 179–80; Minart, *Le Drame*, 105.

112. Cited by Laroche to Flandin, 2 Mar. 1936, DDF, II, 1:379.

improve its vulnerable position in the west.[113] Beck seemed dubious about the possibility of maintaining the demilitarized zone. Legal advisers at Brühl Palace were divided in their opinions on Poland's obligations to France with regard to a coup in the Rhineland.[114] General Sosnkowski, who had been told by Georges Mandel in Paris that France would mobilize, urged Beck to assure the French in advance that Poland would mobilize simultaneously with France. Beck allegedly agreed to do so but did nothing until after the event occurred.[115] The foreign minister doubted French determination and may have been peeved by the exclusion of Poland from Franco-British conversations bearing on the Rhineland.[116]

During his exchanges on 5 February with Chłapowski, Flandin had expressed his resolution to use "all means foreseen in the Locarno pact." He emphasized that a remilitarized Rhineland would immobilize the French army allowing Germany to embark on a major operation in the east, a dangerous perspective not only for the eastern allies but also for France wishing to honor its commitments.[117] During the important conversation twelve days later, Flandin, as mentioned, expressed doubts, whether in case of a German coup, Poland would mobilize. Ambassador Chłapowski recalled, by way of a reply, all the past instances when a resolute stand by a French foreign minister vis-à-vis Germany was followed by concessions. Flandin repeated that with a remilitarized Rhineland "France would be obliged to abandon its historic role of co-shaping the fate of Europe. Central Europe and Poland would then be forced to count on their resources." This threat failed to move Beck, who saw no reason to commit himself, especially since he thought that a close reading of the Franco-Polish alliance would show that a violation of the zone did not constitute a *casus foederis* for Poland.[118] Pursuing his free-hand policy, Beck went to Brussels (1–5 March) where his attempts to strengthen Belgium's independence of France could be hardly viewed by Paris as an amicable move.[119]

The alarming reports, which also included Polish intelligence material

113. See DDF, ii, 1:108–109, 320, 361–62.

114. See DTJS, ii, 71–72, 93, 106; DDF, ii, 1:173–74.

115. See Kirkor letter in *Zeszyty Historyczne*, 32 (1975), 231; compare Noël, *L'Agression*, 129.

116. Bargeton's denial that François-Poncet had warned Berlin that a violation in the Rhineland would trigger an immediate mobilization gave food for thought in Warsaw. See Chłapowski report, 27 Jan. 1936, AAN, MSZ, P.ii, w.102, t.1 (old classification).

117. Chłapowski telegram, 5 Feb. 1936, HIA, Amb. Paryż, box 6.

118. Chłapowski report, 21 Feb. 1936, DTJS, ii, 392–96; see also ii, 94.

119. On Beck's visit and its background, see Noël and Laroche to Flandin, 21, 23 Dec. 1935, 24, 27 Feb. 1936, MAE, Z 698.1, Pologne 2101; intelligence report May 1936, SHA, EMA/2, Pologne 43; DTJS, ii, 108–10; Jackowski, *W Walce*, 404–405; speech, 4 Mar., Beck, *Przemówienia*, 220–21.

passed to the French, seemingly failed to make the Quai d'Orsay or François-Poncet realize fully that only days, and then hours, separated them from the German move.[120] On 6 March, Sarraut told the senatorial army commission that France would not accept the remilitarization of the Rhineland and would act not in isolation but together with Britain, Italy, and Belgium. Awaiting the action of the League, the government would bring the Maginot Line troops to their full strength, augment the "couverture," move reserve units to the frontiers, and alert antiaircraft defenses.[121] The government conveyed the impression of calmly awaiting a situation that it was fully prepared to handle.

On Saturday morning, 7 March, some twenty-two thousand German troops entered the Rhineland and were joined there by the local paramilitary *Landespolizei*, roughly fourteen thousand strong. Hitler's justification for the move was the Franco-Soviet treaty, which he represented as a violation of Locarno. The latter was now null and void. The chancellor proposed, however, a new accord in the West, nonaggression pacts in the East, and hinted at German interest in rejoining the League.

In Paris three consecutive meetings were held to deal with the situation: the first of armed services ministers, accompanied by Gamelin and the chiefs of staff and presided over by Sarraut; the second, at three o'clock between Maurin as war minister and the chiefs of staff; finally at six o'clock a skeleton cabinet session comprising Sarraut, Flandin, the armed services ministers, Paul-Boncour, and Mandel. The German coup did not make the government or the army revise their former thinking. Gamelin rejected any limited offensive operations unless general mobilization was decreed. His main argument was that the entry of the French army into the demilitarized zone meant war. Hence, it was not so much the absence of troops ready for a lightening operation—two light mechanized cavalry divisions and the mainly colonial "forces mobiles" were available—that determined Gamelin's stand, as his conviction that the Germans would not withdraw at a show of force.[122] Indeed, the existing evidence tends to confirm the opinion that the Germans would not have withdrawn without offering resistance. A risk of war there was; the ultimate question was whether the French government was willing to take it. To do so, it would have had to overcome the resistance of army chiefs by using the argument that time was not working in France's favor. Mandel apparently held this position.[123]

120. Conflicting appraisals in DDF, II, 1:311, 314, 323–24, 344, 375; compare DBFP, II, XIII:843; Straus to Secretary of State, 7 Mar. 1936, SDNA, 740.011 Mutual Guarantee/364, Locarno. On Polish warnings, Noël, *L'Agression*, 125–26.

121. 6 Mar. 1936 session, CA/Sén.

122. Compare Neré, *Foreign Policy*, 190.

123. Mandel cited in Jeanneney, *Wendel*, 252. For the Wehrmacht, see Emmerson,

Although ex posteriori assertions about what might have happened are risky, it appears that the chances of a victorious war were good. Le Goyet's opinion that it "could have been won without the help of England, but with that of Poland and Czechoslovakia," sounds very plausible.[124] The combined armies and air forces of the three states were superior to the Wehrmacht. The deployment of fewer German divisions on the western front than opposite Poland and Czechoslovakia[125] indicates that the German high command considered the possibility of a two-front war. The morale of Polish and Czechoslovak troops was good; fortifications in Bohemia were already completed. What was lacking was Paris's resolve to galvanize the system of alliances and its will to act.

The Czechoslovak government did not believe that France would respond militarily to the Rhineland coup, but Krofta immediately informed the French envoy that in this grave situation Czechoslovakia would make its "attitude conform exactly to that of France."[126] Flandin summoned the Polish ambassador at half past one—that is, after the first of the three meetings held in Paris on 7 March. In Chłapowski's absence (he was in Lyon) Counselor Feliks Frankowski arrived at the Quai d'Orsay, having learned by telephone from Warsaw that Beck had asked Noël to come in the afternoon. France, Flandin explained, had "no intention of reacting now by military dispositions," but it rejected unilateral denunciations of treaties, refused to negotiate with Berlin, and proposed to initiate "legal action" to force Germany to withdraw. Flandin hoped he could count on Polish support. Mentioning that Beck had summoned Noël, the counselor said that Poland would always remain true to its engagements. Whether it could define its position before the meeting of the Locarno signatories, he did not know. Asking about Britain's stand, he was told that it would probably be clarified by Monday, 9 March. London was not to be rushed. By the evening of 7 March, the British knew that a French mobilization or military measures—before a meeting of the League Council—were out of

---

Rhineland Crisis, 98–99; Weinberg, *Foreign Policy*, 252; Watt, "German Plans." For de Gaulle's arguments and their rebuttal, see *Mémoires*, 17–18, and Adamthwaite, *France*, 39. On military figures Parker, "First Capitulation," 364–66; also Le Goyet, *Mystère*, 121–25; Gamelin, *Servir*, 2:201–202; Flandin, *Politique*, 198–199; Duroselle, *Décadence*, 167–69, which largely supersedes his "France and the Crisis of March 1936"; Evelyn M. Acomb and Marvin J. Brown, eds., *French Society and Culture since the Old Regime* (New York, 1969); Gauché, *Le 2e Bureau*, 45–47. A good deal of material can be found in DDF, II, I and II, and in depositions of the principal actors of the drama in *Evénements survenus en France*.

124. *Mystère*, 130.

125. See Defrasne, "L'Evénement," 252–53.

126. Monicault to Flandin, 7 Mar. 1936, DDF, II, 1:419; also Kvaček, *Nad Evropou*, 225.

the question. The Poles reported that Britain was assuming the position of a "mediator rather than a guarantor."[127]

In Warsaw, Beck, having learned of the Rhineland occupation, conferred with President Mościcki and Rydz-Śmigły prior to his conversation with Noël.[128] The French ambassador came at five o'clock. Recalling his warnings about the likelihood of a brutal German riposte to the Franco-Soviet pact, Beck characterized the situation as grave. He proposed that the French and Polish governments, acting in the spirit of the alliance, keep each other closely informed about the developments and their intentions.[129] The way in which Beck phrased his remarks made a profound impression on Noël. Never before had he heard the minister speak of the alliance so emphatically. He understood that it meant full Polish adhesion.[130]

Because Beck did not believe that France would counter the German fait accompli with military might—a view shared by most European capitals— was his declaration a mere gesture, made possibly under the pressure of the military as Noël subsequently assumed?[131] Rydz-Śmigły, who had conferred with Beck by telephone and face to face, later asserted that he believed in French forcible reaction and regretted that it did not occur. He regarded Beck's statement to Noël as a declaration of readiness to make war against Germany, and approved it as such.[132] This series of events does not necessarily mean that the foreign minister had to be coerced or acted against his better judgment. Beck deliberately took the initiative without

127. Frankowski telegram, 7 Mar. 1936, HIA, Amb. Paryż, box 5; Chłapowski report, 14 Mar., AAN, MSZ, P.II, w.102, t.1 (old classification). Also DBFP, II, XVI:49–50, DDF, II, I:414, 427–28, 431, 501–503; Emmerson, *Rhineland Crisis*, 131–45.

128. Noël's information that Beck also consulted Premier Zyndram-Kościałkowski, repeated by Slávik on 9 Mar. (CPP) and Cudahy to Secretary of State on 12 Mar. (SDNA, 740.0011, Mutual Guarantee/520, Locarno), is not confirmed by other sources.

129. Beck to Chłapowski, 7 Mar. 1936, AAN, MSZ 3769.

130. See Noël in DDF, II, I:415–16 and *L'Agression*, 125; DBFP, II, XVI:57; FRUS 1936, I, 239–41; Slávik report, 9 Mar. 1936, CPP. Also DTJS, II, 110, and Beck, *Dernier rapport*, 113 (which lists the wrong time of the meeting with Noël). Beck's resolve is stressed by Paul-Boncour, *Entre deux guerres*, 2:374, 3:36; and grudgingly by Bonnet, *Quai d'Orsay*, 159, and Gamelin, *Servir*, 2:214. Kváček accuses Beck of duplicity, *Nad Evropou*, 229. The fullest treatment appears in Bułhak, "Polska deklaracja," 286–87. Also Zacharias, "Strategia," 73–86.

131. Noël to Flandin, 14 Apr. 1936, DDF, II, II:120–21. On views at Brühl Palace, see Schimitzek, *Drogi*, 392.

132. For Beck–Rydz-Śmigły encounter, 7 Mar. 1936 Agenda, PI, Akta Edwarda Rydza-Śmigłego. See also Rydz-Śmigły's remarks to Chastenet and Noël cited in DDF, II, I:588 and II:319. In notes he dictated during World War II, Rydz-Śmigły said, "Beck renews the proposal of waging a preventive war against Germany by telling the French ambassador that if France would actively reply to the German venture, Poland would be immediately on its side." Rydz-Śmigły, "Czy Polska," 130.

awaiting a French inquiry in order to reestablish his credentials as an ally. By recalling his warnings, he was telling the French that Poland was a more valuable partner than Russia, and that Paris having wooed Moscow had proceeded along a false route. Hitler's repudiation of Locarno de facto restored Franco-Polish relations to what they had been prior to 1925—a relationship that Warsaw prefered. Thus, Beck, using this opportunity to enhance Poland's standing as an ally of France, was trying to revive the old military alliance. In view of the suspicions prevailing in Paris, this attempt was surely important.[133]

Whether the Polish foreign minister wished France to respond militarily is uncertain. Retrospectively he regretted—as a "great tactical error"—the absence of a quick diplomatic intervention, possibly backed by a military demonstration that could have forced Germany to retreat.[134] But he also told the Belgian minister in April that Paris was right in not having resorted to force.[135] Whichever represented his real feelings, his alleged remark to the Belgian diplomat on 7 March that if Belgium marched, Poland would march too, is apocryphal.[136]

One thing is clear. Having taken a firm position, Beck had to guard himself against being used as a pawn by Paris in a diplomatic showdown with Berlin. He was careful to remain within the bounds of alliance obligations that Germany had recognized as legitimate in 1934. By the evening of 7 March, it was evident that France would not engage in any military moves, and Beck dictated a statement that appeared the next day in *Gazeta Polska* in the form of a communiqué of the semiofficial news agency Iskra. It said that if Germany's reaction to French and Czechoslovak pacts with Russia could have been anticipated, the form it took was somewhat unexpected. Berlin's move primarily affected Locarno, German-Polish relations having been regulated by bilateral agreements. Nevertheless, Poland had to follow most attentively the developments, because they bore on "the system of

133. See DTJS, II, 110; also DDF, II, 1:436–37. Beck's remarks in Paternotte de la Vaillée to van Zeeland, 8 Apr. 1936, Archives du Ministère des Affaires Étrangères, Brussels. I am indebted to Rector Jerzy Lukaszewski for a photocopy of this document. See also MS, OSS, Wysocki, III, 2, 193, and his *Tajemnice*, 490–91. The retrospective view of Beck's chef de cabinet, Michał Łubieński, that the minister was motivated by soldierly honor, is only partly convincing. DTJS, II, 403–404.

134. See memo in Biddle to Roosevelt, 19 June 1938, FDR, Presidential Secretary File, Box 65, Poland 1935–1936. The relevant passage is cited in Cannistraro, Wynot, and Kovaleff, *Biddle*, 222. Compare Beck, *Dernier rapport*, 273–74; DTJS, IV, 216.

135. Paternotte to van Zeeland, 8 Apr. 1936, photocopy from Archives du Ministère des Affaires Étrangères, Brussels.

136. The story appears in a footnote in Beck, *Dernier rapport*, 114n. and goes back to Michał Sokolnicki who allegedly heard it from Paternotte himself. But neither of Paternotte's reports, 8 (unpublished) or 9 Mar. (DDB, IV, 129–30), refers to a meeting with Beck on 7 Mar. or to such a conversation.

political relations in Europe toward which the Polish government, despite its restrained foreign policy, could not remain indifferent."[137]

The ambiguous wording of the communiqué was attacked by the opposition, which said that it almost justified the remilitarization. Rydz-Śmigły apparently disliked it; the Czechoslovak envoy spoke of Beck's duplicity; the next day Noël protested to the foreign minister, who feigned ignorance.[138] The French ambassador riposted by revealing at a press conference his conversation with Beck on 7 March. Ambassador Kennard, whom he also informed, passed the news to London where it was made public by the Reuter and Havas agencies. Noël's motive was partly to pin down Beck, partly to influence Britain, which was interested in the question of Polish and Czechoslovak involvement in the crisis.[139]

On 8 March the French cabinet met for the first time as a whole, and after a stormy session agreed not to treat the remilitarization as a "flagrant violation" of Locarno. Paul-Boncour appears to have been the only one to mention the eastern allies, but he spoke of the aid that France owed them rather than vice versa.[140] French public opinion was unprepared for any drastic measures against Germany. When in the evening, Sarraut attempted to galvinize it by a rousing speech on the radio—"we are not prepared to let Strasbourg be placed under the fire of German guns"—he was dubbed "Sarraut-la-guerre."[141]

Flandin hoped for success through diplomacy. If in the days to come the general staff was instructed to prepare limited operations under the aegis of the League and the Locarno guarantors, this was but a futile exercise.[142] As part of the diplomatic campaign, Paris sought to utilize the eastern allies. Flandin wanted the Little Entente to meet as soon as possible and take

137. See DTJS, II, 111 and text 404–405; also DDF, II, 1:528. Compare Bułhak, "Polska deklaracja," 276.

138. See Noël to Flandin, 13 Mar. 1936, MAE, P.A. Noël 200; Slávik report, 14 Mar. in Berber, *Europäische Politik*, 57–58; also *Kurjer Warszawski* and *Robotnik*, 10 Mar.

139. See DDF, II, 1:487, 526–28; compare DTJS, II, 403; Bułhak, "Polska deklaracja," 273–75; Emmerson, *Rhineland Crisis*, 141.

140. See Paul-Boncour, *Entre deux guerres*, 3:32–34, and his "Le Coup," 23–33; Flandin's views on East European repercussions appear in Straus to Secretary of State, 8 Mar. 1936, SDNA, 740.0011, Mutual Guarantee/377, Locarno; Bonnefous, *Histoire*, 5:385–86; Duroselle, *Décadence*, 172–73; Zay, *Souvenirs*, 66–67.

141. See Emmerson, *Rhineland Crisis*, 116–17; Flandin, *Politique*, 199–200; Reynaud, *Mémoires*, 477. Also Chłapowski report, 18 Mar. 1936, AAN, MSZ, P.II, w.102, t.1 (old classification).

142. See DDF, II, 1:501–506. The "prises de gages" were to involve an occupation of Luxembourg (*sic!*) and of the left bank of the Saar, a naval demonstration near Heligoland, and some warlike preparations of Poland and Czechoslovakia. Compare Hughes, *Maginot Line*, 256–57, who takes these measures fairly seriously, Gamelin, *Servir* 2:205–11; Bonnefous, *Histoire*, 5:454. For Flandin, see DDB, IV, 125–27.

a formal stand that could have a beneficial influence on Britain.[143] Prague agreed, but Stojadinović first tried to delay a meeting and then, acting together with the Greeks and the Turks, repudiated a joint communiqué of the Little and Balkan Ententes issued arbitrarily by Titulescu on 12 March.[144] Prague, like Paris, placed its faith in diplomatic and possibly economic sanctions against Germany. Beneš even believed, although Krofta did not, that this would suffice to make Germany back down or even cause Hitler's fall. Osuský was pointing out forcibly to Léger the dire consequences for Central Europe of a permanent German presence on the Rhine, and urging firmness. But Czechoslovakia refrained from any provocative moves vis-à-vis Germany; Mastný maintained a low profile in Berlin. Faucher reported that there was only increased vigilance along the German border, Prague having been informed by the French general staff that its military measures were "purely defensive." Still, Beneš was aware of the gravity of the situation, and subsequently spoke of March 1936 as a moment "when the European war could really have broken out."[145]

The Poles continued to demonstrate their adherence to the military alliance. On Monday, 9 March, Chłapowski read to Flandin a statement of Beck that was both more precise and more limited in scope than that previously made to Noël, Beck declared that "in case of an attack against France, in conditions that constituted under the Franco-Polish agreements a *casus foederis*, Poland would naturally and without fail honor its signature and fulfill its obligations of any ally."[146] Was the wording so constructed as to draw the attention of Paris to article 1 of the military convention according to which *casus foederis* arose when Germany mobilized or constituted a threat to peace?[147] Possibly, but when Beck asserted that the Rhineland remilitarization per se did not activate the alliance—and stressed that aggression had to be "against French territory"—he was refusing to be drawn into sanctions against Germany in the defense of Lo-

143. Osuský report, 8 Mar. 1936 in Berber, *Europäische Politik*, 55. For an appraisal of the catastrophic consequences of the remilitarization by Jan Masaryk and Prague circles, see Corbin and Monicault reports in DDF, II, 1:547–49.

144. See Deák, "Siedmy marec," 330–31.

145. Beneš, *Message*, 8. Also DDF, II, 1:454, 496–97, II:277–79; FRUS 1936, I, 246–47; Wright to Secretary of State, 18 Mar. 1936, SDNA, 740.0011, Mutual Guarantee/543, Locarno; exchange of telegrams between generals Gerodias and Faucher, 9, 10, 12 Mar., SHA, EMA/2, Tchécoslovaquie 3; Deák, "Siedmy marec," 328–31; Kvaček, "Německá," 323.

146. Instructions read by Chłapowski to Flandin, 9 Mar. 1936, HIA, Amb. Paryż, box 8.

147. Wojciechowski, Noël, and d'Arbonneau incline to this interpretation. See Bułhak, "Polska deklaracja," 279–83. Massigli believed Beck to be sincere. See Gen. Schweisguth memento, 9 Mar. 1936, Archives Nationales, Dossier 351 AP 3. I am obliged to M. Henry Rollet for the transcript of this document.

carno, the disappearance of which he could only welcome. Wishing to remain the judge of what constituted Polish obligations, he was emphasizing that military alliance alone offered real guarantees. His hope to restore Franco-Polish relations to what they were before 1925 appeared, however, unrealistic to Szembek; after all, at that time no Franco-Soviet pact existed.[148]

The insistence on the military aspect of the Franco-Polish relationship emerges also from the visit of the Polish military attaché at the French general staff, effected simultaneously with Chłapowski's call on Flandin. Colonel Gustaw Łowczowski came to announce Poland's army readiness to assist France in case of a showdown. He saw the deputy chief of staff, General Paul Gerodias, and two days later Colonel Gauché. It is difficult to imagine that Gerodias did not immediately inform Gamelin. In fact, two days earlier, the other deputy chief of staff, General Victor Schweisguth, noted in his diary (7 March) that "in Poland declarations were made to the effect that Poland would be on France's side." In these circumstances Gamelin's assertions that he did not know about the Polish attitude sound unconvincing.[149]

Chłapowski, Mühlstein, and Łowczowski received assurances that although France placed its trust in the Geneva procedure, it would be ready to take military measures if necessary. The high command was in full control of the military situation. In the absence of any mobilization orders, these statements rang hollow.[150] But there was more. Gamelin presided over a lunch for the military attachés (including the German) on 10 March, which took place in an atmosphere of "real military camaraderie."[151] Consequently, it is difficult to see Gamelin's invitation two days later of the Polish attaché (the same day the military attachés of the Little Entente were received) as an attempt to coordinate French strategy with the eastern allies. Gamelin told Łowczowski another half-truth, namely that the French army was transformed into a force capable of offensive operations. But no hints of joint military operations were dropped, although a note of the French general staff did mention them on 11 March.[152] Moreover, a governmental declaration read by Flandin in the chambers said that France

---

148. See 10 Mar. 1936 conversation and telegram, DTJS, II, 122–13, 403.

149. See Gamelin, *Servir*, 2:213; Łowczowski report in Bułhak, "Stanowisko Polski," 456–59; compare Łowczowski, "Jeszcze o stosunkach," and his "Przymierze," and letter to the editor of *Bellona*, 42, 4 (1960), 310–11. Col. Łowczowski spoke to Gerodias on 9 Mar. and Gauché on 11 Mar. See also Gauché, *Le 2e Bureau*, 44. Also Schweisguth memento, Archives Nationales, Dossier 351 AP 3.

150. Chłapowski telegrams, 9, 10 Mar. 1936, HIA, Amb. Paryż box 5. Also 14 March report, AAN, MSZ, P.II, W.102, t.1 (old classification).

151. See Le Goyet, *Mystère*, 124. Also Defrasne, "Evénement," 256.

152. Łowczowski report in Bułhak, "Stanowisko Polski," 457–58. DDF, II, 1:506.

had no allies. The Poles objected, and Sarraut explained that the term "alliances" had the connotation of prewar alignments from which France wanted to dissociate itself. Paul Bargeton, the director of political affairs at Quai d'Orsay, argued that the 1925 treaty was only a guarantee pact, and when reminded of the 1921 alliance, described it as "less precise."[153] It looked as if Paris, in order to justify its inaction, wanted to create the impression of an isolated France, although by doing so it was questioning its whole eastern system.

French diplomatic efforts were singularly ineffective. The Council of the League censored Germany rather perfunctorily for its violation of a treaty obligation, and the London meeting that lasted until the second half of March was characterized by "incertitude, depression, skepticism and anger."[154] Even Beneš found it hard at times to follow the weak and vacillating French leadership. In retrospect, he blamed Flandin for contributing to the "decay and tragedy of France."[155] As the Yugoslav Božidar Purić told Osuský: "When France could do nothing without the British for itself, surely it would do nothing without the English for Austria, Czechoslovakia or Yugoslavia."[156] Krofta worried that a complicated situation might arise if the Franco-German arbitration treaty signed at Locarno became invalid, for this would also affect the German-Czechoslovak accord. Yet the French showed little interest in a possible reformulation of the pact between Paris and Prague.[157] In brief, as Daladier later admitted, "our attitude on 7 March . . . had shaken the Little Entente."[158]

Beck's performance in London was based on a sharp differentiation between the Franco-Polish alliance, which he wished to strengthen, and sanctions against Germany, which he deemed ineffective and opposed.[159] The Poles lectured the French on their foreign policy, which had led inexorably to the remilitarization of the Rhineland. They insisted on making the 1921 alliance obligations more precise. The French balked, however, at the Polish interpretation of "immediate aid" as meaning "sans retard" and given

153. Chłapowski reports, 14, 18 March 1936, AAN, MSZ, P.II, w.102, t.1 (old classification).

154. Jan Masaryk's words cited in Kvaček, *Nad Evropou*, 323–33.

155. Beneš, *Memoirs*, 13. Compare Krofta's speech at the foreign affairs commission, 17 Mar. 1936, ANM, Pů zostalost Krofty, IV, 1; also Beneš's views in Deák, "Siedmy marec," 234–36, 238; DDF, II, 1:633–35; Osuský report, 14 Mar., in Berber. *Europäische Politik*, 56–57.

156. Cited in Kvaček, *Nad Evropou*, 233.

157. Krofta telegram, 20 Mar. 1936 (excerpts shown to author).

158. 3 Aug. 1936, DDF, II, III:110. Compare Mastný's remark of 18 Oct., that 7 Mar. had "changed all the bases of Czech policy," in Weinberg, "Hitler–Beneš Negotiations," 368.

159. A good contemporary analysis cited in DTJS, II, 410.

before a decision of the League Council.[160] Flandin suspected Beck of wishing to clarify the alliance as a reinsurance while pursuing policies at odds with those of France.[161] A Belgian diplomat wrote: "The attitude of Poland had been appreciated, and one renders homage to its loyalty, but the hatred of Beck is such that people immediately hasten to add that Warsaw is playing a double game."[162] The Czechoslovak envoy in London likened Beck to a "dishonorable intriguer from a bad detective film," making cynical faces and sabotaging the London conference.[163]

The hatred of Beck made Paris play down publicly his stand on 7 March, which incensed the Poles and was viewed as contrary to French interests by Noël.[164] Privately General d'Arbonneau opposed the thesis that Poland had no right to criticize France over the Rhineland affair, because its own support "would have been absent *a fortiori*, had we taken a firm stand." He termed this reasoning logical but false. If Paris had acted with firmness, Warsaw would have stood by its ally. It was obvious that at the London meeting of the Council, Poland was ready "to associate itself with *action* but not with *pin-pricks*"; it was ready to knock out its dangerous neighbor, but not to annoy the neighbor to the point of being "bitten." D'Arbonneau assured Gerodias that he was not telling all this to the Poles, but he wanted a Frenchman to understand Polish psychology. And he concluded: "There is a tremendous lack of comprehension between us, reciprocal no doubt, but certain on our part, although it is much less marked among the military than the diplomats."[165]

The point that the Rhineland crisis may have represented the last chance to save peace has been made by many, including Bonnet and Gamelin.[166] Even Pope Pius XI opined that a French advance with 200,000 men into the Rhineland would have rendered a great service to humanity.[167] Léger allegedly exclaimed: "We have lost Central Europe and we have lost the peace!"[168] The American attaché in Berlin remarked that by "a single move on the diplomatic chess board, he [Hitler] has cut the military basis

---

160. See DTJS, II, 112, 116, 120–21, 436–38; Beck, *Przemówienia*, 222. Compare DDF, II, II:22, 57–58, 191–92, 249.

161. Flandin to Noël, 23 Mar. 1936, DDF, II, I:641.

162. Kerchove to van Zeeland, 14 Mar. 1936, DDB, IV, 149.

163. Masaryk report, 27 Mar. 1936, Berber, *Europäische Politik*, 59–60.

164. Noël to Flandin, 13, 19 Mar. 1936, MAE, P.A. Noël 200 and DDF, II, I:608.

165. D'Arbonneau to Gerodias, 15 Apr. 1936, SHA, EMA/2, Pologne 12. He authorized Gerodias to show the letter to Colson and Gauché (underlined in text). Compare Schweisguth's mementos, 13 Mar. 1936, Archives Nationales, Dossier 351 AP 3.

166. Bonnet, *Quai d'Orsay*, 152; Gamelin, *Servir*, 2:194, 215. Defrasne speaks ironically of Gamelin's "real self-criticism," "Evénement," 267.

167. Charles-Roux to Flandin, 17 Mar. 1936, DDF, II, I:574–76.

168. Léger in Apr. 1936 cited by Pertinax, 244.

from under the whole series of French post war alliances." In 1937 Herriot admitted that France could "no longer regard itself as a great power of sufficient military strength or human resources to maintain its position in Central and Eastern Europe and bring effective support to its allies in those regions."[169]

It was generally agreed that once Germany fortified the Rhineland effective French military aid would be seriously hampered.[170] Yet, the allied evacuation of that province in 1930 and French defensive strategy had already undermined this aid. Beck astonished the Belgian envoy by saying that from a military viewpoint it mattered little "whether fortifications were constructed fifty kilometers closer or farther from the Maginot wall [because] this would not greatly influence the operations of the French army in case it sought to intervene in Central Europe."[171] While the minister may have wished to minimize the consequences of the remilitarization, it was undoubtedly easier for the Germans to penetrate a demilitarized Rhineland than for the French army to advance into it. This consideration may explain the relative equanimity of the French military leaders during the 1936 crisis.[172]

The decade from 1926 to 1936 had run its full circle. Beginning with Locarno, it ended with the German denunciation of the pact. Starting with an early evacuation of the Rhineland, it ended with the Wehrmacht in full control of the zone. The consequences for East Central Europe were tragic, but for France too there was writing on the wall. In the summer of 1936, the new French envoy in Prague asked whether "France, eliminated from Central Europe, would remain a great power?"[173] This was not an academic question.

The Epilogue

Two years separated the remilitarization of the Rhineland from Anschluss; three from the occupation of Prague; three and a half from the outbreak of World War II. The events of 7 March brought only a temporary awak-

---

169. Report, 20 Mar. 1936, FRUS 1936, I, 260. The view that 7 Mar. sounded the "death knell of the eastern pacts" (Adamthwaite, *France*, 42) is shared by Kvaček, "Situation," 294; Bloch, "La Place," 23; Reynaud, *Mémoires*, 475. Herriot is cited in FRUS 1937, I, 97.

170. See Kremer, "Polska," 151–52. Allegedly Piłsudski had once said that "Poland need not fear Germany . . . as long as the Rhineland is demilitarized." See Juliusz Łukasiewicz, "Okupacja Nadrenii i Rambouillet," *Wiadomości*, 115 (24 May 1942), 3.

171. Paternotte to van Zeeland, 8 Apr. 1936, photocopy from Archives du Ministère des Affaires Étrangères, Brussels.

172. This point is made in Neré, *Foreign Policy*, 192.

173. Lacroix to Delbos, 17 July 1936, DDF, II, II:724. Hubert Ripka raised a similar question in *Lidové Noviny*, 15 Sept. 1936.

ening. Franklin-Bouillon, as could be expected, demanded that, reciprocal mistakes notwithstanding, France "return to the Polish friendship" and "strengthen the ties with the Little Entente."[174] The premier of the Popular Front cabinet, Léon Blum, assured Prague that 7 March would not be repeated in the future. Was the French system, however, which Bargeton termed "incoherent,"[175] capable of being made operative? In the summer of 1936, Massigli suggested a comprehensive plan designed "to furnish our allies with a tangible proof that we intend to put our economic relations in harmony with our political, and practice our alliances."[176] Such grandiose ideas had no sequel. Only a fraction of the 800 million francs armament loan to Poland, agreed upon at Rambouillet during Rydz-Śmigły's visit to France (6 September 1936) reached the country. French armament industries proved unable to thrive, as the German did, on orders from East Central Europe, or to compete effectively with the Reich.

In the political-military sphere the old problems remained unresolved. Paris failed to extract any promises from Warsaw to change its attitude toward Prague. Beneš's efforts to make the Little Entente operative against a great power failed, as did the endeavors to conclude an alliance between France and the Little Entente as a bloc. Such radical proposals came too late to be acceptable to the Yugoslavs, Romanians, and indeed the French. The grouping became in the words of a Yugoslav diplomat "une blague politique"; its 1937 meeting in Belgrade was "a first class funeral."[177]

The trip of the foreign minister Yvon Delbos to the capitals of East Central Europe in late 1937—a faint echo of Barthou's tour—was devoid of deeper political significance. In the era of appeasement, the French system was becoming a relic of the past. In tow of London, Paris followed almost passively the Anschluss and suffered the humiliation of Munich. France's acquiescence in the partitioning of its faithful ally—in which Poland played an inglorious part—showed how low the country had fallen. Beneš said later that he had known what was happening in France from Laval to Daladier, but he could not desert Paris, and he still clung to the hope that a governmental change might redress the situation.[178]

After Munich French diplomacy seriously considered whether it ought not to abandon the debris of its system. When Ribbentrop denounced the eastern alliances during his Paris visit in December 1938, he could assume

174. Radio speech, 4 Apr. 1936 cited in AAN, MSZ 3705.

175. See note of Bargeton, 30 June 1936, DDF, II, II:563–64.

176. Cited in Kaiser, *Economic Diplomacy*, 199.

177. The expressions are respectively of Purić and Stojadinović cited in Wandycz, "Little Entente," 561, 563.

178. Beneš's letter to Karel Čapek in Josef Domaňský, "Několik poznámek k otázce politického zápasu o tzv ČS vojenskou doktrínu po r. 1945," *Historie a Vojenství*, 1 (1964), 4n.

from Bonnet's attitude that France was ready to grant Germany a free hand in the region. In the last months preceding the war, France was more a second than a partner in the British-Polish negotiations that culminated in the long-coveted Polish alliance with London. It was also symptomatic that when Germany attacked Poland on 1 September, France declared war only after Britain did, and stood by idly as Poland fell. It was without the benefit of its eastern alliances that France engaged in the phony war and went to its own debacle in the spring of 1940.

Appraisal: A Pattern of Relations

At the beginning of this study certain basic questions were raised about the French system of eastern alliances. Did it represent an important option for the preservation of peace and status quo? What was its place in the French, Polish, and Czechoslovak diplomacy? How was it affected by domestic political, military, and economic considerations? Did it correspond to the existing set of values, traditions, and behavioral patterns of the French, Czechs, Slovaks, and Poles?

These questions may well appear to have been submerged in the chronological survey of the Franco-Polish-Czechoslovak relationship during the post-Locarno era. In my presentation I avoided a rigid structuring of the developments. But if the story of diplomatic moves and countermoves, Czech-Polish squabbles, recurrent malaise, search for French credits, and military planning may have appeared repetitive, nay tedious at times, one must remember that dramatic events grow out of the slowly evolving changes in the day-to-day intercourse. Attention to minutiae was not dictated by pedantry but inspired by the French saying: "la vérité est dans les nuances." Having patiently followed the intricate story with its reappearing themes, the reader is now entitled to an overview, a sketch of the emerging pattern revealing the profound forces at work.

Analyzing the French system in 1930, a British diplomat opined that it represented the hope that France, grouping around her "the secondary states which she protects," will "secure their alliances by their interests" and become "the head of a defensive coalition sufficiently strong to discourage all ambition. Thus surrounded she will remain a first-class Power, and Europe will aid her to maintain that rank."[1]

The French alliances made sense geographically—hemming in Germany on the west and the east—and historically as a new version of the *barrière de l'est* and a revived *alliance de revers*. The combined populations of France, Poland, and Czechoslovakia exceeded that of Germany; their armies during the decade remained superior to the Reichswehr. The eco-

---

1. Tyrrell's historical analysis in DBFP, 1a, VII:458.

nomic potential of the three allies was, however, definitely inferior, taking steel and iron production as an indicator.[2] According to one calculation, relying exclusively on its own industrial potential France could in 1929 equip 200 divisions, Germany 250, Czechoslovakia 38, and Poland 20. The respective figures for 1937 were 160, 260, 42 and 24.[3] The weakness of Poland especially was striking. How could France communicate with the eastern region in wartime? The Mediterranean-Balkan route was long and difficult.

The alliances aimed to contain Germany in peacetime, serve as a deterrent to war, and ensure Berlin's defeat if it risked the use of force. As a historian put it: "The demotion of Germany was the essential condition, and not only the aim of the French system." He added, "If this condition was not fulfilled, the interests changed to such an extent that a solid system of alliances in the original sense was no longer conceivable."[4] But the evolution that occurred in 1924 and 1925 made the working of the alliances largely conditional on Locarno and the League "without which," Paul-Boncour observed, "they were burdensome and uncertain."[5] This change was important. The alliances were neither to resemble the prewar blocs nor to be discarded, but reflecting France's "noble passion of guaranteeing the independence and integrity of the small nations on the continent," were to assist France in its European task.[6] While it was the German threat that kept the alliances together, it constituted, paradoxically, the focus of dissension, as each of the three states tried at various times to establish its own direct relationship to Berlin, potentially at least, to the detriment of the others. This was true for France and Czechoslovakia in the Briandist era, and for Poland after 1934. Thus the common denominator was simultaneously a source of weakness.

The impact of the other great continental power, the Soviet Union, was particularly adverse for the Franco-Polish relationship in the 1930s and complicated the eastern policy of Paris. The dilemma of reconciling the Paris-Moscow alignment with that between Paris and Warsaw appeared insoluble. French and Czechoslovak interests, as in the case of relations with Germany, were largely convergent.

France's dependence on Great Britain grew significantly in the post-Locarno decade. Because London favored a policy of appeasing Germany and refused to underwrite French eastern commitments, the British connection halted and impeded French initiatives. Nevertheless, a Franco-

2. See Appendix IV.

3. Kostrba-Skalicky, "Bewaffnete Ohnmacht," 478.

4. Krüger, "Politique extérieure," 271.

5. *Entre deux guerres*, 2:193.

6. Flandin, *Politique*, 119.

British united front appeared most desirable not only to Paris but also to Prague and Warsaw, which hoped for a change of Britain's policies. We shall return to this issue later. Italy also offered a possibility of strengthening France against Germany, even though its policies and the ambitions of the duce aroused profound mistrust at the Quai d'Orsay. A Franco-Italian alignment was on the verge of materializing in 1933 and in Laval's era; each time, however, it either hurt or complicated the relations between Paris and Warsaw (the Four Power Pact) or alarmed the Little Entente. The Italian connection was not to be.

The perception of the policy of eastern alliances varied with the geographic perspective. For Prague, the French alliance was, together with the League of Nations and the Little Entente, one of the three pillars of its foreign policy.[7] The fate of Czechoslovakia appeared inextricably linked with democracy and collective security, the country itself being, in Beneš words, "an indispensable state for the equilibrium of Europe"[8]—hence, the constant involvement in international schemes, which earned Beneš's diplomacy the name of "pactomania." French alliances were seen more as a diplomatic than a military device, and in this respect the views of Prague were close to those of Paris. Beneš's support of Briandism was to dull the edge of German aggressiveness; later, the introduction of Soviet Russia into European councils was to serve as a counterweight to the Third Reich. The Little Entente as an instrument of regional policy was not only useful militarily and politically against Hungary, but also represented an alternative to Habsburg restoration and to a Danubian union under Rome's aegis. Prague agreed with the need for a Franco-Italian cooperation in the region, provided it resulted neither in a condominium nor in a sacrifice of the Little Entente's interests. Czechoslovak relationship with Poland was largely determined by all these considerations: Prague's aspiration to a dominant role in East Central Europe, justified by its strong economy and political stability, went counter to Warsaw's ambitions of leadership. Czechoslovakia and Poland were rivals, and each regarded itself as *the* ally of France east of Germany. Beneš favored good neighborly relations with Poland but not an involvement necessitating a reorientation of diplomatic goals. Moreover, "if Czechoslovakia did not seek a military alliance with Poland," wrote Ripka, "this was because she did not want to undertake any commitments toward a state which had so many unsettled disputes to

7. For an overview, see Wandycz, "Foreign Policy." Compare Krofta, "Le Président Masaryk et la politique étrangère de la Tchécoslovaquie," *L'Europe Centrale*, 11 Mar. 1933, and his introductory essay in Beneš, *Boj o mír*, 3–229; also his *Zahraniční politika*.

8. Beneš, *The Problems of Czechoslovakia*, 33. Compare Gajanová, "Ke Vzniku," 44–46. "I believe that peace is only possible through democracy," Beneš asserted in another major speech (*Problémy*, 276) and Gajanová counted that the words "democracy" and "democratic" appeared fifteen times in this address.

resolve both with Germany and with Russia."[9] The argument that it was difficult for a genuine democracy to cooperate with Piłsudski's authoritarian regime was also advanced, although it was downplayed vis-à-vis the dictatorial monarchies of Yugoslavia and Romania.

Military planning assumed Czechoslovak participation only in a general war in which France was involved. Even so, an emphasis on eliminating Hungary first only slowly receded, under French pressure, into the background. Defensive strategy led to the construction of a local version of a Maginot Line.[10]

If *sécurité* was the key word for France, and the stress on multilaterialism characteristic for Czechoslovakia, the Polish watchword was independence (*niepodległość*). Piłsudski's two canons of foreign policy—alliances with France and Romania, and balance between Germany and Soviet Russia—did not mean unqualified endorsement for the French eastern system. In fact, the marshal viewed the latter as anchored on Prague and based on a patron-client relationship, and opposed to it a bilateral Franco-Polish alliance that he wanted to make as close to a union between equals as possible. Indeed, one of the considerations for the nonaggression pact with Berlin was to enhance the value of the Polish connection in the French eyes.

Claiming a certain freedom of action for Poland in the diplomatic field, Piłsudski conceived Franco-Polish solidarity as related mainly to military objectives. The convention of 1921 was the essence of the Warsaw-Paris relationship, and the marshal opposed any attempt to weaken it. In 1936 Beck hoped to restore it to a central place in the Franco-Polish alignment. France was to assist Poland in a conflict with Germany and partly protect it against Russia, for in the late 1920s and early 1930s it was assumed that Moscow would fight on the German side. The French defensive strategy was likely to expose Poland to the brunt of a German attack; hence the ideal scenario, which would ensure a two-front war, was a German offensive in the west rather than the east. In that sense the détente with Berlin aimed to reduce the risk of Poland becoming the first and possibly an isolated victim of German aggression. One had to maneuver so as not to antagonize Berlin too soon but still not lose the French ally. This policy could not be popular in Paris, Prague, or Moscow. With regard to the latter, Piłsudski favored correct relations but no more than that. If the Russian threat seemed greater than that of Germany, it was partly because Piłsudski believed that one could always find allies against Germany but not against Russia.

Italy represented a potentially useful factor but was generally a second-

9. Ripka, *Munich*, 427.

10. See Ota Holub, "Československá opevněni 1935–1938," *Historie a Vojenství*, 6 (1981), 62–73; 1 (1982), 91–110.

ary element in Polish foreign policy. As for Britain, it was obvious to Piłsudski, as it had been to Skrzyński, that a rapprochement with London would be most beneficial from Warsaw's viewpoint. But chances of involving Britain were still slender.

Cooperation with Czechoslovakia never claimed priority during this period, even though its importance from a military point of view was recognized, and Skrzyński and Lasocki went far in their attempts to win over Prague. Their experiences were disappointing, and after May 1926 Warsaw became ever more dubious and suspicious of the southern neighbor. By 1933 close collaboration was feasible only on Polish terms, which were unacceptable to Czechoslovakia. From the perspective of Brühl Palace, Czechoslovakia was increasingly perceived as a state that stood in the way of Polish diplomatic designs and policies.

The fact that the French eastern alliances were seen as both a diplomatic and a military instrument produced certain internal contradictions. A ranking French staff officer wrote retrospectively about "the exclusively defensive French army, which rules out any action outside of [France's] borders, while the policy it supports obligates it to intervene almost everywhere in Europe to assist countries threatened with aggression." Another author spoke of the "mortal danger implied in the incompatibility between the external and military policy of France."[11] These points are valid, and yet it would be incorrect to assume that the military cooperation between the French and the east European armies was a pretense or a farce. Poland and Czechoslovakia were seen by the high command as "forming an important maneuvering space east of Germany,"[12] even though they could not offer room for an in-depth strategy, as could Russia, for example, with its huge *Hinterland*. The French military considered on several occasions the modes of assistance that France could render, short of an offensive, to its allies in the east. Planning was taken quite seriously. The French army pressed Warsaw and Prague to give priority to the German rather than Russian or Hungarian threat and to develop mutual cooperation. Even the Franco-Russian alignment was viewed in terms of the relief it could bring to East Central Europe by alleviating France's burden, as was to some extent a military alliance with Italy. In view of the geographic distance, transit issues assumed great importance, and air force cooperation reached, in the Czechoslovak case, the form of an actual convention. Yet coordinated planning, not to mention a joint command in wartime, never went beyond theoretical memoranda. The French side never gave precise information on its mobilization plans; the foreign ministry did not allow the general staff, despite the latter's requests, to ask the allied armies what

11. Respectively, Gauché, *Le 2e Bureau*, 233 and Chastenet, *Histoire*, 6:192–93.

12. See Dutailly, *Problèmes*, 41.

their needs would be in case of war.[13] It was at the express orders of the government that the French command had to press Poland twice to consent to a dilution of the military convention.

The absence of a sustained and consistent effort to strengthen the military capabilities of the allies (especially Poland) through systematic and large-scale material aid was striking. Recommending such an effort, General Weygand wrote to the minister of war that "our policy is of a meanness that is prejudicial to our highest interests. What are some dozens of millions of francs if they could help to eliminate the risk of war."[14]

Here we are touching on what may be the crucial and the least explored aspect of the French eastern alliances, namely their economic base. The lament of Flandin about the "ruinous support accorded by French finance" to East Central Europe, which, together with 'imprudent engagements," inexorably led France to a catastrophe, hardly represents a balanced judgment.[15] Referring to French loans to Romania and Yugoslavia, a deputy characterized them as niggardly and extended on conditions that "smacked of usury."[16] A large loan for armament purposes, advocated by d'Arbonneau, did not materialize during the period, and the general, recapitulating French assistance, commented that such "aid had not been considerable from a financial point of view. In sum, one could say that there had been no investments of capital by France [in Polish armament industries] but only credit efforts, which, while useful to Poland, had at the same time profited the French industry."[17] The French cabinet showed on at least one occasion an awareness of the "incompatibility between foreign policy of France and [its] agricultural policy. The first urged the development of exchanges with Central Europe; the second imposed rigorous protectionism."[18] There were divergences between the Quai d'Orsay, which wanted France to play a bigger international role, and the finance ministry, which did not believe such a policy practicable.

The fact that economics played a largely negative role in the French system appears fairly clear. Be it loans, trade, or investments, one can see that East Central Europe did not occupy a prominent place in French economic policies.[19] Except in 1935, the balance of trade with Poland was favorable to France, and except for some years, notably 1931 and 1932, the same was true for Czechoslovakia. Paris did not appreciate the argument that

---

13. See Soutou, "L'Alliance," 312.

14. On 11 Jan. 1935 cited in Dutailly, *Problèmes*, 296.

15. Flandin, *Politique*, 121.

16. Ybarnegaray, 7 May 1931, J.O. Chambre, 2634.

17. D'Arbonneau report, 3 Feb. 1936, SHA, EMA/2, Pologne 13.

18. Zay, *Souvenirs*, 288, recalling cabinet debates.

19. See Appendix IV. See also the conclusion of Segal, "French State," 335–59.

its allies needed a favorable trade balance to equalize their balance of payments. A sound policy of investments might have alleviated this difficult situation, but Poland especially, as a weaker partner, did not succeed in attracting enough French capital or, when it did, make it benefit the country's economy. According to Adam Koc, "cooperation with French capital was the aim of our economic policy . . . up to the beginning of 1933." Thereafter, the Poles lost entirely their illusions.[20] French investments, many of them predating the reemergence of the Polish state, were, of course, considerable. Second only to American investments, they constituted 19.5 percent of total foreign investments,[21] and could have cemented the alliance. Yet they produced friction more than a feeling of solidarity. The Żyrardów clash epitomized the difficulties and had an adverse effect on the policy of the Banque de France, which in Moreau's days showed a good deal of understanding of Poland's economic and political problems.

The issue of Polish workers in France further aggravated the Franco-Polish malaise. Attracted to the province of the Nord, and needed to rebuild and work its mines and factories, the Poles formed a separate group, with their own schools, churches, and emigré organizations. As such they "offended people in France, a country that extends a welcome to newcomers in proportion to the rate at which they become assimilated."[22] These workers were unprotected against summary dismissal and deportation at times of economic hardship. Their sizeable repatriation to Poland in 1934 was bitterly resented, and gave rise to accusations of French chauvinism and treatment of Polish laborers as subhumans.[23]

On the whole, French investments fitted much better into the Czechoslovak economy. Occupying a second place, with over 20 percent of total foreign investments, French capital concentrated in economically strong enterprises. The most notable French presence was of course that of Schneider, the major shareholder in l'Union Industrielle et Financière, which ran a veritable empire in East Central Europe, based largely on Czechoslovakia and extending into Poland. The Schneider establishment controled Škoda, and the French 1932 loan, it will be recalled, was partly connected with this huge concern. Because the partners were more equal, with the Czechs being able to drive a harder bargain, the amount of friction was less than in Poland.[24] Still, there were complaints about French

20. Koc's testimony, 23 Oct. 1934, AAN, BBWR, t.115, k.56. This information was received from Professor Zbigniew Landau, which I gratefully acknowledge.

21. See Appendix IV: Pietrzak-Pawłowska, "Les Investissements," 319–24.

22. Neré, *Foreign Policy*, 134–35.

23. For a passionate statement, see Marius Moutet at 16 Jan. 1935 session, CAE/Ch. Compare article in *Kurjer Poranny*, 2 Mar. 1936.

24. Figures in Appendix IV. See Teichová, *Economic Background*, 94–95, 194, 139–

practices, and attempts at domination of Czechoslovak economy. Even the difficulties of Škoda in the 1930s were partly due to its exclusion from several markets to the advantage of the Creusot plant in France.

The point, made some thirty years ago, that if Paris "could have employed similar amounts of money [as loaned to and invested in Czarist Russia] to set the new eastern states on the road toward prosperity, the system of French eastern alliances might have become a strong underpinning of the European status quo," is still valid.[25] The reason this was not done can be found in a combination of international and domestic factors—economic, political, and psychological.

France was able to practice briefly a financial diplomacy in the early 1930s, but the economic structure of the country and policies pursued did not generally assist its foreign policy goals. Up to 1929, the French economic growth of 5.8 percent compared favorably with 5.7 percent for Germany and 2.7 for Britain.[26] A rigid adherence to the gold standard, the maintenance of the overvalued franc, and a tightening of the traditionally protectionist trade policies, however, contributed to economic stagnation. French share in the expanding world trade was diminishing. Tourism and foreign investments—60 percent of which were in Europe—counted as the main assets in the balance of payments. France, together with its colonial empire, being almost self-sufficient in the agricultural domain, imported on a larger scale only during bad harvest periods. Its major trading partners were Britain, the United States, Germany, Belgium, and Switzerland. Pursuing classical economic policies, the country suffered from diminishing revenues (increased taxes could only provoke domestic upheavals), unbalanced budgets, and constant financial problems. These difficulties, as well as vested interests of various groups in the society, harmed the relations with the eastern allies.

A great deal has been written about the political instability of the Third Republic. During the period from November 1925 to March 1936 there were twenty-six cabinets, most of them based not on a consensus of views among their members, but resulting from combinations meant to satisfy diverse political and personal interests. This situation may help to explain why governmental changes did not result in the adoption of strikingly new policies. Naturally, the eight foreign ministers (Briand, Laval, Tardieu, Herriot, Paul-Boncour, Daladier, Barthou, and Flandin) tried to put their own stamp on French diplomacy, but except for Briand and the phenomenon of Briandism, none stayed long enough to succeed fully. Duroselle has judged severely the political leaders of the period when he wrote that

217, 374–76 and her "Les Investissements," 331–38; Claude Beaud, "Interests" (with excellent graphs); and Bussière, with Crouzet, "The Interests."

25. Hajo Holborn, *The Political Collapse of Europe* (New York, 1954), 118.

26. Figures from R.A.C. Parker, *Europe 1919–45* (New York, 1969), 170.

they frequently "manquent de sérieux," ignored economics, and lacked "grands desseins."[27] Most of them had empathy for Czechoslovakia; few, with the possible exception of Paul-Boncour and Barthou, had any real liking for or understanding of Poland. The same was true for Berthelot whom Monzie blamed for "installing Czechoslovakia in the heart and confidence of the French."[28] Léger was allegedly even more anti-Polish and hated Beck (with reciprocity), regarding him as a German agent.[29] Sumner Welles once described Léger's mind as "typical of that kind of French mentality which is logical, and mathematically precise, and very clear, but which makes no allowances for the imponderables of human nature such as human emotion."[30] There was little common ground here for a true Franco-Polish meeting of minds.

The two secretaries general and the bureaus assured the continuity of French foreign policy, and the Quai d'Orsay line was characterized, in the words of a French historian, by *juridisme, immobilisme, and suivisme.* This meant an exaggerated attachment to legal formulas, a reluctance to rush matters, and a tendency to follow, or at least not to alienate, London.[31] Naturally, the Quai d'Orsay was not a free agent, nor did its viewpoint always predominate over that of other concerned ministries. A greater coherence was assured when the minister was simultaneously president of the council (as was the case with Briand, Herriot, Laval, and Tardieu) or when a strong premier could make his will felt like Poincaré or Doumergue. There were, of course, other loci of power, and Mussolini once said that France had six ministers in charge of foreign policy: Quai d'Orsay, the two presidents of the commissions of foreign affairs, the Comité des Forges, the general staff, and the Grand Orient.[32] This is obviously an exaggeration but structural problems did exist.

The rift between the Left and the Right was real enough, and the elections of 1924, 1928 and 1932 did have an impact on the country's external policy, although perhaps less profound than often asserted. The divergence between the two camps "was inherent in their respective outlooks upon life: realistic pessimism on the one hand, idealistic optimism on the

27. *Décadence,* 17–18. For Briand, in addition to earlier-cited works, Siebert, *Briand*; for an amusing verbal duel between him and Mandel, see 24 Dec. 1929, J.O. Chambre, 4649.

28. See Planté, *Monzie,* 260–64.

29. See Noël, *Polonia,* 131.

30. Report 7 Mar. 1940, FRUS 1940, I, 66.

31. See conclusion of Vaïsse, *Sécurité.* On Quai d'Orsay relations with the parliament, commerce, propaganda, etc. see Lauren, *Diplomats,* 196. Compare Vaïsse, "L'Adaptation du Quai d'Orsay aux nouvelles conditions diplomatiques," *Revue d'Histoire Moderne et Contemporaine,* 32 (Jan. Mar., 1985), 145–62.

32. See Drummond to Simon, 9 Dec. 1933, DBFP, II, VI:181–82.

other."[33] Yet reconciliation with Germany, for instance, was pursued by both leftist and rightist ministries, even though the means and the styles differed. Pacifism, usually equated with the Left, transcended party lines. There were pure pacifists, especially among the intellectuals; pacifists for whom peace meant security; those willing to sacrifice the lesser allies to avoid war; and those who stood for peace because France, in their view, could not fight a war without Britain. Did pacifism adversely affect foreign policy? In some ways, especially as combined with the antimilitarism of the French socialists, it undoubtedly did.[34]

A direct impact of socialists on the government of Daladier was significant, but perhaps never decisive as far as foreign policy was concerned. Their emphasis on the struggle against fascism at home rather than the German threat abroad acted as a brake on French diplomacy. The communist input was important mainly in the sphere of disarmament and in decisions that involved the USSR. The Center was occupied by the radical socialists, a "buffer party" between the Right and the Left, and characterized by "a factor of inertia."[35] The radicals frequently split on foreign issues, the Daladier–Herriot controversy providing a good example. The Young Turks, seeking to introduce an ideological element, added to the complicated picture. In these circumstances, one could speak of an outlook on matters international of the Left, but hardly of a single and consistent foreign policy.

In turn, the image of an intransigent Right—insistent on the fulfillment of treaties, nationalistic, defiant vis-à-vis Britain, and tough towards Germany and Russia—is not without flaws. The Right comprised such different groups as the traditional and the moderate wings, as well as the antiparliamentary and violently nationalistic extremists. The traditionalists put stronger emphasis on armaments, alliances, territorial status quo, anticommunism, and anti-Germanism. The name of Louis Marin comes readily to mind as symbolic of this trend. The moderates, whom Poincaré may well have epitomized, were more inclined to stress the League and the negotiating process. On such grave issues as the reduction of the military budget in February 1933, Ethiopia in September 1935, and the ratification of the pact with the USSR, the Right split.[36]

Close ties existed between the Right and the financial and business world, to mention only François-Poncet, Wendel, Henry de Jouvenel, or

---

33. Micaud, *French Right*, 14; also 19.

34. See Vaïsse, "Der Pazifismus und die Sicherkeit Frankreichs 1930–1939," *Vierteljahrshefte für Zeitgeschichte*, 34, 4 (1985), 590–616. Also Wilhelm von Schramm, . . . *Sprich von Frieden, wenn du den Krieg willst; die psychologischen Offensiven Hitlers gegen die Franzosen 1933 bis 1939* (Mainz, 1973).

35. See Serge Bernstein, *Histoire du parti radical* (Paris, 1980–1982), 596, 597.

36. See Rémond, *La Droite*, 1:197, 207.

Reynaud.[37] Yet the image of the Comité des Forges speaking with a single voice and directing policy hardly squares with the realities.[38] Was there a financial, industrial, or agricultural lobby promoting the eastern alliances? Not really. As pointed out in the Background, French economic expansion to the east was more government-sponsored than spontaneous, and the capitalists in Czechoslovakia and Poland proved to be more concerned with narrow interests than with the strengthening of the countries in which they operated. Too frequently they cared little about supplanting the Germans or reinvesting their gains in Polish economy. Exploiting their priviledged position, based on higher profits than in France, and having technical material imported from the mother country under a preferential treatment, they demanded that France's might be placed behind them. Noël, who like all the representatives in Warsaw, had to speak often on behalf of the French businessmen in Poland, commented on the Żyrardów–Boussac case: "Never did I feel as much as here the influence of certain economic interests on our policy."[39] French farmers had no incentive to assist East European peasantry; the wine-growers, an important factor in the radical party, had every interest to see their product accepted by Eastern Europe.

The Right controlled more journals than the Left. Wendel and Peyerimhoff held large shares in such papers as *Journal des Débats* and *Le Temps*; Boussac, according to Noël, had influence over Elie Bois of *Le Petit Partisien*.[40] But it would be erroneous to assume that the Right dominated French public opinion, or that the latter's outlook was decisively shaped—as far as foreign policy was concerned—by the press. Given the multitude of papers and the myriad of opinions, a simple correlation is almost impossible to establish. Moreover, "foreign policy issues have never been good war horses of the electoral battle,"[41] and the French press was not only frequently manipulated but was notoriously venal. Deliberate leakages appeared to the British to be part of French diplomatic practices. Stresemann, the Poles, even Beneš had occasion to complain about these intended indiscretions.[42] The somewhat irresponsible forays of

37. See Schor, "Etude d'Opinion," 23.

38. See Vaïsse, *Sécurité*, 6. On the powerlessness of Wendel, see Jeanneney, *Wendel*, 618–25.

39. Noël, *Polonia*, 169.

40. See Tyrrell to Henderson, 14 Apr. 1930, FO 371 146916 W 3802/3802/17. On Boussac, see Noël, *Polonia*, 168.

41. Pierre Miquel, *La Paix de Versailles et l'opinion publique française* (Paris, 1972), 560.

42. See Emmerson, *Rhineland Crisis*, 278n; DBFP, 1a, III:362; DTJS, I, 219; DDF, I, VII:824–25. On corruption see Łaptos, *Francuska opinia*; Jeanneney, "Sur la venalité"; also Claude Bellanger et al., *Histoire générale de la presse française* (Paris, 1972), 3:498–

French journalists into the foreign domain contributed on occasion toward the poisoning of Franco-Polish relations. To counter the effect of such articles, the Poles and the Czechs subsidized French newspapers and periodicals on a substantial scale.[43]

References to Czechoslovak democracy and heroic Poland were almost de rigueur in many French public pronouncements. Stemming partly from an old tradition of polonophilia in certain quarters and more recent sympathy for the Czechs, they need not necessarily reflect real involvement in the interests of eastern allies. A stress on the community of interests and the invocation of the Sadova-Sedan syndrome belonged to the repertory of a minority of speakers, usually, although not always of the Right or Center: Louis Marin, Franklin-Bouillon, and in the late 1920s Jouvenel. The radicals, especially the Young Turks, became increasingly critical of Poland. Jacques Bainville jeered that "in order for their love to revive, it may be necessary for [Poland] to be partitioned again."[44] The evolution of Warsaw's regime toward authoritarianism awakened the hostility of the socialists. "At the bottom of their hearts," Daladier told the Belgian ambassador, they may have "perhaps less aversion for Hitler and his partisans than for Piłsudski and the Polish nationalists whom they consider the hangmen of socialists."[45] Beck became the favorite target of attacks, and if those by Pertinax or Geneviève Tabouis did not exceed the limits of good taste, mudslinging campaigns were waged by leftist organs.[46]

Czechoslovakia enjoyed a better press. Masaryk was exalted as a great humanitarian; Beneš as the unflinching ally and collaborator. The kind of open relationship, unencumbered by a military convention, appealed more to the French public than secret alliances.[47] Generally, the French Left had

---

509. On the interests of the reader, see Pierre Albert, "Remarques sur la stagnation des tirages de la presse française de l'entre deux-guerres, "*Revue d'Histoire Moderne et Contemporaine,* 18 (Oct. Dec., 1971), 544–46.

43. These included *L'Ere Nouvelle, Journal des Débats, L'Europe Nouvelle, L'Ordre, Paris Soir, Petit Parisien, Le Temps,* and *Volonté* subsidized by the Czechoslovak foreign ministry. See Urban, *Tajne fondy,* 14. For Czech efforts to curb Jules Sauerwein, see Urban, *Tajne,* 68. Czech subsidies are mentioned by historians Carmi and Launay and in Chłapowski 15 Nov. 1927 report, AAN, MSZ 5421. For Polish subsidies, see, among others, Lipski–Chłapowski conversations, 9–13 Oct. 1930, AAN, MSZ 3762. As for propaganda in general, France was spending annually 74 million francs, Poland 26, Czechoslovakia 18. The corresponding figure for Germany was 256. See Dariac report, 9 Mar. 1933, J.O. Chambre, Annexe 2725.

44. *L'Action Française,* 14 April 1932.

45. Gaiffier in DDB, III, 123. Compare polemic with Blum in *La République,* 28 May 1932.

46. Noël, *Polonia,* 71 and 73, wrote that the "russophiles, the sovietophiles, the anticlericals, the intellectuals of the Left and extreme Left manifested generally an antipathy toward Poland." For criticism of the press campaigns, see Laroche, *Pologne,* 266.

47. True to its juridical mentality, the Quai d'Orsay insisted that Noël not use the

a better rapport with Czechoslovakia than the Right, the opposite as compared with Poland. Critics of Czechoslovakia included those who regretted the passing of the Habsburg monarchy, such as d'Ormesson, Marin, and Paul Deschanel. Monzie disliked the Czech who "was always right"—"the spoiled child" of the West.[48]

The French public was fairly ignorant about East Central Europe, its languages, history, and geography. Laroche commented that the anti-"corridor" revisionist campaign was singularly facilitated by the fact that people in France neither knew nor understood the issues involved.[49] Lieutenant Colonel Julien Filipo of the military mission in Prague pointed out that articles in the prestigious *France Militaire* contained "childish errors" and fantastic stories.[50] Constant misspelling of Czech names, Masaryk included, was almost a norm, but *České Slovo* rebelled (25 October 1929) when *L'Illustration* printed a map on which Yugoslavia was marked Czechoslovakia. Ignorance mingled with condescension. General d'Arbonneau wrote that "when one moves a little in other countries, he realizes that the Frenchman is not particularly amiable toward the foreigners who come to see him, because he believes that he had already granted a special honor by receiving them."[51] Still, Laroche thought that the Poles tended to be hypersensitive and preoccupied with prestige. On one occasion, he exclaimed that "the subleties of the Slav soul are inaccessible to us."[52]

Did freemasonry offer a platform for a meeting of minds and constitute a subsidiary channel for Franco-Czechoslovak-Polish communication? The documentation is fragmentary, and the connection between freemasonry and foreign policy so hazy that it is difficult to draw even tentative conclusions. To explain the Briand–Stresemann relationship by freemasonic ties is to oversimplify or even to distort facts.[53] Masaryk's adherence to freemasonry has been disputed. The ties between the Grand Orient and the Scottish Rite on the one hand, and such Czechoslovak lodges as 28 Řijna, Pravda Vítězi, and Comenius (to which Beneš allegedly belonged) on the other were unstable.[54] Zaleski's connection with the freemasonry,

---

term *alliance* when presenting his letters of credence in Prague. See Noël, *Tchécoslovaquie*, 9–10, 18.

48. See Planté, *Monzie*, 260–64.

49. Laroche to Briand, 12 Apr. 1929, MAE, Pologne, 114:103–104.

50. Filipo's private letter, 9 July 1934, SHA, EMA/2, Tchécoslovaquie 3.

51. D'Arbonneau report, 29 May 1935, SHA, EMA/2, Pologne 12.

52. Laroche in DDF, I, V:222.

53. For a denial that Briand was a freemason, see Castex, "Briand." On the incompatibility of French and German masons, see Margerie reports, 8 June 1927 and 6 June 1929, MAE, Allemagne 381:44 and 292:208.

54. See Noël, *Tchécoslovaquie*, 72; Papée report, 24 Apr. 1937, AAN, MSZ, Z.4, w.5, t.39 (old classification); Michel, "Milieux dirigeants." Also Hass, "Wolnomularstwo."

which he denied, and the alleged membership of Beck, which Noël is the only one to affirm and consider important, even if true, does not help to explain any of their policies.[55] When Monzie and the radical deputy Gaston Martin (both of the Grant Orient) visited Warsaw in 1935, Beck regarded this as a deliberate move of international freemasonry.[56] To achieve what? While politicians sharing a common liberal-rationalist outlook may have found it easier to have a common language, their affiliation or non-affiliation to masonic lodges appears somewhat irrelevant. The freemasonic component of the Franco-Polish-Czechoslovak relationship has thus to remain, at least temporarily, in the realm of conjectures, which all too often are colored by prejudice and a "conspiratorial" view of history.

Conjectures are not needed when we consider the army as a factor in the triple relationship. The existence of eastern alliances allowed the French high command to intervene "more or less directly in foreign policy."[57] The alliances constituted, in Flandin's words, "a dogma for the general staff,"[58] but given the antimilitarist atmosphere and the strict subordination of the military to the political, the high command was usually on the defensive. True, between 1928 and 1932—the last year representing a veritable army "revolt"—Foch, Weygand, and to a lesser extent Pétain tried to challenge policies they regarded as exceedingly dangerous on military grounds. Worried by the manpower issue, the high command had to accept a reorganization and a shortened military service, restored to two years only in 1935. It agreed on political and strategic grounds, to budget vast sums for the Maginot Line. One might argue, however, that the parliament never refused military credits if their need was fully demonstrated.[59] Nor must one forget that the high command itself never promoted new and bold concepts. Its obsession with strategic mass led to the perpetuation of a large force on paper that was more of a "skeleton" of an army, a cadre top-heavy with officers, than an effective fighting machine. A mobile *armée de métier* gained no support. The organization of defense suffered from confusion and lack of effective central authority. Despite the existence of the CSG, CSDN with all its important commissions of studies, and the Haut Comité Militaire, military-civilian cooperation was not fully integrated. In the absence of proper planning of industrial mobilization, armaments tended to become obsolete. Modern rearmament required a

---

55. See Noël, *Polonia*, 132, on Beck.

56. Leon Chajn, *Polskie wolnomularstwo 1920–1938* (Warszawa, 1984), 134.

57. See Dutailly, *Problèmes*, 25.

58. Flandin, *Politique*, 111

59. See d'Hoop, "La Politique"; Le Goyet, "Evolution"; and Vaïsse, *Sécurité*. Compare Gauché, *Le 2ᵉ Bureau*, 236. Military expenses constituted around twenty-five percent of the budget in the 1924–31 period, around twenty in 1931–34, and up to thirty and then thirty-four percent in the late 1930s.

greater industrial power than France possessed. Slow technical progress affected badly the air force whose role in an interallied effort could be of major importance.

The three separate ministries of war, navy, and air force—as well as the dualism present in the roles of the chief of staff and the vice-president of CSG—did not make for a coordinated effort. The evolving mobilization plans (A to D) were less and less compatible with serious planning of joint action with the East European allied armies, which may help explain why the latter were kept in the dark. Paradoxically, the French army was both a major factor in the perpetuation of the alliances and the Achilles heel of their practical functioning in wartime. The role of military representatives abroad was beneficial in smoothing differences but could not be of decisive importance. General Faucher, "our general Faucher" as the Czechs referred to him, enjoyed a special standing in Prague but this diminished somewhat his influence in Paris, where he was suspected of identifying too closely with the Czechoslovak viewpoint.[60] The relations of the Polish military attachés in Prague, successively Colonel Jan Bigo and the Lieutenant Colonels Andrzej Czerwiński and Bogdan Kwieciński, with the Czechoslovak army were apparently correct. So were seemingly those of their counterparts in Warsaw, Colonel Rudolf Viest and General Kamil Holý. In Paris the Czechoslovak army was represented by Colonel Silvestr Bláha and General Vladimír Klecanda; the Poles by Colonel Jerzy Ferek-Błeszyński (who replaced Colonel Juliusz Kleeberg in the late 1920s) and finally Colonel Gustaw Łowczowski. The last attaché seemed more important than his predecessor. In Warsaw, General d'Arbonneau was an important factor, an astute observer whose counsels Paris did not always heed.

The functioning of Czechoslovak foreign policy indicated a high degree of control, unusual in a parliamentary democracy, exerted by Beneš. It provided for continuity in a foreign ministry that lacked tradition and was forced to improvise. Beneš's deputy, the historian Krofta, occupied a position similar to that of the secretary general at the Quai d'Orsay. Occasionally referred to as undersecretary, he never participated in cabinet meetings. Diplomats accredited to Prague found it useless to seek clarifications at Czernin Palace during the absence of Beneš, who "as foreign minister" was "his own salesman."[61]

---

60. See Noël, *Tchécoslovaquie*, 26: Marès, "La Faillite," 57–58.

61. Mackenzie, *Beneš*, 133. A typical appraisal in Mack to Carr, 14 Sept. 1934, FO 371 18382 R 5171. Compare Gajanová, "Ke vzniku," 52–53; Noël, *Tchécoslovaquie*, 72. For the organization of the ministry, Krofta, *O Zahraniční službě*, 5–18. I am indebted to Beneš's parliamentary secretary and a friend of Krofta, the late Hubert Masařik, for sharing with me illuminating comments and stories.

Combining the "methodical Cartesian rationalism" with the practical approach of a hard-bargaining, down-to-earth Czech peasant," Beneš was the grand master of compromise. In Geneva he acquired the habit of advancing "suitable formulas for resolving diplomatic deadlocks."[62] Politics, he regarded as "a practical application of sociology," and he prided himself on having developed an art and science of foreign policy based on "the constant, the regularly occurring." Already in 1923, he asserted that "we have created a political system supported by a philosphical approach and scientifically proved."[63] Beneš had a tendency to lecture, to propagandize, and to win at all cost. The writer Karel Čapek compared his diplomacy to his favorite game of tennis, where no ball was too high or too low, and where the elegance of style mattered less than the determination to score.[64] The American envoy called him "a born propagandist" who was "quite unable to meet anyone, however insignificant, without trying at once to win him over to his point of view."[65] A British diplomat characterized Beneš as "an unconscious opportunist" apt to "lose himself in his own volubility" when giving "loose general assurances" that he could not "otherwise implement."[66] This trait, noticed also by Charles-Roux, led to accusations of duplicity by British, Polish, Italian, and German diplomats.[67] Beneš was also described as "a busybody" determined to "have his finger in every pie," and "a little, astute, scheming" man "who wanted to play at being a Metternich."[68] The nickname "little Jack Horner" bestowed on him by the British frequently occurred in dispatches from Prague.

Was the Czechoslovak foreign minister "a dogmatic ideologist," whose "mental reactions are ever of the head, never of the heart," or as the American envoy put it "unconsciously the truest romantic I have ever known"?[69] Beneš's chief of cabinet during World War II inclined to the

62. Taborsky, "Beneš," 669–70.

63. Cited in Opočenský, *Beneš*, 133.

64. See *Prager Presse*, 27 May 1934. Bruce Lockhard also commented that Beneš's tennis "was like his languages, more efficient than stylish"; Opočenský, *Beneš*, 88.

65. Gelfand, *Einstein*, 200.

66. Clerk to Curzon, 5 Oct. 1922, cited in Kunstadter, "Czechoslovak-Italian Relations," 94.

67. See Charles-Roux to Briand, 13, 17 July 1928, MAE, Tchécoslovaquie 39:81–84 and 70:241–43. For criticism by Bardonaro, see Kunstadter, "Czechoslovak-Italian Relations," 93; for Addison's scathing remarks, see his letter to Sargent, 25 Jan. 1932, FO 371 15900 C 1088.

68. The quotes are respectively by Lampson cited in Campbell, *Confrontation*, 141; Mussolini in *Popolo d'Italia*, 24 Aug. 1922; Schubert in Charles-Roux to Briand, MAE, Tchécoslovaquie 39:81–84.

69. Quotes respectively from Vlastimil Kybal, "Czechoslovakia and Italy: My Nego-

former view, calling him "a machine for thought and work, without human feeling, but with human weaknesses." He added that "Masaryk was a leader, Piłsudski was a leader, and they not only established the course, but could inspire their followers. Beneš, unfortunately, only established the course."[70] Regardless of how one characterizes Beneš, there is no doubt that he had usually common language with the French, whom at times he flattered in extravagant terms, and was on intimate terms with their leaders. Seydoux recalled how he would enter "without having to be announced the room of the minister [Briand] in Geneva, and the office of the secretary general in Paris."[71] To them he was normally "dear friend" and "cher Beneš."

The foreign minister was invariably on a different wavelength from the Poles, whom he disliked and mistrusted. His personality and style helped to exacerbate the existing estrangement between Prague and Warsaw, for Piłsudski and Beck reciprocated this antipathy. His self-assurance and belief in his own cleverness irritated them. Indeed, Beneš had cause to be pleased with his career and achievements, even though many of his predictions, possibly colored by wishful thinking, proved wrong. He hoped for, and foretold, an imminent fall of Mussolini, Hitler, and Piłsudski. He underestimated the determination of Paris not to become dependent on London, and he insisted that Poland and not Czechoslovakia would be the primary object of German expansion.

Although Beneš regarded foreign policy as a preserve of experts, he duly delivered long and professional-sounding speeches in parliament, and submitted to rough questions in the chamber and attacks in the press. The brutality of the criticism somehow obscured the fact that, as the French chargé stressed, "the Czechoslovak press generally followed, in quite a docile way, the directives which were given by high quarters." Naturally this "facilitates singularly the action of the government in diplomatic affairs."[72]

The absence of a real challenge to Beneš's diplomatic course stemmed partly from Czech mentality (admittedly an elusive concept), partly from the stability of the Czechoslovak political model. Beneš spoke on occasion against "great romantic political conceptions," which he associated with an "eastern" (Polish) outlook, and contrasted with a sustained, day-to-day effort.[73] The latter proved to correspond better to the views of the Czechs,

tiations with Mussolini 1922–23," *Journal of Central European Affairs*, 13 (1954), 363; Hitchcock, 328; Gelfand, *Einstein*, 199.

70. Othalová and Červinková, *Dokumenty*, I, 91.

71. See Seydoux, *Mémoires*, 56.

72. Seguin to Briand, 25 July 1929, MAE, Tchécoslovaquie 49:240–41.

73. See Beneš, *Problemy*, 45. For contrast of Czech and Polish mentality, see Fiala, *Soudobé Polsko*, 162–63. Also my *France and her Eastern Allies*, 374–75.

who, as the German envoy put it, "always see only things next to them." Hodža complained once about the thankless task of putting forward great ideas in Czechoslovakia.[74] Moreover, Beneš's foreign policy was "supported by the majority of the parliament" and "all the governments in the republic agreed with it."[75] This fact can be explained by the Czechoslovak system based on the Hrad, the governmental coalition, and the financial-economic establishment.

Whether cabinets assumed the form of an "all-national coalition" up to 1926, a "gentlemen's coalition" to 1929, or the "bourgeois-socialist" coalition thereafter, they relied on an ongoing collaboration of party leaderships, especially the agrarian, the socialist, and the national socialist. At moments of crisis, nonpartisan cabinets of officials were appointed as stopgap arrangements. The Slovak populists participated only in the "gentlemen's coalition"; the Germans were represented in the government by 1926. Their presence, however, was not tantamount to a solution of the German question in Czechoslovakia. The idea of a Central European Switzerland, advertised during the Paris Peace Conference, was never tried and it did not correspond to the Czech (Czechoslovak) view of the country as a national and historic homeland in which they were the masters. In the 1920s and early 1930s the Germans tried to be a bridge between Czechoslovakia and Germany and a channel for German influences in the country. The situation changed after the Depression, Hitler, and the victory of the Sudeten German party in 1935. A time bomb was installed under the very structure of the republic. The Slovak issue in turn, especially as seen by the Hlinka party, was both constitutional (the Slovaks were co-rulers in principle) and connected with German, Hungarian, and Polish minority problems that presented a potential challenge to the Czechoslovak state. No solution was readily available under the existing circumstances.

Another challenge came from the Right, which the financial-economic establishment—inclining to the Right but retaining sufficient ties to the Hrad—tended to mitigate. Such leaders as Jaroslav Preiss of the Živnostanská Banka or Karel Loevenstein of Škoda, exerted considerable influence. Except for two serious challenges (the anti-Beneš campaign from 1926 to 1929 and the 1935 election), the rightist opposition never really menaced the regime. Reinforced by special laws for the defense of the Republic, Czechoslovakia resembled a "directed democracy," something the Poles vainly tried to achieve. Masaryk had said once "that without a cer-

74. See Mareček, *Št'astnější Evropa*, 33; and Koch to Schubert who wrote on 3 June 1928: "Die Tschechen sind kleine Leute, die immer nur das Nächstliegende sehen; grosse Gesichtspunkte und grosse Zusammenhänge vergangen bei ihnen nicht." ADAP, B, IX/126.

75. Rudolf Bechyně, *Pero mi zůstalo 1938–1945* (Praha, 1948), 34.

tain degree of dictatorship a democracy is no more,"[76] and a well-func-
tioning administration supported by an efficient police force made sure
that challenges to the state by political or national groups would be contained. The system could operate best in an international context of stability and economic prosperity, and Prague was interested in both for
international as well as domestic reasons.

The country was the most industrialized and Western-like in its socioeconomic structure in East Central Europe, and it depended heavily on
foreign trade. Its reorientation after 1918 notwithstanding, Germany and
Austria continued to be Czechoslovakia's most important partners. Attempts to increase commercial exchanges with France produced, as mentioned, little result. This failure, plus an unfavorable balance of trade, produced occasional protests against French egoism.[77] Both economic and
political factors tend to explain why Beneš's French orientation "never
enjoyed the full support of the Czechoslovak financial community," and
Preiss for one was calling for improved relations with Germany.[78] Vested
interests of the agrarians in turn militated against too close a cooperation
with the Little Entente. Opposition to cheap imports and demands for
higher tariffs were the slogans of the agrarian party; reluctance to guarantee armament credits to Romania and Yugoslavia was visible on the part
of the Živnostanská's Banka.[79]

The Polish economic angle was of limited interest to Prague. The trade
balance was generally unfavorable to Czechoslovakia, except for 1935.[80]
True, the largest part of exports was of industrial products, and imports
from Poland comprised mainly cattle and raw materials. The use of
Gdynia as a transit port held some attraction but never assumed a large
scale. Attempts by Czechoslovak capital to penetrate Poland in the 1920s
produced meager results. In some cases Czechoslovak firms acted in conjunction with the French, although Schneider opposed mixing Polish and
Czechoslovak holdings, and Preiss shared his viewpoint.[81] When the agrarians clamored for cooperation with Poland on political grounds, the economic aspects tended to undermine their position.

Czechoslovakia generally followed orthodox economic methods, bor-
rowing little abroad and devaluating the crown only to a small extent in
1934. A major shift in production from light manufacturing (mainly textiles) to heavy (principally metallurgical and machinery industries) was re-

76. Cited in Ripka, "Le Fondateur," 1–47.

77. See Olšovský, *Světový obchod*, 271; for an overview, Romanow-Bobińska, "Polityczne aspekty."

78. See Campbell, "The Castle," 251.

79. See Černý, "Wirtschaftliche Voraussetzungen."

80. See Appendix IV.

81. See Horejsek, *Snahy československé*, 89–95. Compare *Češi a Poláci*, 2:542–43.

flected in external trade. The sizable foreign capital, present in a wide range of enterprises and banks, on the whole operated to the advantage of the Czechoslovak economy. The problem of agriculture, however, in a state of chronic maladjustment during the 1920s and 1930s, had unfavorable economic and political repercussions.

The Czechoslovak army did not constitute a separate determinant of the country's foreign policy. The position and standing of the military establishment was rather low. Historical traditions and popular outlook operated against militarism. The officer's corps, deprived of the aura that surrounded it in Poland, was fully subordinate to the civilian authorities. Top generals lacked the charisma and will to challenge governmental policies.[82] General Gajda's episode left a residue of distrust of letting the military meddle in politics. The general staff might believe that without cooperation with Poland it had no viable strategy—and the French constantly said the same—but this was not enough to override Beneš's position on a military alliance with Poland.

Neither Masaryk nor Beneš, for all their antimilitarism, espoused pacifism; the president disliked Jaroslav Hašek's *Good Soldier Švejk* and all it stood for. Beneš was largely responsible for the increase in Czechoslovak defense capabilities, and saw to it that over twenty-two percent of the budget went for defensive needs. In a series of lectures on the military in a democratic society that he delivered to the officers (and later published as a book), Beneš emphasized that he viewed the army as an essential instrument, albeit one that he hoped would never be used.

The contrasts between Masaryk's Czechoslovakia and Piłsudski's Poland were striking. The personality of the marshal, which often baffled the foreigners, was undoubtedly stamped with charisma. He was both a romantic and a realist, a man of great vision and a skillful tactician—a pragmatist who believed in imponderables. His sudden moves and faits accomplis—as Laroche, for one, realized—were not impulsive decisions but the result of long meditations.[83] An ardent patriot imbued with glories of the past, Piłsudski was no doctrinaire nationalist. Raised in a tough conspiratorial school, he relished secrecy.

82. See Jan Anger, "Postavení armády v politickém systému buržoazní ČSR na počátku 30 let," *Historie a Vojenství*, 2 (1980), 74–100. Criticism of Syrový and Krejčí in Noël, *Tchécoslovaquie*, 121–22. A sympathetic survey appears in Gen. Louis Faucher, "La Défense nationale tchécoslovaque 1918–1939," *L'Année Politique Française et Étrangère*, 14 (1939).

83. Laroche in DDF, I, v:222. Compare also perceptive analyses of Piłsudski in DDF, I, I:590–91 and VI:66–68; Leeper to Chamberlain, 26 Dec. 1927, FO 371 13300 Hm 03282, and Savery in Kennard to Simon, 20 May 1935, 18899 C 4198.

Piłsudski rejected fascism as alien to Polish psyche,[84] but he also believed that parliamentary democracy as practiced by the Poles spelled disaster. Parties had to be curbed, as done in the Brześć affair, and the country ruled by his followers who had earned this right by their services to the cause of Poland's independence. To perpetuate their regime, the authoritarian 1935 constitution was enacted.

The marshal's stress on the internal strength of the country was inextricably linked with his insistence on its external independence. The conviction that only a fully independent Poland could count for something in the international society was characteristic for Piłsudski's foreign policy. So was the emphasis placed on its dynamic character and inner consistency. Passive diplomacy was seen as inviting defeat.[85] Piłsudski strove to emancipate external matters from domestic politics and make his voice in diplomacy and military affairs supreme. The input of President Mościcki, poorly versed in international problems, was negligible. Piłsudski "well knew how much Poland owed to the victorious Allies" and he "was not blind either to the strength of the Western Powers or to the fact that their own interests prompted them to help Poland to achieve a place in the sun, despite pressure from her neighbours to the East and West. But he was more inclined to rely on his own resources than on the good-will of Allies whom he lacked either the means or the inclination to know more closely."[86] The marshal understood the East better than the West. His dislike of the Czechs, going back at least to the period 1919–20, colored his attitude toward the southern neighbor. He recognized, however, the high stature of Masaryk.

Piłsudski affected the execution and the style of Polish diplomacy indirectly and more discreetly under Zaleski and more openly and directly under Beck. Zaleski's somewhat accommodating manner corresponded both to the tug-of-war between the government and the political parties after 1926, and to Piłsudski's belief that the time was not propitious for attempts to seize the diplomatic initiative. Piłsudski showed himself more clever—as Laroche acknowledged—than his national democratic opponents during the Briandist era, by avoiding to defy Briand in the hope of support by the French Right.[87] Brześć and the Ukrainian "pacifications" on one side and The Hague Conference on the other marked the end of this phase. Piłsudski now needed a disciple and an executor rather than a collaborator to shift Polish diplomacy into a higher gear. His choice for

84. See Baranowski, *Rozmowy*, 206; Jędrzejewicz, *Kronika*, 2:144; several entries in AAN, Akta Świtalskiego.

85. See the excellent analysis in Zacharias, *Polska*, summarized on 32–33.

86. Raczyński, *In Allied London*, 162.

87. See Laroche's comments, 26 Oct. 1932, DDF, I, 1:591.

foreign minister was Colonel Beck, whose toughness, dynamism, and utter devotion to his "commander" went hand in hand with a sharp intelligence, a prodigious memory, and supreme self-confidence. Beck could be trusted to follow Piłsudski's course caring little whether it made him unpopular at home and abroad.[88] Ambitious and proud, he tended to translate Piłsudski maxim of not bowing low to anyone into an exaggerated preoccupation with his own and Poland's prestige. Beck's suave manners and a certain air of cynicism and mystery were reminiscent of the old-style diplomacy, although paradoxically he was also attracted by the "new" dynamic diplomatic drive of a Count Galeazzo Ciano or even a Ribbentrop. They were young like he was, and he found them easier to deal with than the aged Western diplomats.[89]

Indeed, the majority of foreign diplomats regarded Beck as disingenuous, untrustworthy, and unscrupulous. Only a few Americans and British took a more positive view of him. Sir Samuel Hoaze (later Lord Templewood) expressed the opinion of many when he wrote that "Beck remained aloof, suspected and suspicious, only too ready both to take offense and to assert his claims with little regard for the dangers and susceptibilities of his neighbours. These personal failings undoubtedly damaged his credit." Which is not to say, Templewood concluded, that "even the wisest of ministers would have prevented Germany and Russia from making another partition of Poland as soon as the opportunity was given them."[90]

Between 1932 and 1934 Piłsudski became less concerned with making Polish policies palatable to Paris and more with showing the French through a determined course that they needed Poland just as much as Poland needed them. Beck executed this policy with gusto and perhaps a touch of arrogance. Did not a policy of alliances and equilibrium, within Poland's reach at that moment, require a delicate balancing act accompanied by concern for public relations and an attempt to assuage the French through minor concessions? If so, Piłsudski and Beck ignored it. Noël said that it was not so much the Polish détente with Germany that worried France, but the fact that it was in the hands of Beck "in whom we do not have confidence" and who "gives the impression of directing it

88. Lack of political support at home made Beck's position delicate. See Mackiewicz, *Beck*, 115; compare his secretary's pleas for improved public relations, in Starzeński, *Trzy lata*, 92. For a view of nationalist foe, see MS, BJ, Rymar, II, 15.

89. Noël to Flandin, 2 Feb. 1936, DDF, II, 1:179–80.

90. Templewood, *Nine Troubled Years*, 346–47. For other views, see Laroche, *Pologne* 78, 116; Noël, *L'Agression*, 20–23, and his obsessively anti-Beck *Polonia*; Vansittart, *Mist Procession*, 536; Cudahy to Secretary of State, 24 Feb. 1934, SDNA, 760C.6212/24; Biddle report in Cannistraro et al., *Biddle*, 206–207; Slávik report in Berber, *Europäische Politik*, 55; Kennard to Hoare, 16 Dec. 1935, FO 371 18896 HM 04023, and Col. Charles Bridge, 27 Dec. 1927, FO 371 13300 N 14/c.

against us."[91] Beck's style influenced the foreign ministry, which Piłsudski had criticized in the past and which had no chance yet to develop its own characteristics.[92] It became fashionable at Brühl Palace to display military-like toughness and cynicism and to show contempt for the powerless League and idealistic multilateral schemes. The aristocratic undersecretary did not succumb to this trend, but Szembek's influence was limited.

Piłsudski's basic goal, as mentioned, had been to free diplomacy from domestic party politics. A prominent Piłsudskiite spoke of an "equilibrium between foreign and domestic policies" by mid-1930s, meaning the marshal's unchallenged supremacy in both. Naturally he denied that the diplomatic course was in any way a function of internal power struggles,[93] but can one accept this view uncritically? A connection between the shift from Zaleski to Beck on the one hand and the domestic transition toward authoritarianism has already been suggested. Indeed, the opposition pointed to a link between the limitation of democracy at home and Poland's increased involvement abroad with those opposed to collective security. Beck's sporadic and occasionally cryptic enunciations in parliament were contrasted with Zaleski's much fuller reports on the international situation; this seemed symptomatic of the changing situation. Although criticism of foreign policy in the parliament and the press continued freely, its effect was minimal.

Major political parties, driven into opposition, had, of course, no direct influence on the government's conduct of external relations. But they could and did shape public opinion. The Left, motivated by ideological considerations kept advocating cooperation with the Western democracies, even though the Polish socialist party (PPS) was somewhat reserved about capitalist France, and had been opposed to the Weimar Republic less than other parties. The socialists stressed the League and collective security; they gradually became more pro-Czechoslovak and even pro-Soviet. Their criticism of foreign policy centered on Beck, with the implication—after Piłsudski's death—that he was departing from the marshal's line by leaning too much toward Berlin.[94] The populist Center, tradition-

91. Noël, *L'Agression*, 118–19.

92. See especially Michel, "La Formation"; Wandycz, "MSZ widziane oczyma amerykańskiego dyplomaty," *Zeszyty Historyczne*, 32(1975) 153–57; "MSZ w okresie międzywojennym," *Zeszyty Historyczne*, 35 (1976) 3–6; and "MSZ w okresie międzywojennym. Odpowiedzi na ankietę," *Zeszyty Historyczne* 38 (1976) 120–54; also Tomasz Drymer, "Wspomnienia," *Zeszyty Historyczne*, 27–30 (1975). The predominence of ex-Galician Poles in the ministry, stressed among others by Král, *Spojenectví*, 24, as an explanation for anti-Czech prejudices, must not be exaggerated.

93. Ignacy Matuszewski, "W Dniu 19 marca," *Polityka Narodów*, 5 (1935), 261–64. Compare Zacharias, *Polska*, 20.

94. See Żarnowski, *Polska Partia Socjalistyczna*, 120–21, and sections in Faryś, *Koncepcje*. Articles by Mieczysław Niedziałowski in *Robotnik* represented the party line.

ally less involved with diplomatic matters, was generally pro-French and anti-German, and it favored détente with Russia. With the party leader Wincenty Witos in political exile in Czechoslovakia, the populists were critical of Warsaw's anti-Prague line, although they were less outspoken than the Christian democrats, whose organ *Polonia* pursued a consistently pro-Czechoslovak course.[95]

The national democrats (officially the National Party since 1928), with their wide following particularly among the younger generation, were moving away from a parliamentary tradition toward an authoritarian and chauvinistic stance. They believed that European evolution tended toward a victory of nationalism and the "rebirth of heroic ideals."[96] Despite a certain attraction exerted by the Nazi model, especially on the more radical splinter groups, the party remained staunchly anti-German. Its equally strong and traditional francophilia was colored by distrust of any but the *genuine* nationalist France, which they wanted strengthened by cooperation with fascist Italy.[97] A common Slav solidarity against Germany dictated the national democrats pro-Czechoslovak line, although they disliked the regime in Prague and regarded Beneš as anti-Polish. Their violent anticommunism did not prevent the nationalists' advocacy of a rapprochement with the USSR.[98]

During the Zaleski period, the national democrats criticized too great a dependence on Geneva and Britain, an underestimation of Germany, a lukewarm attitude toward Italy, and a lack of positive initiatives toward Russia. Beck, in turn, was attacked for weakening the alliance with France, his anti-Czechoslovak line, and allegedly collaborating with Berlin against Russia.[99] There was some demagoguery in the nationalist stance—for instance, their demand that the foreign policy be securely anchored on the Polish nation[100]—for in concrete cases (the Four Power Pact or Eastern Pact, for example) their views did not appreciably differ from those held by the policy makers.[101]

The impact of the influential rightist press on public opinion was facili-

95. See Jachymek and Szaflik, "Myśl polityczna," 4:239–43; Borkowski, "Stronnictwo ludowe," 162–65; also Faryś, *Koncepcje.*

96. *Myśl Narodowa*, 11 Aug. 1935.

97. See, for instance, Laroche to Briand, 3 Dec. 1927, MAE, Pologne, 9:164–66.

98. Once a month prominent rightist journalists lunched at the Soviet mission in Warsaw. See MS, BJ, Kozicki, III, p. VII, 165.

99. Kozicki believed seriously that Piłsudski and Beck aimed at "a political and possibly military offensive against Russia in cooperation with Germany." MS, BJ, Kozicki, III, p. VII, 50.

100. See a statement in *Gazeta Warszawska*, 16 Sept. 1934.

101. See Stroński-Moltke talk, 3 Jan. 1936, in Wojciechowski, *Stosunki*, 225. Compare Stanisław Stroński, "Polityka zagraniczna 1933–39," *Horyzonty* (Apr. 1963), 12.

tated by a certain lack of sophistication about the nature of international relations.[102] Public thinking tended to oscillate between "naive faith and mistrust," moving easily "from uncritical enthusiasm to unjustified feelings of disappointment."[103] Far too often public opinion reacted to external matters in an emotional way, colored by prejudice and a belief in dark forces plotting Poland's downfall. Burdened with the heritage of partitions, the Poles were prone to perceive threats and slights where none may have been intended, displaying a mixture of inferiority complex and megalomania. Some governmental quarters, to boost the national morale, cultivated a great-power image that distorted reality and irritated the better informed Poles.[104] If one can speak of a definite climate of opinion in Poland, it is much more difficult to show where it affected concrete cases; considerations of prestige, for instance, were often inseparable from other factors. It is interesting that Beck's policy underwent no changes after 1935, although his line obviously enjoyed precious little public support in Poland.

Piłsudski's control over Brühl Palace and the armed forces eliminated the danger of dualism, a feature that was perceptible before 1926 and seemed to grow after the marshal's death.[105] Was Poland ruled by the army? The cult of the uniform, the prominence of high-ranking officers in the country's life, and the growth of a military-type mentality would seem to point in this direction. Yet it would be "misleading to talk of a 'militarization' of the Government offices," wrote the well-informed British consul, for it "would be a great mistake to think of these men" as "'military' in the ordinary sense of the word."[106] Such top politicians as colonels Sławek, Aleksander Prystor, or Beck were hardly representatives of an established professional officers' corps. The Polish army was too recent a formation, Laroche opined, for "these colonels to have lost the remembrance [of the days] when, although still young, they had had civilian oc-

102. See Andrzej Paczkowski, "'Geografia polityczna' prasy polskiej 1918–19," *Rocznik Historii Czasopiśmiennictwa Polskiego*, 9, 4 (1970), 524, and his "Prasa." Also see the stimulating Aleksander Bregman, "Opinia polska a sprawy zagraniczne: uwagi o niemocarstwowości myślenia," *Przegląd Współczesny*, 36 (Mar. 1931); Fiala, *Soudobé Polsko*, 163.

103. Sokolnicki, "Polacy," 483.

104. To mention only Łukasiewicz, *Polska jest mocarstwem* (Warzawa, 1939), criticized in Starzeński, *Trzy Pata*, 37–38. Compare Stanisław Głąbiński, *Wspomnienia polityczne* (Pelplin, 1939), 23, and Raczyński, *In Allied London*, 162–63.

105. On the "politicization" of the army, see comments in Adam Krzyżanowski, *Dzieje Polski* (Paris, 1973), 196, and Piotr Stawecki, *Następcy Komendanta: wojsko a polityka wewnętrzna Drugiej Rzeczypospolitej w latach 1935–1939* (Warszawa, 1969).

106. Savery's note in Leeper to Collier, 27 Dec. 1927, FO 371 13300 N 14/C. Compare Laroche report, 10 Apr. 1935, MAE, P.A. 200.

cupations," even if they did acquire a mentality of obedience to their leader and a habit of despising public opinion.[107] A militarism of sorts blended well with the general atmosphere in Poland, where pacifism was a marginal phenomenon. "It was war and not peace that had brought us freedom," a paper reminded its readers.[108]

The sizable national minorities of interwar Poland weakened the cohesion of the state, yet one can hardly speak of their direct impact on the country's external policy. Naturally, Weimar's propagation of the cause of the German minority did on occasion produce Polish concessions (the optants' issue), or led to a confrontation at the League (the Lugano incident) that France deplored. But the concern was more about international public opinion than about the minority population itself.[109] The Ukrainian "pacifications," for instance, tarnished Poland's image abroad, but the same was true about the Brześć affair, which had nothing to do with minorities. If the German minority figured large in the Warsaw-Berlin relationship until 1934, the Ukrainians were a constant irritant in the relations between Poland and Czechoslovakia, although there was also a German angle and potentially a Soviet.[110] The national minority problems acquired special significance when connected with territorial revisionism: the "corridor," Upper Silesia, or the eastern confines. The urgency of this problem abated somewhat in the early 1930s and the feeling of stabilization that stemmed from the nonaggression accords with the two great neighbors grew. The Poles greeted with relief Beck's denunciation of the Versailles minority treaty procedures in 1934, hailing it as emancipation from international tutelage.

Seen as a determinant of foreign policy, the state of the Polish economy deserves special emphasis. Poland, as two specialists have asserted, was a "terrain of exploitation by foreign enterprises and states [rather] than a country actively sharing on a footing of equality in the international division of obligations and privileges."[111] Underdeveloped, with a majority of the population living—often unproductively—in the countryside and contributing to the "hidden unemployment," Poland badly needed to be modernized and industrialized. In view of the dearth of native capital, foreign credits, investments, and loans were eagerly sought, and the United States and France were the objects of such solicitations. Yet, the already invested foreign capital that Poland did attract was used in a way that made Poles

107. See Laroche to Briand, 15 Nov. 1928, MAE, Pologne, 55:248–49.

108. *Głos Prawdy*, June 1928 cited in Barbier, *Un Frac*, 336.

109. See discussions in DTJS, I, 269–71, 275–77, 279.

110. See Lewandowski, *Sprawa ukraińska*, and Torzecki, *Kwestia ukraińska*.

111. Landau and Tomaszewski, *Polska*, 236.

complain of a semicolonial type of exploitation.[112] Its consequences for the Franco-Polish relationship have been stressed throughout this study.

Foreign trade showed a negative balance in the period from 1927 to 1929; favorable balances thereafter were largely achieved through limitations of imports. The structure of trade changed somewhat, but the raw materials continued to predominate among the export items. Poland gradually sought to diversify the directions of its commerce, emancipating itself from Germany and concentrating on overseas partners. The size and the pattern of the trade with France was a source of constant disappointment; we have alluded to only partially successful efforts to reverse the trend of a negative balance. By contrast, commercial relations with Czechoslovakia were more advantageous to Poland, not only because of an active balance, but because even in 1933 imports from Czechoslovakia occupied the sixth place and exports to Czechoslovakia the seventh.[113]

Despite strenuous efforts, the Depression was not fully overcome by the mid-1930s. The economy remained sluggish; perennial problems found no ready solution. It is hardly surprising that in this state of affairs, the weak industrial-financial establishment represented by the so-called Lewiatan (Centralny Związek Polskiego Przemysłu i Górnictwa, Handlu i Finansów) played no noticeable role as either a pressure group or a determinant of foreign policy. Similarly, for all the talk of the great landowning class in interwar Poland, one can hardly see its vested interests influencing the direction of Polish diplomacy.

Poland's economic weakness limited the country's international position placing it frequently in the role of a suppliant, obliged to pay for economic favors with political concessions and for political gains with economic sacrifices. At no time was Poland able to imitate France's financial diplomacy or serve, like Czechoslovakia, as an arsenal to its friends. Poverty circumscribed Poland's industrial-military potential. In 1935 there was only one car in the country per 1250 inhabitants, as compared to one car to one hundred fifty in Czechoslovakia and seventy-five in Germany.[114] While expenditure for defense (from the late 1920s on) never fell below one-third of the budget, it did not resolve the country's problems. Territory and population placed Poland among the leading states of Europe; underdeveloped economy pulled it back to a much inferior rank.

112. See Fiala, *Soudobé Polsko*, 184–85; MS, OSS, Wysocki, II, 136; see Grabski cited in Landau and Tomaszewski, *Gospodarka*, 1:315. Also see the mid-Apr. 1935 articles in *Gazeta Polska* by Oeconomicus (I. Matuszewski).

113. See Landau and Tomaszewski, *Gospodarka*, 2:288–92, 388; 3:380–82, 390. Survey of Czechoslovak trade in AAN, PPRM, LXXXI, 458; LXXVIII, 600.

114. Figures cited in Polish senate, 1 Mar. 1935, Sprawozdania stenograficzne senatu, LXXIIII/69.

The functioning or malfunctioning of the eastern alliances, affected, as we have seen by so many factors, was also influenced by the activities of the diplomatic representatives of the three states. While, the role of ambassadors and envoys had been steadily dwindling, they remained the necessary intermediaries. Their mentality and behavior affected international relations, whose edges they could smooth or sharpen.

In Paris, Štefan Osuský, a Slovak Protestant raised in America, was regarded as a proven friend of France, a capable diplomat with wide contacts. His sympathies lay more with the Right than the Left, and perhaps Poincaré had this in mind when he said that Osuský exerted a most felicitous influence on Beneš.[115] Actually, the two men differed considerably, and Beneš seemingly preferred to have Osuský abroad than engaged in politics at home. His Polish counterpart, Ambassador Alfred Chłapowski, a scion of a wealthy landowning family and a descendant of an aide de camp of Napoleon, entertained in his salon many members of the high society but—as the French director of Skarboferm claimed—few individuals who had a decisive influence on the shaping of French policy toward Poland. Neither Piłsudski nor Beck had a particularly high opinion of Chłapowski, and placed a good deal of important work in the hands of embassy counselors, particularly Colonel Tadeusz Schaetzel and Mühlstein.[116]

There were four successsive French envoys in Prague. Joseph Couget who had come to Prague in 1920 retired in the autumn of 1926. François Charles-Roux, who had collaborated with the prominent Slovak leader Milan Štefánik during World War I and enjoyed the reputation of a high-calibre diplomat, served from 1926 to 1932. His successor, Léon Noël, not a professional diplomat, did not disguise the fact that he regarded his appointment as a stepping stone in an administrative career.[117] A forceful personality, he believed in being vis-à-vis Beneš "an adviser—not to say a tutor—which was proper for representatives of France in these little countries." Noël thought that France had too often neglected "to guide them for their own good," but he recognized that statesmen other than Beneš would not have been so tolerant.[118] In early 1935 Noël was replaced by

115. Cited in Wurm, *Die französische Sicherheitspolitik*, 59. Compare Laroche to Couget, 4 Apr. 1925, MAE, Tchécoslovaquie 27:12; Noël, *Tchécoslovaquie*, 90n.; Břach, "Československá zahraniční politika: politické proměny Evropy 1924," *Československý Časopis Historický*, 18 (1970). Also Paul Valéry, *Stefan Osusky* (Paris, 1937).

116. See MS, OSS, Wysocki, III, 488; DTJS, I, 282, 417; Laroche on Schaetzel, 19 Jan. 1929 report, MAE, Pologne 12:221. Also James S. Pacy, "Polish Ambassadors and Ministers in Berlin, Moscow and Paris, 1920–1945," *Polish Review*, 30, 3 (1985), 249–50.

117. See Guerney to Foreign Office, 12 Jan. 1934, FO 371 18381 R 189/189/12.

118. Noël, *Tchécoslovaquie*, 92–93.

Paul-Emile Naggiar, who, however, was destined to remain there for less than a year. All these envoys had excellent relations with the Hrad and Beneš; all displayed genuinely pro-Czech feelings; and all tried to improve Prague's relations with Poland.[119]

Warsaw was a more exacting post than Prague, as the Poles increasingly rebelled against the patronizing and tutorial tendencies of the French diplomats. The days when a simple secretary had easy access to leading Polish personalities were fast disappearing under the Piłsudski regime.[120] Jules Laroche, whose ambassadorship almost coincided with the post-1926 era (his predecessor Panafieu left in the spring of 1926), made an effort to learn Polish and to cultivate the Piłsudskiite circles. Although he became very familiar with the country, and his reports were accurate, even penetrating, his standing at the Quai d'Orsay was on the decline, and his input lesser than it would have been otherwise.[121] Whereas Laroche had the reputation of a polonophile, the same could not be said about Noël, who succeeded him in 1935. His criticism of Laroche for permitting a diminution of France's prestige in Poland was accompanied by proconsular leanings, evident from his previously mentioned views. Soon he became a sworn enemy of Beck, whose downfall he tried later to engineer.[122]

French diplomatic dispatches frequently referred to the unfortunate choice of Prague in nominating Václav Girsa as envoy to Poland in 1927, to replace Robert Flieder. The minister's hostility toward the Piłsudski regime and his undisguised support for the opposition and the national minorities undermined his standing. Criticism of Piłsudski's Poland colored his reports at the expense of their objectivity. Girsa's close ties to Beneš probably reinforced the latter's prejudices against Warsaw. Piłsudski never received Girsa, and his successor, Juraj Slávik, came at a moment when little could be salvaged from the Czechoslovak-Polish relationship.[123]

Girsa's opposite number in Prague, Wacław Grzybowski, succeeded the

119. For changing tone of accreditation speeches by French envoys, see Mareš, "La Faillite," 55.

120. See Barbier, *Un Frac*, 288. For rudeness of French consul, Zaleski telegram, 6 Apr. 1929, HIA, Amb. Paryż, box 1.

121. For Aveling's view, see DTJS, I, 382; compare Cudahy to Secretary of State, 12 May 1935, SDNA, 751.60C/75; also MS, OSS, Wysocki, II, 356. The introduction to the Polish translation of Laroche's memoirs is unjustifiably critical.

122. Noël later wrote that the nomination of Beck was "a snub to France that ought never to have been tolerated" (*Polonia*, 86). For views on Noël and Laroche by Davignon, see DTJS, II, 83, and the previously cited references to Aveling and Cudahy (n. 121).

123. See Laroche dispatches, 16 Nov. 1932, 6 Mar., 30 Oct. 1933, 16 Aug. 1934, MAE, Z 864.5 and 10, Tchécoslovaquie 2586, 2587, 2602; Noël dispatches, 19 July 1934, 18 June 1935, Tchécoslovaquie 2587. Also Girsa report, 7 Apr. 1934, and 22 June 1933 briefing, KV, CPP.

strongly-pro-Czechoslovak Zygmunt Lasocki, and stayed at his post for the major part of this period. Enjoying Piłsudski's trust, Grzybowski, a refined man who looked like a diplomat from a fashions journal, had little sympathy for the Czechs but no personal animosity. He adhered strictly to instructions, which made Naggiar comment that he had been czechophile before Beck and czechophobe after 1932. Prague viewed Grzybowski as "a permanent obstacle to the reestablishment of good [Czechoslovak-Polish] relations."[124] Grzybowski was then relieved by Marian Chodacki who served as chargé d'affaires. Coming from the army, Chodacki adopted rather a defiant attitude.[125]

Relations between French, Czechoslovak, and Polish diplomats in the key European capitals varied. In Berlin, François-Poncet presided over periodical meetings of the Little Entente and Polish representatives, until the German-Polish declaration of 1934 led to the exclusion of Lipski from this informal club.[126] Periodic encounters of French, Polish, and Little Entente diplomats were also held in Rome, where Ambassador Charles de Chambrun often antagonized his colleagues.[127] A good deal of cooperation in Geneva—although Tytus Komarnicki, the Polish delegate, aroused at times the criticism of Noël—gave the appearance of a united Franco-Polish-Little Entente front on many an occasion.

What is a plausible verdict on the French eastern alliances during the crucial post-Locarno decade? One can say that they had great potentialities and did correspond to genuine pro-French feelings in Poland and Czechoslovakia. However, everything we have examined thus far would also indicate that they lacked cohesion, solid economic bases, and a consistent and inspired French leadership. The system was often incoherent because French diplomatic, economic, and military policies did not fully complement each other. From the perspective of Warsaw there were two distinct diplomatic alignments: the Franco-Polish alliance and the French eastern system based on Prague. To bridge the Czechoslovak-Polish gap and to make the system cohesive was surely one of the objectives of

124. Monicault and Naggiar in DDF, respectively I, XII:284, XIII:106.

125. On Lasocki, see Clerk to Chamberlain, 1 Feb. 1925, FO 371 11232 C 1254/1254/12; also MS, PAN, Teki Lasockiego, 4091; on Grzybowski: Guerney to Foreign Office, 12 Jan. 1934, FO 371 18381 R 189/189/12; Einstein to Secretary of State, 28 May 1929, SDNA, 760.60F/129; Laroche to Paul-Boncour, 16 Nov. 1932, MAE, Z 864.5, Tchécoslovaquie 2586; Noël to Delbos, 17 June 1936, MAE, P.A. Noël 200; also Noël, *Tchécoslovaquie*, 134; Wandycz, *Zaleski*, 129; MS, OSS, Wysocki, III, 2, 68. Comments on Chodacki are from personal reminiscences he shared with me in New York.

126. On Lipski, see especially a note, 19 Dec. 1924, MAE, Pologne 12:46; Laroche to Paul-Boncour, 30 May 1933, Z 698.1, Pologne 2099; François-Poncet in DDF, I, XII:6; Seydoux, *Mémoires*, 52; Smutný in Kozeński, *Czechosłowacja*, 64.

127. See MS, OSS, Wysocki, III, 33–36.

France's eastern policy, but it was not pursued consistently and imaginatively. Of course, Prague and Warsaw cannot be absolved. They could not overcome their differences and had at times a narrowly egotistical vision of their interests. Could France have coerced them? Flandin found it difficult to understand why France did not demand, in exchange for its guarantee of Czechoslovak borders, Prague's alignment with Warsaw, a "more reasonable" policy toward Austria, and a less egoist view of Danubian problems. Noël felt that France "sinned far too often" in its relationship with the East European allies by an "'excessive reserve." The obligations Paris had assumed "should have silenced the scruples, which if they did honor to our tender feelings were in this domain excessive and unjustifiable."[128]

There is something to this argument, but it is not absolutely convincing. To be firm, dynamic and resolute abroad, France had to be a different state from the declining, "decadent" Third Republic. To adapt the alliances to the new post-Locarno realities, without emptying them of content, required a grandiose vision and élan, which were conspicuously absent, for Briandism was like a shadow without substance. Any bold vision naturally carries with it a risk, and as Robert Aron wrote in 1931: "A fear of risk" seems "the greatest danger."[129] Perhaps, in the final analysis, this was the main cause for the decline and fall of French eastern alliances.

128. Respectively Flandin, *Politique*, 114; and Noël, *L'Agression*, 64.

129. Robert Aron and Arnaud Dandieu, *Décadence de la nation française* (Paris, 1931), 10.

Appendix I

Presidents, Premiers, Ministers of Foreign Affairs
and of War, 1926–36*

	France	Czechoslovakia	Poland
1926	DOUMERGUE	MASARYK	WOJCIECHOWSKI
	Briand PF	Švehla P	Skrzyński PF
	Painlevé;	Beneš F	Żeligowski W
	Guilaumat W (June)	Stříbrný W	
		Černý P (March)	Witos P (10 May)
		Beneš F	Morawski F.
		Syrový W	Malczewski W
			Bartel P (15 May)
			Zaleski F
			Piłsudski W
	Herriot PF (19 July)		MOŚCICKI (June)
	Painlevé W		
	Poincaré P (28 July)		
	Braind F		
	Painlevé W		
		Švehla P (October)	Piłsudski PW (October)
		Beneš F	Zaleski F
		Udržal W	
1927			
1928			Bartel P (June)
			Zaleski F
			Piłsudski W
1929			Świtalski P (April)
			Zaleski F
			Piłsudski W
1929	Briand PF (July)		
	Painlevé W		
	Tardieu P (November)		
	Briand F		
	Maginot W		
		Viškovský W (December)	Bartel P (December)
			Zaleski F
			Piłsudski W

Appendix I (cont.)

	France	Czechoslovakia	Poland
1930	Chautemps P (February) Briand F Besnard W Tardieu P (March) Briand F Maginot W Steeg P (December) Briand F Barthou W		 Sławek P (March) Zaleski W Piłsudski W Piłsudski PW (August) Zaleski F Sławek P (December) Zaleski F Piłsudski W
1931	Laval P (February) Briand F Maginot W DOUMERGUE (June)		 Prystor P (May) Zaleski F Piłsudski W
1932	Laval PF (January Tardieu W Tardieu PF (February) Piétri W LEBRUN (May) Herriot PF (June) Paul-Boncour W Paul-Boncour PF (December) Daladier W	 Malypetr P (October) Beneš F Bradáč W	 Beck F (November)
1933	Daladier PW (January) Paul-Boncour F Sarraut P (October) Paul-Boncour F Daladier W		 Jędrzejewicz P (May) Beck F Piłsudski W

Appendix I (cont.)

	France	Czechoslovakia	Poland
	Chautemps P (November)		
	Paul-Boncour F		
	Daladier W		
1934	Daladier PF (January)		
	Fabry W		
	Doumergue P (February)		
	Barthou F; Laval F (October)		
	Pétain W		Kozłowski P (May)
			Beck F
			Piłsudski W
	Flandin P (November)		
	Laval F		
	Maurin W		
1935			Sławek P (March)
			Beck F
			Piłsudski W; Kasprzycki W
	Buisson P (1 June)	Machník W (June)	
	Laval F		
	Maurin W		
	Laval PF (7 June)		
	Fabry W		
		Hodža P (November)	
		Beneš F	
		Machník W	
		BENEŠ (December)	
		Hodža PF (December)	
		Machník W	
1936	Sarraut P (January)		
	Flandin F		
	Maurin W		
		Krofta F (February)	

ᵃ Capital letters for president,

P for premier,

F for foreign minister,

W for minister of war or national defense.

Appendix II

Diplomatic Representatives 1926–36

French Ambassadors in Warsaw
Hector de Panafieu (to April 1926)
Jules Laroche (to April–May 1935)
Léon Noël

French Ministers in Prague
Joseph Couget (to October 1926)
François Charles-Roux (to May 1932)
Léon Noël (to March 1935)
Paul-Emile Naggiar

Czechoslovak Ministers in Paris
Štefan Osuský

Czechoslovak Ministers in Warsaw
Robert Flieder (to February 1927)
Václav Girsa (to 1935)
Jaromír Smutný (chargé d'affaires to November 1935)
Juraj Slávik

Polish Ambassadors in Paris
Alfred Chłapowski

Polish Ministers in Prague
Zygmunt Lasocki (to April 1927)
Jan Karszo-Siedlewski (chargé d'affaires to August 1927)
Wacław Grzybowski (to October 1935)
Marian Chodacki (chargé d'affaires)

Treaty Obligations: Excerpts[1]

A. French-Polish Political Agreement, 19 February, 1921[2]

Article 1. In order to co-ordinate their endeavours towards peace, the two Governments undertake to consult each other on all questions of foreign policy which concern both States, so far as those questions affect the settlement of international relations in the spirit of the Treaties and in accordance with the Covenant of the League of Nations.

Article 3. If, notwithstanding the sincerely peaceful views and intentions of the two Contracting States, either or both of them should be attacked without giving provocation, the two Governments shall take concerted measures for the defence of their territory and the protection of their legitimate interests, within the limits specified in the preamble.

B. Secret French-Polish Military Convention, 21 February, 1921[3]

Article I. In case the situation in Germany would become menacing to the degree of involving a danger of war against one of the [two] countries, and especially in case of German mobilization and when the execution of the Treaty of Versailles would necessitate common action on their part, the two Governments undertake to reinforce their preparations so as to be able to lend to each other effective and rapid help, and act in common. In case of German aggression against either country, the two countries are also bound to help each other following a common accord. . . .

Article II. In case Poland would be threatened by the Soviet Republic or in case of an attack by the latter, France undertakes to act on land and on sea to contribute to insure Poland's security vis-à-vis Germany . . . and to help it in its defense against the Soviet army.

1. Unless otherwise indicated, translations from the French are by the Secretariat of the League of Nations.

2. League of Nations, Treaty Series, 18 (1923), 13.

3. My translation. French text in Wandycz, *France and her Eastern Allies*, 394–95; Ciałowicz, *Polsko-francuski sojusz*, 403–405; Kazimiera Mazurowa, "Przymierze polsko-francuskie z roku 1921," *Najnowsze Dzieje Polski 1914–1939*, 11 (1967), 212–14.

Article III. In either contingency envisaged in Articles I and II above, the direct aid which France undertakes to provide to Poland may consist in sending of war material and rolling stock as well as technical personnel but not of French troops fighting as reinforcement of the Polish army. France also undertakes, as far as its circumstances permit, to assure the security of lines of communication between it and Poland, maritime lines included.

C. French-Czechoslovak Treaty of Alliance and Friendship, 25 January, 1924[4]

Article 1. The Governments of the French Republic and of the Czechoslovak Republic undertake to concert their action in all matters of foreign policy which may threaten their security or which may tend to subvert the situation created by the Treaties of Peace of which both parties are signatories.

Article 2. The High Contracting Parties shall agree together as to the measures to be adopted to safeguard their common interest in case the latter are threatened.

D. Exchange of Letters between Raymond Poincaré and Edvard Beneš, 26–31 January 1924[5]

. . . It is understood that, through the application of article 2 of the Treaty of alliance and friendship dated 25 January, the General Staffs of both countries will continue to maintain and tighten, in a constant manner, their entente, in the same spirit and for the same aim as concerns the drawing up of concerted plans to stave off an aggression directed against one of the two countries by a common enemy.

E. The Treaty of Locarno, October 16, 1925[6]

Article 2. Germany and Belgium, and also Germany and France, mutually undertake that they will not attack or invade each other or resort to war against each other.

This stipulation shall not, however, apply in the case of

(1) The exercise of the right of legitimate defence, that is to say, resistance to a violation of the undertaking contained in the previous paragraph or to a flagrant breach of articles 42 and 43 of the said Treaty of Versailles, if such breach constitutes an unprovoked act of aggression and by reason of the assembly of armed forces in the demilitarized zone immediate action is necessary. . . .

4. League of Nations, Treaty Series, 23 (1924), 165–69.

5. My translation. Texts of identical letters in Wandycz, "L'Alliance," 331–33.

6. League of Nations, Treaty Series, 54 (1926), 291–97.

Article 4.

(1) If one of the high contracting parties alleges that a violation of article 2 of the present treaty or a breach of articles 42 or 43 or the Treaty of Versailles had been or is being committed, it shall bring the question at once before the Council of the League of Nations.

(2) As soon as the Council of the League of Nations is satisfied that such violation or breach has been committed, it will notify its finding without delay to the Powers signatory of the present treaty, who severally agree that in such case they will each of them come immediately to the assistance of the Power against whom the act complained of is directed.

(3) In case of a flagrant violation of article 2 of the present treaty or of a flagrant breach of articles 42 or 43 of the Treaty of Versailles by one of the high contracting parties, each of the other contracting parties hereby undertakes immediately to come to the help of the party against whom such a violation or breach has been directed as soon as the said Power has been able to satisfy itself that by reason either of the crossing of the frontier or of the outbreak of hostilities or of the assembly of armed forces into the demilitarized zone immediate action is necessary.

F. French-Polish Treaty of Mutual Guarantee [Identical to French-Czechoslovak Treaty], 16 October, 1925[7]

Article 1. In the event of Poland or France suffering from a failure to observe the undertakings arrived at this day between them and Germany with a view to the maintenance of general peace, France, and reciprocally Poland, acting in application of Article 16 of the covenant of the League of Nations, undertake to lend each other immediate aid and assistance, if such a failure is accompanied by an unprovoked recourse to arms.

In the event of the Council of the League of Nations, when dealing with a question brought before it in accordance with the said undertakings, being unable to succeed in making its report accepted by all its members other than the representatives of the Parties to the dispute, and in the event of Poland or France being attacked without provocation, France, or reciprocally Poland, acting in application of Article 15, paragraph 7, of the Covenant of the League of Nations, will immediately lend aid and assistance.

7. League of Nations, Treaty Series, 54 (1926), 335–57 and 361–63.

Selected Economic Data

Production of Steel and Iron
(in thousands of tons)

	1929		1936	
	Steel	*Pig Iron*	*Steel*	*Pig Iron*
France	9,800	10,364	6,703	6,237
Czechoslovakia	2,145	1,645	1,559	1,140
Poland	1,377	704	1,141	584
Germany	16,246	13,401	19,208	15,303

Source: Teichová, *Economic Background*, 68.

Czechoslovak and Polish Shares of French Trade, 1928, 1933–36
(in percentages)

	1928	1933	1934	1935	1936
Czechoslovakia					
Import share	0.4	0.8	0.8	0.9	0.9
Export share	0.4	1.0	1.3	1.3	1.7
Poland and Danzig					
Import share	0.4	0.7	0.8	0.7	0.8
Export share	0.8	0.9	1.0	0.8	1.3

Source: Kaiser, *Economic Diplomacy*, 324.

Value of French Trade with Poland and Czechoslovakia, 1928, 1933–36
(in millions of francs)

	1928	1933	1934	1935	1936
Poland and Danzig					
Imports from	210	204	177	153	205
Exports to	432	173	159	128	142
Czechoslovakia					
Imports from	218	219	190	193	231
Exports to	199	191	231	199	264

Source: Kaiser, *Economic Diplomacy*, 321.

German, British, and French Shares of Czechoslovak and Polish Trade, 1928, 1933–36
(in percentages)

	1928	1933	1934	1935	1936
Czechoslovakia					
Exports					
German share	22.1	17.7	21.5	14.9	14.5
British share	7.0	6.1	6.4	6.9	9.0
French share	1.3	5.5	4.1	4.0	4.3
Imports					
German share	24.9	19.8	19.4	17.3	17.5
British share	4.3	4.6	5.2	5.4	6.0
French share	4.3	6.2	6.4	5.6	6.0
Poland and Danzig					
Exports					
German share	34.2	17.5	16.6	15.1	14.2
British share	9.0	19.2	19.7	19.6	21.6
French share	1.7	5.5	4.2	3.5	4.3
Imports					
German share	26.9	17.6	13.6	14.4	14.3
British share	9.3	10.0	10.8	13.6	14.1
French share	7.4	6.8	5.8	4.9	4.3

Source: Kaiser, *Economic Diplomacy*, 326.

Poland's Share of Czechoslovak Foreign Trade (in percentages)

	Of Total Export	Of Total Import
1926	2.0	7.1
1927	3.3	5.7
1928	4.0	6.6
1929	4.3	6.5
1930	3.6	5.6
1931	2.9	5.3
1932	2.4	4.6
1933	2.6	3.1
1934	1.9	3.7
1935	3.2	3.7

Source: Horejsek, *Snahy Československé*, 80.

Czechoslovak Share of Polish Foreign Trade (in percentages)

	Of Total Import	Of Total Export
1926	5.0	8.8
1927	5.8	10.0
1928	6.3	11.7
1928	7.2	10.5
1930	7.5	8.8
1931	6.7	7.5
1932	5.3	8.3
1933	4.3	5.0

Source: Horejsek, *Snahy Československé*, 86.

Balance of Czechoslovak-Polish Trade (in millions of Czechoslovak Crowns for Czechoslovakia)

Year	Balance of Trade
1926	−732
1927	−360
1928	−413
1929	−411
1930	−254
1931	−240
1932	−194
1933	−32
1934	−94
1935	+7

Source: Horejsek, *Snahy Československé*, 57.

Share of French Capital in Foreign Investments in Poland, 1933 (in percentages)

State loans	20.4
Municipal loans	7.3
Credits	9.2
Joint stock companies	31.1
Total	19.5

Source: Pietrzak-Pawłowska, "Les Investissements," 322.

Direct French Capital Investment in Czechoslovak Enterprises, 31 December 1937
(in percentages of foreign investment)

Banks	44.5
Mining and metallurgy	15.0
Mineral and vegetable oil industry	10.5
Chemical	25.3
Textiles	15.6
Engineering	73.8
Sugar refining	33.7
Glass, porcelain, ceramics	14.2
Others	12.7
Total	21.4

Source: Teichová, *Economic Background*, 48.

Bibliography

This study is based mainly on French, Polish, and, to a lesser degree, Czechoslovak archival materials. They are supplemented by relevant British, American, and German unpublished documents. In view of the multitude of secondary works only those most directly relevant are included in this bibliography.

Archival Sources

FRENCH. The French archives had suffered grevious losses during World War II, but large collections have been preserved or reconstituted. Those used here were as follows. At the Quai d'Orsay, Ministère des Affaires Étrangères, Archives Diplomatiques, Série Europe 1918–40. At the time of the completion of my research, documents bound in volumes went only up to 1929 (inclusive). They are cited by country, volume number, and page numbers (for example, Pologne 78:151–58). The post-1930 documents are cited by series (z) number followed by country and file number. Because they are now also bound, to obtain the relevant volume number one can use a conversion table in the archives. Thus, Z 698.1, Pologne (for the years 1930–32) would now be in Pologne 333, and Z 864, Tchécoslovaquie (for Jan. 1930–Apr. 1932) could be found in Tchécoslovaquie 142. The number of citations for the post-1930 period has been too great for me to try to convert them from old classification to the new without increasing the risk of technical mistakes, not to mention the labor involved. Série Y 1918–40 covers international conferences. The collection called Papiers d'Agents comprises papers of individuals; those of Aimé de Fleuriau, Edouard Herriot, Alexandre Millerand, Léon Noël, Joseph Paul-Boncour, Gabriel Puaux, André Tardieu, and René Massigli (the last one with the permission of Ambassador Massigli) were consulted. At the Château de Vincennes, Service Historique de l'Armée, I examined the documentation of the État Major de l'Armée de Terre—deuxième et troisième bureau—Conseil Supérieur de Guerre (procès-verbaux), and Conseil Supérieur de la Défense Nationale (procès-verbaux and some studies) as well as papers from Cabinet du Ministre. Because no printed catalogue was then available, I had to describe the documents by titles on boxes. Only those materials I examined at a later date, and which come mainly from the troisième bureau files, are cited here by file numbers, for instance 7 N 3446/3.

Selected documents from Marshal Ferdinand Foch papers, now deposited at the Service Historique de l'Armée at Vincennes, I consulted when still in possession of Colonel Henri Fournier-Foch.

Parliamentary documentation was examined at Palais Bourbon and Palais Luxembourg: in the former, Archives de la Chambre des Deputés, proceès-verbaux des Commissions des Affaires Etrangères; at the latter, Archives du Sénat, remnants of procès-verbaux of the Commissions des Affaires Etrangères, and Armée. Most of the minutes were destroyed during the war. These materials were examined by special permission.

At Rue Rivoli, Archives du Ministère des Finances, Série, F^{30} was consulted. Among the French materials deposited in the United States, I perused the Louis Loucheur Papers at the Hoover Institution Archives at Stanford. They proved to be of limited value for this particular topic.

POLISH. The War and occupants devastated the archives, and many collections are abroad. In Warsaw at Archiwum Akt Nowych the following materials were used: Archiwum Ministerstwa Spraw Zagranicznych and the badly depleted (except for the embassy in Berlin) archives of the missions abroad. Their classification was changed during the course of my research, and I have not always been able to give the new numbers. In the old numeration, P followed by a Roman numeral stood for a department in the ministry while Z meant mission abroad (Z.4 equals legation in Prague). In the same archive Prezydium Rady Ministrów (acts and protocols), and such individual collections as Archiwum Ignacego Paderewskiego, Akta Józefa i Aleksandry Piłsudskich, and Akta Sprawy Płk. Kazimierza Świtalskiego. A copy of "Dziennik Kazimierza Świtalskiego" is at the Piłsudski Institute in New York. Biblioteka Narodowa in Warsaw contains the manuscripts of Zofia z Grabskich Kirkor-Kiedroniowa, and of Zygmunt Karpiński, both called "Wspomnienia." In Cracow, Archiwum Biblioteki Polskiej Akademii Nauk has "Dziennik Juliusza Zdanowskiego" and "Teki Zygmunta Lasockiego." In the manuscripts division of Biblioteka Jagiellońska, I consulted "Papiery Stanisława Kozickiego" and his "Pamiętnik 1876–1939," Stanisław Rymar," Pamiętnik," and Konstanty Skirmunt," Moje wspomnienia." (A copy of the latter is in the Piłsudski Institute.) The Ossolineum in Wrocław (Manuscripta Instituti Ossoliniani) contains the Alfred Wysocki, "Dzieje mojej służby." Of all the minutes of the foreign affairs commissions, only one, for 16 January 1936, has survived the war; it is in Archiwum Sejmowe, Diariusze z posiedzeń komisji spraw zagranicznych.

The archive of the Józef Piłsudski Institute of America in New York has the part of the secret files of the Polish embassy in London that had survived the war, the Józef Lipski papers, the Edward Rydz-Śmigły papers [microfilm copies of all these papers are at Yale University Sterling Memorial Library], and Jan Weinstein Collection, which comprises also photocopies (from British and German archives) of papers relevant for Polish diplomacy. At the Hoover Institution Archives are the Polish Embassy in Paris files of decoded messages and the August Zaleski Papers. The Polish Institute and General Sikorski Museum in London has some of the foreign ministry papers (MSZ, Wydział Zachodni) and the files of decoded messages of the Polish Embassy in London, as well as the fragmentary Papiery Jana Szembeka and a Tytus Komarnicki Collection.

CZECHOSLOVAK. Archives of the foreign ministry, as most Czechoslovak archives, have survived the war much better than those of France or Poland. During my stay in Prague, I was allowed, however, to examine only certain collections, namely in Archiv Národního Muzea: Půzostalost Kamila Krofty, Kramářův Archiv, and the small but most valuable Vojtěch Mastný Archiv. My access in the Státni Ustřední Archiv, Ministerstvo Zahraničních Věcí, was limited to the Výstřižkový Archiv, a most useful collection of press cuttings from Czechoslovak and foreign newspapers thematically arranged. As for foreign ministry documents properly speaking, I was assisted by the fact that they usually exist in more than one copy. Hence, I was able to see copies of many reports from the legation in Warsaw, of several circular notes of Beneš, and notes of the weekly briefings by Beneš's deputy Kamil Krofta. Called at various times Kroftový zápisy, porády u p.vysl.Dr.Krofty, or Kroftový výklady na porádach, they are cited here as Kroftový výklady. All these documents have to be described somewhat cryptically as copies in private possession. They are complemented by Czechoslovak diplomatic documents translated by the Germans, which are now part of the T 120 collection of captured German documents in the National Archives in Washington. The Štefan Osuský Papers at the Hoover Institution Archives contain only a few items relevant for this study.

OTHERS. Relevant British documents consulted here come from the Public Record Office in London. Foreign Office Papers, group 371 and 800 (private papers, especially of Henderson, Simon, Lord Cushendun, Sargent, Balfour, and Austen Chamberlain); German from the Bundesarchiv in Bonn (mainly photocopies were used). Two photocopies of Belgian archival documents were consulted. American material consists of State Department decimal files at the National Archives, especially dispatches from Warsaw and Prague; John C. Wiley Papers; and the Presidential Secretary File, Franklin Delano Roosevelt Library, Hyde Park; also papers in Herbert Hoover Presidential Library, West Branch, Iowa; and Henry L. Stimson Papers at Yale University Sterling Memorial Library. The fragment of

the William C. Bullitt Papers that has remained at Sterling (microfilm) was
of some interest.

Published Sources: Documents, Diaries, Speeches, and Pronouncements

Ajnenkiel, Andrzej, ed., "Rozmowa marszałka Piłsudskiego z posłem pol-
skim w Berlinie Alfredem Wysockim 7 czerwca 1932," *Dzieje
Najnowsze*, 5, 2 (1973), 133–38.

Akten zur deutschen Auswärtigen Politik: 1918–1945 (Göttingen,
1966–   ). Series B (1925–1933) and C (1933–1937). All references are
to this version rather than the *Documents on German Foreign Policy*.

Aloisi, Baron Pompeo, *Journal: 25 juillet 1932–14 juin 1936* (Paris,
1957).

Archiwum politvczne Ignacego Paderewskiego, Polska Akademis Nauk,
Instytut Historii, 4 vols. Edited by Halina Janowska et al. (Wrocław,
1973–74).

Bacon, Walter B., *Behind Closed Doors: Secret Papers on the Failure of
Romanian-Soviet Negotiations 1931–1932* (Stanford, 1979).

Balcerak, Wiesław, ed., "Legenda bez pokrycia" [Beck–Beneš conversation January 20, 1934], *Studia z Dziejów ZSRR i Europy Środkowej*, 9
(1973), 201–206.

———, "Pogląd Beneša na polską politykę zagraniczną w 1934 roku,"
Studia z Dziejów ZSRR i Europy Środkowej, 7 (1971), 179–82.

Beck, Józef, *Przemówienia, deklaracje, wywiady* (Warszawa, 1939).

Beneš, Edvard, *Boj o mír a bezpečnost statu* (Praha, 1934).

———, *Demokratická armáda, pacifismus a zahraniční politika* (Praha,
1936).

———, *Message de Noël 1936* (Sources et documents tchécoslovaques
37; Prague, 1937).

———, *Polsko a Československo: kde hledati příčiny rozporů polsko-
československých* (Praha, 1934). Published anonymously.

———, *The Problem of Central Europe and the Austrian Question*
(Czechoslovak Sources and Documents 7; Prague, 1934).

———, *The Problems of Czechoslovakia* (Czechoslovak Sources and
Documents 11; Prague, 1936).

———, *Problémy nové Evropy a zahraniční politika československá*
(Praha, 1924).

———, *Le Sens politique de la tragédie de Marseille* (Sources et documents tchécoslovagues 27; Prague, 1934).

———, *The Struggle for Collective Security in Europe and the Italo-
Abyssinian War* (Czechoslovak Sources and Documents 8; Prague,
1935).

———, *Vers un regroupement des forces en Europe?* (Sources et documents tchécoslovaques 26; Prague, 1934).

Berber, Fritz, ed., *Europäische Politik 1933–1938 im Spiegel der Prager Akten* (Essen, 1942).

Bułhak, Henryk, "Rozmowy polsko-francuskie w Paryżu, październik-listopad 1924," *Przegląd Historyczny*, 61 (1970), 680–83.

————, "Stanowisko Polski wobec Francji na tle remilitaryzacji Nadrenii w marcu 1936 r. w ujęciu polskiego attaché wojskowego," *Wojskowy Przegląd Historyczny*, 11, 2 (1966), 456–59.

Bullitt, Orville H., ed., *For the President: Personal and Secret. Correspondence between Franklin D. Roosevelt and William C. Bullitt* (Boston, 1972).

Cannistraro, Philip V., and Edward D. Wynot, eds., "Polish Foreign Policy in 1934: An Unpublished Document from the Italian Archives," *East Central Europe*, 1, 1, (1974), 71–81.

Cannistraro, Philip V., Edward D. Wynot, and Theodore P. Kovaloff, eds., *Poland and the Coming of the Second World War: The Diplomatic Papers of A. J. Drexel Biddle, Jr., United States Ambassador to Poland 1937–1939* (Columbus, Ohio 1976).

D'Abernon, Lord, *The Diary of An Ambassador*, 3 vols. (New York, 1929–1931).

Degras, Jane, ed., *Soviet Documents on Foreign Policy 1917–1941*, 3 vols. (London, 1951–1953).

Diariusz i teki Jana Szembeka, 4 vols. (London, 1964–1965). Volumes 1–3 edited by Tytus Komarnicki. Vol. 4 edited by Józef Zarański. The French version, Jean Comte Szembek, *Journal 1933–1939* (Paris, 1952), is incomplete and not properly edited.

I Documenti diplomatici italiani. Commissione per la pubblicazione dei documenti diplomatici. 7th series. (Roma, 1952–).

Documents diplomatiques belges 1920–1940, 4 vols. Académie royale des sciences, des lettres et de beaux arts de Belgique. Edited by Ch. de Visscher and F. VanIangenhove (Bruxelles, 1964–1966).

Documents diplomatiques français 1932–1939. Ministère des Affaires Etrangères, Commission de publication des documents relatifs aux origines de la guerre 1939–1945 (Paris, 1963–). Série I (1932–36), II (1936–39).

Documents on British Foreign Policy 1919–1939. Foreign Office. Edited by E. L. Woodward and R. Butler (London, 1946–). Series Ia (1925–29), II (1930–37).

Dodd, William E. Jr. and Martha, eds., *Ambassador Dodd's Diary 1933–38* (New York, 1941).

Dokumenty a materiály k dějinám československo-sovětských vztahů. Akademie Věd SSSR, Československá Akademie Věd (Praha, 1975–).

Dokumenty i materiały do historii stosunków polsko-radzieckich. Polska Akademia Nauk, Akademia Nauk ZSRR (Warszawa, 1962–).

Dokumenty vneshnei politiki SSSR. Ministerstvo inostrannykh del SSSR (Moskva, 1957–   ).

Les Evénements survenus en France de 1933 à 1945. Temoignages et documents, recueillis par la Commission d'enquête parlementaire, Assemblée Nationale, 1946 (Paris, 1951).

Flandin, Pierre-Etienne, *Discours. Le ministère Flandin: Nov. 1934–mai 1935* (Paris, 1937).

Foreign Relations of the United States (Washington, D.C., 1861–   ).

Hanak, Harry, ed., "The Visit of the Czechoslovak Foreign Minister Dr. Edvard Beneš to Moscow in 1935 as seen by the British Minister in Prague, Sir Joseph Addison," *Slavonic and East European Review*, 54 (1976), 586–92.

Hodža, Milan, *Články, reči, štúdie*, 7 vols. (Praha, 1930–34).

Jędrzejewicz, Wacław, ed., *Diplomat in Berlin 1933–1939: Papers and Memoirs of Józef Lipski, Ambassador of Poland* (New York, 1968).

Jędrzejewicz, Wacław, ed., "Rozmowa Marszałka Piłsudskiego ze Stresemannem w Genewie w 1927 roku," *Niepodległość*, 10 (1976), 139–44.

Journal Officiel de la République Française. Débats parlementaires; Chambre des deputés/ Sénat (Paris, 1918–   )

Krofta, Kamil, *Zahraniční politika československá a její kořeny* (Praha, 1937).

Łaptos, Józef, ed., "Dwa listy marszałka Focha w sprawie polsko-francuskiego układu wojskowego z 1921 r.," *Studia Historyczne*, 18 (1975), 381–87.

League of Nations, Official Journal (Genève, 1920–)

———, Treaty Series (Genève, 1920–)

Łopatniuk, Stanisław, ed., "Nieznane dokumenty archiwalne z historii polsko-radzieckich rokowań o pakt o nieagresji," *Z Dziejów Stosunków Polsko-Radzieckich*, 5 (1969), 177–200.

———, "Przed Lokarnem: archiwalne dokumenty z historii stosunków polsko-radzieckich w okresie Lokarno," *Z Dziejów Stosunków Polsko-Radzieckich*, 6 (1970), 247–63.

Loucheur, Louis, *Carnets secrets 1908–1932.* Edited by Jacques de Launay (Bruxelles, 1962).

Masarykův Sborník, 6 vols. (Praha, 1925–30).

Nixon, Edgar M., ed., *Franklin D. Roosevelt and Foreign Affairs 1933–1937*, 3 vols. (Cambridge, Mass., 1969).

Othálová, Libuše, and Milada Červinková, eds., *Dokumenty z historie československé politiky 1939–1943* (Praha, 1966).

Piłsudski, Józef, *Pisma zbiorowe*, 10 vols. (Warszawa, 1937–38).

Rataj, Maciej, *Pamiętniki 1918–1927* (Warszawa, 1965).

Skrzyński, Aleksander, *Dwie mowy* (Warszawa, 1927).

Sprawozdania stenograficzne sejmu / senatu RP (Warszawa, 1922–39).

Stresemann, Gustav, *Vermächtniss*, 3 vols. Edited by Henry Bernhard (Berlin, 1932).

Těsnopisecké zprávy o schůzích poslanecké sněmovny/senátu Národního shromáždění Republiky Československé (Praha, 1920–38)

Turner, Henry A., ed., "Eine Rede Stresemanns über seine Lokarnopolitik: Dokumentation," *Vierteljahrshefte für Zeitgeschichte*, 15 (1967), 412–15.

Wandycz, Piotr S., ed. "L'Alliance franco-tchécoslovaque de 1924: un échange de lettres Poincaré-Bénès," *Revue d'Histoire Diplomatique*, 3–4 (1984), 328–33.

——, "Jeszcze o misji Jerzego Potockiego w 1933 r.," *Zeszyty Historyczne*, 18 (1970), 81–83.

——, "Listy Piłsudskiego do Masaryka i Focha," *Niepodległość*, 15 (1982), 108–12.

——, "Louis Barthou o swej wizycie w Polsce w kwietniu 1934 r.," *Niepodległość*, 18 (1984) 107–21.

——, "Ocena traktatów sojuszniczych polsko-francuskich [pro-memoria]," *Niepodległość*, 16 (1983), 61–74.

——, "Rozmowa Marszałka Piłsudskiego z Marszałkiem Franchet d'Esperey 17 listopada 1927 r.," *Niepodległość*, 15 (1982), 130–36.

——, "Trzy dokumenty: przyczynek do zagadnienia wojny prewencyjnej," *Zeszyty Historyczne*, 3 (1963), 7–14.

——, "Wypowiedzi Marszałka Piłsudskiego na konferenceji b. premierów 7 marca 1934 r.," *Niepodległość*, 9 (1974), 345–50.

Zaleski, August, *Przemowy i deklaracje 1926–1931*, 2 vols. (Warszawa, 1929–31).

Memoirs, Reminiscences, Contemporary Accounts

Avon, Anthony Eden, Earl of, *Facing the Dictators 1923–1938* (Boston, 1962).

Baranowski, Władysław, *Rozmowy z Piłsudskim 1916–1931* (Warszawa, 1938).

Barbier, Jean-Baptiste, *Un Frac de Nessus* (Rome, 1951).

Beck, Joseph, *Dernier rapport: politique polonaise 1926–1939* (Neuchatel, 1951).

Beneš, Edvard, *Paměti: od Mnichova k nové válce a k novému vítězství* (Praha, 1947).

——, *Memoirs of Dr. Beneš: From Munich to New War and New Victory* (London, 1954).

Bérard, Armand, *Un Ambassadeur se souvient: au temps du danger allemand* (Paris, 1976).

Berezowski, Zygmunt, *Polityka zagraniczna: wskazania programowe O.W.P.* (Warszawa, 1927).

Bláha, Silvestr, *Branná politika a demokracie* (Praha, 1936).

Bonnet, Georges, *Le Quai d'Orsay sous trois républiques* (Paris, 1961).

Bregman, Aleksander "Opinja polska a sprawy zagraniczne: uwagi o nie-mocarstwowości myślenia," *Przegląd Współczesny*, 36 (1931), 398–420.

Brinon, Fernand de, *Mémoires* (Paris, 1949).

Churchill, Winston S., *The Gathering Storm* (Boston, 1948)

Difreville, Jacques, ed., "De Lattre chez Weygand," *Revue des Deux Mondes*, (June 1970) 558–78, (July 1970) 70–92.

Fiala, Václav, *Soudobé Polsko* (Praha, 1936).

Flandin, Pierre-Etienne, *Politique française 1914–1940* (Paris, 1947).

Franchet d'Esperey, Louis, "Souvenirs de mon voyage en Pologne en 1927: Pilsudski intime," *La Pologne Littéraire*, 15 juillet 1935.

François-Poncet, André, *De Versailles à Potsdam* (Paris, 1948).

———, *Souvenirs d'une ambassade à Berlin* (Paris, 1946).

Gamelin, Général Maurice, *Servir*, 3 vols. (Paris 1946–47).

Gaulle, Charles de, *Mémoires de guerre*, 3 vols. (Paris, 1954–59)

Gawroński, Jan, *Moja misja we Wiedniu 1932–1938* (Warszawa, 1965).

Gelfand, L. E., ed., *A Diplomat looks Back: Louis Einstein* (New Haven, 1968).

Günther, Władysław, *Pióropusz i szpada: wspomnienia ze służby zagranicznej* (Paryż, 1963).

Heidrich, Arnošt, *International Political Causes of the Czechoslovak Tragedies of 1938 and 1948* (photo offset, Washington, D.C., 1962).

Herriot, Edouard, *Jadis: d'une guerre à l'autre 1914–1936*, 2 vols. (Paris, 1952).

Hilger, Gustav, *Wir und der Kreml: Errinerungen eines deutschen Diplomaten* (Frankfurt, 1964).

Hodža, Milan, *Le Problème agricole en Europe Centrale* (Prague, 1935).

———, *Federation in Central Europe: Reflections and Reminiscences* (London, 1942).

Jackowski, Tadeusz Gustaw, *W Walce o polskość* (Kraków, 1972).

Kahánek, Ferdinand, *Beneš contra Beck: reportáže a dokumenty* (Praha, 1938).

Krofta, Kamil, "E. Beneš a československá zahraniční politika 1924–1933" in Edvard Beneš, *Boj o mír a bezpečnost státu* (Praha, 1934), 3–324.

———, "Le Président Masaryk et la politique étrangère de la Tchécoslovaquie," *L'Europe Centrale*, 11 mars 1933.

———, *Československo v mezinárodní politice* (Praha, 1934).

———, *O Zahraniční službě; vznik, cíle a význam Malé dohody* (Praha, 1933).

———, *Z Dob naší první republiky* (Praha, 1939).

Kutrzeba, Tadeusz, "Wpływ układów w Locarno na warunki obrony Polski," *Przegląd Współczesny*, 16 (Jan. 1926), 118–26.

Laroche, Jules, *Au Quai d'Orsay avec Briand et Poincaré 1913–1926* (Paris, 1957).

———, *La Pologne de Pilsudski: souvenirs d'une ambassade* (Paris, 1953).

Łowczowski, Gustaw, "Jeszcze o stosunkach polsko-francuskich przed drugą wojną światową," *Wojskowy Przegląd Historyczny*, 10, 4 (1965), 437–38.

———, "List do redakcji," *Bellona*, 42, 4 (1960), 310–11.

———, "Przymierze polsko-francuskie widziane z attachatu paryskiego," *Bellona*, 33, 1, 2 (1951), 44–54.

Mareček, K. *Šťastnější Evropa v Hodžove plånu* (Praha, 1937).

Miedziński, Bogusław, "Droga do Moskwy," *Kultura*, 6/188 (1963), 74–84. English version in Leopold Tyrmand, ed., *Kultura Essays* (New York, 1970), 76–101.

———, "Pakty wilanowskie," *Kultura*, 7/189–8/190(1963), 113–32.

Monnet, Jean, *Memoirs* (London, 1978).

Montfort, Henri de, and André de Piasecki, *La France et la Pologne après Locarno* (Paris, 1926).

Moreau, Emile, *Souvenirs d'un gouverneur de la Banque de France: histoire de la stabilisation du franc 1926–1928* (Paris, 1954).

Mühlstein, Anatold, "Świadectwo amb. Laroche'a," *Kultura*, 6/68 (1953), 127–32.

Niedziałkowski, Mieczysław, *Położenie międzynarodowe Polski i polityka socjalizmu polskiego* (Warszawa, 1925).

Noël, Léon, *L'Agression allemande contre la Pologne: une ambassade à Varsovie 1935–1939* (Paris, 1946).

———, *La Guerre de 39 a commencé 4 ans plus tôt* (Paris, 1979).

———, *Les Illusions de Stresa: l'Italie abandonnée à Hitler* (Paris, 1975).

———, *Polonia Restituta: la Pologne entre deux mondes* (Paris, 1984).

———, *La Tchécoslovaquie d'avant Munich* (Paris, 1982).

Paul-Boncour, Joseph, "Le Coup de force de la Rhénanie (mars 1936)," *Revue de Paris*, 5 (1946), 23–33.

———, *Entre deux guerres: souvenirs sur la Troisième République*, 3 vols. (Paris, 1945–46).

Poincaré, Raymond, *Au Service de la France*, 11 vols. (Paris, 1926–74).

Raczyński, Count Edward, *In Allied London* (London, 1962).

———, *Od Narcyza Kulikowskiego do Winstona Churchilla* (London, 1976).

Reynaud, Paul, *Au Coeur de la mêlée 1930–1945* (Paris, 1951). English version *In the Thick of the Fight* (London, 1955).

———, *Mémoires*, 2 vols. (Paris, 1960–63).

Ripka, Hubert, "Le Fondateur de la Tchécoslovaquie; pionnier de la nouvelle Europe," *Le Monde Slave*, (Jan. 1936), 1–47.

———, *Munich: Before and After* (London, 1939).

Rydz-Śmigły, Edward, "Czy Polska mogła uniknąć wojny?" *Zeszyty Historyczne*, 2 (1962), 125–40.

Schimitzek, Stanisław, *Drogi i bezdroża minionej epoki: wspomnienia z lat pracy w MSZ 1920–1929* (Warszawa, 1976).

Schmidt, Paul, *Statist auf diplomatischer Bühne* (Bonn, 1949).

Seydoux, François, *Mémoires d'outre-Rhin* (Paris, 1975).

Sforza, Count Carlo, *The Totalitarian War and After* (Chicago, 1941).

Sikorski, Władysław, "Ferdynand Foch," *Przegląd Współczesny*, 29 (May 1929), 177–90.

———, *Polska i Francja* (Lwów, 1931).

Sokolnicki, Michał, "Polacy wobec zagadnień międzynarodowych," *Sprawy Obce*, 3 (1930), 483–94.

Starzeński, Paweł, *Trzy lata z Beckiem* (London, 1972).

Studnicki, Władysław, *Ludzie, idee i czyny* (Warszawa, 1937).

Templewood, Samuel Hoare, Viscount, *Nine Troubled Years* (London, 1954).

Vansittart, Robert, Lord, *Lessons of My Life* (New York, 1943).

———, *The Mist Procession* (London, 1958).

Weygand, Maxime, *Mémoires*, 3 vols. (Paris, 1950–57).

Witos, Wincenty, *Moja tułaczka* (Warszawa, 1967).

Wysocki, Alfted, *Tajemnice dyplomatycznego sejfu* (Warszawa, 1974).

Zabiełło, Stanisław, *W Kręgu historii* (Warszawa, 1970).

Zaufall, Jan, "Misja Ludwika Hieronima Morstina," *Niepodległość*, 8 (1972), 161–66.

Zay, Jean, *Souvenirs et solitude* (Paris, 1945).

Secondary Works

Ádám, Magda, "Confédération danubienne ou Petite Entente," *Acta Historica*, 25 (1979), 61–113.

———, "Les pays danubiens et Hitler: 1933–1936," *Revue d'Histoire de la Deuxième Guerre Mondiale*, 25, 98 (1975), 2–26.

Adamthwaite, Anthony P., *France and the Coming of the Second World War 1936–1939* (London, 1977).

Artaud, Denise, "Les Dettes de guerre de la France 1919–1929," in Maurice Lévy-Leboyer, ed., *La Position internationale de la France: aspects économiques et financiers XIX–XXe siècles* (Paris, 1977), 313–18.

Auffray, Bernard, *Pierre de Margerie et la vie diplomatique de son temps* (Paris, 1976).

Balcerak, Wiesław, "K Československo-polským vztahům w letech 1921–1927," *Slovanský Přehled*, 54 (1968), 448–55.

———, *Polityka zagraniczna Polski w dobie Locarna* (Wrocław, 1967).

———, "Sprawa polsko-czechosłowackiego sojuszu wojskowego w latach 1921–1927" *Studia z Dziejów ZSRR i Europy środkowej*, 3 (1967), 207–26.

———, "Wizyty Min. Barthou w Bukareszcie i Belgradzie w prasie europejskiej: czerwiec 1934 r," *Studia z Dziejów ZSRR i Europy środkowej*, 8 (1972), 127–40.

Bankwitz, Philip, *Maxime Weygand and Civil–Military Relations in Modern France* (Cambridge, Mass., 1966).

Bariéty, Jacques, "L'Appareil de presse de Joseph Caillaux et l'argent allemand," *Revue Historique*, 247 (Apr.–June 1972), 375–406.

———, "Finances et relations internationales: à propos du 'plan de Thoiry'; septembre 1926," *Relations Internationales*, 21 (1980), 51–70.

———, *Les Relations franco-allemandes après la première guerre mondiale* (Paris, 1977).

———, "Der Tardieu-Plan zur Sanierung des Donauraums (February-Mai 1932)," in Josef Becker and Klaus Hildebrand, eds., *Internationale Beziehungen in der Weltwirtschaftskrise 1929–33* (München, 1980), 361–87.

———, "Der Versuch einer europäischen Befriedung: Von Locarno bis Thoiry," in Helmuth Rössler, ed., *Locarno und die Weltpolitik 1924–1932* (Göttingen, 1969), 32–44.

———, and Charles Bloch, "Une Tentative de réconciliation franco-allemande et son échec 1932–33," *Revue d'Histoire Moderne et Contemporaine*, 15 (1968), 433–65.

Bartlová, Alena, "Przyczynek do historii stosunków słowacko-polskich w okresie międzywojennym," *Studia z Dziejów ZSRR i Europy Środkowej*, 9 (1973), 181–98.

Batowski, Henryk, *Austria i Sudety 1919–1938* (Poznań, 1968).

———, "Sojusze wojskowe Czechosłowacji 1918–1938," *Przegląd Zachodni*, 12, 2 (1961) 289–306.

———, "Z pol'sko-slovenských vztáhov v období rokov 1931–1939," *Historické Štúdie* 15 (1970), 227–43.

Baumont, Maurice, *The Origins of the Second World War* (New Haven, 1978).

Beaud, Claude, "The Interests of the Union Européenne in Central Europe," in Alice Teichova and P. J. Cottrell, eds., *International Business and Central Europe 1918–1939* (New York, 1983), 375–97.

Bennett, Edward W., *German Rearmament and the West 1932–1933* (Princeton, 1979).

Bennett, Edward W., *Germany and the Diplomacy of the Financial Crisis 1931* (Cambridge, Mass., 1962).

Binion, Rudolph, *Defeated Leaders: The Political Fate of Caillaux, Jouvenel and Tardieu* (New York, 1960).

Bloch, Charles, "Great Britain, German Rearmament and the Naval Agreement of 1935," in Hans W. Gatzke, ed., *European Diplomacy between Two Wars 1919–1939* (Chicago, 1972), 125–51.

———, "La Place de la France dans les différents stades de la politique extérieure du Troisième Reich," in *Les Relations franco-allemandes 1933–1939* (Colloques internationaux du Centre National de la Recherche Scientifique, no. 563; Paris, 1976), 15–32.

Bonnefous, Georges, *Histoire politique de la Troisième République*, 7 vols. (Paris, 1956–67).

Borejsza, Jerzy W., *Mussolini był pierwszy . . .* (Warszawa, 1979).

Borisov, Iu. V., *Sovetsko-francuskie otnosheniia 1924–1945* (Moscow, 1964).

Borkowski, Jan, "Stronnictwo ludowe wobec polityki zagranicznej 1931–1939," *Roczniki Dziejów Ruchu Ludowego*, 8 (1966), 144–83.

Bosl, Karl, et al., eds., *Die "Burg,"* 2 vols. (München, 1974).

———, *Gleichgewicht–Revision–Restauration: die Aussenpolitik der Ersten Tschechoslowakischen Republik im Europasystem der Pariser Vororteverträge* (München, 1976).

Bourgin, Georges, Jean Carrère, and André Guérin, *Manuel des partis politiques en France* (Paris, 1928).

Bournazel, Renata, *Rapallo: naissance d'un mythe* (Paris, 1974).

Břach, Radko, "Francouzský alianční system a Československo na počátku roku 1924," *Historie a Vojenství*, 1 (1968), 1–21.

———, "Locarno a ČS diplomacie," *Československý Časopis Historický* 8 (1960) 662–95.

Břachová, Věra, "Francouzská vojenská mise v Československu," *Historie a Vojenství* 6 (1967), 883–910.

Bréal, Auguste, *Philippe Berthelot* (Paris, 1937).

Bruegel, J. W., *Czechoslovakia before Munich: The German Minority Problem and British Appeasement Policy* (Cambridge, 1973). German version, J. W. Brügel, *Tschechen und Deutsche 1918–1938* (München, 1967).

Budurowycz, Bohdan B., *Polish-Soviet Relations 1932–1939* (New York, 1963).

Bułhak, Henryk, "La Pologne et les relations franco-allemandes 1925–1932," *Acta Poloniae Historica*, 45 (1982), 141–58.

———, "Polska a Rumunia 1918–1939," in Janusz Żarnowski, ed., *Przyjaźnie i antagonizmy: stosunki Polski z państwami sąsiednimi w latach 1918–1939* (Wrocław, 1977) 305–44.

Bułhak, Henryk, "Polska deklaracja sojusznicza wobec Francji w czasie remilitaryzacji Nadrenii, marzec 1936 r.," *Wojskowy Przegląd Historyczny*, 19, 4 (1974), 272–90.

———, "Polsko-francuskie koncepcje wojny obronnej z Niemcami z lat 1921–1926," *Studia z Dziejów ZSRR i Europy Środkowej*, 15 (1979), 69–96.

———, "W Sprawie oceny strategicznego zagrożenia Polski z maja 1934 r.," *Wojskowy Przegląd Historyczny*, 15, 4 (1970), 370–72.

———, "Z Dziejów stosunków wojskowych polsko-czechosłowackich w latach 1921–1927," *Studia z Dziejów ZSRR i Europy Środkowej*, 5 (1969), 115–45.

———, "Z Dziejów stosunków wojskowych polsko-czechosłowackich w latach 1927–1936," *Studia z Dziejów ZSRR i Europy Środkowej*, 11 (1975), 97–146.

Bussière, Eric [with commentary by François Crouzet], "The Interest of the Banque de l'Union parisienne in Czechoslovakia, Hungary and the Balkans, 1919–30," in Alice Teichova and P. J. Cottrell, eds., *International Business and Central Europe 1918–1939* (New York, 1983), 399–413.

Bystrický, Valerian, "Pokus o politické a hospodárske upevnenie Malej dohody, 1933," *Slovanské Štúdie*, 18 (1977), 163–66.

———, and Ladislav Deák, *Európa na prelome: diplomatické a politické vzt'ahy v rokoch 1932–1933* (Bratislava, 1974).

Cairns, John C., "March 7, 1936, Again: The View from Paris," in Hans W. Gatzke, ed., *European Diplomacy between the Wars 1919–1939* (Chicago, 1972), 172–92.

Cameron, Elizabeth R., "Alexis Saint-Léger Léger," in Gordon A. Craig and Felix Gilbert, eds., *The Diplomats 1919–1939* (Princeton, 1953), 378–405.

Campbell, F. Gregory, "The Castle, Jaroslav Preiss, and the Živnostenská Bank," *Bohemia*, 15 (1974), 231–55.

———, *Confrontation in Central Europe: Weimar Germany and Czechoslovakia* (Chicago, 1975).

Campus, Eliza. *Mica Inţelegere* (Bucureşti, 1968).

Carmi, Ozer, *La Grande Bretagne et la Petite Entente* (Genève, 1972).

Cassels, Alan, *Mussolini's Early Diplomacy* (Princeton, 1970).

Castellan, Georges, "Le Réarmement clandestin de l'Allemagne dans l'entre-deux guerrres," in *Les Relations franco-allemandes 1933–1939* (Colloques internationaux du C.R.N.S. no. 563; Paris, 1976), 277–96.

———, *Le Réarmement clandestin du Reich 1930–35 vu par le 2e bureau de l'état major français* (Paris, 1954).

Castex, H., "Aristide Briand et la franc-maçonnerie," *Information Historique*, 36 (Jan.–Feb. 1974), 36–38.

Černý, Bohumíl, "Wirtschaftliche Voraussetzungen der tschechoslowak-ischen Politik zwischen den Weltkriegen: Beitrag zur Wirtschaftspolitik der Agrarpartei," *Historica*, 11 (1965), 177–215.

César, Jaroslav, and Bohumil Černý, *Politika německých buržoazních stran v Československu v letech 1918–1939*, 2 vols. (Praha, 1962).

Češi a Poláci v minulosti, 2 vols. (Československá Akademie Věd; Praha, 1964–1967). [Interwar parts authored by Jaroslav Valenta.]

Challener, Richard D., "The French Foreign Office: The Era of Philippe Berthelot," in Gordon A. Craig and Felix Gilbert, eds., *The Diplomats 1919–1939* (Princeton, 1953), 49–85.

Chastenet, Jean, *Histoire de la Troisième République*, 7 vols. (Paris, 1952–63).

Ciałowicz, Jan, *Polsko-francuski sojusz wojskowy 1921–1939* (Warszawa, 1970).

Cienciala, Anna M. "Nastawienie Austena Chamberlaina do Polski w latach 1924-1933" in Antoni Czubiński, ed., *Polska, Niemcy, Europa, studia z dziejów myśli politycznej i stosunków międzynarodowych* (Poznań, 1977), 482–94.

———, "The Significance of the Declaration of Non-Aggression of January 26, 1934 in Polish-German and International Relations," *East European Quarterly*, 1 (1967), 1–30.

Cienciala, Anna M., and Titus Komarnicki, *From Versailles to Locarno: Keys to Polish Foreign Policy 1919–1925* (Lawrence, Kan., 1984).

Čuláková, "Pakt Čtyř," Diplomove prace, Univ. Karlový, Praha, 1967.

Deák, Ladislav, "Die Kleine Entente und die kollektive Sicherheit in den Jahren 1933–1936," *Studia Historica Slovaca*, 10 (1978), 113–52.

———, "Siedmy marec 1936 a Malá dohoda," *Československý Časopis Historický*, 17 (1969), 323–49.

Defrasne, Colonel Jean, "L'Événement du 7 mars 1936: la réalité et la portée de l'opération allemande; la réaction de la France dans le cadre des ses alliances," in *Les Relations Franco-Allemandes 1933–1939* (Colloques internationaux du C.R. N.S. no. 563; Paris, 1976), 247–76.

Dell, Robert, *The Geneva Racket* (London, 1941).

Deutscher, Isaac, *Stalin: A Political Biography* (New York, 1949).

D'Hoop, Jean Marie, "Frankreichs Reaktion auf Hitlers Aussenpolitik 1933–39," *Geschichte in Wissenschaft und Unterricht*, 15, 4 (1964), 211–23.

———, "La Politique française de réarmement 1933–39," *Revue d'Histoire de la Deuxième Guerre Mondiale*, 4, 14 (1954), 1–26.

Dobrý, Anatol, *Hospodářská krize československého průmyslu ve vztahu k Mnichovu* (Praha, 1959).

Duroselle, Jean-Baptiste, *La Décadence 1932–1939* (Paris, 1979).

Duroselle, Jean-Baptiste, "Louis Barthou et la rapprochement franco-soviétique en 1934," *Cahiers du Monde Russe et Soviétique*, 3, 4 (1962), 526–45.

———, "The Spirit of Locarno: Illusions of Pactomania," *Foreign Affairs*, 50 (1972), 752–64.

Dutailly, Henry, *Problèmes de l'armée de terre française 1935–1939* (Paris, 1980)

———, "Programmes d'armement et structure modernes dans l'armée de terre 1935–1939," in Klaus Hildebrand and Kurt F. Werner, eds., *Deutschland und Frankreich 1936–1939* (München, 1981).

"Dyskusja o wielkim kryzysie 1929–1935," *Dzieje Najnowsze*, 7, 2 (1975), 1–72.

Emmerson, James T., *The Rhineland Crisis* (London, 1977).

Fabry, Philipp, W., *Die Sowjetunion und das Dritte Reich* (Stuttgart, 1971).

Faltus, Józef, "Rozwój gospodarczy Słowacji w burżuazyjnej Czechosłowacji 1918–1938," *Studia z Dziejów ZSRR i Europy Środkowej*, 6 (1970), 51–86.

Faryś, Janusz, *Koncepcje polskiej polityki zagranicznej 1918–1939* (Warszawa, 1981).

Feller, J., *Le Dossier de l'armée française: la guerre de 'cinquante ans' 1914–1962* (Paris, 1966).

Fink, Carole, "Germany and the Polish Elections of November 1930: A Study in the League Diplomacy," *East European Quarterly*, 15 (1981), 181–207.

Frankenstein, R., "A Propos des aspects financiers du réarmement français 1935–1939," *Revue d'Histoire de la Deuxième Guerre Mondiale*, 26, 102 (1976), 1–20.

Gajan, Koloman, "Die ČSR und die deutsche Frage 1918–1925," *Die Entstehung der Tschechoslowakischen Republic und ihre international-politische Stellung* (Acta Universitatis Carolinae, Philosophica et Historica 2–3, Praha, 1968), 183–207.

———, "Die Rolle der Tschechoslowakei in Mitteleuropa 1918-1945," *Oesterreichische Osthefte*, 8 (1966), 183–91.

Gajanová, Alena, *ČSR a středoevropská politika velmocí 1918–1938* (Praha, 1967).

———, *Dvojí tvář* (Praha, 1962).

———, "Entstehung und Entwicklung der internationalen Beziehungen der ČSR," *Die Entstehung der Tschechoslowakischen Republik und ihre international-politische Stellung* (Acta Universitats Carolinae. Philosophica et Historica 2–3; Praha, 1968), 135–61.

———, "Ke Vzniku a úkolům československé zahraniční politiky a k metodam a charakteru československé diplomacie," *Mezinárodní Vztahy*, 4, 1 (1969), 43–54.

Garlicki, Andrzej, *Od Brześcia do maja* (Warszawa, 1986).

———, *Przewrót majowy* (Warszawa, 1978).

Gasiorowski, Z. J., "Did Pilsudski Attempt to Initiate a Preventive War in 1933?" *Journal of Modern History*, 27, 2 (1955), 135–53.

———, "The German-Polish Nonaggression Pact," *Journal of Central European Affairs*, 15 (1955), 4–29.

———, "Polish-Czechoslovak Relations 1922–1926," *Slavonic and East European Review*, 35, 85 (1957), 473–504.

———, "Stresemann and Poland after Locarno," *Journal of Central European Affairs*, 18 (1958), 292–317.

Gauché, Général, *Le 2ᵉ Bureau au travail 1935–1940* (Paris, 1953).

Gehl, Jürgen, *Austria, Germany, and the Anschluss 1931–38* (London, 1963).

Girardet, Raoul, "Litvinov et ses énigmes," in J. B. Duroselle, ed., *Les relations germano-soviétiques de 1933 à 1939* (Paris, 1954).

Girault, René, "Crise économique et protectionisme hier et ajourd'hui," *Relations Internationales*, 16 (1978), 365–82.

———, "L'Europe centrale et orientale dans la stratégie des hommes d'affaires et des diplomates français," in *Les Relations financières internationales, facteurs de solidarités ou de rivalités* (Centre d'Etudes Européennes; Bruxelles, 1979).

———, "Korreferat zu Jacques Bariéty," in Josef Becker and Klaus Hildebrand, eds., *Internationale Beziehungen in der Weltwirtschaftskrise 1929–33* (München, 1980), 389–92.

———, "Les Relations franco-soviétiques devant la crise économique de 1929," *Revue d'Histoire Moderne et Contemporaine*, 27 (1980), 237–57.

Giurescu, Dinu C., "La Diplomatie roumaine et le pacte des quatre 1933," *Revue Roumaine d'Histoire*, 8 (1969), 77–102.

Goguel-Nyegard, François, *La Politique des partis sous la IIIe République* (Paris, 1968).

Gorodetsky, Gabriel, *The Precarious Truce: Anglo-Soviet Relations 1924–27* (London, 1977).

Gregorowicz, Stanisław, *Polsko-radzieckie stosunki polityczne w latach 1932–1935* (Wrocław, 1982).

Gromada, Thaddeus V., "Piłsudski and the Slovak Autonomists," *Slavic Review*, 28 (1969), 445–62.

———, "Polish-Slovak Relations between the Wars 1918–1939," in Joseph M. Kirschbaum, ed., *Slovakia in the 19th and 20th centuries* (Toronto, 1973), 243–64.

Grosfeld, Leon, "Polska wobec sprawy ewakuacji Nadrenii 1926–1929," *Dzieje Najnowsze*, 7, 1 (1975), 187–98.

La Guerre polono-soviétique de 1919–1920 (Collection historique de l'Institut d'Études Slaves 22, Colloque; Paris, 1975).

Gwido (Wacław Lipiński), *Polityka zagraniczna Piłsudskiego i Becka* (Warszawa, 1943).

Hartmann, Peter C., "Ein Aspekt der französisch-tschechoslowakischen Beziehungen von 1919 bis 1938; der Vertrag von 1924," in Karl Bosl, ed., *Gleichgewicht–Revision–Restauration* (München, 1976), 61–84.

Hass, Ludwik, "Wolnomularstwo w międzywojennej republice czechosłowackiej," *Studia z Dziejów ZSRR i Europy Środkowej*, 10 (1974), 25–74.

Helbich, Wolfgang J., "Between Stresemann and Hitler: The Foreign Policy of the Brüning Government," *World Politics*, 12 (1959), 24–44.

Hemmerling, Zygmunt, "Ludowcy wobec węzłowych problemów polityki zagranicznej II Rzeczypospolitej," *Ruch ludowy a sprawa niepodległości* (Zakład historii ruchu ludowego przy NK ZSL; Warszawa, 1969), 127–40.

Herman, Karel, and Zdeněk Sládek, *Slovanská politika Karla Kramáře* (Praha, 1971).

Hildebrand, Klaus, *The Foreign Policy of the Third Reich* (Berkeley, 1973).

Hitchcock, Edward B., *"I Built a Temple for Peace": the Life of Eduard Beneš* (New York, 1940).

Hoentsch, Jörg K., "Polen und die Tschechoslowakei—oder das Scheitern der slawischen Solidarität," in Karl Bosl, ed., *Gleichgewichts–Revision–Restauration* (München, 1976).

Höhne, Roland A., "Die Aussenpolitische Neuorientierung Frankreichs 1934–1936," in *Les Relations franco-allemandes 1933–1939* (Colloques internationaux du C.N.R.S. no. 563; Paris, 1976), 209–34.

Höltje, Christian, *Die Weimarer Republik und das Ostlocarno-Problem 1919–1934* (Würzburg, 1958).

Holzer, Jerzy, *Mozaika polityczna drugiej Rzeczypospolitej* (Warszawa, 1974).

Horejsek, Jaroslav, *Snahy československé buržoazie o hospodářskou expanzi do Polska v letech 1918–1929* (Praha, 1966).

Houštecký, Miroslav, "Plán rakousko-německé celní unie v roce 1931 a postoj Československa," *Československý Časopis Historický* 4 (1956), 27–51.

Hovi, Kalervo, *Alliance de Revers: Stabilization of France's Alliance Policies in East Central Europe 1919–1921* (Turku, 1984).

———, *Cordon sanitaire or barrière de l'est: the Emergence of the New French Eastern European Policy 1917–1919* (Turku, 1975).

Hughes, Judith M., *To the Maginot Line: the Politics of French Military Preparation in the 1920s* (Cambridge, Mass., 1971).

Iordache, Nicolae, *La Petite Entente et l'Europe* (Genève, 1977).

Iordan-Sima, Constantin, "La Roumanie et les relations franco-italiennes dans les années 1926–1927: une page d'histoire de la diplomatie roumaine," *Revue Roumaine d'Histoire*, 14 (1975), 327–40.

Jachymek, Jan, and Józef R. Szaflik, "Myśl polityczna ruchu ludowego wobec bezpieczeństwa granic państwowych w II Rzeczypospolitej," in *Polska myśl polityczna XIX i XX wieku: 4, Na warsztatach historyków polskiej myśli politycznej* (Wrocław, 1980), 223–54.

Jäckel, Eberhard, *Hitler's Weltanschauung: A Blueprint for Power* (Middletown, 1971).

Jacobsen, Hans-Adolf. *Nationalsozialistische Aussenpolitik 1933–1938* (Frankfurt, 1968).

Jacobson, Jon, *Locarno Diplomacy: Germany and the West 1925–1929* (Princeton, 1972).

———, and John T. Walker, "The Impulse for a Franco-German Entente: The Origins of the Thoiry Conference, 1926," *Journal of Contemporary History*, 10, 1 (1975), 157–81.

Jarausch, Konrad H., *The Four Power Pact 1933* (Madison, Wis., 1965).

Jeanneney, Jean-Noël, *François de Wendel en République: l'argent et le pouvoir* (Paris, 1976).

———, "Sur la vénalité du journalisme français entre les deux guerres," *Revue Française de Science Politique*, 25, 4 (1975), 717–38.

Jędruszczak, Hanna and Tadeusz, *Ostatnie lata Drugiej Rzeczypospolitej 1935–1939* (Warszawa, 1970).

Jędrzejewicz, Wacław, *Kronika życia Józefa Piłsudskiego 1867–1935*, 2 vols. (London, 1977).

———, *Piłsudski: A Life for Poland* (New York, 1982). Polish version, *Józef Piłsudski 1867–1935: życiorys* (London, 1982).

———, "The Polish Plan for 'a Preventive War' against Germany in 1933," *Polish Review*, 11, 1 (1966), 62–91.

Jíša, Václav, and Alois Vaněk, *Škodový závody 1918–1938* (Praha, 1962).

Johnson, Douglas, "The Locarno Treaties" in Neville Waites, ed., *Troubled Neighbors: Franco-British Relations in the Twentieth Century* (London, 1971), 100–24.

Jouvenel, Bertrand de, *D'Une guerre à l'autre*, 2 vols. (Paris, 1941).

Juhász, Gyula, *Hungarian Foreign Policy 1919–1945* (Budapest, 1979).

Jurkiewicz, Jarosław, *Pakt wschodni* (Warszawa, 1965).

Kaiser, David E., *Economic Diplomacy and the Origins of the Second World War: Germany, Britain, France and Eastern Europe 1930–1939* (Princeton, 1980).

Kalvoda, Josef, *Czechoslovakia's Role in Soviet Strategy* (Washington, 1978).

Káňa, O., and R. Pavelka, [Stefania Stanisławska], *Těšínsko v polsko-československých vztazích 1918–1939* (Ostrava, 1970).

Keeton, Edward D., "Briand's Locarno Policy: French Economics, Politics and Diplomacy 1925–1929," Ph.D. Dissertation, Yale University 1975.

Kemp, Tom, *The French Economy 1913–1939* (London, 1972).

Kennedy, Paul, *The Realities behind Diplomacy: Background Influences on British External Policy 1865–1980* (Glasgow, 1981).

Kindleberger, Charles, *The World in Depression 1929–1939* (Berkeley, 1973).

Kirkor, Stanisław, "Próby dozbrojenia Polski," *Zeszyty Historyczne*, 20 (1971), 34–42.

Kirkpatrick, Ivone, *Mussolini: A Study in Power* (New York, 1968).

Kiszling, Rudolf, *Die militärischen Vereinbarungen der Kleinen Entente 1929–1937* (München, 1959).

Knipping, Franz, "Frankreich in Hitlers Aussenpolitik 1933–1939," in Manfred Funke, ed., *Hitler, Deutschland und die Mächte* (Düsseldorf, 1976), 612–27.

Komarnicki, Tytus, *Piłsudski a polityka wielkich mocarstw zachodnich* (London, 1952).

Komjathy, Anthony T., *The Crises of France's East Central European Diplomacy 1933–1938* (Boulder, Colo., 1976).

Korczyk, Henryk, "Locarno i jego geneza," *Dzieje Najnowsze*, 11, 3 (1979), 85–112. .

———, "Polska dyplomacja wobec traktatu berlińskiego w świetle dokumentów," *Przegląd Historyczny*, 74 (1983), 301–30.

Korpalska, Walentyna, *Władysław Sikorski* (Wrocław, 1981).

Kostrba-Skalicky, Oswald, "Bewaffnete Ohnmacht: die tschechoslowakische Armee 1918–1938," in Karl Bosl, ed., *Die Erste Tschechoslowakische Repubik als nationaler Parteienstaat* (München, 1979).

Kovrig, Bennett, "Mediation by Obfuscation: The Resolution of the Marseille Crisis, October 1934 to May 1935," *Historical Journal*, 19 (1976), 191–221.

Kozeński, Jerzy, *Czechosłowacja w polskiej polityce zagranicznej w latach 1932–1938* (Poznań, 1964).

———, "Próby zbliżenia polsko-czechosłowackiego w latach 1926–31," *Przegląd Zachodni*, 20, 2 (1964), 310–27.

———, "Rokowania polsko-czechosłowackie na tle niebezpieczeństwa niemieckiego w latach 1932-1933," *Przegląd Zachodni*, 18, 2 (1962), 253–75.

Král, Václav, *Spojenectví československo-sovětské v evropské politice 1935–1939* (Praha, 1970).

Krasuski, Jerzy, *Stosunki polsko-niemieckie 1919–1932*, 2 vols. (Poznań, 1962–64).

Kremer Jan, "Polska wobec remilitaryzacji Nadrenii w 1936 r.," *Zeszyty Naukowe Uniwersytetu Jagiellońskiego*, 71: *Prace Historyczne*, 12 (1963), 135–63.

Krüger, Peter, *Die Aussenpolitik der Republik von Weimar* (Darmstadt, 1985).

———, "Beneš und die europäische Wirtschaftskonzeption des deutschen Staatssekretärs Carl v. Schubert," *Bohemia Jahrbuch*, 14 (1973), 320–39.

———, "Der deutsch-polnische Schiedsvertrag im Rahmen der deutschen Sicherheitsinitiative von 1925," *Historische Zeitschrift*, 230 (1980), 578–612.

———, "Das europäische Staatssystem und die deutsche Politik gegenüber der Tschechoslowakei in den 30er Jahren," in Karl Bosl, ed., *Gleichgewicht–Revision–Restauration* (München, 1976), 235–52.

———, "Friedenssicherung und deutsche Revisionspolitik: die deutsche Aussenpolitik und die Verhandlungen über den Kellogg Pakt," *Vierteljahrschefte für Zeitgeschichte*, 22 (1974), 227–57.

———, "La Politique extérieure allemande et les relations franco-polonaises 1918–1932," *Revue d'Histoire Diplomatique*, 2/3/4 (1981), 264–94.

Kühl, Joachim, *Die Föderationspläne in Donauraum und in Ostmittel-Europa* (München, 1958).

Kukiel, Marian, *Generał Sikorski* (London, 1970).

Kukułka, Józef, *Francja a Polska po traktacie wersalskim 1919–1922* (Warszawa, 1970).

Kunstadter, John, "Czechoslovak-Italian Relations 1915–1922: The Roots of Enmity," M.A. Dissertation, Yale University, 1978.

Kupferman, Fred, "Diplomatie parallèle et guerre psychologique: le rôle de la Ribbentrop Dienststelle dans les tentatives d'action sur l'opinion française, 1934–1939," *Relations Internationales*, 3 (1975), 79–95.

Kuźmiński, Tadeusz, *Polska, Francja, Niemcy 1933–1935: z dziejów sojuszu polsko-francuskiego* (Warszawa, 1963).

———, "Wobec zagadnienia wojny prewencyjnej w 1933 r.," *Najnowsze Dzieje Polski 1914–1939*, 3 (1960), 5–49, with Henryk Batowski's comments in *Najnowsze Dzieje Polski 1914–1939*, 5 (1962) 225–28.

Kvaček, Robert, "Boj o Rakousko 1933–1938 a československá zahraniční politika," *Sborník Historický*, 22, 12 (1964), 241–86.

———, "Hodžův plán," *Slovanský Přehled*, 6 (1967), 347–53.

———, "Jednání o východní pakt v letech 1934–1935," *Acta Universitatis Carolinae, Philosophica et Historica* 3 (1966), 5–47.

————, "K Francouzsko-sovětsko-československým vztahům po květnu 1935," in *Z Českých dějín: sborník prací in memoriam prof. dr. Václava Husy* (Praha, 1966), 269–87.

————, "Ke Genezi návrhu na jednotný pakt Malé dohody," in *Československo a Juhoslávia: z dejín československo-juhoslovanských vst'ahov.* Edited by Jozef Hrozienčik (Bratislava, 1968), 301–11.

————, *Nad Evropou zataženo: Československo a Evropa 1933–1937* (Praha, 1966).

————, "Německá likvidace demilitarizovaného porynského pasma," *Československý Časopis Historický*, 11 (1963), 306–30.

————, "Situation de la Tchécoslovaquie dans la politique internationale des années trente du xxe siècle," *Historica*, 11 (1965), 217–72.

————, and Václav Vinš, "K německo-československým sondážím ve třicátych letech," *Československý Časopis Historický*, 14 (1966), 880–96.

La Gorce, Paul-Marie de, *The French Army* (New York, 1963).

Landau, Zbigniew, "The Great Depression in Poland, 1929–1935, and its Consequences," *Studia Historiae Oeconomicae*, 8 (1973), 337–54.

————, *Plan stabilizacyjny 1927–1930, geneza, założenia, wyniki* (Warszawa, 1963).

————, *Polskie zagraniczne pożyczki państwowe 1918–1926* (Warszawa, 1961).

Landau, Zbigniew, and Jerzy Tomaszewski, *Anonimowi władcy: z dziejów kapitału obcego w Polsce 1918–1939* (Warszawa, 1968).

————, *Gospodarka Polski międzywojennej* (Warszawa, 1967–   )

————, *Kapitały obce w Polsce 1918–39, materiały i dokumenty* (Warszawa, 1964).

————, *Polska w Europie i świecie 1918–1939* (Warszawa, 1984)

————, *Sprawa żyrardowska: przyczynek do dziejów kapitałow obcych w Polsce międzywojennej* (Warszawa, 1983).

Lapter, Karol, *Pakt Piłsudski-Hitler* (Warszawa, 1962).

Łaptos, Józef, *Francuska opinia publiczna wobec spraw polskich w latach 1919–1925* (Wrocław, 1983).

Lauren, Paul G., *Diplomats and Bureaucrats: The First Institutional Responses to Twentieth-Century Diplomacy in France and Germany* (Stanford, 1976).

Leczyk, Marian, *Polityka III Rzeczypospolitej wobec ZSRR w latach 1925–1934* (Warszawa, 1976).

————, "Polityka zagraniczna rządów pomajowych w Polsce w świetle raportów posła czechosłowackiego w Warszawie," in Antoni Czubiński, ed., *Polska, Niemcy, Europa: studia z dziejów myśli politycznej i stosunków międzynarodowych* (Poznań, 1977).

Leffler, M. P., *The Elusive Question: The American Pursuit of European Stability and French Security 1918–1933* (Chapel Hill, N.C., 1979).

Le Goyet, Colonel Pierre, "Evolution de la doctrine d'emploi de l'aviation française entre 1919 et 1939," *Revue d'Histoire de la Deuxième Guerre Mondiale*, 19, 73 (1969), 3–41.

———, *Le Mystère Gamelin* (Paris, 1975).

Lewandowski, Krzysztof, *Sprawa ukraińska w polityce zagranicznej Czechosłowacji w latach 1918–1932* (Wrocław, 1974).

———, "Stosunki polsko-czechosłowackie w latach 1919–1939," in Janusz Żarnowski, ed., *Przyjaźnie i antagonizmy* (Wrocław, 1977), 217–61.

L'Huillier, Fernand, "Allemands et Français au temps de Locarno: accords, dialogues et malentendus, 1924–1929: un aperçu," *Revue d'Allemagne*, 4 (1972), 558–68. Polish version, "Francuzi i Niemcy w oczach Locarno: umowy, dialogi i nieporozumienia," *Dzieje Najnowsze*, 5, 2 (1973), 45–55.

———, *Dialogues franco-allemands 1925–1933* (Strasbourg, 1971).

Link, Werner, *Die amerikanische Stabilisierungspolitik in Deutschland 1921–1932* (Düsseldorf, 1970).

Łopatniuk, Stanisław, "Przed przewrotem majowym i po przewrocie: z historii stosunków polsko-radzieckich," *Studia z Dziejów ZSRR i Europy Środkowej*, 6 (1970), 147–78.

Łossowski, Piotr, "Stosunki polsko-niemieckie w latach 1933–39 a klęska wrześniowa," *Wojskowy Przegląd Historyczny*, 8 (1963), 132–62.

Łukasiewicz, Juliusz, *Polska w Europie w polityce Józefa Piłsudskiego* (London, 1944).

Lundgreen-Nielsen, Kay, *The Polish Problem at the Paris Peace Conference* (Odense, 1979).

Lungu, Dov B., "Nicolae Titulescu and the 1932 Crisis concerning the Soviet-Romanian Pact of Non-Aggression," *East European Quarterly*, 18 (1984), 185–213.

Mackenzie, Compton, *Dr. Beneš* (London, 1946).

Mackiewicz, Stanisław (Cat), *Colonel Beck and His Policy* (London, 1944).

———, *Polityka Becka* (Paris, 1964).

Maier, Charles S., *Recasting Bourgeois Europe: Stabilization in France, Germany and Italy in the Decade after World War I* (Princeton, 1975).

Marès, Antoine, "La Faillite des relations franco-tchécoslovaques: la mission militaire française à Prague," *Revue d'Histoire de la Deuxième Guerre Mondiale*, 28, 111 (1978), 45–71.

Maxelon, Michael O., *Stresemann und Frankreich: deutsche Politik der Ost-West-Balance* (Düsseldorf, 1972).

Mazur, Zbigniew, *Pakt czterech* (Poznań, 1979).

Mazurowa, Kazimiera, *Skazani na wojnę* (Warszawa, 1979).

Mencl, Vojtěch and Menclová, Jaromila, "Náčrt podstaty a vývoje vrcholné sféry předmnichovské československé mocensko-politické struktury," *Československý Časopis Historický*, 16 (1968), 341–63.

Micaud, C. A., *The French Right and Nazi Germany* (Durham, N.C., 1944).

Micewski, Andrzej, *W Cieniu Marszałka Piłsudskiego* (Warszawa, 1969).

Michel, Bernard, "La Formation du Ministère des Affaires Etrangères et le personnel diplomatique en Pologne de 1918 à 1939," in Ulrich Haustein, Georg W. Strobel, Gerhard Wagner, eds., *Ostmitteleuropa: Berichte und Forschungen, Festschrift für Gotthold Rhode zum 65 Geburtstag* (Stuttgart, 1981), 403–21.

———, "Millieux dirigeants et franc-maçonnerie en Europe centrale: l'example de la Tchécoslovaquie," *Bulletin de la Société d'Histoire Moderne*, no. 19, *supplément à la Revue d'Histoire Moderne et Contemporaine*, 110 (1977) 3–9.

Michowicz, Waldemar, *Genewska konferencja rozbrojeniowa 1932–1937 a dyplomacja polska* (Łódź, 1986).

———, "Realizacja przez ZSRR leninowskich koncepcji rozbrojenia a dyplomacja polska 1927–1934," *Z Dziejów Stosunków Polsko-Radzieckich*, 7 (1970), 107–38.

———, "Rozbrojeniowy plan Herberta Hoovera z 1932 r. a dyplomacja polska," *Historia i Współczesność*, 1 (1977), 175–86.

———, *Walka dyplomacji polskiej przeciw traktatowi mniejszościowemu w Lidze Narodów w roku 1934* (Łódź, 1963).

Mikhutina, I. V., *Sovetsko-polskie otnosheniia 1931–1935* (Moskva, 1977).

Minart, Jacques, *Le Drame du désarmement français 1918–1938* (Paris, 1959).

Namier, Lewis, *Europe in Decay* (Gloucester, 1966).

Neré, Jacques, *La Crise de 1929* (Paris, 1968).

———, *The Foreign Policy of France from 1914 to 1945* (London, 1975).

Novotný, K., "Několik poznatku ze cvičení a manevrů v československé armádé z let 1930–1938," *Historie a Vojenství*, 6–7 (1968), 1046–1077.

Nowak-Kiełbikowa, Maria, "Anthony Eden w Warszawie, 2–3 kwietnia 1935 r.," *Dzieje Najnowsze*, 15, 1 (1984), 81–96.

———, "Wizyta Augusta Zaleskiego w Londynie w grudniu 1931 r." *Dzieje Najnowsze*, 4, 1 (1974), 19–33.

O *Československé zahraniční politice: sborník stati* (Praha, 1956).

Olivová, Věra, "Československo-sovětská smlouva z roku 1935," *Československý Časopis Historický*, 13 (1965), 477–99.

———, *The Doomed Democracy: Czechoslovakia in a Disrupted Europe 1914–1938* (London, 1972).

Olivová, Věra, and Robert Kvaček, *Dějiny Československa od roku 1918 do roku 1945* (Praha, 1967).

Olšovský, R., *Světový obchod a Československo 1918–1939* (Praha, 1961).

——, et al., *Přehled hospodářského vývoje Československa v letech 1918–1945* (Praha, 1961).

Opočenský, Jan, ed., *Edward Beneš: Essays and Reflections presented on the Occasion of his Sixtieth Birthday* (London, 1945).

Orde, Anne, *Great Britain and International Security 1920–1926* (London, 1978).

Orlof, Ewa, *Dyplomacja polska wobec sprawy słowackiej w latach 1938–1939* (Kraków, 1980).

——, *Polska działalność polityczna, dyplomatyczna i kulturalna w Słowacji w latach 1919–1937* (Rzeszów, 1984).

Ormos, Maria, Sz., "A Propos de la sécurité est-européenne dans les années 1930," *Acta Historica*, 16 (1970), 307–21.

——, *Le Problème de la sécurité et l'Anschluss* (Studia Hungarica 124; Budapest, 1975).

——, "Sur les causes de l'échec du pacte danubien 1934–35," *Acta Historica*, 14 (1968), 21–81.

Ort, Aleksandr, "Dvacáté výročí československo-sovětské smlouvy o vzájemné pomoci 1935–1955," *Sovětská Věda: Historie*, 5, 3–4 (1955), 375–89.

Paczkowski, Andrzej, "Prasa w życiu politycznym Drugiej Rzeczypospolitej," *Dzieje Najnowsze*, 10, 3 (1978), 29–53.

Parker, R. A., "The First Capitulation. France and the Rhineland Crisis of 1936," *World Politics*, 8 (1955–56), 355–73.

Perman, Dagmar, *The Shaping of the Czechoslovak State: Diplomatic History of the Boundaries of Czechoslovakia 1914–1920* (Leiden, 1962).

Pertinax (Géraud, André), *The Gravediggers of France* (New York, 1944).

Pietrzak-Pawłowska, Irena, "Les Investissements français en Pologne," in Maurice Lévy-Leboyer, ed., *La Position internationale de la France: aspects économiques et financiers* (Paris, 1977), 319–24.

Planté, Louis, *Un Grand seigneur de la politique: Anatole de Monzie* (Paris, 1954).

Pobóg-Malinowski, Władysław, *Najnowsza historia polityczna Polski 1864–1945*, 3 vols. (London, 1963–81).

Polonsky, Antony, *Politics in Independent Poland 1921–1929: The Crisis of Constitutional Government* (Oxford, 1972).

Polskie siły zbrojne w drugiej wojnie światowej, 3 vols. (London, 1951–75).

Ponty, Janine, "L'Attitude des milieux politiques français envers la Pologne à l'époque de Locarno," *Relations Internationales*, 4 (1975), 81–90.

Post, Gaines, Jr., *The Civil-Military Fabric of Weimar Foreign Policy* (Princeton, 1973).

Prasolov, Sergej I., "Československo-sovětská smlouva o vzájemné pomoci z roku 1935," *Studie z dějin československo-sovetských vztahů 1917–1938* (Praha, 1967), 79–126.

Přehled dějin československo-sovetských vztahů v údobí 1917–1939 (Praha, 1974).

Preissig, Erhard, *Die französische Kulturpropaganda in der ehemaligen Tschechoslowakei 1918–1939* (Stuttgart, 1943).

Pryor, Zora P., "Czechoslovak Economic Development in the Interwar Period," in Victor S. Mamatey and Radomír Luža, eds., *A History of the Czechoslovak Republic 1918–1948* (Princeton, 1973), 188–215.

Przewłocki, Jan, *Stosunek mocarstw zachodnioeuropejskich do problemów Górnego Śląska w latach 1918–1939* (Warszawa, 1978).

Pułaski, Michał, "Projekty paktu naddunajskiego 1934–1935," *Historia i Współczesność* 1 (1977), 213–26.

———, *Stosunki dyplomatyczne polsko-czechosłowacko-niemieckie od roku 1933 do wiosny 1938* (Poznań, 1967).

Radice, Lisanne, *Prelude to Appeasement: East Central European Diplomacy in the Early 1930s* (Boulder, Colo., 1981).

Rakowski, Bogusław, "Pierwsze reakcje polskie na propozycje paktu czterech mocarstw," 20, *Zeszyty Naukowe Universytetu Łódzkiego; Nauki Humanistyczno-Społeczne*, 20, z. 76 (1971), 69–83.

———, "U Źródeł paktu czterech," *Zeszyty Naukowe Uniwersytetu Łódzkiego; Nauki Humanistyczno-Społeczne*, ser. 1, 10, z.67 (1970), 71–88.

———, "Polsko-radzieckie aspekty paktu czterech mocarstw z 1933 r.," *Z Dziejów Stosunków Polsko-Radzieckich*, 10 (1973), 97–120.

Ránki, György, *Economy and Foreign Policy: The Struggle of the Great Powers for Economic Hegemony in the Danube Valley 1919–1939* (Boulder, Colo., 1983).

Raupach, Hans, "The Impact of the Great Depression on Eastern Europe," in Herman van der Wee, ed., *The Great Depression Revisited* (The Hague, 1972), 236–45.

Rémond, René, *La Droite en France de la première Restauration à la Vᵉ République*, 2 vols. (Paris, 1968).

Renouvin, Pierre, "Aux Origines de la Petite Entente: les hésitations de la politique française dans l'été 1920," in *Mélanges offerts à Victor-Lucien Tapié* (Publications de la Sorbonne, sér.Etudes, t.6 études européennes; Paris, 1973), 489–500.

Ressel, Alfred, "Mnichov ve vzpomínkách a v kritice důstojnika generálního štába československé armády," *Historie a Vojenství*, 2 (1969), 302–58.

Riekhoff, Harald von, *German-Polish Relations 1918–1932* (Baltimore, 1971).

Roberts, Henry L., "The Diplomacy of Colonel Beck," in Gordon A. Craig and Felix Gilbert, *The Diplomats 1919–1939* (Princeton, 1953), 579–614.

Rollet, Henry, "Deux mythes des relations franco-polonaises entre les deux guerres," *Revue d'Histoire Diplomatique*, 3/4 (1982), 225–48.

Romanow-Bobińska, Klara, "Polityczne aspekty handlu zagranicznego Czechosłowacji w okresie międzywojennym," *Studia z Dziejów ZSRR i Europy Środkowej*, 12 (1976), 127–54.

Roos, Hans, "Jozef Pilsudski und Charles de Gaulle," *Vierteljahrshefte für Zeitgeschichte*, 8 (1960), 257–67.

———, *Polen und Europa: Studien zur polnischen Aussenpolitik 1931–1939* (Tübingen, 1957).

———, "Die Präventivkriegspläne Pilsudskis von 1933," *Vierteljahrshefte für Zeitgeschichte* (1955), 344–63.

Rostow, Nicholas, *Anglo-French Relations 1934–1936* (London, 1984).

Rothschild, Joseph, *Piłsudski's Coup d'Etat* (New York, 1966).

Sander, Rudolf, "Přehled vývoje československé vojenské správy v letech 1918–1939," *Historie a Vojenství*, 3 (1965), 359–404.

Sauvy, Alfred, "The Economic Crisis of the 1930s in France," *Journal of Contemporary History*, 4, 4 (1969), 21–36.

———, *Histoire économique de la France entre les deux guerres*, 2 vols. (Paris, 1965–67).

Schor, Ralph, "Une Étude d'opinion: la droite française face à la crise mondiale de 1929," *Information Historique*, 36 (1974), 23–27, 64–70.

Schuker, Stephen A., *The End of French Predominance in Europe* (Chapel Hill, N.C., 1976).

Scott, William E., *Alliance Against Hitler: The Origins of the Franco-Soviet Pact* (Durham, N.C., 1962).

Segal, Paul H., "The French State and French Private Investment in Czechoslovakia: A Study of Economic Diplomacy," Ph.D. Dissertation, Columbia University, 1983.

Senn, Alfred E., *The Great Powers, Lithuania and the Vilna Question 1920–1928* (Leiden, 1966).

———, "The Polish-Lithuanian War Scare, 1927," *Journal of Central European Affairs*, 21 (1961), 267–84.

Siebert, Ferdinand, *Aristide Briand* (Zürich, 1973).

Sieburg, Heinz-Otto, "Les Entretiens de Thoiry, 1926," *Revue d'Allemagne*, 4 (1972) 520–46.

Sierpowski, Stanisław, *Stosunki polsko-włoskie w latach 1918–1940* (Warszawa, 1975).

Skrzypek, Andrzej, "Polsko-radziecki pakt o nieagresji z 1932 r.," *Z Dziejów Stosunków Polsko-Radzieckich*, 13 (1976), 17–40.

———, *Strategia pokoju* (Warszawa, 1979).

———, "Zagadnienie rumuńskie w stosunkach polsko-radzieckich w latach 1932–1938," *Z Dziejów Stosunków Polsko-Radzieckich*, 11, 189–207.

Sládek, Zdeněk, "Akce československých a polských vládních kruhů proti sovětskoněmecké neutralitni smlouvě v dubnu 1926," *Slovanský Přehled*, 61 (1975), 255–64.

———, *Hospodářské vztahy ČSR a SSSR 1918–1939* (Praha, 1971).

———, *Pozycja międzynarodowa, koncepcje polityki zagranicznej i dyplomacja państw Europy środkowej i południowo-wschodniej w okresie międzywojennym* (Warszawa, 1981).

———, and Jerzy Tomaszewski, "Próby integracji gospodarczej Europy środkowej i południowej w latach dwudziestych xx w.," *Roczniki Dziejów Społecznych i Gospodarczych*, 40 (1979), 1–23.

———, "Próby integracji gospodarczej Europy środkowej i południowo-wschodniej w latach trzydziestych xx w.," *Sobótka* 34 (1973), 377–401.

Soulié, Michel, *La Vie politique d'Edouard Herriot* (Paris, 1962).

Soutou, Georges-Henri, "L'Alliance franco-polonaise 1925–1933 ou comment s'en débarasser?" *Revue d'Histoire Diplomatique*, 2/3/4 (1981), 295–348.

———, "L'Impéralisme du pauvre: la politique économique du gouvernement français en Europe Centrale et Orientale de 1918 à 1929," *Relations Internationales*, 7 (1976), 219–39.

———, "Les Mines de Silésie et la rivalité franco-allemande 1920–1923: arme économique ou bonne affaire?" *Relations Internationales*, 1 (1974), 135–154.

———, "La Politique économique de la France en Pologne 1920–24," *Revue Historique*, 509 (1974), 85–116.

Stambrook, F. G., "A British Proposal for the Danubian States: The Customs Union Project of 1932," *Slavonic and East European Review*: 42 (1963), 64–88.

———, "The German-Austrian Customs Union Project of 1931," *Journal of Central European Affairs*, 21 (1961), 15–44.

Starzewski, Jan. *Zarys dziejów polskiej polityki zagranicznej* (mimeographed; London, 1944).

Stawecki, Piotr, "L'Attitude de l'état-major polonais face au problème du désarmement au cours des années 1920–1934" in *Histoire militaire de la Pologne: problèmes choisis. Publié à l'occasion du XIIIe Congrès international des sciences historiques à Moscou* (Varsovie, 1970). An enlarged Polish version in *Acta Universitatis Lodziensis: Folia Historica*, 28 (1986).

Steyer, Donald, "Stosunki polsko-francuskie w zakresie gospodarki morskiej w latach 1919–1939," *Zapiski Historyczne Towarzystwa Naukowego Toruńskiego* 29 (1964), 39–67.

Suarez, Georges, *Briand*, 6 vols. (Paris, 1938–52).

Suval, Stanley, *The Anschluss Question in the Weimar Era* (Baltimore, 1974).

Szklarska-Lohmannowa, Alina, *Polsko-czechosłowackie stosunki dyplomatyczne w latach 1918–1925* (Wrocław, 1967).

———, "Z Raportów dyplomatów czechosłowackich w Polsce, 1935–1938," *Historia i Współczesność*, 1 (1977), 104–12.

Taborsky, Edward, "The Triumph and Disaster of Eduard Beneš," *Foreign Affairs*, 36 (1958), 669–84.

Taylor, A.J.P., *The Origins of the Second World War* (New York, 1962).

Teichman, Miroslav, "Titulescu a rumunská zahraniční politika 1933–36," *Československý Časopis Historický*, 14 (1966), 667–84.

Teichová, Alice, *An Economic Background to Munich: International Business and Czechoslovakia 1918–1930* (Cambridge, 1973).

———, "Les Investissements directs français en Tchécoslovaquie entre les deux guerres," in Maurice Lévy-Leboyer, ed., *La Position internationale de la France, aspects économiques et financiers* (Paris, 1977), 331–38.

Thimme, Annelise, "Stresemann and Locarno," in Hans W. Gatzke, ed., *European Diplomacy between Two Wars 1919–1939* (Chicago, 1972), 73–93.

Tomaszewski, Jerzy, "Miejsce Polski w Europie środkowej w koncepcjach polityków," in *Polska myśl polityczna XIX i XX w.*, 4: *na warsztatach historyków polskiej myśli politycznej* (Wrocław, 1980), 173–90.

———, and Jaroslav Valenta, "Polska wobec Czechosłowacji w 1933 roku," *Przegląd Historyczny*, 70 (1979), 695–721.

Tournoux, Gén. Paul-Emile, *Haut commandement, gouvernement et défense des frontières du Nord et de l'Est 1919–1939* (Paris, 1960).

Torzecki, Ryszard, *Kwestia ukraińska w polityce III Rzeszy* (Warszawa, 1972).

Truelle, J., "La Production aéronautique militaire française jusqu'en juin 1940," *Revue d'Histoire de la Deuxième Guerre Mondiale*, 19, 73 (1969), 75–110.

Tucker, Robert C., "The Emergence of Stalin's Foreign Policy," *Slavic Review*, 36 (1977), 563–89.

Turner, Henry A., "Continuity in German Foreign Policy: The Case of Stresemann," *International History Review*, 1 (1979), 509–21.

Urban, Rudolf, *Tajne fondy III sekce: Z archivů ministerstva zahraničí Republiky Česko-slovenské* (Praha, 1943).

Vaïsse, Maurice, "Le Désarmement en question: l'incident de Saint Gothard 1928," *Revue d'Histoire Moderne et Contemporaine*, 22 (1975), 530–48.

———, *Sécurité d'abord: la politique française en matière de désarmament 9 décembre 1930–17 avril 1934* (Paris, 1981).

Valenta, Jaroslav, *Česko-polské vztahy v letech 1918–1920 a Těšínské Slezsko* (Ostrava, 1961).

———, "Československo a Polsko v letech 1918–1945," in *Češi a Poláci v minulosti*, 2 vols. (Československá Akademie Věd; Praha, 1962), 2:431–668 [except chapter 7, authored by A. Měštan].

———, "Vývojové tendence československo-polských vztahů v nejnovějsích dějinách, 1918–1945," in *Československo-polské vztahy v nejnovějsich dějinách* (Ustav pro mezinárodní politiku; Praha, 1967), 9–36.

Vondracek, Felix J., *The Foreign Policy of Czechoslovakia* (New York, 1937).

Wandycz, Piotr S., *August Zaleski: minister spraw zagranicznych RP 1926–1932 w świetle wspomnień i dokumentów* (Paris, 1980).

———, "Colonel Beck and the French: Roots of Animosity?" *International History Review*, 3 (1981), 115–27.

———, "Foreign Policy of Edvard Beneš," in Victor S. Mamatey and Radomír Luža, eds., *A History of the Czechoslovak Republic 1918–1948* (Princeton, 1973), 216–38.

———, *France and her Eastern Allies 1919–1925; French-Czechoslovak-Polish Relations from the Paris Peace Conference to Locarno* (Minneapolis, 1962).

———, "French Diplomats in Poland 1919–1926," *Journal of Central European Affairs*, 23 (1964), 440–50.

———, "The Little Entente: Sixty Years Later," *Slavonic and East European Review*, 59 (1981), 549–64.

——— "Pierwsza Republika a Druga Rzeczpospolita," *Zeszyty Historyczne*, 28 (1974), 3–20.

———, "La Pologne face à la politique locarnienne de Briand," *Revue d'Histoire Diplomatique*, 2/3/4 (1981), 237–63.

———, *Polska a zagranica* (Paris, 1986).

Wapiński, Roman, "Myśl polityczna narodowej demokracji wobec problemów bezpieczeństwa II Rzeczypospolitej," in *Polska myśl polityczna XIX i XX w.*, 4: *na warsztatach historyków polskiej myśli politycznej* (Wrocław, 1980), 201–16.

———, *Władysław Sikorski* (Warszawa, 1978).

Warner, Geoffrey, *Pierre Laval and the Eclipse of France* (London, 1968).

Watt, Donald C., "The Anglo-German Naval Agreement of 1935: An Interim Judgement," *Journal of Modern History*, 28 (1956), 155–75.

―――, "German Plans for the Reoccupation of the Rhineland: A Note," *Journal of Contemporary History*, 1, 4 (1966), 193–99.

Weinberg, Gerhard L., "Czechoslovakia and Germany 1933–1945," in Miloslav Rechcigl, ed., *Czechoslovakia Past and Present* (The Hague, 1968), 760–69.

―――, *The Foreign Policy of Hitler's Germany: Diplomatic Revolution in Europe 1933–1936* (Chicago, 1970).

―――, "Secret Hitler-Beneš Negotiations in 1936–37," *Journal of Central European Affairs*, 19 (1960), 366–74.

Władyka, Wiesław, *Działalność polityczna polskich stronnictw konserwatywnych w latach 1926–1935* (Wrocław, 1977).

Wojciechowski, Marian, "Polska i Niemcy na przełomie lat 1932–1933," *Roczniki Historyczne*, 19 (1963), 105–180.

―――, *Stosunki polsko-niemieckie 1933–1938* (Poznań, 1965). German version, *Die polnisch-deutschen Beziehungen* (Leiden, 1971).

Wroniak, Zdzisław, *Polska–Francja 1926–1932* (Poznań, 1971).

Wurm, Clemens, *Die französische Sicherheitspolitik in der Phase der Umorientierung 1924–1926* (Bern, 1979).

Wynot, Edward D., *Polish Politics in Transition: The Camp of National Unity and the Struggle for Power 1935–1939* (Athens, Ga., 1974).

Young, Robert J., *In Command of France: French Foreign Policy and Military Planning 1933–1940* (Cambridge, Mass., 1978).

Zacharias, Michał J., *Polska wobec zmian w układzie sił politycznych w Europie w latach 1932–1936* (Wrocław, 1981).

―――, "Strategia polityczna Józefa Becka a przesilenie marcowe 1936 roku," *Dzieje Najnowsze*, 5, 4 (1973), 73–86.

Żarnowski, Janusz, ed., *Dyktatury w Europie środkowo–wschodniej 1918–1939* (Wrocław, 1973).

―――, *Polska Partia Socjalistyczna w latach 1935–1939* (Warszawa, 1965).

Zgórniak, Marian, "Sytuacja międzynarodowa Czechosłowacji i niektóre aspekty stosunków czechosłowacko-polskich w latach 1919–1937," *Najnowsze Dzieje Polski 1914–1939*, 9 (1965), 5–36.

―――, "Sytuacja międzynarodowa Polski w latach 1931–1934," *Przegląd Historyczny*, 66 (1975), 198–215.

Ziaja, Leon, *PPS a polska polityka zagraniczna 1926–1939* (Warszawa, 1974).

Zieliński, Antoni, "Stosunki polsko-rumuńskie, grudzień 1933–maj 1935," *Studia z Dziejów ZSRR i Europy Środkowej*, 12 (1976) 157–92.

Zinner, Paul E., "The Diplomacy of Eduard Beneš," in Gordon A. Craig and Felix Gilbert, eds., *The Diplomats 1919–1939* (Princeton, 1953), 100–22.

Zorach, Jonathan, "The Enigma of the Gajda Affair in Czechoslovak Politics in 1926," *Slavic Review*, 35 (1976), 683–98.

Guides and Bibliographies

Among the many existing auxiliary tools, the following may be singled out as especially useful:

Dějiny Československa v datech (Praha, 1968), for chronology.

Łoza, Stanisław, ed., *Czy wiesz kto to jest?* (Warszawa, 1938), a Polish who's who.

Nowak, C. M., *Czechoslovak-Polish Relations 1918–1939: A Selected and Annotated Bibliography* (Stanford, Calif., 1976).

Young, Robert J., ed., *French Foreign Policy 1918–1945: A Guide to Research and Research Materials* (Wilmington, Del., 1981).

Index

Addison, Sir Joseph, 331
agrarian bloc, 199, 200; and Czechoslovakia, 175, 191, 255; and Warsaw conference, 175–76
agrarian party, Czechoslovak, 29, 56, 57, 318, 465; and Little Entente, 466
air force, French, 462; and Czechoslovakia, 263; and Poland, 11, 110, 144, 263
Air Locarno, 386
Alexander, King, 370, 381
Alexandrovsky, Sergei, 398
alliance, Czechoslovak-Soviet. See Czechoslovak-Soviet treaty of mutual assistance
alliance, French-Czechoslovak: Czechoslovak view of, 10–11, 30–31, 190–91, 450; French view of, 10–11, 353; mutual guarantee treaty, 14, 31; and Poland, 10–11, 450–51; signed, 8, 10
alliance, French-Polish, 53, 69–70, 121, 232, 235, 295; alleged expiration of, 187, 235; ambiguity of, 26, 35, 142, 397n, 443; and attack on Czechoslovakia, 397, 402; and flagrant aggression clause, 146, 152–53; and French-Soviet pact, 296, 394–97; and German-Polish nonaggression, 321, 326, 335, 427–28; and Germany, 71–72; and Locarno, 14–15, 33, 335; as mutual guarantee treaty, 14–15; and remilitarization of the Rhineland, 435, 438–39, 441, 442–44; and Romania, 232–33; signed, 8
alliance, French-Soviet. See French-Soviet pact of mutual assistance
alliance, Polish-Romanian, 112, 113; and Little Entente, 250; renewed, 39, 45; signed, 9, 232. See also Romania
alliances, French-Eastern (Eastern barrier), 3, 167, 253, 255, 449, 453; and

Britain, 13, 19, 411–12; economic component of, 453–55, 458; and Four Power Pact, 276–78, 287, 298–99, 446; French views on, 10, 11, 14, 75, 107, 155, 156–57, 253, 360, 412; and Germany, 156–57, 449; and Italy, 452; and Kellogg-Briand, 121–23; and Locarno, 14–15, 16, 25, 35, 156, 449; and remilitarization of Rhineland, 435; and Soviet angle, 452
Aloisi, Pompeo, 275
Alphand, Charles, 298–99, 305, 377
Amis de la Pologne, 27n
Anschluss, 445, 446; and Briand, 192; Czechoslovak view of, 88–89, 115–16, 118, 192, 291; and French, 10, 65, 89, 104, 109, 159, 291; and German-Polish rapprochement, 311; and Hodža plan, 424; and Little Entente, 90; and Mussolini, 31, 113; Polish view of, 102–3, 113, 159, 294; and Rhineland evacuation, 103, 108, 126; and Schubert, 116
Antonov-Ovseienko, Vladimir, 311
arbitration treaties, 14–15, 25, 27, 31, 443
Arciszewski, Mirosław, 81, 128–29
Argentina, 224
Armádní poradní sbor, 303
armaments: Czechoslovak, 240, 303; French, 345, 396, 416–18; Polish, 239–40
Armengaud, General Paul, 263
army: Czechoslovak, 30, 35n, 84, 99, 154–55, 240, 303, 467; French, 8, 22, 28, 35n, 66, 71, 108, 110, 144, 156, 168, 185–86, 196–97, 233, 239, 242, 248, 253, 262, 346, 389, 395–96, 432–33, 436–37, 442, 449, 461, 462; Polish, 8, 35n, 55, 56, 433, 437, 442, 472–73. See also Reichswehr

Aron, Robert, 478
Association, France-Pologne, 415
Austria, 200–201, 222, 339, 382; and
Beneš, 114, 291; and Danubian coop-
eration, 102, 222; and German cus-
toms union project, 192–201; and
Hodža plan, 422–24; and Stresa front,
392. *See also* Anschluss

Badoglio, Marshal Pietro, 394
Bainville, Jacques, 22, 158, 235, 459
Balkan Entente, 339, 411, 441
Baltic countries: and agrarian bloc, 176;
and Beck, 362; and Eastern pact, 357;
and nonaggression treaties with USSR,
211; and Soviet-Polish relations, 39,
50, 136, 210, 333–34
Banque de France, 415, 454; advances
from, 23; and East-Central Europe,
93–95; and Polish stabilization loan,
94
Banque des Pays de l'Europe Centrale,
235
Barbusse, Henri, 22
Bargeton, Paul, 443, 446
Bariéty, Jacques, 324, 354, 358, 366, 367
Bartel, Kazimierz, 47, 51, 86
Barthélemy, Joseph, 79
Barthou, Louis, 8, 60, 335, 336, 337–39,
340–42, 357–61, 364, 369–71, 378,
428, 455; and Beck, 347–49, 350, 354,
358, 366; and Beneš, 341, 350–53,
361; and Chłapowski, 341, 353; and
Czechoslovakia, 342–46, 349–53; and
Eastern Pact, 349, 356, 358, 361, 362,
366; and Four Power pact, 277, 341;
and Franco-Polish relations, 341, 353–
54, 456; on German revisionism, 62,
179; and Italy, 339, 341, 381; and Laroche, 364–65; and Litvinov, 357–58;
and Piłsudski, 341, 348–49, 354, 355,
388; and Russia, 341, 367; and visit to
Poland, 341, 347–50, 353, 354
Bartoš, Colonel F., 85
Baumont, Maurice, 324
BBWR, 47–48, 111
Beck, Colonel Józef, 90, 199, 210, 212,
228, 270, 276, 295–96, 307, 309,
320–21, 326, 334–35, 349, 358, 362,
373, 386, 391–92, 395–96, 400–401,
405, 413, 421, 425, 461, 469–70; and
Anschluss, 294, 311; and Barthou,
341, 347–50, 354, 358, 366, 367; and
Beneš, 282–83, 308, 317, 321–23,
402, 406, 464; criticism of, 414, 444,
469, 470; and Curtis-Schober project,

194–95; and Czechoslovakia, 203,
246, 286, 419, 420, 425; and Danubian pact, 384, 392; and Eastern pact,
358, 362–63, 366, 375–78, 389; on
foreign policy, 247, 318–19, 321–22,
430; and Four Power pact, 279, 283,
286; and French alliance, 265, 295,
319, 321, 335, 347, 384, 385, 416,
427–28; French views of, 231, 246–
47, 266, 310, 367, 414, 415, 417; and
German-Polish nonaggression pact,
307, 308, 320, 321, 384; and Germany, 261, 284, 358–59, 405; and
Hitler, 301–2, 318, 325, 405–6; and
Laval, 376–77, 378, 384, 401–2, 406–
7, 413, 421; and Little Entente, 250–
51, 279; and national minority treaty,
347, 366–68, 473; and remilitarization
of the Rhineland, 435, 437, 438–39,
441, 445; and Romania, 230, 231,
358, 362
Beer, Max, 115, 116
Belgium, 37, 62, 435, 439, 455
Beneš, Edvard, 5, 10, 12, 15, 38, 45–46,
57, 68–69, 71, 85–87, 114, 115–16,
118, 121, 127, 130, 147–48, 173–75,
190–91; and Anschluss, 89, 103, 115–
16, 339, 340–41; and Austria, 114–15,
212, 291, 294, 351, 408–9; and Beck,
282–83, 285, 317–23; criticism of,
317, 332, 350, 471; and Curtius-
Schober project, 194, 196; and Danubian project, 212, 291–92, 382, 383,
384, 393, 408–9, 422; and Eastern
Pact, 352, 356, 359–60, 361, 369,
378–79, 383; economic plan of, 198–
201; and Four Power pact, 276, 278–
79, 280–81, 285, 288; and France, 7,
10, 11, 352, 360, 426, 443, 446; on
Franco-German relations, 180–81,
190, 198, 238, 314, 351, 413; and
Franco-Italian cooperation, 291–93;
and French-Soviet pact, 398–400, 431;
and Germany, 83, 84, 104, 115–16,
118, 201, 261–62, 393; and Hodža,
134, 420, 423, 424–25; and Hungary,
91, 114, 115, 197, 212, 226; and Italy,
249, 278, 294; and Kellogg-Briand,
121; and Little Entente, 68, 90, 114,
135, 174–75, 201, 241, 249–51, 254,
281, 339, 383; and Locarno, 30, 97,
114–17, 235; and 1926 crisis, 29–30,
57–58; and Piłsudski, 118, 197, 254,
322, 341, 379, 464; and Poland, 42,
44, 58–59, 68, 85–87, 103, 104, 118–
19, 156, 182, 191, 229, 244, 254,

282–83, 285, 287, 290, 316, 319–23,
381, 388, 450–51; and revisionism,
14, 191, 264, 281; and Russia, 31–32,
399; and Tardieu Plan, 222–27; and
Treaty of Berlin, 40–42; views of, 104,
242, 248, 322, 378–79, 399, 540
Beneš-Skirmunt pact, 9
Béranger, Henry, 277
Berlin, treaty of (arbitration and friend-
ship), 36, 40–42, 46, 50, 62, 207
Berthelot, Philippe, 4, 8, 28, 38, 52, 64,
67, 74, 78, 103–7, 118, 124, 128, 134,
146–47, 171–72, 216
Bessarabia, 102, 210
Bethlen, István, 137, 147
Bienaimé, Georges, 28
Bigo, Colonel Jan, 43, 462
Bláha, General Silvester, 316, 462
Bloch, Charles, 324
Blum, Léon, 187, 267, 301, 406, 421,
446
Bohemia and Moravia, 261
Bois, Elie, 314, 367, 458
Bokanowski, Maurice, 116
Bonnefous, Georges, 152
Bonnet, Georges, 25, 35, 148, 277, 315,
361, 444, 446
Borah, William E., 218
Bortnowski, General Władysław, 416
Boussac, Marcel, 124, 417, 458. *See also*
Żyrardów
Bradáč, Bohumír, 368
Brazil, 38
Bressy, Pierre, 237
Briand, Aristide, 9, 19, 24–26, 37–38,
52, 59, 63, 74, 75–76, 140–41, 149,
179, 183, 188, 199–200, 203, 214,
223, 230, 234, 364, 455; and "corridor," 102, 189; and Curtius-Schober
project, 192; and eastern alliances, 98,
103, 107, 108, 167, 188; and European Union, 116, 167, 170–71, 172,
187–88; and Franklin-Bouillon, 150–
51, 204; and German nationalism,
166–67, 204; and the Hague Conferences, 145–46, 148, 149, 169; and Interallied Control Commission, 74; on
Locarno, 24–25, 77, 92–96, 130; and
Poincaré cabinet, 60, 64, 65; policies
of, 156–57, 158; and Rhineland evacuation, 69, 92, 97, 106, 108, 120, 126,
127, 129, 149; and Treaty of Berlin,
40; and USSR, 209; and Young Plan,
133
Briandism, 24, 36, 191, 223, 332, 450,
458, 478

Brockdorff-Rantzau, Ulrich von, 95, 111
Brühl Palace, 247, 320, 326, 332–33,
435, 452, 470, 472
Brüning, Heinrich, 165, 179–80, 195,
205–6, 216, 219, 222, 234, 252, 262
Brześć Affair, 164–65, 180, 246, 468,
473
Bulgaria, 176
Bullitt, William C., 268, 426
Bülow, Bernhard von, 165, 193, 319, 407
Buré, Emile, 78, 216, 242, 367, 427

Caillaux, Joseph, 24, 107, 272, 277
Cambon, Jules, 235
Canada, 202
Čapek, Karel, 463
Carol II, King, 174
cartel des gauches, 12, 19, 22
Catholic People's Party (Czechoslovak),
29, 57
Cat-Mackiewicz, Stanisław, 326
Central European Locarno: and Austria,
159; Beneš on, 31, 91, 114; and Cham-
berlain, 31; and French, 102; and
Hungary, 159; and Poland, 159; and
Schubert, 68–69. *See also* Danubian
cooperation
Centrolew, 164
Černý, Jan, 29, 44
Chalupa, General Vladimír, 182
Chamber of Deputies. *See* Parliament:
French
Chamberlain, Sir Austen, 13, 19, 128,
156; and Briand, 101; and Central Eu-
ropean Locarno, and Piłsudski, 101;
and Poland, 37, 97; and revisionism,
14, 157; and treaty of Berlin, 40; and
Young Plan, 133
Champetier de Ribes, Auguste, 79
Charles Habsburg, 9
Charles-Roux, François, 82, 90, 154–55;
and Beneš, 82, 84–87, 198, 229, 463;
as envoy in Prague, 58, 137, 198, 475;
on Polish-Czechoslovak relations, 103,
119, 155, 177, 182, 199, 203
Charpy, General Charles, 55–56, 95
Chautemps, Camille, 300
Chicherin, Georgi V., 49, 73, 74, 95
Chłapowski, Alfred, 36, 69, 75, 113,
145, 153, 154, 218, 232, 236, 264,
280, 341, 347, 365, 401, 415, 423,
475; as ambassador in Paris, 36, 53,
80, 109, 121, 205, 244, 406, 413, 427,
441, 475; and Beneš, 126, 316, 318;
and Briand, 61–63, 64, 78, 91; and
eastern alliances, 429–30; and Franco-

Chłapowski, Alfred (*cont.*)
  Soviet pact, 209, 232, 304, 396, 401;
    and French-German rapprochement,
    74, 216, 412; on Herriot cabinet, 236;
    and Laval, 218, 375, 377–78, 422; and
    the Rhineland, 69, 435, 437, 442
Chodacki, Marian, 400, 419, 421
Churchill, Winston, 13, 267–68
Citroën, 216
Clemenceau, Georges, 336
Coblenz zone, 146
Colbert, Jean-Baptiste, 215
"colonels," Polish, 414, 472–73
Colson, General Louis, 417, 433
Comité des Forges, 60; and foreign pol-
    icy, 456, 458; and François-Poncet,
    207; and Germany, 412; and Poland,
    125
Comité des Houillières, 60, 412
Commission of Verification and Concilia-
    tion, 127, 141, 143, 145
communists: Czechoslovak, 29; French,
    28, 66, 361, 398, 457; German, 180;
    Polish, 47
Compagnie Franco-Polonaise de Chemin
    de Fer, 202
Confederation of the Rhine, 99
Conference of Ambassadors, 76
Conseil Supérieur de Guerre (CSG), 108,
    188, 262, 461, 462
Conseil Supérieur de la Défense Natio-
    nale (CSDN), 66, 239, 337, 461
conservatives. *See* Right
Convention for the Definition of Aggres-
    sor, 295–96
Corbin, Charles, 67, 124
cordon sanitaire, 3
"Corridor," Polish: American views on,
    217–18; and Czechoslovaks, 89; and
    demography, 186, 205; and Eastern
    Locarno, 102; and Franco-German
    talks, 60, 234, 266; and the French,
    68, 77, 124, 168, 185–86, 187, 206,
    217, 234–36, 266, 267, 274; and Ger-
    many, 20, 21, 153, 473; and Musso-
    lini, 274–75, 279; and Piłsudski, 53,
    101, 206; and Schacht, 62, 64; and
    Schubert, 68–69; and Zaleski, 206. *See
    also* revisionism
Cot, Pierre, 264, 304; and disarmament,
    186; and eastern loans, 235; and Four
    Power pact, 277; and French-Soviet
    pact, 429; and Kellogg-Briand, 122–
    23; and Popular Front, 406; and revi-
    sionism, 189, 219, 235; and Soviet
    Russia, 296, 361; and Zaleski, 235

Couget, Joseph, 57, 82, 475
Coulondre, Robert, 77, 166
Creditanstalt, 195
Croix de Feu, 219, 300
Cudahy, John, 377
Curtius, Julius, 115, 165, 166, 187, 193,
    206, 209, 216
Curtius-Schober Project, 203, 225; and
    Britain, 193; and Czechoslovakia,
    193–96, 201; and the French, 192,
    194, 195, 202, 252; and Italy, 193;
    and Little Entente, 198, 201; and Per-
    manent Court of International Justice,
    196; and Poland, 194–95; and USSR,
    207
Cushendun, Lord, 127
Czapiński, Kazimierz, 152
Czechoslovakia: diplomats, 475–77;
    economy of, 164, 465–67; of the late
    1930s, 407–8; military estabishment,
    467; and political crisis (1925–26),
    29–30, 56; political model, 465–66;
    postwar, 3
Czechoslovak-Soviet treaty of mutual as-
    sistance, 398–400
Czernin Palace, 278, 310, 319, 329, 353,
    380, 387, 423, 424, 462
Czerwiński, Lt. Colonel Andrzej, 462
Częstochowa, 125

D'Abernon, Lord, 40
Dąbski, Jan, 43
Daladier, Edouard, 260–62, 280, 297,
    304, 311, 315; cabinets of, 262, 288,
    300, 302, 314; and Four Power Pact,
    276, 277, 287, 288–89; and Germany,
    277, 296, 314; and Poland, 187, 288–
    89, 290, 314; and Popular Front, 406;
    and preventive war, 269–70, 272; and
    socialists, 443, 459
Danubian cooperation (Union), 5, 68–69,
    88–89, 158, 174; and Beneš, 88, 221;
    and British, 22, 193; and Four Power
    pact, 290–93; and France, 200–201,
    212, 221, 290–94; and Little Entente,
    291–92. *See also* agrarian plan; An-
    schluss; Central European Locarno
Danubian pact, 369–70, 381–84, 394,
    408
Danzig (Gdańsk), 42, 68, 88, 236–37,
    405
d'Arbonneau, Colonel (General) Charles,
    271, 295, 328, 345, 367, 390, 396,
    431, 444, 453, 460; and arming of Po-
    land, 345, 396, 416, 418; and Czecho-
    slovak-Polish relations, 282, 330, 418–

19; and Piłsudski, 234, 246, 311–13, 328, 349, 356, 462
Dawes Plan, 12, 64, 67, 130, 133
Debeney, General Marie-Eugène, 22, 66, 98, 110, 119, 144; and Poland, 354–56, 360
de Brinon, Fernand, 296
de Broglie, duke, 60
debts, interallied, 4, 203
de Castellane, Stanislas, 130, 189
de Castelnau, General Edouard, 76
de Chámbrun, Charles, 477
de Gaulle, Charles, 48, 158, 338
de Jouvenel, Bertrand, 35, 335
de Jouvenel, Henri, 96, 273, 277–78, 458; and Eastern Locarno, 65, 80, 107, 274, 459; and Italy, 273, 292–93; and revisionism, 274–75
de Kérillis, Henri, 427
de Laboulaye, Andre Lefebvre, 179, 189, 209
de Larson, Major Geoffrey du Perier, 234
Delbos, Yvon, 361, 421, 446
de Margerie, Pierre, 61
de Monzie, Anatole, 277, 415, 417, 456, 460–61
Denain, General Victor, 144, 168, 185, 361
de Panafieu, Hector, 52, 476
de Peyerimhoff, Henri, 60, 77, 458
Depression, Great, 159, 163–65
de Rothschild, Diane, 79
de Rothschild, Edouard, 415
Deschanel, Paul, 460
Desticker, General Pierre, 64
de Talleyrand, Charles de Perigord, 266
de Tessan, François, 235
de Vienne, Mathieu, 90–91
de Wendel, François, 260, 377, 415, 458
Diamand, Herman, 50
disarmament: French and allied, 36, 108, 159, 239–40, 244–46, 336–37, 361; and equality of rights, 238, 241, 243, 246, 264, 275, 375; and Germany, 4, 34–36, 66, 81, 238, 241, 243, 269; and Little Entente, 240, 249; and Nazi Germany, 263, 267; and Poland, 81, 240–47; and USSR, 207, 239–40
Długoszowski, Colonel Bolesław Wieniawa, 271–72
Dmowski, Roman, 52, 260
Dolfuss, Engelbert, 339, 369–70
d'Ormesson, Wladimir, 60, 76–77, 97, 179, 188–89, 216, 260, 403, 460
Doumergue, Gaston, 108, 137, 140, 192, 333–38, 365, 371, 378, 456

Dovgalevsky, Valerian, 208, 356
Duchemin, René, 266
Dufour, General Gaston, 176
Dupont, General Charles, 28, 53
D'určanský, Ferdinand, 164
Duroselle, J. B., 324, 456
Dzierzykraj-Morawski, Kajetan, 326

East Prussia, 68, 74, 134, 168, 179, 205
Eastern Locarno, 27, 95, 97, 105, 158; and Briand, 92, 96, 101, 106, 339; and French, 107, 158, 305; and Jouvenel, 80, 96; Polish plans of, 81, 91–92, 96, 97, 141–43, 158, 205. *See also* Rhineland
Eastern Pact, 344, 357–58, 361, 362, 375; and Britain, 361, 386–87; and Czechoslovakia, 359–60; failure of, 404, 408–9; and Germany, 357, 361, 363, 366, 376, 378; and Laval-Litvinov protocol, 377, 378, 389; and Litvinov, 358, 376, 392; and Poland, 355, 362–63, 366, 369, 370, 375, 376–77, 392
economic relations. *See* investments; loans; trade
Eden, Anthony, 310, 386, 391–93, 432–33
Eliáš, General Alois, 182
Englicht, Colonel Józef, 373, 380
Erskine, Sir William, 321
Estonia. *See* Baltic countries
Ethiopia: Italian conflict with, 409–11, 421–22, 457; Laval-Mussolini deal, 382
Eupen and Malmédy, 21, 62, 65, 69
European Union, 170–72, 175, 225

Fabre-Luce, Alfred, 434
Fabry, Jean, 270
Fabrycy, General Kazimierz, 365, 385
fascists (and extreme Right): Czechoslovak, 29–30; French, 22; and Piłsudski, 47, 49, 468
Faucher, General Louis-Eugène, 30, 59, 84, 154, 196–98, 282, 379, 441, 462
Faure, Jean-Louis, 303
Faury, General Louis, 373
Federal Reserve Bank, 94
Fédération interalliée des anciens combatants (FIDAC), 373, 415
Fédération Républicaine. *See* Right: French
Ferek-Błeszyński, Colonel Jerzy, 462
Fiat, 216, 233
Filipo, Lt. Colonel Julien, 460

Filipowicz, Tytus, 217
Finland, 211
Flandin, Pierre-Etienne, 24, 184, 189,
    206, 207, 215, 225, 260, 423–24, 428,
    444, 461, 478; cabinet of, 371, 372,
    406; and eastern alliances, 428–29,
    453; as foreign minister, 421, 455; on
    Franco-Soviet treaty, 428–29; and
    pacts, 382, 412; and remilitarization of
    the Rhineland, 433–36
Flieder, Robert, 58, 476
Foch, Marshal Ferdinand, 8–10, 75, 98,
    302, 461; and evacuation of the Rhine-
    land, 64, 66, 108, 128, 146; and Inter-
    allied Control Commission, 35, 74;
    and strategy, 22–23
fortifications: Czechoslovak, 303, 437,
    451; French, 22, 108, 112. See also
    Maginot Line
Four Power Pact: antecedents to, 246,
    252, 274; and the British, 275–76; and
    Czechoslovakia, 278–79, 283, 285,
    288–89; and France, 276–78, 284,
    287–90; and Germany, 275; impact of,
    on French-Czechoslovak-Polish rela-
    tions, 294, 298–99, 450; and Italy,
    246, 248, 274, 290–94; and Little En-
    tente, 279, 281, 288, 298; and Poland,
    279, 283, 285–86, 288–89, 292, 295,
    374, 471; and Titulescu, 280, 288
France, 3, 163, 336, 458, 460; economy
    of, 23, 163, 455; envoys, 475–76; and
    foreign ministry and ministers, 253,
    455–56; and Left-Right rift, 253, 457–
    59; and Locarno, 22–24; and military
    establishment, 461–62; and Popular
    Front, 406–7
Franchet d'Esperey, Marshal Louis, 98–
    101, 105, 109, 176–77, 180
François-Marsal, Frédéric, 76, 188
François-Poncet, André, 107, 189, 204,
    206–7, 209, 271, 305, 329, 337, 406,
    432, 436, 458; and Germany, 24, 260,
    286, 296–97, 307, 310, 315, 327–28,
    413; and Lipski, 309–10, 327, 477
Franklin-Bouillon, Henry, 27, 37, 107,
    187–88, 192, 260, 270, 372; and alli-
    ances, 204, 245, 299, 301, 446, 459;
    and Briand, 150–51, 204; and Four
    Power Pact, 277–78, 289; on Polish se-
    curity, 77, 277–78
Frankowski, Feliks, 437
freemasonry, 29, 456, 460–61
French-German committees, 60, 77, 139,
    216, 234, 266, 412
French mutual guarantee treaties with

Poland/Czechoslovakia. See alliances
French-Romanian treaty of friendship,
    62n, 63
French-Soviet pact of mutual assistance,
    304, 341, 357, 409, 431; French view
    of, 361, 395–96; and Laval, 395, 422;
    and Locarno, 304, 406, 436, 492–93;
    Polish view of, 400–401, 422; ratifica-
    tion of, 422, 427, 429–31, 457; signed,
    397–98
French-Yugoslav treaty, 31, 104
Fromageot, Henri, 92
Frot, Eugène, 28

Gajda, General Rudolf (Radola), 30, 56–
    57, 83, 181
Gamelin, General Maurice, 188, 242,
    277, 360–61, 368, 373, 389–90, 394,
    412, 417–18, 427; and remilitarization
    of the Rhineland, 432–33, 436, 442,
    444
Gąsiorowski, General Janusz, 302, 312,
    316, 326
Gauché, Colonel Maurice, 416, 442
Gdańsk. See Danzig
Gdynia-Silesia railroad, 168–69, 184,
    202, 233
general staff. See army
Geneva Protocol: on Austria (1922), 193,
    196; for the pacific settlement of inter-
    national disputes, 12–13, 97–98, 170,
    241
Genoa, Conference of, 9
George v, King, 417, 423
George of Poděbrady, King, 45
Germany, 9, 97, 121, 165, 192, 253,
    335, 365, 449; announces conscrip-
    tion, 390–91; at Geneva, 293, 300,
    307; and Poland, 385, 431. See also
    disarmament; Reichswehr; revisionism
Gerodias, General Paul, 442, 444
Ghika, Dimitri, 211
Girsa, Václav, 57–58, 87, 155, 250, 287,
    289, 295, 317, 319–20, 400, 476; and
    Beck, 280–81, 308, 318; and Piłsudski,
    87, 244, 369, 380, 476; and regime,
    138, 244
Gleichberechtigung (Equality of rights).
    See disarmament
Glogau. See fortifications
Goebbels, Joseph, 307, 331, 365
Goering, General (Marshal) Hermann,
    331, 384–85, 404, 430
Gömbös, Gyula, 372
Górecki, General Roman, 373–74, 380,
    415

Gottwald, Klement, 134
Grandi, Dino, 136, 167
Great Britain, 49, 140, 148, 216, 224, 252, 386, 381, 411; and France, 9, 238, 301; and French eastern alliances, 13, 19, 157, 450; and Locarno, 13, 19–20
Greece, 239
Green International, 43
Grzybowski, Wacław, 86, 271, 288, 318, 333, 400, 477; and Beck, 283, 285, 289; and Beneš, 155, 329, 332; and Czechoslovakia, 283, 289–90, 332–33; as envoy in Prague, 86, 120, 286, 369, 387; on German-Polish nonaggression, 329, 381
Guitry, General Jean, 110, 144

Habsburg Restoration, 10, 167, 174, 351, 381, 409, 424, 450
Hague (The) Conferences, 145–50, 152, 159, 468
Haller, General Stanisław, 11–12, 100
Hammerstein, General Kurt von, 234
Hašek, Jaroslav, 467
Haushoffer, Albrecht, 323
Haut Comité Militaire, 390, 412, 433, 462
Havas Agency, 84, 209
Headlam-Morley, Sir Charles, 13
Heidrich, Arnošt, 282
Henderson, Arthur, 140, 145, 240
Henlein, Konrad, 407–8
Herbette, Jean, 95
Hering, General Pierre, 129
Herriot, Edouard, 6, 12, 60, 186, 231–32, 238, 253, 267, 336–37, 445, 456; and Barthou, 354, 357; cabinets of, 12, 227, 231, 236; and disarmament, 241, 243, 246–47; and foreign policy, 204, 243; and Four Power pact, 277, 287, 289; and Germany, 139, 238, 337; and USSR, 232, 295, 304, 361, 429
Hervé, Gustave, 187–88
Hesnard, Oswald, 64
Hindenburg, Paul von, 166, 259
Hirtenberg Affair, 250
Hitler, Adolf, 166, 187, 259, 275, 286, 298, 307, 368, 386, 390, 392, 404–6, 413; and Czechoslovakia, 261–62, 379; and disarmament, 263, 267; and France, 259–60, 305, 314, 350, 377; and Lipski communiqué, 308–9, 333; on Locarno, 404, 413, 431, 436; and Poland, 260–61, 309, 324, 385n; and preventive war, 269, 272–73

Hlinka, Father Andrej, 33, 134, 419
Hlinka Populist party, 244, 333, 407; in cabinet, 57, 465; meetings of, 164, 244
Hlond, Cardinal August, 402
Hoare, Sir Samuel, 411, 421, 469
Hodža, Milan, 43, 175, 420–25, 465; and Beneš, 134, 420, 423, 424, 425; Central European policy of, 422–23
Hodža Plan, 422–26
Hoesch, Leopold von, 75, 78, 134, 140, 157, 171, 189, 193, 204; and Zaleski, 123–24
Hohen-Aesten, Wiegand von, 306
Holý, General Kamil, 462
Hoover, Herbert, 203, 217, 241
Horák, General J., 85
Hotchkiss Co., 79
Hrad (castle), 211, 244, 255, 261, 272, 353, 465, 475; and crisis of 1926, 29–30, 56–57. *See also* Masaryk, Tomáš Garrigue
Hugenberg, Alfred, 165
Hungary, 212, 381; and agrarian bloc, 175–76; and Czechoslovakia, 83, 89, 91, 115, 181, 197; and Danubian union, 5, 31, 90–91, 159; and France, 212, 226; and Italy, 89, 226, 291; and Poland, 89–90, 113, 126, 136–37, 372, 384. *See also* revisionism; Szentgotthárd Affair
Husárek, General Karel, 360

Interallied Military Control Commission, 34–35, 65, 71, 73–74, 82
investments: Czechoslovak, 466; French, 6–7, 53–54, 79, 124–25, 203, 233, 345, 349, 454–55
Iskra Communiqué, 439
Italy, 13, 89, 339, 450; and Austria, 31, 113, 291, 369; and France, 52, 104, 273, 290–94; and Hungary, 89, 291; and Little Entente, 291–94, 339; and Poland, 112–13, 167, 452; and Warsaw embassy, 113, 150

Jagiellonians, 45
Japan, 254, 359; and Mukden incident, 209–10
Javorina, 9, 87
Jędrzejewicz, Janusz, 307
Jews, 29, 48
Junga, Karol, 178

Karszo-Siedlewski, Jan, 177
Kasprzycki, General Tadeusz, 144, 326
Kayser, Jacques, 219, 235

Keller, General René, 408
Kellogg, Frank, 121
Kellogg-Briand pact (pact of Paris), 121, 123–24, 136, 142, 208, 324; and Four Power pact, 275, 277; and French-Polish alliance, 152–53; and Poland, 121–22, 125, 129. *See also* Litvinov Protocol
Kennard, Sir Howard, 363, 416, 440
Klecanda, General Vladimír, 462
Kleeberg, Colonel Juliusz, 462
Knoll, Roman, 50, 58
Kobylański, Tadeusz, 425
Koc, Adam, 215, 415, 417, 454
Koch, Walter, 116, 191, 272
Koeltz, Colonel Marie, 263, 301–2
Komarnicki, Tytus, 477
Königsberg. *See* fortifications
Kościałkowski, Marian Zyndram-, 414
Köster, Roland, 412
Kozicki, Stanisław, 149
Kozłowski, Leon, 366
Kramář, Karel, 56, 134, 248, 407, 419
Krejči, General Ludvik, 331, 360
Krofta, Kamil, 97, 126, 133, 172–73, 181, 289, 369, 380, 397, 405, 407, 409, 420, 424; and Beck, 280, 283; as Beneš's deputy, 57–58, 198, 306, 462; and France, 103, 181–82, 202, 214, 336, 340, 387; and German-Polish nonaggression, 330, 335; and Germany, 114, 443; and Little Entente, 90, 135, 293; and Poland, 104, 155, 194, 248, 282, 316, 318, 351–52, 369, 387–88; and remilitarization of the Rhineland, 434, 437, 441; and revisionism, 248, 264; and Tardieu Plan, 224, 227
Krüger, Peter, 253
Kutrzeba, General Tadeusz, 110, 143, 416
Kvaček, Robert, 324
Kwiatkowski, Eugeniusz, 180
Kwieciński, Lt. Colonel Bogdan, 462

Lagardelle, Hubert, 278
L'Alliance Republicaine Democratique, 107
Lamoureux, Lucien, 353
Laroche, Jules: as ambassador in Warsaw, 52, 55, 95, 137, 155, 169, 247, 272, 279, 284, 286, 302, 363, 372, 375, 385, 391, 460, 476; on Anschluss and "corridor," 89; and Beck, 190, 231, 247, 266, 286, 320, 373, 388; and Beneš, 86–87, 199; on colonels, 472–73; on Eastern Galicia, 177–78; and evacuation of the Rhineland, 81, 93, 125, 128; and French business in Poland, 78–79, 94, 131; and Goering, 385; and Kellogg-Briand pact, 121–22, 125; and Little Entente, 118; on Locarno, 28, 82; and Piłsudski, 52–54, 234, 247, 254, 311, 373, 388; and Polish alliance, 8, 70, 295–96, 373; and Polish attitude toward French, 265–66, 297, 364–65; and Polish attitude toward Russia, 396, 400; and Polish-Czechoslovak relations, 58–59, 103, 177, 199, 203, 243; and Polish-German nonaggression pact, 82, 307–9, 311, 314, 328; and Polish-Romanian relations, 230–31; and Polish-Soviet rapprochement, 295–96; and revision of military convention, 98, 109, 146–47, 152–53; on Tardieu Pact, 228; visited by Barthou, 342, 347; visited by Debeney, 355–56; on Zaleski, 53, 111, 125, 128
Lasocki, Zygmunt, 42, 59, 84–85, 452, 456
Latvia. *See* Baltic countries
Laurent, Théodore, 60
Lausanne Conference, 237–38
Lautier, E., 276
Laval, Pierre, 206, 216, 230, 253, 271, 371–72, 376–77, 390–91, 394, 396, 398, 401, 404, 408–13, 415, 422, 426, 428; and Beck, 376–78, 401, 414; and Beneš, 378, 383; and Briand, 188, 371; and Britain, 372, 385–86, 410; cabinets of, 40, 188; and "corridor," 206, 217–18, 402; and Danubian pact, 372, 383, 422; and Eastern Pact, 358, 372, 375–76, 386, 402, 406; and Ethiopian crisis, 410, 412; as foreign minister, 234, 371, 455–56; and Franco-Polish relations, 313, 375, 378, 380; and Germany, 204, 207, 375, 394, 407–13; and Hitler, 412–13; and Little Entente, 372, 383, 422; and Litvinov Protocol, 377–78, 389; in London, 385–86; policy of, 372, 421–22; in Moscow, 392, 404; and Polish-Czechoslovak relations, 387, 402, 420; in Rome, 381–82, 394; in Warsaw, 392, 401–3; in Washington, 216–18
League of Nations, 26, 36–39, 57, 63, 71, 113–14, 130–31, 296, 298, 300, 304, 357, 366–67, 381–82, 390, 410, 413, 431–33, 443–44
Le Creusot. *See* Schneider

Leeper, Reginald, 179
Left: Czechoslovak, 29, 56–57, 465;
  French, 9, 14, 23, 66, 76, 149, 186,
  188, 207, 214, 245, 253–54, 262, 269,
  277, 301, 398, 410, 457–60; Polish,
  32–33, 47, 260–61, 470
Léger, Alexis, 149, 172, 296, 309, 341,
  356, 385, 413, 456; and Four Power
  pact, 274, 288; and remilitarization of
  the Rhineland, 432, 441; as secretary
  general, 274, 378
Le Goyet, Pierre, 437
Lémery, Henry, 77, 107, 121
Lenin, Vladimir I., 4
Lersner, Kurt von, 189, 198
Lévy, Paul, 28
Lewiatan, 474
Leygues, Georges, 60, 62, 216
Lichtenberger, Henri, 60
Lipski, Józef, 146, 189, 307–9, 312–13,
  320, 326–27, 373, 385, 391, 403–4
Liquidation Accord, German-Polish, 146
Lithuania, 50, 73–74, 101, 111, 177,
  358, 363. See also Memel
Little Entente, 5, 38, 90, 112, 114, 136–
  37, 175, 201, 250, 339, 424, 450; and
  agrarian bloc, 176–77; cohesion of,
  89, 129, 174; conferences of, 31, 90,
  135, 174, 201, 227, 249–50, 294, 370,
  383, 446; and Danubian cooperation
  plans, 212–13, 292–94; and Danubian
  Pact, 369–70, 383–84, 408; and Eastern Pact, 376, 383; economic problems
  of, 58, 135; and Four Power pact,
  278–81, 284, 288–89; and France, 5,
  8, 117, 129, 137–38, 159, 174, 190,
  278, 339; and Franco-Italian relations,
  292–94; and Hungary, 113, 126, 137,
  174, 175; and Italy, 291–93; and military accords, 175, 197; Organizational
  Pact of, 250–52; and Poland, 5, 8, 90,
  118, 131, 135, 159, 174, 283, 425;
  and remilitarization of the Rhineland,
  440–42; and Romania, 114, 118; and
  Russia, 31, 136, 359; and Tardieu
  Plan, 226, 227
Litvinov, Maxim, 49, 230, 304, 334,
  357–59, 377, 392, 395, 399; and
  France, 39, 208; and Germany, 50, 95;
  and nonaggression pacts, 73, 96; and
  Poland, 334–35
Litvinov Protocol, 135–36, 207
Lloyd George, David, 9
loans: international, 227, 339; Polish stabilization, 94
loans and credits, French: to Czechoslo-

vakia, 201, 213–15, 223, 254, 454; to
  East Central Europe, 227, 253; to Poland, 8, 11, 141, 147, 154, 168–70,
  184–85, 215, 233, 345–46, 374, 415–
  16, 418, 430, 446; to Romania, 184,
  453; to Yugoslavia, 453
Locarno, 13–14, 19; and Briand, 24–25;
  and Czechoslovakia, 14, 30, 83; denounced, 431, 438; and eastern alliances, 14–15, 25, 27, 300, 374; and
  Four Power pact, 290; and Franco-Soviet pact, 397, 406, 429–30; and
  French, 14, 24–28; and German-Polish
  nonaggression, 335, 439; and Germans, 20, 41, 42; and Poland, 14, 33–
  34, 158, 441–42; ratified, 27–28; and
  revisionism, 14, 20, 25; violation of,
  431, 440. See also arbitration treaties;
  Eastern Locarno
Loevenstein, Karel, 465
Loizeau, General Lucien, 360
London Conference, 12, 226–29, 253
London Economic Conference, 298
Longuet, Jean, 410
Loucheur, Louis, 79, 170, 173–74, 189,
  191
Louis XIV, 215
Łowczowski, Colonel Gustaw, 442, 462
L'udáks. See Hlinka Populist party
L'Union Européenne Industrielle et Fi-
  nanciere. See Schneider
L'Union Républicaine Democratique. See
  Right: French

MacDonald, Ramsay, 12, 140, 206, 245–
  46, 267, 275–76, 338
Maginot, André, 149, 185
Maginot Line, 108, 140, 146, 436, 445,
  461
Mainz zone, 146
Malhomme, Leon, 332
Mandel, Georges, 76, 151, 270, 435
Margerie, Pierre de, 61
Marin, Louis, 27, 37, 60, 107, 361, 427,
  457, 459–60; and Four Power pact,
  278, 289; and Germany, 24, 27, 303;
  on Locarno, 27–28
Martel, René, 168
Martin, Gaston, 461
Marx, Wilhelm, 115
Masaryk, Jan, 227
Masaryk, Tomáš Garrigue, 10, 57, 82,
  118, 134, 154, 173, 178, 180, 261,
  272, 303, 317, 331, 352, 407, 420,
  459–60, 466; on Anschluss and "corri-

Masaryk, Tomáš Garrigue (cont.)
dor," 88, 181, 284, 340; and German
revisionism, 87–88, 155; Hungary, 89,
181, 274; and 1926 crisis, 29, 56–57;
and Poland, 59, 88, 119, 180. See also
Hrad
Massigli, René, 64, 74, 92, 128, 146,
171, 223–24, 240, 251, 310, 313, 343,
388, 446
Mastný, Vojtěch, 306, 309, 319, 441
Maurin, General Louis, 129, 389–90,
418, 432–36
Maurras, Charles, 22
Mayr-Harting, Robert, 83
Mayrisch, Emile, 60
Mein Kampf, 259–60, 269
Memel (Klaipeda), 21, 61, 69, 77, 101,
106–7, 189, 266
Metternich, Klemens, 463
Miedziński, Bogusław, 294
military convention, French-Polish; 8,
11–12, 35, 54, 98, 100, 109–10, 142–
47, 168, 185, 297, 345–48, 354–56;
apocryphal, 135n, 187n. See also alliance, French-Polish
military cooperation: Czechoslovak-Polish, 43, 46, 58–59, 86, 120, 155, 182–
83, 191, 196–97, 242, 255, 282, 316–
17, 331, 400; Czechoslovak-Soviet,
399; and France, 10–11, 119–20, 155,
176–77, 182, 196, 282; French-Czechoslovak, 10–11, 263, 361, 452–53;
French-Italian, 394; French-Polish, 9,
11–13, 110, 143–44, 328, 390, 403,
452–53; French-Soviet, 404; German-
Soviet (Secret), 180, 182, 239, 248;
and Little Entente, 175, 197, 339, 360.
See also Pact of Perpetual Friendship
military expenditure: Czechoslovak, 84,
119, 303, 467; French, 24, 457, 461;
Polish, 56, 119, 474
military mission, French, 5–6, 30, 83–84,
98, 154, 233–34, 254
military strategy, Czechoslovak, 10, 99,
160, 197, 316–17, 360; French, 8–12,
22, 100, 108, 144, 185–86, 242, 262,
390n; French-Czechoslovak, 22, 144,
262–63, 360–61; Polish, 8–11, 55–56,
100, 197, 403, 451–52
Millerand, Alexandre, 8, 12, 26–27, 39,
76, 128, 150, 272
Mittelhauser, General Eugéne, 30, 36,
176
model D. See tripartite pact
Molotov, Vyacheslav, 428
Moltke, Hans von, 271–72, 308

Monnet, Jean, 94
Montigny, Jean, 124
Moravská Ostrava, 178, 332
Mordacq, General Henri, 76
Moreau, Emile, 93–94, 158, 454
Moret, Louis, 94
Morstin, Ludwik Hieronim, 302
Mościcki, Ignacy, 47, 111, 155, 279,
373, 403, 438, 468
Mouget, Rear-Admiral Georges, 110
Mouvement General des Fonds, 94
Mühlstein, Anatol, 79–80, 204, 206,
209, 216, 265, 272, 287, 310, 313–15,
342, 375, 401, 415–16, 442, 475
Mukden Incident, 209–10
Müller, Hermann, 121, 125, 127, 165
Munich Conference, 446
Mussolini, Benito, 31, 104, 161, 268,
274, 278, 368, 409, 422, 456; and
Austria, 340, 368; and Beneš, 104,
464; and "corridor," 167, 274–75; and
Danubian Cooperation, 293, 381–82;
and Four Power pact, 246, 248, 274;
and France, 274, 369; and Hodža plan,
424; and Zaleski, 112–13

Naggiar, Paul-Emile, 413, 419, 434, 475,
477
Namier, Lewis, 323
Napoleon, 475
Národní Banka, 94
Národní Sjednocení. See Right: Czechoslovak
national Democrats, Polish, Czechoslovak. See Right: Polish
national minorities: in Czechoslovakia,
465; and Poland, 131, 243, 347, 366–
68, 473; and Weimar Republic, 20,
178, 473
national socialists, Czechoslovak, 30,
134, 155, 465
National Union (L'Union nationale), 56
naval agreement, British-German, 404–5
naval mission, French, in Poland, 99–
100, 234, 254
navy, Polish, 53–54
Nazi Party (NSDAP), 165, 180, 183, 242.
See also Hitler, Adolf
Nejvyšší rada obrány statů, 303
Neré, Jacques, 324, 433
Netherlands, the, 262
Neurath, Konstantin von, 243, 266, 307,
320, 358, 360, 404
Niessel, General Albert, 238
Noël, Léon, 353, 369, 458, 475–76,
477–78; and Beck, 414, 417, 428, 430,

461, 469–70, 476; and Czechoslovak-Polish relations, 380–81, 419; as envoy in Prague, 282, 322, 352, 360; and remilitarization of the Rhineland, 437–38, 440–41, 444

Nollet, General Charles, 22

nonaggression pact: Czechoslovak-German, 91, 305–6; Finnish-Soviet, 211; French-Soviet (treaty), 95, 112, 207–10, 221, 229–32, 295; general, 97; German-Polish (declaration), 82, 91–92, 97, 108–9, 305–8, 312, 320–21, 323–35, 341–42, 366, 375, 427–28; Latvian-Soviet (treaty), 211; Polish-Soviet (treaty), 39, 50, 73, 95–96, 112, 136, 207–11, 221, 229, 231–32, 349, 366, 374

Norman, Montagu, 94

Novák, Ladislav, 155

Oberkirch, Alfred, 77

Olivová, Věra, 324

Osuský, Štefan, 40, 69, 172, 200, 214, 248, 253, 284, 293, 309, 356, 382, 441, 443, 475; and Four Power pact, 278–84, 289; and French-German relations, 314, 408; and French trends, 303–4; and Little Entente, 137, 251–52

Ottawa Conference, 224

pacifism: Czechoslovak, 303; French, 22–23, 457; Polish, 473

Pact of Perpetual Friendship (Czechoslovak-Polish), 282–83, 318–19, 322–23, 330, 381

Painlevé, Paul, 60, 71, 110, 189, 216

Palacký, František, 90

Paléologue, Maurice, 5, 91

Papen, Franz von, 189, 236–38, 260, 314

Paris Peace Conference, 3–4

parliament: Czechoslovak, 29–30, 407, 464–65; French, 12, 26–28, 37, 66, 120, 124, 150–52, 187–88, 214, 218, 223, 227, 235, 245, 254, 276–78, 284, 288–89, 295, 372, 390, 421–22, 429–31; Polish, 33, 111, 151, 165

Parti Democrate Populaire. *See* Right: French

Patek, Stanisław, 210

Paul-Boncour, Joseph, 27, 98, 248, 262, 271, 278, 296–301, 327, 339, 364, 418; and Beneš, 251, 264, 316; and disarmament, 245–46, 264–65, 305; on eastern alliances, 299–301, 321; as foreign minister, 251, 253, 262, 300,

455; and Four Power pact, 276–77, 279, 287–88, 290, 294; and Germany, 296, 300, 305; and Italy, 273, 291–92; and Little Entente, 251, 288, 293–94; and Piłsudski, 52, 101; and Poland, 44, 216, 250, 264–65, 297, 313–14, 321, 456; policies of, 339, 364; and preventive war, 269–70, 272; and revisionism, 264, 267, 275; on Rhineland evacuation, 79–80, 107; and Soviet pact, 296–97, 304, 361, 398

peasant party, Polish, 260

Pełczyński, Colonel Tadeusz, 197

Pergler, Karel, 181

Pernot, Georges, 169

Pertinax (André Geraux), 26, 75–76, 236, 266, 279, 291, 298, 338, 361, 364, 414, 427, 459

Pétain, Marshal Philippe, 22, 64, 154–55, 169, 188, 336, 361, 404, 418, 429, 461

Pétin, General Victor, 339, 348, 354

Pezet, Ernest, 427

Pfeiffer, Edouard, 235, 310

Pieracki, Bronisław, 368

Piétri, François, 418

Piłsudski, Marshal Józef, 4, 32, 47, 55–56, 81, 87, 90, 101, 122, 138, 164, 167–69, 206–8, 220, 230, 233, 271, 290, 302, 311, 319, 368–69, 385, 392, 403, 475; and Anschluss, 220, 294; and Barthou, 348–49, 354–56, 378, 386, 388; and Beck, 190, 302, 312, 403, 468–69; and Beneš, 290, 464; and Britain, 48–49, 392, 452; and Czechoslovakia, 5, 56, 58–59, 86, 127n, 180, 197, 220, 281, 283, 468; and d'Arbonneau, 234, 311–13; death of, 403–4; and Debeney, 354–56; and disarmament, 243, 246, 348; and Eastern Pact, 363, 388; and foreign policy, 50, 52, 111, 232, 403, 451, 472; and Four Power pact, 279, 287; and France, 8, 33, 51–53, 55–56, 78–79, 148, 245, 356, 367, 468–69; and Franchet d'Esperey visit, 98–101, 109; on French alliance, 50, 143, 234, 294–95, 325, 348, 362, 403; and French loans, 168–69, 184; and Gdynia-Silesia railroad, 168; in Geneva, 101, 111; and Germany, 50, 70, 102, 143, 242, 308, 320, 325–26, 328, 348, 418, 451; and Hitler, 183, 286, 311–12, 348; illness of, 101, 280; and Laroche, 52–54, 234, 247, 311, 467–68; and League of Nations, 254, 348; and Lipski, 307–8;

Piłsudski, Marshal Józef (*cont.*)
  and Lithuania, 73, 138; and Locarno,
  33, 54–55, 99; and Masaryk, 5, 468;
  and model D, 143, 152; personality
  and outlook of, 47–50, 99, 158, 348,
  467–70; on Poles in Teschen, 212,
  220; as premier, 72, 177; and preventive war, 269–73, 280; and Romania,
  111, 126–27, 138, 230–31; and
  Skrzyński, 51, 54; and Soviet Russia, 4,
  49–50, 52, 74, 95, 96, 135, 138, 232,
  294, 319n, 325–26, 348–49, 451; on
  strategy, 100, 144; and USSR, 210–11,
  230–32
Piskor, General Tadeusz, 182
Pius xi, Pope, 444
Podhajský, General Alois, 83
Poincaré, Raymond, 8–12, 36, 63, 66,
  77, 120, 126, 133, 137, 140, 336,
  456–57, 475; and Briand, 60, 64, 67;
  and financial diplomacy, 93–94, 158;
  on German revisionism, 61–62, 179;
  and radical socialists, 130, 158; and
  Thoiry, 64, 66–67, 70
Poland, 3, 32, 47–48, 468; economy of,
  164–65, 473–74; foreign ministry and
  envoys, 470, 475–76; military establishment, 472–73; political opposition
  and public opinion, 470–72; and Soviet war, 4–5
Politis, Nicholas, 434
Populists, Polish. *See* peasant party
Populist party, Slovak. *See* Hlinka party
Potocki, Jerzy, 270–71, 279
Prchala, General Lev, 197, 242, 282
Preiss, Jaroslav, 134, 465–66
Press: Czechoslovak, 43–45, 83, 155,
  180, 196, 244, 261, 329, 369, 422,
  464; French, 51, 56, 75, 179, 246–47,
  264, 266, 276–77, 314, 328–29, 342,
  364, 367, 372–73, 400, 414, 424,
  458–59; Polish, 43, 233, 236, 244,
  331–32, 343, 345, 364, 367–68, 402,
  431, 471–72
Prystor, Aleksander, 471
Purić, Božidar, 443

Quai d'Orsay, 456
Quesnay, Pierre, 79, 204

Raczyński, Edward, 265–66, 281, 287
Radek, Karl, 49, 248, 294–95
radical socialists, French, 23, 120, 130,
  158, 186, 188, 236, 398, 457; Con-
  gresses of, 107, 186, 219; revisionist

views of, 70, 107, 218–19, 235–36;
  split among, 277, 296
Radziwiłł, Janusz, 51, 150–52, 189–90,
  326, 375
Rambouillet agreement, 446
Rapallo, treaty of, 9, 20, 39, 41, 210
rearmament: Austrian, 393; Bulgarian,
  393; and Eastern Pact, 361, 363, 376,
  378; French views on, 337, 386; German, 239, 298, 337; and note of 17
  April, 337–39, 385
Rechberg, Arnold, 60, 139, 187
Regedanz, Wilhelm, 190–91, 201
Regnier, Marcel, 415
Reichswehr/Wehrmacht, 165, 236, 239,
  242–43, 275, 436–37
René, Carl, 77
Renondeau, General Gaston, 315
reparations, 3, 12, 23, 62, 64, 93, 106,
  145, 147, 222, 238
revisionism, German (territorial), 13,
  264; and Americans, 217–18; under
  Brüning, 165, 178–80, 191, 218,
  221; and Czechoslovakia, 15, 88, 129,
  180, 264, 284, 290; and the French,
  14, 70, 77, 102, 150, 157, 168, 179,
  187–88, 206, 218, 234–36, 252, 264,
  266–67, 279, 284; and Hitler, 166,
  385n; and Italy, 167, 274–75; and
  Luxembourg meeting, 234–35; moratorium on, 205–6, 236, 252; and Poland, 34, 37–38, 61–62, 129, 131,
  264; and Young Plan, 134
revisionism, Hungarian (territorial), 114,
  173, 274–75, 360
Reynaud, Paul, 139, 151, 215, 276, 389,
  421, 427, 458
Rhineland, 12, 418; and Anschluss, 103,
  108, 126; and Beneš, 129, 148; evacuation of, 4, 64, 65, 81, 130, 140–41,
  145–46, 148, 163, 166–67; French
  views on, 66–69, 76–78, 80–81, 92–
  93, 107–8, 146; and Kellogg-Briand
  pact, 122; and Poland, 68, 71, 81–82,
  91–92, 123, 125–27, 141–47, 151,
  374; the Quai d'Orsay and, 67–68; remilitarization of, 427, 431–45; and tripartite pact, 142–43, 145; and Stresemann, 21, 73, 80, 106, 130. *See also*
  Coblenz zone; Eastern Locarno; Mainz
  Zone
Rhineland pact. *See* Locarno
Ribbentrop, Joachim von, 296, 376, 446
Riga, treaty of, 4, 8, 50, 366
Right: Czechoslovak, 30–31, 56–57,
  196, 317–18, 465; French, 5, 9, 22,

27, 76, 107–8, 113, 139, 149, 188, 207, 253, 277, 296, 303, 361, 369, 382, 398, 410, 427, 457–58; Polish, 5, 32–33, 48, 51–52, 78, 127, 149, 151, 190, 196, 260–61, 471
Ripka, Hubert, 317, 451
Roche, Emile, 235
Rolland, Romain, 21–22
Rollin, Louis, 215–16
Romania, 31, 63, 80, 136–37, 399; and Eastern Pact, 356, 362, 383; French loan to, 184, 453; and Italy, 249n; and Little Entente, 5, 135, 174; and Poland, 9, 118; and USSR, 39, 50, 210–11, 229–32
Rome Protocols (Italo-Austro-Hungarian), 340
Romier, Lucien, 22, 390
Roosevelt, Franklin D., 298
Rothermere, Lord, 114
Roux, Colonel Henri, 416
Ruhr, 8, 10, 12, 23
Rumbold, Sir Horace, 165–66
Russia. *See* Soviet Union
Rydz-Śmigły, General (Marshal) Edward, 326, 403, 414–17, 438, 440, 446

Saar, 64–65, 145, 166, 187, 315, 389
Sadova, 27, 80, 187, 218, 245, 298, 459
Saint-Brice, 28
Šámal, Přemysl, 155
Sarraut, Albert, 216, 270, 300–301, 422, 430, 433, 440, 443
Sauerwein, Jules, 28, 39, 42, 51, 61, 65, 103, 168
Schacht, Hjalmar, 62, 64–65, 94, 134
Schaetzel, Tadeusz, 142, 152, 475
Schleicher, General Kurt von, 190, 236, 246, 260, 262
Schlesser, Major, 328
Schneider, Eugène, 6, 53, 79, 125, 139, 214, 233, 345, 454–55, 466
Schubert, Carl von, 20, 68–69, 72, 121, 136, 139, 159, 171, 193
Schuschnigg, Kurt von, 423
Schweisguth, General Victor, 442
Seipel, Ignaz, 114
Sejm. *See* parliament: Polish
Senate. *See* parliament
Serruys, Daniel, 116
Seydoux, François, 464
Seydoux, Jacques, 67, 139
Sforza, Carlo, 411–12
Sidor, Karol, 164, 333, 419
Siegfried, André, 60
Sikorski, General Władysław, 9, 12–13,

15, 100, 128, 139, 233, 356
Simon, Sir John, 219, 223, 275, 300, 368, 391–92
Skarboferm (Société Fermière des Mines Fiscales l'État Polonais), 7, 53, 79, 124, 131
Skirmunt, Konstanty, 9
Škoda, 7, 42, 84, 154, 213–14, 303, 454–55, 465
Skrzyński, Aleksander, 12, 21, 37–38, 169; and Britain, 49, 158, 452; and Czechoslovakia, 12, 36, 42–46, 452; and Locarno, 15, 32–34; in Prague, 44–45; and Treaty of Berlin, 40–41
Slávik, Juraj, 425, 476
Sławek, Walery, 403, 472
Slovaks, 86, 134, 317–18, 333, 402, 465
Smeral, Bohumír, 30
Smutný, Jaromír, 400
Socialists. *See* Left
Sokal, Franciszek, 171
Sosnkowski, General Kazimierz, 326, 385, 388, 417–18, 427, 431, 435
Soukup, Colonel Jaroslav, 197
Soulier, Edouard, 28, 77
Soutou, Georges-Henri, 6, 7, 335
Soviet Union (USSR): Czechoslovakia and, 11–12, 169, 211, 359–60; and Far East, 207, 209–10, 357; and French, 4, 12, 73, 295–96; and Piłsudski, 49–50; and Poland, 294–95, 334
Spain, 38
Spina, Franz, 83
Stachiewicz, General Julian, 431
Stalin, Josef V., 20, 49, 207, 399, 427
Stavisky (Serge) Affair, 300
Steel Cartel, 63
Stefánik, Milan, 475
Stein, Ludwig, 34
Stimson, Henry L., 206, 217
Stojadinović, Milan, 420, 424, 441
Stresa Conference, 392–95, 404, 409, 432
Stresemann, Gustav, 39, 63, 88, 101–2, 111, 126, 131, 133, 136, 148, 156, 165–66, 170, 238–39, 458; and Briand, 80, 93, 126; and evacuation of the Rhineland, 20–21, 65–66, 73, 80, 120, 130; and Locarno, 13, 20, 65; policy goals of, 20–21; and revisionism, 20–21, 61, 65, 72, 102; and Soviets, 20, 74; and Treaty of Berlin, 63, 65, 69
Stříbrný, Jiří, 30, 57, 181
Stroński, Stanisław, 33, 190

Subcarpathian Ruthenia, 402
Sudeten Germans, 15, 57–59, 83–84, 116, 118, 130, 154, 164, 181–82, 261, 407, 465
Suvich, Fulvio, 268, 391, 432
Švehla, Antonín, 29, 42, 44, 57, 85, 353
Syrový, General Jan, 30, 99, 197, 263, 316, 331, 394; and cooperation with Poland, 59, 85–86, 119, 182
Szembek, Jan, 247, 312, 325–26, 356, 385, 415, 425, 442, 470
Szentgotthárd Affair, 113–14

Tabouis, Geneviève, 459
Tardieu, André, 60, 149, 172, 188, 214, 228, 230, 234, 269, 277, 336–37, 361; cabinet of, 149, 223, 230, 234; characterization of, 149, 253, 456; and cooperation with Poland, 153–54; and disarmament, 239–41, 245; and Germany, 165, 189, 234; and non-aggression with the USSR, 230–31
Tardieu Plan, 223–29, 252, 292, 294, 303
Templewood. *See* Hoare
Teschen (Cieszyn, Těšín), 7, 86, 164, 178; dispute, 3, 5, 87, 401; and Poles, 85, 134, 164, 178, 212, 317, 323, 368, 387, 465; tension over, 331–32, 387
Theodoli, Alberto, 340
Thoiry, 63–70, 92, 106, 127. *See also* Rhineland
Thorez, Maurice, 406
Titulescu, Nicolae, 231, 420, 422–23; and the Eastern Pact, 356, 362, 383; and Four Power pact, 280, 288; and France, 280, 339, 360
Toynbee, Arnold, 218
trade: Czechoslovak, 7, 42–43, 58–59, 85, 116–17, 133, 155, 178, 213, 353, 409, 466; French, 7, 24, 54, 63, 92, 116–17, 125, 213, 215, 345, 353–54, 374, 453–54; Polish, 42–43, 54, 58–59, 85, 125, 141, 155, 178, 215, 345, 374, 474
Transit war, 11, 43, 85, 86, 262, 304, 339, 345
Treaties, 50, 89, 177. *See also* alliances, French-Eastern, arbitration treaties; Locarno; nonaggression pact; Rapallo, treaty of
Treviranus, Gottfried, 179–80
tripartite pacts: and alliance obligations, 142–43, 145; Czechoslovak-Austrian-Hungarian, 222–23; Franco-British-Belgian, 13; Franco-Czechoslovak-So-

viet, 367, 383, 393; Franco-Italian-Yugoslav, 31, 269; Franco-Polish-German, 141, 234; Franco-Polish-Romanian, 10–11; and model D, 141–43, 152, 158; Polish-Romanian-Soviet, 362. *See also* Rome Protocols
Tuka, Vojtech, 134
Turkey, 150, 339
Tyrrell, Sir William (Lord), 188, 269, 275, 299

Udržal, František, 59, 85, 119, 134, 164
Ukraine and Ukrainians, 119, 165, 311, 319, 368–69, 468, 473
United States, 150, 216–18, 224, 252, 298. *See also* Hoover, Herbert; Roosevelt, Franklin D.; Stimson, Henry L.
Upper Silesia, 7–9, 55, 69, 89, 218, 266; French industrialists in, 7, 79, 215; and Germany, 20, 64, 153, 473

Vaïsse, Maurice, 324
Valois, Georges, 22
Vansittart, Sir Robert, 166–67, 239, 412, 432
Vatican, 408
Versailles, Treaty of, 4, 35, 65, 140, 217, 259; and disarmament, 238–39, 243, 246; and Rhineland evacuation, 91–92. *See* disarmament, revisionism
Vienna, 89, 115, 159, 329, 413
Viénot, Pierre, 60, 300
Viest, Colonel Rudolf, 462
Voikov, Pyotr, 95
Voldemaras, Augustinas, 101
Voroshilov, Kliment, 399

Wagener, Otto, 183
Walkó, Lajos, 126
Wall Street Crash, 156
war, Soviet-Polish, 4–5, 8, 100, 110
Weinberg, Gerhard, 324
Weizsäcker, Ernst von, 165
Welles, Sumner, 456
Wendel, François de, 260, 377, 415, 458
Westerplatte Incident, 271–73, 307
Weygand, General Maxime, 4–5, 8, 42, 188, 230, 233, 239, 242, 245, 262, 267, 269, 296, 301–3, 316, 337–38, 348, 361, 389, 429, 453, 461
Wicher Incident, 236–37, 247, 254
Wilson, Woodrow, 206
Witos, Wincenty, 47–48, 470
Wojciechowski, Stanisław, 47
World War I, 3
World War II, 445

Workers, Polish, in France, 374, 401–2, 454
Wysocki, Alfred, 165, 286, 271, 310

Ybarnegaray, Jean, 278, 287
Young, Owen D., 133
Young Committee and Plan, 133–34, 140, 145–48, 183
Yugoslavia, 3, 5, 104, 112, 339, 398, 451, 453

Zagórski, General Włodzimierz, 246
Zaleski, August, 50–52, 71–72, 79, 85–86, 89, 97, 112, 127, 131, 133, 138, 142, 147, 158, 167, 179, 184, 200, 202, 205, 208, 210, 215, 227, 229–31, 235, 237, 246, 326, 431, 461, 470; and Beck, 190, 246, 297; and Beneš, 60, 71, 119; and Briand, 70–71, 112; criticism of, 75, 78, 111, 149, 219, 471; and Curtius-Schober project, 194–96, 202; and Czechoslovakia, 58, 86, 112–13, 203, 229; and diplomatic offensive, 74–75; and disarmament, 81, 240–41, 243; and European Union, 171–72; and evacuation of the Rhineland, 82, 123, 128, 138; as foreign minister, 50–51; on Franco-German rapprochement, 60, 70, 123, 126, 138–39, 150–52, 189; and German revisionism, 50, 61, 72, 123, 179, 195, 205, 235–36; and Kellogg-Briand, 112–23; in London, 219–20; in Paris, 71, 123–24, 215; in Rome, 112–13, 119–20; and The Hague, 141, 145–47
Živnostanská Banka, 134, 465–66
Żyrardów, 124–25, 233, 345, 364, 375, 401, 454, 458